Nietzsche's Corps/e

POST-CONTEMPORARY INTERVENTIONS   *Series Editors: Stanley Fish and Fredric Jameson*

NIETZSCHE'S CORPS/E

Aesthetics, Politics, Prophecy, or,

The Spectacular Technoculture of Everyday Life

Geoff Waite

1996 DUKE UNIVERSITY PRESS *Durham & London*

© 1996 Duke University Press
All rights reserved
Printed in the United States of America on acid-free paper ∞
Designed by Cherie H. Westmoreland
Typeset in Galliard by Keystone Typesetting, Inc.
Library of Congress Cataloging-in-Publication Data appear on the last
printed page of this book.
This book is published with the aid of a grant from the Hull
Memorial Publication Fund of Cornell University.

for N

Let the dead bury their own dead. — Matthew 8:22

Il n'y a que les morts qui ne reviennent pas.
(It is only the dead who do not return.) — Bertrand Barère, 1794

There is no reason, which compels me to maintain that a body does not die,
unless it becomes a corpse; nay, experience would seem to point in
the opposite direction. — Benedict de Spinoza, 1675

Wir leiden nicht nur von den Lebenden,
sondern auch von den Toten. *Le mort saisit le vif!*
(We suffer not only from the living, but also from the dead. *The dead man
grabs the living!*) — Karl Marx, 1867

Your dead are buried ours are reborn
you clean up the ashes we light the fire
they're queuing up to dance on socialism's grave
this funeral is for the wrong corpse. — The Mekons, 1991

Plate 1. Mark Tansey, *Utopic,* 1987, oil on canvas, 68 × 70 inches. Private collection.
Courtesy Curt Marcus Gallery, New York, © *Mark Tansey.*

Contents

Plate 2. Mark Tansey, *Derrida Queries de Man,* 1990, oil on canvas, 83¾ × 55 inches. *Collection of Michael and Judy Ovitz, Los Angeles. Courtesy Curt Marcus Gallery, New York,* © *Mark Tansey.*

Prologue

Many people have contributed directly and indirectly to this book, none to the basic position taken by it. Written between the two historical events it articulates — communism's alleged death that it contests and the sesquicentennial of Nietzsche's birth that it decelebrates — it shows the historical and theoretical necessity of this articulation by producing the concepts "Nietzsche/anism" and "Nietzsche's corps/e." At issue is the relationship of the dead Nietzsche (corpse) and his written work (corpus) to subsequent living Nietzscheanism on the Right and the Center, but most especially to a leftist corps that is unwittingly programmed and manipulated, perhaps irredeemably, by intentionally concealed dimensions of Nietzsche's thinking and writing that remain exo/esoteric and un/readable.

The hypothesis and polemic: Neither "conservative," "proto-fascist," nor "proto-Nazi," Friedrich Nietzsche is in fact the revolutionary programmer of late pseudo-leftist, fascoid-liberal culture and technoculture. Here his deepest influence is subconscious and subcutaneous. If any one person or thing is responsible for the death of communism as imagined fact or "the death of communism" as ubiquitous concept, then it is the concept "Nietzsche," the man Nietzsche. Whom else should we then acknowledge? Whom else should we thank . . . or curse?

Neither user-friendly nor necessarily Marxist, this book advances its argument and polemic by bringing communist theory — especially Leninist, Gramscian, and Althusserian — to bear on the concept of Nietzsche's corps/e. But it strains beyond this ideological and political conviction, beyond this concept and theory, in order to address and settle accounts with "Nietzschean" problems that range more or less bovine throughout the marketplace of contemporary philosophy, political and literary theory, cultural and technocultural criticism. So it shuttles back and forth between philosophy and popular or junk culture, arguing that both are equally important, and equally infected by Nietzsche sub rosa. Particularly this book asks whether the postcontemporary age already upon us will continue to be dominated and oriented by Nietzsche's corps/e. Resolutely communist at root, it makes its address in ways equally — though not entirely — hostile to continental philosophy, cultural studies, deconstruction, hermeneutics, neoliberalism, new historicism, postanalytic philosophy, postmodernism, poststructuralism, structuralism, and — not least — Western Marxism.

It is impossible, therefore, that all colleagues, friends, and enemies — or any other readers — will be entirely pleased with the result, and possible that none will be pleased at all. The fact that this book is intended to be infuriating (*infuriare:* of the Furies; to anger, incense, madden, make fanatic) in part does not weaken the further possibility that it will be infuriating only.

Be the proof of this pudding as it may, and leaving out the names of far too many — including those involved with this press and students from whom one learns more than one teaches — it is only the most immediate and warmest thanks that go to Nora Alter, Louis Althusser, Stanley Corngold, Cyrus Hamlin, Anne Barnett Waite and Robert Waite, Peter Waite, Benjamin Waite.

The inadequate dedication speaks for itself.

Ithaca, New York — September, 1995

1 Nietzsche,
The Only Position as Adversary

The Only Position

Nietzsche's position is the only one outside of communism.[1]

What if this were true literally — this claim bringing into fateful constellation *Nietzsche* and *communism* and nothing else besides? How could we know this today, when communism exists no longer . . . or has not yet really existed? Unlike Nietzsche. For whether or not the living movement is dead, the dead man, the corpse, definitely lives on — as corpus and as corps. Put as another question: If the term "postmodern" ought to be replaced by "post-Nietzschean,"[2] if the precontemporary and the contemporary alike are fundamentally, hegemonically Nietzschean, then what about the postpostmodern, postcontemporary future? Asking this question, consider the possibility that Nietzsche's — relative — success and communism's — apparent — failure are global events intimately imbricated.

This book proposes, in terms minted in another context by Fredric Jameson, that the extensive albeit — in the global scheme of things — comparatively "isolated landscape" of "Nietzscheanism" can serve "allegorically" to access the geopolitical aesthetic "in the present age of a multinational global corporate network."[3] This landscape requires illumination by a "conspiratorial hypothesis" in order to make it visible in its full complexity and effectivity. But neither the New World Order of "late capitalism" nor "Nietzscheanism" can be "represented" or even "perceived," strictly speaking, since totalities of this empirical extent and simultaneous level of abstraction can never be fully represented or perceived, only mapped and triangulated with other forces. In these matters there is no "closure" at the end of the twentieth century — sooner a "closure-effect."[4] On the macrolevel of the history of consciousness, Nietzscheanism must be mapped by triangulating it in the one direction with the ostensible "victory of capitalism" and in the other direction with the "defeat of communism." On the microlevel Nietzscheanism must be mapped by triangulating Nietzsche's reception by Nietzscheans across the ideological spectrum with his published and unpublished writings, showing that Nietzsche programmed his reception in unconscious, subliminal ways to produce what will here be called "Nietzsche/anism" and "Nietzsche's corps/e." While mapping contemporary literary theory and philosophy, the ultimate adversary here is stronger than Nietzscheanism, and nothing less than neocapitalist totality *en marche*.

If, as Jameson argues, "it is indeed the new world system, the third stage of capitalism, which is for us the absent totality, Spinoza's God or Nature, the ultimate (indeed perhaps the only) referent, the true ground of Being of our time," then "only by way of its fitful contemplation can its future, and our own, be somehow disclosed."[5] Slavoj Žižek, too, notes that "it seems as if today we live in an age of new Spinozism: the ideology of late capitalism is, at least in some of its fundamental forms, 'Spinozist.'"[6] Whereas for the Slovene Žižek, Spinozism *is* "the ideology of late capitalism," the North American Jameson takes a middle ground between this position and the communist Antonio Negri's more elaborated one that Spinoza is "the savage anomaly" both of his time but also for ours.[7] But another referent and synonym in the overviews of Jameson, Žižek, and Negri is not "Spinoza" but "*Nietzsche.*" His is the name that comes quicker to mind and lips.

It is widely thought that Nietzsche was a proper follower of Spinoza, the greatest modern Spinozist, even that the two names are synonymous. This is the position held, for example, throughout the later work of Gilles Deleuze and Félix Guattari, indeed its philosophical core.[8] For his part, Negri aligns himself against "triumphant capitalism" in a genealogy of "radical democracy": namely, "the line that in the modern era goes from Machiavelli and Spinoza to Marx, and in the contemporary period from Nietzsche and Heidegger to Foucault and Deleuze."[9] This book stands shoulder to shoulder with this Negrian genealogy with two major exceptions. It argues that the names Heidegger and Nietzsche must be *radically* excised from the lists. And the same goes for Louis Althusser's depiction of his own "materialist" lineage: "Epicurus, Spinoza, Marx, of course, Nietzsche . . . Heidegger."[10] Even the greatest communist philosopher must be extracted from Nietzsche's web. Following Althusser and Negri, it is indeed necessary to pit Spinoza — the "savage anomaly" — *against capitalism* both at its inception and perhaps nearer its termination; but this entails also pitting oneself *against Nietzsche and Nietzscheanism*. Taking the possibility that Nietzsche's position may indeed be the only one outside of communism literally[11] requires neo-Spinozist work of "fitful contemplation": that is, hypothesis and polemic, speculation and science, argument and passion.

In response to "the death of socialism," The Mekons sing their "dinosaur's confession": "How can something really be dead when it hasn't even happened? . . . this funeral is for the wrong corpse."[12] The Mekons' question and response, barely audible in the Society of the Spectacle as it morphs toward a fully technocultural everyday, even while retaining elements of a still remarkably modernist global mode of capitalist production and consumption — Ulrike Meinhof aptly referred to *Konsumterror* — is equally rare in "high" literature and philosophy.[13] Nonetheless, paraphrasing Mike Davis, it is (still) possible to argue that, although the project of communism may lie in ruins, the best overlook is provided precisely from the ruins of alternative futures.[14] In the phrase of dub musician Linton Kwesi Johnson, even if most people (still) regard socialism as a "ghost," this need not prevent others from seeing it (again) as a "seed."[15] Alternatively, world communism has always come into being at moments of counterrevolution and defeat (as exemplified by the USSR and by Gramsci's Italy of the early twenties). Born in defeat, communism never guarantees victory, only ongoing struggle. As such, it may be the most realistic countermovement against Capital Triumphant in postcontemporary times, "when the proclaimed end of history has not terminated the problems that brought Communism into being as a political movement: the eradication of Hell from Earth, not the construction of Heaven upon it,"[16] and when "the character of the capitalist mode of production . . . is that of a structure which dissimulates itself in presenting itself."[17] But in these times, to paraphrase Chris. Marker's *The Last Bolshevik* (1993), the sometimes dangerous choice would appear to have come to this: be either a pure communist in a land of would-be communists, or an impure communist in a land of no other communists. As for all communists being dinosaurs today, the last image in *The Last Bolshevik* is precisely that of a child hugging a cuddly toy dinosaur, accompanied by the voice-over remark that although communists are now indeed dinosaurs, the latter are loved by children — the next generation.[18]

To grasp — and combat — celebrations of the "death" of communism, and to grasp — and build — *proper* communism, it is crucial to grasp in philosophy and mass or junk culture the causes and effects of this death. Nietzsche and Nietzscheanism among the vanguard. This grasp is simply impossible from the today commonplace position of much self-described "post-Marxism" if it always already defines itself as "Nietzschean." The author of *New Reflections on the Revolution of Our Time* (1990) blithely affirms that his own approach to political philosophy and to politics "is but the continuation of a multiple intellectual tradition which becomes manifest, for example, in a philosophy such as Nietzsche's."[19] Symptomatically for "our" times, however, such "post-Marxists" offer nothing remotely like a careful analysis of Nietzsche's work — a fact that does not preclude this particular author from claiming — in megalomaniac Nietzschean fashion — that his own brand of "post-Marxism" is not merely *"Nietzschean"* but is as a consequence poised to "reformulate the materialist programme in a *much* more radical way than was possible for Marx."[20] Far more radical, in any case, *either* than capitalism's — entirely predictable and reasonable — boast that communism has died once and for all *or* the — at least debatable — proposition that "real" socialism never existed in the first place (certainly a disastrous command economy has proven historically to be *one* socialist possibility) is neocapitalism's proleptic, preemptive strike against even the possibility that communism might ever exist in the future.

No single strike in human history is — potentially if not actually — more totalitarian, fascist, racist, sexist, classist, or national socialist than this arguably Nietzschean one. Any power of "postmodernism" and "postcontemporaneity" as analytic tools depends on their capacity to expose contemporary capitalism's own capacity to foreclose all significant *alternatives* to itself. As a consequence, even utopian visions — especially utopian visions — are no longer so readily informed by the possibility of transforming the repressive economic structures of global capital, whose self-representation becomes the ultimate "utopian" vision; rather, they become mere fantasies continuously recoded by, and into, the deformed but considerable pleasures of free-market consumerism and its concomitant cultures.[21] For its part, socialism can never rightly claim to have achieved what ought to be achieved and what Nietzsche categorically rejected: namely, proper communism. Any socialist claiming that socialism, when it is arrested in one country or region, *is* communism is an idiot or a criminal.[22] This is certainly not an argument against socialist-inspired revolution, nor a deprecation of the struggles to build communism by means of socialism under horrific internal and external pressures. Rather it is to say that communism is in principle dynamic and international — still the only major international ideology that might combat and destroy capitalism's patented brand of internationalism.[23]

It follows, then, that the more radical question than The Mekons' "How can something really be dead if it hasn't even happened?" is the question passed on by all great communists from Marx and Engels to Lenin, Trotsky, Luxemburg, Mao, Gramsci, and Althusser to us: How can something really be dead when it is supposed to happen in the future? The "higher phase of communist society," as envisioned by Marx in his late text, *Critique of the Gotha Program* (1875), comes only *after* "the enslaving subordination of the individual to the division of labor, and therewith also the antithesis between mental and physical labor. . . . " And he concludes: "only then can the narrow horizon of bourgeois right be crossed in its entirety and society inscribe on its banner: From each according to his ability, to each according to his needs!"[24] The current triumph of capital and the related if different power that is Nietzscheanism would be total and ineluctable if they can kill not merely all alternatives yesterday or today but also what might exist hypothetically or tomorrow. Then what Georges Bataille calls "Nietzsche's position," in tandem with the neocapitalist New World Order, would be "the ultimate (indeed perhaps the only) referent, the true ground of Being of our time." With Nietzsche and communism, two rival future-oriented systems collide; "synthesis" — at least for the time being — is neither possible nor desirable.

Note with regard to communism: It is likely impossible to be either "melancholic" and "fixated about" *or* in "mourning for" and "working through" a death that a priori is not allowed to exist even theoretically, let alone empirically. Even if communism *were* dead, it is still possible to *refuse* to "mourn" it, *refuse* to "work it through," even *refuse* to work at all.[25] It would still be possible and desirable to continue to "*act out*" communism's best features, especially if there are no better alternatives. This does not mean — thinking with William S. Burroughs of two basic traumas — that we necessarily "get beyond death and conception by reexperience any more than you get beyond heroin by ingesting larger and larger doses."[26] And Nietzsche is a *type* of H/Meth, arguably *the* major type of the post/narcotic "quiver between history and ontology."[27] The resulting Nietzschean text is precisely "immunopathological": that is, "fantasmatically producing antibodies against the auto-immune community it has established within itself (a within that is constantly leaking, running an exscription machine, exposed precisely to a contaminating 'outside')."[28] This text is designed to inculcate proleptically the notion that what has not yet lived precisely *can* be dead. But why and to what end? What precise functions might Nietzsche's immunopathological textual machine serve, and to whose short- and long-term benefit? Who can even ask such questions?

It is possible: Nietzsche's position might just *be* the only position outside of communism. Globally the most influential philosopher professionally *and* popularly since Plato, Aristotle, and Confucius — excluding perhaps Moses, Jesus, Buddha, Mohammed, Zoroaster (Zarathustra), and Marx for not being mainly philosophers — is Friedrich Nietzsche (1844–1900).

One need not accept this assertion (N.B.: first proclaimed by a right-wing historian at Nietzsche's funeral to inaugurate the twentieth century)[29] as true absolutely in order to recognize the historical and sociological truth that others accept it as true and act accordingly. As an experiment, take the thesis that "Nietzsche's position is the only one outside of communism" literally, on the principle that what is said either is or is not meant, either is or is not to be taken at its word. If, as Žižek and Jameson seem to concur, "nobody seriously considers possible alternatives to capitalism any longer,"[30] then what is most needed today is the point of view precisely of "nobody" — a point of view as old as Odysseus, as new as we can make it. In this sense the point of view of the book at hand is nobody's.

Strange as it may seem, both to grasp — *critically* — celebrations of the death of communism and to grasp — *positively* — the possibility of preparing a genuinely communist alternative to capitalism requires — as a necessary if insufficient condition — the grasp of Nietzsche and Nietz-scheanism. This multiple grasp cannot depend exclusively on empirical work, no matter how important that also is; theoretical grasp is supplementally required. In the resulting methodology, the term "grasp," like all keywords, is used advisedly. "An object cannot be defined by its immediately visible or sensuous appearance, it is necessary to make a detour via its concept in order to grasp it (*begreifen*, to grasp, *Begriff*, concept)."[31] By way of a linked series of more or less direct confrontations and detours, it is necessary to grasp — and thus to get "after" — the adversarial "objects" and "concepts" that are Nietzsche, Nietz-scheanism, and their interrelationship as the only position outside of communism.

Incorporation as Adversary

You run to me, run to me, run to me . . .
You try to fly but you cannot fly
You try to hide but I'm by your side
You run from me, run from me, run from me . . .
I am the adversary, I am the adversary
I am the ad-vers-ary . . .
I grow and grow and grow
Between ideals and fact,
Between the thought and the act,
You sink without trace . . .
Run to me, run to me, run to me
Try to run from me, run from me, run from me. . . . [32]

You better run, you better run and run and run . . .
You better run, you better run
You better run to the City of Refuge . . .
You'll be working in the darkness
Against your fellow man . . . [33]

. . . and the City of Refuge was *blueprinted* by Nietzsche, as were all paths running *to* and *from* it. . . . All blueprinting in the postmodern condition is difficult because the privileged arena of combat is no longer defined by nature and built environment exclusively, but by "architecture" combined with "video" — compressed together conceptually as "videodrome."[34] This is where the adversary Nietzsche hangs out today. Precisely because the blueprint of the Nietzschean "city" is so complex, it is both necessary and possible to describe it using *otherwise incompatible discourses.*

Required is the untimely attempt to grasp, to settle accounts with the uncanny phenomena of the endlessly attractive-repulsive adversary and paranoia that is Nietzsche's corps/e: that is, the living corpus of a dead man's work and the living corps of people it informs, incarnates, embodies, incorporates. "We all carry part of him within us"[35] — *unconsciously* as well as consciously. This possibility or fact was recognized already by 1904 and not nearly enough in the remainder of the century. Which means, however, that the adversary is expected to be among other things *us.* Nietzsche's may be the fundamental "hauntology" of our times: that is, the way Being conceals itself and ends history by haunting living beings who are more dead than they know.

"Incorporation," *Einverleibung,* and its several cognates was a key-term for Nietzsche himself in his attempt to disseminate what he called "my thought" — Eternal Recurrence of the Same. It was predicated, extraordinary to say, on the possibility that it would be surreptitiously *einverleibt* in the distant future, indeed millennia away, by people who would not necessarily ever have read a word of his writing.[36] Surely he would have agreed that "In order to be truly alive, philosophy cannot but contain light, sounds, energy, vibrations of the soul and the body: when all of these are weak, philosophy stops being the plan of a grand flight and becomes an academic discipline. . . . And if philosophy has a place of its own, it is not the mind alone: it is mind, heart, skin, cells, neurochemical receptors, senses."[37] The term "incorporation" "encompasses at once themes of *integration* — the integration of human life forces into the larger-than-human systems of social and technical organization; as well as the finer-grained processes of *embodiment* — those strategies through which human life combines with, and assimilates, the minute, shifting, often invisible patterns and rhythms of the concrete historical milieus within which it unfolds."[38] Incorporation also can mean cannibalism — the literal and figurative ritual communion involving ingesting one's own or one's others.[39] Noting the link between cells in biology and politics, David Cronenberg remarks, "An institution is really like an organism, a multi-celled animal in which the people are the cells. The very word 'corporation' means body."[40] And of course "incorporation" is a concept in economics, having its *economic-corporate* mode.[41] So it is that the Nietzsche Industry, Inc. has long been an incorporation in the *economic* sense as well, producing and reproducing the fetishized commodity "Nietzsche" for capitalist markets and for capital. No book is exempt from this rule.

"Incorporation" need not refer to conscious processes; indeed just as often it operates unconsciously. Antonin Artaud — a particularly astute Nietzschean, who developed his "theater of cruelty" from a theory of "contagion" along properly Nietzschean lines — observed in 1938: "I will not say that philosophical systems must be applied directly and immediately: but of the following alternatives, one must be true: Either these systems are within us and permeate our being to the point of supporting life itself (and if this is the case, what use are books?), or they do *not* permeate us and therefore do not have the capacity to support life (and in this case what does their disappearance matter?)."[42] But, with regard to politico-philosophical "incorporation," Nietzsche's corps/e must be grasped not merely as protopostmodern but as post-Socratic and post-Platonic, even Hegelian. Finally, because the body is radically finite, incorporation can be exceedingly painful,[43] although the immediate physical pain of embodiment can also be repressed, deferred until later, or displaced and savored as pleasure.

In his extraordinary analysis of the trial of Socrates in his *Lectures on the History of Philosophy*, Hegel argued that the reason Socrates consented to drink the hemlock was that the Athenians were ironically punishing, in effect cannibalizing, "an element that was their own."[44] In his *Lectures on the Philosophy of History*, Hegel described the moment Socrates was condemned to death as follows: "the sentence bears on the one hand the aspect of unimpeachable rectitude — inasmuch as the Athenian people condemns its deadliest foe — but on the other hand, that of a deeply tragic character, inasmuch as the Athenians had to make the discovery, that what they reprobated in Socrates had already struck firm root among themselves [bei ihnen schon festen Wurzel gefaßt hat], and that they must be pronounced guilty or innocent with him."[45] Hegel is quite precisely describing before the fact *Nietzsche's* incorporative, cannibalizing *intent for and influence on* contemporary and postcontemporary culture. Which includes "even" (read: most especially) the Nietzschean "Left." Not necessarily just as Nietzsche might have wished, of course, but often good enough.

For their part, in Hegel's crucial analysis, the Greeks themselves came to realize only later, and then at best partially, that the Socratic principle of subjective freedom, on which the next stage of history was predicated, had already been *incorporated* into the Athenian public sphere, with the result that the latter was in properly tragic fashion being disintegrated and virused from within by the power of thought over mere practice. This thought subsequently rose to ever higher levels of historical self-consciousness and self-realization, culminating definitively in the Hegelian system. "Socrates" thus became in ancient Greece — at the imagined incept date of Western philosophical culture — a biological organ, a pineal eye of the body politic (to speak Bataillese), about which, ironically enough, it is impossible to have fully self-reflective, transcendental knowledge. The Hegelian Socrates thus was the first to authorize the bourgeois thesis that "Bodies may be governed, but embodiment is the phenomenological basis of individuality."[46] The principle of sub-rosa incorporation, according to Hegel, "constitutes the content of *all* subsequent history," and is the reason that "the later philosophers withdrew themselves from the affairs of the State, restricted themselves to cultivating their inner world, separated off from themselves the universal aim of the moral culture of the people, and took up a position contrary to the spirit of Athens and the Athenians."[47] *This,* then, was the Socratic, Platonic, and premodern paradigm of *incorporation* — as directly or indirectly mediated through Hegel — that, after having passed through Machiavelli's Renaissance, the political philosophy of Nietzsche would later emulate.[48]

Hegel's analysis of the trial of Socrates — and *mutatis mutandis* the entire legacy of *philosophia perennis* — provides a key to unlocking the Nietzschean corps/e. "Socrates" was for the Athenians, and for the subsequent philosophical legacy of Greece, at once a corpus of works — as his words began to be written down and reworked by Plato — and a corpse kept alive by and as a corps which, by reading and rewriting him, embodied him, knowingly or unknowingly, exoterically and esoterically. In the Hegelian view, the Platonic Socrates was the *first* modern political philosopher precisely because he was the first incorporative esotericist. And this thesis could be confirmed by going directly to Plato's account of the trial of Socrates.[49] By analogy, Friedrich Nietzsche was the *last* modern political philosopher. Strictly speaking, Martin Heidegger's was not a political *philosophy* but a political *ontology*. According to Nietzsche's plan, *we* were to be—may actually be—*his* corps/e. And thus not his adversary after all, but his friend or lover.

What is—or ought to be—particularly disturbing today is the hegemonic, *Heideggerian* version of Nietzschean "incorporation," a version that has been too innocently imbibed by hermeneuts and deconstructors alike. Heidegger's profound affinity with Nietzsche has to do with the way the principle of *Einverleibung* (incorporation or embodiment), which both men saw in post/Christian terms, was not merely *thematized* but *rhetorically actualized* in *Thus Spoke Zarathustra*. Specifically at stake is Eternal Recurrence of the Same. In 1937 Heidegger argued of this thought: "What is embodied or incorporated [das Einverleibte] is that which makes the body—the bodying—strong, sure, and erect, and is simultaneously that by means of which we have become complete and that which conditions us in the future, the juice from which we draw our strengths. The incorporation or embodiment of [Nietzsche's] thought means in this regard: to complete the thinking of the thought in such a way that it becomes *in advance the fundamental* position with regard to beings *in their totality* and as such is hegemonic [durchherrscht] *in every individual thought*. Only when the thought has become the *fundamental* stance of *all* thinking is it then, in *conformity* with its essence, taken into *possession*, in-corporated [in Besitz genommen, ein-verleibt]."[50] These hyperbolic phrases are nothing if not also *totalitarian*—with strong undercurrents that are masculinist, phallocentric, fascoid, and capitalist. Heidegger was fairly explicit that his own take on Nietzschean incorporation must be further incorporated into *our* physical bodies projected onto death. *These* bodies as we write and read.

In his *Arts de faire* (arts of making, 1974), former Jesuit priest, historian, ethnologist, and student of everyday life Michel de Certeau paraphrases "the voice of the Law" in a way that also describes what can be called The Law of Nietzsche's Corps/e: " 'Give me your body and I will give you meaning, I will make you a name and a word in my discourse.' " De Certeau continues, "the law would have no power if it were not able to support itself on the obscure desire to exchange one's flesh for a glorious body, to be written, even if it means dying, and to be transformed into a recognized word."[51] The corps/e is today a common theme in the visual arts in their turn to masochism and abjection.[52] But in philosophy the "recognized word" is "*Nietzsche's corps/e*." In his *Ethics* Spinoza had entertained the thought that "There is no reason, which compels me to maintain that a body does not die, unless it becomes a corpse; nay, experience would seem to point in the opposite direction."[53] *In fine:* the core of the corps as corpse; the core of the corpse as corps. Ghost in the machine. *Esprit de corps.*

It may come as a surprise that Nietzsche did not necessarily reject the notion of "life after death." As he formulated the problem privately: "*Life after* death. — Whoever has grounds for believing in his 'life after death' must learn to bear his 'death' during his life."[54] The weight of this aphorism is equally distributed on its two halves. Not only is this an admonition to bear one's suffering — including one's "little deaths" — in life stoically, "like a man"; it is also a way of thereby shaping one's "life after death." Nietzsche pursued this train of thought further: "You believe in your 'life after death'? Then you must learn during your life *to be dead.*"[55] Nietzsche's works are letters addressed from the dead to the living. In his notes while composing *Thus Spoke Zarathustra,* the word *Einverleibung* appears in one context especially. Zarathustra's overall goal is to induce readers to "incorporate opposites" that are depicted in the text, with the specific aim of instilling in readers the notion that all "human beings are only practice runs" in his "monstrous project" to "show the sacrifices [or victims: *Opfer*] that are necessary . . . to breed . . . the higher man."[56]

The subtitle of *Zarathustra, A Book for Everyone and No One,* is crucial to Nietzsche's construction or "breeding" of the modern and postmodern self.[57] On the one hand self must appear to be liberatory to and for "everyone" or what Heidegger calls "Anyone" (*das Man*) — in spite and because of its being couched in a rhetoric that is Janus-faced: that is, often only "appearing" to be stridently elitist so that readers can think that it can be easily "deconstructed." This is an enormously powerful rhetorical strategy since it gives the appearance of empowering "every" reader as self-reflective and self-reflexive transcendental subject and agent. On the other hand, however, Nietzsche intended his writing to have an effect and affect that lies much deeper and is "authentic" or at least radically different. His elitism could not *logically* be a theme of his writing merely, it had also to be a rhetorical strategy. In his subtitle he indicated the existence of this other mode of self in negative terms for "those in the know" (Machiavelli) in saying that *Zarathustra* was also for "no one." This "other" mode of self was produced in such a way as to be "present" to readers "out of the know" only unconsciously, subliminally, subcutaneously — so as to control and manipulate their thoughts and actions as far as possible. So it is that a properly esoteric, intentional, "political" self and agent is produced by Nietzsche as supplement to the "phenomenological" or "existential" self and agent that is exoterically produced. Again, this is *not* to say that Nietzsche was entirely successful in producing exactly the political and social effects he had in mind; this *is* to argue that he may have been comparatively successful in ways that — logically and by definition — no reader could ever know for sure.

According to a dominant Western tradition, the human "self" — formerly *psyche* or soul — is imaged as a "center" articulating "subject" and "agent." From this self *centripetal* and *centrifugal* forces flow: "subject" invoking internal or psychological processes, and "agent" signaling the issues of practice and ethico-political intervention in history. This metaphor can be charted with the help of Spinoza's thesis that there are "two enemies" of the human race on the plane of immanence: "Hatred and Repentance."[58] As paraphrased by Gilles Deleuze, "all the ways of humiliating and breaking life, all the forms of the negative have two sources, one turned *outward* and the other *inward,* resentment and bad conscience, hatred and guilt."[59] Nietzsche's powerful attacks against *ressentiment* are obviously directly related to this analysis, but what is unrelated is his affirmation of hatred for many kinds of people. Nowadays, in technocultural terms, humankind is arriving into a videodrome — perhaps morphing into a new cyborg self — that is at once "beyond good and evil" and yet one in which we are uncannily and sometimes murderously very much at home. In and against this arena the Nietzschean self is constitutive of modernity and postmodernity alike as their unstated tertium quid. In much of the Western tradition, the human subject has been commonly held to be more a *limit* than a *part* of the world. In his *Tractatus-Logico-Philosophicus* (1921), for example, Ludwig Wittgenstein adopts Arthur Schopenhauer's thesis that the subject or I — including its perceiving eye — is never itself an object of experience. For Schopenhauer, "We never know it, but it is precisely that which knows wherever there is knowledge."[60] For Wittgenstein, the I and eye are extensionless points: "The subject does not belong to the world but it is a limit of the world. . . . From nothing *in the field of sight* can it be concluded that it is seen from an eye."[61] For its part, the Nietzschean self (eye and I) can appear to be a single — albeit self-deconstructing — subject, to adapt essentially one subject-position, while in fact several are "interpellated" or "hailed" (Althusser). Alternatively, several subjects or subject-positions can be constructed in the illusion, say, of democratic pluralism, while in fact only one Self is ever actually being produced sub rosa. Nietzsche thought himself to be influenced in his theory of self–subject–agent by Spinoza; and Deleuze has accepted this belief at face value, claiming that Nietzsche is the quintessential post/modern Spinozist philosopher. Yet in fact Spinoza (*pace* Deleuze) was in *no* sense proto-Nietzschean, ideologically speaking. The great political problem posed by Spinoza is why people consent to, even fight to the death for, their own oppression — branding this self-destructive willingness "superstition." Spinoza sought to *destroy* such superstition, Nietzsche to *exploit* it. As Étienne Balibar has pointed out, Spinoza's formula is "surprising" because "this inversion of the natural *conatus* [energy, striving] of individuals goes so far as to give substance, in the fury of mass movements of the desire for their own death, to self-destruction."[62] If the Spinozist anomaly is savage, it is because "it is the radical expression of a historic transgression of every ordering that is not freely constituted by the masses; it is the proposition of a horizon of freedom that is definable only as a horizon of liberation."[63] Nietzsche — who is an "anomaly" no longer but part of our second nature — is also "savage" but against the masses in his willingness to induce some of the multitude to will their own self/destruction. Hence a philosophically coherent and politically emancipatory philosophy must forge its way *back* to Spinoza *past* the Nietzschean self and only then, through communism, *into* the future.

Nietzsche's gradually-to-be-incorporated thought of Eternal Recurrence of the Same is thus intended to "break humanity in two" by keeping slaves out of the know, elites in the know — a polarization that is increasingly global.[64] While writing *Thus Spoke Zarathustra*, Nietzsche codified his doctrine of incorporation into a single abstract phrase, understating but implying the human cost involved: "All beings [are] only rehearsals in the unification (incorporation) of opposites."[65] In Nietzsche's terms, to *read* and/or *rewrite* his corpus may also mean to *be* dead as the incorporation of his corpse, whether one knows it or not. Like his ancient Greeks (e.g., Pindar), Nietzsche believed that one lives on in the hearts and minds of those who would speak about him and, most especially, think his thoughts without being aware *that* they are thinking his thoughts. When Nietzsche's reader has most thoroughly incorporated a thought as he desired, then the thought will not appear to stem from Nietzsche at all, but rather be the reader's own. As Nietzsche put this principle in a private, unpublished collection of short aphorisms entitled "On the Doctrine of Style" (1882): "The more abstract the truth is that one wants to teach, the more one must first seduce the *senses* to it. . . . It is not well-mannered and clever to take away the easier objections of one's readers in advance. It is well-mannered and *very clever* to allow one's readers *themselves to utter* our ultimate wisdom."⁶⁶ Nietzsche is the ultimate adversary of communists because he designed his writing subliminally to program his readers to act in ways and for a single ultimate purpose that in theory they (we) can never fully grasp, and that works against the best interests of most of them (us). This goal includes especially the "death" of communism: that is, the perception, if not yet fact, that something that *never* existed, *could* not exist, is *dead*.

Let the dead bury their own dead, indeed; and if they cannot do the job, the trick, then let the living do it for them — but on *living* terms.⁶⁷ But to bury Nietzsche is not going to be easy, perhaps not possible. It requires hard labor — labor of the kind defined by Marx as "the living, form-giving fire; it is the transitoriness of things, their temporality, as their formation by living time."⁶⁸ It also requires hard combat of a particular kind: namely, "to imagine and explore seemingly fantastic potentials in any situation, while at the same time giving equal consideration to prosaic and practical aspects," to develop "an attitude at once probing and impersonal, remote and alert."⁶⁹ In postindustrial times, however, the problem in grasping or combating the Nietzschean adversary is that "he" has become android, a "psychoplasmic brood" or "avatar," in senses to be developed eventually. Nietzsche's readers were always already supposed to become what they look at, but never actually see. In *this* sense, "Nietzsche" *is* TV and its mass-media equivalents. He *is* the latest hardware on which national and transnational economies and militaries depend: including interfacial, high-definition TV or HDTV.⁷⁰ Which is also to say that Nietzsche is an "influencing machine" (Victor Tausk) — the technological medium of television that uses "psychology in reverse" (Leo Lowenthal and Theodor W. Adorno) in order to reproduce "totalitarian creeds even if the explicit surface message . . . may be antitotalitarian."[71] Similarly, since today architecture and audiovisualizing media are related, Nietzsche might seem to be not only TV but L.A. As such, he requires "excavation" as well as just "viewing." Not only is Nietzsche a "mass medium," he is — like Davis's City of Quartz, the mass-media capital of the world and of terrible socioeconomic polarity — an "architecture of the future."[72] That is, he is an uncanny "city of refuge" that is already "everywhere," in part thanks to the electronic media. Nietzsche, too, "dreams of becoming infinite," and, as a "shape of things to come," he is "a mirror of capitalism's future."[73] More precisely put: If L.A. displays "the paradox of the first 'postindustrial' city in its preindustrial guise,"[74] then Nietzsche displays the paradoxes of the major *premodern* philosopher in *postmodern* drag, even though he can equally well appear in *modernist* disguises when the need arises.

But all claims about "Nietzsche" being simply synonymous with technoculture or its various sites need to be made precise. As Jonathan Crary has noted — in a scathing criticism of the theoretical tendency that joyfully embraces postmodern, postcontemporary technoculture as having achieved the "decisive exceeding of modernity" — it is "striking how much critical writing on virtual reality [VR], cyberspace, and interactive computer networks is riddled with enduring myths of modernization."[75] "Generalizing language of the following sort is depressingly pervasive: 'In the near future we may all be on-line.' Beyond the curt and brutal exclusions of the words 'we' and 'all,' this class of statement, in its sweeping untruth, resonates with both a complacent faith in the certainty of modernization and a banal anticipation of its posthistorical fulfillment" (p. 59). Such thoughts are exactly what capitalism — late or other — always wants the world to think. In point of global fact, "much of the preoccupation with VR and cyberspace is merely a sign that we are at another of those recurring moments in the twentieth century when one of the masks of political failure and paralysis is an eager avowal of the transformative force and cultural centrality of technological innovation" (p. 59). For the vast majority of the world's population in the immediate or even distant future, the event — or hope and fear — of being "on-line" is not merely premature but likely *impossible*. At a time when other kinds of attempt to subtend

Nietzsche to a technocultural problematic are already well under way, it is particularly important to argue that his work is *also* one of the many masks of political failure and paralysis. Merely to equate Nietzsche with HDTV, VR, or L.A. and leave it at that is to mask in particular the fact that what is most characteristic of the global situation is not reducible to *any* technological innovation. Instead it is part and parcel of "an intensifying process of global *polarization,* segregation, and impoverishment" — all of which is visible not only in political and economic terms but also "in the phenomenon of radically dissimilar perceptual and cognitive lifeworlds" (p. 59; emphasis added). And precisely here it is crucial to show that Nietzsche was a firm and consistent advocate of nothing so much as *polarization* in all walks and modes of life. Witness his persistent, seductive appeal to archaic notions of "pathos of distance" (*Pathos der Distanz*) and "order of rank" (*Rangordnung*). Nietzschean polarization thus overrides any distinction not only between the postmodern and the modern but also between them and the premodern. But polarization also opens up the possibility, the necessity, of struggle. As Negri has interpreted Marx on "catastrophism":

Capitalist growth may indeed urge the compression of its quantity, it can indeed multiply the productive force of labor, but after all the surplus value that can be extorted is limited: there is still the rigidity of necessary labor (necessary part of the labor day) to constitute the limit to valorization. . . . [T]he quantity of value of the necessary part of the working day is *not only* more and more rigid but also tends towards higher values and therefore tends to diminish — subjectively, actively — the surplus labor that can be extorted. The sum of necessary labor is rigid and it is precisely on this rigidity that are based the possibilities for a higher valorization on the part of the class, *for a self-valorization of the working class and the proletariat.* In sum, for this Marx, the devaluation of labor power, in that it is a compression of the necessary part of the labor day, not only is not indefinite, but is, on the contrary, limited and reversible. Necessary labor can valorize itself autonomously, the world of needs can and must expand. There emerges an aspect of the law of the tendency of the profit rate to decline which combines the proportionality of the decrease of value of capital with the independent valorization of the proletariat. The law of the tendency to decline represents, therefore, one of the most lucid Marxist intuitions of the intensification *of the class struggle* in the course of capitalist development.[76]

17

Bearing Crary's caveat and Negri's hope in mind, the possibility and plausibility of a link between — modern and premodern — philosophy and — postmodern — technoculture makes it possible to theorize a link between the "death" of communism and the triumph of Nietzschean-ism. The first link is suggested by remarks of Jameson: "in the new dimensionality of postmodern cultural space, ideas of the older conceptual type have lost their autonomy and become something like by-products and after-images flung up on the screen of the mind and of social production by the culturalization of daily life. The dissolution of philosophy today then reflects this modification in the status of ideas (and ideology), which itself retroactively unmasks any number of traditional philosophical 'concepts' as having been just such consciousness-symptoms all the while, that could not be identified as such in the culturally impoverished, pre-media, and residually 'natural' human societies (or modes of production) of the past. . . . Or are we to draw the more sober conclusion that all abstract philosophical concepts were always 'media concepts' in some deeper way without our being aware of it?"[77] This critical probe is salutary at a time when even revolutionary Marxists are speaking of "the general deflation of philosophy that is so striking a feature of late twentieth-century intellectual life"[78] — as if the real question were ever the "dissolution," "deflation," or "inflation" of something called "philosophy," as opposed to its many, more or less perceptible, sociocultural embodiments.[79] Jameson's line of inquiry is also salutary at a time when a defining feature of postmodernism is increasingly becoming the conflation of "high" or "avant-garde philosophy" with "popular" or "junk culture"; or, more exactly stated, at a time when philosophy in the form of *Nietzscheanism* is being incorporated into junk culture in high-tech alloys such as "Avant-Pop." It goes without saying that, were he physically alive today, Nietzsche would likely wax indignant *against* junk culture, much as he did against the nascent culture industry of his late nineteenth century.[80] It *also* ought to go without saying, however, that secretly he desired nothing more than to see his *own* version of high philosophy and social transformation occupying — prophylactically when not aggressively — every nook and cranny of all *possible* future societies and cultures.

Just as it is crucial to bring problems concerning the definition and periodization of Nietzsche/anism up to technocultural and technosocial speed, however, it is important to keep open the question of how "new" this speed actually is, how "postmodern" and "postcontemporary" the future capitalist mode of production is really. The thesis that a postindustrial, postideological economy is totally, globally, irreversibly superseding the hammer of traditional industry and the sickle of agriculture has long been a right-wing argument (e.g., Daniel Bell in the early 1970s).[81] As such it tends to serve, either immediately or as a kind of self-fulfilling prophecy, the interests of late or neocapitalism. It seems at least theoretically possible — not to mention politically vital — to argue that what is happening around the world may be less a postindustrial break with the past than the continuing industrialization of premodern, precapitalist enclaves. Nonetheless, in the words of Fourth-International communist Ernest Mandel (writing at the same time as Bell), "industrialization of the sphere of reproduction constitutes the apex" of late or neocapitalist development.[82] For Mandel, the incept date of "late capitalism" was the immediate postwar period (1945), the ending of the "long wave" of postwar economic expansion occurred with the "second slump" (1974–1975), and he warned against overestimating the multinational component of contemporary capitalism at the cost of underestimating continuing interimperialist rivalries. But for Mandel, as paraphrased by Davis, the "hypertrophic expansion of the financial sector is not a new, higher stage of capitalism — even in America speculators cannot go on endlessly building postmodernist skyscrapers for other speculators to buy — but a morbid symptom of the financial overaccumulation prolonged by the weakness of the U.S. labor movement and productive capital's fear of a general collapse"; finally, "the crucial point about contemporary capitalist structures of accumulation [is] that they are symptoms of global crisis, not signs of the triumph of capitalism's irresistible drive to expand."[83] Davis's own position with regard to Mandel's thesis — at least during the mid-1980s — highlights the way momentary upturns in the economy — Reaganomics and the Contract with America — "dramatically accelerated the transformation of American hegemony away from a Fordist or mass-consumption pattern" and toward a general global drift of capital in three directions at once: (1) "interest incomes, with the resultant strengthening of a neo-rentier bloc reminiscent of the speculative capitalism of the 1920s"; (2) "volatile high-profit sectors like military production and financial services"; and (3) "the virtually systematic dislocation of dominant trade relationships and capitalist-flows, as the locus of accumulation in new technologies has been displaced from Atlantic to Pacific circuits of capital."[84]

Actually, *both* lines of argument can be applied to Nietzsche and Nietzscheanism. The philosophical *ur-rentier* Nietzsche grasped and attempted to harness manifestations of capitalist imperialism better than he was able to appreciate more complex aspects of political economy. (Though Nietzsche was quite interested in the latter as well, mainly through repeated reading of the work of Henry Charles Carey, the American political economist, protectionist, and "harmonizer," who also surfaces in Marx's *Grundrisse, Capital,* and *Theories of Surplus-Value.*) Partly as cause, partly as consequence of this in/ability, Nietzsche's personal tastes in terms of philosophy, culture, economics, and politics ran much more to the premodern than to the modern—let alone postmodern. But his strategies of *writing* political philosophy were quite modern in the incorporative sense developed in Hegel's analysis of the death of Socrates. As for Nietzscheanism today, it is a global phenomenon played out in the changing and crisis-fraught arena described by Davis. Yet things are more complicated than this, if for no other reason than because, "from the first moment to the last, the lonely hour of the 'last instance' never comes."[85]

It is also important to stress that if Nietzsche's corps/e can be located, however roughly, within the—perhaps ultimately morbid but still remarkably resilient and rambunctious—reproductive cultural and philosophical systems of capitalism, then this is partly because Nietzsche himself had bridged significant conceptual gaps between the premodern and the postmodern. He did so with modernist strategies, tactics, and flair of communication and incorporation. These have gone undetected by his modernist and postmodernist readers alike. And for this reason what is required is, in part, a resolutely *negative* act. Visually and conceptually speaking, it is an act of radical exposure to illuminate the more darkly concealed, palimpsest "TV" and "L.A."—and thus "spectacular" and "everyday"—Nietzsche, at least for the world's powerful minority. This visual metaphoric of spotlighting something otherwise hidden in darkness must be substantially complicated; but it is best to admit up front that this book is pro-"Enlightenment"—and hence also Euro- and technocentric—*in its way.* But this way is ultimately extratextual. That is, if this way is ever going to be built, it entails collective, communal work and global recreation of a kind that texts by themselves can at best only assist in promoting, and that the world hardly knows yet. Thanks, in not insignificant part, to the very dangerous and ubiquitous adversary here called "Nietzsche/anism."

Nietzsche/anism as Concept (Spinoza)

The concept is an incorporeal, even though it is incarnated or effectuated in bodies.[86]

"Nietzsche/anism" designates a problematic relational structure, not an essence simply. But to speak this way — "against essentialism" — is all too common currency today. What is crucial to identify is the specific *kind* of relation involved.[87] To reemploy a key distinction drawn by Henri Lefebvre, the relation is not "bipartite." It is not as if two opposing terms — here "Nietzsche" and "Nietzscheanism" — ought to be bathed in some mutual illumination, "so that each becomes a signifier instead of remaining obscure or hidden." Rather, the relation in Nietzsche/anism is closer to what Lefebvre, borrowing from musicology, terms a "formant," whereby two terms "imply one another *and* conceal one another."[88] The shift implied here from an essentially visual problematic — the in/visible — to an even harder-to-detect aural problematic — in/audibility — is required to grasp the full power and multiplex spatiotemporality of Nietzsche's philosophemes and ideologemes. Nietzsche's abiding fascination with Richard Wagner has much to do with "formant" in the musicological sense. Lefebvre further suggests that when interrogating formant relationships it is insufficient merely to locate their empirical existence or to theorize them in the abstract. Rather, it is necessary to push on to ask: "where does a relationship reside when it is not being actualized in a highly determined situation? How does it await its moment? In what state does it exist until an action of some kind makes it effective?" (p. 401). And when Lefebvre speaks of the formant as a relational structure in which two or more terms simultaneously "imply" and yet also "conceal" one another, he has in mind the theoretical and empirical requirement not passively to find ready-made but actively to *produce* "things/not-things" or "concrete abstractions" (p. 402). For Hegel, this was *der Begriff*: concept, notion, grasp. For Marx, turning idealism on its head, the role of *der*

Begriff tended to be played by *die Ware* or commodity because it, as both use- and exchange-value, simultaneously "embodies" and "conceals" social relations and modes of production. Which it does in exemplary fashion at the precise intersection of economics, society, and culture. In this sense, then, Nietzsche/anism itself qualifies not only as a set of philological and social incorporations — though it clearly is these — but also as a formant, a thing/not-thing, a concrete abstraction, a concept . . . and a commodity.[89]

For his part, Nietzsche was "Hegelian" (even "Lefebvrean") at least in his concern with incorporation and in the matter of *der Begriff.* In his notebooks he wrote that philosophers "must no longer merely permit themselves to accept concepts as gifts [die Begriffe nicht mehr sich nur schenken lassen], merely purifying and polishing them, but rather first of all *make* them, *create* them, present them and render them convincing [zu ihnen überreden]. Hitherto one has generally trusted one's concepts, as if they were a wondrous *dowry* [*Mitgift*] from some sort of wonderland. . . . " This passage is cited approvingly near the beginning of Deleuze and Guattari's last cooperative book, *What Is Philosophy?* (1991). Indeed, their answer to the question "What is philosophy?" is: "To create concepts that are always new."[90] ("We can at least see what philosophy is not: it is not contemplation, reflection, or communication" [p. 6].) But in the process of citing Nietzsche's text verbatim, the two Nietzscheans suddenly stop, choosing instead to "paraphrase" — that is, *incorporate* — the continuation of his argument. They go on: "but trust must be replaced by distrust, and philosophers must distrust most those concepts they did not create themselves (Plato was fully aware of this, even though he taught the opposite)" (pp. 5–6). But this is not quite what Nietzsche said. Generally speaking, to paraphrase him is not merely to say something slightly different from what he openly said — *all* paraphrase does this — but also potentially to incorporate unwittingly something *else* he said between the lines. Actually, the last part of this notebook text breaks down, as his notebooks frequently do, under a certain pressure. Often it is the pressure of coming dangerously close to putting in print what ought not to be uttered. His text ends: "At first what is necessary is absolute skepticism with regard to all inherited concepts (as *may* have been possessed once by One philosopher — Plato: naturally [he] *taught the opposite*—— ——)." Exactly here Nietzsche's text stutters, becomes unintelligible.[91] Whenever one's handwriting breaks down completely—becomes illegible to others or to oneself—this is not necessarily by chance, nor necessarily *un*consciously motivated. It is this breakdown that is smoothed over by Deleuze and Guattari's paraphrase. They *trust* Nietzsche, who gives them their basic definition of philosophy as the creation of new concepts. But why, returning to Nietzsche's elided words, is it *"natural"* that perhaps the "One" philosopher before Nietzsche would have "taught the opposite" of what that philosopher believed: that is, only give off the *appearance* of skepticism with regard to all inherited concepts. Plausibly, because Plato had some hidden agenda in mind that neither he nor Nietzsche is going to state publicly. If so, what is this agenda in Plato and Nietzsche? Plausibly, it has something to do with a shared elitism with regard to *politics*. In this context, Nietzsche's attack against Plato's *metaphysics* is *too* well known. And it has to do with the concomitant requirement to speak simultaneously to those both "in the know" and "out of the know." This requirement logically entails the subliminal incorporation of concepts, as emerges between the lines— with Hegel's help—from Plato's depiction of the death of Socrates and its transformative effect on Athenian society. But then it would also follow *against* Deleuze and Guattari, that if we are philosophers in their Nietzschean sense, then among the newly created concepts we must *most* distrust are those created by *Nietzsche*. His gifts would be always poisoned. The trust Nietzsche most *betrayed* is *ours:* namely, our trust that the object of philosophy—its joy and its terror, as Deleuze and Guattari say—is the creation of concepts that are always new, when in fact Nietzsche's concepts were created to serve surreptitiously ideological interests and agendas that are premodern, *archaic.* Nevertheless, this book is *itself* Nietzschean in the Deleuze-Guattarian sense that it, too, must *create* the concept of "Nietzsche/anism"—in order to expose Nietzsche's *radical* betrayal of philosophy and trust.

In *What Is Philosophy?* Deleuze and Guattari proceed to argue that a concept has "three inseparable components: possible world, existing face, and real language or speech."[92] Translating this thesis, it can be said that the concept "Nietzsche/anism" is the product of two subconcepts: (1) "Nietzscheanism"—the reception and appropriation of Nietzsche, pro and contra—defined as Nietzsche's "existing face," *plus* (2) "Nietzsche"—the man and his work—defined as what Nietzscheanism commonly imagines to be—but is not—his "real language or speech." "Nietzsche/anism," then, is the overdetermined, created concept of a "possible world." As such, still within the Deleuze-Guattarian metaphoric, Nietzsche/anism may often appear "incorporeal, even though it is incarnated or effectuated in bodies" (p. 21). Nonetheless (now paraphrasing Althusser and Balibar), philosophy defined as "the production of concepts" never occurs — wholly — in isolation but — eventually if not immediately — "as class struggle in the specific element of theory."[93] And so it is with the concept — the possible world — of "Nietzsche/anism."

To be more precise, using the language of traditional metaphysics, it is not that "Nietzsche" is *real* whereas "Nietzscheanism" is *possible* or vice versa. According to this position, the task would be to "rescue" against "misinterpretation" and "misappropriation" the "true" or "real" Nietzsche from *other* interpreters and appropriators — producing an endless, irresolvable debate about what he "really meant." And analysis, as Freud knew, is interminable. This debate about Nietzsche and analysis of his work have been particularly futile to date because most readers basically *trust* him. Alternatively, the question of the "real" or "true" Nietzsche would be presented as *itself* false or inadequate, a mere possibility. It is replaced — or rather displaced — by another, not radically different, question about which *interpretation* or *appropriation* is more real or possible, no longer with regard to Nietzsche's intentions, but to current or future historical contingencies, social conjunctures, and so forth. Yet it is still assumed that Nietzsche himself, who is still cited and/or whose authority is taken for granted, stands behind this move. These two positions often exist in mixed form. For example, a dominant consensus holds — more or less a priori — that Nietzsche's intentions — to the rare extent that these are reconstructed painstakingly if at all — indicate that he was a radically polysemous thinker, and *therefore* that all *possible* interpretations and appropriations are, in theory at least, equally *real*. Against this problematic of traditional metaphysics, accept the proposal (stemming from Henri Bergson as read by Deleuze via Leibniz and especially Spinoza)[94] that the constitutive metaphysical distinction between the *real* and the *possible* ought to be recalled in favor of a distinction between the *actual* and the *virtual* — both of which, however, are held to be real, or rather different modes of the Real. This relationship is at once temporal and spatial. Whereas the possible, by definition, is imagined to be not real but can be actual — in the sense of *contemporary* — the virtual may not be actual — in the same sense — and nonetheless quite real. (Following a bon mot of Marcel Proust, Deleuze defines the virtual as "real without being actual, ideal without being abstract.")[95] Applied to the cases of Nietzsche/anism, this means that "Nietzsche" and "Nietzscheanism" remain at once *actual* and *virtual:* Virtual Reality. In other words, "he" is both a virtuality that can always be actualized in the present as well as real in the past, in "memory." Alternatively, "he" is at the same time a contemporary actuality that is always poised to become realized in the future — as Nietzscheanism.

When it is working correctly Nietzsche/anism has nothing to do with new *possibilities*. Everything has *always already* been said, but we *think* otherwise. The task here is to shatter this paradigm. The result is less a *book* than an *actual-virtuality* contesting that of Nietzsche/anism.

As a nonbipartite relational structure or formant, the concept "Nietzsche/anism" also "cannot be thought within the category *subject*," if the latter term is understood either as some imagined agency existing outside of social and historical determinations or as a completely unified, noncontradictory totality.[96] (For this reason, the agent-as-author of this book is mostly irrelevant and will seldom speak *as* author.)[97] "Nietzsche/anism" and "Nietzsche's corps/e" have nothing ultimately to do with any Cartesian or metaphysical dualism; the constitutive principle involved is sooner a type of materialist monism of a certain Spinozist stamp.[98] Formulated in Spinozist terms, the concept "Nietzsche/anism" compresses into an ugly neologism something more ungainly still: namely, the problem of the *causal* relationship between Nietzsche's original intention and the subsequent appropriation of his works by Nietzscheans and others. The precise mechanism of articulation between Nietzsche and Nietzscheanism is surprisingly undertheorized and invisible in the vast field of Nietzsche studies.[99] To really think causality as it applies to the adversary called Nietzsche/anism requires appeal through Louis Althusser to Benedict de Spinoza.

For Spinoza, the notion of causation is not necessarily, if at all, a *temporal* relation but rather a *logical* one. This means that, as important as historical, sociological, *or* ideological perspectives may be to grasp Nietzsche/anism in part, they are ultimately inadequate to grasp its distinctive logic, its power to replicate itself in virtually any contingency. Nietzschean/ism is less a phenomenon of history than *trans*historical: "neither historical, nor eternal," but existing across space and time "nomadically."[100] Logic cannot be *reduced* to history, sociology, or ideology, even though its modes and effects are obviously *conditioned* by such pressures. Nor does any "new historical" perspective help ultimately, either; all more or less historicistic approaches, whether provided by "interdisciplinarity" or by "cultural studies," only defer addressing the problems posed by logic.

"Nietzscheanism" is always already contained in "Nietzsche." The basic general equation remains "Nietzsche + Nietzscheanism = Nietzsche/anism," though it, too, will have to be rendered more complicated and nuanced. Imagined to exist (in Spinozist terminology) as the continuing presence of a cause *indwelling* "his" effects, "Nietzsche" exists not as something hidden beneath or invisible outside "his" manifestations, but rather as the mobile structuring and incorporating relation within, and of, these more or less visible and audible manifestations themselves — present in them but as a "determinate absence": that is, as an absence that can be seen and heard — though typically is *not* seen or heard — as limited in its determined and determining effectivity. The term "corps/e" is in *logical* terms a cause of itself (*causa sui*). In other words, the corps *follows* the corpse not in a temporal sense, necessarily, but rather logically, from the nature of the corpse and its corpus of writing. Similarly, the *nature* of Nietzsche's corpse and corpus logically and definitionally *entails* the *existence* of his corps. While this might be said of *any* corps/e, Nietzsche/anism *is* exemplary historically in three ways: the lucidity of Nietzsche's intent, the magnitude and nature of its influence, and the possibility — or actual-virtuality — that it is literally "the *only* position outside of communism."

With regard to Nietzsche's intentions — concealed *within* his texts *between the lines* — and Nietzscheanism — the *embodiment* of that textually informed intent — the task at hand coexists in complex solidarity to Spinozism and its greatest philosophical inheritor to date, Althusserian Marxism. Here it is never a question of *reducing* Nietzsche/anism to Nietzsche's own intentions, but rather to take those intentions *into account* so that the truly radical and alien force of his writing might be *grasped* and *accounts settled* with it. Althusser followed Spinoza in rejecting any "hermeneutic" reading either of texts (in Althusser's case, mainly those of Marx and of the history of philosophy; in Spinoza's, primarily of biblical Scripture) or of Nature. "Hermeneutics" is defined here as the search to see some "hidden presence" imaged to be "beyond" or "beneath" surface texture. Rather, for Althusser, as for Spinoza, "Like nature, a text is entirely coincident with its actual existence, it is a surface without depth, without a reservoir of hermeneutic potential."[101] This type of "hermeneutic" procedure—it is not the only possible definition—is understood by Spinozism as a form of "superstition." This is so because "In the same way that superstition adds to nature the anthropomorphic projections that are nowhere to be found in it, so superstition adds to Scripture profound mysteries to justify the despotism that it upholds."[102] Thus at ultimate stake in the question both of superstition *and* of any type of hermeneutics that collaborates with it is nothing less than the intricate power that Antonio Gramsci, following Lenin, called "hegemony." In Spinoza's own uncompromising terms, the ultimate theologico-political role of superstitition is "to hoodwink the subjects, and to mask the fear, which keeps them down, with the specious garb of religion, so that men may fight as bravely for slavery as for safety, and count it not shame but highest honor to risk their blood and their lives for the vainglory of a tyrant. . . . "[103] From such a perspective, then, it is necessary to be "after" hermeneutics. If, in Spinoza's terms, the notion of God Creator as distinct from His Creation is an evident contradiction, then surely this must be true also of the nominally more mortal Nietzsche.

The effort to probe more carefully and deeply than ever before into Nietzsche's original intentions may itself appear to be "hermeneutical," searching as it must for signs of disease and potential contagion—influenza—if not in the cavernous depth, then all along the labyrinthine surface of Nietzsche's fluent corps/e—signs that *by definition* are never going to be immediately or clearly observable. And *by definition* there will be much opposition today from many quarters against looking for such signs in the first place. Pierre Bourdieu has therefore said of Heidegger something that must be said a fortiori of Nietzsche: "An ideological production is all the more successful the more capable it is of *putting in the wrong* anyone who tries to *reduce* it to its objective truth: enunciating the concealed truth of a discourse causes a scandal because it speaks what was 'the last thing that was to be said.' "[104]

Whether or not this scandalously "reductive" procedure, when applied to Nietzsche's corps/e, can ever really be awarded the distinction—some will say curse—of being "Spinozist" or "Althusserian" is hardly of genuine concern, for only something *like* this procedure, whatever one calls it, is prerequisite to grasp Nietzsche/anism. Althusser's controversial notion of "symptomatic reading" was nothing if not supremely attuned not only to what words *say* but also to what they precisely do *not* say; and Spinoza remarked—with whatever reservations and irony—that "it is evidently necessary to know something of the authors of writings which are obscure or unintelligible, if we would interpret their meaning; and for the same reason, in order to choose the proper reading from among a great variety, we ought to have information as to the versions in which the differences are found, and as to the possibility of other readings having been discovered by persons of greater authority."[105] The "only" problem today is that there are few— if any—greater authorities than . . . Friedrich Nietzsche. In short, we—too many of us—*believe* in him, and therefore would do well to entertain the possibility that "belief is an affair of obedience to the dead, uncomprehended letter."[106]

Another, rather more current, way of defining "Nietzsche/anism" as concept would be to say that it is a "difference-engine." Such machines (formerly, in more modernist times, called "general problem solvers") have the following three distinctive features: "A difference-engine must contain a description of a 'desired' solution. It must have subagents that are aroused by various differences between the desired situation and the actual situation. Each subagent must act in a way that tends to diminish the difference that aroused it."[107] But, for many current theorists of technosociality, a difference-engine projects something *merely* illusory: It only appears to be "goal-driven" but in actuality is not. For instance, such a machine only gives "the *impression* of having a goal"; it "does not *seem* to react directly to the stimuli or situations it encounters" but instead "treats the things it finds as objects to exploit, avoid, or ignore, *as though* it were concerned with something else that doesn't yet exist"; and, finally, when "any disturbance or obstacle diverts a goal-directed system from its course, that system *seems* to try to remove the interference, go around it, or turn it to some other advantage."[108] By contrast, there are two basic distinguishing features of the specific difference-engine that is Nietzsche/anism: first, "Nietzscheanism" functions as an unacknowledged consensus under the cover of the production of apparently maximum difference of opinion; and, second, this deeper, largely unacknowledged consensus, in the form of a corps of subagents, works — directly or indirectly — to ensure that the deepest levels of desired solution and directive proposed by the agent known as "Nietzsche" are disguised from view and/or subconsciously embodied by his subagents, as though his solutions and directives ought automatically to be their own.

Nietzsche himself was fascinated by the phenomenon of "*collective hallucinations*" and was prepared to produce them with his work.[109] William Gibson defines cyberspace as "consensual hallucination."[110] And, as Althusser noted laconically, "hallucinations are also facts."[111]

Nietzsche/anism is particularly serious business in two circumstances: first (in the words of one of the greatest technocultural Nietzscheans), "man *has* no future unless he can throw off the dead past and absorb the underground of his own being";[112] and, second, when that underground being always already is, or significantly includes, *Nietzsche*. While it is an ancient hermeneutic adage that *theoretically* "a god can be carved out of any piece of wood" (*e quovis ligno Mercurius*),[113] nonetheless it is striking, in spite of their apparently great diversity, how *few* Nietzsche-gods have *actually* been carved historically out of the man Nietzsche's work. Indeed, it is precisely the vast *apparent* diversity that occludes deeper levels of unacknowledged consensus, the most concealed effects of the difference-engine that is Nietzsche/anism.

No matter what other analogy is chosen, the term "Nietzsche/anism" images Nietzsche and Nietzscheanism: first, in their mutual interdependence with, and yet also distinction from, one another; and, second, in the *relative* independence of both from political economy. As Jameson argues in *Postmodernism, or, The Cultural Logic of Late Capitalism* (1991), under current conditions of "postmodernity" and/or "late capitalism" (each exhibiting the tendency to become a term convertible with the other), the "cultural" and the "economic" "collapse back into one another and say the same thing, in an eclipse of the distinction between base and superstructure that has itself often struck people as significantly characteristic of postmodernism in the first place." But, Jameson justly continues, the upshot of this conflation need not necessarily be to celebrate it nor to give up such distinctions entirely. Rather, the force of this argument "is also to suggest that the base, in the third state of capitalism, generates its structures with a new kind of dynamic."[114] And *one* keyterm for this relentless cultural-economic dynamic — this neo-Spinozist variant on the oneness of Mind, or super-structure, and Body, or base, and at the very least its allegory or symptom — is "Nietzsche/anism."

The phenomenon of Nietzsche/anism is *of course* always overdetermined by other, vaster social, psychological, and intellectual forces in addition to Nietzsche's specific, conscious intentions. *Nonetheless* the problem that must be recognized is that his effectivity and reception were to a significant extent already anticipated by Nietzsche, already programmed into his writing and proleptically *"handicapped"* by it.[115] It should go without saying that neither Nietzsche — as "cause" — nor Nietzscheanism — as "effect" — is wholly *reducible* to the other. Nonetheless, his original intentions can and must be known better than they ever have been; and if these intentions cannot be known absolutely, this is not only because of standard methodological or epistemological caveats about authorial intention — caveats applicable to nearly *any* object of study — but also because he operated to a significant extent within an *esoteric* tradition of political philosophy that had principled objections against ever communicating ultimate aims. Had he communicated these aims fully he would have expected himself to be much more persecuted than he has in fact ever been. Moreover, Nietzsche *should* be persecuted if it has come to pass that his position is actually and virtually the only one outside of communism. It remains to know how to read his writing.

Between the Lines

. . . the influence of persecution on literature is precisely to develop a peculiar technique of writing, the technique which we have in mind when speaking of writing between the lines. The expression is clearly metaphoric. Any attempt to express its meaning in unmetaphoric language would lead to the discovery of a terra incognita, a field whose very dimensions are as yet unexplored. . . .[116]

There is no surer protection against the understanding of anything than taking for granted or otherwise despising the obvious and the surface. The problem inherent in the surface of things, and only in the surface of things, is the heart of things.[117]

It is crucial to grasp Nietzsche's distinctive use of the exoteric-esoteric distinction from several angles, particularly in respect to his political agenda. But it is especially important to bear in mind—because it cannot be repeated at every point in the argument—that the most significant aspect of Nietzsche's esotericism occurs *not* at the level of *content* and the *what,* but rather at the levels of the *form* and *aim,* the *how* and *why.* Nietzsche had good, *logical* reasons to hide his intentions. And while he certainly did *not* conceal many of his elitist opinions, he did conceal *some* of the most draconian of them and, far more important, he concealed *how* he was going to implement them with his writing, *how* he was going to re/vitalize his corps/e. While the Left presumably has read or could have read Nietzsche's elitist remarks, published and un- published by him, it has most often chosen to ignore them, sooner or later embracing him as the Left's own. *Precisely* this effect (or *méconnais- sance*) flows from Nietzsche's esoteric design. This design is related to the notoriously problematic notion of "reading between the lines," to which there is never any fully adequate approach. "The making of meaning is a mysterious business, which historians are only beginning to understand and which can hardly be reduced to a formula like 'read- ing between the lines.'"[118] Especially not when—as in Nietzsche's case—readers are to be influenced and "make meaning" beneath the level of their conscious understanding.

Treatment of Nietzsche qua esoteric writer is quite foreign to the Left, which has no deep understanding of esotericism generally.[119] For years, a cadre of the Right has followed Leo Strauss in assuming that Nietzsche was operating essentially within an esoteric problematic. But, understandably enough, the same Right—including Strauss him- self—has also been reluctant—for reasons of "decorum"—to address this problematic directly and has no good reason to expose it too fully. Increasingly, however, the internal logic of this problematic *requires* that it be addressed ever more explicitly *and* ever more deceptively. The most systematic claim to date by a Right-Nietzschean and neo- Straussian to analyze Nietzsche as an esoteric thinker pulls up way short of full exposure, whether on purpose or not. In *Nietzsche and Modern Times: A Study of Bacon, Descartes, and Nietzsche* (1993), Lau- rence Lampert uses Nietzsche, as his title suggests, as the bookends of philosophical and social modernity, treating him explicitly as an eso- teric writer in the alleged esoteric—not Enlightenment—tradition of Francis Bacon and René Descartes. Here is Lampert's initial take on the basic problem: "Study of Nietzsche's writing brings appreciation of his own brand of esotericism. It differs from Bacon's and Descartes's partly because they succeeded: Nietzsche lived in times dominated by public science and hence by 'the youngest virtue,' honesty or intellectual probity. Nietzschean esotericism does not consist in some masking process of noble lying. It consists, first, of insight into the distance separating perspectives, a distance of rank; and, second, of communicating that insight in such a way as to elevate to the high, to school in the esoteric. . . . One of the tasks of Nietzschean esotericism is to school in the unavoidability of esotericism, to demonstrate a fact unwelcome to a democratic age: philosophers like Plato, Bacon, and Descartes are so sovereign that they could presume to become educators of humankind—and succeed."[120] Now, this argument may sound illogical: that is, Nietzschean esotericism does *not* consist in noble lying *and yet* in the promotion of esotericism. But it is not *just* illogical, any more than it is tautological, circular, or intransitive. For it is certainly transitive in terms of its social—political and economic—implications, notably the critique of democracy. Critiques and criticism of democracy are of course salutary. Liberal democracy often needs to be criticized, indeed itself *appears* to demand self/criticism. The general problem, however, is whether the criticism comes from the Right—to manage or anchor democracy, conserving its elitist tendency—or from the Left—to radicalize it, launching it onto unknown seas. The concomitant specific problem with Lampert's argument is that it conceals, esoterically, a basic principle of its own technique of reading. For if a writer *mentions* esotericism, it is possible, even likely, that the writer is also *using* it. At least this *must* be true for the Right *in principle;* if true also for the Left, it *ought* to be due to *contingent* circumstances. One implication is that one must be prepared to read the *opposite* of what is being read, as Strauss often suggests, though one is also reminded of the controversial Freudian principles of self-legitimation called "resistance" and "denial." Hence, the Straussian Lampert would be saying that Nietzscheanism *does* consist of a kind of noble lying *precisely.* For how *else,* according to Lampert's own argument, could "sovereign" thinkers yesterday (Nietzsche definitely, though without full success) or today (Lampert perhaps, though without full success either) *not only* "become educators of *mankind*" (read: exoterically) *but also* maintain social, as well as philosophical, "pathos of distance" and "order of rank" *for the few* (read: esoterically)? Thus, when Lampert demands—rightly—that we take Nietzsche's advice and read him "philologically," we must not do so in the way suggested *either* by the Right, which does so duplicitously or incompletely, *or* by the Left, which refuses to do so or does so at an exoteric level only. Particularly blind, even dangerous, however, is the dominant perception today on the Left, of Left-Nietzscheans, that the mature Nietzsche somehow "abandoned" rhetoric.[121] Finally, if as Lampert suggests, Nietzsche is to be embraced by "us"—that is, by the Right—as *the* leading guide for "*modern* times," then the Left must be prepared to spurn him as a leading guide for *post*modern, *post*contemporary times. But to do so effectively the Left must spurn him on philological as well as social—political and economic—grounds. *If* there is a time to "appropriate" Nietzsche—including in any Hegelian or even Marxian "dialectical" manner—it is at once *long past* and in the *distant future.*

To read Nietzsche carefully—philologically—requires something like "reading between the lines." But not quite in the Straussian sense. One of the most interesting theories and critiques of "reading between the lines" was advanced by Jean Genet in his last major work *Un captif amoureux* (a prisoner of love). Genet distinguished between "reading between the lines," which he called "a flat, linear art," and "reading between the words," "a steep, vertical art."[122] Genet developed this distinction from his experience living in the Near East and of grappling with the problem of how, as a European writer, most effectively to re/present the struggle for the liberation of Palestine. His time spent "among" the fedayeen (he does not presume to live "with" them) he regarded as being recorded, if at all, *between* his words: neither *in* words themselves, since these were written "so that the reality would disappear," nor even "between the *lines.*" The former notion implies essentialism, while the latter implies that something might ever be successfully captured qua narrative. Thus, *any* meaning Genet's text might produce would be located, at best, "between each word claiming to give an account of a reality that cannot be accounted for, since it was folded in upon itself to the point of self-espousal" (p. 11). What Genet seems to be saying (he admits his theory is at a very preliminary stage) is that the struggle for the *representation of reality* on behalf of the right of people (it is better to say not *a* people but simply *people,* to prevent internationalism from being too easily engulfed by nationalism) *to represent itself* takes place not (only) at the level of larger narrative units, in linearity, but (also) between words that resist narrativity in their more or less desperate search not (only) to capture or understand the real but (also) to appropriate and change it. Applied to the esoteric and elitist thinker Nietzsche, the grasping and resisting of his encoded esoteric moods and messages must transpire not (only) between the lines but (also) between the words, not (only) in linearity but (also) in verticality, not (only) in narrative but (also) in diction, not (only) in time but (also) in space. In other words, in fields of historical *and* theoretical struggle.

Just here it is well to recall with Althusser the old adage that "philosophy is as close to politics as the lips are to the teeth,"[123] but also that it is often difficult to know which are the teeth, which the lips. The full extent of the teeth and lips of Nietzsche/anism—its castrating vagina, its putrefying penis, so to speak—can also be known better but not absolutely—not only because of the contingent, empirical fact of the sheer magnitude of Nietzsche's influence, but also because the latter, too, was significantly esoteric and subconscious—by definition and design—when it was projected into the future just before the turn of our century. And if it is true that Nietzsche, as he himself claimed and his many readers have believed, created a new language of philosophy and literature, then we are justly reminded by James Baldwin that "a language comes into existence by means of brutal necessity, and the rules of the language are dictated by what the language must convey."[124] But before looking for and/or producing Nietzsche/anism between the lines, before interrogating Nietzsche for what he conveyed, we have to figure out how we are going to do so in *our* brutal necessity.

Structural Causality (Althusser versus Heidegger)

The "attempt" to act (for good or evil) begins *always already* "within" thought; it is "implied" in it.[125]

Regarding several of the most intentional writers of previous times, I suspect that even centuries later they are being ironical with their most believing devotees and disciples. Shakespeare has so infinitely many depths, ruses, and intentions; ought

he not also have had the intention to conceal ensnaring nooses
in his works for the most creative artists of posterity, in order
to deceive them so that they, before they realize it themselves,
have to believe they are virtually like Shakespeare? Certainly,
he could likely be far more intentional also in this
retrospect than one surmises.[126]

Nietzsche is to us postromantic postmoderns almost exactly what Shakespeare was to the romantics standing at the other end of modernity and modernism. Friedrich Schlegel's suggestion, in his essay "On Incomprehensibility" (1800), that Shakespeare "ironically" intended to manipulate—to cause—his posthumous reception in concealed, subliminal, identificatory ways was itself meant "parodically" or "ironically." As a general rule of thumb, however, whenever premodernism and modernism take something only as a possibility, metaphorically or ironically, true postmodernism must take such possibilities unironically and literally, at their word. Nietzsche is our Shakespeare—far greater than Shakespeare actually—in precisely this regard, and not merely, say, because he functions as our point of strongest articulation between "high" and "low" culture, though this also is true. But if we are the "effects" of Nietzsche's "cause," it is in a way that has yet to be determined and grasped, let alone combated.

There are three basic modes of causality, and thus of grasping the articulation of authorial intent alongside its appropriation by others. This Althusserian argument is derived from Spinoza's opposition to Cartesian metaphysics. While the question of "influence" in common senses of the term is largely irrelevant in the case of Nietzsche/anism, indeed represents a conceptual schema rejected by Spinozism and Althusserianism alike, nonetheless *causality* remains crucial, as does Nietzsche's *intent* to have an influenzalike impact on the future. Nietzsche/anism is an exemplary instance of what Althusser calls "structural causality," even as the latter term's significance as an empirical problem and analytic tool extends beyond Nietzsche/anism. Hence, a technical discussion of structural causality is demanded, and for at least two reasons. First, this is not really a diversion from the more immediate topic at hand, at least not if any useful form of *communist* theory and analysis is still to be salvaged from oblivion in the New World Order of capitalism. If this salvage operation is going to have any *philosophical* basis, it must take account of Althusser.[127] To be sure, today on the Left an old political slogan of May '68 has returned with political-ontological vengeance: *"Althusser à rien!* [Althusser, you *are* nothing!]" For the *pragmatic* reason that: *"Al, tu sers à rien!* [Al, you're *useless!*]"[128] Yet *without* Althusser the Left risks being left with *nothing* to use, to think.

But before developing a theory and application of causality, it must be said that the most philosophically significant, and currently far more influential, rival account of causality was advanced by arguably the greatest and most influential Nietzschean: *Martin Heidegger.* In one of its methodological and ideological aspects, this book is pitted throughout not only *against* Nietzsche *for* Althusser but also *against* Heidegger. This is the second reason why the following diversion — a diversion within a diversion — is required.[129]

In *The Question Concerning Technology* (1953), Heidegger charts with breathtaking concision the entire impacted trajectory of Western metaphysical thought, in an attempt to open up the possibility of what he calls "another thinking." This call is both formally salutary *and* politically obscurantist. Heidegger makes it on the basis of an intricate critique of the way causality from the pre-Socratics through Aristotle onwards ostensibly has been reduced, without alternative possibility, to four types: material causes (*causae materiales;* following Greek *hyle* and *hypokeímenon,* matter and substratum); formal causes (*causae formales;* following *eidos,* idea); final causes (*causae finales* or *causa ut;* following *telos,* end); and efficient causes (*causae efficientes* or *causa quod*). The so-called "four-fold root of causation" — and hence, in this tradition, all explanation — is commonly attributed to Aristotle. Its long history Nietzsche came to know through Schopenhauer.[130] Aristotle was actually synthesizing a prior philosophical canon. From his perspective (eventually adapted, critically, by Spinoza against Descartes), a basic failure of previous thinkers had been to stress one type of causation at the expense of the other three and thus at the expense of a more properly complex and overdetermined paradigm. For instance, the Milesian pre-Socratics had been overly concerned with material cause — fire, water, air, and so on — and Plato with formal cause — the Ideas.[131] Most Anglo-American philosophers today, under the influence of empiricism and the history of science, likely dismiss the entire

Aristotelian model of causation as merely metaphysical and tend to define a cause simply as "that which produces, and to that extent explains, change." From this "commonsense" point of view, Nietzsche would be seen as obviously having produced Nietzscheanism, which can then be explained fairly easily by recourse to his work without necessarily having to be anything like identical to it. The problem, however, is that Nietzsche's work turns out to be surprisingly elusive to empirical survey and analysis; furthermore, it is — arguably — elusive by Nietzsche's conscious design as efficient cause. In any case, Nietzscheanism has — demonstrably — never probed very deeply into Nietzsche's intent as the former's "cause," perhaps precisely because this intent, by esoteric definition, has been too well concealed ever to be exposed fully. But, as the "empiricist" David Hume showed in his seminal account of causality, the fact that something never happens does not necessarily mean that it cannot happen. And perhaps this is all the logical opening that is needed here. In more recent terms, it is also possible to appeal to Kurt Gödel's "existential proof": namely, a method proving (for Gödel mathematically) that an object *exists* without the necessity of actually producing it. In this case, the object is Nietzsche's corps/e — and to hell with habeas corpus.

"Cause" or *aíton* was further distinguished by Aristotle from "accidental cause" and "accidental effect" (*symbebekós*). According to him, the latter type of cause is subdivided into causes in which there is no aspect of deliberation or spontaneity whatsoever (*autómaton*), as opposed to those in which there is at least some aspect of rational and deliberate choice (*proaíresis*), the latter also comprising "chance" (*tyche*).[132] In protocyborg, but still Aristotelian terms, then, Nietzsche/anism operates in a site of *ontological* "interest" (Latin *inter-esse*) between *aíton, proaíresis,* and *autómaton:* never *being* one or the other — fully spontaneous or fully programmed — but *using* all three modes, more or less elusively, whenever necessary. For causation has to do, eventually, with *political* causes, and vice versa. It is also absolutely critical to remember — as Heidegger tends to "forget" but as this book will recall all along but most especially at its conclusion — that Greek "cause" (*aíton, aitía*) once also meant "culpability," "responsibility," "accountability."[133] Were the Greek Erinyes to reawaken under postmodern conditions, Hélène Cixous suggests, they would tell us: "Formerly, with us, everything was simple. The guilty were guilty. Here, with you, there is terrible complexity. The guilty are not guilty."[134] Nietzsche has contributed mightily to our loss of accountability; his complexity is terrific.

Supremely aware of the Greek problematic in its full complexity, Heidegger argues that the concept of causality, along its errant way, has taken many — apparently very different but essentially equivalent and always metaphysical — forms: for example, as "creator God," "man," *homo faber*, "technology," and "technicity." All of which are predicated on prior, but never adequately questioned, assumptions about the Being that encompasses and interpenetrates them equally. According to Heidegger's Master Narrative, flickers of pre-Socratic thought contained a radically antiproductivist — as well as antitheological and antihumanist — notion of "making," one which lets things be what they are, indeed allowing the Being of beings to disclose Itself at least momentarily. While the pre-Socratics are said by Heidegger to have had words and concepts for matter or material (*hyle*), form or idea (*eidos*), and aim or purpose (*télos*), it is implied that what they did not have, in *this* matrix at least, was an analogous term for what — in the derivative and blinded, Aristotelian, Latin, Scholastic, Jewish-Christian, and metaphysical tradition (Indic and Arabic thought is not used) — became known as *causa efficiens*, Divine Maker, human or industrial producer.[135] (Of course, as Heidegger knew very well, the Greeks did have *other* concepts for "efficient cause," "mover," or "agent"; in Aristotle, for example, there was *kinoún* and its derivatives, as eventually in English "kinetics.") Heidegger's variation on "Let It Be" argues for the necessity of re/opening this allegedly originary — albeit subsequently circumvented — antiproductivist, antisubjectivist, antimetaphysical way of conceptualizing cause-and-effect relations in the darkest, most occluded passageways of our age of technological modernity, productivist mastery, efficiency, and humanist hubris — all supremely exemplified in Nietzsche's Will to Power.

To be sure, as Félix Guattari remarks, the "Heideggerian mode of philosophy entrusts *techné*, in its opposition to modern technicity, with the mission of 'unveiling the truth,' thus setting it solidly on an ontological pedestal — on a *Grund* — that compromises its definition as a process of opening."[136] Clearly Heidegger "rejected" neither technology nor even technicity simply; rather, he strove "to appropriate" each one — including in the sense of making them appropriate and answerable to Being as an event of Being in very specific social conjunctures.

But the point here is that Heidegger's tendency to downplay efficient causality and agency is suspect because it disallows even *inquiry* into Nietzsche's role in the production of his corps.

Heidegger's ontological antihumanism is only superficially related to Althusser's attack on what the latter is careful to emphasize is *"theoretical* antihumanism." (Which, however, though influenced by Heidegger, was *never* antihumanitarianism.)[137] That is, such concepts as "man," "human essence," and "subjectivity" are tangled up in their specific historical inception with the post-Renaissance European bourgeoisie, and it is not in any case "man" that "makes history" but rather socially, economically, culturally, and historically determined masses of women and men, classes, class struggles — all of the type against which Heidegger pitted his awesome intellect. Heidegger's antiproductivism is understandably attractive to many people today, as the remaining rain forests are relentlessly obliterated along with the ozone shield, lead poisoning is still disguised as atmosphere in the former Workers' Paradise of Eastern Europe, and acid rain from the Home of the Brave, Land of the Free rapidly becomes Canadian lakes and Mexican rivers, and so forth.[138] But enthusiasm for Heidegger/ianism eventually runs up against the embarrassingly muscular fact that Heidegger himself ultimately was concerned far less with *any* mere epiphenomenon (e.g., the global environment) than with Being: a Being that inscrutably, effortlessly, and indifferently can manifest itself, say, as metaphysics, productivism, fast food, megamalls, death camps, AIDS, or black lung. Especially embarrassing for Heideggerians, however, is or ought to be the fact of Heidegger's insistence — doubly suspicious because it was expressed more often and extensively secretly than in public — that postmetaphysical thinking can be — indeed sometimes has to be — harnessed to a fascoid but above all Nietzschean sociopolitical solution to fundamental ontological questions as well as to, for him, mere epiphenomena like the global environment. Suffice it to say for the purposes at hand that the Heideggerian ontological account of causality is at the very least *politically* objectionable, and that another account is required to get after the peculiar brand of productivism that is Nietzsche/anism.

Now, according to Althusser, there are three basic modes of causality: (1) expressive, or essentialistic, causality; (2) transitive, or linear, causality; and (3) structural causality, or determinate absence.[139] Althusser rejects the first two notions of causality in part because they are reductive, their ultimate philosophical and political consequences similar, whereas the third is affirmed as suitably complex. He did not locate Heidegger or Nietzsche in the following schema, so this has to be done on a more or less ad hoc basis.

Expressive causality (1) is traced by Althusser in its modern and current form back to Leibniz, and from him on to Christian Wolff, Kant, Hegel, Benedetto Croce, to vulgar Marxism including Stalinism, and also to the botched mess that is almost all Western Marxism.[140] It "presupposes in principle that the whole in question be reducible to an *inner essence* of which the parts are no more than the phenomenal forms of expression, the inner principle of the essence being present at each moment in the whole, such that at each moment it is possible to write the immediately adequate equation: *such and such an element* (economic, political, legal, literary, religious, etc., in Hegel) = *inner essence of the whole.*"[141] Applied to the case of Nietzsche/anism, the overdetermined phenomenon of Nietzscheanism — in all the humanist "disciplines" such as philosophy, anthropology, theology, intellectual history, art and architectural history, literature, cultural theory — would be not merely traced but *reduced* to Nietzsche, in this case to the inner essence or immanent cause of an intent that is always already assumed to be known and accessible. This type of historicistic reduction also entails a form of *relativism,* making it appear as if Nietzsche, like the Zeitgeist Itself, would accept more or less equally, anarchistically, nihilistically, pluralistically, or democratically each and every part of the legacy he — somehow — predetermined. But investigation into the *specific* mechanisms of this predetermination is imagined to be so obvious, so basically liberatory and identical to the reader's own, as to obviate the need for further scrutiny. The result is that — basically — Nietzsche is one of us, whoever "we" may be. At the end of the day we rest in peace, confident that he's on "our side" — whatever that side is, no matter where it leads. And so, finally, we also Rest in Peace.

Transitive causality (2) is traced by Althusser in its modern form back to Descartes, and from him on to John Locke, David Hume, Thomas Reid, John Stuart Mill, and to contemporary Anglo-American empiricism, pragmatism, eclecticism, economism, and liberal democracy. The obverse of expressive causality in some respects but related in others, it entails a linear teleological view of history and a concomitant view of causality as an "effectivity which reduces the whole to the result of the sum of its parts" — the latter understood as a potentially infinitely regressive chain of cause-effect-cause.[142] An underlying fallacy of transitive causality has been summed up in the remark by theoretical physicist and cosmologist Evry Schatzman that "climbing sufficiently far back into the past, the idea of origin ends up by losing its meaning."[143] As Althusser argues in *For Marx* — in his analysis of different ways of reading Marx's relationship to his sources, notably Hegel — transitive causality is inscribed by either "a theory of sources or a theory of anticipation."[144] As a view of human history, transitive causality rests on a tripartite set of not always closely related and typically more or less concealed presuppositions. Applied to the case of Nietzsche/anism, transitive causality's first presupposition (2.1) is *analytic.* It would reduce "the theoretical system" of Nietzscheanism "to its elements; a precondition that enables one to think any element of the system *on its own,* and to compare it with *another* similar element from another system" (p. 56). One effect of analytic relativism would again be to make Nietzscheanism appear to be more pluralistic, more a matter of genuine debate, more open-ended, more loosely articulated than otherwise might be perceived to be the case. The reader is apparently free to pick and choose what of Nietzsche to accept, what to reject, what to read, what not to read. The concomitant effect would once again be that the possible existence of a deeper consensus or difference-engine unacknowledged by "debaters" would be a priori denied by them, thereby forfeiting the possibility of any really exact inquiry into the extent to which Nietzsche did indeed somehow "cause" the tendency known as Nietzscheanism. Transitive causality's second presupposition (2.2) is *teleological and axiological,* because it "institutes a secret tribunal of history which *judges* the ideas submitted to it, or rather, which permits the dissolution of (different) systems into their elements, institutes these elements as elements in order to proceed to their measurement according to its own norms as if to *their truth.* " Whereupon Althusser adds this elaboration: "In the theory of sources it is the origin that measures the development. In the theory of anticipation it is the goal that decides the meaning of the moments of the process" (pp. 56–57). Applied to the case of Nietzsche/anism, there would reign self-serving and permanent confusion about whether what is at stake are sources or aims. And this confusion effectively masks its own tacit determinations and valorizations. Nietzschean/ism would thus again be a matter of relativistic historiography—yet precisely inattentive, under the false banner of ideological neutrality and sociological objectivity, to its own ideology.[145] Once again, the question of Nietzsche's intended influence on Nietzscheanism is then either ruled out of court a priori or, alternatively, the Nietzschean uncritically assumes that s/he *knows* what his intent was and that no further inquiry is needed. Finally, these two presuppositions of transitive causality depend upon a more general third (2.3), "which regards the history of ideas as its own element, and maintains that nothing happens there which is not a product of the history of ideas itself and that the world of ideology is *its own principle of intelligibility.*"[146] Meaning among other things that with Nietzsche/anism one can disregard the politico-economic aspect of Nietzsche's work along with his plan to implement it rhetorically.

All eclectic, idealistic, intellectualist forms of causality encourage and motor the today commonsense proposition that Nietzsche himself was not primarily—nor even at all—a political, practical philosopher with a *specific* social agenda, and that when he said certain more or less objectionable things he didn't *really* mean them, or would have come to revise them on further, more "dialectical," "deconstructive," or "dialogical" inspection.

This unacknowledged consensus is almost perfectly illustrated by a discussion of the uses and abuses of Nietzsche's thinking that took place in 1950, nearing the fiftieth anniversary of his death, and was broadcast on West German radio.[147] The participants in the Frankfurt studio represented supposedly rival wings of then current German philosophy: Max Horkheimer and Theodor Adorno for Marxian critical theory, and Hans-Georg Gadamer representing Heideggerian philosophical hermeneutics. In spite of other differences, with regard to Nietzsche there turned out to be remarkably few. At general stake for Horkheimer, Adorno, and Gadamer was the question of *whether*—not how and why—to take any utterance "literally or figuratively." Gadamer and Adorno both quickly accepted Horkheimer's basic premise that the problem not only with reading Nietzsche—that is, solving the enigma of whether he was a good Enlightenment liberal or a rather bad fascist elitist—but also with modernity *tout court* occurs when the reader "takes what Nietzsche wrote literally." For Horkheimer, it is specifically *American* and *Russian* society that takes things "too literally," with properly *German* thought suspended in between. Remarkably, this is a philosophical version of "convergence theory" that had deep and problematic roots in nineteenth-century Germany; as recently as the 1930s, with the Nazis and Heidegger alike, it had held that the United States and the USSR were developing into an "essentially identical" syndicotechnical form of society, which entails the proposition that Germany, "the heart of Europe," must seek the "third way" between the "pincers" of Americanism and Bolshevism.[148] The three panelists concurred that Americanism — Fordism, Taylorism, pragmatism, and so on — necessarily entails the instrumentalization of language, its "reduction to statements and propositions," as Horkheimer put it, whereas, under Soviet communism, "every word is a thesis for which one can die, if taken at one's word." In either case, however, the tendency is "to take language literally," making it "simply impossible" to read a Nietzsche who — as Horkheimer, Adorno, and Gadamer all simply *presuppose* — used language in a "radically different" manner. Gadamer preferred to say that Nietzsche was a "parodist," whereas Adorno here preferred "ironist," but it amounted to the same thing. And more to the point anyway is Adorno's own technical definition of "parody": that is, "the use of forms in the era of their impossibility" in order to "demonstrate this impossibility and thereby altering the forms."[149] On this consensus assumption, Nietzsche never quite meant what he said. Thus, for example, both the Nazi "misappropriation" of Nietzsche and the "whitewashing" of his elitism by well-meaning liberals (notably Walter Kaufmann, whose influential "existentialist" interpretation of Nietzsche was just then appearing)[150] were equally misguided, equally *literal* and hence "totalitarian" even. Here, in the cold war, the notorious "third period" line of the 1928 Commintern, with its nihilistic and suicidal doctrine of "social-fascism," its denial of any distinction between bourgeois-democratic regimes and military-police dictatorships as instruments of capitalist rule, resurfaces in the German heart of continental philosophy — *nachträglich*. Paradoxically, however, this unacknowledged ideological consensus holds that in *one* matter we *can* read Nietzsche literally: that is, that his remarks ought never to be taken . . . literally. To be precise: *Sometimes* we can read Nietzsche literally, *sometimes* figuratively, or we can conflate the two, but in *any* case we don't need to get exercised about his *intentions,* because the *one* thing we *can* take at face value is his own claim to be a "free spirit," "smasher of all idols," "perspectivist," "parodist," "ironist," "Enlightener," "the great emancipator of humankind," and so on. This a priori "logic" vis-à-vis Nietzsche is thus at root benevolent about what he intended to say, in spite of the subsequent "misrecognition" by all others who take him too literally in one literal direction or another. Yet this "logic" also remains binary and dualist, rendering it impossible for Nietzsche ever to have said something different or more radical than the consensus can see and hear. This "German consensus" of Left, Right, and Center — there are equivalent national variants everywhere — *tacitly* embodies Nietzsche/anism, worrying why "we" ought to take him literally *only* when he might ordain it. Overly committed as it commonly is to ideology-criticism (*Ideologiekritik*), the "German" approach to Nietzsche — a fortiori in the case of Adorno's epigones — fails because Nietzsche's mode of textual production is impervious to it. At most Nietzsche's is a "totalitarian ideology" in Žižek's terms: that is, one of the fundamental forms of a cynicism that — *esoterically* speaking — "is no longer meant, even by its authors, to be taken seriously — its status is just that of a means of manipulation, purely external and instrumental; its rule is secured not by its truth-value but by simple extra-ideological violence and promise of gain."[151] *Exoterically* speaking, of course, one admits nothing of the kind.

Generally, binary or "Cartesian" views of causality — and hence of Nietzsche/anism to date — would maintain that, preceding from a clear and distinct knowledge of an effect (i.e., "our" Nietzscheanism), we can render clear and distinct knowledge of the cause it implies more or less faithfully, transitively or expressively (i.e., "our" Nietzsche), demonstrating tautologically that the effect on us would not be what we know it to be were it not to have the cause upon which it depends. By contrast, in confrontation with Descartes, Spinoza argued in his *On the Improvement of the Understanding* (1661) that by assuming a clear and distinct knowledge of an effect — we know what Nietzscheanism is — we may think we arrive at a clear and distinct knowledge of its implied cause — what Nietzsche really meant. But we will know nothing of any cause or effect *beyond* what we have *already* taken to be its effect and cause.[152] In short, another type of causality is at work in Nietzsche/anism and is required to grasp it.

Structural causality (3) is traceable in its modern form back to Spinoza (his realist and materialist aspect, not the rationalist and metaphysical), and from him on to Marx, Lenin, Gramsci, Mao, and not merely to Althusser himself but to the latter's proposal for *future* communist thought and action. The problem of causality is at once political and philosophical. The political aspect, in Gramsci's terms, is to avoid two twin perils: namely, "to presenting causes as immediately operative which in fact only operate indirectly, or to asserting that the immediate causes are the only effective ones. In the first case there is an excess of 'economism,' or doctrinaire pedantry; in the second, an excess of 'ideologism.'"[153] The philosophical aspect of causality, in Althusser's terms, "can be entirely summed up in the concept of '*Darstellung*,' the key epistemological concept of the whole Marxist theory of value, the concept whose object is precisely to designate the mode of *presence* of the structure in its *effects*, and therefore to designate structural causality itself."[154] It is in no sense a "synthesis" of the other two main modes of causality, opposing both. What is most attractive here is that the category of Nietzsche's "intent" — as the "efficient cause" of Nietzscheanism, and hence as "responsible" for it — is preserved at a more appropriately complex level of efficacy.

Of course, Althusser had a larger target in mind than any one philosopher's reception. Structural causality was incepted to negotiate between economic determination *in the last instance* and that *relative* autonomy from the economy, mode of production, or "structure" that obtains throughout ideological, theoretical, literary, political, and philosophical "superstructures," including social relations and formations generally — all these being sites of class and other struggles. Balibar has shown what critics of Marxism and post-Marxists both ignore: namely, that for Marx himself "*class struggles organized as class struggles* (with the corresponding institutions) in history are not the rule, they are the exception. . . . But the 'basic' structure underlying the conjunctures, which is able to take a number of different forms (including ethnic, national, and religious forms, none of them a single 'essence,' but on the contrary with infinitely many varieties) is precisely "mass conflict,' whose *matter*, so to speak, is precisely *ideology*."[155] Marx emphasized in 1852 that "I do not claim to have discovered either the existence of classes in modern society or the struggle between them," for both had already been discovered by bourgeois historians and economists; rather, his contribution was to show "that the existence of classes is merely bound up with certain historical phases in the development of production"[156] — including, presumably, all postmodern and postcontemporary "phases" of production and reproduction. *La lucha continúa.*

Now, as heuristic, the concept of structural causality — a vision of structures as existing dynamically in their effects — tries to grasp all actual contradictions and oppositions — in their uneven development and as struggle for and against the dominant mode of production — which inform all social relations and which the latter help to reproduce or contest. In this regard it is important to contradict and oppose the widely held belief that Nietzsche himself had little or no sense of economics, and therefore that his own concept of struggle did not extend to anything like class struggle. This impression is misguided or simply mistaken. On the contrary, Nietzsche recognized in his notebooks that "The battle against *great* men for *economic* reasons is *justified*. For these men are dangerous, contingent, exceptions, storms, and strong enough to put into question what has been built and grounded slowly."[157] He then added that the "explosive" aspect of the class struggle against the great must not merely be "defused" and "made harmless" but also positively anticipated, redirected, and prevented from occurring in advance of its eruption. Indeed, such proleptic, preemptive, prophylactic strikes (*vorbeugen* is Nietzsche's verb for this attempt) constitute "the basic instinct of civilized society."[158]

Leaving Nietzsche's own take on political economy aside for now, structural causality has to do with determination by "determinate absence" or "absent cause." For Althusser, "The structure is not an essence *outside* the economic phenomena which comes and alters their aspect, forms and relations"; rather, "the structure is immanent in its effects in the Spinozist sense of the term, that *the whole existence of the structure consists of its effects,* in short that the structure, which is merely a specific combination of its peculiar elements, is nothing outside its effects."[159] To use Spinoza's own concept, the cause "indwells" its effects as *causa immanens.*[160] For this reason, while "expressionism" is an absolutely fundamental term and concept for Spinoza, as Deleuze shows, it has nothing to do with expressive causality as outlined earlier; rather, "expression in general *involves* and *implicates* what it expresses, while also *explicating* and *evolving* it."[161] And this is a precise definition of the way Nietzsche is "expressed" in Nietzscheanism, dynamically informing one another. Nietzsche himself would have affirmed this thesis. His terms were slightly different from Spinoza's, but his point was essentially the same when noted to himself: "Coordination instead of *cause and effect.*"[162] It is this coordinate and coordinating structure of Nietzsche/anism (Spinoza's term is *complicatio,* Deleuze's *pli*) that Althusser might call the "authorless theater." Here, "the ordinary distinctions between outside and inside disappear, along with the 'intimate' links within the phenomena as opposed to their visible disorder."[163] So it is, finally, that while it is impossible to see or depict "living conditions," "social relations," or "the relations of production or the forms of class struggle in a given society," it is possible to see and depict "the *determinate absence* which governs them."[164]

Applying structural causality to the cases of Nietzsche and Nietzscheanism, Nietzsche/anism becomes a problematic of structural causality and determinate absence in the following two — somewhat eccentric — ways. First and more generally, it becomes possible to see Nietzscheanism — heuristically — as "the contradictory effects of a single cause," in this case of Nietzsche himself. Seemingly "serious" and "interesting" "contradictions" or "aporias" that have defined the intellectual marketplace for some time now — including seemingly irreconcilable differences of opinion intestine to Nietzscheanism about *what* Nietzsche really meant, *where* exactly he stood politically, and *whether* his overall influence has been good or bad — would then become considerably devalued, unmasking the unacknowledged consensus or difference-engine motoring them all. At this point, for example, Left-Nietzscheans and Right-Nietzscheans find themselves in the same bed together, as day breaks and the Dionysian revel of the night is transformed into hangover, and no owl of Athena has taken flight. Since, in Gramsci's terms, under neocapitalism a general law legislates that political and economic questions "are disguised as cultural ones, and as such become insoluble,"[165] the apparent contradictions that are Nietzscheanism tend never to be "superseded" or "sublated" but rather only "perpetuated," leaving both the economic base of capital and Nietzsche himself not merely intact but positively rejuvenated.[166] Second and more specifically, Nietzscheanism is grasped by the theory of structural causality as the more or less overtly militant *corps* that has incorporated or embodied the *corpus* of Nietzsche's writing in such a way that this corps exists as the effect of a now apparently absent cause or *corpse.*

Not only is Nietzsche/anism not just any old form of structural causality, however; it may be, following Bataille's bon mot, *the* dominant intellectual form in what has become the postcontemporary world of purportedly postideological, post-Marxist, and postsocialist neocapitalism. What must be particularly highlighted now, however, and recalled throughout this book, is that it is *not* the author — let alone Althusser — who is making the truly scandalous paradigmatic substitution of "Nietzsche" and its equivalents for "economic determination in the last instance" and its equivalents. Strange to say, this is precisely the substitution or displacement always already made — in fact or in effect — *by Nietzsche/anism.* Which is what is really behind the commonly made observation that at least since the early 1970s, long before the "defeat of socialism," Western intellectuals have been drifting away from Marxism to Nietzscheanism, even though this time- and space-frame turns out to be far too restricted.

Nevertheless, it is necessary to *depart* from a stricter Althusserian paradigm in several ways.[167] *Elements* of both transitive and expressive causality still can and must be used to grasp Nietzsche/anism in its *relative* autonomy from economic determination and influence. The reason for this partial departure is fairly straightforward. Nietzsche's *own* notion of causality — including his related notions of intentionality and responsibility, rhetorical strategy and tactics, esoteric and subconscious influence — contains traces of all three main modes. The bottom line was always *pragmatic;* thus he noted, for example, that *causa efficiens* and *causa finalis* were "both only means" to an end — be that end epistemological or other.[168] Anticipating a fuller discussion later of Nietzsche's "esoteric semiotics," it is notable already that Nietzsche's interest in *all* merely philosophical, theoretical critiques of causality was overridden by practical interests, by his refusal on explicitly political grounds to reliquish expressive control over linear processes of causality. It is imperative to have realized this before rushing either to reject Nietzsche out of hand or — even worse — to embrace him as a Dionysiac drinking buddy, as is done by Nietzschean *gauchisme,* of the type that few have theorized against more vigorously than Althusser himself. It is true that Nietzsche/anism can be fully grasped neither (as with transitive causality) by *reducing* it to an infinite regress of causes and effects called "Nietzscheanism" — in which case Nietzsche drops out of the equation along with any other cause — nor (as in expressive causality) by *reducing* Nietzsche/anism's effectivity to reflections of an essence or first cause called "Nietzsche" — in which case now it is Nietzscheanism that drops out of sight and mind.

In *abstract principle,* then, it ought to be possible to grasp Nietzsche/anism as a nonreductive structural causality in Althusserian terms. But the stubborn *historical and sociological fact* remains that the two main terms in the equation of Nietzsche/anism are not really as equal as they appear. In the equation "Nietzsche + Nietzscheanism = Nietzsche/anism," therefore, the term "Nietzsche" has really always been "Nietzscheanism +n" and "Nietzscheanism" has always been "Nietzsche −n": where "n" is that esoteric aspect of "Nietzsche" which to date is unknown simply or known inadequately (a Lacanian might refer to *l'objet petit a*). Much more may appear known about Nietzscheanism than about Nietzsche, but this is also to say that what is not known about Nitetzscheanism is how Nietzsche might have programmed it in ways we do not see, perhaps cannot see.

Obviously, it would make no sense whatsoever to write a book about a single individual from a perspective influenced by Althusser, or by any other Marxist for that matter, were the person in question not a displaced and condensed structure of *much* larger intellectual and social forces. There is no doubt, for example, that the great success Nietzsche/anism has in achieving hegemony over the broad ideological spectrum of intellectuals is conditioned or determined by the way, under capitalism and neocapitalism, the notion of "the individual" is at once openly — exoterically — *promoted* as a positive value (Nietzsche is commonly understood to have promoted nothing if not "individuality") and yet also surreptitiously — esoterically — *demoted* by "abstract" market forces that opened up vast possibilities for Nietzsche to operate beneath the surface of thus demoted consciousness. As put succinctly by Lucien Goldmann,

> The most important consequence of the development of a market economy is that the individual, who previously constituted a mere partial element within the total social process of production and distribution, now becomes, both in his own consciousness and in that of his fellow men, an independent element, a sort of monad, a *point of departure.* The social process of course continues and implies a certain regulation of production and exchange. This

process was not only objectively present in the earlier social structure but also *consciously realized* in the traditional, religious and national rules governing people's behaviour; these rules now begin to fade from consciousness. The regulation of the market is now *implicit,* governed by the blind forces of supply and demand. The total process is seen as resulting from the action of countless autonomous individuals on each other and in response to each other, behaving as rationally as possible for the protection of their private interests and basing their actions on their knowledge of the market with no regard to any trans-individual authority or values.[169]

The problem here, however, is that such general sociological and structural categories apply eventually to nearly *every* intellectual and cultural phenomenon — as their determinate absence — and do not help very much in grasping the more specific philosophical and philological problems involved with Nietzsche and Nietzscheanism.

Marx wrote *The Eighteenth Brumaire of Louis Bonaparte* (1852) in part to demonstrate that an ostensibly "great hero" of history was in fact a function of objective historical forces, most notably of class struggle. Lest this point be lost, in his preface to the second edition, Marx warned of any contrary approach to history that "makes this individual great instead of little by ascribing to him a personal power of initiative such as would be without parallel in world history."[170] And certainly *mere* hagiography-in-reverse is a major risk taken in this book. To that extent, it would be — in theory — the most Nietzschean book *possible.* But the problem is that hagiography is *already* firmly in place in the case of Nietzsche, who for too many people is precisely "without parallel in world history," and who has replaced not merely Marx/ianism and Actually Existing Socialism but even the possibility of communism, even the desire for it. Alluding again to Althusser's allegory of structural causality as an "authorless theater," it is important once and for all to stop throwing out at least this one author with the cleaning water after the performance of "objective history," precisely *because* of the need in the final analysis to *reject* what has been justly derided as "any historical causality other than seminal individuals attempting to materialize their dreams."[171] Finally the problem will arise as to *Nietzsche's* responsibility and accountability for his corpse, and as to how communism might grasp this problem, settle accounts with it. The issue is obviously not Nietzsche's responsibility and accountability for "real

history" *in its entirety,* as its purported "Origin," but rather responsibility and accountability for that *part* of history which is Nietzsche's
corps, and which has demonstrably handicapped the circumstances
wherein which groups might freely and effectively contest — including
by means of class struggle on behalf of the laboring and unemployed
poor — capitalist economic coercion and cultural hegemony in their full
complexity and power. It is in this spirit, then, that one must *lire le
Nietzsche* and do so very closely and cautiously. *Especially* if "Nietzsche's
position is the only one outside of communism."

What any one person intends to do and then does in history is never
absolutely decisive, but nonetheless it can be important. What Friedrich Nietzsche intended to do and did is very important, if not decisive absolutely. It should also go without saying that the alleged "voluntarism" and "humanism" of a Gramsci are insufficient to fight against
the peculiar rival brands of "voluntarism" and "humanism" on the real
Right and fake Left alike — both of which are *radically* structured by
Nietzsche/anism. But, properly grasped, doses of Gramscian and Leninist "voluntarism" and "humanism" are nonetheless necessary when
struggling in a world in which "the truth is that one cannot choose the
form of war one wants."[172]

Corps/e

HAMM: All is . . . All is . . . all is what? (Violently.) All is what?
CLOV: What all is? In a word. Is that what you want to know?
Just a moment. (He turns the telescope on the without, looks,
lowers the telescope, turns towards Hamm.) Corpsed.[173]

. . . the dead
are never as dead as one believes.[174]

But have we a right to assume the survival of something that
was originally there, alongside of what was later derived
from it? Undoubtedly.[175]

The corpse/corpus/corps nexus obtains not only in the case of Nietz-
sche/anism but also *generally* as a major motor of *all* intellectual and —

to a lesser extent—social history. This is to say that the existence of a "corps" (e.g., adherents to a principle or Leader of some sort, whether philosophy or Philosopher, politics or Politician, art or Artist, and their equivalents) presupposes the existence of the death, the "corpse" of that same principle or Leader, and this for two basic and related reasons. First, the corpse is recalled—sporadically or continually—to remind the corps of the radical finitude of human—even planetary—life. This material life—appearances sometimes to the contrary—is factually devoid of ultimate metaphysical consolation or transcendence as it is projected toward death. This is the harder meaning behind the otherwise lugubrious-sounding formula of Horkheimer and Adorno: "The body cannot be remade into a noble object: it remains the corpse however vigorously it is trained and kept fit."[176] Second, the corpse is recalled to reaffirm the corps's own existence as the relative posthumous existence of the principle or Leader after death. Qua corps, the body can be made to think itself noble—as somehow outrunning time. So it is that the body does not die but undergoes an "alternate" or "false" death, in J. G. Ballard's terms, in order to become the "university of death" or even "assassination weapon" known as Nietzsche studies.[177]

So it also is that the corps legitimates itself by reassuring itself that the corpse to which it swears fealty—whether uncritically or more critically—is precisely not dead entirely but rather keeps living on as its more or less conscious embodied and reincarnate corps, and in a more or less polysemous corpus of "works." At the same time, the principle's or Leader's corpus or corpse—prior to death, so to speak—presupposes the core existence of the corps to come, in order to outlive itself and to give itself the only actual transcendence available to the radically material and mortal aspect of all life. It is in this sense, then, that philosophies and Philosophers, political ideologies and Politicians, art forms and Artists attempt—more or less consciously, rigorously, and successfully and under various types of internal and external constraint—to control their posthumous influence, to handicap it esoterically or exoterically in such a way that their subsequent embodiments are predetermined as much and as far into the future as possible. This dimension of structural causality—as corps/e—is *among* the most significant motors of human history. Emphatically to be stressed, however, is that the proleptic desire of the corpse and corpus—which are not strictly equivalent — to handicap the corps has no *guarantee* of success. "In one sense the writer cannot die, for 'he is already dead'; in another, the notion that his body will die contentedly is only a hopeful surmise."[178]

As in any attempt to introduce a keyterm into intellectual let alone social history, the danger exists that the term "corps/e" can easily become yet another shibboleth to keep at bay genuinely radical, passionate criticism of the nearly overwhelming number of clichés that tyrannize human existence. To counteract this danger, or at least to manage it as long as possible, it is useful to recall that one of the meanings of the word "corpse" — and by extension "corps/e" — is buried in the term "hocus-pocus." Which is a compressed form of the Christological slogan "Hoc est enim corpus meum [here is my body]," which is in turn a verbal reformulation not only of the imagined miracle of transubstantiation but also of Jesus' refusal by silence to respond to Pontius Pilate's question "What Is Truth?" since Jesus' tacit but lived claim — as Christ, not Jew; as not God or man but demigod — was that his physical corpse, his spoken corpus, and disciple corps — *all* as the precise intersection of the divine and the human — *are* the Truth. At least since modernism, Jean-Luc Nancy argues, this notion of corpus is also a principle of *writing* that entails not the presence of a body but rather a form of bodily "discharge" like blood: "A body is what cannot be read in a writing."[179] Of course this thesis is straight out of Nietzsche, though Nancy neglects to say so. One of Zarathustra's many patented valorizations, this time "on reading and writing," is that "I love only That which one writes with one's blood." "Write with blood," he prescribes, "and you will experience that blood is *Geist.*"[180] If applied to Nietzsche's own corps/e, however, the Nancy-Nietzsche thesis must not obviate the need to interrogate *either* the body affecting this supposedly "pure fluidity" and what Nancy also likes to call "senseless joy" *or* the bodies more or less unwittingly affected by it. It is easy to forget that Zarathustra himself appends a darker, bloodier, and more consequential thought to "On Reading and Writing": "It is not through anger but through laughter that one kills" (6/1:45).

The general notion of the corps/e is, in one sense at least, post-Christian as well as post-Nietzschean, since Nietzsche himself obviously worked within a Christian problematic to some extent. As is well known, there are at least two fundamental and competing traditions in

Christianity about the status of the corps/e, depending on whether the corps of disciples understands the Eucharist either figuratively, mnemonically, and representationally — bread and wine being recollectively *like* the corpus of Christ Jesus — or literally and ontologically — bread and wine *as* the individual and collective body.[181] Wars have been waged over the difference. On the one hand, then, there is the "sacrificial" corps/e: the figurative restaging of the supreme sacrifice — in order to atone for something called "sin," in the case of Jesus; in the case of Nietzsche, to obviate it. On the other there is the "eschatological" corps/e: the proleptic pullulation of the *corpus Christi* by a corps identifying itself not in name only but in actual body with the corpse and its corpus of works. As far as Nietzsche was concerned — concerned, that is, with the pullulation of his own corps/e — this was a nondebate. *Both* responses to him and his works were possible and necessary, exoterically *and* esoterically. In this, he was pragmatic, political. Nietzsche's last great rhetorical question, "Dionysus or the Crucified One?" — posed when he broke down, identifying with both men or terms equally — does not deny this tripartite claim; it reverses it, extending it simultaneously back into the deeper past and forward into the distant future. Finally, it is commonly forgotten that Nietzsche's last signatures included not only "Dionysus" and "The Crucified One" but also "Nietzsche Caesar."[182]

Discussion in Christological terms of Nietzsche's corps/e, its hegemony today, and the relation in the corps/e of cause and effect can also be converted, up to a point, into the psychoanalytic concepts developed out of Lacan's notion of "the Thing" by Žižek to include "the national Thing." Žižek argues in *Tarrying with the Negative* that "the national Thing exists as long as members of the community believe in it; it is literally an effect of this belief in itself. The structure is here the same as that of the Holy Spirit in Christianity. The Holy Spirit *is* the community of believers in which Christ lives after his death: *to believe in Him equals believing in belief itself*, i.e., believing that I'm not alone, that I'm a member of the community of believers. I do not need any external proof or confirmation of the truth of my belief: by the mere act of my belief in others' belief, the Holy Spirit is here. In other words, the whole meaning of the Thing turns on the fact that 'it means something' to people."[183] Similarly, in the case of Nietzsche's corps/e, the corps does not normally need confirmation by Nietzsche's corpus or by its author. The corps *assumes* that it has this confirmation from Nietzsche, however, and reads his writing continually as granting it. What is more, he and his writing *do* grant this confirmation—but exoterically, not esoterically. Thus it is that the corps re/*incorporates* itself, in all senses: that is, qua community and qua Nietzsche Industry. One might say that Nietzsche/anism *is ideology,* insofar as a mode of "national identity" poses here as "international." And so is obviated the need or desire for *communism.* But it is in terms of the problematic of cause and effect that it is important to differ with Lacan and Žižek, insofar as they wish merely to "invert" cause and effect, focusing on the latter at the expense of the former. What Žižek calls the "paradoxical existence of an entity which 'is' only insofar as subjects believe (in the other's belief) in its existence is the mode of being proper to ideological causes: the 'normal' order of causality is here inverted, since it is the Cause itself [read: Nietzsche's corpse and corpus] which is produced by its effects (the ideological practice it animates [Nietzscheanism as corps])" (p. 202). Lacan and Žižek, in explicit opposition to both "deconstruction" and "discursive idealism," are right not to want to *"reduce . . .* Cause to a performative effect of the discursive practices that refer to it," since Cause must be allowed to retain "its positive ontological consistency, the only substance acknowledged by psychoanalysis" (p. 202). Nonetheless—precisely *in* and *as* this psychoanalytic system—the Cause, defined as *"real,* nondiscursive kernel," turns out to have much more to do with affects than with causes or effects: namely, with the category Lacanians call "enjoyment," as the basic element of social cohesion, and what Gramscians call "hegemony," which includes the problem of why it is that people "enjoy" their own oppression. But what limits this argument, for the purposes at hand, is that the problem of Nietzsche's corpse and corpus as "cause" tends to get lost in the shuffle. *Within the problematic of Nietzsche's corps/e,* it is *Nietzsche* that is "the Real" in the sense of "that which 'always returns to its place' (Lacan), the kernel that persists unchanged in the midst of the racial upheavals in the society's symbolic identity."[184]

The mark / inserted throughout *Nietzsche's corps/e* between "Nietzsche" and "Nietzscheanism," between the former's "corpse" and the latter's "corps," is to be read in several ways—as premodern, modern, and postmodern. It makes the title into a gestalt that is impossible to pronounce—much as Nietzsche's corps/e is, so to speak, *unspeakable*. On the one hand the slash disruptively recalls that for too long the relation between Nietzsche and Nietzscheanism, the corpse and the corps, has been only reductively figured: either (1) as being too porous or too quickly fusing—as if the two binary terms within each set were really always already one and the same (an anthropologist might refer here to the law of alternation); or (2) as being too rigid; or (3) as being too castrating—as if between the two terms in each set there were no essential connection, no influence, no transmission of power (the law of juxtaposition). (A central feature of bourgeois and idealist thought, as correctly noted by Georg Lukács, is that any significant relationship tends to be expressed in terms of a false antinomy: namely, "only as an insoluble antagonism or an eclectic amalgam.")[185] On the other hand, changing the descriptive imagery now from the modern to the pre/postmodern, the virgule designates a minimally perceptive "surface" of "interface" (Greek *prosópon:* interface, face-to-face personification). According to what Paul Virilio in *The Lost Dimension* (1984) terms "the new scientific definition of surface," " 'each surface is an interface between two environments that is ruled by a constant activity in the form of an exchange between the two substances placed in contact with one another.' "[186] This definition "demonstrates the contamination at work: the 'boundary, or limiting surface' has turned into an osmotic membrane. . . . The limitation of space has become commutation: the radical separation, the necessary crossing, the transit of a constant activity, the activity of incessant exchanges, the transfer between two environments and two substances. What used to be the boundary of a material, its 'terminus,' has become an entryway hidden in the most imperceptible entity. From here on, the appearance of surfaces and superficies conceals a secret transparency, a thickness without thickness, a volume without volume, an imperceptible quantity" (p. 17). It is important, however, not merely to apply these globally geophysical terms to a specific case study such as Nietzsche/anism but also to allow the latter to speak back to the former, modifying their global abstraction with microanalysis. The virgule between "Nietzsche" and "Nietzscheanism," "corps" and "corpse," is intended to suggest that both terms work as structural causality, osmotically, *interfacially* in tandem: Nietzsche with and within Nietzscheanism; the corpse with and within the corps. The more polite, euphemistic, housebroken, everyday term for "Nietzsche's corps/e" is "Nietzsche/anism." The two would be synonymous, except that the former is less abstract, more precise, concrete, and fully adequate to the ultimate violence and embodied terror that was and is Nietzsche's own intent. More important, a therapeutic lesson is that as soon as *any* keyterm — whether it be "corps/e," or "communism," or whatever — becomes a mere conjurer's or juggler's hocus-pocus, a mere ontotheological shibboleth, it must be immediately interrogated and, if need be, blown into disgraced, desecrated, dysfunctional bits.[187] Including this book.

Put in global and historical perspective, and with this caveat, the case of Nietzsche/anism is obviously one example *inter alia inter pares*. But the distinction of Nietzsche/anism and Nietzsche's corps/e is not merely relative but also a matter of magnitude (*quanta*) and of kind (*quala*). Here a particular distinction between theory and historical practice needs to be drawn.

In theory it is possible — indeed desirable — to substitute for "Nietzsche" any number of proper or improper names into that structural causality that is intellectual and social history. Think of *any* proper name "X" & its assumed movement, period, or genre "x": "Jesus" or "Reverend Moon" & "christianity" or "religion"; "Velázquez" or "Bach" & "culture of the baroque"; "James Yorke" & "chaos theory"; "Machiavelli" & "machiavellianism" or "political philosophy"; "Freud" or "Juliet Mitchell" & "psychoanalysis"; "Cavour" & "moderate politics"; "Ghandi" & "politics"; "Lévi-Strauss" & "anthropology"; "Valie Export" or "Alfred Hitchcock" or "Chris. Marker" or "Derek Jarman" & "cinema"; "Shakespeare" or "David Wojnarowicz" & "world literature"; "Georg Cantor" & "mathematics"; "Ranke" & "historiography"; "Gabriel García Márquez" & "the novel"; "Kiyoshi Miki" & "the Kyoto school" or "philosophy"; "Patti Smith" or "Beethoven" & "music"; "Manfredo Tafuri" & "architecture"; "Langston Hughes" or "Sylvia Plath" or "Aimé Césaire" or "Mahmoud Darwish" & "poetry"; "Fernando Pessoa" or "Jackson Pollock" & "modernism"; "Marx" or "Tosaka Jun" & "Marxism"; "Stalin" or "Pol Pot" or "Gramsci" or "Althusser" & "communism," and so forth. Each case includes the entire, interactive history of the reception or appropriation of these people or categories, both in professional scholarship and more popularly. And, in each case, the theory of the corps/e should be applied.

Yet Nietzsche/anism is distinct *in historical practice* from many, if not all, of these other examples. This relative but real distinction has two aspects: qualitative and quantitative. Nietzsche's conscious mastery of the modes of multiple causality, in the form of a proleptic rhetorical gesture that was designed to handicap the posthumous incorporation of his written corpus by informing it more or less surreptitiously, was — independent of its actual success — qualitatively greater around the world than that of *most* other writers, thinkers, politicans, or artists in history. All things considered, this impact has been remarkably positive and uncritical. Second, and as important, the quantitative extent of this impact on intellectuals and the intelligentsia has in fact proven to be greater than that of Nietzsche's *major* rivals, both beginning in his own historical conjuncture and continuing in today's — when his corps/e is more alive than ever.

Polemic and Hypothesis

Truly not the least attraction of a theory is that it can be contradicted.[188]

Where two principles meet, which cannot be reconciled with one another, then each calls the other a fool or a heretic. . . . If people did not sometimes do silly things, nothing intelligent would ever get done.[189]

When debating with an opponent, try to put yourself in his shoes: you will understand him better, and may end by recognizing that there is some truth in what he says, and perhaps a lot. For some time I myself followed this sage advice. But my adversaries' shoes got so filthy that I was forced to conclude it's better to be unfair than risk fainting from the stink they give off.[190]

The philosopher must be content with proposing theses without ever being able to verify them himself. He must always anticipate the effects of his philosophical theses without even knowing when, or how, these effects will be able to manifest themselves![191]

Given the actual power and apparent timeliness of Nietzsche/anism, what is necessary is a *polemic* in the common sense of the term. Not the least function of polemic is to combat *boredom*. Leonard Cohen could be singing for the reader of Nietzsche who tries to turn not merely against the Nietzsche Industry but against Nietzsche himself: "They sentenced me to twenty years of boredom for trying to change the system from within. I'm coming now, I'm coming to reward them."[192] For Nietzsche *is* the system, *is* maximum boredom in the guise of maximum excitement — a principle surreptitiously entailed by Eternal Recurrence of the Same. Yet this book also strives to be *scientific* in the sense that *philology* matters: namely, not only as devotion to what a writer says but also as critical analysis of what s/he intends to say but for some reason precisely does not write, except between lines and words. Hence, this is an experiment in what will be defined as *anexact* philology.

Now, for a sophisticated, quite powerful wing of the Nietzschean tradition — inaugurated by Nietzsche but led most brilliantly by Heidegger — *common* polemic is disparaged as a sign of philosophical failure, "the failure from the outset to take the posture of thinking."[193] Disclaimers aside, however, for the Nietzscheo-Heideggerian tradition, "thinking" never thereby sacrifices its *ultimate* combativity. On the contrary. According to this canon, origin-ary *pólemos* and *agón* never refer to simple battles in which the fronts and antagonists could ever be entirely clear. For all *open* battles (be they wars of maneuver or position)[194] can be considered an admission of not only philosophical but also military failure. This thesis would be confirmed by most tacticians and strategists, from Sun Tzu to Jeanne D'Arc, Clausewitz, Gandhi, Che Guevara, Truong Son, Vo Nguyên Giap, Carlos Marighela, Ulrike Meinhof, Kwame Nkrumah, Oliver North, and Paul Virilio — though each with a different constituency and aim in mind. And pick your side, you're on one already.[195] Speaking of philosophy, Althusser clarified Kant's famous image (with its ultimate source in Plato) that metaphysics is a "battlefield" (*Kampfplatz*) to argue that "A philosophy does not make its appearance in the world as Minerva appeared to the society of Gods and men. It exists only in so far as it occupies a position, and it occupies this position only in so far as it has conquered it in the thick of an already occupied and bloody world. It therefore exists only in so far as this conflict has made it something distinct, and this distinctive character can be won and imposed only in an indirect way, by a detour involving ceaseless study of other, existing positions."[196] More specifically, Althusser noted: "No, philosophy is not, as the young Marx still wanted it, on this point a faithful disciple of Hegel, 'the self awareness of an historical epoch'; rather, it is the site of a class struggle [le lieu d'une lutte de classe] that repeats itself and that reaches it most approximate forms at certain moments of history and in certain thinkers: for us, above all, Epicurus, Machiavelli, Spinoza, Rousseau, and Hegel, authentic precursors of Marx."[197]

But in most fields sooner or later one encounters a position always already occupied by *Nietzsche/anism*. Althusser has succinctly paraphrased three basic concepts of Spinoza and Machiavelli that bear directly on this phenomenon: that is, on Nietzsche as "cause" and Nietzscheanism as "effect." In specific, Althusser highlights two Spinozist concepts: first, the theory of "third-level knowledge," that is, knowledge of a case that is simultaneously "singular and universal," precisely as Nietzsche/anism is or strives to be; and, second, the theory of the way it is that thought, or rather "thinking with the body," comes to be "reconstituted" or "embodied" — both in oneself and in the work of others. Finally, there is Machiavelli's "astonishing" and "radical" idea to the effect that Chance (*Fortunà*) "is in essence no more than the void, and par excellence the interior void of the Prince, which foregrounds, in the equilibrium and play of his passions, his role as fox, allowing him to introduce a crucial distance between these passions and the Prince-qua-Subject, so that being can appear as nonbeing and nonbeing as being."[198] With these three concepts, mediated by Althusser, we catch a deep insight into the world of Nietzsche's corps/e and *its* battlefield.

In the direct aftershock of World War II, Wittgenstein defined philosophy as "a battle against the bewitchment of our intelligence by means of language [Die Philosophie ist ein Kampf gegen die Verhexung unsres Verstandes durch die Mittel unserer Sprache]."[199] Wittingly or not, his definition is informed by a disturbing ambivalence, insofar as it is rather unclear whether "the means of language" serve our "understanding" or rather its "bewitchment," and hence, appropriately enough, this definition of philosophy not only constates but also performs its certain bellicosity. Be this ambivalence as it may, also relevant for the case of Nietzsche/anism is a philosopheme of the later Wittgenstein. What entraps us, even more profoundly than language, is "an image" or "a picture" (*ein Bild*) deeper within it. "A picture held us captive. And we could not get outside it, for it lay in our language and language seemed to repeat it to us inexorably."[200] "Nietzsche" is "a picture" or "an image" — not an "idea," which could be effectively combated by logic — in this Wittgensteinian sense: namely, an image inexorably *lying* — in both senses of the word — in/visibly and in/audibly within contemporary language, including at least initially any language with which one attempts to dissociate oneself from the "bewitchment" of Nietzsche's corps/e. And the notion that Nietzsche's work, by itself, is the "battlefield" (*Schlachtfeld*) on which the intellectual and creative life of modernity must be contested had been claimed in pre–World War I Germany.[201]

The distinctly Nietzschean tradition of thinking about polemics has long traced — or rather produced — its self-legitimating genealogy to the pre-Socratic philosophers. Philosophical "origins" — and the possibility of return or turning, rupture and reintegration that they logically entail — are claimed by the sophisticated Nietzschean tradition in Parmenides' slogan, "the same thing exists for thinking and for being," but, precisely for this reason, also potential conflict between them (*tò gàr autò noein estín te kaì einai*); in Empedocles' slogan about the ontological interaction between Love and Strife, to the effect that "things never cease from shifting continually — at one time or another coming together, through Love [*Philóteti*], into one, yet each borne apart, at another time, from the others through Strife [*Neíkeos*]"; and especially in Heraclitus' slogan — often alluded to by Nietzsche — that "war is father of all things [*pólemos pánton mèn patér esti*]."[202] According to this agonistic view of the world, peace forever brings disunity, war unity — a thesis related to the simple observation of everyday life that "a Frosty Dairy Dessert™ [Heraclitus himself knew only *kykeon*: an apparently savory mixture of wine, barley, and cheese] begins to separate if it is not stirred,"[203] or quickly *consumed*.

Heidegger among mortals strove hardest to recapture what he took to be the premetaphysical, preproductivist instant of pre-Socratic thinking. For him, the only authentic philosophico-military polemic would be "a confrontational act of setting one thing apart from another" (*pólemos* as *Aus-einander-setzung*), but so that the master thinker/leader might bring these things together, uniting and engaging them in the more proper and noble battle royal that is profound thinking: namely, disclosive of Being. In this context, Heidegger says that Heraclitian *pólemos* and *lógos* "are the same thing." This is to say, in part, that any capacity "to bind together" — including but not only by means of more or less systematic speech or discourse — is always radically combative as well as combinative. *Pólemos* is further imagined by this tradition and by Heidegger himself as *the* cosmological, ontological, but also political principle. It is both unalterable and determining — at once ultimately beyond human control and yet decisive in organizing any human society, but especially one authentically open to the way things supposedly really *are*.[204] So it is that, for Heidegger, polemic — as a way of "revealing" (*deichnúmai*) and also "producing" (*poiein*) — is originary: cosmologically and ontologically, but also socioeconomically and politically, since after its inception polemic is "carried on by creators, poets, thinkers, statesmen."[205] Because Heidegger is the dominant Nietzschean philosopher of the twentieth century, his grasp of polemics needs to be pursued to its lair.

Heidegger's combative, political-ontological way of thinking presumes to see the radically "conflictual way" it is that Truth (even Being Itself, which *is* not but rather *happens*, "*events*," or "*advents*") "tragically" reveals itself as *alétheia:* that is, discloses itself in the fundamental "mutation in the essential way to be of truth," which is "the technicity of modern technique" and which we in our fallen, post-Platonic, mathematico-productivist age commonly reify as "technology."[206] Very roughly it can be said that, according to Heidegger, originary — pre-Platonic — Truth (Greek *alétheia*) is composed of the privative *a*- and a verb *léthein,* "to conceal," but also, more sinisterly — as Heidegger's readers almost never seem to grasp — "to dissemble," "to purloin," "to make esoteric."[207] And as it is with epistemological matters of truth and falsity, so is it also with ontological matters of being and nonbeing (not to mention also aesthetic, erotic, moral, and political questions) — all have exo/esoteric dimensionality.

In 1943–1944, for example, Heidegger took from Heraclitus' phrase that "nature loves to conceal itself" (*phusis kruptesthai phiei*) the fundamental lesson that Being Itself as *phusis* "is the play of emergence in self-concealment, playing that hides in the act of emancipating that which emerges into the open. . . . "[208] The supreme import in terms of the history of philosophy or metaphysics of this claim for Heidegger is succinctly formulated by Stanley Rosen. After citing Heidegger's interpretation of the Heraclitian play of concealment and unconcealment in and as *phusis,* Rosen paraphrases Heidegger's overarching position: "Plato initiates the shift in attention from awareness of Being as the play of presence and absence to a conception of Being as pure or genuine (*ontós on*) presence, namely, as the presence of the look, that by which we identify what a thing is: the *idea*. From this point on, philosophy is defined by the Platonic standard."[209] *Until* Heidegger, or at least until his *preparation* for "another way of thinking." But it is equally important to note that—in Heidegger's own view, though he would never say so exactly—Being Itself must obey the logically prior law of the exo/esoteric. It is this iron law—unrepealable and unappealable—that also propels the thought of Nietzsche, no matter what comparatively superficial difference might separate him from Heidegger.

Heideggerian Truth qua unconcealment is not the negative obverse of untruth qua concealment, mere linguistic proximity aside. What *is*—or *can be*—unconcealed are things, entities, objects, and technologies perceptible by the senses, and hence generally the exoteric world that the Greeks called aesthetics or *aisthetón*.[210] By crucial contrast, what pertains to concealment is Being qua Being specifically and absolutely. Hence, (esoteric) Truth and (exoteric) untruth are not only asymmetrically balanced but also opposed—ludically and militarily—in irreconcilable fashion. Their primal relationship—such as the eventful isomorphic relationship within Being Itself between expropriation and appropriation that Heidegger calls *Enteignis/Ereignis*—is endlessly belligerent. Compare also, crucially, *apókryptein*, "to conceal," with *apókalyptein*, "to uncover"; in this conceptual world, ultimately it takes apocalypse to decode cryptograms, to expose apocrypha. But this belligerency obtains not just with Heidegger's vision of *ontology*—the way things are—but also with his vision of *political ontology*—the way things ought to be. With regard to the way things ought to be—and in *this* proleptic sense always already are—Heidegger was opportunistic. His description of polemics could be and was normally adjusted according to historical contingencies. But he preferred to keep his views as secret, as esoteric as possible . . . and hence maximally preparatory for ever-renewable "other beginnings" and "another thinking" in the future.[211] It was from Nietzsche most directly that Heidegger inherited this entire problematic.

Living at a more preliminary stage of modern industrial, technological, and political development, the young Nietzsche had launched his own bellicose intellectual and social itinerary by speaking of "the Dionysian worldview," of truth as *páthos,* and of deepest thinking in terms of "tragedy" and "tragic ages," "struggle" and "war," *agón* and *pó-*

lemos.[212] Later, in "On Reading and Writing," Zarathustra teaches that "wisdom is a woman: she loves only a warrior"—desiring him "courageous, unconcerned, mocking, brutally violent."[213] Among other things, Wisdom "is just asking to be raped"—*date raped,* as it were. *On the Genealogy of Morals* was Nietzsche's most rigorous, sustained, and interesting work by the standards of Anglo-American analytic philosophy; it bore the subtitle *A Polemic.*[214] According to Heidegger, but only when his own Nietzschean and national-socialist political ontology was in disarray, Nietzsche, like one tendency of national socialism, sold out this more authentic, properly agonistic, and warlike vision to a less authentic, historically contingent, productivist Will to Power; though Heidegger continued to share with Nietzsche the same fascoid social agenda and the same *base* commitment to esoteric speech and subliminal influence.

Aware of this sophisticated tradition of polemic, and of its subtle internal quibbling, it is nevertheless important to engage Nietzsche's corps/e with polemics of a comparatively commonsense, common, and base sort: a form of struggle that has no intention of uniting what ought not to be joined except in maximally communal and globally egalitarian combat. Gandhi was right: *They* started it their way, let *us* strive to finish it in ours, using their bad conscience, if they have one, against them. In this effort do not forget, as Heidegger and Nietzsche knew intimately, that Heraclitus' oft-cited slogan "war is father of all things" (Fr. 53) reads in full: "War is father of all things, king of all, and some he shows as gods, others as men; some he makes slaves, others free [*pólemos pánton mèn patér esti, pánton dè basileús, kaì toùs theoùs édeixe toùs dè anthrópous, toùs mèn doúlous epoíese toùs dè eleuthérous*]." For once, *let* women and men bury the gods, and the slaves the slavemasters. Let us try to bury Nietzsche's corps/e. In this effort, the baser, slam-dance polemic pays tribute to Bertolt Brecht's affirmation of the necessity sometimes for "crude-and-lewd thinking" or "mindfuck" (*das plumpe Denken*).[215] For there are excellent reasons to mistrust radically the underlying intent behind the sophisticated wing of the Nietzscheo-Heideggerian tradition, and *its* mindfuck, or, as Gramsci might say, "rape of the intelligence."[216]

Related to "polemics" is "hypothesis." Nietzsche's own esoteric take on hypothesis characteristically involves social and rhetorical—beyond merely epistemological or thematic — considerations. Specifically, hypothesis has to do with his project in *Thus Spoke Zarathustra* to produce a text for an increasingly secular and modern age that would have an at least equivalent power to the one enjoyed by the Bible in previous premodern times — reversing most but not all of its effects. What Nietzsche wanted most to preserve was the capacity of the Bible, indeed religion generally, for social cohesion and the maintenance of hierarchy. In this vein, Nietzsche wrote to himself: " — just as lower humans looked up to God, it is appropriate that someday we *look up to my Overman.* "[217] He continued: " — the contradiction of atheism and theism is *not:* 'truth' or 'untruth,' but rather that we no longer allow ourselves a hypothesis *that we gladly allow others to have* (and more!) [.] *Piety is the only bearable form of common people: our desire* is that the people [das Volk] becomes religious, so that we do not experience nausea when facing it: as now, when the appearance of the masses is nauseating."[218] Nietzschean hypotheses, in other words, are not merely pragmatic tools in any abstract sense; instead, they are part of an overarching polemic and pragmatic intent that is to function differently for two basic groups — the elite and the masses, "us" and "them" — whose absolute social difference is thereby to be perpetuated. This properly, quintessentially Nietzschean perspective cannot be exposed enough today, under postmodern global conditions in which the discrepancy between hyperrich and hyperpoor escalates by the hour.

It should go without saying that what is therefore at stake is not only an *"interpretation"* of Nietzsche but also (in words that have been used to describe the "influence" of Spinoza on Althusser) "an *intervention* in the relationship of forces that governs his text, taking the side of certain hypotheses against others, pushing these hypotheses to extreme conclusions, towards the dismantling of a theoretical apparatus."[219] In any case, the adversary is bigger and more extensive than just one tributary of the Nietzschean current in Europe and the United States. (Though North Americans from Canada to Mexico especially are reminded that what appear as mere "tributaries" of major rivers may actually be incorporating "invaders," each with its own directive dynamic.)[220] Required is a war of maneuver and of position pitted against Nietzsche/anism *simply and in its entirety.*

This is a polemic not out of perversity, exactly, but in the conviction that Nietzsche and Nietzscheanism — both of which are commonly and falsely regarded today as "leftist"—are grasped inadequately even today, especially today. This polemic will try to wrest the mention and especially the use of Nietzsche away from the Left—as well as from the Right and Center—at long last, for as long as possible. Quixotic, yes. All writing and reading—and not just qua corps/e—is undoubtedly a way of dying "a little death," more or less erotic, just as writing/reading is a way of living alternating or alternative lives, borrowed lives.[221] "One of the most important quixotic acts, more obtrusive than fighting the windmill, is: suicide. The dead Don Quixote wants to kill the dead Don Quixote; in order to kill, however, he needs a place that is alive, and this he searches for with his sword, both ceaselessly and in vain. Engaged in this occupation the two dead men, inextricably interlocked and positively bouncing with life, go somersaulting away down the ages." So said Kafka in 1917.[222] Since 1994—that is, since the 150th anniversary of Nietzsche's birth, and registering an end of the legacy of 1917—the fight against his corps/e entails a form of intellectual death, of suicide, not just of life.

The less gymnastic, ostentatious, and more scientific term for "polemics" is "hypothesis," following Francis Bacon's great maxim—not only for science but for esoteric writing—that "truth comes more easily from error than from confusion," in the likelihood that the best scholarship can achieve is not truth, anyway, but rather "competitive plausibility." (The related keyterm in Aristotle's *Poetics* had been "possible probability.") And of course the problem with any attempt to grasp an esoteric mode of writing such as Nietzsche's is that "A demonstrably esoteric text is a contradiction in terms."[223] Besides, esoteric writers are precisely that: *writers*. That is, they must obey what Socrates in Plato's *Phaedrus* called "the logographic necessity": the requirement to write in different ways—ways no longer monitored by verbal/aural strategies and confidences—to different readers in the present and future.[224] And the number of rhetorical *prestidigitations* that result, effective or not, is virtually endless. Which is to say that a person's *prestige* is often based on invisible sleights of hand and other tricks (Latin *prestigiae:* tricks). To *this* extent, if no other, Nietzsche was *pre*modern, a *Platonist*.[225]

A remark once made by Arnold Schoenberg, though not about Nietzsche, sums up part of the problem with Nietzsche/anism qua hypothesis. "So it always goes with very great men," Schoenberg said;

"at each are fired all those accusations of which the opposite is true. Yes *all*, and with such accuracy that one must be taken aback by it."[226] It is necessary to take the risk that "the opposite" of its accusations against Nietzsche may be true, that Nietzsche may really be a true leftist, and that Bataille's dictum is simply wrong. But Schoenberg's unquestioning, quintessentially Nietzschean solidarity with "great men," with the philosophical version of the "cult of personality" must be called to account, must be made to feel taken aback, must be targeted accurately—not because genuine human greatness is to be derided but because its possibility must be made available to the maximum number of people, people mobilized against false human greatness and pretense. In opposition to this liberatory project Nietzsche's own writing was informed by conspiracy theory and can only be exposed in its full complexity, can only be mapped cognitively, by a strong *rival* conspiratorial hypothesis. The intent here is not to persuade the reader that this hypothesis is *definitive*, as a totally accurate representation either of Nietzsche's original intent or relative effectiveness, but rather to persuade the reader that this hypothesis or cognitive mapping is *necessary*. "Nothing is gained by having been persuaded of the definitive verisimilitude of this or that conspiratorial hypothesis," Jameson notes, "but in the intent to hypothesize, in the desire called cognitive mapping—therein lies the beginning of wisdom."[227]

Yet another name for "polemics" is "blasphemy," especially if the latter, combining seriousness and irony, "protects one from the moral majority within, while still insisting on the need for community."[228] The problem in the case of Nietzsche/anism, however, is that nowadays—as "we" enter and engage the postcontemporary—it is blasphemy only to blaspheme *Nietzsche*—formerly the great blasphemer—and *his* community. Postcontemporary interventions must respond accordingly. The *right* to blaspheme, to advance *strong* hypotheses, to fight *ex hypothesi* is earned only when the subject or object to be studied is (1) *apparently very well known*, and/or (2) *in fact inadequately known*, and/or (3) *designed to be esoteric*. All three conditions apply very exactly, in symptomatic and exemplary fashion, to Nietzsche/anism.

Only if it were possible really to settle accounts with Nietzsche/anism might one speak of polemics also as a kind of *"ecstasy"*—in the technical sense proposed by the Nietzschean Jean Baudrillard: namely, "a passage at the same time into the dissolution and the transcendence

THE ONLY POSITION AS ADVERSARY

67

of a form."[229] And only then could one really "close the eyes" of Nietzsche's corps/e, in the sense proposed for corpses generally, for "death in human form," by a different type of Nietzschean, Roland Barthes: "to close the eyes of the dead is to exorcise whatever life remains, to make the dead die for good, to make the dead totally dead."[230] Finally, in this context, there is the answer given by psychoanalytic systems from Freud to Lacan to Žižek to the haunting question "Why do the dead return?" It is *because they were not properly buried,* i.e., because something went wrong with their obsequies. The return of the dead is a sign of a disturbance in the symbolic rite, in the process of symbolization; the dead return as collectors of some unpaid symbolic debt."[231]

Given the extensive explicit—and tacit—hegemony of Nietzsche/anism over contemporary discourse, any conceivable "empirical" or even "phenomenological" account would be insufficient; especially strong counterhypotheses are demanded. If, first, Nietzsche/anism *is* our consciousness, our subconscious, our political unconscious, our geopolitical aesthetic, and, second, if Nietzsche's position *is* the only one outside of communism, then it is particularly urgent to recall the great principle of historical and dialectical materialism that "consciousness does not accede to the real through its own internal development, but by the radical discovery of what is *other than itself.*"[232] The effort to be—to produce—this other is an act not only of polemics but of philology. Qua hypotheses books are what Althusser calls "the theoretical laboratory" (*le laboratoire théoretique*),[233] in which are produced and elaborated *new*—or at least *different*—thoughts in opposition to thoughts as usual, business as usual, Nietzsche Industry as usual.

Outline of the Argument, Anexact Philology

Yet the question of politics has not been hammered into place, and, because of that there is a small space in which the possibility exists that Nietzsche was not the moral monster that he could so easily have been and be—perhaps too, along with this, necessarily, is the possibility that the horror of his politics is still not fully accounted for.[234]

All the capitalized keywords both in the title of this not quite ecstatic but blasphemous polemic-hypothesis—*Nietzsche's Corps/e*—and in its subtitle — *Aesthetics, Politics, Prophecy, or, The Spectacular Technoculture of Everyday Life* — are more than words, concepts, or even signs. They are also rallying cries — slogans — drawn from the interminable debates of post-Enlightenment history: that is, the modernist and postmodernist period — from Taylorism and Fordism to postindustrial neocapitalism — during which "Sign becomes an arena of class struggle."[235] In this complex and — when need be — violent history, Nietzsche pitted himself to the death against the democratic tendencies of the Enlightenment — with remarkable success — by waging war with an esoteric semiotics that must be grasped with an appropriate kind of anexact philology. That is, it must be, following in the tradition of Lucretius, "rigorous, anexact" — "essentially and not accidentally inexact."[236]

Eventually, each of the main slogans of this book needs to be defined, each situated in its context. Attention must also be given sometimes to Kant and especially Spinoza. For Nietzsche worked within a basically neo-Kantian and neo-Spinozist epistemological "problematic," in the Althusserian sense.[237] Nietzsche's "Kantian" opposition to Hegel was prompted by Schopenhauer, who regarded himself as post-Kantian and who despised Hegel. This highly mediated opposition makes it impossible for Hegelian Marxists, of which there are many kinds, to grasp what Nietzsche was about, but *also* for those who reject Nietzsche's Hegelianism out of hand. Kant was one of the few professional philosophers whose work Nietzsche knew fairly well, though far less directly than through Schopenhauer and secondary accounts. Spinoza — whom Nietzsche cited as early as 1878 but waxed enthusiastic about only comparatively late in his career and read even then in highly mediated form — illuminates several obscurities not only in his conceptual world and in Nietzscheanism but also in what is rapidly becoming the "everyday life" of postmodern technoculture. In Spinozist terms, to both recall and anticipate, the *ideal* influence ("effect") of a thinker ("cause") like Nietzsche would be "hidden to the degree that he is socialized and inserted in a vast and adequate cultural society."[238]

There has been to date no adequate leftist — or rather *communist* — analysis of Nietzsche or his legacy, and this book attempts to promote such analysis.[239] The one slogan that systematically refuses definition, however, is "communism" itself, since "communism is for us not a *state of affairs* which is to be established, an *ideal* to which reality [will] have to adjust itself. We call communism the *real* movement which abolishes the present state of the things."[240] A tall order any time, now more than ever when communism has been widely declared dead. Provisionally, however, it is crucial "once again to begin to define communism as the collective struggle for the liberation of work," where work is redefined as "a project and a process of liberation."[241] The phrase or genitive metaphor "liberation *of* work" is intentionally double. This is to say that communism must both *empower* those forms of work that are maximally liberatory for humanity and also *refuse* work when necessary, disempowering those forms of work that are not maximally liberatory, so as to liberate ideal work from its actual oppressive aspect. This liberatory project was exactly what Nietzsche himself—when viewed properly—not only *implicitly and consciously problematized*—as is proper—but also *explicitly and surreptitiously combated*—as is improper, from a communist perspective, and so must be exposed to light. An objective here is to attack the "Spinozist" claim to universality and totality made by global capitalism, its New World Order. To that end, communism is broadly defined "as the assortment of social practices leading to the transformation of consciousness and reality on every level: political and social, historical and everyday, conscious and unconscious."[242] This definition is not as pointlessly vague as it seems, if capitalism has defeated communism, and if "Nietzsche's position is the only one outside of communism."

In the more limited terms of its own "question of style," this book re/produces a communist position qua text in two opposed ways dialectically linked by labor: in one way by work in the form of philological and archival research and logical argument (*science*); in the other by the *refusal* of such work and the affirmation of *other* kinds: speculation, spectacle, and performance (*ideology and politics*). If the modernist problematic, as expressed by one of the earliest and greatest literary Right-Nietzscheans, was that "the best lack all conviction, while the worst are full of passionate intensity," then the postmodernist problematic may be that the very distinction not only between "the best" and "the worst" has evaporated, for better or worse, but also between "conviction" and "passion."[243] Even the *possibility* of having genuine intellectual, moral, and political convictions and passions is fading fast, at least in academic prose. So the aim must be to articulate passion with scholarship once again, on the Left for the Left.

The bottom line always has to do with *labor*, with the ultimate irreconcilability and consequent class and other *struggles* between those women and men who work versus men and women who exploit them, appropriating all the products of work. This is the notorious Marxist "last instance," and it is not "reductionism" but the simple truth to grasp history in such terms, *among others.*

More specifically, "communism is the establishment of a communal life style in which individuality is recognized and truly liberated, not merely opposed to the collective. That's the most important lesson: that the consciousness of healthy communities begins and ends with unique personalities, that the collective potential is realized only when the singular is free."[244] These last phrases may *sound* to us exactly like Nietzsche talking; but he is not really.[245] Rather, these phrases are only *superficially* one of Nietzsche's many contributions to contemporary critical and artistic discourse, his exoteric message only. His esoteric message is quite the opposite, more morally monstrous and horrific: namely, to elevate the few by enslaving the many, *but* with the latter's more or less willing approval and enjoyment, including with the substantial support of gullible intellectuals — self-described Left-Nietzscheans being unwitting vanguards among them. Communism — including communist parties as ideal and potential, though not necessarily as current actualities — may be the *only* alternative ethico-politico-economic force of consequence against capital and its consequences, which includes Nietzsche's corps/e. In other words, Bataille's claim that "Nietzsche's position is the only one outside of communism" now cuts at least two ways, depending of course on what one means not only by "communism" but also by what must be called Nietzsche's *"fascoid-liberal* position."

The term "fascoid" is for preferable in Nietzsche's case to either "protofascist" or certainly "Nazi." As the problem is commonly posed about Nietzsche, these terms entail irrelevant questions of "source" and "anticipation" on which valuable time has been wasted over the years. Besides, Nietzsche could hardly have exerted such extensive positive influence on the Left were matters this simple, and their complexity is trivialized by the originally Lukácsian — later dissenting left-liberal and social democratic — slogan "Actor Hitler, Thinker Nietzsche." The phrase *"Wiederkehr eines Philosophen: Täter Hitler, Denker Nietzsche* [return of a philosopher: actor (even murderer) Hitler, thinker Nietzsche]" was emblazoned on the cover of the influential liberal West German weekly *Der Spiegel* in June 1981. This Lukácsian slogan was superimposed over a drawing of Hitler's head, shoulder, and hand anachronistically brandishing a modern Walter PPK pistol — all morphing from Nietzsche's hair, shoulder, and head, the last supported, as on Auguste Rodin's *The Thinker,* on his clenched fist.[246] A more appropriately complex image of the alleged relationship between Nietzsche and national socialism was produced by Joseph Beuys (1921–1986). *Sonnenfinsternis und Corona* (solar eclipse and corona, 1978) is a two-tier vertical montage: the top three-quarters is a photo-reproduction of Hans Olde's etching in 1889 of the totally insane but docile, hugely mustached Nietzsche staring "heroically" into space; the bottom quarter reproduces a photograph taken of a trashed interior urban space. A shelf has crashed down upon a table, along with a broken picture frame, and so on. Outside — across the street and visible through huge windows — one sees a business-district building with the names of two "Jewish" firms: "Bab & Fleischer" and "Julius Kaufmann." The original photograph was taken November 9, 1938, the night of the first systematic Nazi pogroms (*Reichskristallnacht*). But sprayed diagonally across Beuys's black-and-white montage are two patterns of white disks — or, alternatively, holes — each edged slightly in brownish-red oil paint. They evoke a complex set of references, reinforced by Beuys's double title: the eclipse of one (celestial) body by another and the corona or crown worn in classical antiquity to distinguish important personages or victors to show their proximity to the gods. Beuys thus articulates the philosopher, Nazism, and public collaboration with barbarism. Finally, the holes can be read as having been made by bullets, as someone having taken aim to destroy four images: Olde's hagiographic and obscurantist image of Nietzsche; evidence of the pogroms; the connection between the two; and, not least, Beuys's own composite picture.[247]

Nietzsche — like Heidegger later — was not a "nationalist" or a "socialist" or a "racist" or even an "imperialist" in any conventional or vulgar senses of these terms, even though there are certainly *aspects* of these tendencies in his thinking. And his quite duplicitous doctrine of relativism — which, to say the least, did nothing to restrain his own concept and use of *power* — gives no firm or sufficient grounds for *resisting* imperialist national socialism or fascism. The "fascoid" refers to four things primarily: (1) to a combative political ontology based on more or less permanent overt and covert warfare against democratic values in general and against the possibility of radical democracy in particular; (2) to an unquestioned commitment to some form of "Leader Principle" (i.e., strong—predominantly male—leaders and neo-aristocratic elites as the real motor of history, able to function, when need be, under the guise of individual rights, anarchism, libertarianism, populism, even social democracy—but theoretically By Any Means Necessary); (3) to a concomitant, enthusiastic socioeconomic commitment—not necessarily capitalist, but certainly capitalist if need be—to the maintenance of a gullible, pliable, and—if at all possible—willing workforce, up to and including slave labor; and (4) to a consciously manipulative, duplicitous practice of writing, speaking, and acting grounded in esotericism and other strategies of speaking to two audiences at once—those in the know, and those out of the know who are to be kept out of the know. The Nietzschean fascoid, too, is a "real movement" that is profoundly anticommunist, both historically and right now, independent of the question of whether it is *literally* "the only position outside of communism."

How the fascoid articulates itself to the term "liberalism"—in both its neoliberal and neoconservative variants—is a particularly difficult and crucial question, even more than the fascoid's equally likely but less subtle—and hence more easily combated—articulation with more overt forms of National Socialism or national socialism, Fascism or fascism. Nietzsche's own, often critical, position with regard to liberalism was obviously determined by the versions available to him in Europe and especially Germany in the 1870s and 1880s, including, at the end of his sane life, his embrace of the program of the short-term (one-hundred-day) "liberal" Emperor Friedrich III (1831–1888), and so forth.[248] But the fascoid-liberal articulation will be defined more fully from a Gramscian perspective in the last main section of this book.

Precisely because communism is, among other things, "the *real* movement which abolishes the present state of the things," it is required to operate in untimely, isolated, preliminary, preparatory fashion to bury Nietzsche's corps/e: that is, it works far more in terms of theory and superstructure than of economics and practice. Whereas generally "in discussing a problem, we should start from reality and not from definitions," as Mao taught, and whereas especially "Marxism teaches that in our approach to a problem we should start from objective facts, not from abstract definitions," the actual reality of Nietzscheanism—"the facts at present"—is that it has become virtually indistinguishable from such "abstractions" as cyberspace as well as from less technological everyday life as it is still more normally lived by most of the globe.[249] And though this book is part analysis of the resulting virtual reality, it is also part *performance*. This is to say that it attempts to take seriously the compact or nexus between philology and enactment, "fact" and "fiction," "philosophy" and "literature" that Nietzsche decisively, seminally reformulated, retooled, remobilized. But then this nexus must be radically turned against him. This is not to assume, however, that philosophical performance is *necessarily* subversive, nor is the gesture of "[descending] into evil in order to defeat it from within."[250] Sooner it is the case that "performativity describes the relation of being implicated in that which one opposes, this turning of power against itself to produce alternative modalities of power to establish a kind of political contestation that is not a 'pure' opposition, a 'transcendence' of contemporary relations of power, but a difficult labor of forging a future from resources inevitably impure."[251] Which does not, however, preclude the heuristic possibility that a pure break with Nietzsche/anism *might* occur.

As for Nietzsche himself, he has been taken both *too* seriously and not seriously *enough*. *Too* seriously, in light of the hyperbolic, quasi-mythic, and a priori nature of the claims often made about his absolute significance for "us," including the "Left"—claims that are best taken at face value, initially, for the sake of eventual counterargument; not seriously *enough,* because these claims remain ignorant not so much about *what* his basically horrific ideas "really were"—though this ignorance, too, remains a big problem—but of *how* he intended to implement them with language and in society.

Exactly like Sherlock Holmes's Watson, "readers" of Nietzsche-Moriarty look, but they—quite literally—do not see; and if and when they do see, they do not observe. Sir Arthur Conan Doyle appears to have been one of the early readers of Nietzsche and, in spite of his bourgeois opposition to him, to have modeled both Sherlock Holmes and Prof. Moriarty—Holmes's equal—on him.[252] Alternatively—in postlinguistic, cyberpunk parlance—Nietzschean viewers have *become* what they *perceive*—without knowing what it is they perceive and how it works. The consequences of this particular dialectic of insight and blindness are grave as well as "comic," in the complex senses of the

term. Nietzsche's ideas should be viewed, in part, not only in a protocyborg context but also as profoundly fascoid-liberal. To repeat, they
are *not* strictly Nazi or fascist. But this is fascoid-liberalism of no common garden variety, either, and of a type not yet grasped by the vast,
productive, and comparatively lucrative Nietzsche Industry, at least not
as it most commonly presents itself.

Arguably *the* constitutive paradox of post/modern intellectual, artistic, and political life — thinking with Gramsci of *all* women and men
as intellectuals, artists, philosophers — is that Nietzsche seems to attack
nothing more vehemently than democracy, socialism, feminism, popular culture, and the Left in general. Yet nowhere and at no other time
has he enjoyed a warmer, more uncritical — hence more masochistic —
welcome than today from precisely this same Left — warmer and more
uncritically than ever even on the Center or the Right. And so is incepted and reproduced the Left-Nietzschean corps.

What must never be forgotten, however, is that this paradoxical situation arose — in part — because it was self-proclaimed "*anti-
Nietzscheans*" holding power in East Bloc countries who helped make
Nietzsche/anism appear as a progressive, viable alternative to Actually
Existing Socialism and "communism," there and elsewhere around the
world. This was sometimes done — unforgettably, unforgivably, *and*
counterproductively — by suppressing, even criminalizing free debate
about Nietzsche's thought and writing.[253] But this brutal fact unfortunately cannot fully explain the phenomenon of Left-Nietzscheanism,
and especially not in the capitalist world, where the existence of an
extensive, complex — albeit lopsided toward the Right — discussion of
Nietzsche in the former East Bloc is still virtually unknown, and where
an elaborate Left-Nietzscheanism was firmly in place long before Stalin or even the incomparable October Revolution, *both* of which are
now — for opposing but related reasons — of unfortunately distant collective memory. In addition to *moral* and *legal* questions associated
with the atrocities committed by Stalinism and its equivalents, there is
the intransigent *philosophical* fact that these crimes were committed not
only against human beings but also against fundamental *communist*
principles. As Althusser showed in 1962 — *definitively,* to the extent that
such matters can ever be so decided — what he called "*the overdetermination of any contradiction and of any constitutive element of a society*" means
two things that bear directly on Stalinism. First, "a revolution in the

structure does not *ipso facto* modify the existing superstructures and particularly the *ideologies* at one blow (as it would if the economic was the *sole determinant factor*), for they have sufficient of their own consistency *to survive beyond their immediate life context,* even to recreate, to 'secrete' substitute conditions of existence temporarily."[254] Applied to Nietzsche/anism, Althusser's thesis means that we must expect — "predict" even — Nietzscheanism to continue to live on after *any* revolution, *if* that revolution occurs at the level of structure and nowhere else. And so Nietzsche/anism did in fact live on, "even" in the Union of Soviet Socialist Republics and its satellites, as one of Nietzsche's corps/es — theoretically one of the most significant viruses possible. Second, still following Althusser, "the new society produced by the Revolution may itself *ensure the survival, that is, the reactivation, of older elements* through both the forms of its new superstructures and specific (national and international) 'circumstances'" (pp. 115–116). And this second Althusserian thesis, too, is exactly confirmed in the case of Nietzsche/anism. For nowhere today is there *more* vitality in Nietzsche's corps/e — there is equal vitality in many other places — than in the *former* USSR.

The truly uncanny — virtually global — paradox of Left-Nietzscheanism can only be grasped as such — namely, as an *apparent* contradiction — by means of substantial infusions of scholarly and philological labor. This includes sustained, sometimes even respectful attention to what John Locke called "philosophical underlaborers," to secondary literature more or less like one's own; and it includes taking seriously the disquieting possibility that every bit, every microchip of critical writing contains within itself — like it or not — a program for all criticism: criticism's more or less rational or demented categorical imperative, so to speak. And so it is that a counter-Nietzschean — and thus quasi-megalomaniac — gesture must provide a map of the major tendencies of contemporary philosophical, literary, literary-critical, and popular-cultural theory and practice by means of reference to their Nietzsche/anism. Philological and scholarly work and their methodological precautions are untimely, no longer much in fashion nowadays. And the specific problem they confront in the case of Nietzsche's esoteric semiotic is that esotericism in its strictest and most logical form would leave *no* trace for philology to read. By itself, philology is never sufficient. Nonetheless, its labor — in the form of sometimes heavy endnotes—is required to help steer and, when need be, anchor the performative, hegemonic, cyberspatial navigations (Greek *kybernetes* meant "navigator"; *hegemonikón* meant "directive faculty of the soul") that take place "above" the more "base" labors, and in opposition to Nietzsche's own scholarly and not so scholarly, more or less hidden agendas.

As offensive as it may sound to current aesthetic and academic ears alike, the *ideal* mixture of a democratic offensive against Nietzsche and Nietzscheanism might be exactly *half text, half endnotes*. The concept is Gramscian: two different kinds of text working together as a "bloc"— vanguard and base recruiting from one another—for a single destructive and constructive end. The reader should also be warned—and has noted already—that it is committed to at least two "postmodern" rhetorical techniques, demanding the extensive use of two things. First, there is pastiche—often long quotations—as a way of rivaling or paralleling the postmodern "schiz."[255] This use is intended to complicate more or less parodically the notion of authorship and ownership but also to give the reader the chance to read texts against the grain of this one book's views. Second, there are various forms of apparently parenthetical remarks—or rather remarks set off by dashes—as a way of qualifying, critiquing, or extending arguments.[256] If all these might appear in the abstract to be "Nietzschean" strategies, now they are turned against Nietzsche's corps/e. There are several important *formal-technological* as well as *politico-ideological* aspects of endnote-pastiche.

Technologically speaking, pastiche is a representation—limited in this case to the medium of print—of what in computerese is called hypertext; actual hypertexts can include visual and audio materials. In the words of Michael Heim, hypertext software is "nonsequential writing with free user movement," "a dynamic referencing system in which all texts are interrelated," where endnotes "enfold subordinate parts of the system as well as the references to other books," and where "all texts are virtually coresident. The whole notion of a primary and a secondary text, of originals and their references, collapses."[257] But while this collapse may actually occur in electronic media—though this is certainly debatable—this not quite what is supposed to occur, even metaphorically, in *Nietzsche's Corps/e* qua book; nor, much more important, is this collapse what really occurs in Nietzsche's corps/e qua historical phenomenon and movement. Heim suggests that in "magnetic code there are no originals, no primary, independently existing documents. All texts are virtually present and available for immediate access. The original text is merely the text accessed at the moment, the current center of focus" (p. 35). But note that this possibility — taken here already in Heim as actuality — is also a weak and unwitting description of structural causality, of Nietzsche/anism. Nietzsche's intention, embodied in the hypertext of his written corpus, lives on in embodied concealment, indwelling its effects silently and invisibly — virtually identical with them as corps/e, perhaps, but as yet never quite *really, totally* identical. The possibility that we might publicly access Nietzsche's original, primary, esoteric text or hypertext is not denied by the principle of structural causality. Rather, it is kept open methodologically by a form of pastiche porous to critical commentary. If it is true of computer software generally that, in Heim's words, "it *hides* within it *specific* notions about how we do and how we should think within a digital environment" (pp. 53–54), then we had better begin to access that software Nietzsche/anism that has been surgically implanted in us by reading Nietzsche's corpus — so as to access all that is hidden in and by Nietzsche's corps/e. But Nietzsche's own medium was *writing*, and we must (also) be able to *read* him.

For the *ideological* purposes at hand, pastiche is the rhetorical equivalent of communal, communist response to problems falsely posed to look as if individual, singular responses would be sufficient. This is also to say that pastiche is the rhetorical wing of what in political theory is called — though, alas, seldom in actuality is — "democratic centralism": namely, maximum disagreement *in camera;* maximum solidarity *in praxis.* This analogy, too, is derived from Gramsci, who defined "philology" (which includes, as its initial operation, the precise accumulation of different, accurately established "texts") as "the methodological expression of the importance of particular facts understood as definite and specific 'individualities.'" Trained as a philologist, Gramsci had in mind a rejection of all types of merely "sociological" and "historical" approaches to complex topics — including especially approaches claiming to be "historical materialist" and "Marxist" — whenever they culminate only in driving yet another wedge between the experiences of lived, conflicted everyday life — and in this sense obliterate "facts" and "individualities" — by means of the cold wedge of abstract, impersonal "laws." But Gramsci also had in mind, even more unusually and admirably, not only an equation of "philology" and communist *scholarship* but also of "philology" and communist *action* within but also beyond the academy. For Gramsci, a truly democratic communist party, or "collective organism," must come to its knowledges and practices "through 'active and conscious co-participation,' through 'compassionality,' through experience of immediate particulars, through a system which one could call 'living philology.' "258 This may be the highest possible standard against which to judge any text.

There is obviously nothing *easy* about grasping such notions or their deployment, such attempts to articulate the science of "philology" in all senses of the word with political "intervention." And particularly there is nothing *easy* about such attempts in a postcontemporary, Nietzschean culture that has long ago lost its taste for "philology." Widely forgotten today is the fact that Nietzsche himself was trained not as a philosopher or literary theorist but as a *philologist*, and that in certain circumstances he explicitly favored the "text" over its "explanation." Further ignored is the likelihood — indeed the *logical requirement* — that he incorporated his training as a textual critic into his *own* politico-rhetorical practice.259 But, as the young Gramsci emphasized in 1918 to fellow communists: "In order to be *easy* we would have had to falsify and impoverish a debate which hinged on concepts of the utmost importance, on the most fundamental and precious substance of our spirit. Doing that is not being easy: it amounts to fraud, like the wine merchant who passes off coloured water as Barolo or Lambrusco. A concept which is difficult in itself cannot be made easy when it is expressed without becoming vulgarized. And pretending that this vulgarization is still the same concept is to act like trivial demagogues, tricksters in logic and propaganda."260 It is in these Gramscian terms, then, that one must attempt to grasp Nietzsche/anism — all its new wine in old bottles. To this end, one also joins that tradition of *uneasy* materialist-communist thought extending from Spinoza through Gramsci and Althusser to Negri, which insists that "philology" and "militant politics" are *profoundly* related terms.261 And because the corps/e always has to do with death, the fight against it must be ferocious as well as anexact.

This tradition is pitted in a sometimes life-and-death struggle with another, vaster and more powerful tradition that encompasses, in the Jewish-Christian-Islamic variant at least, *Scriptural* interpretation. This tradition encompasses the veritable Scripture Industry that the Nietzsche Industry has become. But the drift of the "hermeneutic" tradition, in Warren Montag's paraphrase, is "based on a fundamental denial of objective material existence" of the texts in question, in so far as it seeks meaning "beneath" or "behind" or "above" texts or "between" texts and readers; and hence "its very reason for being is to explain away the antagonisms and inconsistencies that the text all too openly displays."[262] One of Nietzsche's own key notions, emerging from his earliest reflections on "the birth of tragedy out of the spirit of music," was that the Greeks appeared "superficial" only because they had the "good taste" to withhold their deeper (read: more esoteric) sense of "depth." But Nietzsche used many decorous euphemisms (e.g., The Dionysian, The Apollinian, The Socratic) to conceal the precise *social consequences* that he intended, today, to emerge from the interaction between this particular metaphoric of "surface" and "depth."[263]

This surface/depth metaphoric is the most basic formant (Lefebvre) already of Nietzsche's first book, *The Birth of Tragedy Out of the Spirit of Music* (1872). A decade and a half later—having completed *Thus Spoke Zarathustra* and as part of his attempt to republish all his previous work with new guides for the perplexed—Nietzsche reissued this book under the revised title *The Birth of Tragedy, or, Hellenism and Pessimism* (1886). He now added a new preface modestly entitled "Attempt at a Self-Criticism," in which he staked out some critical distance between himself and his earlier mentors, most notably Wagner and Schopenhauer. In fact, however, this preface constitutes the—ultimately very successful—attempt to guide certain kinds of reader away from its rhetorical excesses, to the extent that these might blow the cover off the most subtle layers of Nietzsche's own underlying elitist political and social agenda, which remained essentially the same as before. In both its versions *The Birth of Tragedy* showed two aspects to the world, the first of which has been accepted at face value, the other roundly ignored. The first argued, famously, that "the existence of the world is *justified* only as an aesthetic phenomenon" ("Attempt at a Self-Criticism," 5)—a remark all the more extreme given the strong Lutheran sense of "justification," which entails the absolute priority of faith. Since there is apparently no room for morality in this post-Schopenhauerian ontology "beyond good and evil," Nietzsche's readers have commonly assumed that he himself was not attempting to promote any really specific political or moral agenda, for good or ill. The second and concealed aspect of *The Birth of Tragedy*, as only Nietzsche's notebooks make clear, is frankly pragmatic and indeed "moral," not "extramoral." In 1881, for example, he emphasized, privately, with reference to his first book that it was directed "against Schopenhauer and the moral interpretation of existence," but quickly changed the stress: "I place ABOVE IT THE AESTHETIC, *but without denying the moral* or altering it."[264] Thus Nietzsche secretly left himself plenty of room to promote certain *kinds* of moral agenda, both exoteric and esoteric. And the surface/depth metaphoric, as well as the related one of proximity/distance, is almost always inscribed by essentializing assumptions about "woman" — both in masculinist discourse generally and specifically in Nietzsche.[265]

The precise philological problem is that the esoteric level of Nietzsche's texts must be imaged not as something hidden "beneath" or "behind" its exoteric level as a problem of representation or reference; rather, the esoteric can flit somewhere along the material surface, between the lines or words — for all to look at and for few actually to see, in what Althusser, following Spinoza, calls "the opacity of the immediate."[266] Nietzsche and his texts have long seemed "natural" and "reasonable" to many readers, too many. Insofar as Spinoza "rejects the reduction of the Scripture to nature or reason (much as he rejects the reduction of nature to Scripture), he speaks of an object, an objective existence that the others do not, cannot, or will not see."[267] This is true of the way most Nietzscheans read Nietzsche's texts. In a sense, this way is Hobbesian, when Spinozist would be more appropriate. Montag usefully compares and contrasts Spinoza's grasp of Scripture with the better known and cruder one of Thomas Hobbes in *Leviathan*.[268] On the one hand their antihermeneutic, materialist positions are comparable, since "For Hobbes as for Spinoza the words and sentences of which the Scripture is comprised no longer reveal or conceal meanings deeper than themselves. Instead, they congeal into objects which can be investigated." On the other hand the Hobbesian and Spinozist positions on the radically self-contradictory character of Scripture appear politically and ideologically at odds. For Hobbes, "the radical absence of organic unity necessitates the mediating function of the Sovereign who, through the institution of the established church, will bring textual conflicts and antagonisms into an artificial unity possessed finally of a (artificial) meaning. Hobbes therefore needs mystery. He must suspend his search for an interpretive method in *Leviathan* at this point because to proceed any further towards a rationality proper to Scripture would undercut the very authority whose existence the mystery of Scripture justifies and makes necessary."[269] The Nietzsche Industry — especially its supposedly "left-wing," "hermeneutic," *and* "deconstructive" branches — functions more or less "ironically," more or less against its own intentions, precisely as a mediating "Sovereign" in this Hobbesian sense. Fetishizing and mystifying the imagined "polysemy" (hermeneutics) or "undecidability" (deconstruction) of Nietzsche's text only allows the latter's impact to be all the more socially effective surreptitiously. In contrast to Hobbes, "Spinoza, enemy of mysteries and opponent of servitude, was free from the constraints that prevented Hobbes from developing a method of reading proper to Scripture." "Rather than attempt to distort" any of the "counterposed doctrines" that one finds in any text — Scriptural or Nietzschean — "into agreement through a hermeneutic procedure (which adds to the text what it claims to discover in it), Spinozism accepts the contradiction as irreducible and proceeds to explain it by seeking its cause."[270] This is a properly materialist *and* communist philological procedure for reading Nietzsche and the many apparent "contradictions" in his texts.

Morphing the communist problematic thus defined back into a more traditional metaphoric, one result is a piece of "masonry," as described by Bataille. "The work of the mason, who assembles, is the work that matters. Thus the adjoining bricks, in a book, should not be less visible than the new brick, which is the book. What is offered the reader, in fact, cannot be an element, but must be the ensemble in which it is inserted: it is the whole human assemblage and edifice, which must be, not just a pile of scraps, but rather a self-consciousness."[271] Or rather, in the present case, a possible, alternative self- *and* collective-consciousness must be pitted against the dominant "self"-consciousness — really an *unacknowledged* collective-consciousness — that already exists as a profoundly anticommunist Nietzsche/anism. Hence the necessity for a premodernist and post-postmodernist — and properly *communist* — methodology of pastiche. And, as such, a postcontemporary intervention.

Pastiche or not, communist or not, *some* type of performative procedure is necessary alongside the scholarly and philological in order to grasp Nietzsche. It is no longer enough merely to talk *about* him—pro *or* con, seriously *or* playfully. This is because his influence—by his design—has never been merely rational or logical in nature and hence is not wholly susceptible to reasoned, "clear and distinct" definition, argument, or scholarly demolition alone. In Hegelian terms, the aim of any philosophic act "by itself is a lifeless universal, just as the guiding tendency is a mere drive that as yet lacks an actual existence; and the bare result is *the corpse* [*Leichnam*] which has left the guiding tendency behind it."[272] What counts more in this system (according to Left-Hegelians, in opposition to their right-wing counterparts who announce and desire "the end of history") is the movement of thought and its effectivity. On the other side of the same token, however, this book is non- or anti-Hegelian in its refusal to respect Hegel's own—contradictory—insistence that philosophical logic never conflate "speculative" and "ratiocinative methods."[273]

It would have been impossible for Nietzsche to become a post-Enlightenment thinker of such consequence had he *merely* constated and not also successfully *enacted* his attack on Reason because of its egalitarian impulsion. This is certainly not to say that Enlightenment had no ideological deformations or totalitarian impulsions. But it is to say that Nietzsche's corpse would not have lived on as corpus had he merely produced rhetorical acts by himself and not also resulting actions by subsequent others. In such matters it is less *content* than *form* that matters. As Nietzsche's contemporary Émile Zola exclaimed: "Form! Form is the great crime."[274] "Whatever is formal instead of thematic always contains the possibility of its future tradition within itself."[275] In the Nietzschean way of waging warfare, "the secret is no longer a content held within a form of interiority; rather, it becomes a form identified with the form of exteriority which is always external to itself."[276] The secret of Nietzsche's future-oriented warfare must not be reduced to his common, obvious thematicization of war and violence, for this is mere content, mere signified. The secret subsists, much more paradoxically, as a form of exteriority in which an affective charge of violence is produced that logically entails but is not fully conflatable with any signifier, including "warfare," just as what Deleuze and Guattari call "the war machine" is not reducible to any particular manifestation of war, nor to any state apparatus that thinks it can contain it. "To place thought in an immediate relation with the outside, with the forces of the outside, in short to make thought a war machine, is a strange undertaking whose precise procedures can be studied in Nietzsche (the aphorism, for example, is very different from the maxim, for a maxim, in the republic of letters, is like an organic State act or sovereign judgment, whereas an aphorism always awaits its meaning from a new external force, a final force that must conquer or subjugate it, utilize it)."[277] And so, like most Left-Nietzscheans, Deleuze and Guattari rush on to utilize Nietzsche *without* having studied his precise procedures.

One might refer here also to the "rhetoric of the empty secret" as a fundamental category of post-turn-of-the-century discourse. The structure of the "empty secret" — as opposed to that of the "public" or "open secret" — embraces "the cluster of aperçus and intuitions that seems distinctively to signify 'modernism' (at least, male high modernism)," and further "delineates a space bounded by hollowness, a self-reference that refers back to — though it differs from — nineteenth-century paranoid solipsism, and a split between content or thematics on the one hand and structure on the other that is stressed in favor of structure and at the expense of thematics."[278] But this formulation of the perennial "form/content" paradigm, which shadows so many attempts to define the "esoteric/exoteric" distinction, leaves open the question of what the full political point of the empty secrets of modernism might be. As Jaques Derrida noted in a Nietzschean fashion, "*form* fascinates when one no longer has the force to comprehend force from within itself."[279]

Images of extracting "rational kernels" from "mystical shells" — or vice versa: mystical kernels from rational shells — have bedeviled historical materialism since Marx and Engels, and are hardly any improvement.[280] In any case, it is a grave mistake to reduce the Nietzsche/an esoteric to "content," the exoteric to "form." But how, then, did Nietzsche think that people would actually be produced by means of his writing; what are our precise functions to be in the social hierarchy; and to what degree might these have been proleptically programmed? If form is a kind of crime, perhaps this is why Nietzsche was fascinated by criminals, on occasion declaring himself to be one. This assertion, too, must be grasped *literally*.

Nietzsche was *almost* a philological "cynic" in Peter Sloterdijk's meaning of the term in his *Critique of Cynical Reason* (1983). "Nietzsche's decisive self-characterization," Sloterdijk writes, "often overlooked, is that of a 'cynic' [*Cyniker*]; *with this*, next to Marx, the most momentous thinker of the century, Nietzsche's 'cynicism' [*Cynismus*] offers a modified approach to 'saying the truth': It is one of strategy and tactics, suspicion and disinhibition, pragmatics and instrumentalism — all this in the hands of a political ego that thinks first and foremost about itself, an ego that is inwardly adroit and outwardly armored."[281] Sloterdijk's formulation is characteristically at once *right, wrong,* and *imprecise.* It is *right* in its stress on the *pragmatic* aspect of Nietzsche, leaving aside the rather ambiguous comparison or conflation with Marx, who was arguably *not* a cynic in this sense. It is *wrong* because Nietzsche's political ego did *not* think primarily or exclusively of itself but rather of its replication in the future, its embodiment in and as corps/e. Finally, it is *imprecise* because Sloterdijk, who is something of a Left-Nietzschean himself, fails to account for *how* Nietzsche intended this proleptically projected corps/e to be produced — to be steeled for combat by being at once "inwardly adroit and outwardly armored."[282]

The philological difficulty that the Left — that Left-Nietzscheanism — has always had in settling accounts with Nietzsche can be glimpsed nowhere more clearly than in an analysis advanced by Horkheimer in 1933, in his essay "Materialism and Morality."[283] This was one of the most significant attempts to bring neo-Kantian and Marxist analysis to bear on a critical contemporary historical moment, and established the basic position on Nietzsche that was to inform *Dialectic of Enlightenment* (1944), coauthored with Adorno but with Horkheimer's take on Nietzsche dominating. In "Materialism and Morality" Horkheimer attempted to take the measure of Nietzsche's demolition of moral values in order to democratize what Horkheimer thought of as Nietzsche's elitist *aspect,* not essence. Horkheimer argued critically *and* naïvely that Nietzsche had merely "failed to recognize that the characterization of the present which he so detested derives precisely from the dearth of propitious conditions for society at large. With the spread of reason that he feared, with its application to all of the relationships of society, those characteristics — which in truth rest upon the concentration of all the instincts on private advantage — must be transformed, as must ideas and indeed drives themselves" (pp. 30–31). With this quintessentially neo-Enlightenment end in sight, Horkheimer appealed — with the help of Freud as well as Kant and Marx — to an edified Nietzsche, clarified of his elitist "dross." A dominant trend of Left-Nietzscheanism informs this tack. What is so problematic here is less the naïvely optimistic imperialism of Horkheimer's claim for Reason — a claim long since abandoned by most Left-Nietzscheans — than the concomitant triple imputation concerning Nietzsche: first, that he somehow "failed" to give Reason, and hence democracy, its due; second, that he himself would have recognized this failure for what it was, rectifying it as soon as he had been shown the light; and, finally, that, when he had done so, Nietzsche would have been on "our" side, in this case the side of radical democracy and Enlightenment against the Fascist Eclipse of Reason. Obscured by this assumption is that Nietzsche was operating all along in terms of *another* kind of Reason, one that would preserve *another* kind of society — for the few — precisely by transforming a corps of his readers — including Horkheimer and the rest of critical theory — in ways inaccessible to Reason alone. This transformation entails persisting in the belief that Nietzsche is *basically* on "our" side. When in fact he is not.

In Nietzsche's own words, in his *Gay Science* (1882), "young men" are "explosives": *"Therefore,* subtle seducers know the art of getting them to expect explosions and not to see the reasons behind the political cause: One does not recruit powder kegs with reasons!"[284] Since post-Enlightenment recruitment is exactly a matter of subtle seduction, there is no good reason why Nietzsche would do more — in public — than say *that* his "gay science" exists in principle. But, reasonably enough on logical and pragmatic grounds, he never says — up front or even quite in private — *how exactly* he would put this science to work to recruit his young Marines, his Few Good Men, his fellow demolition experts. It may be impossible ever to *answer* this question adequately because, for Nietzsche, it is ultimately a matter of esotericism and logographic necessity; but it is still possible to *ask* it.

With regard to the post-Enlightenment implications of Nietzsche's writing on all his readers, Bataille was right in 1937: "When Nietzsche said he wanted to be understood in fifty years, he could not have meant it in only the intellectual sense. That for which he lived and exalted himself demands that life, joy, and death be brought into play, and not the tired attention of the intellect. This must be stated simply and with an awareness of one's own involvement. . . . [I]t is vain and unbearable to try to address those who have at their disposal only a feigned comprehension of the teachings of Nietzsche."[285] Not to mention a comprehension based exclusively on his exoteric themes.

Certainly there is good reason to be intolerant, angry, or bored with any reading of Nietzsche that attends only to the thematic, *locutionary,* and hence exoteric — and translated — level of his work and not also to its *illocutionary* and *perlocutionary,* and hence more esoteric, dimension. Thematic reading — at times under the guise of fixating on "the question of style" — finds in Nietzsche's works only always "contradictions" that can be more or less easily deconstructed; and, for precisely this reason, thematic reading has long been a bankrupt response, and it makes no difference whether it flows from the pen of an Adorno and Horkheimer, a Habermas or Sloterdijk, a Gadamer or Foucault, a Deleuze, a Rorty, or — appearances to the contrary — a Derrida.

Following J. L. Austin's philosophy of "speech acts" and what Brecht might have called "social gest," distinctions must be made between three discursive events.[286] These can be analytically distinct but are often empirically intertwined: (1) The "performance of an act *of* saying something." *Locution:* "He said, 'Eternal Recurrence of the Same will divide us into two castes: a higher noble and a lower base' " — meaning by "divide" *divide,* and referring by "us" to *us.* (2) The "performance of an act *in* saying something." *Illocution:* "He urged us to divide into two castes after incorporating into ourselves the doctrine of Eternal Recurrence of the Same." And (3) saying something that produces "certain consequential effects upon the feelings, thoughts, or actions of the audience, or of the speaker, or of other persons." *Perlocution:* "We have been persuaded to divide ourselves into two castes." Better yet, at the maximum level of effectivity — which will later be called the properly Nietzschean Channel 4 — the prophylactic quotation marks disappear: We have divided ourselves into two basic castes but we neither say nor know that we have. And so the statement "We have divided ourselves into two basic castes" is never in fact uttered, even thought. But *lived.*

The perlocutionary system of Nietzsche's corps/e is thus related to what has been called "vivification," a way of making vivid that is always slightly in excess of cognition. "Vivification is not identical to persuasiveness, though it may be an essential part of it"; it is a way of "rendering *felt* what representations only allude to," so that "affective ties" are "forged" — albeit "obliquely" — "between viewer and representation."[287] Nietzsche's corpse and corpus are particularly vivid but always slightly in excess of clearly identifiable representation, persuasive without the corps being fully aware of the precise nature and source of Nietzsche's peculiar technique of vivification. Vivification is a way of theorizing a matrix of questions directly relevant to the phenomenon of Nietzsche's corps/e: "How . . . can the body be both an agent and an object? How can it be testimony to life and evidence of death? How can a person live, subject to the vicissitudes of history, and yet be remembered as somehow transcendent, available for mythic representation? How can an economic system that destroys its environment not destroy itself? How can what appears to be difference and equity on one level become hierarchy and control on another?" (pp. 234–235). A general answer is: by means of perlocutionary incorporation.

The theory of the speech-act system must also be expanded and sharpened to include *desire*. Russian philosopher Valery Podoroga draws the further distinction within the category of the "performative" between "performance" and "performativity" — and thus between "Language as that which instantaneously performs an utterance as an action, and language as the activity of performance — activity as the pure act of desire."[288] Linking "performance" to the parallel and to some extent interpenetrating movement of the "tragic" — that is, a centrifugal force away from what is mimetically depicted in representational language — and "performativity" toward the "comic" — that is, a centripetal force toward what is thus depicted — Podoroga provides what are, in effect, the conceptual tools for a description not only of Nietzsche's own "tragicomic" illocutionary force but also its perlocutionary effect, its corps/e. In any case, in order to get after the "designs, intentions, and purposes" of Nietzsche's own "gestic performance" — that is, to "choose" our caste or "forget" we have one, and then act accordingly — it is always appropriate, even necessary, to fight back with a gestic counterperformance and counterproduction.

The science to which anexact philology aspires does not just find what it seeks waiting to be discovered, by a gesture that is either hermeneutically circular or positivistically linear. Sciences are among other things modes of simultaneously producing — valid but never absolute — knowledge *of* their object "in the specific mode that defines it," while also producing knowledge *from* their object in the process of constituting it.[289] To that end, counterperformance and counterproduction must engage Nietzscheanism with several tactics on several fronts at once — including but also beyond those he himself chose to contest. For Nietzsche's impact is powerfully in effect not only among professional philosophers, critics, and artists. It operates equally deep,

implicitly when not explicitly, within popular, mass, or junk culture —
which he found beneath his refined personal taste, though was not
loath to use to promote his larger social ends, and where he has been
eagerly accepted and loved.

Sociologically speaking, there is no *necessary* or *ultimate* ideological or
political "essence" — Left, Right, Center, or Other — of either high culture or mass/popular/junk culture. Nor *even* of Nietzsche/anism. But
politically speaking, the *best* — which is also to say the most potentially
communist — junk-cultural production is un- or even anti-Nietzsche/
an, whereas the *worst* is exactly that. This might be described as a *pro-
Jamesonian* and *anti-Adornoan* perspective, marking as it does the sea
change between national Fordist modernism and its critique on the one
hand, and multinational post-Fordist postmodernism and its critique
on the other. As Colin MacCabe suggests, "For Adorno the commodification of art marked the final abolition of any autonomous perspective from which to criticize the dominant forms of economic development. For Jameson the moment at which cultural production is
fully integrated into economic production opens out the possibility of
a cultural politics which would fundamentally intervene in the economic."[290] MacCabe's adverb "fundamentally" is bad, however, since
fundamental intervention can come *only* when cultural politics forms
blocs with *other* politics and at moments of *economic* crisis. Nonetheless,
what is demanded is just such a Trojan horse — indeed, *the* Trojan
horse — within Nietzsche/anism. As such, this effort must also be "allegorical," as *one* — smaller and less lethal — Trojan horse to intervene in
postmodern, postcontemporary politics, in order to liberate it from the
Nietzsche/anism that has at once besieged, infiltrated, and virused it.

Points of compromise and merger were negotiated some time ago
between the Nietzsche Industry and the Culture Industry, and Avant-
Pop — the late twentieth-century fusion of Avant-Garde and Pop — is
only one of the resulting hybrids. Nietzsche is encountered philosophically and rhetorically within the entire postmodern Society of the Spectacle, the spectacular technoculture of everyday life. Sensory overload is
one problem in grasping Nietzsche/anism, as the impossibility ever to
map cognitively the full extent of Nietzsche's corps/e. This is what
Kant called "the mathematical sublime": if the part is overwhelmingly
awesome or complex, then the whole must be even more so. For Nietzsche's corps/e inhabits not merely the *thematic* Nietzscheanism of films

such as (picking almost randomly) Stephen Frears's 1991 film *The Grifters*—where Nietzsche's Will to Power outmaneuvers Freud's Oedipus Complex, not to mention Marxism, with remarkable ease—but also the *techno-formal* Nietzscheanism of David Cronenberg's *Videodrome*. The horizontally and vertically integrative Nietzsche Industry or Corporation—in its competitive, in its monopoly-imperialistic, and in its postindustrial, neocapitalist, postmodern phases alike—includes a left wing, right wing, and center. But it is not by chance that it was not the Left but the Right that first attempted—around 1930—to develop Nietzsche's scattered and contradictory remarks about the actual and potential relationship between the human and the technological into a coherent theory of what Georg Förster called a properly Nietzschean "supernatural" or "hypernatural reality" (*übernaturhafte Realität*)[291]—today's hypertext, virtual reality, or cyberspace. It is high time for the "Left" to catch up to the Right in this regard as in so many others. Increasingly, the most important site of Nietzsche's more popular or mass sphere of influence is "situated" (i.e., qua Situation, qua Spectacle) not only within the "everyday life" of the audiovisual media such as cinema but also in cyberspace and virtual reality. Here, terms like "cyberspace" and "virtual reality" must be grasped less as sites of *technological innovation*—though they are also this, or will be—and more as modes of *interpreting* the past and present, and then of changing the future.

The common slogan "interpretation" is invoked often by Nietzsche as a riposte to positivism, historicism, and psychologism, as in the obsessively recited slogan: "There are no facts, only interpretations." But this is a most misleading concept with which to grasp his work, in settling accounts with him and his influence direct and indirect. For Nietzsche/anism is a function of a semiotic system that is programmed to be concealed from view. Hence, the requirement to go "beyond interpretation."

To anticipate further, in a note written while working on *Beyond Good and Evil* in 1885–1886, as part of his neo-Heraclitian attempt to replace explanation (*Erklärung*) with interpretation (*Auslegung* or *Ausdeutung*), Nietzsche wrote: "Interpretation *not* explanation. There is no stock of facts [Thatbestand], everything is fluid, ungraspable, elusive; the most enduring is but our opinions. Projective meaning

[Sinn-hineinlegen] — in most cases a new interpretation over an old interpretation that has become incomprehensible and that is itself only a sign."²⁹² What Nietzsche characteristically is silent about here, however, is the specific *use* to which such a semiotics-as-power can be put; in any event, hermeneutics alone is never the only thing that is at stake for him. Versions of the philosopheme that "there are no facts, only interpretations" are ubiquitous throughout his notebooks and published writing alike from the mid-1880s on, although they are perhaps best known through one truncated aphorism in *Beyond Good and Evil*: "There are no moral phenomena at all, rather only a moral interpretation [Ausdeutung] of phenomena. . . . "²⁹³ But it is crucial to raise suspicions about this slogan's *specific* use-value — which is neatly occluded by Nietzsche's ellipsis — and about what in his notebooks Nietzsche calls its "exploitation." To this end, it is enough for the time being to cite an unpublished remark from the same period: "N.B. *Against* the doctrine of the influence milieu and external causes: inner strength is infinitely *superior*. Much that looks like influence from outside is only its adaptation from within. Exactly the same milieus can be interpreted [ausgedeutet] and exploited [ausgenutzt] in opposite ways: there are no facts. — A genius is *not* explained [erklärt] from such conditions of origin — [.]"²⁹⁴ In short, the notion of "genius" — and, as it turns out, the social system prerequisite to it — is somehow outside *mere* "interpretation" and is a matter of "exploitation" — in all senses of the word. And thus is the reader thrown off the scent of *this* particular "genius." It is emblematic of Left-Nietzscheanism generally that even when readers "see" this problematic explicitly stated in the works Nietzsche published — namely, his precise articulation of interpretation *and* domination — they simultaneously mystify and depoliticize it, folding it back on itself as an imagined hermeneutic or deconstructive moment only.²⁹⁵ In short, readers don't really see, like Holmes and Moriarty; they just look, like Watson; *and* in so doing they absorb what they do not (ever) see.

Whatever the reason, there usually appear to be many different options for interpretation — or rather channels — available to the interpreter. But far fewer channels are really open than s/he is commonly led to believe. In fact, there exist only three basic channels for most of us: (1) "objectivist," (2) "subjectivist," and (3) "hermeneutic" or "dialectical," especially when "dialectics" entails not Marxist struggle but

"Hegelian" synthesis.[296] To the Big Three, however, Nietzsche contributed an equally, if not more basic, fourth. Channel 4—part vitally serious, part deadly comic—involves the esoteric attempt to deliver messages beneath the surface of consciousness, even of the skin. This is a channel beyond (1) locution, (2) illocution, and (3) perlocution, to the effect that (4) "We certainly don't agree with everything he says, but we can still safely use the rest of it, anyway"—where this belief is both *untrue* and *dangerous*. Nietzsche's, then, is an "information" matrix, formant, or medium that both trans-mits messages more or less sub rosa and also in-forms, inter-pellates their recipients subcutaneously, in-corporates them. Recognizing this problematic is an important step toward grasping the paradoxical existence of a Left-Nietzscheanism in the flushed face of Nietzsche's hatred of the Left.

Nietzsche was perhaps the greatest "interpellator," "hailer," and "summoner" of the modern and postmodern subject, recalling Althusser's famous scenario. According to it,

> ideology "acts" or "functions" in such a way that it "recruits" subjects among the individuals (it recruits them all), or "transforms" the individuals into subjects (it transforms them all) by that very precise operation which I have called *interpellation* or hailing, and which can be imagined along the lines of the most commonplace everyday police (or other) hailing: "Hey, you there!" Assuming that the theoretical scene I have imagined takes place in the street, the hailed individual will turn round. By this mere one-hundred-and-eighty-degree physical conversion, he becomes a *subject*. Why? Because he has recognized that the hail was "really" addressed to him, and that "it was *really him* who was hailed" (and not someone else). Experience shows that the practical telecommunication of hailings is such that they hardly ever miss their man: verbal call or whistle, the one hailed always recognizes that it is really him who is being hailed.[297]

Whenever Nietzsche has shouted "Hey, you there!" all heads tend to snap round on their neural stalks. When telecommunication systems rather more advanced than verbal calls and whistles are informed by Nietzsche/anism, heads don't even have to turn, *can't* turn.* For in-

---

*The earliest versions of Nietzschean interpellation were no less spectacular, for all their apparent lack of technological sophistication. During the heyday of the Nietzsche Archive in Weimar before Nietzsche's death in 1900 — or is it 2000? — his sister Elisabeth

stance, in direct interfaces between cathode ray tubes and eye stalks, including already nascent technologies enabling people born blind to see by having their optic nerves hardwired to TV and video. So it is always already—paradoxically and uncannily—that one is made to accept the "humanist" delusion that the origin of messages lies deep within "human nature"—within ourselves qua creating, rebelling, programming subjects (*natura naturans:* substance and cause) rather than qua created, programmed, mentally and socially subjected subject-formations (*natura naturata:* effect, mode, and medium).[298] The truth of the matter likely is that "we" and "nature" are both. But whenever "*natura naturata* wins a total hegemony over *natura naturans,*" Negri asks rhetorically: "What could be the work of the devil if not this?"[299]

It is necessary to add—*pace* Lukács and various Stalinists—that Nietzsche/anism is not—never was, likely never will be—"*the* dominant ideology of the ruling class," no matter how many self-described "Nietzscheans" are near, at, or in centers of power in capitalist countries or in the few socialist countries still in existence. The reason Nietzsche's corps/e could not have this role is hardly due to any lack of desire on Nietzsche's part to be dominant. Rather, there is no such thing as "*the* dominant ideology of the rulers," not even "capitalist." Elaborating a central thesis of Althusser, Étienne Balibar explains: "The dominant ideology in a given society is a specific universalization of the imaginary of the *dominated:* what it elaborates are such notions as Justice, Liberty and Equality, Effort and Happiness, etc., which draw their potential universal meaning from their belonging to the imaginary of the individuals who live the masses' or the people's conditions."[300] It is *this* multiplex ideology—in an "everyday" aspect that is increasingly technocultural—that Nietzsche/anism most successfully informs, directly or indirectly. And it does so either negatively, by closing off effective options to capitalism, or, more positively, by transforming even the *possibility* of collective revolt against capitalism into various ostensibly

---

Förster-Nietzsche staged dinner parties in the Villa Silberblick which housed both the madman and the Archive, later a Nazi think tank. The dinners were served in an elaborately carved *Jugendstil* (art nouveau) room, at the end of which was a drawn curtain. After dessert the curtain was parted to reveal Nietzsche, draped in a togalike outfit sitting in the chair where he had been all during the meal. The guests spontaneously stood and applauded the dully staring, corpselike, but still-living philosopher.

"individual" agendas. Political economy *before* Marx, in other words. To expose this "everyday" aspect of Nietzsche's corps/e becomes all the more pressing if, as Balibar also points out (again *pace* Lukács), "No class is the absolute 'Subject of History,' but there is no doubt that only the masses really 'make history,' i.e., only they can produce political changes" (p. 13). Finally, Balibar (following Gramsci) makes another basic point that bears directly on all current obituaries for the "death" of communism: "a fatalistic view of the revolutionary conditions merely reflects the 'subordinate' position of a divided working class" (p. 16). *Nietzsche* can be viewed—at least theoretically and *ex hypothesi*—as having esoterically effected this globally disastrous division *and* our incapacity to perceive it or do much about it. Certainly this was his illocutionary *desire,* his social gest. And the joke is on us.

Subconscious, subcutaneous influence—whereby the Sublime becomes subliminal and vice versa—involves techniques of employing and deploying language not as a linguistic or even semiotextual system per se, but rather in its imag-inary and aural-musical potential for suasion, reception, and self/deception. It is in this sense only that Althusser—indeed all consistent communism—proposes that ideology is never fully conscious, nor even subconscious, but unconscious. These techniques or technologies are exactly appropriate ways of waging war in a world that today is simultaneously preliterate and postliterate, but no longer—perhaps never again—significantly or predominantly literate. The fantasy of posthumous, subconscious influence and transformation—which is what "politics" has always been about at least since Aristotle, whenever the term means more than yet another academic mantra chanted to ward off, repress, and suppress more radical thought or action—has enjoyed a long, complex, sometimes bizarre history. The empirical impossibility of controlling the future appropriation of one's writing absolutely is often overridden by two factors: (1) by the *empirical possibility* of exerting at least *weak* performative control over this appropriation, and (2) by the *theoretical dream* of exerting *total* control. This possibility and this dream were further encouraged in Nietzsche's case by the thought of Eternal Recurrence of the Same, which suggests that the future will be essentially similar if not literally identical to the past and the present. The phantasmagorias of idealism help overdetermine ideological, political, economic, artistic, theoretical, and other practices. And few philosophers or artists or critics or other people have taken this im/possible fantasy of posthumous, sub-rosa effectivity more seriously — and have been more successful, comparatively speaking, in realizing it — than has the Nietzsche who developed both his esoteric semiotics and his rhetorico-politics of euthanasia — his "process of weeding out" — accordingly.

As is evident from its headings, an organizing principle of *Nietzsche's Corps/e* is of the type "from X to Y." That is: "From Bataille to Nietzsche"; "From Gramsci to Dick." Furthermore, the section on Nietzsche's theory and practice of esoteric semiotics argues that to get *after* (in both senses: *hot pursuit* and *temporal*) this theory and practice of sign systems, and its coterminous process of weeding out, it is necessary to think Nietzsche after Nietzscheans like Derrida and Pierre Klossowski, just as it is necessary to get beyond interpretation, but even further than they do, at least with regard to Nietzsche. It must be emphatically stressed, however, that all proper names — but *most* especially "Nietzsche" — are both authorizing "signatures" or "name-effects" and im/proper names. In other words, these nominal names, these slogans, stand in not only for many other people or subjects but also for specific problems, forces, and technologies. The current "crisis of exnomination" — the perceived inability to find new or even any names for political, economic, and cultural practices after Fordist modernism and after the conterminous "defeat of communism" and "triumph of capitalism" — can be said to be a result of the supposedly "Nietzschean" proposition that *all* names are ultimately arbitrary. The headings "From Bataille (Channel 3) to Nietzsche (Channel 4)" and "*Trasformismo* from Gramsci to Dick, or, The Spectacular Technoculture of Everyday Life" do not represent a simple chronological argument or development but also not something wholly achronological, let alone "eternally recurrent." Rather, since *temporal* causal relationships in Spinozist and Althusserian systems are — often — less important than *logical* causal relationships, it is necessary to cut away from all *simple* teleologies so as to produce politico-philosophical non/synchronicities, spaces, or matrixes. This quasi-sequential organizing principle is designed to expose what turns out in "Left-Nietzschoids, Right-Nietzscheans" to be a comparatively small space between a significant "Left"-Nietzschean ("Richard Rorty," who seems to affirm cheerfully that he is a Nietzschean) and a significant "Right"-Nietzschean ("Stanley Rosen," who seems to deny ironically that he is one) — both of whom are compatible, if in significantly different ways, with the state-terrorist fantasy of neocapitalism that "North Atlantic Postmodern Bourgeois Liberal Democracy" and its neoliberal cognates are our absolute, untranscendable horizon of thinking and being. It is theoretically possible, certainly, to have android Nietzscheans — Nietzschoids — on the Right; but Right-Nietzscheans *tend* to be more conscious Nietzscheans and truer to Nietzsche's intentions than not, and certainly more conscious and truer than Left-Nietzscheans. If it is on the right track and scent, however, this hypothesis is not ideologically reversible simply: that is, it is virtually impossible, taking Nietzsche's designs into account, to have genuine Nietzscheans on the Left, *only* Nietzschoids. Hence the otherwise rather arbitrary-sounding — not necessarily insulting — distinction between Right-Nietzsch*eans* and Left-Nietzsch*oids,* with its echo of programmed *androids.* Just as it is important not to place too much stock in any im/proper names, however, it is equally important to avoid overinvestment in mantras such as "left-wing" or "right-wing." As the filmmaker and writer — and communist — Pier Paolo Pasolini suggested about literature: "There is a tendency to the Right and a tendency to the Left even in literature, and for reasons 'purely' literary. Those on the Left in literature, however, are not always on the Left in politics, and so forth: Thus there exists a double play of relations between the political and the literary."[301] The differences between a liberal-democratic, North Atlantic Rorty and a neoliberal, cosmopolitan Rosen are real enough in significant respects. The latter is a much finer reader of Nietzsche than the former, for instance, yet also much less acceptable to the philosophical establishment. But they are not that different in the larger scheme of Nietzsche's intent. His double-play intent — which Rosen comes much closer to grasping and turning than does Rorty — was from the beginning to produce apparently opposing virtualities of reading him, in the desire proleptically — prophetically — to handicap and manipulate this unacknowledged consensus, this difference-engine. *All* of it and us.

A larger chronological, but also ideological, space or matrix separates Nietzsche from Georges Batailles. Especially when the latter is read not only as the important thinker and great — Left- or is it Right- or just liberal? — Nietzschean he was, but also as the one who, when carefully unpacked, best illustrates the absolute horizon of a merely "hermeneutic" or even "dialectical" — that is, "synthesizing" — approach to a Nietzsche whose personally programmed Channel 4 may have always already anticipated all future, more or less Bataillean Channel 3s, just as it has Channels 1 and 2. Bataille is especially important because he and his readers are among those most responsible for the still current perception not only that Nietzsche was "misunderstood" *by fascism,* and hence could be appropriated positively in the struggle *against* it — which is one thing, and perhaps possible — but also that *Nietzsche himself and his work* were intended and designed to be antifascoid — which is quite another thing, and false absolutely. Most important, however, is that Bataille originated today's virtually axiomatic slogan that "Nietzsche's position is the only one outside of communism." And even Nietzscheans like Pierre Klossowski and Jacques Derrida, no matter how different and important they may be in other respects, have hardly managed to get beyond or after *this* Bataillean problematic.

Finally, the largest ideological space or matrix separates the American "science fiction" writer Philip K. Dick from the communist theorist and imprisoned militant Antonio Gramsci, and separates especially their opposing visions of the politico-historical transformation or *trasformismo* of intellectuals in "our" times: from the Left to the Center and then the Right of the ideological spectrum — an ongoing transformation of which Nietzschean *gauchisme* is the single most significant instance. Dick opened up the possibility — already by the 1960s and early 1970s — for a confrontation between older modernist, paranoid technologies of post/Fordist nationalisms and multinationalisms on the one hand, and on the other the newer — but overlapping and intersecting — postmodernist, schizoid, cyborg technoculture of "our" current advance toward total and global, fiberoptical and cyberspatial neocapitalism. Against this New World Order there is still time and space for effective communist combat, using combinations of older and more conventional tactics and strategies with ones that are newer and more unconventional. But what Nietzsche/anism most effectively resists is *any* possible — but *especially* communist — *alternative* to itself. Herein lies a measure of Nietzsche's genius and a major reason for his popularity in many quarters. Gramsci — the exemplary communist theoretician and militant after Lenin[302] — provides help to would-be communists today only if his thinking can both inform new technocultures and work against the grain of their dominant current use. This use includes technologies of warfare that Gramsci—for all his deep fascination with Taylorism and Fordism—did not quite foresee—very unlike the self-described "fascistic" Dick—and in the face of which neither technophobia nor technophilia are adequate or progressive responses. Viewed globally, the more traditional working class and the peasantry still exist, still are exploited, and still might become (again) very powerful, even communist agents of historical change. But new forms of labor—including the more "autonomous" New Social Subject or New Social Worker—have been emerging for years as actual or virtual vanguards in the World Picture, so as to make Integrated World Capital impossible to combat with orthodox or traditional means or agents only.[303] But in that event it is especially necessary—not sufficient—to know which side *Nietzscheanism* is on and which matrix *Nietzsche* has already informed and handicapped. The matrix is huge and intricate, including as it does not only its two major rival discourses—*Marxist political economy* and *Freudian psychoanalysis*—but also all the most significant attempts to *fuse* them.

Utopic: Nietzsche versus Freud versus Marx

> In the reign of "freedom" thought and ideas can no longer be born on the terrain of contradictions and the necessity of struggle. At the present time the philosopher—the philosopher of praxis—can only make this generic affirmation and can go no further; he cannot escape from the present field of contradictions, he cannot affirm, other than generically, a world without contradictions, without immediately creating a utopia. This is not to say that utopia cannot have a philosophical value, for it has a political value and every politics is implicitly a philosophy, even if disconnected and crudely sketched.[304]

Since before World War I, Nietzsche has been read and discussed as part of what can be called "The Marx-Nietzsche-Freud nexus." Much has been speculated about what Nietzsche's relationship to Marx and Freud was, or rather might have been. Actually, he had come across both their names in print, though very much in passing; he had no firsthand knowledge of Marx's work, and Freud's was of course just beginning. But, even as the nexus was incepted, Nietzsche was evolving into the most important member of this hegemonic troika. A burning — or at least smoldering — question for postcontemporary thought is whether this privilege will continue to be extended to him as Marx and even Freud fade increasingly into obscurity or are treated more critically than is Nietzsche. It is important here to draw some clear distinctions between the modus operandi of the three Master Thinkers, the three greatest critics *and* producers of utopian thought in our era.

What is the aim — so common — in reading a thinker like Nietzsche, who was trained — far beyond current, if not all future standards[305] — in philology and textual scholarship without attempting to be philological and scholarly? When dealing with purportedly the epoch's greatest and most influential thinker, what is the point of reading only or primarily the thoughts that he himself made public, and not also triangulating his books with his letters and, especially, his unpublished notebooks? Reading only the fragments collected in *The Will to Power* does not qualify as taking him seriously, let alone scientifically; nor does reading what exists of his corpus only in translation. *Freud* and even *Marx* are commonly read in a philologically complex and critical way, so why not extend the same courtesy to *Nietzsche?* After all, he himself sometimes asked to be read this way. Lacan demanded that Freud be read exactly, ignoring the distorting encrustations of his reception, and Althusser demanded the same of his "return" to Marx. Yet, in spite and because of his greater influence, no one of equal stature has made the same demand when appropriating Nietzsche. Of course, one sometimes *talks* about doing this with all three men. Cornelius Castoriadis is not wrong to quip that "It is not just that one talks on and on of Freud, Nietzsche, and Marx; one talks less and less about them, one talks about what has been said about them, one compares 'readings' and readings of readings."[306] But the peculiar logic of the nexus legislates that these days one is really "talking about" or "reading" Marx himself very rarely, Nietzsche mainly.

The possibility of a philologically informed intervention that would be at once postcontemporary *and* communist must confront the fact that Althusser's relationship to the nexus appears remarkably positive and uncritical at first glance. "However paradoxical it may seem," Althusser wrote in *Reading Capital* (1965), "I venture to suggest that our age threatens one day to appear in the history of human culture as marked by the most dramatic and difficult trial of all, the discovery of and training in the meaning of the 'simplest' acts of existence: seeing, listening, speaking, reading—the acts which relate people to their works, and to those works thrown in their faces, their 'absences of works.' And contrary to all today's reigning appearances, we do not owe these staggering knowledges to psychology, which is built on the absence of a concept of them, but to a few people: Marx, Nietzsche and Freud."[307] In "Freud and Lacan" (also 1965), Althusser granted the troika similar distinction: "To my knowledge, the nineteenth century saw the birth of two or three children that were not expected: Marx, Nietzsche and Freud. 'Natural' children, in the sense that nature offends customs, principles, morality and good breeding: nature is the rule violated, the unmarried mother, hence the absence of a legal father. Western Reason makes a fatherless child pay heavily. Marx, Nietzsche and Freud had to foot the terrible bill of survival: a price compounded of exclusion, condemnation, insult, poverty, hunger and death, or madness. I speak only of them (other unfortunates might be mentioned who lived their death sentences in colour, sound and poetry). I speak only of them because they were the births of sciences or of criticism."[308] Nevertheless, and any personal persecution aside, it is clear from his overall argument that Althusser regulates Nietzsche to the realm of "criticism," not "science." For in "Freud and Lacan," just as in *Reading Capital,* Nietzsche quickly drops out of Althusser's extended comparisons of Freud and Marx. For whatever reason, and external pressures from the French Communist Party likely contributed, Nietzscheanism turns out to be refreshingly and atypically absent in Althusser in two respects: from his *published* work, and, more important at the end of the day, *compared to the standard of the times.*

In *private,* however, Althusser—*even* Althusser—was haunted by a certain uncanny presence of Nietzsche. According to Derrida, conversations at Althusser's bedside before he died in 1990 turned as much to Nietzsche and Heidegger as to Marx and Lenin, though the gist is not recorded.[309] In Althusser's two remarkable attempts at objective "self-analysis," the presence of Nietzsche is felt in three related ways: *existentially* (both men were diagnosed as having *dementia praecox* and both suffered from the symptoms of manic depression and hypomania); *thematically* (the appeal to "will to power" to take control of one's life and to produce knowledge); and to some extent *stylistically* (repeated slippage from real to imagined or screen memories, experimentation with hyperbolic formulations).[310] Althusser had begun reading Nietzsche with interest already during the time of his incarceration in a German prison camp in World War II.[311] It was in the stalag that Althusser was "metamorphosed" not into a Nietzschean but rather "from a royalist caterpillar into a communist butterfly."[312] Nonetheless, Althusser was also deeply moved — to the point of partial identification — by the figure of Nietzsche as a tragic, solitary philosopher. This uncanny, unpublished relationship is made clear in an unrequited letter to Lacan in 1963, after the latter had not responded to an earlier letter in which Althusser had attempted to establish deeper levels of philosophical and human contact.[313] But, as his conversations and letters with Mexican philosopher Fernanda Navarro make clear, Althusser struggled with Nietzsche, and with Heidegger, particularly hard in 1984 during his confinement as criminally insane. He did come to terms with Heidegger, he said, whom he concluded was "an extraordinary historian and interpreter of philosophy" *and* "a sort of unctuously refined *curé.*" Nietzsche, whom Althusser regarded as having "edified philosophy with his critique of language and signification," and whom he found (à la Freud) to have anticipated aspects of his own work in this regard, he found comparatively easier to grasp.[314] None of this would be particularly significant, were not Althusser arguably the only hope of communist philosophy and Nietzsche the only position outside of communism.

Be all this as it may, the absence of detailed and explicit critical discussion of Nietzsche in Althusser's published work has done communist philosophy no good, indeed has unwittingly given Nietzsche's corps/e considerable aid and abetment. To appropriate Althusser's own metaphor of the father, one might say that this is one reason Nietzsche has become a father figure to precisely those contemporary intellectuals who would *deny* the Father and his *non et nom* — whether explicitly or implicitly — by failing to settle accounts with "him." This problematic is familiar, of course, to all those who struggle to understand the power not only of Nietzsche but also of Freud and Marx, indeed of the monotheistic God, over disciples: that is, one *ends up by idolizing* the God or a god (Marx, Freud, Nietzsche) who, in principle at least, *began by prohibiting idolatry* and precisely for that reason attracted the disciples. The problem is that Nietzsche has become more influential than either Freud or Marx in this regard as well.

Althusser notwithstanding, the notebooks of philologist Nietzsche indicate that he did not say in public what he intended to say, could have said differently had he wished, but chose not to say in order to have maximum subconscious, subcutaneous effect. It is in this one absolutely crucial respect that Friedrich Nietzsche differs *radically* from the remainder of the troika—though less from Sigmund Freud than from Karl Marx.

The problem of duplicity in the case of the supposedly radically honest and self-analyzed Freud is not merely *personal,* thinking of his hanky-panky with Dora and Her Sisters.[315] It is also *institutional.*

It was as a direct result of the defections of [Alfred] Adler, [C. G.] Jung, and [Wilhelm] Stekel that Ernest Jones proposed the institution in 1912 of a "strictly secret" committee of loyal adherents who could be charged with safe-guarding the future of psychoanalysis. The principle inspiration for this idea, as Jones tells us in his biography of Freud, was his acquaintance with "stories of Charlemagne's paladins from boyhood, and many secret societies from literature." The committee's appointed tasks were to share the burden of replying to Freud's critics; to direct the ever-widening movement according to a "preconcerted plan" (which included controlling the International Association and its publishing house); and, in Freud's own words, to "defend the cause against personalities and accidents when I am no more." . . . Freud presented each committee member with a special gold ring upon which was mounted an antique Greek intaglio from his private collection. The committee remained a secret organization until 1927, when it was merged with the official board of the International Organization.[316]

By contrast, while many more or less Stalinist Central Committees of communist parties around the world have at one time or another embraced analogous secrecy, for good reasons of survival as well as bad reasons of duplicity and terror, esotericism is not in communism by design. Indeed, communism—both as "the *real* movement which abolishes the present state of the things" and as the maximum possible empowerment all people—is in principled though not suicidal opposition to such secrecy.[317] According to Walter Benjamin, the *ideal*—if often impractical, even suicidal—situation of the Marxist, her or his "revolutionary virtue par excellence," would be to live in a fully transparent house, visible to all.[318] Intending to throw some very heavy stones, Nietzsche had no intention of living in any glass house. Despising the maximum empowerment of all people in principle as Freud and Marx did not, lacking any substantial institution or movement in his own time as Freud and Marx also did not, and seeing Nietzscheanism's nascent germ cells — particularly in Austria, initially — as deficient, Nietzsche felt he had no choice but to produce his corps duplicitously and proleptically with his written exo/esoteric corpus.

Marx's multiplex way of analyzing capitalist society — virtually the only society he knew, and at a relatively straightforward state — was remarkably free from the assumption that ideology entailed duplicity or esotericism. *Too* free, in practical and theoretical terms. As summarized by the philosopher Richard W. Miller, Marx's position was: "If a belief is ideological, then in the final analysis, its currency is not due to mere intellectual limits in evidence gathering and theorizing." Miller continues: "At some point, people must advance the belief as true when they ought, rationally speaking, to know better than to believe in its truth. Are they lying? The claim that lying is essential seems the sort of Enlightenment cynicism that Marx avoids as being too cheap. For all the impoliteness of his attacks on ideological economists, Marx surely did not think that they were literally lying for pay. It would be just as bizarre to suppose that the controllers of means of production who are at the origins of the ideological process lie when they say that major business people possess good evidence for a different view of the interests of the majority. Because most of these purveyors of ideology are neither stupid nor mentally disturbed, there is an urgent need for a psychological mechanism likely to sustain their supposed nonrationality."[319]

Gramsci was duly suspicious of conspiracy theories as an adequate explanation of history or society, even though he and his Party were the victims of a conspiracy.[320] He tried to provide a better explanation without recourse to psychology with his notions of *egemonia* (noncoercive coercion or hegemony) and *trasformismo* (ideologico-political transformation, more or less gradually and unknowingly over time, from the Left to the Right). Today, at a stage of postmodernist technoculture when conspiracies are not just a "specific political secret" but, as Jameson puts it, "the very secret of the world system itself," all sites where the representation of conspiracy occurs undergo a shift, at least for "our" Nietzschean consciousness: "the cognitive or allegorical investment in this representation will be for the most part an unconscious one, for it is only at that deeper level of our collective fantasy that we think about the social system all the time, a deeper level that also allows us to slip our political thoughts past a liberal and antipolitical censorship. But this means on the one hand that the cognitive function of the conspiratorial plot must be able to flicker in and out, like some secondary or subliminal after-image; while by the same token the achieved surface of the representation itself must not be allowed to aspire to the monumental status of high art as such."[321] Nietzsche/anism can thus be defined, in Marxist terms, as the precise albeit flickering point of articulation between "high" and "low" art—but far surpassing both Freud and especially Marx in intended duplicity.

It is instructive to note that arguably the first person seriously to propose the Marx-Nietzsche-Freud nexus as a central event of intellectual and social history is *also* a major example of ideological *trasformismo:* that is, the transformation *from* Marx *to* Freud and finally *to* Nietzsche. This drift in the *political* sphere from Marx to Nietzsche had begun already in the nineteenth century, including among Nietzsche's personal acquaintances and obviously without Freud.[322] And neither Freud nor Freudianism stemmed the Nietzschean tide, to say the least.

The psychologist Alfred Adler (1870–1937) was a member of the Austrian Social Democratic Party, joined Freud in 1902, and in 1910 became chairman of the Vienna Psychoanalytic Society. Not long thereafter Adler broke with Freud—a split in evidence between the lines of the minutes of the society that were kept from 1906–1915. Soon after signing up with Freud's group, Adler had, by his own admission, "tried to establish a direct line from Schopenhauer, through Marx and [Ernst] Mach, to Freud." In 1908 he regretted that he had "omitted Nietzsche" from this genealogical tree, stressing—to the evident discomfort of Freud, who repeatedly waffled on how much he himself owed to Nietzsche[323]—that "among all great philosophers who have left something for posterity, Nietzsche is closest to our way of thinking."[324] After Adler's decisive rupture with Freud, Nietzsche's notion of Will to Power arguably became the single most important inspiration for his own account of dysfunctional neurosis. In any case, the Nietzsche/an brood is chock full of "Alfred Adlers"—whose commitment to socialism, never mind communism, is never really very deep, never really of the heart in addition to the mind. Never when compared to their commitment to Nietzsche.

Returning to the problematic of lying as adumbrated by Richard Miller for Marx, it must be added that certain pre-, post-, or anti-Enlightenment wordsmiths *are* cynical in the Enlightenment sense — much like their patron Ares-Mars-Eris-Enyo-Bellona, like Nietzsche himself, and like some Nietzscheans. This is to say that they *do* lie literally. Certainly they have *good reason* to forge lies both "public" and "noble"; and they have no internally, philosophically imposed prohibition *not* to. What is more important is that they get away with lying — precisely because they are read so often — and yet so seldom between the lines *or* literally. Conspiracies *do* exist. They are matters of both individuals and structures; their significance must be neither over- nor underestimated; nor should they automatically be dismissed as "paranoid." Paranoia can be recuperated as a critical tool in terms of ideology, if the latter is "a form of 'identity thinking' — a covertly paranoid style of rationality which inexorably transmutes the uniqueness and plurality of things into a mere simulacrum of itself, or expels them beyond its own borders in a panic-stricken act of exclusion."[325] In any case, to deny the existence of conspiracies out of hand can be suicidal. So it is, too, that to settle accounts with Nietzsche/anism, communists must develop a theory of esotericism — and intentionality — that Marx apparently could not, or did not, himself provide. *Nietzsche's Corps/e* is a failure — as concept and as book — if it does not contribute to this end.

In the event of failure, perhaps it will at least be piquant. Exactly this is suggested by the Neapolitan character actor Totò near the end of Pasolini's film *Uccellacci e uccellini* (the hawks and the sparrows, 1966). Totò and his filmic son Ninetto are preparing to eat Marxist crow. The Crow had introduced himself to them at the beginning of the film: "I come from far away; from the Land of Ideology, the City of the Future, Karl Marx Street." And now, preparing to eat him, Totò legitimates his act: "Professors are meant to be eaten with *salsa piccante.*"[326] In this spirit, it is necessary to brew up some red-hot sauce in which others may really cook Nietzsche/anism's goose, some day. Some of that spirit flows from Pasolini who wrote perhaps the most fitting epitaph to the very existence and concept of the Marx-Nietzsche-Freud nexus. "It has been said that I have three heroes: Christ, Marx, and Freud. This is reducing everything to formulae. In truth, my only hero is *reality.*"[327]

One might quibble, as Pasolini implies, about the inclusion of *any* im/ proper names in such lists. If there is one demand, however, it is to remove *Nietzsche's* name from them, as Pasolini did in his own way. As early as 1967 he wrote: "I'm no longer really so interested in the subject of the research of Freud and Marx. . . . I want to stress the fact that now, at age forty-five, I've emerged from the wilderness of Freudian and Marxian dogma. *But where have I got to go?*"[328] This is a difficult — today perhaps even impossible — question to answer. At least Pasolini, unlike so many transformed others, did not answer: "To Nietzsche!"[329]

The fundamental points so far are two: that Nietzsche was unlike Freud and especially Marx in the matter of theorizing and practicing conspiratorial esotericism, *and* that this fact has been missed completely by the elaborate history of the Marx-Nietzsche-Freud nexus. The Big Three have been compared and contrasted, when not conflated, only either *thematically* — for example, for their imagined decentering of the human subject in terms, respectively, of *political economy,* of *power quanta,* and of the *unconscious* and its *everyday symptoms* — or in terms of their approaches to *interpretation,* but not their *illocutionary practices.* Following the work in the mid-1940s and early 1950s of the rather heterogeneous group called the Frankfurt School (which, though influenced profoundly by Marx, Nietzsche, and Freud, never articulated the nexus *as such*),[330] *explicit* hermeneutic-thematic analysis of the nexus was re/ inaugurated by Paul Ricoeur in 1961. Ricoeur famously depicted Marx, Nietzsche, and Freud as "masters of the school of suspicion" in opposition to a hermeneutics of "interpretation as recollection of meaning."[331] This was Ricoeur's way of taking his partial distance from the hermeneutic tradition influenced by Heidegger, insofar as the latter had inadequately incorporated Marx and Freud while fully incorporating Nietzsche. Yet if Nietzsche was an esoteric writer, then Ricoeur's easy attribution to him of "suspicion" is one of *the* most misguided categories to describe what Nietzsche *intended.* At most this could describe how the *reader* should approach his work. Nonetheless, Ricoeur's naïve fantasy set the table for many subsequent roundtable and cocktail discussions of the troika. Thus, when Hans-Georg Gadamer, in his programmatic 1962 essay, "The Philosophical Foundations of the Twentieth Century," dismissed — implicitly and not by name — the principle of structural causality for being an insignificant aspect of the history of philosophy, this dismissal — which constituted one of *the foundational acts of philosophical hermeneutics* — again appealed, explicitly, to Nietzsche as the most significant member of the Marx-Nietzsche-Freud nexus. For Gadamer, Nietzsche was "the great, fateful figure who fundamentally altered the task of the critique of subjective spirit for our century." Gadamer then asserted: "If we are concerned with Nietzsche's real and epoch-making significance, . . . we do not have to decide whether philosophy is the expression of an event or the cause of it. For his criticism aims at the final and most radical alienation that comes upon us from out of ourselves — *the alienation of consciousness itself.* Consciousness and self-consciousness do not give unambiguous testimony that what they think they mean is not perhaps a masking or distorting of what is really in them. Nietzsche hammered this home in modern thought in such fashion that we now recognize it everywhere, and not merely in the excessive, self-destructive and disillusioning way in which Nietzsche tears one mask after another from the I, until finally no more masks remain — and also no more I."[332] Immediately, Gadamer proceeded to map Nietzsche onto Marx and Freud: "We think not only of the plurality of masks, represented mythologically by Dionysus, the god of masks, but also of the critique of ideology that, since Marx, has been applied increasingly to religious, philosophical, and world-orienting convictions that are held with unconditional passion. Above all, we think of the psychology of the unconscious, of Freud, whose interpretation of psychological phenomena is dominated by his insight that there can be powerful contradictions in man's psychic life between conscious intention and unconscious desire and being and that in any case what we believe ourselves to be doing is in no way identical with what is in fact transpiring in our human being" (pp. 116–117). But this today commonplace view — both of Nietzsche and of what might distinguish him from Freud and Marx — makes any firm theoretical or practical grasp of Nietzsche/anism and Nietzsche's corps/e simply impossible.[333]

Also in 1962 appeared — wholly independent of Gadamer's hermeneutic intervention — Deleuze's very influential book in France, *Nietzsche and Philosophy,* in which Nietzsche was portrayed as a profoundly non- or antidialectical thinker — and hence, implicitly at least, anti-Freudian and anti-Marxist.[334] This thesis was to be constitutive for the poststructuralist or "French" appropriation of Nietzsche; but it must be revised, certainly, in terms of Nietzsche's intent, his willingness to use all forms of dialectical incorporation when it suits his pleasure.[335] Furthermore — as Deleuze, Foucault, and Paolo Caruso at the time and as Peter Dews more recently have all stressed — it is insufficiently understood that so-called poststructuralism never really developed, beginning in the early 1960s, as a *negative, reactive response to structuralism*. More properly still, however, poststructuralism must be defined as the *overwhelmingly positive, assimilative embrace of Nietzsche*.[336] And it is as such that it persists today.[337]

In 1967 literary critic and theorist Paul de Man, just then coming on the scene, appeared to attack the Marx-Nietzsche-Freud nexus in an early attempt to deconstruct what he called "the demystifiers" by comparing them rather unfavorably to the European romantics, notably to his own great troika: Jean-Jacques Rousseau–Friedrich Hölderlin–William Wordsworth. A year earlier, at the seminal "Structuralist Controversy" conference attended by de Man, philosopher Jean Hyppolite had attempted, against all odds and unsuccessfully, to use Hegel to hold back the tidal wave of the Marx-Nietzsche-Freud nexus. Hyppolite suggested that the nexus had merely "written the criticism" of what remains a basic Hegelian problematic.[338] Within that year, de Man was writing: "Our great demystifiers, Freud, Marx, and Nietzsche, are much more naïve than their romantic predecessors, especially in their belief that the demystification can become a praxis beneficial to the personality or to the society."[339] In other words, de Man at once accepted the neo-Hegelian critique of the centrality of the nexus while denying to that same critique any salvific power of its own. On the one hand this nihilist and quietist position on the nexus was hardly widely shared; on the other de Man himself very quickly came to reverse himself on *Nietzsche*. For complex reasons, neither Freud nor Marx were ever significant touchstones to him, but Nietzsche was soon elevated by de Man to the status of a "romantic" in his positive, hyperbolic, deconstructive sense of the term: namely, a producer of radically self-referential, cognitively transcendental, but at the same time self-effacing, "literary" or "allegorical" texts that rigorously and perpetually deconstruct *any* affirmative claim made on behalf of what has remained for too many de Manians *mere* "empiricity," "personality," "history," and "society." The irrevocable turn to Nietzsche by de Man meant that a great opportunity for radically deconstructing the Marx-Nietzsche-Freud nexus was lost.

Now, within the parameters of this ubiquitous pro-Nietzschean bias or problematic—firmly entrenched in European thought already by the early 1960s at least—only three basic "logical" responses to Nietzsche seemed possible: *affirmation, rejection,* or an ostensibly *neutral* and/or *synthetic* stance. Heidegger's position is the great exception, being too complex for reduction to such schematization. The first, affirmative, valorization of the nexus was that of Michel Foucault— beginning around 1964, though he had encountered Nietzsche in earnest over a decade earlier.[340] According to Foucault, Nietzsche's "semiology"—in ways anticipating Freud's and surpassing Marx's—had been precociously pitted with exemplary and definitive force against all structuralism and phenomenology. Both of which vainly, power-trippingly search as they do for "deep," "first," or "communicating" structures.[341] Henceforth Nietzsche would remain by far the most important member of the troika for Foucault, who also had absolutely *no* interest in reading Nietzsche in any philologically exacting or accurate way, including with regard to the problem of esotericism. In one of the interviews conducted soon before his death, Foucault looked back: "I have never been too concerned about people who say: 'You are borrowing ideas from Nietzsche; well Nietzsche was used by the Nazis, therefore . . .'; but, on the other hand, I have always been concerned with linking together as tightly as possible the historical and theoretical analysis of power relations, institutions, and knowledge to the movements, critiques, and experiences that call them into question in reality."[342] None of Foucault's august and supposedly diverse body of interviewers—Paul Rabinow, Charles Taylor, Martin Jay, Richard Rorty, and Leo Lowenthal—pressed Foucault to wonder whether the questioning he rightly demanded might be more radical were it not so uncontestedly "Nietzschean." But then the interviewers are themselves members of the corps/e.

Turning the Foucauldian valorization on its "dialectical" head, Jürgen Habermas took the rejective position, nearly unique within the trajectory of Frankfurt School Western Marxism. Earlier Adorno and Horkheimer had sucked Marx-Nietzsche-Freud into one more or less positive breath, beginning in the 1930s and 1940s, as would Marcuse for the next generation. Habermas's lame spin on this aspect of his philosophical inheritance was to say that Nietzsche represented the culmination of a dominant tendency of post-Enlightenment thought— if not of this thought in its entirety because, like negative dialectics of the Adornoan stamp, "Nietzsche—and this puts him above all others—denies the critical power of reflection with and only with *the means of reflection itself.*"[343] The resemblance between this thesis and that of Ricoeur or Gadamer is due to the common source in Heidegger. (And thus is light also shed on Sloterdijk's subsequent attempt, in the early 1980s, to use the concept "critique of cynical reason" to rescue the best of critical theory, to go beyond the naïveté of Habermas, and to sublate the Marx-Nietzsche-Freud nexus by what Sloterdijk, in a move more naïve than anything in Habermas, embraced as "Left-Heideggerianism."[344] Thinking he had dispatched Nietzsche in 1968— of all years—Habermas promptly delivered himself of the opinion that "Nietzsche is no longer contagious."[345] A decade and a half later, he had to admit in an interview that this claim had been "mistaken," at least with regard to the French reception of Nietzsche.[346]

In the event, within the decade in France, by 1977–1978, the quickly mediatized and commodified "New Philosopher" André Glucksmann, a lapsed student of Althusser and former '68er, was excoriating Marx and Nietzsche, and even "a certain Freud," as totalitarian *Maîtres penseurs.*[347] By contrast, the second foundational treatise of "new philosophy" published the same year, Bernard-Henri Lévy's *Barbarism with a Human Face* (1977), was equally hostile to Marx, equally reticent to engage Freud, and yet was at the same time also—symptomatically enough for the underlying legitimation of neocapitalism that was and is "new philosophy"—much more positively disposed to Nietzsche.[348] At almost exactly the same time, across the Rhein in Germany, Marx, Freud, and Nietzsche were being analyzed by the quasi-renegade Catholic theologian Hans Küng in *Does God Exist?* (1978) as the veritable Trinitarian base of contemporary atheism and nihilism.[349] Finally, across the Channel in England, simultaneously and more neutrally, Freud and Marx were being trivialized by a literary critic as the main, implausibly polite "company" at a veritable Oxbridge high-table dinner given in Nietzsche's honor—as if by his own invitation.[350] In sum, the philosopher Alex Callinicos, a Trotskyist and no friend of Nietzscheanism—though Trotsky is often accused of making too many concessions to Nietzsche—is right to suggest that already by the late 1970s, largely for political reasons, Marxism had "lost the contest with Nietzscheanism." The reasons mentioned by Callinicos include: "the reflux of class struggle in the West after the great upturn of 1968–76, the crisis of the Communist Parties, caught between 'really existing socialism' and a reinvigorated social democracy, the disintegration of Maoism."[351]

In the context of the relative *Eurocentrism* of the Marx-Nietzsche-Freud nexus, Edward W. Said, in *Culture and Imperialism* (1993), is not entirely unjustified to contrast the perspective of Frantz Fanon, whom he regards as the intellectual descendent of the nexus. According to Said: "The difference between Freud, Marx, and Nietzsche on the one hand and Fanon's 'native intellectual' on the other is that the belated colonial thinker fixes his predecessors geographically — they are *of* the West — the better to liberate their energies from the cultural matrix that produced them. By seeing them antithetically as intrinsic to the colonial system and at the same time potentially at war with it, Fanon performs an act of closure on the empire and announces a new era."[352] The deep problem with Said's analysis, however, is not so much the inclusion of *Marx* in the problematic of Eurocentrism — from which, arguably, he took significantly more distance than either Freud or Nietzsche — but rather the a priori assumption that *Nietzsche's* project was liberatory at root and that it is possible, simply by contextualizing and historicizing Nietzsche, to unlock that potential in a new era, as if the old could thereby be left behind. Said's own basic and uncritical "Nietzschean," non-Marxist orientation is well documented.[353]

Nowadays — the end of the twentieth century and the turn to the twenty-first — it seems simply "obvious" to have reunions of the Central Committee of a remarkably unified, democratically centralized Party of left-liberalism: Marx (secretary of politics, though seldom of *economics* any longer); Freud (secretary of everyday life, though rarely of *social* pathology); and Nietzsche (secretary of virtually everything, especially aesthetics, though not in connection to *other* forms of power).[354] Note, however, that this same division of labor not only tacitly favors Nietzsche but also, as such, meshes remarkably well with the three major institutions, instances, or practices fundamental to *any* social formation — the political, the economic, and the ideological — but *particularly* to the production and reproduction of capital.[355]

In his painting *Utopic* (1987), Mark Tansey has inserted into a representation of Anna Freud's consultation room a Roman sculpture of a naked hermaphrodite reclining obliquely on the analytic couch—both major sexes fused as one body extending backward and forward in perspectival depth and into history (see plate 1).[356] The sculpture can be imagined to be alive or dead: *It is a corps/e.* On the wall behind the nude—in a room otherwise decorated only with books and an oriental rug and mysteriously illuminated by a brilliant white, shroudlike tablecloth beneath dying flowers in a vase—are three portraits in descending order of size, as if they were establishing a peculiar vanishing point: both spatially *out* of the u-topic, "no-where," twilight/dawn-blue room, as well as temporally *into* the past/future. Appropriately, Tansey creates by subtraction, producing images "by wiping or pulling the paint away,"[357] "working against time across space."[358] Nonchronologically and monochronistically arranged in terms of biological birth, the quasi-orthogonal of this high-modernist triptych interpellates the postmodern viewing subject: a large Freud, of course; a smaller Marx, snared in the pincers of his two greatest intellectual rivals; and finally Nietzsche, the smallest, most distant, most dimly illuminated. *And just so.* In the world of Nietzsche's corps/e, the truest and greatest degree of influence and power is typically in inverse proportion to apparent size and perspective. Whereas Freud and Marx seem to make eye contact with the viewer, Nietzsche does one of three things. Either he looks *back at the other men,* his gaze boring through his predecessor Marx to get at his successor Freud, informing their gaze from within—and hence also the Nietzschean viewer's gaze at them. Or Nietzsche is *absorbed into himself,* and hence by extension ourselves, his visionary near-blindness becoming our own. Or he casts his visual net into some unrepresentable space and time *other* than the contemporaneous, into the deep azure past and postcontemporary. In any case, the body exposed to view on the couch of analytic desire is the embodiment, the incorporation of both Freud and Marx *as* Nietzsche's corps/e: as hermaphrodite, if not also as android, as cyborg. As *"our"* postcontemporaneity.

Something of the same absolute—albeit more tacit and less complex—priority of a Nietzsche who is independent of relative size is also compressed by Baudrillard's "cool memory" in 1987—the same year as Tansey's *Utopic*—that "ours" is *"l'âge nietzschéen, marxiste-freudien."*[359] Thus Marx-Freud remains for postmodernity either a single articulated figure or a fused alloy, whereas only Nietzsche retains the semblance — adverbially, outside the iron cage of the Marxo-Freudian simulacrum — of imaginary uniqueness.[360] Symptomatically, Baudrillard had abandoned adherence to and analysis of "modernity" to embrace "postmodernity" at exactly the same time — 1980 — that he explicitly rejected all of Marx and Freud and one half of Nietzschean "nihilism": that is, Nietzsche's "active" as opposed to Baudrillard's own increasingly "passive" brand.[361] And hence only Nietzsche possesses whatever might remain of real power. If Baudrillard is no longer on the Left, however, his continuing "weak" allegiance to a Nietzsche imagined to be *without* Marx (and Freud) at least has the virtue of being more honest and coherent than the persistent attempt by the Left to incorporate Marx *into* Nietzsche by using Nietzschean categories. Here, Marx plays "Apollo" to Nietzsche's "Dionysus"[362] — without having a clue about what would happen to this disingenuous equation were not Nietzsche's but Marx's terminology used. This position on their relationship is symptomatic of the state of Left-Nietzscheanism today, signaling as it does Nietzsche's triumph over Marx by his corps/e.

The hypermodern incorporation of Marx and Freud into Nietzsche is not exactly new, however. It occurred not only in Alfred Adler but also over the tragic lifespan of Wilhelm Reich (from 1897 in Austrian Galicia to Lewisburg Federal Penitentiary in 1957). Reich's courageous attempt, called SEX-POL in the late 1920s and early 1930s, rigorously to link Freud to Marx without the interference of Nietzscheanism was rewarded by expulsion from both the German Communist Party in 1933 and from the Freudian International Psychological Association in 1934, *and* by his own flipped-out subsequent period which was informed by virtually every manner of Nietzschean delusion, eventually landing him in jail.[363] More proximate to Baudrillard — and more willingly than in the case of Reich — the incorporation of Marx and Freud into Nietzsche was anticipated already a decade and a half earlier in Deleuze and Guattari's *The Anti-Oedipus* (1972). This seminal text was modeled both formally and argumentatively on Nietzsche's *The Anti-Christ* (1888). In the words of a commentator, it is "no mere Marxo-Freudian synthesis," but rather "subsumes Marx and Freud within a Nietzschean framework."[364]

By the early 1970s Derrida — having in the 1960s very uncritically embraced "Nietzschean *affirmation*" against "the saddened, *negative,* nostalgic, guilty" aspect of both romanticism and current structural-ism[365] — had entered into the Marx-Nietzsche-Freud nexus at least obliquely: first, by comparing Marx and Nietzsche in terms of the irreducibly "metaphorical" nature of philosophy; and, second, by bringing Freud and Nietzsche together in terms of the problem of "influence," particularly Nietzsche's on Paul Valéry and Freud.[366] But Derrida generally has resisted conflating Marx, Nietzsche, and Freud, and, compared with his detailed separate readings of both Freud and especially Nietzsche, maintained a symptomatic silence about Marx until 1993.[367] Yet, as a resolute post-Heideggerian, Derrida has remained, in his own mind, far more *Nietzschean* than either Freudian or Marxian. And this position is widely shared.

More recently, Lacanian media theorist, philosopher, and political analyst Žižek repeats the today obligatory reference to "the great triad of Marx-Nietzsche-Freud," which is said by him to exemplify "the very essence of theoretical modernism, the revelation of the 'effective contents' behind the 'false consciousness' (of ideology, of morality, of the ego)." Then, on this basis and in spite of his profound critical commitment to both Freud and Marx, "even" Žižek proceeds to distinguish Nietzsche for having inaugurated the purportedly post/modernist, ostensibly "self-ironic, self-destructive gesture by means of which reason recognizes in itself the force of repression and domination against which it fights."[368] Despite other differences with Derrida, in the matter of Nietzsche, Žižek appears willing to link arms and dance.

And so it also has come to pass that the Nietzscheanization of the Marx-Nietzsche-Freud nexus, in current philosophy and cultural studies alike,[369] is a textbook example of the "discursive construction of secondariness." Which is the way imagined "universals" typically are saturated by ideology. Thus, the term "Nietzsche" widely comes to function, and dominate, as the "universal" for the term "Marx-Freud." This more or less surreptitious move is "based on a difference between the terms, where one maintains its specificity, but where this specificity is simultaneously presented as equivalent to that which is shared by both of them."[370] So it is also that "Marx-Freud" — along with so much else — is defined (only) in relation to "Nietzsche," which is (always) taken to be something less accidental, more essential, and just plain better. It is this benevolent, knee-jerk universalization of Nietzsche that must be challenged: thus to pry him away from whatever positive contribution Freud and especially Marx may have made to modernism and postmodernism alike; and thus potentially to free the postcontemporary from the influence of Nietzsche's corps/e, in search of a different Utopic.

Clearly, in the Marx-Freud-Nietzsche troika, Nietzsche remains by far the most currently "in." Somehow, an academic classical philologist became the popcult phenom the talent scouts are always looking for. He is the jerk-off, wet dream role model of kids and academics alike — not only males, though he typically hooks adolescent boys first, starting with the first page of *Thus Spoke Zarathustra*. The Nietzsche Industry as circle jerk. If "orgasm is identification with the body," and if "death is the enforced separation from the body," then "death at the moment of orgasm literally *embodies* death. It would also yield an earth-bound spirit — an incubus dedicated to reproducing that particular form of death."[371] In other words, the avatar brood that is Nietzsche's corps/e. The mandarin guru — from Hermann Hesse's many magi to *Karate Kid, Dead Poets Society,* and beyond — becomes globally popular — especially in modes of male bonding — when guided by what are imagined to be Nietzsche's most extreme, most arcane, most "experimental" thoughts. Yet while the erotic is clearly linked to death, as Eros to Thanatos, they are rarely the same thing exactly. *Thus Spoke Zarathustra* would disseminate less than it does were it only stroke literature.

Throughout the writing of this dead man who keeps living on, he persists in using *violent military* terminology and tones of voice. Ought we not, in theory, to take our acclaimed geniuses at their *every* word, if we do so *once*? How can we know when, or if, they are saying what they mean? Does it not make sense that a fundamentally bellicose thinker like Nietzsche would have put to work not merely *themes* — which can be idiotically easy to accept or reject — but also more or less and otherwise covert, anamorphic rhetorico-military *strategies and tactics* to communicate across enemy and to friendly lines?

"In every strategical critique," Clausewitz advised, "the essential thing is to put oneself exactly in the position of the actors; it is true that this is often very difficult."[372] Well over two thousand years earlier, Sun Tzu had noted: "It will not do for the army to act without knowing the opponent's condition, and to know the opponent's condition is impossible without espionage."[373] Dealing with Nietzsche, espionage is needed. He is a very difficult thinker to read, to put oneself in his place, in part because one must not read his published words only. His most popular book, *Thus Spoke Zarathustra,* ought to be the *last* thing read, most meticulously programmed as it is. His private letters were his tracer-bullets and his scouts—his avant-garde in the present and his android space-probes into the future. His unpublished notebooks were his battle plans, as he intimates often enough. And for his sake just maybe once too often. No field commander in his right mind ever makes his ultimate battle plan public, or at least not entirely public; but what if Nietzsche really was just a little bit crazy or sick, sometimes? Perhaps this is why it is possible to access his codes. His notebooks, working alongside the correspondence, tested adversary troop movements, actual and potential; they felt out the resolve and combat-readiness of comrades and allies, the weather conditions, and the general and specific lay of the "land." Text, soil, or computer chip; new or outmoded.

No polemic or hypothesis by itself is ever enough to combat successfully Nietzsche and his influence. And these days traditional philological and/or communist counterrigor to Nietzsche's philology would be particularly naïve without supplemental openness to alternative, new-fangled ideas and practices—whenever they can be appropriated and activated to forge new conceptual alliances, new "historical blocs." But this will happen only if and when it is possible, in Lenin's words, to "master and *refashion*" the positive achievements of alternative, rival ideas and practices, but without allowing mere *"fashion* to *become us.*"[374] This means renewed, appreciative attention to the work of important—non- or even anticommunist—Nietzscheans such as Bataille, Deleuze, Foucault, Derrida, Klossowski (also Baudrillard and Virilio), and it means a certain solidarity with what remains of international situationism and Italian *operaismo* and the *movimento autonomo.*[375] It should go without saying that all explicitly political sympathies and allegiances are relevant at best indirectly to the intellectualist arguments of a book such as this. But remaining leftists and would-be communists should pay at least equal attention to Nietzscheans on the *Right.* This includes North American neoliberals, if for no other reason than that some of the latter—from Leo Strauss to Stanley Rosen—are among the most perceptive readers of Nietzsche, more perceptive than any way of seeing produced by the Left to date.[376] These days, to say the obvious, the Right hand knows better than the Left hand not merely what the Right itself is doing but what the Left is doing as well. This is the situation throughout the Nietzsche Industry but also outside its gates, its lockouts.

One of many self-anointed "neutral" historians of the phenomenon of Nietzscheanism has written recently that the "often-confused attempt to combine Nietzsche with Marx still continues, but as far as the organized socialist movement of the left is concerned, the Nietzschean influence was never central. Although it bore various manifestations and functioned as a protean and re-evaluative irritant, it could not become part of the mainstream."[377] But the apparent fact that no "organized" and "mainstream" socialism exists any longer — if it ever did — hardly entails that Nietzsche/anism ought therefore to be either uncritically embraced or historicized out of existence. On the contrary, it means only that Nietzsche/anism has been remarkably effective in ensuring that a properly organized socialist Left has been always already handicapped by Nietzsche/anism, even before it can ever get off its mark. In the immediate and distant future, any properly organized Left needs to settle accounts with this hypothesis, if not fact, and in this sense it is Nietzsche's corps/e that is "central."

There can be today no simple assurance that one can extricate oneself easily, or even at all, from the problematic of Nietzsche/anism and its global context.[378] In this regard, one can be either depressed or heartened by Althusser's remark in his 1976 autobiography that "the crux of the problem of all philosophical (and political and military) problems [is] to know how to exit well from a circle while remaining within it."[379] Within or against capital and within or against Nietzsche/anism; and someday, perhaps, beyond them both for communism. In 1984 Althusser wrote in private correspondence that he appreciated Freud's famous claim that he had consciously refused reading Nietzsche so that he might come to his own thoughts independently of him, of his too-strong influence. Of Nietzsche, Althusser added: "Had I truly known him, I believe I would have passed by on the side of certain things that I more or less 'discovered.'"[380] As Althusser also discovered, it is not possible to avoid Nietzsche. Sooner or later one either reads him consciously or realizes that one has been reading him unconsciously. What one must do, if one wants to make discoveries against and after Nietzsche in the age of Nietzsche, is while reading him to read "beside" him. To the extent that we are all unwittingly part of Nietzsche's corps/e, it is necessary also to be "besides ourselves" with anger, repulsion, and revulsion.

Our local task here and now is to begin producing a more dexterous, precise, firmer, properly communist grasp of Nietzsche, Nietzschean-ism, and Nietzsche's corps/e in some of their historical detail and theo-retical precision. In the last instance, however, the task set here could only approximate success if it became part of a larger social praxis that is truly communal as well as truly singular. But this also means a praxis that is *anti-* and *post-*Nietzschean: that is, a praxis radically *besides* and *after* Nietzsche's uncannily still living corpse, corpus, and corps. And beyond *any* book, program, and practice — no matter how polemically, hypothetically, blasphemously, or scientifically effective — that engages them exclusively. In other words: Utopic.

Caveat on the Un/canny

What's outside? The videoworld.
(What's outside the videoworld?)
What's outside? The heart of the nation.
(What's outside the heart of the nation?)
What's outside? Retaliation.
(What's outside Retaliation?) . . .
What's outside? The oppression of the daylight.
(What's outside the oppression of the daylight?)
What's outside? Nothing to be afraid of.
(What's outside Nothing to be afraid of?) . . .
The future of the human race . . .
What's inside? The rhythm of time.
(What's inside the rhythm of time?) . . .[381]

. . . as a Hollywood beatnik turned on to Nietzsche would say,
"Man, that cat's so far out, he's in!"[382]

According to Adorno's *Aesthetic Theory* (unfinished at the time of his death in 1969), "what everybody takes to be intelligible is what has become unintelligible; what people who are manipulated repulse from themselves is secretly all-too-intelligible to them. This is by analogy with Freud's dictum that the uncanny *is* uncanny *as* the cannily all-too-familiar."[383] Or, as the situationist René Viénet had said more crisply and sharply a bit earlier (in May '68), "the *familiar* in alienated life, *and* in the refusal of that life, is not necessarily *known*."[384]

So it is that Nietzsche/anism and Nietzsche's corps/e are uncanny in the strict sense of being all too familiar and yet unknown: at once or by turn *heimlich* and *unheimlich*. The relationship between the two German terms is neatly summed up by the nineteenth-century social critic and dramatist Karl Gutzkow, a key witness in Freud's 1919 essay "The 'Uncanny'": "'*Heimlich?* . . . What do you understand by *heimlich?*' Well . . . , they [a local family] are like a buried spring or a dried-up pond. One cannot walk over it without always having the feeling that the water might come up there again.' 'Oh, we call it *unheimlich;* you call it *heimlich.*'"[385] For its part, *un/heimlich* also refers to what is *eso/exoteric*. But it has a meaning overlooked in work fixated on the unconscious. It can mean *canny* in the Scottish sense of cautious, crafty, cunning — particularly with regard to *consciously* withheld but *used* secret information. In philosopher Friedrich Schelling's phrase, perhaps the most important clue in Freud's attempt to shed light on the uncanny, though Freud quickly gave it a spin away from canny manipulation: "*Unheimlich* is the name for everything that *ought* to have remained . . . secret and hidden but has come to light."[386] The fact that Nietzsche's corps/e has not come to light sooner — and may not now — serves as a warning sign on the quicksand terrain of the un/canny.

Leftists have had two "options" or antinomies in getting after un/canny corps/es: *abstentionism,* as represented by the Western Marxist Adorno, or situationist *activism.*[387] Yet *both* positions have been as complicitous in making Nietzsche's corps/e all too familiar. Nor can anyone claim easy exemption from this rule. Nietzsche has long become un/cannily ir/relevant. That is, it seems unnecessary — is indeed rare — that anyone would feel the need to justify yet another mention or use of his work or name, yet another conversation, lecture, seminar, symposium, article, or book about him. Unlike almost any other Dead White Male who might come to mind, Nietzsche is astonishingly *un*controversial — at least in global context and in the sense that no one seems required to defend mentioning or using him once again; no one seems to object, not really. Nietzsche studies have become Culture Industry and vice versa: that is, unthinkably *boring* under the guise of *maximum* excitement. Essays in virtually all disciplines of the human, even social sciences are sprinkled with uncritically cited quotations from Nietzsche's work like input/output jacks on a cyborg. Appearances to the contrary, Nietzsche's writing is commonly treated not as material object but as Scripture, as gospel. Of course, Nietzsche waxed fearful in his autobiography that his name might one day be pronounced "*holy.*"[388] And this fear has been dutifully taken as genuine, not as a calculated strategy; and so his name has become precisely holy, just as he secretly wanted. A few sentences earlier, he had also claimed to be not a man but "dynamite," and far too few have questioned what this meant, where the explosive was placed, and when the timing device was set to go off. If he is a fully esoteric writer — hence canny, not just uncanny — we might never know.

"Nietzsche" is too easily said. His name and ideas have become virtually real or, if you prefer, "second nature," "common sense," part of "practical consciousness, in effect a saturation of the whole process of living."[389] Which is to say, part of the atmosphere and the subconscious of professional philosophers, other academics, and more popularly as well; part of the electrical, fiberoptical current into which, by means of which, one jacks in and out of apparent realities and real appearances. His refined disgust with popular culture notwithstanding, Nietzsche might even savor the moment in Wes Craven's film *Shocker* (1989) when an electrocuted man develops the posthumous capacity to interact electronically with the mass media. Nietzsche's own physical body has long since decomposed in the grave in his birthplace in Röcken bei Lützen, eastern Germany — of all places.[390] Yet Nietzsche seems very much at home — thank you — in the otherwise desperately homeless modern, postmodern condition into which he has already always been *ein-ver-leibt, em-bodied, in-corporated.* It is not that some Nietzschean specter is merely haunting the world, outside people. On the contrary, it is as if Nietzsche, or some part of him, is alive *in* people *as* them, as a zomboid, Neitzschoid brood. When Nietzsche claimed that he was not a man but dynamite, he was preparing to be a posthuman cyborg, having already exploded the point of conceptual articulation, the effective difference, between "everyday life" and "consensual hallucination" — a "semiotic ghost" in the nascent cyberspatial, global matrix.

It should be unnecessary to repeat that not all Nietzsche's effects are exactly what he wished necessarily. It is necessary to add that the entire vision of *Nietzsche's Corps/e* is hyperbolic, an exaggeration, a myth, a leftover fragment of Eurocentric, pre/modernist, "molar" paranoia in a supposedly "molecular" schizophrenic, post/modern, postindustrial world. Nietzsche has long had a powerful impact on intelligentsia in the so-called Second and Third Worlds, an impact as heterogeneous as these different regions. This book does not deal systematically, or at all, with Nietzsche/anism in most of the world—Africa, Australia, China, Eastern Europe, Latin America, India, Indonesia, Japan, Korea, the Near East, Pakistan, Turkey, the former Union of Soviet Socialist Republics—and deals with only a fraction of Western Europe, England, and North America.[391] Its argument can thus be read as intestine merely to part of the so-called First World—even as it attempts to disrupt it "parodically" from within, on behalf of a possible or virtual communist perspective globally. Nonetheless, the basic problematic of Nietzsche's corps/e is unlikely to change radically on account of the different empirical geophysical locations or times in which it must operate. Nietzsche anticipated postmodernism in his intuitive grasp of what might be called his *philosophical rhetoric of flexible accumulation on a global scale.* Flexible accumulation, the basic economic principle of post-Fordism, couples "maximum financial control with flexible and interchangeable deployment of producers and sellers across variable national landscapes."[392] Nietzsche's patented control is the proleptic deployment of a corps/e constructed by his illocutionary power and perlocutionary effect. Fighting against this corps/e anywhere, one can never be sure that Nietzschean/ism is not somehow one step ahead, that apparent contestation is not already always part of his program, that fightback, too, is not merely "the sweet revenge of a bitter enemy."[393] Nietzsche's un/canny elusiveness resides in the fact that he's so far out that he's always already *in*, so far in that he appears out.

On the one hand it would be both intellectually irresponsible and simply counterproductive to "demonize" or "Satanize" Nietzsche once again, as has been done often enough by the Right, the Center, and the Left. When all is said and done, demonization is ultimately indistinguishable from canonization.[394] As important, a "consequence of demonization is that it sets unacceptable limits to the range of inquiry into problems of history and human personality."[395] On the other hand with Nietzsche all is *not* said and done. He has been so thoroughly and so uncritically incorporated today into so many otherwise antagonistic discourses, that a controlled, figurative dose of "demonization" and "exorcism" is not always counterindicated to test the limits of the dominant range of his uncritical reception and appropriation. The ultimate caveat remains that "we" — readers and writer of this book — may be already always immune to radical self-criticism. *In fine* we may be always already Nietzsche/anized, corps/ed. Information may want to be free[396] — yet can't be. Foucault warned in his "final interview" before his death in 1984 that even *anti*-Nietzschean utterances are in effect always already *Nietzschean.*[397] Foucault did not elaborate this crucial point — himself long a member of the corps/e.

Sometimes it's necessary to fight one myth with another. No doubt Che Guevara was also talking about war in Nietzsche/an cyberspace: "In order to carry on warfare in country that is not very hilly, lacks forests, and has many roads, all the fundamental requisites of guerrilla warfare must be observed; only the forms must be altered. The quantity, not the quality, of guerrilla warfare will change."[398] All wars involve questions of responsibility. But, in the postmodern condition "beyond good and evil," we are constantly warned that it is unclear against whom we are fighting, to whom and for what, if anything, we are accountable. *"Des enfants dans le dos, c'est lui qui vous en fait."*[399] So if and when we do fight Nietzsche's corps/e — as we must — then under what banner, with which slogans?

2 Channeling beyond Interpretation

On Slogans: Aesthetics, Politics, Prophecy

> Every particular slogan must be deduced from the totality of
> specific features of a definite political situation.[1]

If Lenin's dictum is true and binding, it includes the slogans aesthetics, politics, prophecy. A book is not like a political pamphlet or rallying call, in that the "definite political situation" in which its slogans are written and read tend to appear far less "specific." This hardly means that the definite political situation is any less specific or important, only that it becomes more elusive in the case of reading and writing books than in many other forms of activity. Here keep in mind, however, Ernst Bloch's assertion that Nietzsche's "impulse" more than that of any other philosopher was to "grasp his times in *slogans,*" and hence also the "heritage" of "our time" supposedly in its totality.[2] The only historical event of his own time that ever really put a holy fear into Friedrich Nietzsche, decisively shaping his way of responding to current events, was the Paris Commune.[3] And this was a great time of slogans with specifically proleptic desire, their efficacy intended to be measured not only today but tomorrow. In the slogans of the Paris Commune, "affectivity destabilizes semantic content; what is transmitted is not a precise meaning but rather the desires that mobilized a particular situation, and that have survived, in a compressed or frozen, lapidary form, only to be reawakened and reanimated decades later."[4] So it is also with Nietzsche's own slogans and with those required to grasp his corps/e.

Aesthetics

"Aesthetics" means not only a theory of beauty or art applied to the exquisite corpse of Nietzsche's written corpus — though his writing, sometimes, is nothing if it is not also surpassingly *sublime* as well as *beautiful*. For the romantic-Kantian problematic within which Nietzsche/anism was incepted, "beauty" (*Schönheit*) — or, more precisely, "the aesthetic act" (*der aesthetische Akt*) — was the crucial mediating link between epistemology and "truth" (*Wahrheit*) on the one hand, and pragmatics and "the good" (*die Güte*) on the other.[5] In Nietzsche's own words to himself: "My direction of *art:* Not to write any longer where its *limits* are! but rather the *future* of man! Many *images* have to exist according to which one can *live*."[6] Which also means where one can *die* — hence the link to "the Sublime" (*das Erhabene*). In late classical philosophy, notably Plotinus, the function of beauty had been to conceal "evil"; in Nietzsche's beyond-good-and-evil world, evil is replaced by such categories as "the terrific" or "horrific" (*das Furchtbare*).

Aesthetics is also the sector of interface between mortal organism and im/mortal environment, the world either perceptible to the human sensorium (*aisthetón*) or — simultaneously or by turns — anaesthetically imperceptible to it. Nietzsche synchronized his writing with the principle that, as he put it, "The greatest portion of our experiences is *unconscious* and [as such] effective."[7] As interface, aesthetics means *prosthesis*. Which is the logo-erotic extension of the material body and mind propelled onto death, an extension nonetheless of all — increasingly mass-mediatized — senses and organs, in theory to infinity and immortality.[8] As Marshall McLuhan put it in 1964: "after more than a century of electric technology we have extended our central nervous system itself in a global embrace, abolishing both space and time as far as our planet is concerned. Rapidly, we approach the final phase of the extensions of man — the technological simulation of consciousness, when the creative process of knowing will be collectively and corporately extended to the whole of human society, much as we have already extended our senses and our nerves by the various media."[9] In the condition that Baudrillard calls the "cybernetic peripeteia of the body," it is not so much that "passions have disappeared," it is rather that they "have materialized."[10] In Haraway's terms, "By the late twentieth century . . . we are all chimeras, theorized and fabricated hybrids of machine and organism; in short, we are cyborgs. The cyborg is our ontology; it gives us our politics."[11] It gives us our "technological *polis*" — a polis of "technobodies."[12] Attempts to read a cyborg problematic directly back into Nietzsche's texts, notably *Thus Spoke Zarathustra*, are already underway.[13] Such attempts must be continually reminded that the original Greek polis required slave labor for its architecture, institutions, philosophical leisure, and virtually all its other masculinist activities — doing so more or less *openly*. *Unlike* any Nietzsche/anized "social space" or "public sphere," cyberspatial or other.

In the New World Order of neocapitalism, Nietzschean aesthetics is taking shape as *psychoplasmics* and vice versa. "Psychoplasmics" (also called "the shape of rage") refers to a transferential psychoanalytical operation involving the self-replicating — including posthumous — body-free projections of unconscious and conscious fears, hatreds, and desires into an embodied, materialized corps of transsexually generated beings or "broods."[14] It has certain salutary benefits for the projecting individual, with immediately disastrous consequences for the latter's victims and potentially for society at large. Psychoplasmics is not of recent conceptual origin, however, even though its technological representation, if not imminent realization, may be. In premodern Spinozist terms, psychoplasmics is a version of the anti- or non-Cartesian principle that Body and Mind — physical Extension (*res extensa*) and mental Thought (*res cogitans*) — are neither distinct and clear, nor more or less parallel, nor even coordinated, orders of things or events. Rather, they are the same order of things, events, or causes within one Substance, although they are commonly grasped under different Attributes of this single Substance. Spinoza held that "whether we conceive nature under the attribute of extension, or under the attribute of thought, or under any other attribute, we shall find the same order, or one and the same chain of causes — that is, the same things following in either case."[15] Nietzsche, staking out claims to be Spinozist himself, has long ago become a brood, an organ/ism on us, within us, as us. Thus does his corps/e become a mind-body brood of psychoplasmic Nietzscheans or Nietzschoids.

Other contemporary terms applicable to Nietzsche's aesthetics include "actants," borrowed from narrative semiotics, and "avatars," borrowed from cyberpunk. The actant, as defined by A. J. Greimas in *Sémantique structurale* (structural semantics, 1966), is part of a deep semantic structure that underlies the surface content of all narratives and depictions of characters.[16] Operating beneath this level of "enunciation spectacle," the actant — or, more properly, actantial *function* — can be dispersed among several — otherwise different, even rival — agents in a narrative; alternatively, a single agent can shift from one surface role to another — perhaps contradictory — role, yet while retaining its concealed identity. Thus can Nietzsche's corps/e be grasped traversing its way through history. Nietzschean actants come and go, believing themselves to be free agents, but their basic function for Nietzsche remains remarkably intact. For its part, the term "avatar" uploads, as many cyberpunk notions do, ancient religious notions for maneuver in cyberspace. In Hinduism, the avatar is the embodiment or incorporation of a deity. The avatar is also the software form taken in cyberfiction by hackers in the computer-generated universe or "Metaverse," becoming "audiovisual bodies that people use to communicate with each other."[17] You can Taylorize your avatar to suit any need and fantasy — but only within your technological, aesthetic, ideological, and financial limitations. Nietzsche, admirer of the Indic caste system and Laws of Manu, proleptically Taylorized his psychoplasmic avatars in strange and mysterious ways.

Nietzsche's corps/e, in the form of psychoplasmic broods and their cognates, is analogous — if not formally identical to — what Virilio in *The Lost Dimension* calls the "emergence of the incorporeal" that comes with the rapid development of cyberspatial technologies.[18] What this means is that Nietzsche's corpse — long ago re/incorporated and re/embodied cannibalistically as a mental image or *imago* of many people — is now also becoming part of the quasi-four-dimensional space of interface between the human mind and/or the computer matrix. This is part of what Nietzsche himself seems to have had in mind, proleptically, by the fantasy often recorded in his notebooks that people would not actually have to *read* his masterpiece, *Thus Spoke Zarathustra*, in order to be *influenced* by it. For they — via what Spinoza and Nietzsche both called *actio in distans* — would *always already* be enfolded in the matrix of (his) exo/esoteric thought. If and when this point is ever actually reached, memory of Nietzsche's original hard copy will be but a distant memory, at best. Contemporary technomusic intuits Nietzsche's presence without knowing it is he. His books threaten to be what Thin White Rope calls the trace of a "whirling dervish" or "dust devil": "I realize it's two or three comparisons away, / But somewhere in the background of the calmest of your days, / A scrap of paper floats a thousand feet up in the air, / Abandoned by some dust devil that died and left it there."[19] Put even more un/cannily, Nietzsche himself would then be what Front Line Assembly calls a "TACTICAL Neural Implant."[20] Then doctrines such as Eternal Recurrence of the Same would be irremovable, overlapping neural implants, such as the ones depicted in the film *Total Recall* (1990); though, as Philip K. Dick's original text makes clearer, actual hardwiring is not the issue, indeed detracts from the more complex and effective concepts employed by Nietzsche/anism.[21] It is as if Nietzsche uploaded archaic theories of chaos to produce an early version of chaos theory. Nietzschean chaos would then be "the production of significant appearances."[22] From Nietzsche's posthumanist point of view, however, the most significant appearances are only those exo/esoterically manipulated.

On a more upbeat note, Virilio speaks — in remarkably modernist, Enlightenment fashion — of the promise of the new technology called "ideography," which (à la Chris. Marker's 1962 film *La jetée* or Wim Wenders's 1991 *Until the End of the World*) would permit the observation of "the figurative action of cerebral air — the positron camera capable of detecting photons, or quanta of light, thanks to the multitude of photosensitive cells distributed around the cranium of the conscious subject."[23] Virilio also cites affirmatively Jean-Pierre Changeux's famous claim in *The Neuronal Man* (1983) that "It is not utopian to think that one day we will be able to see the image of a mental object appearing on a computer screen"[24] — and, as such, almost infinitely manipulatable. *Nietzsche's Corps/e* might be read, then, as a preliminary, grainy *ideograph* of Nietzsche/anism and Nietzsche's corps/e, in the aesthetic attempt to head off at the pass their incorporeal cyberspatial inception before it is too late. The problem today with all metaphors derived from or related to photography, however, is that digital image manipulation and synthesis has made images alterable or "reconfigurable" in undetectable ways, with the result that "photorealistic synthesized images" are virtually indistinguishable from "actual photographs."[25] It is as if Nietzsche "predicted" this technocultural development: both in terms of *producing* an "image" of himself that would give off different signals to different viewers, but also at the level of *consumption,* allowing different viewers the "freedom" of themselves producing any image they might desire of Nietzsche, while in fact surreptitiously programmed and handicapped by that production.

The aesthetic theater of operations of Nietzsche's corps/e can be conceptualized as what David Cronenberg calls "Videodrome."[26] It is the site in which the Nietzschean brood hallucinates realities and realizes hallucinations. Recall not only philosopher Althusser's remark that "hallucinations are also facts," but the fine distinction drawn by porn star Marilyn Chambers: "My dream *is* reality and reality is *like* a dream."[27] In general, Videodrome might be described, recalling Virilio's terminology, as the properly postmodern site of interface between "architecture" and "mass communication." As an architecture, it can also be a *mood,* speaking with The Mekons: "We know we should feel a fraud / But the whole place never moves / And nothing will change."[28] Videodrome, using Virilio's terms, is "more than an array of techniques designed to shelter us from the storm. It is an instrument of measure, a sum total of knowledge that, contending with the natural environment, becomes capable of organizing society's time and space."[29] But today this "geodesic capacity to define a unity of time and place for all actions now enters into direct conflict with the structural capacities of the means of mass communication. The two processes confront each other. The first is primarily material, constructed of physical elements, walls, thresholds and levels, all precisely located. The other is immaterial, and hence its representations, images and messages afford neither locale nor stability, since they are the vectors of a momentary, instantaneous expression, with all the manipulated meanings and misinformation that it presupposes."[30]

The Nietzsche/an Videodrome is *assuredly* — that is, it *insinuates* itself *reassuringly as* — the postmodernist arena of combat constituted by mind-body-cyborg-psychoplasmic interfaces and metamorphoses within and by means of which the struggle for total capitalist hegemony is sadomasochistically played out on and as the "reverse-psychology" site of "public-access" TV. *Nietzschean* public-access TV, HDTV. Aesthetics à la Nietzsche. According to Bianca O'Blivion, not-so-distant relative of Marshall McLuhan, in the Videodrome that is North America, "the tone of the hallucinations is determined by the tone of the tape's imagery. But the Videodrome signal, the one that does the damage — it can be delivered under a test pattern, anything. The signal induces a brain tumor in the viewer; it's the tumor that creates the hallucinations." Finally, "Videodrome has a *philosophy* . . . *that's* what makes it dangerous."[31] *Nietzschean* philosophy, it is necessary to add. Therefore, as high philosophy is relentlessly morphed under post-Fordist conditions, Nietzsche's corps/e simultaneously becomes an ever more significant aesthetic dimension of the spectacular technoculture of everyday life.

Not fortuitously, "everyday life" is a concept that came into existence as an object of philosophical inquiry and of more or less Nietzschean political struggle, after World War II, only with the advent of the spectacularizing media and with the concomitant transformation of high philosophy and mass culture together into technoculture. Everyday life is in some respects the hardest slogan of all to define. In the words of Maurice Blanchot in 1959, it "is no longer the average, statistically established existence of a given society at a given moment; it is a category, a utopia and an Idea, without which one would not know how to get at either the hidden present, or the discoverable future of manifest beings."[32] In other words, everyday life includes a more or less Nietzsche/an, proleptic aesthetics. Today it is situated on, and as, the "everyday" articulation of "high philosophy" and "junk culture." If, as Jameson argues—retrospectively from a hypothetically already attained postpostmodern, postgenre, and postcontemporary vantage point—"the ideologeme of elegance and glossiness, expensive form, in postmodernism, was also dialectically at one with its opposite number in sleaze, punk, trash and garbage art of all kinds,"[33] then this dialectic between the sublime and the ridiculous characterizes nothing more accurately than Nietzsche's own mature written production and its initial consumption from their incept date in the 1880s onwards. The fact that Nietzsche had to *write* his aesthetic was a contingent, contemporary, modernist technological constraint. But the *theoretical drive and desire* behind that writing—namely, to become everyday—was as proto-postmodernist and postcontemporary as it was nostalgic for premodernity.

Whatever its precise location may be called—Videodrome or other—Nietzsche's corps/e is the psychoplasmic brood of the modern and the postmodern, the precontemporary and the contemporary aesthetic. The remaining questions would be whether this corps/e will *remain* our political postcontemporary, and how in this context conceptual and political *alternatives* to neocapitalism might be found.

Politics

"Politics" is among the most overused words in contemporary cultural studies, where virtually everything is "political" to such a degree that the term loses signifying or analytic clout. Therefore, the less *said* about politics here the better, the more actually *done* with it the better. In brief, politics means not only the attempt to *transform* life as it—both the definition and the life—has been since at least Aristotle. For politics is also the more or less successful, more or less dangerous transformation of life *without people's awareness that their lives have been transformed.* So it is that in the Nietzsche/an world politics always eventually eludes logical definition.

Benedetto Croce systematized a modernist position that conceptually undergirds much liberalism to the effect that politics is at root a "passion": that is, that it falls outside the four major discourses or "distinctions" extrapolated from the Kantian Enlightenment: aesthetics (the beautiful), ethics (the good), logic or epistemology (the true), and economics (the useful), and hence is of no philosophical merit. Nietzsche is commonly perceived as being non- or antipolitical in this liberal tradition. Therefore, it is thought, either his work is *not* political *at all,* or a certain political *aspect* is *inessential* to it. Lenin's and Gramsci's warning that precisely this form of liberalism is always poised to collaborate with fascism goes unheeded.[34] Nietzsche's politics is indeed a "passion" in the sense that it was designed to influence by eluding rational detection—but this hardly renders it any less aesthetic, logical, useful, or political for his fascoid-liberal purposes.

Nietzsche's aesthetico-political hyperinfluence is sub-missive: sub-conscious, sub-rosa, sub-terranean, sub-liminal, sub-cutaneous. We've got him under our skins: he is the real prototype for *The Silence of the Lambs.*[35] For, according to Zarathustra, it is the thoughts in our "most silent moments," it is the "thoughts that come with the feet of doves that guide the world."[36] A beautiful and a chilling thought. Nietzsche's sometimes "megalomaniac" rhetorical mode has, as its concomitant, its comrade-in-arms, its distinctive "minor literature" equivalent: namely, a site of operations deep within the most subtle, intricate, and overlooked levels of common language.[37] It is only Nietzsche's most beautiful and unobtrusive thoughts that are the most chilling—when we slow reading down to measure the pulse rate of his an/ aesthetic ideology and coterminous modern political philosophy, its future-orientedness, its futurative desire. To the extent that Nietzsche's corps/e was intended to be at once aesthetic and political it was as prophecy.

Prophecy entails prolepsis. Prolepsis (prior grasp, preconception, or anticipation) is a privileged grammatical and rhetorical device or figure for many writers. As the "trope of anticipation," it is used in all genres of narrative to propel the imagination of the reader—or listener or viewer—into a future from which the initial "prophecy" can be affirmed or rejected. It was a particular favorite of Nietzsche's. The full title of his major work between *Thus Spoke Zarathustra* and *On the Genealogy of Morals* was *Beyond Good and Evil: Prelude to a Philosophy of the Future.*[38] He remarked in private, "I write for a breed [Gattung] of humans that does not yet exist: for the 'Masters of the Earth.'"[39] Whether or not these masters have materialized *exactly* as Nietzsche desired them to be is certainly debatable; the problem, however, is that too many people have assumed that they already are, or ought to become, Nietzschean masters—but without knowing *exactly* what Nietzsche desired of them. There can be no answer to Agnes Heller's question, "How can the past absorbed in the fabric of our present be recognized as past at all?"[40] if that absorption is *total* or if Nietzsche's corpse has become *totally* corps.

Referring to Nietzsche but without pursuing the matter, Lacan once implied that prolepsis is related to what Plato called "logographic necessity." "There is a danger in public discourse," Lacan told his listeners in Seminar XI (1964), "precisely in so far as it is addressed to those nearest—Nietzsche knew this, a certain type of discourse can be addressed only to those farthest away."[41] But of course what seems farthest away is often what is closest to home as *das Unheimliche.* Prolepsis, then, is a way of consciously, shrewdly anticipating and manipulating unconscious phenomena, making prophecy serve particular aesthetic and political ends. Particularly apposite is Adorno's description of Richard Wagner's un/canny innovation in opera staging, the Wagnerian "world of *gestures.* " According to Adorno, writing in 1937–1938 with the paradigm of Josef Goebbels and the Nazi rallies immediately before him: "Wagnerian gestures were from the outset translations onto the stage of the imagined reactions of the public—the murmurings of the people, applause, the triumph of self-confirmation, or waves of enthusiasm. In the process their archaic muteness, their lack of language, proves its worth as a highly contemporary instrument of domination that fits the public the more exactly, the more high-handedly it confronts it. The conductor-composer both represents and suppresses the bourgeois individual's demand to be heard. He is the spokesman for all and so encourages an attitude of speechless obedience in all."[42] In this respect Nietzsche remains to date the greatest Wagnerian *writer.*

There is nothing especially novel about the recognition that the *effect* of Nietzsche's work has been proleptic, prophetic. Already before World War I, one of his biggest fans, Thomas Mann, asserted that what will always endure of Nietzsche — for generation after generation of future youths but without their necessarily knowing it — is Nietzsche's "purified aftereffect." According to Mann in 1910, for each successive generation Nietzsche will be "a prophet one does not know very exactly, whom one hardly needs to have read, and yet whose purified results one has instinctively in one."[43] What has not been grasped, however, is that Nietzsche *incepted* his writing to have precisely this aftereffect, handicapping it in ways that are anything but pure.

Prolepsis is related to "typology" in the technical (Christian) sense of the way two significant events are imagined to exist in a mutual relationship of anticipation (Old Testament) and fulfillment (New Testament); jazzers and rockers call the oscillatory forward thrust of such call-and-response systems "swing." Rather more is at stake in prolepsis than a retroactive way of reading, viewing, or listening to earlier artifacts so as to anticipate later ones, especially one's swinging own. Prolepsis has also to do with mechanical reproducibility — fast-forward (anticipation) and fast-reverse (memory). It is the way that video technologies become *embodied* — metaphysically if not physically — as organs within the human sensorium so that the most intense and hence ephemeral experience (e.g., the erotic) can be artificially "advanced . . . in time to give it stillness and coherence, to make it a memory of shape and grace caught unaware."[44] In these techno-aesthetic terms, there is graceful shape in Nietzsche's writing, but hardly any Grace theologically or socially.

The most obsessive concern with aesthetico-political prolepsis by a philosopher after Nietzsche has been Heidegger's, who molded his political ontology around it.[45] Heidegger's project sheds some light on Nietzsche's by both similarity and contrast. Paradoxically, political ontology is a pragmatic project revealed and/or concealed exclusively as a nonpragmatic theory of *Being;* yet, conversely, in historical conjunctures deemed favorable, political ontology is also the theory of Being revealed and/or concealed exclusively as a *pragmatic* project. The question is whether this labile amalgam must *necessarily* be fascist or national socialist. It does *not*. But a variant of this question would be whether Heidegger himself ever *thought* this necessity to be the case. He *did*. Under Nietzsche's influence Heidegger demonstrably believed that a proper political-ontological conjuncture had been reached in Germany around 1929–1934; arguably, he never stopped believing it.

The political-ontological project, in the strict Heideggerian sense, is informed by at least five specifically *pre*modern and *modern* — as distinct from *post*modern — features: (1) It was to be realized not in the present but proleptically in the future. (2) It was to be esoterically hidden from exoteric view. (3) It was not to be realized rationally, cognitively or consciously only, but also subliminally incorporated and embodied. (4) It was elitist at root and required a social base of more or less willing slaves, or their updated equivalent, to support it. (5) It was dependent upon a nation and national language, and thus the *Dasein* it presupposed was also social, rather than just individual. In sum, political ontology would or could be national socialist (writ small, not large necessarily).[46] At stake, with Heidegger's political ontology *as* with Nietzsche's political philosophy, is not only a fascoid political project but also the illocutionary techniques for implementing it. Nonetheless, this book can afford not to engage Heidegger's powerful and influential reading of Nietzsche in otherwise demanded detail. Nietzsche was more cosmopolitan in inclination than Heidegger and was not a national socialist in the sense of political ontology. Furthermore, Heidegger's aim with political ontology became politico-*theological*, for which Nietzsche had little taste. The mature Heidegger was obsessed with what he mysteriously called "Das Letzte" (The Final, Last, Ultimate, Most Extreme).[47] This supreme project had to do with no one else but *Friedrich Hölderlin*. In his most esoteric text published to date, Heidegger wrote simply: "The historical determination of philosophy reaches its apex in the realization of the necessity to create a way of harkening to Hölderlin."[48] *Not*, for Heidegger, *to Nietzsche*.[49] Heidegger's reading of Nietzsche is crucial in many respects. Nonetheless, political ontology does not help crack the code of Nietzsche's esoteric semiotics; indeed — likely by design — it conceals it.

Properly Nietzschean prolepsis is an illocutionary way of representing future acts or developments as being always already *almost* present, a way of taking beforehand, of preempting possible objections and oppositions to weaken their perlocutionary force. Here Nietzsche could appeal to a complex tradition of antiquity that was theological and economic as well as rhetorical and philosophical. In Greek mythology and in the German intellectual tradition, Dionysus is the proleptic god par excellence. He is "the coming god," not merely in the sense that his coming is anticipated in the future — for example, every destructive-creative springtime — but also in the strong sense that his primary attribute — his corps/e, as it were — is defined in terms of coming and recoming, not actual arrival. The true essence of the demigod consists in perpetually coming toward humanity from the future but not necessarily ever arriving.[50] Also since the Greeks, prolepsis was a keyterm of political economy, with specific legal reference to *property*. In Roman law, for example, prolepsis related to the *nexum:* that is, the nexus of ownership relations, which included the principle of preemption, the right to appropriate property to the future exclusion of other owners.[51] In the Epicurean, and to some extent Stoic, epistemology that Nietzsche knew, while there is only one ultimate criterion of truth, namely sensation, there are subsidiary criteria that include not only emotions (*páthos, hedoné*) but also a peculiar mental apprehension, a form of "being known," called *notitia* (Lucretius) or *prólepsis* (Epicurus himself). Since it refers to a conception or belief not derived directly from sense perceptions, it is not necessarily true epistemologically; nonetheless it is important *pragmatically,* functioning as a standard of social order against which the truth of subsequent apprehensions can be judged and held accountable. But not only does prolepsis anticipate these standards, it also helps produce them in the first place, in the form of a *self-fulfilling prophecy.* So it is that prolepsis *works.* It works *incorporatively* (recalling Hegel's take on the trial and death of Socrates), *hegemonically* (in the Stoic sense of *hegemonikón:* the soul's "directive" or "guiding" function), and also *cybernetically* (*kybernetes:* "navigator").[52] Thus, not only does prolepsis work, it *navigates* and *guides* by *producing:* Latin *pro-ducere.* Translated into German political theory, prolepsis becomes "Leader-Principle" (*Führerprinzip*).

According to Heidegger, this "Latin" moment of thinking enfolds Roman imperialism. For worse *and* better it has been fulfilled in the history of Being twice: *conceptually* and *definitively* with Nietzsche's Will to Power, and *socially* and *momentarily* with German national socialism. In other Heideggerian terms, the "Latin" moment represents a major *aesthetico-political* stage of productivist mentality, a stage that had been always already latent *even* in Greek pre-Socratic *thought* but avoided in the Greek *social formation* — which both Heidegger and Nietzsche admired equally for its elitist "order of rank." For Heidegger, productivism had been *radically* avoided *not* by the History of Being, which demonstrably can adapt productivist form, but only in certain moments in "works," most notably in philosophical texts of pre-Socratic Greece; in Hölderlin's language; in Heidegger's own thought; but also in a recent, necessarily ephemeral social formation: that is, national socialism in its unfulfilled "ideal" form, if not reality. According to Heidegger, Nietzsche is the absolute culmination of productivism in thought. But Heidegger stopped short of talking about Nietzsche as a site of *textual* production — quite simply because he did not want to expose Nietzsche's elitist *social* agenda, which was also Heidegger's. If the challenge of communism following Marx, Lenin, Gramsci, and "the death of socialism" is to think and reorganize the relationships between "hegemony" and "production" in the premodern senses under global and residual national, postmodern conditions, then this is something communism must do in ways *radically* incompatible with the overall agenda of Heidegger and Nietzsche's corps/e, but as aware as possible of the corps/e's full extent, complexity, and combative will.

Heidegger remained "Greek" in that he mistrusted the Roman-Imperial aspect of Nietzsche's expressed concept of Will to Power as counterproductive to achieve the social cohesion conducive to disclosure of Being. Nietzsche, by contrast, admired Epicurean thought for its materialist, antitheological, and — most of all — political implications. From his "pathos of distance" Nietzsche viewed the entire sweep of modern social and intellectual history as one in which, he wrote, "Christianity had accommodated itself to a preexisting, generally implanted *anti-heathendom,* to cults that had been combated by Epicurus: more precisely, to *religions of the lower mass of women, of slaves, of NON-NOBLE castes.*"[53]

Nietzsche's self-appointed task was to prepare new "accommodations" for the higher caste and for the slaves who will work, more or less willingly, more or less androidly, for it. To this end, prolepsis is an illocutionary mode of *military strategy,* and Althusser's description of Lacan's proleptic style is uncannily applicable *mutatis mutandis* to Nietzsche's: "the language of a man of the besieged vanguard, condemned by the crushing strength of the threatened structures and corporations to forestall their blows, or at least *to feint a response to them before they are delivered,* thus discouraging the opponents from crushing him beneath their assault."[54]

Prophecy, then, means proleptic transmission in an un/canny way. The final E on the ideograph *Nietzsche's Corps/e* is conceived (of) as a silent "e" of the corpse ventriloquizing the corps. It is the purloined letter indicating the secret agent, the fifth column, the ghost in the machine, the armed men from dragon's teeth, the Trojan horse, the esprit de corps. "Acoustically," by activating the *ps,* the silent *e* morphs the rebus from "corps" [kōr] to "corpse" [kôrps], living or dead.

No matter how it is spelled or spoken, however, Nietzsche's corpse has been continuously re/embodied in and as corps. Like the "Latin" Machiavelli, Nietzsche was one of the greatest of the political-philosophical "captains without an army who had to recruit only by means of books."[55] This proleptically and then actually recruited corps can take several basic forms and many more minor ones. This corps/e of artist-warriors, his "centurions," he called them, his hundred men, his Few Good Men, his Marine Corps — Nietzsche = *amante marine,* marine lover *and* lover of Marines[56] — was to march, if need be, as broods over corpses. If Nietzsche's privately expressed "decision" is to be believed, "There will have to be countless *dead bodies* [*Opfer:* offerings or sacrifices]."[57] Or is another part of Nietzsche, a deeper core perhaps, already within the corpses themselves, giving their murder the appearance of suicide, as he also said? What exactly was the prophecy — *la télématique,* the tele-vision, the fore-cast — of this self-described weatherman and fisherman? What *is* prophecy?

According to Spinoza's *Theologico-Political Treatise,* "to suppose that knowledge of natural and spiritual phenomena can be gained from prophetic books, is an utter mistake, which I shall endeavor to expose, as I think philosophy, the age, and the question itself demand."[58] But if Nietzsche's writing, his corpse, is in fact prophetic, having been actually incarnated and embodied — and Nietzsche savored the thought that *Thus Spoke Zarathustra* would prove to be most effective if it were *not* necessary to read it — then how has this "utterly mistaken" incorporation come about, aided by the Nietzsche Industry and culture industry alike? This, too, is an un/canny matter demanding attention not only in terms of high philosophy and junk culture but also in terms of everyday common sense—and all the circulations and articulations between them. There also remains the problem of how to *read* prophecy, for which Gramsci provides invaluable clues.

One of the reasons Gramsci was a passionate rereader of Dante Alighieri, by common definition the first modern European writer, was the concern to explain how communists could continue to have "faith" (*fedes*): that is, to continue to struggle for the egalitarian "city of the future" (*la città futura*) in the post-Nietzschean absence of belief in God, to struggle for ethical values and social aims that are not tangibly measurable in the present and will likely never again be groundable in terms transcendent to human thoughts and actions. Gramsci's programmatic slogan was "Pessimism of the intelligence, optimism of the will."[59] Which reiterates the basic point that communism—born in defeat—does not necessarily promise success, only struggle. Hence, its relevance for the twenty-first century. Too, Gramsci in prison became painfully concerned about the existential toil to mind and body that collective projects exact from individuals. In an essay published in 1918 in his column entitled "Il cieco Tiresia" (the blind Tiresias) in the socialist newspaper *Avanti!*, Gramsci had exhibited the first scholarly indications of what was to be a lifelong preoccupation with Canto X of the *Inferno*.[60] The trained linguist and philologist focused particular attention on Dante's depiction of the total ignorance that some of the damned have of the present, due, paradoxically, to their capacity or desire to predict the future. In the *Inferno* author Dante is warned of his own coming exile. According to Gramsci, this particular circle of Hell's two principle occupants—namely, the atheist Epicureans Farinata delgi Uberti (a family enemy of Dante) and Cavalcante de' Calvacanti (a family friend)—are punished, because they desired not merely sensual pleasure but at the same time to see too far into the world *beyond* the present, by being deprived of all knowledge *of* the present. They also "transcended the bounds of Catholic discipline"—by which the communist Gramsci also meant, in his code, democratic-central Party discipline. Once in prison (from 1926 to his death in 1937), Gramsci's "allegorical" take on Dante's canto became more politically and existentially specific. For example, he now compared the figure of Farinata in Hell, among other things, to his own comrade Amadeo Bordiga's behavior back in the crucial year 1921, since the latter, by "predicting" that a fascist coup d'état was "impossible," attempted to conjure away what he thought he could not control, and thus ended up producing a dangerous *self-fulfilling* prophecy.[61] Nor was Gramsci innocent from this charge, as he also implies. Most poignant and central to Canto X, for Gramsci, is the fate of Cavalcante. For his punishment is particularly "embodied," in that he now "sees into the past and into the future, but does not see in the present, in a specific zone of the past and the future in which the present is included."[62] More specifically, he cannot see his own son and so knows not whether he is dead or alive.

A basic lesson to be drawn from Gramsci's reading of Dante, which is more complex than indicated, is that if *modern* political thinking is "damned" insofar as it sacrifices the ability to interpret and change the present for the ability to see a future in which it can never be present, then *postmodern, postcontemporary* political thinking is damned because of its inability even to imagine alternative futures — and hence radically to interpret and change the present of individuals and collectives. Certainly this is how the dead Nietzsche — as a proper modernist — proleptically handicapped his corps, damned as this corps is from seeing alternative pasts, presents, and futures to those he himself provided. An exact communist philology, following Gramsci, must mediate between such unacceptable antinomies to grasp Nietzsche's corps/e as prophecy.

According to Gramsci in his prison cell, "In literary tradition and in folklore, the gift of foresight [or foreknowledge] is always related to the present infirmity of the seer, who, while he sees into the future, does not see into the immediate present because he is blind."[63] Gramsci then adds this parenthetical remark: "(Perhaps this is linked to the concern with not disturbing the natural order of things. That is why seers are not believed, like Cassandra. If they were believed, their predictions would not come true, since, once alerted, men would act differently and events would unfold differently from the prediction.)"[64] In this sense, then, Nietzsche precisely did not want to be "believed," if that meant that his predictions would not come true. Hence, all his incandescent fulminations against "belief." In other words, Nietzsche strove to be believed, at the deepest level, not exoterically but esoterically. Virilio might add that in postmodern technoculture and technological warfare alike "to govern is more than ever to fore-see, in other words to go faster, *to see before.*"[65] Gramsci also noted: "It is certain that prediction only means seeing the present and the past clearly as movement. Seeing them clearly: in other words, accurately identifying the fundamental and permanent elements of the process. But it is absurd to think of a purely 'objective' prediction. Anybody who makes a prediction has in fact a 'programme' for whose victory he is working, and his prediction is precisely an element contributing to that victory."[66] But what, then, was Nietzsche's own "blindness" — apart from his painful physical shortsightedness? Was his blindness of illocutionary design? Why does he still appear as a seer to so many of us? We must attempt to see him, his corps/e, *otherwise*.

Nietzsche is not merely one of the most important philosophers in history, or so many assume, he is also genuinely popular, just one of the guys, part of everyday life: from the AMOK bookstore in Los Angeles, heading west across the Pacific, before arriving in Ithaca, and not just Ithaca, New York.[67] The phenomenon of Nietzscheana — from various "Nietzsche-cult commodities" to "Nietzscheanisms" in common speech — has been firmly in place since the early 1890s, when Nietzsche, commonly depicted as "martyr" and "prophet," was still alive though no longer sane.[68] Still, it is a remarkable thing: more books have been published about Nietzsche in the last *five* years — to 1995–1996 — than at *any* other comparable length of time previously. The sesquicentennial of his birth, which *Nietzsche's Corps/e* is written to mark in its own way, was in 1994. The year 2000 will be the centennial of his death. Nietzsche's case best illustrates Bataille's thesis that there is a powerful "allurement linked to the corpse's putrefaction"; for "apparently and in principle, the prohibition concerning the dead is not designed to protect them from the *desires* of the living."[69] And vice versa. Because, before they die, the dead have made their own proleptic plans — "aesthetic" and "political" — for the living.

Left-Nietzschoids, Right-Nietzscheans

O, the sharp watchfulness,
the sweet deception,
the lukewarm struggle![70]

See your reflection here,
O proud and foolish age
Who have abandoned the clear path carved out

For us by years of reawakened thought —
Who stumbling backward
Trumpet your retrogression as a gain.[71]

They do not see the evil character of his thought because
they are the heirs of the Machiavellian tradition; because they,
or the forgotten teachers of their teachers, have been
corrupted by Machiavelli.[72]

German criticism has, right up to its latest efforts, never
left the realm of philosophy. It by no means examines its general
philosophic premises, but in fact all its problems originate in a
definite philosophical system, that of Hegel. Not only in its
answers, even in its questions there was a mystification. This
dependence on Hegel is the reason why not one of these
modern critics has even attempted a comprehensive criticism of
the Hegelian system, however much each professes to have advanced beyond Hegel. Their polemics against Hegel and against
one another are confined to this — each extracts one side of the
Hegelian system and turns this against the whole system as well
as against the sides extracted by the others.[73]

Standing on the shoulders of giants
Leaves me cold.[74]

The phenomenon of the "Nietzsche cult" has already been analyzed —
as early as 1897.[75] In the face of an already then established leftist
appropriation, arguably the first major sociologist, Ferdinand Tönnies
(1885–1936), asserted that Nietzsche's mature thinking — Tönnies remained a lifelong, boundless admirer of Nietzsche's first book, *The
Birth of Tragedy* — was, *appearances* very much to the contrary, *"pseudo-
emancipatory."* This insight was *never* adequately to be developed in the
subsequent century. Instead, Right-Nietzscheans have "stumbled backwards, trumpeting their retrogression as a gain"; and even the most
Argus-eyed leftist criticism of Nietzsche, when it exists, turns out at the
end of the day to serve struggle that is merely "lukewarm." Like the
unwitting heirs of Machiavelli, Left-Nietzschoids, more than Right-
Nietzscheans, do not see the character of Nietzsche's thought because

they are his corrupted students: that is, students of his students.[76] In short, following Marx and Engels, our "Hegel/ianism" is Nietzsche/anism, our problematic.

Tönnies's fundamental claim remains correct: Nietzsche continues to provide only a *veneer* of leftist radicalism for bourgeois intellectuals who, at a time of ongoing class and other struggles, require philosophical self-legitimation for their own *fundamentally* elitist and exploitative socioeconomic positions of power. The ultimate role of Nietzscheanism, for Tönnies, is to legitimate capitalism, to conceal its most radical root and inhuman face. But this challenge to the left wing of Nietzsche's corps/e was largely dropped, including by Tönnies himself. In important respects he remained Nietzschean to his death in the Third Reich, as did German sociology as a profession.[77] The second early attempt to navigate the "Nietzsche cult" took a different tack. A decade later, Wilhelm Carl Becker's book *The Nietzsche-Cult: A Chapter from the Divagations of the Human Spirit* (1908) detected Nietzsche behind German imperialist and colonialist aspirations and policies in Africa.[78] Yet Becker left the precise nature of Nietzsche's role in German expansionism shrouded in mystery. Aijaz Ahmad is surely right that "The Marxist tradition had been notably anti-imperialist; the Nietzschean tradition had no such credentials."[79] Yet, generally speaking, Tönnies's insight is potentially far more valuable than Becker's: What is most peculiar and in/visible about Nietzsche cults is not that they exist on the Right but rather that they exist on the Left.

It is important to imagine the relationship between Right- and Left-Nietzscheans not as extreme manifestations on a spectrum, with Nietzsche's "true" intent somewhere in the middle, but rather as two modes of a single supple but invariable intent that spins its effects out centrifugally. And here the most extravagant figures on the Left or the Right are not the most revealing but the more "centrist" — not in the sense of being in the middle of an ideological scale but of philological proximity to Nietzsche as center. Apparent differences of opinion about Nietzsche on the Left and the Right — represented by the names, or name-effects, "Rorty" and "Rosen" — confirm deeper levels of unacknowledged consensus. This also confirms Althusser's argument that "the philosophy of philosophers assumes the role of unifying the contradictory elements of ideology with which every dominant class is confronted when it comes to power, to form a dominant ideology for both dominant and dominated class."[80] Thus Nietzsche's corps/e always seems poised to be the philosophy *either* of the dominated *or* the dominant, but ultimately is always on the side of the latter. As a rule of thumb, it is best to assume that Right-Nietzscheans grasp not only Nietzsche better than does the Left but also the paradoxical existence of Left-Nietzscheanism.

It is not uncommon to assert that it is *only recently* that the Left, or rather a *faction* of it, has become Left-Nietzschoid. Those making this claim ignore history. Nietzsche's *initial* influence was not on the Right or Center but rather on what many historians of this phenomenon call "the Left."[81] This affirmation began in Austro-Hungary in the mid-1870s when Nietzsche was alive and sane, and continued in Germany and the rest of the world when he was neither. There have *always* been Left-Nietzschoids as well as Right-Nietzscheans, just as there has always been debate about which of the two *Nietzsche* himself was or considered himself to be.

Nor are these questions of recent origin. They were discussed explicitly and publicly in Europe no later than 1902, in a feuilleton entitled "Nietzsche — Socialist in Spite of Himself" appearing in what had been Nietzsche's own favorite periodical, the Parisian *Journal des Débats*.[82] The author, Jean Bourdeau, still editor in chief of this prestigious organ as he had been in Nietzsche's time, was well versed in contemporary German and American as well as French thought on Nietzsche. Years later, "Nietzsche — Socialist in Spite of Himself" would catch the eye of an archivist named Georges Bataille. Noting that "at the present hour there is hardly a writer more commented on than Frédéric Nietzsche," Bourdeau concluded that a transnational, more or less "socialist Nietzscheanism" was already in place all across the continent — but one which, ironically, had inadequately worked through the problematic announced in his title: namely, Nietzsche's own animus against socialism. It turns out that Bourdeau (1848–1928) had been personally contacted by Nietzsche from Turin in December 1888, during the last days of his sanity, in the hope of promoting his fortunes in France.[83] Bourdeau was an early recruit by Nietzsche himself to his corps. A decade and a half later, Bourdeau was dutifully obliging as interpellated corps/e — though only after the "socialist Nietzschean" had already begun entrenching himself alongside the other major ideological camps.

It should also be noted that Nietzsche's readers — particularly the most fanatic — have included considerably more men than women. But this discrepancy has hardly prevented him from exerting a substantial influence even on the most progressive women's movements, also from the late nineteenth century on. Common opinion to the contrary, his influence was thus felt neither first nor most substantially by contemporary French and Anglo-Saxon feminisms.[84] The early phase of his reception, before the turn of the century, found not only male poets creating "Superwoman" (*Überweib*) as Superman's bosom buddy but also women novelists creating "Zarathustrene," who could operate pretty much on her own.[85]

Philosopher and media analyst Heide Schlüpmann has shown that Nietzsche began to have an affirmative impact on German feminism just before the turn of the century — less on conservative feminists such as Helene Lange and Gertrud Bäumer's *Bund Deutscher Frauenvereine* (league of German women's associations) or on radical social democrats such as Clara Zetkin, though she embraced Nietzsche on occasion, than on "radical middle-class feminists" such as Helene Stöcker's *Bund für Mutterschutz und Sexualreform* (league for the protection of mothers and for sexual reform), which was active from 1904 to 1933.[86] Nietzsche's impact on Stöcker (1869–1943) was especially deep, beginning in the early 1890s but especially after 1900.[87] Eventually forced into American exile by the Nazis and aware of Nietzsche's appeal for some of them, Stöcker still could write near the end of her life that she still felt herself more "united" with Nietzsche than "with any spirit among the living."[88] Schlüpmann draws from Stöcker's "Nietzschean" logic — if God is dead, so is Patriarchy — positive lessons for contemporary philosophy and feminism, where Nietzsche has been doing nicely for some time now, particularly in France, Japan, and the United States. Schlüpmann also uses her historical example to open up a new perspective on Jürgen Habermas's *Philosophical Discourse of Modernity* (1985), which attempts to transcend the two kinds of Nietzscheanism that he thinks are particularly hostile to Enlightenment. On the one hand Habermas, who is often weak on women's issues, stodgily opposes what he regards as more or less flippant tendencies of French poststructuralism and postmodernism; on the other he resists the continuing aftershocks of the "global pessimism" in Adorno and Horkheimer's most influential and Nietzschean text, *Dialectic of Enlighten-*

ment (1944). Habermas's own attempted exit from this antinomy is to pit against both "subject-less" and "subject-centered" attacks on Reason an eclectic, intersubjective theory of communicative reason and action. By analogy and contrast, Schlüpmann finds prefigured in Stöcker's early feminist Nietzscheanism a "still unsurpassed" way to transcend the antinomy between "equality with men" and/or "feminist essentialism," and to push for "a critique of the reactionary tendency of the cults of motherhood and femininity."[89] In short, Nietzsche has been alive and well on the feminist Left, including even Germany, for a full century. But the puzzle of a largely uncritical reception by women of a sometimes self-professed hater of women remains unsolved.

Since Bourdeau in 1902, a number of Nietzsche's readers have called attention to the paradox of the existence of any Left-Nietzscheanism in light of the nasty — *not always unjustified* — things Nietzsche said about "socialists." These readers embrace strange bedfellows, however, including Nazi philosopher Alfred Rosenberg. In his 1930 best-seller *The Mythos of the Twentieth Century,* he asserted that "Nietzsche demanded, with passion, a strong personality; falsified demand [falsified by "communists"] becomes an appeal, a letting loose of all the instincts. Around his banner rally the red battalions and the *nomadic prophets* of Marxism, the sort of men whose senseless doctrine has never been more ironically denounced than by Nietzsche."[90] Rosenberg was uncharacteristically right. But then, of course, he quickly folded Nietzsche into his version of Nazi racism.[91]

Obviously it has been more the Left than the Right that has claimed Nietzsche for Marxism.[92] Yet the Right, too, has done this, as demonstrated by no one less than Benito Mussolini — and not only when he was a self-described "socialist." Scrutiny of the affirmative right-wing conflation of Nietzsche and Marx is complicated by the fact that the historian who has studied it in most detail, namely Ernst Nolte, now accepts the proposition that Nietzsche and Marx really were essentially "the same" in terms of both ideology and even political effect. The reason why this former student of Heidegger is making this claim today is murky, though basically right-wing.[93] But, to repeat, it has not been Nazi or neo-Nazi Nietzscheans who have done the most to make Nietzsche appear to be a progressive alternative to the present, *including* to Actually Existing Socialism and "communism." Much of the responsibility lies with anti-Nietzscheans in power throughout former

East Bloc countries. But this fact does not in itself illuminate the paradoxical existence of Left-Nietzscheanism.

Historical arguments linking Nietzsche positively to "the Left" can be compromised by demanding that the historians who make them define what they mean by "the Left" — a term that too often means a cowardly liberalism that has been more part of the *problem* of the relationship between liberalism and not only the welfare state — "bourgeois democracy at its maximum" — but also fascism — "bourgeois democracy at its minimum" — than any *solution* to it.[94] A powerful, even dominant fascoid-liberal tendency has long been more in league with Nietzsche's corps/e than in effective combat against it. But what makes Nietzsche's influence most un/canny is that there has never been adequate resistance from a real Left. Because neither Adorno — and his follower Habermas — nor his rival Lukács — and his Eastern European and Soviet disciples — were inattentive to Nietzsche's illocutionary strategies, Western Marxism has been *particularly* unable to account for Nietzsche's perlocutionary effect. All merely thematic criticism of Nietzsche — including any "ideology criticism" — sooner or later becomes more a part of Nietzsche's corps/e than a radical settling of accounts with it. Finally, unlike the Right, the Left has not considered the possibility that Nietzsche *programmed* "even" "feminist" and "socialist" responses to his work, not "in spite" but *because* of an agenda that was designed to be in/visible, exo/esoteric.

For every person who reads Nietzsche as "the stepgrandfather of fascism" (Leo Strauss)[95] or national socialism's "indirect apologist" (Lukács),[96] at least two people read him as a man of the Left, even of having written one of two of the "last socially accepted philosophies" of our age (Adorno).[97] No one, especially on the Left, has described more sharply the underlying paradox of the existence of Left-Nietzscheanism than has the neo-Straussian philosopher Stanley Rosen. It is a sad commentary on the state of contemporary thinking that his work is so often ignored or maligned by the Philosophy Industry and Nietzsche Industry alike. He begins his 1987 essay "Nietzsche's Revolution" by stating flatly: "Friedrich Nietzsche is today the most influential philosopher in the Western, non-Marxist world."[98]

Interrupting Rosen right off the bat, it is important to note when this remark was written. That is to say, before the Berlin Wall came down and the USSR began to unravel, and without reference to Nietz-sche's decisive influence elsewhere in the world. Nietzsche's impact in Russia and in Japan began almost as early as it did in Europe. Maxim Gorky's autobiography recalls the radical intelligentsia struggling to "synthesize" Marx and Nietzsche along the Volga in the 1890s.[99] By 1901 the Japanese literary scene, which likewise had begun debating Nietzsche around 1893, was speaking less about Marxism than about "Nietzsche fever" (*Niitse-netsu*).[100] Not long thereafter this phenome-non migrated to mainland China, with Chinese intellectuals returning from Japan with "Nietzsche fever."[101] Nor does Rosen mention the exis-tence today of thousands of Nietzsche/an intellectuals all over the "Sec-ond" and "Third" Worlds. Considering this fact (alongside encounters the author of *Nietzsche's Corps/e* had in October 1989 in Moscow at the Soviet Academy of Sciences with many self-described "Nietzschean" philosophers), Rosen may if anything *understate* the extent of Nietz-sche's influence.[102] And one might reasonably guess that he has not heard rock groups like Will to Power or Neue Werte.[103] Nonetheless, Rosen's "Nietzsche's Revolution" proceeds to pose the *fundamental* question.

Rosen continues:

The scope of [Nietzsche's] influence cuts across the traditional lines of the-ory and practice by which intellectuals and political activists are usually divided. Furthermore, in apparent contradiction to Nietzsche's own asser-tion that he does not write for the mob, his doctrines have been dissemi-nated throughout the general public, and not the least among people who have never heard of his name or read a page of his voluminous writings. It is a remarkable fact that Nietzsche — a self-professed decadent, nihilist, atheist, anti-Christ, opponent of academic philosophy, scourge of socialism, egali-tarianism, and "the people," who espoused aristocratic political and artistic views, insisted upon a rank ordering of human beings, and went so far as to advise men to carry a whip when they visit the women's quarters — is today one of the highest authorities, if not *the* authority, for progressive liberals, existentialist and liberation theologians, professors, anarchist speculators, left-wing critics of the Enlightenment and bourgeois society, propounders of egalitarianism and enemies of political and artistic elitism, the advance guard of women's liberationists, and a multitude of contemporary movements, most if not all of which seem to have been castigated by Nietzsche's un-paralleled rhetorical powers.[104]

Notwithstanding the fact that Left-Nietzscheanism has now been around for a full century, Rosen's formulation here is as close as anyone has ever come to formulating *the* problematic of Nietzsche/anism. Rosen is particularly precise in suggesting of Left-Nietzscheanism that it exists in only "*apparent* contradiction" to Nietzsche's intentions.

Now, many otherwise very rational people have been impressed, if not also taken in, by Nietzsche's illocutionary powers. Richard Rorty, claiming Paul de Man for the "American Left" in 1989, quickly dismisses what he calls "Nietzsche's occasional attempts to proclaim himself the superman, and therefore entitled to neglect the needs of mere humans."[105] Rorty then adds that "from my antiessentialistic angle, the hallucinatory effects of Marxism, and of the post-Marxist combination of de Man and Foucault currently being smoked by the American Cultural Left, are just special cases of the hallucinatory effects of all essentialistic thought" (p. 137). Rorty writes from a self-described "American" or "North Atlantic" position; and he is in solidarity — albeit a sometimes skeptical and critical one — with other "American cultural leftists" and their European inspirations — most notably Derrida and Heidegger — all of whom, on both sides of the Atlantic, Rorty thinks should abandon such popular notions of cultural periodization as "the postmodern." According to Rorty, in the 1991 introduction to his *Philosophical Papers,* this "term is so over-used that it is causing more trouble than it is worth" and, as noted, he recommends replacing "postmodernism" by "post-Nietzscheanism."[106] For Rorty, an eminently sensible man, "post-Nietzschean European philosophy and postpositivist analytic philosophy [are] converging to a single, pragmatist account of inquiry" (p. 3). Indeed — not entirely by chance at this moment of "our" triumphant *pax americana* — Rorty imagines a global drift of philosophy toward the theory and practice of what he is pleased to dub "pragmatic recontextualization." It is in this context, then, that Rorty downplays what he regards as Nietzsche's and Heidegger's merely *occasional,* merely fascist-"*sounding*" utterances as mere minor, momentary aberrations. Embarrassingly enough, these utterances are admitted to exist. But somehow they always end up being in/visible, unworthy of serious thought or worry. In "Philosophy as Science, as Metaphor, and as Politics" (1986–1989), Rorty insists, in the face of considerable empirical evidence to the contrary, that "Heidegger was only accidentally a Nazi" — a contingent political fact simply irrelevant to his enormous *philosophical* importance and which can be purged by politely asking both Heidegger and his great predecessor in this regard, Nietzsche, not to take language quite so seriously.[107] This recommendation is reminiscent of the 1950 agreement between Adorno, Horkheimer, and Gadamer that Nietzsche not be read "literally" — except of course when we happen to like what he is saying. According to Rorty, this overseriousness is the main fault shared, though with rather different political valences, by major contemporary post- and Left-Nietzschoids such as Derrida and de Man.

Rorty's most complex arguments about Nietzsche and Heidegger come in *Contingency, Irony, and Solidarity* (1989).[108] Yet precisely here, especially in the essay "Self-Creation and Affiliation: Proust, Nietzsche, and Heidegger," is where Rorty splits post-Nietzschean philosophy — or rather Nietzsche's corps/e — too neatly in binary twain. On the one hand there is for Rorty what might be regarded as the phenomenon's *historical* dimension. This, for Rorty, is merely *contingent* and, in the case of post-Nietzscheanism, often *suspect* both in its grandiloquent pretension and specific political recommendations. On the other hand there is a properly *philosophical* dimension, which remains *pathbreaking* and *valid* — even though modest in initial appearance from the perspective of Anglo-American argumentation. Rorty writes:

> When Nietzsche and Heidegger stick to celebrating their personal canons, stick to the little things which meant most to them, they are as magnificent as Proust. They are figures whom the rest of us can use as examples and as material in our own attempts to create a new self by writing a bildungsroman about our old self. But as soon as either tries to put forward a view about modern society, or the destiny of Europe, or contemporary politics, he becomes at best vapid, and at worst sadistic. When we read Heidegger as a philosophy professor who managed to transcend his own condition by using the names and the words of the great dead metaphysicians as elements of a personal litany, he is an immensely sympathetic figure. But as a philosopher of our public life, as a commentator on twentieth-century technology and politics, he is resentful, petty, squint-eyed, obsessive — and, at his occasional worst (as in his praise of Hitler after the Jews had been kicked out of the universities), cruel.[109]

Structural causality is pitted against this line of "commonsense" or "toolbox" approach to argue that no member of Nietzsche's corps/e can be carved up so easily. Nietzsche's "personal canon" includes his intentions, his proleptic illocutions that cannot be separated from their perlocutionary effect. Rorty's proposal in effect to dissect Nietzsche's corps/e—separating corps from corpse—may even have been promoted by Nietzsche himself and by his most influential follower, Heidegger, but only exoterically, with deeper esoteric motives in mind. To play with Rorty's own image, Nietzsche's "personal canons" were always already also designed as *cannons*. Philosophically, philologically, and politically speaking, Rorty's binary recommendation is thus not *necessarily* "wrong"—since it is undesirable, and in any case impossible, to place *absolute* restrictions on how any body of thought is going to be cannibalized—but rather far too *premature*.

According to Rorty's sometime sparring partner Jean-François Lyotard, in *Discours, Figure* (1971), there are three distinct but related "orders" of vision and visuality. Beneath the order of the contours of the "seen" image, and beneath the "unseen" yet still visible order of the gestalt, operates the order of the invisible proper: not a stable or intelligible structure but rather a "block" or "matrix."[110] "If the matrix is invisible," Lyotard argues, "then it is so not because it arises from the intelligible, but rather because it dwells in a space that is beyond the intelligible, is in radical rupture with the rules of opposition. . . . What characterizes it is to have many places in one place, and together these block what is not compossible" (p. 339). Applied to *Nietzsche's* intent and illocutionary strategy—as Lyotard himself oddly does *not* do—the matrix can be seen as a major source of his suasive power. As Rosalind Krauss has suggested, the Lyotardian matrix also involves an "im/pulse," the invisibility of which "is secured . . . by the very activity of the changes it produces, of the constant nonidentity of its component parts. Yet the product of the matrix is an obsessional fantasy, a recurrence which, in each of its repetitions, is the same."[111] And so do matters stand, precisely, with the obsessional fantasy, the im/pulse, and the matrix that is the invisible but informing presence of Nietzsche in the system of more or less visible effects of Nietzscheanism: in short, in the im/pulsive and pulsating—yet remarkably constant—matrix of Nietzsche's corps/e. In fact, Rorty has no tools to see what he himself might be. For Rorty as for so many other Left-Nietzschoids, Nietzsche's merely fascist-*sounding* utterances are not essential—not to say essentialistic—to Nietzsche's or to Heidegger's "true" thinking. Rorty may reject "essentialism" in principle, yet he claims to know Nietzsche's "personal canon" in its uncontaminated essence even without philological inquiry.

A stronger but related thesis, long fashionable in France, holds that Nietzsche only *"made himself* fascist in order better to fight fascism."[112] This is part of a more general postcontemporary stance that defends its favored object from attack by claiming that it was already an exemplary part of the attack to begin with. (Compare, e.g., the claim that Alfred Hitchcock made patriarchal films only the better to deconstruct patriarchy.) In other words, Nietzsche infiltrated fascism *in advance,* holding up to it its own hidden obverse of identification to subvert it by a process of hypermimesis. The risky strategy of politico-cultural "mimesis" whereby one imitates fascism to the point of total identification with it, but with the intent to expose its covert obverse so as to deconstruct and destroy it from within, is anticipated by Bataille's theory and practice of *"sur-*fascism," and part of what he meant by *"sur-*Nietzscheanism." Today, this practice is best exemplified by the Slovene industrial postpunk rock group Laibach, as interpreted and supported in these terms by Žižek in *LAIBACH: A Film from Slovenia.*[113] It is hardly by chance that members of the audience interviewed in the film after a New York City performance comment explicitly on Laibach's "Nietzschean" root and effect. But without philological analysis we will never know whether Nietzsche himself had such a corrosive effect in mind, or rather something more sinister — particularly so if, as Žižek also suggests, the blood-drenched breakup of Yugoslavia represents not a flashback to the past but the future of the world.[114]

Since so many left-liberal post-Nietzscheans sail with Rorty sooner or later under a Heideggerian as well as Nietzschean flag, it is important to contrast Nietzsche and Heidegger once again. Pragmatically speaking, and some serious philosophical and rhetorical differences aside, Heidegger shared with Nietzsche a virtually identical vision of anti- or nondemocratic society. They differ "only" in terms of metaphysics, ontology, thematics, and illocutionary style. To repeat, Heideggerian political ontology cannot be reduced to Nietzschean political philosophy. But the bottom line, in terms of the implications for postmodern and postcontemporary political economy, is that Nietzsche and Heidegger shared a deep commitment to the esoteric implementation of their social vision. Grasping this fact is made difficult because Heidegger's critique of Nietzsche's Will to Power as "metaphysical" is generally thought to be definitive and sincere politically as well as philosophically, and because there exists no adequate study of Heidegger's version of the exo/esoteric problematic, either.[115] While it is increasingly supposed by know-nothing liberal anti-Heideggerians that "Heidegger never tires of repeating that, as existence, Dasein is prior to a rational approach, which emerges only within existence,"[116] for some reason the next step is not made: that is, away from this ontological *thematic* of "concealing and revealing," which is rationally graspable — for example, by Tom Rockmore — toward the possibility of subrational illocutionary strategies that this very theme necessitates and that, if they were working properly, could not be rationally grasped. This lacuna between ontology and illocution not in Heidegger but his readers opens up the possibility, even likelihood, that Left-Heideggerians will flourish. Several recent Nietzscheo-Heideggerians — Reiner Schürmann and Gianni Vattimo the most notable — have found a certain — homeopathic or is it allopathic? — curative value in the later Heidegger's image of technology as "the danger that 'saves.'" This theory-oriented point of view must be viewed against the backdrop of a rival tradition of historical scholarship that stresses the ambivalent fascination of German "mandarin" or "reactionary modernist" intellectuals with technology — an ambivalence that Heidegger shared fully with other members of the Nazi Party from the top down — and that highlights their consequent struggle never to reject technology per se but rather to develop specific politically, culturally, socially, and always nationally managed *kinds* of technology.[117] It is reasonable to assume that Nietzsche's attitude toward technology would have been roughly the same as Heidegger's; indeed the latter's views are useful because one can read back from them to imagine what Nietzsche's might have been. At the grand opening of the Berlin Automobile Show in 1939, Josef Goebbels proclaimed in no uncertain terms: "National Socialism never rejected or struggled against technology. Rather, one of its main tasks was consciously to affirm it, to fill it inwardly with soul, to discipline it and to place it in the service of our people and their cultural level."[118] From his own — in historical context not so eccentric — perspective, Heidegger developed his fundamental notion of "the danger that 'saves'" out of Hölderlin's slogan that the most extreme "danger" is always already "proximate" to "salvation." When Hölderlin wrote in his poem "Patmos" the lines "Nah ist und schwer zu fassen der Gott, wo aber Gefahr ist, wächst das Rettende auch [near is and hard to grasp the God, but where danger is, grows the salvific also]," he had in mind the botanical curiosity, or so he believed, that in the immediate vicinity of poisonous plants their antidotes grow. The neo-Heideggerian variant of Hölderlin's reassuring slogan for Schürmann and Vattimo — though their positions are incompatible in important respects — is that technological nihilism is both the modernist form of the concealment of the — supposedly — absolute uniqueness and incomparability of Being, and yet also one of Being's "existential" modes or moods of self-disclosure, and hence offers a possibility for some form of "salvation" — however weak — from technological totalitarianism. Schürmann's Heideggerianism seems comparatively technophobic; and even Vattimo's version — which sees some potential albeit unspecified "emancipatory implications" in mass technoculture because of the latter's decentralized nature — has residues of some remarkably old-fashioned "humanist" antipathies to technology. For his part, Schürmann promotes what he regards as a properly "an-archistic" conceptual and practical possibility of resisting, even breaking the stranglehold of what has become normative, mathematico-techno-Reason. By partial contrast, Vattimo accepts, as much as he can, multidimensional information technology — *la télématique* — as a given, indeed as a postmodern, technocultural confirmation of Heidegger's notion of the "enframing" power of technology, as Being's simultaneous self-concealment/disclosure. Vattimo promotes a "weak ontological" alternative to technocentrism, or what he has more recently and precisely called "an ontology of the weakening of Being." With this alternative is supposed to come an expansion of democratic, liberal — or is it libertarian? — values.[119] The problem, however, is that both Schürmann and Vattimo build up their theoretical models on the shaky, seepy, quicksand soil of Heidegger's exoteric thinking only — and therefore, by extension, of *Nietzsche's,* especially in the case of Vattimo, who has written extensively on Nietzsche — initially from an explicitly leftist point of view, before joining the "reflux" of the Italian Left to "weak thought."[120]

In this regard it must be reiterated that Heidegger seriously misrepresented his own long engagement with Nietzsche, including his particularly influential view that Nietzsche's doctrine of Will to Power "succumbed" to the constitutive techno-metaphysical and productivist bias of Occidental thought, whereas Hölderlin—uniquely—had not. When he published his two-volume book *Nietzsche* in 1961, Heidegger claimed that it was the literal transcript of lectures and seminars delivered during the Third Reich, and thus a more or less explicit and ultimately critical *pólemos* or "confrontation" (*Auseinandersetzung*) with Nazism. In fact, however, as the recent publication of the original lectures and seminars show—other essays on Nietzsche he wrote during this period may never see the light of day[121]—Heidegger made some subtle but crucial changes and omissions in 1961 as part of his elaborate attempt to postdate his commitment to Nazism and to backdate his critique—never radical rejection—of "The Movement" in terms of its complex, ambivalent relationship to technological modernity. Heidegger's supposed "turn" both against his earlier adherence to national socialism—his membership in the NSDAP began before he became rector of the University of Freiburg in 1933, and he never formally gave it up—and against Nietzsche's "metaphysical involutions" came only in the late 1930s, *after* national socialism itself had taken one too many self-destructive political, philosophical, and economic "turns." Ultimately, Heidegger's critique of national socialism had to do with its imagined failure to negotiate an appropriately "authentic" response to technological productivism, and not, say, with its direct responsibility for World War II and for its systematic incarceration and murder of Jews, Jehovah's Witnesses, Romany, trade-unionists, homosexuals, socialists, and communists.[122] But national socialism could not be Heidegger's *only* political commitment—not because of any "essence" on the part of national socialism, imagined or real, but *logically*. No *mere* political movement can "represent" the esoteric entirety of political ontology, *its* aspiration to map and be the geopolitical aesthetic of our time. *Nothing* empirical can ever actually re/present or embody Being *totally* or *permanently;* though Heidegger himself sometimes "forgets" this caveat as, also according to him, all mortals tend to do. It is in the same manner that the complexity of Nietzsche's powerful fascoid-liberal impulse is trivialized by such fake leftist bon mots as "Actor Hitler, Thinker Nietzsche." Too many would-be and post-Heideggerians are unaware of this problematic in their masters, or aware of it but for some reason ultimately indifferent to it, unable or unwilling to integrate it radically into their appropriations of Nietzsche's or Heidegger's thought. As if one can just pick and choose, scratch 'n' sniff. Vattimo and especially Schürmann are joined in this studied ignorance by Rorty, however substantial their other differences may be. And in this sense, at least, they are all Nietzschoid members of Nietzsche's corps/e.

Rorty's claim that the nasty passages in Nietzsche and Heidegger need not be taken *so* seriously cannot be easily supported by the *philological* record, though this claim, coupled with a general disinterest in philology, is *philosophically* productive for Rorty and other Nietzschoids, since it immediately relieves them of the task of reading Nietzsche very carefully while making use of him, safe in the a priori belief that *their* "recontextualization," at least, is inoculated from any possibly hallucinatory effects Nietzsche might have. Rorty is with regard to Nietzsche a "nonsmoker" — yet another liberal who doesn't inhale even passive smoke.

In his most sustained analysis of Nietzsche, in *Contingency, Irony, and Solidarity*, Rorty argues that "A culture in which Nietzschean metaphors were *literalized* would be one which took for granted that philosophical problems are as temporary as poetic problems, that there are no problems which bind the generations together into a single kind called 'humanity.' A sense of human history as the history of successive metaphors would let us see the poet, in the generic sense of the maker of new worlds, the shaper of new languages, as the vanguard of the species."[123] This is a *very* selective appropriation of Nietzsche's metaphors, suddenly passing by in uncanny silence what Rorty himself recognizes as moments in Nietzsche that are politically "at best vapid, at worst sadistic." Much like Adorno, Horkheimer, and Gadamer before him, Rorty has no theory or methodology to determine when to read Nietzsche literally, when not. If Rorty's suggestion now has any merit — namely, that there is at least one positive social sense in which we can take Nietzsche literally — one really ought to know what Nietzsche *himself* had in mind by his potentially species-determining vanguardism. Rorty's pragmatic "toolbox" recommendation to take Nietzsche literally sometimes, sometimes not, opens up a huge can of conceptual worms.

Tautological appeals at this point to "poetic license" or "irony" don't help in Nietzsche's case. Again like Adorno, Horkheimer, and Gadamer a half century earlier, *Contingency, Irony, and Solidarity* treats Nietzsche as an "ironist." For Rorty, *this* is what makes Nietzsche unlike all

"Nazi and Marxist enemies."[124] Whereas the latter—always?—take their beliefs too seriously and literally, Nietzsche—sometimes?—did not, and hence is endearing to Rorty, whose own views therefore should be taken less literally and seriously than they commonly are in the profession. But Nietzsche the "ironist" turns out to be just as slippery as the "literalist" to grab hold of, and certainly much more slippery than the workaday toolbox ought to be.

Nonetheless, not all objections to Rorty's Nietzsche are equally valid. There are two basic reasons why it is inconsequential to object to Rorty's appropriation of Nietzsche as "ironist" by quipping that "unlike Rorty, Nietzsche does not conceal his elitism, but admits that in making a choice in favour of an aristocratic polity he is condemning the vast majority to an impoverished life."[125] First, Nietzsche did conceal *the esoteric depth and extent* of his elitism; and, second, this objection does not account for how Nietzsche *implemented* elitism with illocutions that have succeeded in interpellating the very best liberal Nietzschoid ironists—led by Rorty.

But whatever one may think of liberalism politically, the *intentions* behind Rorty's variant are basically benevolent, whereas Nietzsche's were malevolent. It is even dangerous for liberal ironists ever to appeal to Nietzsche until they have grasped what *he* intended. And one of the things Nietzsche intended was to recruit good-natured people to support him against the interests of others—nonelitists, whom good-natured people might otherwise have helped better. The problem is also not that "Rorty's liberal ironism rests on a problematic separation of private self-creation and public justice,"[126] since this is a basic problematic of virtually *all* thinking and acting, but rather how a "Rorty" can become an unwitting tool, an ironic effect of Nietzsche, a Nietzschoid corps/e. As are facile objections *to* Rorty.

Part of Rorty's problem with Nietzsche arises because his overall view of irony is remarkably simplified and fails to make a fundamental distinction—drawn by Northrop Frye via Aristotle and especially by Kirk Rising Ireland—between the *alazon* and the *eiron*. Whereas "the alazon is a pretender to knowledge, a boaster and blusterer," the eiron "pretends to know less than he or she does, pretends not to know that he or she is being ironic even."[127] In Frye's *The Anatomy of Criticism* (1957), the eiron is "a predestined artist, just as the alazon is one of his predestined victims"; further, the eiron "makes himself invulnerable," employs "a pattern of words that turns away from direct statement or its own obvious meaning," "fables without moralizing," and so on.[128] "Nietzsche," Ireland notes, "has qualities of both the eiron and the alazon and even seems to adopt a role like that of an eiron who uses the *pretense* of being an alazon. He also carries attributes of the other comic opposition of buffoon and churl. It should be remembered, too, that in *Ecce Homo* he claims that he gets the sweetest grapes."[129] Ireland has also made the incisive suggestion that, in Nietzsche, the exoteric/esoteric problematic — as opposed to, say, a problematic of the visible/invisible or the conscious/unconscious — might be more fruitfully and rigorously expressed: exoteric/esoteric/exoteric. In other words, the exoteric/esoteric/exoteric, aside from being cumbersome, opens a dimension to "confidence." It allows for the covert to function as the overt in the way that an *eiron* might pretend to be an *alazon:* that is, it could at times be more covert to directly state a desire or fear or murderous impulse but state it in such a way that the listener — like Rorty — is left wondering whether or not to take it seriously. Thus, when *Nietzsche's Corps/e* refers to the exoteric/esoteric problematic it is a shorthand form of the exoteric/esoteric/exoteric in Ireland's sense. Neither is reducible to any "dialectical synthesis," including either the "visible and the invisible," as commonly understood, or, as in Rorty's case, "the serious and the ironic."[130] Ireland contributes especially to the understanding of Nietzsche the notion that it is "confidence," in the multiple meanings of the word, which is the authentically Nietzschean problematic, rather than comparatively epiphenomenal themes — such as, say, "the Dionysian" versus "the Apollinian" — which depend on unquestioned *prior* assumptions about when Nietzsche is telling the truth or lying, being serious or ironic, whenever he speaks about them. Rather it is the *instrumentalization* of confidence by confidence men in order to serve specific socially destructive ends that informs the quintessentially Nietzschean project — a concern often taken up, interestingly enough without Nietzsche's direct mediation, in recent mainstream theater and filmic productions.[131] With an eye on all Nietzsche/anism, it is good to recall Althusser's dictum that "neither amnesia, nor disgust, *nor irony* produce even the shadow of a critique."[132] If, as Žižek has argued, appealing to Laibach, we can no longer assume that "ironic distance is automatically a subversive attitude,"[133] then it would make perfect sense for Nietzsche to have made his own position on irony appear as "undecidable" as possible. Irony has its own history — under certain social conditions it is more effective than others. As Žižek notes, under conditions of neocapitalist postmodernity, "the dominant attitude of the contemporary 'post-ideological' universe is precisely a cynical distance towards public values," and "this distance, far from posing any threat to the system, designates the supreme form of conformism, since the normal functioning of the system requires cynical distance" (p. 72).

It is also instructive to view Nietzsche's corps/e along lines suggested in an argument not about irony but about vision advanced by the "postcontemporary" philosopher Podoroga.[134] In his essay "The Eunuch of the Soul," he develops certain theses about the relation of the visible to the invisible worked out, explicitly, in the philosophical system of Merleau-Ponty,[135] but especially, implicitly, in the later works of the great Soviet science fiction writer Andrei Platonov (1899–1951), author of *Chevengur* (1922–1928, first completely published in the USSR in 1988) and *The Foundation Pit* (1930).[136] From this philosophico-poetic point of departure, Podoroga develops — perhaps communist — possibilities of "seeing" that are opposed radically to all binary oppositions between "the inner" — whether "invisible," as in subjectivism and idealism, or "visible," as in objectivism and realism — and "the outer" — "the visible," from similar perspectives. Podoroga constructs what he variously terms "a gaze," "a special culture of the eye," "an objective nonrelative perception," "a disembodied eye," and, following Platonov, *evnukh dushi* (eunuch of the soul). This gaze typically sees but is not seen, continually mapping what Podoroga calls "a topological measurement of the external available to us — a more complex kind of measurement, whose analysis is not possible on the basis of the old inner/outer opposition."[137] Thus might we see Nietzsche without being seen by him, so to speak, and such a gaze is particularly advantageous to grasp Nietzsche/anism. Platonov's characters are exactly like Nietzsche's corpse in that both seek constantly "to enter into other bodies," are thus "prone to self-destructiveness" and desirous to be "external to themselves as they are." The specificially Nietzschoid corps/e can also be grasped, adapting Podoroga's terms, as "porous" and "covered by ruptures," since "what is inside is expelled onto the skin surface" (p. 362) — just as in Rorty's superficial view of Nietzschean irony. At the same time, however, Nietzsche also *appears* aloof from Nietzscheanism as the latter's *evnukh dushi* — always observing but itself never quite observed.

The Podoroga-Platonov depiction of *evnukh dushi* is remarkably isomorphic with the indescribable—"Sublime"—experience of clinical manic depression, in spite of the fact that Podoroga is refreshingly suspicious of the current hegemony of psychoanalysis on the intellectual marketplace. Nonetheless, as put by William Styron in *Darkness Visible* (1990): "A phenomenon that a number of people have noted while in deep depression is the sense of being accompanied by a second self—a wraithlike observer who, not sharing the dementia of his double, is able to watch with dispassionate curiosity as his companion struggles against the oncoming disaster [of suicide], or decides to embrace it."[138] Nietzsche—his megalomaniac Superman and his deconstructive *eiron/alazon* alike—is not really, appearances often to the contrary, the ego ideal or superego of post/modernity, but rather its wraithlike *evnukh dushi*. Nietzsche was "manic" not just in terms of personal psychopathology—many writers are manic who do not have his illocutionary talents—but because of his fascination with the perlocutionary capacity of writing to uplift and/or depress others, including to the point of suicide. This possibility he consciously built into his rhetoric of euthanasia, with the aim of weeding out certain people and social types from his ideal social formation—with their cooperation. More on this later. For the time being, it is enough to note that, within the structural causality that is Nietzsche's corps/e, the "invisible inside" exists as an effective "outside visibility" in a way that eludes virtually any inside/outside, visible/invisible, or serious/ironic "dialectical" grasp, but that nonetheless motors Nietzsche's corpse, corpus, and corps.

No less misleading—and potentially dangerous—than Rorty's "ironic" or "poetic" but also supposedly "pragmatic" view of Nietzsche is the popular neo-existentialist position, following Walter Kaufmann, that Nietzschean politics "must *first* be individual, and only then social."[139] For his part, Nietzsche had good reason to be royally disinterested in such crude and above all ineffectual binary oppositions or chronologies. To be precise, Rorty does sometimes complicate his view of the Nietzschean relationship between "metaphor," "poetry," and "politics." Nonetheless, his basically cheery view both of Nietzsche and of a culture in which some metaphors can be taken literally, some not, is politically and philosophically naïve; philologically, it is simply inaccurate. And so it is, to repeat Adorno, that "what everybody takes to be intelligible is what has become unintelligible." And if, as Kant argued, the basic criteria of the a priori are necessity and universality, and if Nietzsche is perceived as both necessary and universal as the post-Nietzschean replaces the postmodern, then Nietzscheanism would be virtually total "even" in Rorty's "democratic" and "pragmatic" world, and paranoia would be an objectively appropriate response. All Rorty's "recontextualizations" are of very little hlep, indeed counterproductive. More help in grasping Nietzsche's corps/e comes from the Right-Nietzscheans, specifically the great tradition of *Straussian* political philosophy.

Turning back to Rosen, it is unnecessary to accept his own solution to the paradox or contradiction informing so-called leftist response to Nietzsche. Like all those trained in Straussian exo/esotericism, Rosen offers no certainty in distinguishing when he is speaking openly, when in code; his argument may not be fully graspable in logical terms, to the extent that it is itself quasi-esoteric in design or implication. What is very important remains Rosen's formulation of the questions. Like Rorty, Rosen is not shy about linking Nietzsche to postmodern thought; unlike Rorty, this leads him directly to speak of Nietzschean politics. Rosen argues in *The Quarrel Between Philosophy and Poetry* (1988): "What is today called 'postmodernism' is a version of the teaching of Nietzsche." Part of what Rosen means by "postmodernism" and "Nietzsche" has to do with what he regards as the perennial "quarrel between philosophy and poetry," in which "Nietzsche" and "postmodernism" exemplify "a self-conscious recognition that poetry is triumphant over philosophy."[140] More specifically, for philosopher — or is it poet? — Rosen, "Nietzsche can and must say everything, precisely because where everything is talk — that is to say interpretation — everything is permitted. Philosophy, precisely by transforming itself into art, becomes nihilism."[141]

Quirks of periodization and labeling aside, the Straussian and post-Straussian tradition really objects to Nietzsche not on grounds that are either philosophical or poetic but rather *pragmatic*. It seems Nietzsche blew — or rather almost blew — the cover off the means of communicating the "Noble" doctrine: in other words, the subtlety with which "order of rank" must be transmitted to have maximum transformative and positive effect on the elite, while having maximum hegemonic and negative effect on the supporting, laboring "Base." Support for this hypothesis comes from the exposé of Leo Strauss and Straussians by a hostile reader, the political scientist Shadia B. Drury. She shows some of the extent to which Strauss/ianism is consciously but surreptitiously Nietzschean.[142] But also the philosopher Rémi Brague, who is sympathetic to Strauss as Drury is not, openly states that Strauss remained a Nietzschean, esoterically, even while criticizing him, exoterically, as the "last wave of modernity." According to Brague, Strauss thought that Nietzsche had left moderns with two choices: "either to refuse the possibility of the contemplative grasp of the eternal and to enslave thought to destiny, or to insist on the esoteric character of an analysis of life and thus to return to the Platonic cave of the noble lie. If the first solution was, at least in Strauss's eyes, that of Heidegger, one might ask whether the second was not his own."[143] Hence, perhaps, the certain reluctance of Straussians and post-Straussians — inconsistent in light of their own stated principles of reading, and explicit denials very much to the contrary[144] — to undertake *radically* deep *rhetorical* and especially *illocutionary-perlocutionary* analyses during their otherwise excruciatingly meticulous close readings of many Great Books, but especially Nietzsche's. Strauss himself published only one text explicitly on Nietzsche, and it is not an analysis of the How of Nietzsche, only the What.[145] Yet this goes directly against Strauss's great maxim, formulated for reading Plato: "One cannot separate the understanding of Plato's teaching from the form in which it is presented. One must pay as much attention to the How as to the What."[146] Do not be misled by "metaphysics": In the matters of *philosophical incorporation,* of *logographic necessity,* and of *social elitism,* Nietzsche was *nothing* if not *Platonic.*

Now, it is one thing to admit — as Rosen to his credit has done — that, for Strauss himself, philosophy has esoterically little to do with, say, *ontological* or *epistemological* "truth" but rather is explicitly "*Nietzschean.*"[147] In his context, this argument means that all philosophy is a quintessentially political and, so it is hoped, ultimately effective form of exoteric sociohegemonic constraint: namely, "a passion or desire, i.e., an eros, but hence, too, an act of the will by which we presuppose what we need in order to gratify that eros" (p. 161). Philosophy thus defined has the conscious aim to convince us unwashed masses that we have a voice in determining power — which we *do* have but only in appearance, *exoterically* — when in — *esoteric* — fact we do *not* have real power and never will, if Straussian Right-Nietzscheans can help it. Another thing entirely, however, is a problem not meticulously addressed — conceivably for self-serving reasons — by Rosen or by any other Straussian or post-Straussian, which is that not merely *thematic* and *locutionary* but also *illocutionary* and *perlocutionary* aims must always already be in mind and operation whenever philosopher kings legitimate their vested interests in opposition to the rest of "us citizens."

In Spinozist terms, Nobility (*generositas*) is "a form of disinterestedness, not unlike Aristotle's supreme virtue of magnificence (*megaloprépeia*), and is a rational disdain of particular interests and of small worldly calculations."[148] To grasp Nietzsche's corps/e it must be understood that Nietzsche betrayed the disinterested aspect of Nobility by selling out, in calculated fashion, to elitist political interests, but that he did so esoterically — slightly beneath the cover of the exoteric lip service he often did pay to the "amoral" or "aesthetic" task "beyond good and evil" of smashing or deconstructing all "idols." In Spinoza's true ethical system, by contrast, "The free man never acts fraudulently, but always in good faith."[149] To the extent, and only to the extent, that Nietzsche's own profound betrayal of Nobility (in the Spinozist sense of *generositas*) was not actually effective, even counterproductive, in promoting the worldly interests of elites — which for Nietzsche and proper Nietzscheans are the only human interests that really matter — Right-Nietzsche/ans must go beyond Nietzsche's illocutionary letter while still remaining resolute in his political-philosophical and social spirit. In an analogous way, Heideggerian political ontology can reject Nietzsche's ontology while remaining loyal to his politics.

Rosen sometimes distinguishes Nietzsche from postmodernism, since the latter has some claims to be democratizing and anti-elitist. According to Rosen, Nietzsche's " 'positive' or 'esoteric' teaching — unlike that of his twentieth-century disciples — stands or falls upon the possibility of distinguishing the high from the low, the noble from the base, the deep from the superficial — and not merely the healthy from the sick or the strong from the weak."[150] Because Rosen himself is in basic *favor* of distinction in this multiple sense, he is in his own terms a Platonist *and* a Nietzschean. Rosen is certainly *not* a "Platonist" in scare quotes as *he* uses them; and perhaps he is too aware of Nietzsche's depths ever to be Nietzschoid *fully* — unlike Rorty on their surface.

With regard to all combative discourses on behalf of "Nobility," we are justly reminded by Bataille that the "warrior's nobility is like a prostitute's smile [though hardly only a 'prostitute's']." This is because "War is not limited to forms of uncalculated havoc. Although he remains dimly aware of a calling that rules out the self-seeking behavior of work, the warrior reduces his fellow men to servitude."[151] Nobility, in the tradition to which all Nietzsche/anism allies itself—wittingly on the Right, unwittingly on the Left—requires both nearly *absolute* leisure time for oneself and *always* the surplus labor of others. This political economy is to be sharply contrasted once again with one of Spinoza's key ethico-political theses, though not yet an economic principle: "The free man, who lives among the ignorant, strives, as far as he can, to avoid receiving favours from them."[152] While Nietzsche may seem to affirm this thesis in proto-existentialist terms, he actually does so only exoterically. And, at the same time, his political philosophy is proto-Straussian in its open affirmation of the necessity of the favors provided "free spirits" by slaves and their more modern sisters and brothers. The *only* thing Nietzsche and Right-Straussians always conceal are the precise illocutionary techniques to be used that are most effective in turning potential communists into Left-Nietzschoids.

Rosen has provided his own characteristically intricate remarks on the Straussian problematic in his *Hermeneutics as Politics* (1987). Trained as a Straussian, Rosen says he is no longer one in principle. Unlike many Straussians, Rosen claims interest only in affairs of philosophy, disinterest in affairs of the state. Yet Rosen thus differs with Strauss mainly on pragmatic, strategic, and tactical grounds. He writes elsewhere: "Unfortunately, Strauss's own conception of philosophy was incapable of defending itself against the poetry of Nietzsche and Heidegger."[153] It seems clear from Rosen's take on the history of philosophy as *pólemos*—as a perennial quarrel between philosophy and poetry—that *he* cannot claim to have "defended" himself *philosophically* and *poetically* against Heidegger and Nietzsche, either. But he *could* rightly claim to have shored up that fundamental aspect of their thinking that is *politically* elitist and that "even" (read: *especially*) Strauss may have gone too far in endangering.

On the last page of *Hermeneutics as Politics,* Rosen refers in a related matter to "we Maoists." Rosen writes:

we Maoists understand a deeper theory, one that springs from the identity of theory and practice in the will to power. At this deep level, ten thousand feet *below* good and evil, a level by its nature esoteric, we understand that edifying hermeneutics is the fifth column of the army of future Enlightenment. Edifying hermeneutics is the exoteric doctrine of the will to power, an instrument of the cunning of reason, a stage in the dialectical self-destruction of bourgeois civilization. In political terms, edifying hermeneutics (and perhaps even unedifying hermeneutics) is an expression of middle-class fear of the violent and repressive nature of truth. We close with the prophetic words of a French Maoist of a bygone generation, Georges Sorel: "A social policy on middle-class cowardice, which consists in always surrendering before the threat of violence, cannot fail to engender the idea that the middle-class is condemned to death, and that its disappearance is only a matter of time."[154]

Now, as a former member of a Maoist political party in the mid 1960s, the author of *Nietzsche's Corps/e* is unaware that Sorel, long beloved by both the fascist Right as well as the fake "Left," was in any meaningful sense "Maoist." Sooner was Sorel an open vessel for virtually any ideological fluid that flowed his way: revolutionary syndicalist; proponent of the "myth of the general strike"; sympathizer with the Bolshevik Revolution; but also an anti-Jacobin moralist, near-monarchist, far-right preacher of antibourgeois and authoritarian "rejuvenation," and so on. But not a Maoist. The author also cannot recognize genuine Maoist principles in Rosen's own argument.[155] On the other hand, this same author was not fully aware at the time that the party to which he belonged was "Maoist"; so he may be the worst possible judge of Rosen's exoteric Maoism, let alone its esoteric forms. As a communist still today, he is never quite sure what Nietzsche was about, either, but must try to find out, if "Nietzsche's position is the only one outside of communism." And clearly we all have different "pictures" of Mao, acknowledging from different perspectives that he himself used many proleptic means "to announce his return and demonstrate his vitality, to reinspire the revolution."[156]

Nonetheless, Maoism now aside, it remains vital to appreciate the way Rosen formulates the question of *Nietzsche's* revolution, and to affirm with him that Nietzsche was indeed in no meaningful sense "a political conservative" but a "revolutionary." Nietzsche was also not merely — as he is commonly presented by even the supposedly more critical branch of the current Nietzsche Industry — a "neo-aristocratic conservative": that is, "a conservative looking back to the social orders that developed in Europe between the Renaissance and the emergence of bourgeois political orders, and forward to a time when similar cultural aristocracies might be established."[157] This knee-jerk position, too, is hardly new, formerly shared as it was by thinkers as diverse as Georg Lukács and Sigmund Freud. Lukács pointed out in 1934–1935 that Nietzsche's political thinking was part of a more general ideological matrix that was temporally Janus-faced: on one side nostalgia for precapitalist culture and society, on the other the attempt to construct a future wherein the contradictions of present-day capital were "resolved" — but only for a cultural elite while society as a whole remained exploitative.[158] But Lukács knew neither *how* Nietzsche set out to create such a future with illocutionary strategies and tactics nor *why* he was so successful. And then there is Freud's even earlier — *also* never pursued — suggestion in 1921 that "the father of the primal horde . . . at the *very beginning* of the history of mankind, was the 'superman' whom Nietzsche only expected from the *future*."[159] Part of Freud wanted to be among these Nietzschean supermen, no less than did Lukács.

For his part, Nietzsche could easily prefer, sometimes, a historical scenario according to which he could be, or appear to be, a "neo-aristocratic conservative." But he was neither so naïve nor stupid as to think that the relentless drive of modernity and modernism would tolerate atavistic ideologies for long. Nor would he remain so influential today, were this the exclusive avenue, back alley, or "royal way" open to his political thought. Such interpretations are almost inevitably grounded on at least two bogus assumptions about Nietzsche. First, there is the false — at least debatable — *philosophico-political* premise that "the innovative aspects of his philosophy find little expression in his overt politics [and that] what he does, unsuccessfully, is combine a postmodern philosophy with a premodern politics," which are imaged to be at odds with one another.[160] Second, there is the old and equally false *philological* premise — indeed, combined with the first premise, the self-fulfilling prophecy — that, when reading Nietzsche, "Where there are conflicts between the *Nachlaß* [notebooks never intended for publication by Nietzsche] and published texts," one must "opt" for the latter.[161] Such unexplained leaps of methodological faith are based on the a priori supposition, rarely made explicit or problematized, that Nietzsche always meant what he said when he said it *in print* more than in letters or in notebooks, *and* that what he said in print was sometimes meant literally, sometimes not. Depending on our whim we can take him or leave him.[162]

Sooner than being *any* sort of "conservative" was Nietzsche a *revolutionary* — thus far Rosen is incontrovertibly *right*. At least *Nietzsche* thought of himself this way, not *just* as any varicose "aristocratic radical."[163] Certainly this "untimely skirmisher" *despised* any merely "timely" conservative in his era — *anybody* in *any* era — who had lost the nerve, will, and ability to *rule*.[164] More strongly put in private: "The *decadence of rulers and of the ruling castes* [Die *Entartung der Herrscher und der herrschenden Stände*] has created the greatest harm in history!"[165]

The most "orthodox" of communists are not necessarily wrong about Nietzsche. Georgi Plekhanov knew in 1912 — at a time when "There is not, I think, a single country in the modern civilized world where the bourgeois youth is not sympathetic to the ideas of Friedrich Nietzsche" — that what Nietzsche *really* thought was wrong with virtually all his contemporaries was "that they could not think, feel and — chiefly — act as befits people who hold the predominant position in society."[166] Among the questions never really asked Nietzsche — the "proleptic revolutionary," the *fascoid-liberal* revolutionary — are the following: Revolution of what kind precisely? by what means? on whose behalf, short term and long? and, finally, with what postcontemporary success?

It is in *this* context that it is especially exigent to take to heart Rosen's apparent suggestion — for he waffles — that we must engage such philosophical and political questions with attention to Nietzsche's *rhetorical* strategies and tactics, including the possibility that he was an *esoteric* writer. As a Platonist and Straussian — if not also Maoist — of sorts, Rosen himself is ultimately hostile to rhetoric, finding as he does his own practical benefit — in opposition to the alleged hegemony of mathematical logic and technology — in Plato's salutary way of blurring the distinction between constructive, technological thinking and the contemplative life.

There is *never* any easy answer to the question of esotericism, if only because *totally* esoteric writers would leave *no* trace of this intent, and Nietzsche *did* leave some trace. Nor, as obviously, should one ever assume that what Nietzsche intended to communicate covertly was always expressed with equal finesse or effectiveness. But Rosen in "Nietzsche's Revolution" *points* to what he calls Nietzsche's "double rhetoric," corresponding to "two stages" of Nietzsche's "overall revolutionary strategy." The resulting hypothesis constitutes arguably *the* most significant moment in all Nietzsche criticism.

Rosen writes: "An appeal to the highest, most gifted human individuals to create a radically new society of artist-warriors was expressed with rhetorical power and a unique mixture of *frankness and ambiguity* in such a way as to allow the mediocre, the foolish, and the mad to regard themselves as the divine prototypes of the highest men of the future." And, as Rosen concludes this part of his argument, "Nietzsche intends to accelerate the process of self-destruction intrinsic to modern 'progress,' not to encourage a return to some idyllic past. The more persons who can be convinced that they are modern progressives (or postmoderns), the quicker the explosion." In short, "Nietzsche is a revolutionary of the right in his radical aristocratism and antiegalitarianism," *but* he needs the willing cooperation of a workforce in this bizarre, even murderous and suicidal project. Furthermore, Nietzsche seems to have *succeeded,* for Rosen, at least in part and negatively: namely, "in enlisting countless thousands in the ironical task of self-destruction."[167]

Now, these are *incredible, un/canny, and above all deadly serious* charges. They implicate not only Nietzschoids — such as "Rorty" — and Nietzscheans — such as "Rosen" — but virtually *all of us* — if for no other reason than they are likely impossible to prove or disprove apodeictically, once and for all. There is no choice but to continue trying. But — if not to "Rorty" and the "Left" or to "Rosen" and the "Right" — then where else to turn? Standing on the shoulders of Nietzsche ought to launch a chill up your spine.

From Bataille (Channel 3) to Nietzsche (Channel 4)

. . . But while I possess history,
it possesses me. I'm illuminated by it;

but what's the use of such light?

I'm not speaking of the individual. . . . [168]

As for Bataille, beyond what he says and sometimes apart from what he says, he communicates community itself.[169]

Nietzsche is beyond interpretation. To the extent that "interpretation" is linked to history, to one's own historical and personal pressures, Nietzsche/anism eludes "interpretation" because he designed his corps/e as a transhistorical phenomenon, to remain relatively stable across time, nomadically — no matter how class and other relations and struggles might be organized. Bound to history or not, "interpretation" as it is commonly understood and practiced, and as was grounded for the "interpretive community" of postmodern thought around "Nietzsche" by Georges Bataille, is inadequate to grasp Nietzsche's esoteric semiotic. Nietzsche was the creator-producer, arguably the greatest in history, of a fourth, quasi-prophetic "option" beyond three common modes of "interpretation" that exist either singly or in a consciously accessible "dialectic" between (1) more or less faithful adherence to what an author or text "really means"; (2) more or less willful appropriation of a text on behalf of "current relevance"; and (3) an agnostic position that combines elements of both, mediating them. Grasping Nietzsche's own notion of "community" depends on accessing his way of going beyond interpretation.

What is at stake in reading Nietzsche is never "semantic," "thematic," or "dialogic." All hermeneutic or historicist questions are irrelevant and distracting until one can grasp how Nietzschean illocutions were designed to *work*. At the end of the day Nietzsche's intended meaning returns to have its effect precisely when there is ignorance or lack of clarity about its precise mechanism. The priority of work in this sense is insisted upon not only by Marx but Freud, noting — in the year of Nietzsche's death — that what is "essential" in dreams is less any latent meaning than the "dream-*work*" itself.[170] Illocutions do not necessarily work consciously; they may be most effective when subconscious, unconscious. Nietzsche's way of working, of producing not merely the thoughts but the dreams of his corps, is particularly un/canny. For what appears to individual members of the corps as private dreams is a collective dream manipulated by the corpus of his writing. The problem, then, in Pasolini's terms, is not only to *illuminate* what Nietzsche "really meant" and to demand to know its current *use,* but also to grasp how Nietzsche attempted with such remarkable success to *prevent* his *modus operandi* from ever seeing the light of day, as it surreptitiously interpellates individuals into the *collective* body that is his historical corps/e. *How* it works is by definition beyond interpretation; the fact *that* it does must be prized open to question. In the abstract, "collectivity" is of no interest; interest lies rather in which collective any individual wittingly or unwittingly exists, in which media s/he appears. And this goes a fortiori for what Bataille and Nietzsche each meant by "community."

Traditionally and commonly, there are only the three major "possibilities," "decisions," or "choices" open to the "interpreter." The first two are neatly summarized by Virilio's question: "Do we represent the construction, or construct the representation?"[171] The third option, of course, is that we do both, with several ways of proceeding. But does one really have to be locked into this relentlessly triadic or "dialectical" scheme? *Nietzsche* did not think so, producing according to his principles another medium, less susceptible to illumination, more conducive to individual and collective incorporation.

Call the three main options Channels 1, 2, and 3. This appellation is related to but different from Barthes's theory of "the third" or "obtuse meaning" and Althusser's three major epistemological schemata or Generalities. It is also related to the theory of the "semantic rectangle" elaborated by Greimas and Jameson beginning in the late 1960s and early 1970s.[172] In 1970 Barthes posited a "third meaning" beyond (1) "an informational level" of "communication," which he says is "of no further concern," and which corresponds roughly to Channel 1; and (2) "the symbolic level"—whether the symbolism is referential, diegetic, personal, or historical—or "level of signification."[173] "The symbolic level" combines elements of Channels 1, 2, and 3. Barthes's "third meaning" is "the level of significance." "Evident, erratic, obstinate," it is virtually beyond definition—"it is not in the language system"—and, as emotive supplement and excess, that which it "disturbs, sterilizes, is metalanguage (criticism)" (pp. 318–322). It also "exceeds psychology, anecdote, function, exceeds meaning without, however, coming down to the obstinacy in presence shown by any human body" (p. 319). But this last phrase begins to indicate why "the third meaning" is not quite Channel 4: that is, the way Nietzsche's corpse and corpus is *incorporated* and *embodied* precisely as corps. Note that classical—that is, Freudian—psychoanalysis is simply irrelevant on this terrain, insofar as it maintains a binary distinction between two basic forms of identification. In this case, either the subject is required to identify with Nietzsche as other (heteropathology) or, alternatively, Nietzsche identifies with the same subject as other by being ingested (idiopathology). In and as corps/e, such distinctions are always already moot. Be this as it may, elements of Barthes's "third meaning" could point to Channel 4, if his theory and methodology were not so idealistic and impressionistic, so reluctant to enter into the possibility of an exo/esoteric mode of *manipulation by design*. There is also paradox in Barthes's suggestion that "the third meaning" is beyond language, since his own essay, indeed all his rich critical writings, can be read as its rendering into language and since he persists in retaining the semantic and therefore linguistic category "meaning," "obtuse" though it may be. Barthes remarks of "obtuse meaning" *en passant* that it "has something to do with disguise," but he cannot mean tactically or strategically programmed disguise, since he has already thrown *intention* out the window with levels 1 and 2, and it has no place in level 3 either. *Like* Channel 4, however, "obtuse meaning" eludes conscious detection as "the one 'too many,' the supplement that my intellection cannot succeed in absorbing, at once persistent and fleeting, smooth and elusive" (p. 320). But what is at stake in Channel 4 is not only "my intellection" in Barthes's resolutely subjectivistic and narcissistic sense (Channel 1). The properly Nietzschean Channel 4 is also a problematic that is not only *embodied* but *collective*. This is radically *unlike* Barthean "third meaning" in that the latter does not "extend outside culture, knowledge, information." Rather, "meaning" in Channel 4 strives to *become* all this. Nor does "meaning" in Channel 4 belong so exclusively "to the family of pun, buffoonery, useless expenditure" (p. 320). Channel 4 certainly can take the form of "carnivalesque excess" but in ways that are ultimately deadly serious. In short, Barthes's final allusion to Bataillean "expenditure" needs to be rendered considerably more precise if it is to apply to Nietzsche's corps/e.

Althusser offers nothing if not precision. According to his theory of knowledge production, developed in the early 1960s, in terms of Generalities, Generality I has to do with "concrete" facts. Like Channel 1, it "constitutes the raw material that the science's theoretical practice will transform into specified 'concepts,' that is, into that other 'concrete' generality (which I shall call *Generality III*) which is a knowledge."[174] In the resulting system of "theoretical practice" (from which Althusser later came to take critical distance), Generality II is the *problematique* which is "constituted by the corpus of concepts whose more or less contradictory unity constitutes the 'theory' of the science at the (historical) moment under consideration, the 'theory' that defines the field in which all the problems of the science must necessarily be posed."[175] Generalities II and III thus combine elements of Channels 2 and 3. But — unlike Channel 2 — Generality II is not a tool just lying around for the use of an autonomous subject — though this is often precisely how ideology makes it appear in the production of Generality III — but rather a historically conditioned and conditioning structure functioning within and through the consciousness of more or less porous social subjects. Analogously, Channel 2 — and the most powerful drift of Barthes's "third meaning" — typically *poses* as "subjective" or "individual" in ways that are in fact ideologically and economically determinate "in the last instance." Yet Althusser — like too many other historical materialists, let alone materialist narcissists like Barthes — tends to denigrate the kind of *intentional* and *surreptitious* influence that *Nietzsche's Corps/e* calls Channel 4 to ideological levels that are — in principle, if not always in fact — discernible and disclosable to rational view. Once again, the phenomenon of Nietzsche's corps/e requires grasping post-Enlightenment mechanisms and illocutionary practices of domination that are not reducible to rational illumination. In *this* matter, Althusser effectively critiques elements of Barthes but not of Bataille, who will take us closer to Nietzsche but not all the way.

Whatever name one gives them, three perennial "options" are encountered in dealing with any period of history, event, idea, author, text, or artifactual remain. First, we jack *ourselves* into the *object* of study — go to it, into it, merge with it, and perhaps — more or less coincidentally — are changed by it. Channel 1 is that of the historian, the historicist, the empiricist, the positivist, the enthusiast, the fan, the bureaucrat, the hagiographer. Or, second, we jack the *object* into *us* — letting the current of influence flow in the opposite direction. Now we bring the object to us, milking it, forcing or coaxing it to become one with us more or less quickly, on what we imagine to be "our own terms." Channel 2 is reached through several different circuits (as is Channel 1), and it doesn't really matter with what result: whether to the point of willful, more or less aggressive "misrecognition" or "misprision," where, for example, Nietzsche's name may remain, but transformed beyond "normal" recognition; or, alternatively, to the point of total absorption and "active forgetting," when Nietzsche's name becomes at most a "name-effect."[176] In either case, however, Channel 2 is that of the "appropriation artist," the Bloomian "epigone,"[177] the "original" philosopher, the situationist or populist perhaps, and many modes of more or less political *Umfunktionierung* or *détournement*. It is also the moment when even the historicist scholar is pressed to be "relevant," has to justify his or her interest in the historical past. For, while all Channels may appear to be distinct analytically, empirically they often coexist.

There's always some degree of static, of noise. The first two major Channels — 1 and 2 — tend to drift into, overlap, or override one another, sometimes in confused or confusing ways. Feeble is any semiotic theory, including Umberto Eco's in one of his moods, that sets out to distinguish apodeictically between textual "interpretation" — as an ideal reading situation posited as the proper relation between "model author" and "model reader" or "textual strategy" — from more or less inappropriate textual "use."[178] Not only do historicists smuggle their own ideological presuppositions and prejudices into their comparatively "objective" scholarship; but so also the more "subjectivist" approach commonly depends, in unacknowledged ways, on tacit, a priori historicist or positivist assumptions about what an author "really meant" or what a historical period "really was" or "is."

So it is, then, that one seems logically to require a third, agnostic, mediatory space — a Channel 3 somewhere in the no-man's-land between, above, or outside the other two. This is the Channel of interpretation proper: that is, of hermeneutics ("the fusion of horizons"); of psychoanalytical transference ("working through" versus "acting out" — as if these terms were not mutually imbricated); of phenomenological or structuralist "reduction" (putting into brackets the question of the existence of the object of study); of liberal pluralism and of all bad Hegelian "mediation" or "dialectics" that seeks synthesis where there is or ought to be none. To offer a summation in good Hegelese, as glossed by Hyppolite: Channel 1 corresponds to "*material thought* buried in content, actually egocentric, but unaware of its own involvement in the affair"; Channel 2 is "*formal thought* which builds up frameworks of relationship, for which the object reference becomes an unknowable nucleus and which must always seek its content outside"; and, finally, located in the Hegelian matrix between or beyond formal thought — rationalism — and material thought — empiricism — there is properly "*dialectical* thought" or Channel 3: "the possibility of a style of narrative in which the one who knows is himself involved in the thing that is known" and vice versa.[179] Note, however, that in the Hegelian system self/consciousness and exotericism are *always* privileged over and above the possibility of subliminal influence and esotericism. Including over what Hegel himself called "incorporation." And precisely *this* possibility — or *actual-virtuality* — informs yet *another* channel beyond interpretation. This is Channel 4.

Today the maximally clear technical resolution — the highest pixel-plane — attainable in Channel 3 may seem to be not in philosophy, literature, or literary theory but rather in terms, conceptually if not yet actually, of cyberspace and virtual reality (VR). And hence the transition to some unknown *other* Channel seems unnecessary. This appearance is deceptive in three ways: philosophy, literature, and literary theory have always been powerful "technologies"; the hype about VR is overdetermined by exactly the same ideological hopes and fears that have accompanied the less technologically spectacular media; and in general one ought to be suspicious when one is told that a technology is definitive. Nonetheless, VR technologies are what teach many people today an old truth that must be continually forgotten and then remembered: namely, that "what we have made, makes us."[180] Which is also today "the postmodernist paradox": that is, *"the perceiver literally becomes the perceived"* and vice versa. Takayuki Tatsumi gives the following example regarding the relation between the cyberpunk novels of William Gibson and Japan. "Gibson's Chiba City may have sprung from his misperception of Japan, but it was this misperception that encouraged Japanese readers to correctly perceive the nature of postmodernist Japan. In short, the moment we perceive cyberpunk stories which misperceive Japan, we are already perceived correctly by cyberpunk."[181] "Nietzsche" can be substituted for "Gibson" in Tatsumi's argument — and likely for "Tatsumi" himself — and "Nietzscheanism" for "Japan." And Nietzsche was well familiar with an earlier form of this argument, developed by Schopenhauer, to the effect that when we transcend the strictures of the principle of sufficient reason (i.e., for everything there is, there is a reason or ground why it is) "we no longer consider the where, the when, the why, and the whither of things, but simply and solely the *what*. . . . [I]t is as though the object alone existed without anyone to perceive it, and thus we are no longer able to separate the perceiver from the perceived."[182] To be sure, the allegedly postmodern paradox collides with the objection that all the various mechanisms of knowledge do not *actually* transform "the real object" but rather what Althusser calls "its perception into concepts and then into a thought-concrete."[183] Even in the post-Freudian system of Lacan, who influenced Althusser in this regard, the "Real" retains a certain excessive surplus status, however tenuous, just beyond the clutches of either the "Symbolic" or the "Imaginary." Even cyberspace and VR depend on remarkably traditional materials that must be mined or manufactured (metal, plastic); even cybernauts are anchored in PR — not just the hype of "public relations" but "Primary Reality." The crucial point, however, is that in VR and its equivalents the appearance of interaction with the Real is often precisely that — appearance only. Thus, Channel 4 is (like) virtual reality up to a point. It, too, is a zone interactive with but slightly beyond either *unmediated* reality (viewed in Channel 1), *symbolized* reality (Channel 2), or their *interface* (Channel 3). Yet, if it is beyond interpretation, Channel 4 still remains part of Reality, one of its modes.

In this way, Nietzsche's corps/e under postmodern conditions is a dominant form of "non/consensual hallucination" informing Channel 4, indeed in important respects *is* Channel 4. The paradox that to *perceive* Neitzsche's corpse and corpus is to unwittingly *become* Nietzsche's corps/e is a possibility worth taking literally. The "opposed" Channels 1 and 2 logically imply the existence of one another, and both are the prerequisite for Channel 3 as their imagined "synthesis." In turn, these three channels logically imply *another* channel beyond them — or rather, in Spinozist terms, *one* Channel of which all others are its attributes. Channel 4 stakes out certain claims to be this "Substance, God, or Nature." At its highest level of abstraction, Channel 4 is only the *hypothesis* that a Channel exists beyond 1, 2, and 3 — since these *seem* to cover all possible types of the production and consumption of information, communication, and meaning. Interpretation is like the Hegelian system itself in that it dynamically enfolds even the most radical objections to itself into itself. By definition, Channel 4 cannot be *fully* defined in advance, since it involves levels of transmission beneath the threshold of consciousness, and hence beyond empirical — though not necessarily logical or hypothetical — "falsification" or "verification."

In the premodern high-philosophical terms of Spinoza, as well as

David Cronenberg's postmodern, junk-cultural ones, the human body is modified or transformed by the very act of *imaging* an external body. Spinoza argued in *The Ethics* that "The images of things are modifications of the human body."[184] The idea of this modification — a crucial illustration of structural causality — involves the nature of one's own body as well as that of the external body. "If . . . the nature of the external body be similar to the nature of our body, then the idea we form of the external body will involve a modification of our own body similar to the modification of the external body" (p. 148). This series of reflections led Spinoza to his theory of *compassion* with others, indeed with the *multitude* (*multitudo*). This move was a terrible anathema to Nietzsche. But in Spinozism the imaged and the imaging, natured nature (*natura naturata*) and naturing nature (*natura naturans*), become alternating descriptions of the same process. And this hypothesis provides something like the *formal* "logic" or "ethic" of Nietzschean Channel 4, even as Nietzsche's *ideology* is pitted against Spinoza's to the death.

There exists only the constitutive process, for Spinoza, and no third, neutral, stable, "hermeneutic," or "dialectical" site on which to stand and cast light on it, nor any presumption to see or produce a politically neutral dialectical synthesis. As put long after Spinoza by the idealist philosopher Fichte, though with different ideological valence, absolute self-consciousness is "a power into which an eye is implanted." The Nietzschean "I/eye" is thus always already "in-oculated" in larger conceptual and social matrixes.[185] Fichte's insight is also available in one of the most popular forms of mass culture — detective fiction's "private eye." In its most self-reflexive moments, as in the work of Paul Auster, the postmodern detective/narrator notes that the term "private eye" has three simultaneous meanings: "the letter 'i,' standing for 'investigator'"; "'I' in the upper case, the tiny life-bud in the body of the breathing self"; and "the physical eye of the writer, the eye of the man who looks out from himself into the world and demands that the world reveal itself to him."[186] And of course this same "eye/i/I" — Fichte's as well as Auster's — is also "private" in the *economic* sense. Not only is it part of the matrix of private *property,* but it is such without ever adequately *seeing* this fact. One of the most succinct definitions of "spectacle," that of Guy Debord, is "*capital* accumulated until it becomes *image.*"[187] Precisely *this* insight is seldom available in *any* Channel, and

174

never for long. But the point for now is that, in terms of grasping how Nietzsche/anism works, premodern Spinozism and postmodern cyberpunk suggest that a *perennial* possibility of "channeling" exists, one relatively independent theoretically from empirical and historical contingencies yet informing them. And this Channel is beyond interpretation.

So it is that a hypothetical — if not also actual — synapse is made available to *Nietzsche/an esotericism*. It is *here* that the decisive switch begins — almost imperceptibly — from Channel 3 to 4. But it is impossible to lock into it easily, and considerable patience is required to combat the corps/e's hegemony over its use.

All Channels have been available throughout recorded history, including the comparatively brief history of Nietzsche/anism. Nietzsche is no exception to the general rule of thumb that thinkers — not complex thinkers only but any sort — can be and are received and appropriated differently — at different social, political, and historical conjunctures — by people who may agree or disagree about everything else. In the deceptively simple words of Spinoza, "Different people may be differently affected by the same object, and the same people may be differently affected at different times by the same object."[188] And so it has always been with Nietzsche's corps/e: for every Nazi swine who embraced Nietzsche there was one who spurned him; for every "Walter Kaufmann" there is one "Jacques Derrida"; for every "Martin Heidegger" there is one "you" or "I." And so The Beat Goes On, Same As It Ever Was. More interesting, however, is what occurs when reception in the three dominant Channels begins to oscillate *within* a single interpreter or text. It is the very uncontrollability of this oscillation that indicates the existence of, and the necessity to grasp, Channel 4. And so we come to arguably the most insightful reader of Nietzsche's relation to aesthetics and politics: Georges Bataille.

Bataille's explicit and implicit impact on French thinking about Nietzsche is perhaps most faithfully represented by Pierre Klossowski, and perhaps most betrayed by the equally brilliant, more influential work of Derrida, even at moments when the latter takes his most explicitly hostile stance against Nietzschean "politics." But, as members of Nietzsche's corps/e themselves, they get no further beyond interpretation in the matter of Nietzsche than did Bataille himself. Bataille's intense response to Nietzsche and Nietzscheanism came very close to locking in on Nietzschean Channel 4. It is the fact that Bataille did not—that he remained within the Channel of interpretation—that results in the perception that "Nietzsche's position is the only one outside of communism."

Heidegger in private conversation seems to have been of the opinion that Bataille—whose work Heidegger did not know particularly well, and who was ambivalent about Heidegger[189]—was one of the few contemporary writers in France, indeed Europe, to be taken with utmost seriousness. Heidegger, whom one might think would still be required for getting after Nietzsche's corps/e, given his complex and influential interpretation of Nietzsche, always turns out to be part of the problem, not the solution, since Heidegger so carefully concealed his own esoteric motivations from view, his own vested interests in Channel 4. In his seminal essay on the "economies" of Bataille and Hegel, Derrida noted that "if more than anyone else, more than *to* anyone else, to the point of identification, Bataille thought himself close to Nietzsche, then this was not, in this case, motivated by simplification."[190] Yet Bataille's way of "identifying" is more complex than Channel 2. With regard to Nietzsche, Bataille owns Channel 3. And, as the Black Panthers used to say, "Either you *own* the motherfucker, or you *work* for it," though they never said that's *all* you work for. As can happen with all Nietzsche/ans, Bataille may have worked for what he owned without being fully aware of the fact.

Bataille (1887–1962) began imbibing Nietzsche in earnest by the early 1920s. He claimed in 1951—as he had implied in texts extending back into the later 1930s—that "no one can read Nietzsche authentically without 'being' Nietzsche."[191] This gesture was crucial for Bataille's lifelong critique of what he called "sovereignty," his attempt to explore all the parameters and mechanisms of power in general, Nietzschean power in specific. With this patented gesture of infiltration, incorporation, and identification, Bataille simultaneously adapted Channels 1 and 2. This is to say that Bataille assumed the objectivist position that an authentic reading of Nietzsche does exist (Channel 1), hence the scare quotes around "being" in the phrase " 'being' Nietzsche"; and yet he also reaffirmed the subjectivist position (Channel 2). The latter position Bataille expressed most forcefully in 1954 in *Sur Nietzsche* (*on*

Nietzsche but also *over-*, *hyper-*, *super-*, *excessive*-Nietzsche), when he averred: "I could only write the projected book on Nietzsche *with my life.*"[192] There is nothing really new in this conceit, which is at least as old as 1894, when it was entertained seriously for the first time by Lou Andreas-Salomé.[193] But Bataille gave it its most important philosophical spin to date.

In his essay on Hegel and Bataille, Derrida implies that Nietzsche's *On the Genealogy of Morals* fascinated Bataille not merely for its subtle appropriation of the Hegelian master-slave dialectic but also because, partly due to Nietzsche's influence, this ultimately enslaving dialectic remains so uncannily effective *in us*. Yet Derrida does not follow up on this suggestion. In his 1937 essay "Nietzsche and the Fascists," which Derrida does not consider, Bataille had insisted that "Nietzsche's Doctrine Cannot Be Enslaved"—leaving suitably vague the force of the modal verb "cannot." Did Bataille mean that it is, in fact, *impossible* to enslave it? Or was this merely yet another—more or less futile and problematic—plea or injunction *not* to enslave it? In any event, Bataille concluded "Nietzsche and the Fascists": "Nietzsche's teachings elaborate the faith of the sect or the 'order' whose dominating will creates a free human destiny, tearing it away from the rational enslavement of production [in the sense of the liberal Enlightenment], as well as from the irrational enslavement to the past [as in fascism]. The revealed values must not be reduced to use value—this is a principle of such burning, vital importance that it rouses all that life provides of a stormy will to conquer. Outside of this well-defined resolution, these teachings only give rise to inconsequential things or to the betrayals of those who pretend to take them into account. Enslavement tends to spread throughout human existence, and it is the destiny of this free existence that is at stake."[194] One problem with this particular line of argument, however, is that most of Bataille's defense of Nietzsche against national socialist appropriation operates only at the level of theme and content: for example, Nietzsche *himself* was not an anti-Semite. But what exactly was Nietzsche's opinion of "enslavement" and how does it function across time? How did he want to implement it textually? and did he succeed? To get after Bataille's partial take on this question, it is necessary to grasp the conceptual context in which he posed it, which, like Nietzsche's own, was post-Enlightenment.

Bataille had been revitalizing the ancient philosophical notion of ipseity (*l'ipse, l'ipséité*) to speak of the irreducible, incomparable "self-hood" of human existence, and hence its fundamental incomparability with anything other than itself—but particularly to anything cosmetically overlaid upon its ostensibly origin-ary desire not to produce and acquire, reproduce and conserve, but rather to *expend*. Note immediately the hotline to Nietzsche: Zarathustra's very first discourse or "teaching" is about expenditure and gift-giving. But this important, if obvious, thematic link cannot be the whole story where strategies of illocution are involved. Bataille's notion of expenditure is part of what he calls "the general law of the economy," which has the power to spin off any number of epiphenomenal dualist paradigms, including—most disturbingly to Bataille himself—"profane versus sacred." Crucial, however, is that this "general law of the economy" remains concealed from view, *secret*.[195] Exactly here is where one might expect and demand a link from "economy" to secret modes of *thinking* and *writing*, but here is also where the reader of Bataille is disappointed. The Bataillean categories of ipseity and expenditure *approach* grasping Nietzschean Channel 4 qua medium, because the latter feeds off the illusion that it cannot be *compared* to any other Channel, to any other type of response—in this case to *Nietzsche*. Channel 3 requires *comparison* with Channels 1 and 2 in order to function and legitimate its existence.

Taking his point of departure from "existentialist" ipseity and "Nietzschean" expenditure, Bataille's resulting "hermeneutic" or "dialectical" procedure did not relapse into existentialist solipsism (Channel 2), as some readers might think. Jean-Luc Nancy is right: What is ultimately at stake for Bataille is "community," concealed as well as revealed. Nor, more obviously, did Bataille remain at the level of facts (Channel 1), despite the obsession this professional archivist and librarian had with historical data and exotica. Rather, Bataille's aim was to charge ipseity with unexpected (social) meaning and disruptive (political) desire, as part of a principled post-Enlightenment critique of Reason, Imagination, and the Sublime—all related to the problem of ipseity. It is on these principles that Bataille founded Channel 3—the Channel of ostensibly "Nietzschean" excess and expenditure—*and* where interpretation remains trapped.

In terms of aesthetics, Bataillean ipseity represents one of the deepest and most coherent post-Kantian critiques of the Sublime. Bataille's philosophical and literary project was intended to be a revolutionary response to Nietzsche's aesthetics and politics. Bataille's grasp of Nietzsche's articulation of these two terms, as well as his own interventions into the history of consciousness, depends to a significant extent on not only a post-Hegelian but a post-Kantian framework.[196] If Kant's "Protestant" — as opposed to, say, Catholic, Islamic, Jewish, Buddhist, Hindi, or other[197] — system had its conservative streak, as Bataille will suggest, it was more in its formal problematic than its content. As is well known, Kant supported the French Revolution even comparatively late in the day, given the temper of the times, including its violence; he was in favor, at least in principle, of the abolition of serfdom and so forth. However, Kant's *opus postumous* complicates any simple ideological assessment, since there are hints there of Kantian esotericism, suggesting a mode of "as if" thinking attuned more to heuristic, pragmatic concerns than to any first principles, including fretting about the "existence" of synthetic a priori judgments. Perhaps for this reason, recent scholarship can show that the membranes between Kant's three major critiques — of epistemology, ethics, and aesthetics — are more porous than previously thought.[198] Kant is an obviously important figure to any study of Nietzsche because the latter's own theory of esoteric communication touches on the Sublime, though Nietzsche went less to the source in Kant than to its mediation by Schopenhauer and others.[199] The basic point here, however, is to grasp how, in Nietzsche's corps/e, aesthetics shades into politics of a peculiarly prophetic nature — much as the Sublime shades into pragmatics, into the *subliminal* transmission of social agendas. Full access to Channel 4 is disallowed not only by the Kantian tradition, however, but also by structuralism and poststructuralism. If, as has been suggested by Ricoeur, appropriating Nietzsche, *structuralism* has remained both consciously and unconsciously prisoner within the aporias of *Kantian* epistemology, its failure of nerve to transcend what it only *assumes* cannot be transcended, its inability to imagine anything more than its *own* categories,[200] and if, as has been suggested by Jameson, also appropriating Nietzsche, *poststructuralism,* too, has pressed against the bars of much the same prison without breaking out,[201] then "Bataille" remains *the* exemplary figure of this triple failure. For Bataille impossibly straddles the imagined "transition" from one failure to the next — from Kantianism to structuralism to poststructuralism — all the while under the panoptical auspices of Nietzsche's "prison-house of language." As if Nietzsche did not *want* some people to remain locked in, others locked out . . . and a few others savoring life somewhere else entirely! In a sense, Bataille's approach to Nietzsche might have done better to avoid the Kantian and Enlightenment problematic entirely because even its most radical critique of reason focuses too much on *consciousness* to grasp what Nietzsche was about. Instead Bataille might have begun with Spinoza — "the savage anomaly."[202]

Nearly a century before Kant, Spinoza had mapped out in his *Ethics* what can be considered a critique of the Kantian Sublime before the fact. Certainly Spinoza provided a critique of philosophical "wonder" (*thauma*) for its claim to be "the conception [*imaginatio*] of anything wherein the mind comes to a stand, because the particular concept in question has no connection with other concepts,"[203] and for its presumptive assertion to be totally *beyond comparison* with the rest of Nature, God, Substance. Spinoza surveyed this conceptual matrix in order to get at the power such wondrous claims invariably conceal and to take radical democratic responsibility for alternatives. Though Spinoza waged "a polemic against every anthropomorphic conception of the Divinity, where anthropomorphic is understood as that which adapts a definition of being that is in any way metaphorical or analogical," and though for him "Truth is therefore a sign to itself," Negri has shown that nonetheless, for Spinoza, "the recomposition of truth and the objective order of the world remain unaccomplished," and hence — arguably — it was radically, savagely democratized.[204] How does this position cash out in Nietzschean or Bataillean terms?

Much more than Nietzsche, Bataille often seems close to savage democratization. If he remains in the end far from it, this is due to the fact that he is part of Nietzsche's corps/e and did not quite make the switch when reading Nietzsche from Channel 3 to Channel 4. Certainly if Bataille remained a "materialist dualist,"[205] then this remains a big problem in reading Nietzsche today, given Bataille's direct and indirect influence. Dualists require "synthesis," and "synthesis" is what monists like Nietzsche eat for lunch. No matter whether one considers Bataille himself to be a man of the Left, Right, or something else, this failure to switch Channels is symptomatic of most Nietzsche/anism and all Left-Nietzsche/anism. Nevertheless, Bataille's notion of ipseity does bear directly on the post-Cartesian problem of how to approach *any possible comparison* between two or more things.[206] This problem is vital because the inability to compare Nietzsche with anything else would mean that *his* hegemony is total, including over all *possible* alternatives to his influence — the alternative of *communism* not least among them.

Because Bataille does not adequately consider technological determinations on culture, his reformulation of Kant on the problem of uniqueness and comparability can be profitably supplemented by Walter Benjamin's contemporaneous "Work of Art in the Age of Its Technological Reproducibility" (1935), wherein technology problematizes both the auratic uniqueness or ipseity of things and any ability to compare them to anything else. If mechanically produced simulacra can be distinguished neither from some purported origin nor from one another, being conceptually and commercially — if not actually — "identical," they also cannot be compared *simply*.[207] Thus, by a paradoxical loop of logic and history seldom noted by Benjamin's many readers, the entire *system* of mechanical reproducibility becomes *auratic,* becomes the New World Order. In Spinozist terms, Benjamin never escapes from his a priori valorization of the auratic, which takes on apparently opposed Attributes yet remains essentially the Same. Benjamin's question of mechanical reproducibility and loss of aura obviously bears on the problem of comparing aesthetics, politics, and prophecy as well as comparing "high philosophy" and "technoculture." But the more immediate question is whether Nietzsche's purported ipseity in post/ contemporary culture is so strong that there is nothing left with which to *contrast* "him." It remains to ask if Bataille and interpretation are of any use.

Going beyond the Kant who had defined Enlightenment as "man's emergence from his self-imposed nonage" or "minority" — "the inability to use one's understanding without another's guidance" — Bataille noted laconically that "it is sad to say that *conscious humanity has remained a minor;* humanity recognizes the right to acquire, to conserve, and to consume rationally, but it excludes in principle *nonproductive expenditure.*"[208] According to Bataille — whose critique of Enlightenment predates that of Horkheimer and Adorno in *Dialectic of Enlightenment* and in the matter of Nietzsche is more telling — the long hypocritical exclusion, repression, and suppression of radical expenditure has had disastrous consequences — not only in the dissimulations of bourgeois-liberal culture vis-à-vis the working class as producer of value, but also because, for Bataille, these same dissimulations feed more or less directly into fascism. Which is to say that aspect of liberalism and modernism best able to tap into the darker, nominally more "archaic" recesses of human experience — though precisely not *the* darkest, since these are still only being "managed," at enormous social and individual cost. On this model, the Kantian Sublime is symptomatic of this hypocritical general refusal to confront the fact that classical philosophical, economic, cultural, and political thought in its entirety has not grasped the most radical — supposedly Nietzschean — underbelly of all mere utility qua expenditure, qua potlatch. Following Bataille's logic (read: fervent wish), Nietzsche's thought *cannot* be utilitarian at root; to assume it is is the lethal "mistake" made by fascist and communist appropriations alike. Recalling a thesis of anthropologist Marcel Mauss in the 1920s, "potlatch" means a gift-giving potentially unto death; and the Germanic root *-gift* means "poison" and "wrath" as well as "dowry." For Bataille, it is under this sign that Zarathustra's entire teaching must be understood: that is, as potlatch but also as *Gift*, as *pharmakon*.[209]

Althusser once suggested that "the only possible definition of communism" would be expenditure, in the sense of "spending freely rather than for profit [*la dépense (gratuite, non marchande)*]." He went so far as to link this gratuitous act with Heidegger's notion of *Ereignis* — the way Being itself is said to "eventuate" — and he could have been thinking of Zarathustra as well.[210] But references in this context to either Heidegger or Nietzsche are misleading. Their exoteric notions of expenditure came with considerable esoteric strings attached, and if there was one thing they were not it was communists — neither in Althusser's sense nor even Bataille's. It is important to achor Bataille's concept of expenditure and excess, as Bataille often did not, to a basic mechanism of *capitalist* economy, not just a "general economy." As duly noted by Žižek in another context, an "elementary feature of capitalism consists of its *inherent structural imbalance,* its innermost antagonistic character: the constant crisis, the constant revolutionizing of its conditions of existence. Capitalism has no 'normal,' balanced state: its 'normal' state is the permanent production of an *excess;* the only way for capitalism to survive is to expand."[211] The *political* consequences of this economic problematic, insoluble in terms of capitalism itself, are potentially very dangerous both for the Nietzschean Bataille, since he flirted continually with fascist thought patterns, but also for Nietzsche/anism generally. In Žižek's words, "the fascist dream is to have *capitalism without its 'excess,' without the antagonism that causes its structural imbalance.* Which is why we have, in fascism, on the one hand, the return to the figure of the Master — Leader — who guarantees the stability and the balance of the social fabric, i.e., who again saves us from society's structural imbalance; while, on the other hand, the reason for this imbalance is attributed to the figure of the Jew whose 'excessive' accumulation and greed are the cause of social antagonism" (p. 210). To grasp Nietzsche *and* Nietzscheanism in these terms, "Nietzsche" can be substituted for "Master" and "Leader," "communism" for "Jew." As for Nietzsche — alias "the only position outside of communism" — he was willing and able to make numerous substitutions in the slot that can be filled by virtually *any* political, social, religious, or ethnic designator; but his commitment to elitism and an economy of "slavery," and thus his antipathy to *real* communism, was his *rigid* designator. But apparently a designator invisible and inaudible in Channel 3.

What must not be forgotten with regard to Nietzsche's corps/e is that in the last instance potlatch is a way of acquiring *rank,* which is "conferred," as Bataille wryly put it, "on the one who has the last word."[212] *Anything* Zarathustra says is an "expenditure," albeit "poisoned." "Zarathustra, another loser," as the rock group Roxy Music once rhymed. And what Zarathustra said was therefore designed to winnow out, and in this sense "differentiate," the strong from the weak. Nietzsche noted to himself: "*More is at stake than giving:* rather it is a matter of CREATING, of *overpowering or raping* [*Vergewaltigen*]. . . . Our 'gifts' are dangerous!"[213] Yet Nietzsche wasn't in the business of fucking, but mindfucking.

The auratic Sublime, as that which does not suffer comparison with *anything* else — except, for Kant, the Idea — is *itself* the most sublime euphemism: which is to say, "*censored, euphemized,* i.e. unrecognizable, [yet nevertheless] socially recognized violence."[214] Edmund Burke's originary depiction of the Sublime was as "the master category of aspiration, nostalgia, and the unattainable," but also as having "its fundamental source in *terror*"; at the same time, Burke recognized the equally fundamental *political* point for Nietzsche/anism that "not everything that induced terror was sublime."[215] As paraphrased by Schopenhauer, the Sublime was a sense of compensatory displacement, "tragedy" but also "elevation" (German *erheben:* to raise up), in which, "shuddering, we feel ourselves already in the midst of hell."[216] But if with Schopenhauer we are ever in hell — then it is a position much too passive and resigned for Nietzsche.[217] Beneath Nietzsche's Sublime, as well as beneath all the "lesser" genres and subgenera of his prose — all the media of Channel 4 — still more subliminal terrors can lurk undetected.

Bataille made it part of his lifework to analyze the social effects of the deeply disturbing and shattering human enigma that "the *end* [*fin*] of Reason, which exceeds Reason, is not opposed to the *overcoming* [*dépassement*] of Reason."[218] In other words, there is life after Reason but it is not going to be *known*. Bataille argued that "Kant saw the location of this problem, but there is likely an escape-hatch [une échappatoire] built into his discourse (if he did not see that his position presupposes in judgment a prior agreement on utility, against utility)."[219] Changing the image, one might say that Kant's obsession with "architectural categories" of all kinds, and the sheer techno-philosophical difficulty of making sense of them, especially to the public, tends to deflect attention away from the insight that "*the space of a (social) order is hidden in the order of space.*"[220] For Bataille, Kant had inadequately interrogated the contaminations in philosophy of general economy and utility, on which social cohesion for better or worse depend. Bataille's interpretation of Nietzsche is inspired by the post-Kantian crisis of Reason, and ought to entail interrogating the concomitant crisis in the transmission of Ideas in the public sphere.

Channel 4 as a problem of post-Enlightenment thought is clarified by Sloterdijk's argument in *Critique of Cynical Reason* that Enlightenment has to do not only with power, knowledge, and empowerment but also with the problem of what he calls the "enlightened prevention of enlightenment." Sloterdijk argues that "those in power have always tried to smash the mirrors in which people would recognize who they are and what is happening to them."[221] "Enlightenment, no matter how impotent the mere means of reason seem, is subtly irresistible, like the light, after which, in sound mystical tradition, it is named: *les lumières,* illumination. Light is able to reach only those places where obstacles do not block its rays. Thus, enlightenment tries first to light the lamps and then to clear the obstacles out of the way that prevent the light's diffusion" (p. 77). The first Enlighteners thought they were opposed by three major enemies — three "monsters" — but in fact there was a fourth. The original three were Superstition, Error, and Ignorance. Sloterdijk notes that these "monsters were real powers with which one had to contend and which the Enlightenment took it upon itself to provoke and overcome. Enthusiastically and naïvely, the early enlighteners presented themselves to the powers-that-be in the name of their struggle for light and demanded free passage. However, they never really got a clear view of the 'fourth monster,' the actual and most difficult opponent. They attacked the powerful but not their knowledge. They often neglected to investigate systematically the knowledge of domination in the hegemonic powers. This knowledge always has the structure of a double knowledge: one for the rules of conduct of power and one for the norms of general consciousness" (p. 78). It is within the "order of space" left open by precisely methodological and ideological failure — also discernible as the gap between esoteric and exoteric knowledge — that post-Enlightener Nietzsche's Channel 4 has been able to exploit as a privileged medium. Sloterdijk — who ends up being quite charitably disposed to Nietzsche — unwittingly describes Nietzsche's fascoid-liberal point of entry into the problem of Enlightenment when he continues: "The consciousness of those who rule is that 'reflecting surface' that is decisive for the course and diffusion of enlightenment. Thus, enlightenment brings power truly to 'reflection' for the first time. Power reflects in the double sense of the word: as self-observation and as refraction [Brechung] and return [Zurücksendung] of the light. Those who rule, if they are not 'merely' arrogant, must place themselves studiously between enlightenment and its addressees in order to prevent the diffusion of a new power of knowledge and the genesis of a new subject of knowledge about power" (p. 78). In just these terms, however, Nietzsche was not *merely* arrogant.

Even Bataille ultimately denied to the post-Enlightener Nietzsche the *pragmatic* and *utilitarian* dimension that he teased out of the Enlightener Kant. This singular lack of radicality, this greatest blind spot in Bataille's work, was to be an *exemplary* moment in the history of Nietzscheanism. The question whether this blind spot is debilitating or enabling for Bataille's enormous corpus is important but likely undecidable. Bataille, particularly in his later work, was comparatively free from esotericism; at least he seems to expose himself continually, which may explain his inability or lack of desire to see Nietzsche's esoteric problematic. On the other hand, especially during World War II, Bataille was virtually obsessed with esotericism and secret societies, and it is unlikely that he would not have practiced illocutionary esotericism sometimes. Whatever its cause, however, the consequence of Bataille's blind spot, this black hole in all Nietzsche/anism, was that Bataille's foundational "interpretation" of Nietzsche remained aesthetic even in *Kantian* terms, since for Kant there is a radical difference between a teleological and an aesthetic judgment. In Deleuze's words, even though the latter "already manifests a genuine finality," "it is a finality which is *subjective, formal, excluding any end* [whether objective or subjective]."[222] Bataille's reluctance or inability to grant Nietzsche his own instrumental dimension collides with the fact that Nietzsche's "general" — or rather *"illocutionary"* — economy did not support radical expenditure but rather concealment. And it is this misprision that undergirds Bataille's remark in the wake of World War II that Nietzsche is the only radical alternative to communism. Thus Bataille wrote: "In fact, today there are *only two admissible positions remaining in the world.* Communism, reducing each man to the *object* (thus rejecting the deceptive appearances that the subject had assumed), and the attitude of Nietzsche — similar to the one that emerges from this work [Bataille's *The Accursed Share*] — free the *subject,* at the same time, of the limits imposed on it by the past and of the objectivity of the present."[223] Thus is "communism" figured as Channel 1 and Nietzsche-Bataille is figured not merely as Channel 2 but as a Channel 3 of "freedom" beyond both. But instead of being beyond interpretation in Channel 4, we are listening to Radio Free Nietzsche.

If communism necessarily "reduced each man to the *object,*" then Bataille would be right to criticize and reject it; were Nietzsche really out to "free the *subject,*" for the maximum possible number of people, Bataille might be right to identify with Nietzsche, to see Nietzsche's project in solidarity with his. The fact is, however, that this is *precisely not* what Nietzsche's corps/e is really about.

In Bataille's view, a more or less covert political praxis, or at least theory of praxis, was smuggled into the Cartesian-Kantian notion and practice of Judgment (*Urteil*), as a way of containing the social consequences of radical expenditure. The very possibility of human ipseity under conditions of post-Enlightenment modernity is constructed or, as he says, "composed" psychologically and sociologically more by the irretrievable absence of ipseity than its presence, sooner by hypocritical displacements of expenditure than by fulfillment. This bleak situation entails the *virtual* impossibility of finding ipseity or selfhood anywhere in the "labyrinth" of individual and social experience.

But just here is where *Nietzsche* comes back into focus, since, according to Bataille, we are all wandering deep within the properly Nietzschean labyrinth: a "labyrinth resulting from human inconsistencies," but a labyrinth of which Nietzsche, allegedly first among all other thinkers, was both the exemplary navigator and also the exemplary accuser *"without any hope of appeal."*[224] The resulting nihilism was so strong — if it is taken literally and not as part of a ruse for some still deeper purpose — that Bataille could only waver. On the one hand, particularly deep under Nietzsche's influence in 1937–1939, Bataille toyed briefly with founding a Nietzschean "faith" or even "church."[225] Yet by the mid-1940s, in *Sur Nietzsche,* Bataille seems to reverse himself, imagining that Nietzsche's "destruction of the efficacy of language" is linked to a principled refusal to commit his notion of expenditure to any "city," "God," "church," or "political party."[226] For the rest of us, however, whatever "comes precipitously on the scene strangely loses its way."[227] In this mise-en-abîme, any concept or word is a labyrinth within a larger architecture of labyrinths — labyrinths apparently without entrance, exit, or center. But with a minotaur at every other turn. What, then, is to be done?

It is a commonplace of criticism that Bataille, like the entire Collège de Sociologie in the late 1930s, was simultaneously attracted to and repelled by fascism.[228] But this sweeping generalization fails to unpack the specificity of either Bataille's fascination with Nietzsche or the importance of Bataille's thought for Nietzsche's corps/e. In his 1937 essay "Nietzsche and the Fascists," Bataille freely conceded that the leading neo-Kantian Nazi philosopher Alfred Baeumler's position on Nietzsche had some merit. Along with his many political excesses, Baeumler had written an important study of Kant that is still cited today in the technical literature. But Bataille had in mind an axial moment in Baeumler's *Nietzsche, The Philosopher and Politician* (1931), written after the author had joined the NSDAP.[229] In Bataille's words, Baeumler "draws out of the labyrinth of Nietzschean contradictions the doctrine of a people united by a common Will to Power," into which, according to Baeumler, certain ultimately "secondary" or "mystical" Nietzschean aberrations, such as Eternal Recurrence of the Same, had to be "subsumed." Bataille pricks up his ears here, because of his own abiding search for "community" and because, anticipating a central thesis of Fredric Jameson, he wants to distill positive residues of utopian vision from even — if not especially — their most depraved form, namely, national socialism and fascism. But with regard to Baeumler's Nietzsche, Bataille rather surprisingly remarks that "such considerations" — including the requirement that the Will to Power be realized by a *national* and *socialist* Movement or State — "would be *correct* on the condition that the hypothesis formulated were capable of having a meaning in the spirit of Nietzsche."[230] At this remark the entire reception of Nietzsche holds its breath.

Bataille himself happened to believe that this condition was *not* met or at least *ought* not to be met, though read "between the lines" his own text waffles slightly. "Nietzsche and the Fascists" concludes by shifting from claims about what Nietzsche himself "really meant" (Channel 1) to Bataille's pious wish (on Channel 2) that Nietzsche not be recuperated by either the national socialist or Enlightenment "enslavement of production" (p. 194). But, to repeat, the terrible logical problem with Bataille's interpretation is that it is grounded on the a priori assumption that Nietzsche — with whom Bataille virtually identified — has no pragmatic, utilitarian dimension essential to him. This prejudice about Nietzsche's intentions, so common on programs in Channel 3, is *radically* mistaken according to texts Bataille himself likely read.[231] Hence, the desperate need to grasp Channel 4.

The Bataillean "aporia" is symptomatic of every attempt to date to articulate Nietzschean aesthetics, politics, and prophecy. Whereas, for the ancient Greeks as for Nietzsche, the *aporia* (*a-poros:* no way) was the *beginning* of a way *out* of a problematic, for most intellectuals today it means yet another *dead-end street.*[232] By and large, the uncanny reception of Nietzsche's work — incredibly extensive and detailed though it is — has responded only to its exoteric, not esoteric, surfaces and impulsions, and Bataille is no exception. The labyrinth of Nietzsche/anism winds on and on.

Nietzsche reserved for himself a "possibility," "decision," "option" that is open, in principle at least, to any writer and reader, producer and reproducer. And if you can't pick up Channel 4 on your cable or with your satellite dish, that's because it's already informing even the test pattern of every Channel you do get. There is not necessarily anything "new" about Channel 4 in terms of its intended effects, the major of these being to "guide" culture for distinctive social and economic aims that are designed to remain *concealed.*

Historically, Channel 4 has been available at least since the seventeenth century; which is to say "the culture of the baroque," as it has been constructed by José Antonio Maravall.[233] The term "baroque" may seem unusual thinking of Nietzsche, who took as his basic *social* paradigm the city states of ancient Greece and the Italian Renaissance. But, in terms of how to manipulate culture and "rhetoric" — consciously and conspiratorially — in order to guide an entire society through a time of extreme crisis, the "baroque" provided Nietzscheanism with the most proximate historical paradigm, whether Nietzsche knew it or not. He was not much of a student of baroque culture, though with some notable exceptions since this was the age of Spinoza. Wilfried Barner is right, however, to suggest that Nietzsche's use of "rhetoric" has "baroque aspects," even though Barner hardly follows through on the consequences for Nietzscheanism.[234] Maravall notes that during the seventeenth century not only "baroque cities, triumphal arches, tombs, altars, and artificial fountains," and other large architectural structures, but even "the hieroglyphs and other pictures that were drawn on their surfaces" — all these "reinforced the call addressed to the spectator or listening public, and opened up a *channel* in their attention for the penetration of a doctrine or feeling of amazement, suspension, or stupor that would facilitate the public's captivation."[235] This was the first "modern" cultural formation in which a relatively small number of intellectuals and men of action came to the full awareness — at a time of impending radical economic and cultural transition globally — that society's "ruling classes needed to attract and act upon mass opinion by means of *extrarational channels*" (pp. 256–257; emphasis added). Maravall's description of this turn from the premodern to the modern is remarkably in tune with the key line in the postmodernist film *Videodrome:* "the tone of the hallucinations is determined by the tone of the tape's imagery. But the Videodrome signal, the one that does the damage — it can be delivered under a test pattern, anything. The signal induces a brain tumor in the viewer; it's the tumor that creates the hallucinations." Nietzsche's view of the "baroque" would be that it was less a closed historical period than a recurrent cultural and rhetorical problem — a theory of tropes for use in subliminal persuasion.

One of the themes of Maravall's work on the pre/modern is to draw attention to the substantial parallels between the inception of "guided culture" in the seventeenth century and its full-bore form as "mass culture" in the twentieth. Nietzsche/anism takes on particular significance in this context because it represents the most precise and influential current articulation between otherwise disparate philosophical, cultural, and political concerns, aesthetics, and politics.

For centuries thinkers, major and minor, have entertained the possibility of building prophecy into their work — in the form of posthumous manipulation and handicapping of future readers. Nietzsche's notebooks show that he was obsessed with this possibility. In this regard, formally, he can be considered "baroque" or "Spinozist." In his study of Spinoza as "the Marrano of Reason," Yirmiyahu Yovel has noted: "New Christian intellectuals, whether Judaizing or not, had for many years before Spinoza developed the art of playing the overt meaning against the covert one, deciphering hidden messages, using several voices at a time or (as readers) learning to reverse the declared intention of authors, or to draw illicit information from texts not intended to convey it."[236] Spinoza had good reason to write — perhaps even to think — accordingly. It well behooves post/moderns, post/socialists, and would-be communists to grasp every version of what Lenin calls the "accursed period of Aesopian language, literary bondage, slavish speech, and ideological serfdom"[237] — especially if communists would ever settle accounts with it by appropriating it for more politically egalitarian ends. For, as Negri has argued, the postmodern, neo-capitalist, mass-cultural nuclear state is yet another State founded on secrecy.

Secrecy — or rather, a principle which at first sight is totally ill-adapted to a society of communication — is in fact a principle which functions so well that it is broadened in step with the deepening of the process of expropriation of social communication. *Domination is secrecy.* Expropriation not only mystifies communication and the results of laboring cooperation which such communication produces, it even prohibits communication and destroys its substance. Communication can only exist to the extent that it is selectively used and subordinated to capitalist teleology. The mechanisms which produced subjectivity, therefore, also produce secrecy. Secrecy is the symbol of the capability of destroying the determinations which are constitutive of the processes of communication. The great absurdity of the advanced capitalist societies is that while they claim to be open, secrecy is growing all the time; while they claim to be democratic, secrecy is increasingly protected and defended; while life-enhancing possibilities have grown explosively, secrecy concerning the possibility of death is maintained.[238]

And, though "death is not named" as such under these conditions, "it is written in the discourse of life," of everyday life.[239] It is here that Nietzsche's corps/e, his version of the king's two bodies, would reign supreme, all over the world. Which is not to say that Nietzsche's corps/e *is* already victorious, only that it always strives to be.

This includes all Channels, all Worlds: "First," "Third," and "Second" in between. Writing of his hope for a resurgence of real communism, Negri claims that "what has happened in the East is not foreign to us: indeed we might say, 'de te fabula narratur.' For in the countries where capitalism reigns idiotic and triumphant, corrupt and incapable of self-criticism, arrogant and confused, here as well the subject who constantly proposes to revolt is the same: the new productive subject, intellectual and abstract, students, scientists, workers linked to advanced technologies, university workers, etc."[240] With the phrase *de te fabula narratur,* Negri alludes to Marx's preface to the first German edition of volume 1 of *Capital:* "If . . . the German reader shrugs his shoulders at the condition of the English industrial and agricultural laborers, or in optimist fashion comforts himself with the thought that in Germany things are not nearly so bad, I must plainly tell him, 'de te fabula narratur!' [it's about you that the story's being told!]."[241] From the perspective of Nietzsche's corps/e, however, the problem is that Marx, in turn, was alluding to Horace (*Sat.* 1:12) and thus to a major principle of double-edged, esoteric speech through the ages. Negri's Enlightenment hope to smash "domination as secrecy" thus runs full tilt against communism's greatest, most duplicitous, Nietzsche/an foe. The pressing question of our time in Eastern Europe, in the sphere of influence of the former Soviet Union, is the extent to which it is only Nietzsche/anism that has triumphed. *De te fabula narratur* . . . This Song's About You . . . It Could Happen Here.

Uncannily closer to some of "our" homes than are the East Bloc

Cities of Lead is Southcentral L.A., City of Quartz. Nietzsche's corps/e roams not only the halls of Congress and the academy but the mean streets. In the lyrics of a great progressive punk band, The Clash, in 1985: "Wise MEN and street kids together make a GREAT TEAM . . . but can the old system be BEAT?? no . . . not without YOUR participation . . . RADICAL social change begins on the STREET!! . . . So if you're looking for some ACTION . . . CUT THE CRAP and get OUT there."[242] "Radical social change" from the Left, and "the big problems" for the Right, may not "begin" or "end" in the streets and alleys, or not only there, but they certainly take place there among other places and at specific times. "Youth, after all, is not a permanent condition, and a CLASH of generations is not so fundamentally dangerous to the art of government as would be a CLASH between rulers and ruled."[243] But the problem, once again, is that Nietzsche anticipated this argument, this demand for an alliance between "wise men" and "street kids." Back in '81 — 1881 — there he was in full skinhead kit intoning: "Die grossen Probleme liegen auf der Gasse [the big problems lie in the street]."[244] He didn't say *only* there. He *meant* in Channel 4.

Yes, *Nietzsche's Corps/e* is *paranoid*. Alternatively, it may be more self-legitimating, confident, *and hopeful* than is warranted. But paranoia takes more complex forms than mere psychopathology, mere self-deception, mere semiotextual production and consumption.[245] Not only is paranoia, according to Foucault, "a systematized, coherent delusion, without hallucination . . . crystallizing in a pseudological unity of themes of grandeur, persecution, and revenge,"[246] it is also an often effective mode of *deceiving* others and of *combat*. According to a recent student of paranoia,

> It is a peculiarity of the paranoid structure to combine opposition with doubling; the former is, in fact, a function of the latter. The paranoid sees the visible as a simulated double of the real; it deceptively repeats the real. Or, more accurately, it deceitfully repeats the real: as if such doubleness would not occur if there were not an intention to deceive. Otherwise, so paranoia Itself reasons, we would have the Real Text. Thus the paranoid imagination operates on precisely that assumption which its enemies — *if they existed* — would wish it to operate on: the assumption that simulations belong to the

other side, that doubles have no reason to appear or to exist except to prevent us from seeing the original. The self-protective suspicions of paranoia are, therefore, already a defeat. The paranoid We *must* lose out to the enemy They, and this by virtue of the fact that it authorizes, or creates, the condition of possibility of They-ness by a primary, founding faith in the unicity of the Real. On the basis of that faith, or conviction, all appearances risk being seen as treacherous simulations and other people have merely to fill the slot, or take the structural position of a dissimulating They, in order to have us, at once, in a position characterized by anxiety-ridden suspicions and permanent subordination. In paranoia, the primary function of the enemy is to provide a definition of the real that makes paranoia necessary. We must therefore begin to suspect the paranoid structure itself as a device by which consciousness maintains the polarity of self and nonself, thus preserving the concept of identity. In paranoia, two Real Texts confront one another: subjective being and a world of monolithic otherness. This opposition can be broken down only if we renounce the comforting (if also dangerous) faith in locatable identities. *Only then, perhaps, can the simulated doubles of paranoid vision destroy the very oppositions that they appear to support.*[247]

Thus was Nietzsche's corps/e incepted, thus has it remained in/visible in Channel 3 interpretation, and thus must it be combated as adversary.

If it is impossible to know for certain why Bataille never analyzed the esoteric dimension of Nietzsche's thought, this is due to the *nearly* absolute priority that he and his friends put on silence about things that matter most. During their tenure in the 1930s in Le Collège de Sociologie, Bataille and Roger Caillois had a crucial disagreement about how much of their position on secrets they ought to reveal, undoubtedly since their own thinking was also at stake. This disagreement — about exoteric rhetoric, not esoteric substance — can be read between the lines of a 1938 talk for the college entitled "Brotherhoods, Orders, Secret Societies, Churches," which was drafted by Caillois but read by Bataille, altering its form. Denis Hollier has emphasized that this oddly ventriloquized talk "touches the heart of the College of Sociology, the heart of its project, the heart of its dreams, the heart of its very being. Here we discover the secret, passionate core in which these sociologists, who wanted to unmask society and wrest its secret from it, held their communion."[248] At one point Bataille-Caillois aver, in the most precise and megalomaniac of terms, that "the innermost power of the very principle of the 'secret society' is precisely that it constitutes the sole radical and working negation, the sole negation that does not simply coexist in words, of that principle of necessity in the name of which all contemporary mankind collaborates to waste existence. It is that way, and that way alone, that human aspirations absolutely escape from the real embezzlement and fraud operated by political structures."[249] It is almost as if Adorno's Negative Dialectic were being extrapolated, significantly before the fact, into a principle of political organization on behalf of Expenditure and the Principle of Hope. According to Hollier, Bataille's position, in opposition to Caillois, was that the college ought not to be a "conspiratorial society"; according to Hollier, "its secret is not clandestine in the sense of political underground."[250] This distinction may seem very unclear, itself esoteric. What is clear is that, at one point in the transcript of their talk, Bataille-Caillois cite Nietzsche. They do so without quotation marks, as if he had been absorbed into the guiding principle of the college, no matter how it was being understood by two of its leaders. At one point Bataille cryptically notes: "Nietzsche's words: And especially no secret society, the consequences of your thought must be appallingly ruthless."[251] Bataille had already considered using this "quotation" in another context, having lifted it from the intellectual biography of Nietzsche written by the social democrat Charles Andler.[252] In his semipublic talk, however, Bataille omitted Nietzsche's punch line, as cited by Andler: "infinite numbers of people will find their death!"[253] Several questions are broached by Nietzsche's quotation and Bataille's use of it: How does *Nietzsche* grasp the difference between "secret societies" and the "appallingly ruthless" consequences of his self-described murderous thought? How does *Bataille* grasp Nietzsche's remark? and, not least, Why do Bataille, his colleagues at the time, *and* his later compatriots all choose not to "interpret" Nietzsche accordingly — neither in public nor even in private? Access to Nietzsche's esoteric semiotic has been occluded, is now demanded.

3 *Nietzsche's Esoteric*
Semiotics

Nietzsche

Written over with the signs of the past, and even these signs
painted over with new signs: thus have you concealed yourselves
well from all semioticians![1]

But simulacra are not only a game played with signs; they imply
social rapports and social power.[2]

But how can a man perform the miracle of speaking in a publication
to a minority, while being silent to the majority of his readers?[3]

We're cryin' and we're hurtin'
and we're not sure why . . .
it's almost . . . it's almost as if if you could only crack the code
then you'd finally understand what this all means
but if you could . . . do you think you would trade in
all the pain and suffering?[4]

We now come — at last and at first — to Nietzsche. "Excursus" would be
a proper designation for this arrival at Channel 4, since to read Nietzsche between his lines and words, to attempt to see rather than merely
look, has never been the "proper" or "mainstream" current of Nietz-
sche/anism. Given its concealed nature, the most esoteric code is never
directly accessible. To get at and after the resulting corps/e, to be properly *post*contemporary, it is necessary to be *ex*current.

Umberto Eco argues that the concept of "sign" has always been in a
certain state of crisis, but that recently this "reasonable critical attitude"
has become a mannerism.[5] Just as, since Hegel, it is necessary to begin

discussion of philosophy by announcing its death, and discussion of Freud or Marx by pronouncing theirs, so today "many people have deemed it useful to start out in semiotics by announcing the death of the sign" (pp. 14–15). But, Eco argues, "This announcement is rarely prefaced by a philosophical analysis of the concept of the sign or by its reexamination in terms of historical semantics" (p. 15). In *Nietzsche's Corps/e* the role of "sign" is played by Nietzsche, "historical semantics" by a Nietzscheanism that has never reexamined its own concept radically enough. The cost of such failures can be high. Eco concludes his discussion of the crisis and death of the concept of sign: "The death sentence is therefore pronounced upon an entity which, being without its identity papers, is likely to be resuscitated under a different name" (p. 15). In other words, *as corps/e.*

The notion that Nietzsche's "influence" — his resuscitation or resurrection — was determinate on a wide range of people *without their being aware of it* is not new. Indeed, it was remarked as early as 1906 in passing by the racialist philosopher Raoul Richter.[6] Racialism aside, Nietzsche's *intent* to have *precisely* such an influence — an intent related to his practice of esotericism and order of rank — has never been adequately studied, nor even remarked. It is no accident that it has been almost exclusively intellectuals on the Right who have at least intuited this intent.[7]

Pace his many existentialist, postanalytic, and post-Marxist fans alike, Nietzsche had use neither for "individuals" by themselves nor for "radical pluralism." His was always a full-bore *social* project, as he continually reminded himself: "*Nota bene.* There must be *many* Supermen: All that is good develops only among equals. *One* God would always be a *devil!* A ruling race. Add this to 'the rulers of the earth.'"[8] This is "equality" almost exactly as Mussolini was later to define it. So it was that "art" was for Nietzsche always only an exoteric expression, the *epi*phenomenon, of political and economic esotericism. *This* is what ought to be meant by Nietzsche's "aesthetic," "anaesthetic," or "post-Enlightenment" position, if and when such terms are used.

Even romantic "nature philosophers" like Schelling — whose reaction against the Enlightenment was in some respects even more vehement than Nietzsche's — wrote in 1795, still in his twenties: "It is a crime against humanity to conceal fundamental principles that are communicable to a general public." But Schelling, like all bourgeois revolutionaries, immediately added a proper Nietzschean rider: "But Nature itself has set limits on this communicability; it has preserved a philosophy for the *worthy* that *by its own agency* becomes *esoteric* because it can not be *learned,* not mechanically echoed, not resimulated, and also not repeated by secret enemies and spies—a symbol for the covenant of free spirits, by means of which they all recognize one another and yet which, known only to themselves, will be an eternal enigma to the others."[9] Schelling's rider sheds disturbing light on liberal political philosopher Norbeto Bobbio's assertion—elaborating Kant's dictum that ideas and acts that cannot be made public violate public welfare—that "Whatever sphere it spread to, the metaphor of light and enlightenment (of *Aufklärung* and *illuminisms*) expresses well the contrast between visible and invisible power."[10] Symptomatically, the problematic of esotericism in Schelling is the only significant issue in his work *not* touched on by Heidegger in his 1936 lecture course "Schelling, *On the Essence of Freedom* (1809)."[11] To be precise, Heidegger *does* allude to this problematic. Once. But he does so *obliquely* and by way of *Nietzsche,* whom Heidegger tells his charges in his introductory remarks is "The only essential thinker after Schelling" (p. 3). Heidegger then adds: "During the time of his greatest productivity and his deepest solitude, Nietzsche wrote the following verses in a dedication copy of his book *Dawn of Day* (1881): 'Whoever one day has much to proclaim / Is silent about much / Whoever must one day kindle the lightning / Must be for a long time—cloud (1883)'" (pp. 3–4). If for Nietzsche's corps/e the rest is silence, we can kiss free access to "the essence of freedom" good-bye.

A main reason Nietzsche mistrusted, even hated Socrates—even more than he hated German idealism and romanticism—could have been due to the depiction of him by young Schelling's friend Hegel as the *only* Athenian who refused initiation into the mysteries, because, according to Hegel's logic, Socrates "knew well that science and art are not the product of mysteries, and that Wisdom never lies among arcana" but "much rather in the open field of consciousness."[12] One can also then confront Nietzsche's esoteric semiotics with one of Spinoza's arguments against theology, to the effect that its "most serious error . . . consists precisely in its having disregarded and *hidden* the difference between obeying and knowing, in having caused us to take principles of obedience for models of knowledge."[13] Nietzsche, with all his talk of "freedom" — for the favored few — presumably agreed — in the abstract — with Spinoza that "liberty . . . does not take away the necessity of *acting,* but supposes it,"[14] though Nietzsche and Spinoza had quite different ideological aims and political constituencies in mind. Unlike the Right, the Left has inordinate trouble seeing the difference.

Nietzsche's principle of esotericism is related to the great tradition of Western logographic philosophizing or *philosophia perennis* beginning with Pythagoras and Plato, to the extent that he wrote not only with two basic types of readers in mind — esoterically for the elite, heterodox minority "in the know," exoterically for the unwashed, orthodox majority "out of the know" — but also so that both — particularly the latter — would be influenced and embodied beneath their conscious ability ever *to* know, so as to enchain the many in past and current states of pain and suffering, but to enchain without their being aware of the fact, and to liberate the few, including liberation from any guilty conscience about their privileged status. For every philosopher there must be many underlaborers, Locke noted, and Nietzsche added: for every Superman, many more or less willing Submen, Subwomen. But before continuing with Nietzsche, another excursus — an excursus within an excursus — is required in order to situate Nietzsche's esoteric semiotics within current thought.

Now, terms like "esoteric" can be used in at least two senses — one weaker, the other stronger. The *weaker* sense would mean that Nietzsche wrote for three audiences at once: (1) those *in* the know, to draw them further in; (2) those *out* of the know, to repel them further away; and (3) those *in between* — to recruit or "interpellate" an audience that was not *yet* in the know and yet at the same time *susceptible* to being in the know, *useful* to have in the know.[15] As will be seen presently, this is a comparatively weak sense of "esoteric" to the extent that we are dealing at a *thematic* level only, and hence with something *cognizable* and *expressible,* at least in principle. This Channel 3 in contemporary philosophical terms can be called "Cavellian."

The Cavellian sense is important because it represents the position on esotericism taken by Anglo-American postpositivist and postanalytic philosophy, and hence by one of the most coherent and powerful professional philosophical discourses in the English-speaking world. The struggle of deconstruction and poststructuralism, and their variants, for what they often imagine to be "Nietzschean" hegemony takes place chiefly in the fields of literature, film and media studies, history of art and architecture, religion, intellectual history, and cultural studies — with the partial exception of a small cohort of "continental philosophers," duly marginalized by their mainstream colleagues. Over this terrain, however, the exo/esoteric distinction is rarely an issue — either in general or with regard to Nietzsche in specific. One exception is the vital interest taken in esotericism by the legacy of Leo Strauss in various disciplines. It, too, appeals directly to Nietzsche, precisely *because* he is thought to have been an esoteric thinker, yet "even" among Straussians there is an understandable reticence to analyze him as such. But there is another exception.

In *The Claim of Reason* (1979), Stanley Cavell has applied what he calls — significantly enough — *"logical* esotericism" to his interpretation of Wittgenstein's *Philosophical Investigations,* an exemplary text marking the transition from analytic to postanalytic thought.[16] Alongside Rorty, Cavell is one of a small handful of professional philosophers *not* marginalized from their mainstream and who *are* influenced by "continental philosophy." Under Cavell's influence, it has been suggested that "logical esotericism" might also be applicable to Heidegger, though this has yet to be done, and the implications remain unclear.[17] Nor has it been applied to Heidegger's main philosophical predecessor, Nietzsche.

Cavell argues that throughout history the lack of *explicit discussion* of a body of philosophical work does not mean that it has had no *deeper influence.* On the contrary, some works in particular — for Cavell most notably *Philosophical Investigations,* but Nietzsche's œuvre must come to mind — are at once hermetically obscure *and* yet somehow commonsensical. As such, they are particularly resistant to *either* "professionalization" *or* "popularization." Cavell's thesis can be viewed as isomorphic with Stanley Rosen's notion — independently arrived at from a very different tradition of thought — that Nietzsche's "doctrines have been disseminated throughout the general public, and not least among people who have never heard his name or read a page of his voluminous writings."[18] Such a Janus-faced work's apparent failure to be appropriated, to have what Cavell calls "public or historical effect," might thus mean only that it has been "internalized" by a culture sub rosa, in ways more or less in/visible to it. Hegel and Nietzsche called this "incor-

199

poration." In a sense, as Cavell puts it, philosophical works of this esoteric kind are, in terms of consciousness, "essentially and always *to be* received."[19] Furthermore, in the Cavellian definition, "the major modernist works of the past century at least" are characterized by being "logically speaking, esoteric": "That is, such works seek to split their audience into insiders and outsiders (and split each member of it); hence they create the particular unpleasantness of cults (at best as a specific against the particular unpleasantness of indifference or intellectual promiscuousness, combating partialness by partiality); hence demand for their sincere reception the shock of conversion."[20] This is an exceptionally interesting argument, though Cavell's language is infelicitous in its details and inapplicable in the final analysis to Nietzsche — or, of more particular interest to Cavell himself, to Heidegger — and his corps/e.

Several conceptual imprecisions are betrayed by Cavell's metaphors, the most interesting questions begged. Cavell's use of personification — the claim that "works seek," "create," "demand," rather than authors — might be useful, but in this form the trope passes too quickly over the necessary explanatory steps to grasp structural causality, the way causes indwell effects. The personification of objects always tends to obviate the need to search for intentions and volitions, and can end up providing too easy an escape hatch for the object's producer with regard to philosophical and political responsibility and accountability — in our case *Nietzsche's.* While it is important not to *reduce* philosophical, literary, or historical constructions to authorial intention — which may be impossible to construct in any *ultimate* sense — it is important to be willing to treat the problem of intention as *seriously* as any other topic, especially since our capacity to have and defend our own intentions is ultimately at risk. Needless to say, personificatory slippage to and fro between Channels 1 and 2 — shared by postanalytic philosophers with structuralists, poststructuralists, deconstructionists, and critical theorists such as Adorno — which puts responsibility and accountability at such risk, is out of tune with the intent of Cavell's *The Claim of Reason,* which begins with a ringing humanist credo by Ludwig Feuerbach. Too, Cavell's introduction of the quasi-mystical term "conversion" into his definition of "esoteric" further nudges discussion outside of the question of responsibility and accountability for human actions, and even perhaps, at the end of the day, outside of all rational discussion and debate. As Gramsci argued, much of what appears as "common sense" is "religious" or "superstitious" in origin, and the mutual imbrication of common sense and religion is more intimate, and ideologically powerful, than is the relationship between common sense and professional philosophy.[21] It will be necessary presently to return to Gramsci's way of articulating his critique of common sense with his notion of writing for those "in the know" and those "out of the know." For his part, Cavell certainly does not intend to aid and abet irrationalism, any more than he intends to undermine moral responsibility. Nietzsche savored precisely this dilemma and exploited it.

The more pressing point here, however, is that the term "conversion"—which Cavell sometimes appears to take quite literally—has to be brought together much more precisely with the Cavellian distinction between "insiders" and "outsiders." Who exactly is to be "converted"? By definition, insiders *already are* converted, while potentially rambunctious outsiders, should *never be* converted. As Frank Kermode has remarked about certain esoteric meanings in the Christian Gospels, in many cases "it will be best for the faithful to deny the very existence of a secret vision."[22] Here the stakes are very high. "To divine the true, the latent sense, you must be of the elect, of the institution. Outsiders must content themselves with the manifest, and pay a supreme penalty for doing so. Only those who already know the mysteries—what the stories really mean—can discover what the stories really mean."[23] Just as Cavell's "esoteric" does not take seriously enough the possibility of *intentional manipulation by authors at the level of textual production,* so also it does not suggest a way of analyzing texts appropriately *at the level of consumption.* This failure is unacceptable in dealing with Nietzsche/anism. At least it *ought* to be unacceptable to the tradition of historical materialism from Marx through Gramsci and beyond, which insists on grasping the inextricable relation of production and consumption also in matters of intellectual and cultural history. But there is no adequate category or theory of the "social" or "economic" in Cavell, nor is there in the tradition of Anglo-American philosophy generally; though an unspoken, very productive class-interested theory and practice informs both.

In his analysis of "common sense," Gramsci provided an alternative account of the Cavellian "logical esotericism" that gives the term some sociological, historical, ideological, and political teeth. Gramsci developed this analysis in the early 1930s for communism as a way of articulating this "philosophy of praxis" with popular culture on behalf of a properly "democratic centralist" and "dialectical" philosophy and politics.[24] Gramsci's analysis must be forged into a tool to analyze Left-Nietzsche/anism as it has more or less unwittingly served the reactionary and revolutionary Right. According to Gramsci, "common sense" is hegemonically powerful, and hence resistant to radical change; but it is not entirely static, incorporating into itself elements of religion but also philosophy and science. Thus there is room to negotiate and places to apply political pressure. As with Cavell's "logical esotericism," for Gramsci, "every philosophical current leaves behind a sedimentation of 'common sense': this is the document of its historical effectiveness. Common sense is not something rigid and immobile, but is continually transforming itself, enriching itself with scientific ideas and with philosophical opinions which have entered ordinary life."[25] Gramsci's version of "logical esotericism" follows from his lived experience of mass work as a revolutionary as well as a thinker. Among "Western Marxists," incredibly enough, Gramsci was the only major intellectual figure from an impoverished background, and, arguably, "the one major theorist in the West who was not a philosopher but a politician"[26] — which does not mean that he was not *also* a philosopher. And if he was an esoteric writer, it was mainly because he had to be to elude prison censorship; as he put the matter slyly in a letter: "you refuse to believe that I write what I want to write so as not to write something else."[27] Gramsci had a particularly keen appreciation that "common sense is an ambiguous, contradictory and multiform concept, and that to refer to common sense as a confirmation of truth is a nonsense"; for him it followed that "It is possible to state correctly that a certain truth has become part of common sense in order to indicate that it has spread beyond the confines of intellectual groups, but all one is doing in that case is making a historical observation and an assertion of the rationality of history. In this sense, and used with restraint, the argument has a certain validity, precisely because [the tendency of] common sense is crudely misoneistic [i.e., fearing and hating innovation and change] and conservative, so that to have succeeded in forcing the introduction of a new truth is proof that the truth in question has exceptional evidence and capacity for expansion."[28]

Thus, when initially esoteric philosophical ideas turn up incorporated into a "public or historical effect," this is not necessarily proof, to speak Hegelese, that history is *rational* and that the *rational* is historical, though some of the most basic philosophical dicta — "Know thyself" — can be viewed "as a product of the historical process to date which has deposited in you an infinity of traces, without leaving an inventory."[29] What this description of exo/esoteric effect does suggest, however, is the possibility that common sense can be manipulated by intellectuals in more or less scrupulous ways, which are more or less beneficial to those masses of people who are not professional philosophers, and who are at once full of "common sense" and not "in the know." Because these ways can be subrational, their intended effect subliminal, it is particularly imperative that claims of mere *logical* esotericism be expanded and refined to analyze the full complexity of Nietzsche's corps/e. Gramsci is not sufficient help beyond this point, however, since like many historical materialists he had his reasons to mistrust "conspiracy theory" of all types.

Now, it is simply not enough, even in Cavell's argument in *The Claim of Reason,* for texts to be read only by a tiny number of — already converted? — insiders, and yet rejected by many more — never to be converted? — outsiders. For one thing, the logically esoteric writer would have to guard the deepest level of the text from being read *at all,* since outsiders are at least *potentially* insiders and vice versa, and since — as many logographic writers including Nietzsche have thought — there may be something *necessarily* democratizing, *necessarily* dangerous about putting things better left unuttered into the exteriorized and comparatively public medium of print. Though, to apply a claim by Leo Strauss about Moses Maimonides to this problem, presumably the intention of esoteric writing would be that "the truths should flash up and then disappear again"[30] — *somehow.* But it remains the outsiders who have to *work* so as to allow the insiders the *leisure time* prerequisite to *remain* in the know — in part, by reading texts that are both popular and occult at the same time. But then, in *socioeconomic* terms, the really effective esoteric text would never really "*convert,*" as Cavell thinks, *except exoterically* — appearing to offer transcending escape from the grubby socioeconomic cage. Rather, the really effective esoteric text would *reproduce* social division, hierarchy, and order of rank — without being accessible to full philosophical awareness and political response by those held perpetually out of the know.

Because Cavell's definition of the "esoteric" reflects inadequately on its own metaphoricity and on the social dimension of the problem of esoteric and exoteric production and consumption, Cavellian "logically esoteric works" tend to remain intransitive, rather than transitive, trusting rather than suspicious, conscious rather than subconscious, Sublime rather than subliminal. At the end of the day, it is logically unclear what *specific* content such written works could ever convey, except some sort of "conversion-experience." And such experience, by definition, remains beyond words, subliminally Sublime. At least it does assuming with Alexandre Kojève that "religion is a form of silence, or attribution of genuine speech to an inaccessible deity who cannot be contradicted."[31] But we can *also* assume, with Kwame Nkrumah, that the preferred mode of communication among revolutionaries worth their salt—and Nietzsche is nothing if not also a revolutionary thinker and writer—is *either* by *word of mouth*—oral and without any written trace—*or* by means of *third parties,* who do not know precisely what it is that they are communicating.[32] To which a third category must be added: the long tradition of logographic writing and incorporation leading up to Channel 4.

Finally, Cavell's basically idealist notion of "logical esotericism" is not situated historically or skeptically enough in terms of other competing attempts to define "*modernism.*" Which may be less a discourse at all than the interruption of discourse, the halting, tautologous search for that social order that sustains and legitimates it.[33] *If* modernism *as it is usually employed* is to remain a useful term—which is by no means certain—it must be historicized as an overdetermined conjuncture; as Perry Anderson has suggested, the peculiar modernist moment requires taking account of the way that it, qua cultural phenomenon, entails a "triangulation" of at least three "coordinates": (1) the persistence of older aristocratic and agrarian values codified into a formalized and institutionalized academicism; (2) the emergence, from out of the so-called second industrial revolution, of new technologies and a mass consumption industry; and (3) the imagined proximity and threat of a radical, international, communist revolution.[34] And Anderson is appropriately wary of granting the term "modernism" much explanatory power so long as it remains an exclusively or predominantly *cultural* designation, without economic base or actual revolutionary significance—as does Cavellian "logical esotericism."

Nonetheless, at its more abstract and innocent level, the Cavellian problematic thus calls forth the possibility of a *stronger* definition of "esoteric" that is closer to the stricter Nietzschean Channel 4. In the final analysis, when writing in the esoteric mode, the strong esoteric writer would care less about how either outsiders *or* insiders "read," and still less about "conversion experiences" as they are *commonly* understood. The strong esoteric writer would care much more about how to transmit general *and* specific doctrines *subrationally* — beneath or beyond any "claim of reason" — to readers of various persuasions, with the intent to preserve, produce, or reproduce the socioeconomic division of manual and intellectual labor in a society perpetually divided into classes and/or other groups.

It may not seem possible to grasp Nietzsche's corps/e in terms of this strong definition of "esotericism," for it would hardly have been in Nietzsche's best interest to speak openly of it, even if he may have spoken about it a bit too much. "The silence of a wise man is always meaningful."[35] And "Complete silence is completely invisible."[36] Nietzsche's esoteric semiotics is not *completely* invisible, but invisible or not, in any event it is idiotic to plod on in the attempt to produce an "aesthetics" or "politics" — let alone an "ethics"![37] — in his name, or on the basis of any aspect of his published writings, without settling accounts with the fact that, in his scheme, at least, such projects will always already be manipulated by what he wanted readers to read.

Nietzsche made little secret — publicly as well as privately — that he loved concealment, camouflage, subterfuge. And this fact is related to the way he attacked democratic values of openness. It is not possible to read far in him without seeing that he very positively values "masks," "caves," "labyrinths," "perspectives," even "lies." If Nietzsche admired anything in Christianity, ostensibly his mortal enemy, it was what he called — in his last book, *The Anti-Christ: Curse against Christianity* (1888) — its deep "Oriental" commitment not to Truth, to which it is "totally indifferent," but rather to the archaic and still relevant principle of "every school of *esoteric* Wisdom," according to which what is "of highest importance" is ultimately only "whether something is *believed* to be true."[38] But Nietzsche's valorization of "masks" and "lies" was itself what an anthropologist might call one of Nietzsche's "public secrets," which are essential to the way authority is preserved in societies.[39] He learned of this principle from his philosophical master

ESOTERIC SEMIOTICS

205

Schopenhauer, who followed Plato to hold that "it is the great *árrethon* [the unspeakable], the public secret [das öffentliche Geheimnis] which must never be distinctly mentioned anywhere, but is always and everywhere understood to be the main thing as a matter of course, and is therefore always present in the minds of all. For this reason, even the slightest allusion to it is instantly understood."[40] Nietzsche's readers, alternatively, continue to pretend or mime that they are witnesses to Nietzsche's truths and not lies, even after having been told explicitly by Nietzsche that there are no truths, only lies. By virtue of being made "public," specific lies may be exposed to light, but the *principle* of lying remains intact, and darker lies remain concealed. Or rather in/visible, in/audible. This is an ancient — "Cretan" — paradox of lying, and formal logic spins in its vertigo sooner or later. But it was Nietzsche who gave it its most characteristic, most effective post/modern twist.

In his "transition" book *Day Break: Thoughts About Moral Prejudices* (1881), Nietzsche teased present and future researchers with an aphorism entitled "*Letzte Schweigsamkeit*" (last, final, or ultimate state of silence). It reads in full: "*Ultimate State of Silence.* With some men it is as with treasure-diggers. They uncover by chance things of a stranger's soul that remained hidden, thus acquiring a knowledge that is often difficult to bear! Under certain circumstances, one can know, and know one's way around inside, the dead and the living to such a degree that it becomes painful to talk about them to others: With each word one fears being indiscreet. — I could imagine to myself a sudden silence on the part of the wisest historian."[41] Psychosocial thematic aside, when taken as a directive about *how to read Nietzsche* — or, more accurately, as a prohibition against reading *too* far past his exoteric levels — the reader of this public communication ought to be left wondering not only about what *x* it is that *s/he* is not supposed to know but also about why s/he does not feel any responsibility even to ask what this *x* might *possibly* be. What might *Nietzsche's own* illocutionary "indiscretion" be that he does not want to be made any *more* public than this, even to the wisest among us, assuming for the sake of argument that the historians are wise, their spirit taking flight only after mere day is done? Several hermeneutical choices seem to be offered at this point. Assume, for the sake of argument, that Nietzsche's aphorism does *more* than merely *constate* something about an unnamed person, artifact, situation, or practice: *either* because, as in a roman à clef, the code is relatively easy to crack and so is not *really* an esoteric code at all; *or* because, as a kind of proverb, the abstract principle is more important than any merely contingent, empirical illustration. Of course it is possible to read Nietzsche's aphorisms, such as this one on silence, as "self-deconstructive" or "dialogic" performances, which is exactly what many current readers likely do assume—acts that in the first and final analysis are radically intransitive, without specific content or object. Alternatively, and more interestingly, one might also suggest that this aphorism is constructed precisely so as to conceal some never fully stated transitive object and the possibility of its exposure, using the ostensible deconstruction of silence to maintain silence of a more important kind.

Nietzsche's private correspondence gives some indication of what this occluded content, or rather its intended perlocutionary effect, was programmed to be, or at least that it exists. But even here—reasonably enough, in light of what is ultimately at stake—what he does not say is how he wants to *realize* his locution and illocution as perlocutionary act, nor does he say what the prerequisite *sociopolitical* as well as cultural transformations will then have to be in order that his unstated aim be actualized. But that he *has* one fundamental aim, and that its implications are going to be *horrific for most of humanity*—of this there is, or ought to be, no doubt.

The problem of how to designate this singular thought more precisely is part of its constitutive definition. It has no proper name, all names given it being epiphenomenal to an intent that ultimately must remain publicly nameless. When Nietzsche uses the term "Will to Power," "Eternal Recurrence of the Same," "Superman," or "Nihilism" it is selected for a specific occasion on the basis of an equally unspoken strategic calculation. Heidegger is the philosopher who most extensively and rigorously argued that Nietzsche had "one basic thought"—Will to Power—and that Nietzsche's personality, psychopathology, and historical circumstances are totally irrelevant to grasp this thought and its consequences.[42] The "French" or "new" Nietzsche has evolved out of a deconstruction of Heidegger's claim that Nietzsche had "one basic thought," be it Will to Power or any other. This deconstruction has passed from Derrida to Lacoue-Labarthe and Sarah Kofman, achieving its fullest elaboration in the magnum opus completed before Kofman's death: the two volumes of *Explosion* (1992 and 1993).[43] Kofman begins *Explosion I* by closely following Derrida and Lacoue-

Labarthe to assert that Heidegger's two concomitant claims — that Nietzsche had "one basic thought" and that this thought had nothing to do with his "personality" — were an attempt "to protect Nietzsche from madness" and thus "to blind himself from that madness threatening every thinker and thought, every 'subject.'"[44] In other words, citing Lacoue-Labarthe, Kofman's Heidegger was attempting "'to obliterate' less the subject than the fact that there is no subject ['d'oblitéter' non tant le sujet mais qu'il n'y a pas de sujet]."[45] This "obliteration," for the "new" Nietzsche, is what most "frightens" Heidegger, "because then the suspicion might well arise that, no more than there exists a subject, there cannot be a single thought, a single name, a single history, a single metaphysics, or Beings as a whole" (p. 42). Against this single thought of Heidegger and of Nietzsche — against even the *possibility* that one exists — Kofman substitutes the today familiar, unintentionally boring, ostensibly Nietzschean "desire, laughter, 'eccentricity,' buffoonery, carnivalesque multiplicity," and so forth (p. 42). This thesis is obscurantist. Heidegger was an esoteric thinker who had his own reasons to assert exoterically that radically different in Nietzsche are *thinker,* what Derrida calls the question of Nietzsche's "name" or "politics of signature," and *thought,* what Derrida calls the question of "totality."[46] Heidegger was right to assert that Nietzsche had but one thought. He was misleading about what that thought was and why it remained nameless, Nietzsche's signature withheld. This sleight of hand allowed Heidegger to reject Will to Power exoterically as metaphysical doctrine and yet affirm the unstated thought behind it esoterically in its political-ontological dimension. As for Nietzsche himself, what Kofman passes over in silence is not merely Nietzsche's private assertions that he has "one thought" but his refusal to say what that one thought is. Just as the social function of carnival is ultimately to manage subversion, Nietzsche's "buffoonery" and "explosion" of subjectivity were ruses to prevent the subversion of his one basic thought. Nothing Kofman says about Nietzsche's "explosion" of the subject is really an *argument;* rather, it is an *illustration* of what Derrida and Lacoue-Labarthe assumed a priori to be the case. Everything Kofman then claims about Nietzsche against Heidegger may be true, but only with regard to the exoteric level of both thinkers. In *Explosion II,* Kofman can show how Nietzsche's early works "anticipated" their own "infants." But she means by "infants" only Nietzsche's own later works, not in the sense of other writers, including Kofman herself. Once again Nietzsche-Zarathustra is always already "the deconstructor par excellence," and "we" his epigones.[47] So it is that Kofman, like Derrida and Lacoue-Labarthe, becomes corps/ed. In December 1888 Nietzsche drafted a letter to Jean Bourdeau—whom he was just about to "name ambassador to my court"[48]—in which, before the text becomes illegible, he wrote that "it is highest time that I come into the world again as a Frenchman—for the task on behalf of which I live is ———."[49] Symptomatically, Kofman cites only from this draft what is legible and does not indicate the existence of more that was not.[50]

Toward the end of March 1884, during the period he was working on *Thus Spoke Zarathustra*, Nietzsche wrote to Malwida von Meysenbug (1816–1903).[51] This quasi-confidant was an important writer in her own right, early feminist, and former woman of the Left—a '48er. She served to introduce Nietzsche to her large number of friends and acquaintances across Europe, preventing him from being as isolated as he otherwise would have been. Nietzsche told von Meysenbug that he had experienced much personal humiliation in the last few years. This was likely a veiled reference to Richard Wagner's devastating gossip to his inner circle that Nietzsche had a "small penis," "masturbated excessively," "committed pederasty," and "was homosexual."[52] But this, Nietzsche averred, was not "the main thing." "The main thing," he wrote at this axial juncture in his career, was that "I have things on my conscience that are a hundred times heavier to carry than *la bêtise humaine*. It is possible that I am a destiny [or disaster: Verhängnis] for all future humanity, *the* destiny or disaster—and consequently it is very possible that I will one day become silent out of love for humanity!"[53] But what was it *exactly* that Nietzsche claimed to have on his conscience? Can one ever know this absent signifier, this determinate absence? Other letters echo this sigetic mode—the mode of hinting that something exists that could be said but that remains unsaid. In late 1888, as Nietzsche's conscious mind began to unravel weeks before his definitive collapse, and as his rhetorical defense mechanisms threatened to evaporate along with it, Nietzsche wrote the draft of a letter to his sister, literary executor, and woman of the Right, Elisabeth Förster-Nietzsche (1846–1935). His defenses were still sufficiently strong that he apparently did not mail this particular text, though he did mail similar ones. It reads in part: "what I have to do is *terrible* [*furchtbar*], in every sense of the word: I challenge not individuals, I challenge humanity as a whole with my horrific [entsetzlichen] accusation; no matter how the decision may fall, *for* me or *against* me, in any case an unspeakable amount of destiny adheres to my name. . . . "[54] But, as before, *precisely* what this terrible or horrific act, challenge, and destiny are to be remains shrouded in secrecy. And the unrepresented Sublime tends to become subliminal.[55] At stake is what *Nietzsche's Corps/e* eventually will call "the process of weeding out."

Even as a problematic of sub-limity, the unrepresent*ed* Sublime is not in principle or *ex hypothesi* unrepresent*able*. Nevertheless, some writers struggle to keep their deepest meanings divulged only to some readers, undivulged to the many. They can also attempt to communicate beneath the threshold of consciousness of *anyone*, still in order to influence but not at the level of conscious reception, and opaque to Enlightenment. It is then that the Sublime becomes subliminal. The Sublime is also a radically ambivalent addiction unto death: that is, "that aesthetic satisfaction which includes as one of its moments a negative experience, a shock, a blockage, an intimation of mortality."[56] Dating back to before his death in 1900, it has been common for readers to become addicted to Nietzsche's works, to the Nietzschean Sublime. At the same time, however, there is a virtual consensus that Nietzsche practiced a form of semiotics, a play with signs. It is never immediately evident how *sign systems* relate to the *unsayable*. As Derrida demonstrated in his work on Husserl's phenomenology, even the most radically self-conscious thinkers tend to repress the thought that the very possibility of signs is intimately related to their absence, to silence, indeed to death.[57] So — suspended in the uncanny space between the Sublime and signs — one wonders whether *anything* Nietzsche said can ever be taken at its word: *à la lettre, beim Wort, dead seriously.*

Although the association of Nietzsche with semiotics in the technical sense — where it stakes out certain claims to be a science — may be anachronistic, the term sign (*Zeichen*) and its cognates were favorites of his, and it is not wrong to see him as a forerunner of philosophical semiotics. But to what *end* was Nietzsche a "semiotician" in *any* sense? Was the verbal intent and force of his work *transitive* — as positive project — as well as *intransitive* — as self-deconstructive act? Current philosophical discussions of signs as "simulacra of social power," as "performatives," as re/presentational structures of a subrational "economy," and in terms of the problematic of "the power of the false and the false as power," typically appeal for support, explicitly or implicitly, *to* Nietzsche.[58] Yet this appeal is illegitimate. If these discussions intend to be liberatory in democratic ways *and* appeal to Nietzsche, they can find *no* support in Nietzsche *except* superficially, exoterically, at conscious levels of reception. This is not to say, of course, that Nietzsche did not intend his work to be liberatory in *other* ways, nondemocratically, for some people. Current discussions of Nietzsche in terms of "signs" do not get close to properly Nietzschean sub-limity, even as they skirt round its various modes, particularly when, like Bataille, they simply assume that Nietzsche did not really have any *particular* agenda in mind — beyond a general project for human liberation from all "idols," the celebration of "expenditure," and the like. If Nietzsche did have a more specific agenda, which he called "horrific" or "terrible," it remains shrouded in mystery at the level of both conscious intent and subliminal efficacy.

Nietzsche, unlike the Nietzsche Industry, believed in radically alternative possibilities of reading, whereas most of us postmodern readers — who, in our "schizoid" condition, are fairly laid back about all occasional outbursts of megalomania — tend not to be overly concerned to uncover this or any other intentional act, "challenge," and "destiny" — if for no other reason than that it is assumed beforehand that no speaking or writing voice ever represents a stable subject-position. In our cynical times, such virtually a priori prejudices are not necessarily held on ad hominem grounds: say, because of the fact of Nietzsche's own breakdown or alleged "schizophrenia," itself a highly debatable diagnosis. Rather, *any* voice is always already assumed to emanate from the quintessential protopostmodern subject, the always already *decentered* subject. Paradoxically and tautologically enough, however, it commonly turns out that one appeals to *Nietzsche* as author of this supposedly authorless situation. In *this* case, his subject-position becomes quite centered, his authority unquestioned. Weakness of flesh and mind aside, what Nietzsche's philosophy is *not* in any case philosophically is either dualist or perspectivist and relativist *except* to the extent that these stances are momentarily available exoteric positions that serve his esoteric purposes.[59]

The fact that Nietzschean perspectivism and relativism can inspire baneful political movements — whether Nietzsche would have liked them or not—can be clarified by reference not to German national socialism but to Italian fascism, even though at least one *aspect* of Nazism is also at stake.[60] Mussolini himself and the fascist philosopher Alfredo de Marsico argued that the effective realization of the Nietzschean doctrine of "hierarchy" or "order of rank" (*gerarchia: the* basis, according to Mussolini, of the Fascist State) must not entail the simple suppression of "equality" (*l'ugualianza*)—for that would be stupidly counterproductive. The fascist point, rather, is that order of rank "corrects" "natural inequalities" on behalf of the powerful, who are equal among themselves.[61] Poised to take power in 1922, Mussolini himself went to great lengths—most explicitly in his 1921 article "Relativism and Fascism"—to insist that the "philosophy of force" or "power" (*filosofia della forza*), on which fascism was conceptually grounded, and fascism itself as social "movement" were modes of *relativism.* As his two philosophical authorities, Mussolini appealed to Nietzsche and the leading neo-Kantian Nietzschean. "In truth, we are relativists *par excellence,*" Il Duce emphasized, "[and] the moment relativism linked up with Nietzsche, and with his Will to Power, was when Italian Fascism became, as it still is, the most magnificent creation of an individual and a national *Will to Power.*"[62] In "Relativism and Fascism," Mussolini also argued that left-socialism simply cannot grasp the fact that there are no eternal verities: God is dead, all is permitted; only the strong shall inherit the earth; and so forth.[63] "Socialism" of the Right was thus a direct, conscious response to an epistemological lacuna on the Left and to Nietzschean relativism.

The main point, however, is that Nietzsche's *own* view of subjectivity was radically different from, say, the hegemonic poststructuralist one. He knew that he and his writing had a *center,* a "terrible" and "horrific" one at that.

So it was that on January 3, 1888, Nietzsche noted in a letter to one of his oldest friends—with whom he had almost lost contact—that some German critics who had just begun to be interested in his work were given to characterize it in pejorative medical terms: that is, as "'eccentric,' 'pathological,' 'psychiatric,' *et hoc genus omne.*" But, Nietzsche continued, "These gentlemen, who have no clue as to my center [centrum], as to the great passion in the service of which I live, will have difficulty casting a glance even where I previously have been outside of my center, where I was *really* 'eccentric.'"[64] What and where *is* this uncanny site? This question has less to do with any mental "eccentricity," or the basic romantic trope of "eccentric circle" as a figure of irony or poetic rigor, than with Nietzsche's *principled refusal* fully to reveal this site of destructive passion, in either public or private. Merely to intuit the un/canny presence of his esoteric semiotics is not to know how it works, but it is a start.

Sometime between early summer 1886 and autumn 1887—during the composition of *Beyond Good and Evil: Prelude to a Philosophy of the Future,* and thus at another critical moment in the formulation of his mature philosophy—Nietzsche wrote for his eyes only:

Exoteric-Esoteric

1. —everything is Will against Will
2. There is no Will at all
1. Causalism
2. There is nothing like cause-effect.
1. [65]

This is one of only a small handful of explicit references, unpublished or published, made by Nietzsche to the exo/esoteric problematic. Here, as indicated, a projected series of thoughts breaks off abruptly. Up to this in/visible point—the point of the Lyotardian "matrix"—the note is so fragmentary and preliminary as to render any attempt to read it highly speculative but nonetheless necessary. Context helps. We watch Nietzsche's corpse die in the blank where his thought breaks off, only eventually to be resurrected as his corps.[66] Be this as it may, the next sentence of his notebook, immediately following the truncated series, reads:

All causality goes back psychologically to the belief in *intentions* [*Absichten*]. Precisely the effect of *one* intention is *unprovable.*[67]

"Belief"—as with all "as-if" and "public-secret" structures—is thus clearly important to Nietzsche—not just as something to make risible or to deconstruct, but also more positively and cannily. What is the "intention" behind the last two sentences cited?

It might have been to lay the groundwork for a deconstruction of psychologism: that is, the *reduction* of mental and other phenomena to psychology and thence to intentionality. The postphenomenological reading of Nietzsche developed by Derrida, de Man, and others has pointed, obsessively, in this direction. But today this interpetation comes to us with a knee-jerk velocity that ought to be suspicious, uncanny. "Deconstruction," to the extent that it is a homogeneous movement — which is certainly debatable — like most of the major critical tendencies at the end of the twentieth century, is premised both on a reading of Nietzsche and on an incredibly confused and confusing critique of the relationship between authorial intentions and textual intentions.[68] Deconstruction is nothing if not a technique of reading slowly, and it does not handle the higher — especially esoteric — speeds well.[69] Similarly, philosophical hermeneutics (Gadamer) and existential analysis (Ludwig Binswanger) — which are commonly perceived as being at fundamental odds with deconstruction with regard to the problem of the location or even existence of meaning and the human subject — fully *share* with it the presupposition that Nietzsche was not a system-building philosopher but rather an "experimenter" committed either to "dialogue" or "irony" — one who denied on principle every sort of "coherent whole" or "monologic coercion."[70] And of course the hermeneutic dictum that the *interpreter* (or, in the case of deconstruction, the *text*) knows more than the author hardly encourages interest in problems of authorial intention, getting us nowhere in the case of Nietzsche. A very broad, benevolent, and unacknowledged consensus, fully insightful with regard to Nietzsche's exoteric illocutions only, is wholly blind to his esoteric matrix and perlocutionary force. Which is precisely the playground of structural causality. And hence the consensus is blind to the aesthetics, politics, and prophecy of Nietzsche/anism. This blindness in the guise of insight *is* Nietzsche's corps/e. Programming Channel 4, Nietzsche was after something quite different, more complex, speedier, and much more sinister than either radical deconstruction, existential analysis, or traditional hermeneutics. Thus he spoke as early as 1875 of "the tragic *velocity* of the Greeks" — in reference to the problem that the pre-Socratic philosophers had less *effect* than the post-Socratics.[71]

Returning to the fragment from 1886–1887 entitled "*Exoteric-Esoteric,*" and speaking more pragmatically, the proposition that "precisely the effect of *one* intention is *unprovable*" positively *reassured*

Nietzsche. As he intimated in his letters to his sister and to von Mey-senbug, he was protected by this means from ever having his full inten-tions — *his one* deepest intention — laid bare to prying eyes. If this inter-pretation is at least possible, then the deconstruction or dialogization of intentionality is indeed built into Nietzsche's arguments at their inception, but only as a decoy — a decoy in a politico-philosophical blind, shooting gallery, target range, or battlefield. The subsequent rediscovery by "us" — qua unacknowledged consensus — of this osten-sibly "textual" or "tropical" mechanism of deconstruction would serve to prevent "advanced" or "smart" readers — *even* or *especially* them — not merely from ever grasping Nietzsche's one intention but, more important, from defending them against whatever x was being more esoterically transmitted. It is when the hermeneutic or deconstructive synapses are most under the delusion of either vigilance or dialogue — that is, most locked in Channel 3 — that silent and invisible interference from Channel 4 can begin.

Keeping this polemic-hypothesis in mind, and returning to Nietz-sche's apparently aborted list of exoteric-esoteric distinctions — aborted either because the necessity to continue fleshing it out further em-pirically was beside the main theoretical point or because it was better not to leave any clear trace of his deliberations — it is possible to group his numbered examples in two alternative ways as indicated by his main heading — *"Exoteric-Esoteric"* — depending on whether one takes the first or second numbered examples to be exoteric or esoteric. It is not entirely clear which way to go at this juncture; but what matters more — as his own assertive conclusion indicates — is that Nietzsche is willing to withhold at least *one* intention, *one* philosopheme, from any public purview.

Whatever its name, Nietzsche's im/perceptible "infra-text" or "rigid *designator,"* to employ Saul Kripke's term for "a possibility that cer-tainty exists in a formal modal language," though it does not have to be explicitly stated, or in a "possible worlds" semantics that would "desig-nate the same object" in "any possible world"[72] of a given discourse or narrative trajectory. Whatever the precise identity of such a philo-sopheme may turn out to be, what matters for now — and the closest we might ever come to it, if Nietzsche tells us no more than this — is: first, the existence of an *intent* to make an exoteric-esoteric distinction in the first place; and, second, the requisite illocutionary principles to be used to produce and reproduce this hierarchical distinction, to have it *incorporated* in and as social life.

Perhaps this entire line of analysis of *"Exoteric-Esoteric"* is unnecessarily complicated. Based on the way Nietzsche's fragmentary snippet is arranged, it may be clear enough how he means to order his two sets of examples exoterically and esoterically. He might be stating only that the claim that "everything is Will against Will" — as, say, in the Hobbesian principle that *bellum omnium contra omnes* necessitates and legitimates a Leviathan State founded in equal measure on muscular coercion and subcutaneous, noncoercive coercion — *and* the claim that "causalism exists" are equally exoteric and to be publicly disseminated accordingly. But now turn to the esoteric flip-side of the first statement. What is and presumably will remain secret — or rather comparatively secret — is that "there is no Will at all." This means that, whenever Nietzsche uses the term "Will" what is at stake is only apparently an ontological claim about the way things are, the way nature or society — aka "Will to Power," "Eternal Recurrence of the Same," "Nihilism," "Superman" — just *is*. With the additional implication being that there is nothing we can ultimately do about it anyway, so go with the flow. For we are presumably part of this *phusis,* this All-that-there-is. Heidegger adds, beyond Nietzsche, that what is still occluded, still to be disclosed, is the Being *of* this All-that-there-is, including its re-presentation in and as language. Note also that the statement that "there is no Will at all" might be taken in at least two politico-ideological directions: as a defense either of right-wing "conservatism" or of left-wing "economism" — *both* of which Nietzsche demonstrably influenced at one time or another. But were these really the only kinds of effect Nietzsche had in mind?

Viewed esoterically, things can look rather different from the way they look when viewed exoterically and vice versa. For Nietzsche and for those "in the know" — whose ears he seeks both to reach and to re/produce — nothing like ontology or volition can ever really be at issue, anyway, because "there *is* no Will at all." Nietzsche, in this regard, was thus not a "vitalist" or "life philosopher" à la Henri Bergson or Wilhelm Dilthey, esoterically speaking, any more than he was a "fundamental ontologist," as Heidegger succeeds in showing very well. But what still remains for Nietzsche — and for Heidegger as *political* ontologist—is the exoteric, instrumental *use* to which this particular or any other philosophical argument can be put, more or less surreptitiously. In other terms—exoteric—ontological Will always stands to be superseded by—esoteric—practico-political Will. Or the other way around. It depends on whether "you" happen to be "in the know" or "out of the know," on who "you" already are, were, and are to become. We will return to Nietzsche's way of writing simultaneously for those "in the know" and those "out of the know" presently, but we are not done with the text fragment at hand.

Nietzsche's second example in his purloined aphorism *"Exoteric-Esoteric"*—the example "causality"—initially seems to complicate any pragmatic argument, since the binary—esoteric—term he pits against the—exoteric—notion of causality is not, as might be expected, "effectivity." Rather, it is causality's enabling binary opposition itself: "cause-effect." This, too, is said simply not to exist—not merely as, recalling Althusser's terms, a problematic of transitive or expressive or even structural causality but of any causality imaginable. Yet, not so very paradoxically, the binary opposition *does* continue to exist in one sense at least: namely, *exoterically*. And hence it is salvaged for its *pragmatic* potential. As just seen by analyzing Nietzsche's first example, while this binary may not exist ontologically and esoterically, according to his peculiar practico-logic, it can presumably continue to be *usable:* say, as a political carrier pigeon or computer virus earmarked or coded to convey esoteric as well as exoteric messages. It is just that these messages need not be grounded on any actual, ontological existence— either of "Will" or "cause-effect" relations. The bottom line is that *causality* still must exist for public consumption. And this doctrine of "conscious illusion" (Hans Vaihinger) or "extramoral lie" (Nietzsche himself) is all that matters in the final analysis, when push comes to shove—as it does when one is at war. And Nietzsche is nothing if not (also) at war. And so it is, finally, that esoterically handicapped effects also live exoterically and practically—though Nietzsche does not say so here, nor ought he to when speaking to himself.

It is useful to think back again to the Althusserian theory of structural causality as designating the existence of a cause present only in its effects, and to its precedent, in Spinoza, of the play between "nature viewed as active" or *natura naturans* (substance and cause) and "nature viewed as passive" or *natura naturata* (mode and effect).[73] For

Spinoza, *natura naturata* and *natura naturans* "are interconnected through a mutual immanence: on the one hand the cause remains in itself in order to produce; on the other the effect or product remains in the cause."[74] The theory of structural — as opposed to linear and ex-pressive — causality is the attempt to rescue a materialist kernel from the rationalist husk with which Spinoza himself had protected his het-erodox insight. Nietzsche's critique of causality seems momentarily proximate to both theories, so to speak. But what is more interesting is, first, the rhetorico-political consequences he elicits from them, and, second, his reluctance to relinquish expressive control over linear and expressive processes of causality.

Nietzsche's editor Giorgio Colli rightly called attention to the exem-plary significance of Nietzsche's notebook entry on exoteric and eso-teric causality but fell short of an adequate interpretation. Colli sug-gested, correctly, that after Nietzsche wrote *Thus Spoke Zarathustra* all that was left was time and space for retrospection and self-reflection, a fine-tuning of the exoteric expression of the esoteric doctrines of the text that was for Nietzsche literally unsurpassable. Nietzsche noted in a letter to Peter Gast on September 2, 1884, that he had been outlining what in scare quotes he called his " 'philosophy' " until the development of which, he coyly noted, "Zarathustra . . . has only a wholly personal meaning, as my 'Book of Edification and Consolation' — otherwise opaque and concealed and risible for Everyman."[75] Colli was also cor-rect that thereafter, over the entire extent of his subsequent writing, Nietzsche no longer granted strong — if any — *ontological* or other *philo-sophical* status to such terms as "Will," "Will to Power," "Superman," "Eternal Recurrence of the Same," and so forth. Rather, these were merely exoteric expressions of "something deeper." However, the symptomatic problem with Colli's reading centers on how to describe and interpret what this "something deeper" is and where it is located. It is clearly insufficient to explain it — indeed, to explain it away — as Colli immediately did. For him it is merely Nietzsche's *private, existential,* and *"artistic"* response to otherwise intractable ontological and epis-temological aporias: for example, as "an esoteric, secret, entirely per-sonal immersion of the authentic thought of Nietzsche"[76] — where-upon Colli bails out of the entire problematic as all Left-Nietzschoids tend to do.

What is evident is that Nietzsche will continue speaking to his readers exoterically by way of asserting that both the *bellum omnium contra omnes* and some form of causality (*natura naturans*) really *do* exist. "Christianity," "decadence," and "democracy," for example, are all *caused*, at least in part, by certain factors that Nietzsche regards as historically necessary, and in turn they cause other factors, which he passionately believes to be baneful and in need of radical correction. What Nietzsche will tend *not* to tell his readers publicly—to tell them as seldom as he deems advisable—is that certain specific types of effectivity (*natura naturata*) also continue to exist, even though he knows privately that they are grounded on no ontological or philosophical principle, nor can they ever be. God is dead, all is permitted. Or is it less than before? But the simple strategic and tactical point so far is that, by means of these sleights of conceptual hand, Nietzsche can conceal—or at least hope to conceal—the exact nature of whatever doctrine or intention is being conveyed at any given moment by and in his writing. And there may well be one and only one such doctrine or intent, precisely because it is theoretically impossible, he wants us to believe, to prove that only *one* exists. In *Twilight of the Idols* Nietzsche, ever the moralist as *pragmatist,* almost let one cat out of the bag. In number 36 of his "Dicta and Arrows," he wrote: "Whether we immoralists do virtue any *harm?*—Just as little as anarchists do to princes. Only after they have been shot at do the latter sit again firmly on their throne. Moral: *One must shoot at morals.*"[77] That is, keep the princes on their throne with all the powers of exoteric ruse.

Needless to say, within this virtual reality there is no possibility for Nietzsche himself—nor for anyone else really "in the know"—to suffer anything like a "legitimation crisis" in any post- or neo-Enlightenment, Habermasian sense. This is not to say that Nietzsche—this supposedly most honest and truthful of men—was operating in bad faith, cynically, hypocritically, or irresponsibly—at least not *really* or *esoterically.* It is to say, however, that he could justify and legitimate being hypocritical and telling lies—lies both "Noble" and "Base"—*virtually* or *exoterically.* It is also to say that—in spite of all his attacks on hypocrisy—moral, religious, political, cultural, and other—Nietzsche could and did justify and legitimate to himself keeping very large numbers of people excluded from more esoteric knowledge of the manipulative effects his writing was programmed to have on their thoughts, lives, and deaths. Alternatively, sometimes Nietzsche does *seem* to tell them (us) outright, *and yet* still leaves them (us) wondering whether or not it was said seriously or not. Herein lies the true genius of Nietzsche's "rhetoric."

By definition, of course, the most radically esoteric philosopher would never say that s/he was such. Which is why any discussion of Nietzsche's esoteric semiotics will always remain hypothetical: an indecisive sally, a digression, an excursus. Whenever alternatives to the present seem blocked, a turn to history is warranted. It helps to look back over the long history of esotericism, if only to see what Nietzsche saw and how he might have learned from it.

The ancient principle of sigetics—the rhetoric and practice of silence—is succinctly expressed in a mock dialogue in Boethius's *The Consolation of Philosophy* (523–524 C.E.), months before the author's death in the prison where he had landed for having said too much: "'Now do you recognize that I am a philosopher?' . . . 'I would have, had you remained silent [*si tacuisses*].'"[78] Nietzsche alluded to this Boethian principle—*si tacuisses, philosophus mansisses*—in public: *once* and *indirectly*. At the conclusion of the new, 1886 preface to volume 1 of *Human, All-Too-Human: A Book for Free Spirits*—ostensibly his most "positivistic," "scientific," and "democratic" work, which had first appeared in 1878—Nietzsche asks why, in Germany, his book "has been read most carelessly and *heard* the worst." The answer comes in two parts: the first is that of an imaginary or concealed interlocutor; the second is Nietzsche's own answer or, more precisely, the *refusal* of his narrator to give an answer. Speaking of *Human, All-Too-Human*, Nietzsche's preface ends: "'It demands too much, I have been told, it turns toward people unoppressed by crude duties, it demands refined and spoiled senses, it requires superfluity, superfluity of time, of clarity of sky and heart, of *otium* [leisure, idleness] in the most audacious sense: — only good things that we Germans of today do not have and thus also cannot give.'—After such a tactful answer my philosophy advises me to keep silent and to ask no more; especially in certain cases, as the saying goes, one *remains* a philosopher only by—being silent."[79] What is most especially kept silent by this non/dialogue, however, is less even Nietzsche's tacit support for the *socioeconomic system* alluded to by the imaginary interlocutor—a system lacking in modern Germany, unfortunately for Nietzsche, though mere national questions are hardly what is at ultimate stake—than the measures Nietzsche's *lan-*

guage will take to re/produce this socioeconomic system philosophically and socially—which for him means measures that are surreptitious, subliminal, silent, and—even in textual form—in/visible.

After Boethius, in a tradition known to Nietzsche more indirectly than directly, medieval treatises on rhetoric and the craft of preaching were able to jack into the Jewish-Christian admonitions that he had memorized by heart as a youth that, while speaking, "put your hand on your mouth" (Sirach 5) and that "there is a time for speaking, and a time for silence" (Ecclesiastes 3:7).[80] Henceforth, the doctrine was transmitted over various routes by various couriers to modern philosophers, including Neitzsche, Heidegger, even Wittgenstein. So powerful is this tradition that it is remarkable that any methodology for prizing open the esoteric is even available and unremarkable that it may by necessity appear to be a negative or "paranoid" act. But it is also natural, in the words of one of its finest students, Carlo Ginzburg, that "the existence of a deeply rooted [esoteric] relationship that explains superficial [exoteric] phenomena is confirmed the very moment it is stated that direct knowledge of such a connection is not possible. Though reality may seem to be opaque, there are privileged zones— signs, clues—which allow us to penetrate it."[81] And thus perhaps to penetrate—and countervirus—the virtual reality living on as Nietzsche's corps/e.

Whether it qualifies as a "privileged zone" in Ginzburg's sense or not, Nietzsche's fragmentary note in 1886–1887 on the exoteric-esoteric distinction is significantly different from his longer published discussion of this distinction near the beginning of *Beyond Good and Evil* (finished in July 1886), the first of his retroactive prefaces to the cryptically entitled *Thus Spoke Zarathustra: A Book for All and No Man*. The real difference between these two versions—the former itself comparatively esoteric, the latter comparatively exoteric—lies *not* in their underlying philosophical or social thematic or implication, which remain constant, but rather in the way Nietzsche better armors the logico-rhetorical mechanism informing his attempt to persuade and recruit. The point is also not that the notebook fragment of 1886–1887 bares this mechanism entirely, either; though it does yield somewhat to the kind of analysis just proposed.

In aphorism 30 of *Beyond Good and Evil*, Nietzsche states bluntly that the exoteric-esoteric distinction has existed historically in every society grounded—and he thinks very properly so—on "order of rank [*Rangordnung*]." This, he says, is well known to virtually all major philosophers globally, giving as examples "Indians as well as Greeks, Persians, and Muslims, in short, wherever one believed an order of rank, *not* in equality and equal rights."[82] Since, residing in their own geopolitical aesthetic, many postmoderns *believe* they no longer believe in order of rank but in equality and equal rights, they *think* that they no longer need worry about *authorial intention* and *esotericism*—which is technically beyond thought anyway—and that *therefore* they can read Nietzsche unguarded. And if Nietzsche did not anticipate—"predict"—this elementary development, he was a bad philosopher and bad political philosopher, not just a bad esoteric philosopher.

Note that in aphorism 30 of *Beyond Good and Evil* Nietzsche is careful to draw a small but significant distinction between "*believing*" order of rank and "believing *in*" equality and equal rights. The difference may seem trivial. But the first construction entails a more deeply ingrained and incorporated mode of existence that is appropriate to the hierarchical type of society and hegemonic control toward which Nietzsche—simultaneously "hangman" and "priest"—is working.[83] The second construction is more abstract and metaphysical by comparison, and more appropriate to the age of democratic, egalitarian reasoning that Nietzsche is attempting to combat and/or virus against its own anti-elitist and therefore, for him, most depraved tendency.

Aphorism 30 goes on to argue that the distinction between the exoteric and the esoteric is not that the former comes from "outside," the latter from "inside"; rather, the exoteric is the view from below up, whereas the esoteric is the view from above down. From the executive suite, as it were. Nietzsche prefers, when possible, to shift the directional axis of the exoteric-esoteric from a "horizontal" inside/outside metaphoric, which might entail a *merely* philological problematic, to a "vertical" metaphoric of up/down, which preserves the *political* and *social* problematic of order of rank. But esoterically and rhetorically speaking, this is not the whole picture, either, since Nietzsche's own writing—most especially *Thus Spoke Zarathustra*—is designed *both* to be the view from the top—at the threshold of Zarathustra's cave at the peak of his mountain—*and* to in-form and in-habit his readers in valleys, towns, cities: from the cosmopolitan to the cosmos and back, as it were. Different readers must be moved differently—sorted and weeded out as Zarathustra's "narrative" circles around the thought that here happens to be articulated as "the doctrine of decision": Eternal Recurrence of the Same. This doctrine *appears* in the text to be esoteric, even as it eventually reveals itself exoterically. But, precisely because it *appears* this way, what is kept at deeper levels of esotericism is that *even* this doctrine becomes an ultimately interchangeable part of a semiotic system designed to be incorporated in ways that, in principle, cannot ever be fully known, heard, seen.

Thus, at one level, aphorism 30 in *Beyond Good and Evil* is simply re/translating the abstract exoteric-esoteric-exoteric distinction *thematically* into terms of social hierarchy: the view up from below is that of slaves or other workers needed to support the noble caste or class, its "audacious *otium.*" The latter — in this deformed, but equally masculinist, variant of Hegel's master/slave dialectic[84] — "looks down on" these workers, figuratively *and* literally, but nonetheless obviously needs their more or less willing cooperation to provide the leisure time prerequisite to use and savor the panoptical architectures that this same base-labor both produces and is enslaved by. For this reason, slaves or workers must be handled not only with violent coercion — though violence, too, certainly stands in reserve if needed — but with properly exoteric means, using the noncoercive coercion of bourgeois hegemony. Here we are quite close, perhaps, to *the* most rigid designator of Nietzsche/anism.

In *Beyond Good and Evil,* Nietzsche is also hinting broadly that the exoteric-esoteric distinction ought to inform "our" society again, as it has all the great cultures of the past, from ancient India and Greece to the Italian Renaissance — but not much further. But *how* to do this most effectively is the big problem. Now it may seem surprising, therefore, that at the end of aphorism 30 Nietzsche explicitly insults the base-level of society: "Wherever the *Volk* eats and drinks, even where it worships, it tends to stink." He also insults the kind of books — indeed popular or mass culture *tout court* — that are aimed at this base-level. "Books for all the world are always foul-smelling: the stench of small people clings to them" (*KGW* 6/2:44–45). Most readers undoubtedly assume that *this* book, *Beyond Good and Evil,* at least, is not intended to be a vulgar book. Or is it? Most likely, it *is* such a book, as the vulgarity of this very passage shows, but among *other* things.

Are Nietzsche's insults against the larger populace and its many books at all *effective* means of promoting the kind of more noble society Nietzsche has in mind? Judging from the acclamation his writing has received from the "Left," the ad hominem answer is easy: Apparently so — sadomasochistically and abjectly enough. But Nietzsche's many insults are intended to operate not merely exoterically. If he *talks* about the exoteric-esoteric distinction — though rarely as much in public as he does here — it only stands to reason that he must also *put it to work* by means of his writing. To be avoided at all cost when reading Nietzsche is the tendency of "critics" in the Gramscian sense: namely, those who "assume that certain phenomena are destroyed as soon as they are 'realistically' explained, as if they were popular superstitions (which anyway are not destroyed either merely by being explained)."[85] Nietzsche's position requires the necessity of writing for both those "in the know" and those "out of the know," and is clarified by Gramsci's analysis of Machiavelli's position, which Nietzsche had also studied for his rival purposes.

In his prison notebooks, Gramsci critiqued the "moralist" — as opposed to "political" — reading of Machiavelli exemplified by Ugo Foscolo (1778–1827) in his great poem *Dei sepolcri* (on tombs, 1806–1807). The moralist argument is that Machiavelli's *The Prince* (written 1513; published 1532) provides at least unwitting support for "tyrant haters," since it *exposes* the methods of tyranny even while teaching and encouraging their use. Obviously not only tyrants but democrats can in principle read the text, learning from it how to exert their own power more surreptitiously and effectively. Gramsci objected to this mere moral encouragement to "tyrant haters," in part because it would discredit his own efforts to write *The Modern Prince* on behalf of communists and "the philosophy of praxis," and paraphrased the moralistic argument as follows: "It is commonly asserted that Machiavelli's standards of political behavior are practiced, but not admitted. Great politicians — it is said — start off by denouncing Machiavelli, by declaring themselves to be anti-Machiavellian, precisely in order to be able to put his standard 'piously' into practice. Was not Machiavelli himself a poor Machiavellian, one of those who 'are in the know' and foolishly give the game away, whereas vulgar Machiavellianism teaches one to do just the opposite."[86] Applied to Nietzsche, one asks whether he himself was the first poor Nietzschean, since he *potentially* gave over to those "out of the know" — in this case, forces of socialism and, potentially, communism — the knowledge of how the most complex forms of oppressive hegemony work. The problems remain, however, as to why this *potential* has remained *unrealized,* why "even" the Left have become members of Nietzsche's corps/e, and what the exact illocutionary-perlocutionary media of this structural causality might be. And how would one know? Gramsci also remarks that Benedetto Croce had criticized the Foscoloan interpretation of Machiavelli on the grounds that Machiavellianism was a "science." As such, it was, in effect, "beyond good and evil" and available, in principle, to serve "reactionaries and democrats alike, just as skillful swordplay serves both honest men and brigands, for self-defense and for murder."[87] But Gramsci went beyond Croce's view as well, noting that it was true only "in the abstract" and based on an anachronistic misreading of Machiavelli. Gramsci continued: "Machiavelli himself remarks that what he is writing about is in fact practiced, and has already been practiced, by the greatest men throughout history. So it does not seem that he was writing for those who are already in the know [i.e., 'tyrants']; nor is his style that of disinterested scientific activity; nor is it possible to think that he arrived at his theses in the field of political science by way of philosophical speculation — which would have been something of a miracle in that field at the time, when even today he meets with such hostility and opposition" (p. 135). The conclusion Gramsci draws is again applicable to Nietzsche with the structural and political valences reversed. "One may therefore suppose that Machiavelli had in mind 'those who are not in the know' [i.e., 'the revolutionary class of the time'] and that it was they whom he intended to educate politically. This was no negative political education — of tyrant-haters — as Foscolo seems to have understood it; but a positive education — of those who have to recognize certain means as necessary, even if they are the means of tyrants, because they desire certain ends" (p. 135). For his part, Nietzsche, concerned as he was less to promote "negative" or "passive" nihilism than "positive" or "active" nihilism, desired to write — and has actually written — not only for the forces of tyranny "in the know" but also for those democrats "out of the know" — who are supposed to *believe* that they are opposing tyranny when *in fact* they are supporting its undergirding conceptual and economic system.

One thing Nietzsche is not saying explicitly in aphorism 30 is whether a book like *Beyond Good and Evil* is itself only "for all the world," and hence exclusively exoteric and vulgar, or only for "those in the know," and hence exclusively esoteric and noble. But, interestingly enough, this question, too, is not as easily resolvable as one might think or wish. Again, the best response is likely "both": *Beyond Good and Evil* is for those "in the know" *and* those "out of the know." At least this response jibes best *both* with Nietzsche's original intent *and* with the actual effect his writings have had over the years, especially on the Left. For he intended that a suitably renewed, updated deployment of the exoteric-esoteric distinction might actually produce — or at least help produce — a post/contemporary "order of rank." This can never happen ex nihilo — Nietzsche was no metaphysician in this sense of the term — but rather *mutatis mutandis* from out of the historical realities given him: that is, from out of "our" hostile, vulgar, and inexorable drift toward modernity and modernism, democracy and socialism.

Nietzsche would never assume that socialism or communism were really "dead." Nor do any true right-wing revolutionaries.[88] Nietzsche's concern would be that their inevitable eternal recurrence be as delayed and ineffectual as possible. And the best way to do that was to give exoteric glimpses of Eternal Recurrence of the Same, intimate that these glimpses into its formal structure were esoteric, and thereby occlude access to the radically undemocratic social modes of production and reproduction necessary to perpetuate "eternally" the *otium* of the few against the many in the future. In all this Nietzsche was more *realistic* than is seen by his psychoplasmic brood.

Although it is hardly conventional wisdom to think of Nietzsche as a "realist" — in the high modernist nineteenth-century sense or otherwise — this is what he was in at least one crucial way. Though it does not deal with Nietzsche, an argument by Mark Seltzer about the mind/body relation in industrial society, at the moment of the latter's irreversible inception, helps clarify the realist aspect of Nietzsche/anism in terms both of Nietzsche's intended — esoteric and invisible — effect and in terms of how this intent has been grasped cognitively — exoterically and visibly — and bodily incorporated, as subcutaneous consumption — again esoterically and invisibly.[89] The theory of subliminal or "just noticeable differences" that circle around the threshold of the human sensorium separating the perceptible and the imperceptible — where the mind/body dualism begins to collapse technologically and technoculturally as well as conceptually — had been worked out by several European physiologists, such as Gustav Fechner, by the 1830s and 1840s, and Nietzsche was well aware of this scientific problematic.[90] That the desire for, and result of, subcutaneous effectivity is exactly "realist" — in nineteenth-century and subsequent senses — requires explanation. In *Bodies and Machines,* Seltzer suggests that "the realist desire to see is also necessarily a desire to make visible: to employ, physically or materially, character, persons, and inner states and, collaterally, to 'open' these states to what [Stephen] Crane can calls the 'machines of perception,' what [Émile] Zola calls 'the mechanism of the eye,' and what the turn-of-the-century reformer, police reporter, and photographer Jacob Riis calls the social technologies of an 'eternal vigilance.'" Seltzer interprets this point in terms of a dialectic of "seeing" and "embodiment." Furthermore: "From one point of view, the realist project of making-visible is perfectly in line with the techniques of a certain social discipline, along the lines that Foucault has mapped in detail: the opening of the everyday ordinariness of every body to, and the fabrication of individuals under, the perfect eye of something like the police."[91] And of course Nietzsche is conventionally understood, by Foucault and many others, as having somehow *exposed* exactly this — more or less gendered — "eye/I" to sight with some never proven and vague, but nonetheless always presupposed, *progressive* social project in mind. "But," linking back up with Seltzer's argument, "from another perspective, the requirement of embodiment, of turning the body inside out for inspection, takes on a virtually *obstetrical* form in realist discourse. If the first takes as its model the man-factory and the mechanical reproduction of individuals, the second . . . takes as its model the figure of the mother and the biological making of persons. What the logistics of seeing and embodiment in the realist text entails, then, is a perpetual negotiation between these two models of personation: between the body (specifically, the more radically embodied and embodying maternal body) and the technologies of the social machine."[92]

The desire of Nietzsche's corpse, then, is simultaneously to "father" and to "mother" a social machine of slavery qua Nietzschean corps. This is Nietzsche's patented version circa 1888 of the archaic, mythological desire for what Lévi-Strauss called "*the persistence of the autochthonous origin of man.*"[93] And it is in this context that Nietzsche's famous remark at the opening of *Ecce Homo: How One Becomes What One*

Is must be grasped: "The happiness of my *Dasein,* its singularity perhaps, lies in its destiny: I am, to express it in the form of an enigma, already dead as my father, as my mother I am still living and becoming old."[94] What must be stressed is that this seemingly bizarre proleptic desire is also quite "realistic" — now in the sense that it has been so often and so extensively *realized* — as is proven by the existence of Left-Nietzscheanism: that is, by the uncanny and counterproductive positive influence of Nietzsche, beginning already in the nineteenth century, on would-be leftist movements of women and men alike, people and protocyborgs alike. What Heidegger admired in 1936–1937 as Nietzsche's "masculine aesthetics" (*Mannesästhetik*), in opposition to what Nietzsche himself had reviled in 1888 as "feminine aesthetics" (*Weibs-Aesthetik*), is by no means incompatible with the distinctly modernist version of the ancient myth of the androgynous birth and/ or autogenesis (*homo autotelus*) in the specific form of the "combination of autoerotic sexuality and wielding power over others."[95]

Now, it goes without saying that insulting remarks like the ones at the end of aphorism 30 in *Beyond Good and Evil* might antagonize the great unwashed, *das Volk* and some Christians. On the other hand, however, the ardent desire of most readers — even "socialists" — is likely that they not be interpellated as the "masses" whom Nietzsche constantly, and often effectively, makes risible. Indeed, calculated hermeneutic aversion and abjection is itself one of his more effective — if only preparatory — means of *recruitment* and "weeding out."

"Higher" illocutionary techniques used by Nietzsche, working in tandem with the "base" technique of hurling insults, also involve appeals to refinement and pride, and more generally the attempt to reintroduce premodern Renaissance *Tugend* or virtue: namely, the *virtù* of manly, masculinist courage and resolve in the face of a feminized *Fortunà,* including the resolve to dispense with the effeminizing Jewish-Christian tradition.[96] It is quite another kind of love — that is, *amor fati:* love of fate, destiny, or Eternal Recurrence of the Same — that becomes in Nietzsche a principle for the psychoplasmic pullulation of his brood.

In many respects Nietzsche admired the Italian Renaissance even more than classical Greece. The illocutionary strategy of *Thus Spoke Zarathustra* was duly informed by Machiavelli's theory of the political treatise as a "Mirror of Princes": in Nietzsche's case, a way for the higher man to be continually tested in the future by a textual mirror held up to him to check if he is in reality the esoteric ideal he himself claims and needs to be, if "civilization" and "culture" are to survive, let alone improve. Gramsci argued in his section of his prison notebooks called "The Modern Prince"—that is, the ideal Communist Party— that, in *The Prince,* Machiavelli "merges with the people, becomes the people; not, however, some 'generic' people, but the people whom he, Machiavelli, has convinced by the preceding argument—the people whose consciousness and whose expression he becomes and feels himself to be, and with whom he feels identified. The entire 'logical' argument now appears as nothing other than auto-reflection on the part of the people—an inner reasoning worked out in the popular consciousness, whose conclusion is a cry of passionate urgency. The passion, from discussion of itself, becomes once again 'emotion,' fever, fanatical desire for action."[97] The degree of passion and the fanatical desire for action at any given historical conjuncture has varied greatly in the case of Nietzsche's corps/e. Sometimes passion and the fanatical desire for action have proven to be productive, other times counterproductive in his terms. But Gramsci's analysis of the illocutionary structure and desired perlocutionary effect of Machiavelli/anism describes nothing so well as Nietzsche/anism—though with the mortally opposed political ideals and ideologies at stake.

It is virtually impossible to show *exactly how* Nietzsche's esoteric semiotics works on individual readers or groups of readers, constructs and interpellates them, though perhaps not impossible entirely.[98] It is also absolutely necessary to acknowledge *that* Nietzsche intended readers to be influenced qua corps/e differently, subliminally, esoterically. It is necessary to take account of the tradition in which Nietzsche saw himself working.

Machiavelli confided to a friend words presumably close to Nietzsche's heart: "for a long time I have not said what I believed, nor do I ever believe what I say, and if indeed I do happen to tell the truth I hide it among so many lies that it is hard to find."[99] To which one perhaps ought to respond with Creon (Heideggerians take special note): "You cannot learn of any man the soul, the mind, and the intent until he shows his practice of the government and law."[100] Nietzsche was also a great admirer of the renegade Jesuit thinker Baltasar Gracián—renegade in part because his writing threatened to blow the cover off the

Jesuit order's own way with secrecy—who had instructed: "Mystery by its very arcaneness causes veneration. Even when revealing oneself, avoid total frankness"; and "Write your intentions in cipher. The passions are the gate of the spirit. The most practical sort of knowledge lies in dissimulation"; and simply: "Do, but also seem."[101] Finally, from Machiavelli's contemporary, Castiglione, *Thus Spoke Zarathustra* adapted the technique of the "book of the courtier"—the refinement and fine-tuning of the "taste"—for Nietzsche *the* "virtue" in an ostensibly postmoral world—necessary not only to rule hegemonically, without show of force, but also to nuance and take pleasure in the short span of life allotted to "us," without guilty conscience about the laboring poor.

The tradition of valorizing dissimulation positively, often affirmed by Nietzsche publicly, may seem radically opposed to the supposedly rival tradition of free thought codified by Bacon and his Anglo-Saxon legacy. Alternatively, Nietzsche's critique of "idols," in *Thus Spoke Zarathustra* and *The Twilight of the Idols,* is commonly understood by this same tradition as being isomorphic with Bacon's famous critique of "Idols of the Mind." So where do Nietzsche and this tradition really stand with regard to one another? Actually, it turns out that Bacon's objections to dissimulation were as much pragmatic as they were scientific or moral—not unlike Nietzsche's. "Dissimulation," Bacon argued, "is but a faint kind of policy or wisdom, for it asketh a strong wit and a strong heart to know when to tell the truth, and to do it. Therefore it is the weaker sort of politics [read: politicians] that are the great dissemblers."[102] As interesting, however, is that Bacon, like Nietzsche, recognized the possibilities of subconscious, perlocutionary incorporation of another's thoughts and illocutions, a possibility dear to Nietzsche's heart. Bacon noted, for example: "There is a cunning, which we in England call *The turning of the cat* [cate, cake] *in the pan,* which is, when that which a man says to another, he lays it as if another had said it to him. And to say truth, it is not easy, when such a matter passed between two, to make it appear from which of them it first moved and began."[103] This precisely was also the ambition of Nietzsche and Zarathustra: namely, to make us think *we* are the originators of *their* thoughts.

To repeat the main point for now, however: Nietzsche was among other things *realistic.* Given what he regarded as the depraved temper of the times, its "democratic" and "effeminate" spirit, initial "lower" recruitment was at least as important to him as was "higher" rhetoric and refinement. Besides, in addition to combating the "virus" of Christianity as Nietzsche saw it, he was programming a "virus" and a "disinfectant" against "counterviruses" that continue to replicate themselves semiotextually, expanding throughout the "democratic" and "effeminate" matrix, always adjusting themselves to new circumstances. Quality, not mere size, was the only thing of real consequence to Nietzsche. (Try to forget Wagner's witticisms about Nietzsche's tiny penis.)

It is important to emphasize the mostly preliminary, proleptic nature of the recruiting missions undertaken by the books Nietzsche actually published. His second magnum opus after *Thus Spoke Zarathustra* was unfinished and untitled when he collapsed in Turin. But most readers who are drawn even only a small way into his illocutionary world soon want desperately to take the "subject-position" of the frequent pronoun shifters "we" and "I" inhabiting his pages and to join Nietzsche or his narrators in heaping scorn on all third-person Others who attempt to restrain this "we" and "I" from free flight over the abyss, to clip "our" wings. What Nietzsche sometimes does suggest, in *Beyond Good and Evil* and other later expository writings, is that his texts themselves *are* this recruiting or interpolating process. *Thus Spoke Zarathustra* hardly conceals this fact either: for example, Zarathustra alludes to himself as a post-Christian "fisherman of men." But Nietzsche makes this suggestion in ways that never make fully transparent either its deepest illocutionary mechanism — which remains invisible — *or* its most horrific intent — which remains in/visible — even though he theoretically *could* expose both more openly, as his unpublished notebooks and even letters make sufficiently clear. What better way to get the sweaty, unwashed masses — at least the literate among them and us — to think that they/we, too, are among "those in the know"? In Nietzsche's ideal world they/we would never be allowed to read in the first place, and he really *means* it when he rails against making literacy available to the multitude. At the same time, however, he is usually realistic enough to know that the world is hardly ideal. Hence the requirement to write according to logographic necessity. After all, Nietzscheanism has also had to make its way, like Horatio Alger and Karl Rossmann or Josef K, in two-class First World cultures such as the U.S.A., which have a "top" that can read, and sometimes reads well, and a "bottom" that does not, cannot, and is not *supposed* to read beyond being functionally illiterate. Sometimes there certainly are better ways to recruit than to insult, and Nietzsche tried out many such ways in our Dickensian-Kafkaesque world. But insulting works well enough in the right dosage and circumstance, given the sadomasochistic, abject, and paranoid logic of post/modernity. As Jane Siberry and k. d. lang suggest, people are often not willing to crack codes precisely because they are unwilling to give up the pain and suffering that they think will only be worse when the code is gone. Though Nietzsche says often enough, even in public, that he is not writing with the best interests of everybody in mind, nonetheless only the few take him at his word.

Generally speaking, the best technique of recruitment — and whether it happens to work empirically in aphorism 30 on all readers equally well, or in the same way, is beside the theoretical point — is to open up the reader's synapses with an argument or image that is interesting (Latin *inter-esse:* "between being") and then zap in the esoteric message while the conscious ego defenses are momentarily relaxed in Videodrome. In Nietzsche/anism, *there is no one illocutionary technique or perlocutionary effect.* As all master tricksters, merry pranksters, and wily coyotes know, you can fool some of the people some of the time, but not all of the people all of the time; and sometimes one ends up fooling oneself, duping oneself.

Obviously, "even" Nietzsche could not control or handicap every effect he desired. And there is nothing wrong in assuming that Nietzsche often miscalculated, outfoxed himself. The problem is that there is little way of knowing for sure unless he himself tells us. And this hedgehog-fox rarely does, knowing many tricks and one great trick. But surely Nietzsche was sane, smart, and calculating enough to know that he might miscalculate. This is one way to read, between the lines, the outpouring of new prefaces that he added in 1886 to his previous works, after he had completed *Thus Spoke Zarathustra* and had recalled the fourth, final section from public circulation. Clearly, in it he had exposed too much of *something*.

Just as he implies to von Meysenbug and his sister, Nietzsche does have *one and only one truly basic, remarkably rigid and nonnegotiable center and intent*. It is to re/produce a viable form of willing human slavery appropriate to post/modern conditions, and with it a small number of (male) geniuses equal only among themselves. Such pragmatism might seem to involve hypocrisy on Nietzsche's part, although it need not. After all, in his universe hypocrisy cannot exist if there are no truths, moralities, or wills in reaction to which hypocrisy could ever originate or be compared. But this does not mean that Nietzsche does not believe in at least *one* esoterically concealed truth, morality, and Will. In this sense, too, Nietzsche might be seen as a "Spinozist monist."

The first allusion to Spinoza in Nietzsche's published writing remains the most important. It is a quotation in untranslated Latin; Nietzsche does not attribute it to Spinoza, and he conceals the fact that he has found it ready-made in Schopenhauer's *Parerga und Paralipomena* (1851), where its source is revealed and analyzed in detail as a key to the articulation of law and politics.[104] Thus highly mediated though it is, the allusion bears directly on Nietzsche's way of articulating questions of legality, politics, and epistemology. The reference occurs in volume 1 of *Human, All-Too-Human* (1878) at the end of an aphorism entitled "Rights of the Weaker." Nietzsche argues, via the example of the relation between master (*Herr*) and slave (*Sclave*), that rights or laws (*Rechte*) exist only pragmatically, which is to say as functions of power and at the discretion of the master. But they also exist by virtue of a weak degree of countercondition provided by the slave, who can *kill himself* if the master's conditions of rule become too severe, depriving the master of his mode of production. Obviously, the slave might also *rebel,* individually or collectively, but this is not said. As Nietzsche puts it, rights between master and slave obtain "precisely to the degree that the ownership of the slave is useful and significant to his master." Nietzsche then draws his general conclusion: "*Rights [Das Recht]* originally extend *so far* as one man *appears* to the other as valuable, essential, inalienable, invincible, and the like. In this regard, even the weaker still has rights, but lesser ones. Thence the famous unusquisque tantum juris habet, quantum potentia valet (or more precisely: quantum potentia valere creditur)."[105] Because Nietzsche did not find the two "famous" theses in Spinoza directly but in Schopenhauer, it is beside the point to turn discussion to their original context: that is, Spinoza's analyses of "the good which every man, who follows after virtue, desires for himself" in *The Ethics* and of natural right in *A Political Treatise.*[106] But *Nietzsche's* basic point is clear enough. It is less precise to say "unusquisque tantum juris *habet,* quantum potentia *valet* [each man *has* as much right (over nature) as he *has* power]" than it is to say "quantum potentia valere *creditur* [as he is *believed* to have power]." *In theory,* this precision could cut two ways: against the master or against the slave. Though "slaves" today and in Nietzsche's time generally don't know Latin. For, whenever hegemonic belief is sufficiently shaken, slaves can revolt and/or masters can lose the nerve and will to rule. *In practice,* however, it is understood from the context of Nietzsche's discussion that what he wants to leave intact and unchallenged is *some* version of the master/slave relation and mode of production. This unquestioned persistence is the common — sometimes visible, sometimes invisible — thread throughout Nietzsche's writing and thinking. Nietzsche further took from Schopenhauer the view that this complex of un/concealment is "Machiavellian" in potentially lethal ways, but with the virtue at least of logical consistency.[107]

Saul Bellow's Moses Herzog is almost on to something when he says, thinking explicitly of "Herr Nietzsche," "Any philosopher who wants to keep his contact with mankind should pervert his own system in advance to see how it will really look a few decades after adoption."[108] This seems to be intended as a rebuke to Nietzsche: for losing contact with mankind; for maintaining his elitist ideological purity by refusing to pervert his system; and, concomitantly, for neglecting to reflect on his future reception. There are only three problems with Herzog-Bellow's argument: Herr Nietzsche never lost contact with all of mankind, only with most of it; he intentionally programmed a certain perversion into his system, to keep it maximally dynamic and influential and as immune as possible to interferences; and for these and other reasons he reflected profoundly and obsessively on his posthumous reception, not only a few decades down the road but arching out proleptically over millennia.

The Nietzschean with most insight into Nietzsche's esoteric semiotics is arguably Leo Strauss. In any case, he goes to enormously sophisticated lengths to show that, in the published book *Beyond Good and Evil,* "the doctrine of the will to power cannot claim to reveal what is, the fact, the most fundamental fact[,] but is 'only' one interpretation, presumably the best interpretation among many."[109] Strauss studiously neglected to say at least two things: First, even a very superficial glance at Nietzsche's unpublished notebooks reveals that he himself *began* with the assumption that such doctrines as the Will to Power are not ontologically derived or motivated; and, second, the real reason for this prior assumption, amid all this apparently nihilistic or relativistic "madness," is not some purely intransitive or hermeneutic act, as Strauss appears to suggest in the passage just cited. But nor was Nietzsche's "failure," as Strauss argues explicitly elsewhere in his argument, some covert defense of God or a quasi-Pascalian *homo religiosus* (p. 176). Rather, what was at stake for Nietzsche all along was something more eminently practical. Strauss also claims explicitly—but then passes over with an aura of mystery appropriate both for him and for Nietzsche—that the truly Nietzschean goal was only the *preparation* of "free minds." These are men who "are free of the philosophy of the past but they are not yet philosophers of the future; they are the heralds and precursors of the philosophy of the future" (pp. 175–176). Thus did Strauss himself avoid talking more directly about the precise socioeconomic formation upon which such men—for they *are* males—were, are, and will be free to think, as freethinkers, in more or less democratic, more or less fascist, more or less Stalinist ages that are always hostile to the most radical forms of freethinking (read: intractably *elitist* freethinking).

Exoterically speaking in this mind-set, both the freethinker who supports slavery and the freethinker who attacks it are equally ungrounded in any ultimate or ontological truth; but, esoterically speaking, precisely the fact that there is no grounding means that a Nietzsche is given carte blanche to promote *any* social formation, up to and including the maximum absence of freedom, such as open slavery, though that promotion is rarely required or possible and most often counterproductive.

Strauss's own—ancient and modern *liberal*—reticence to talk either philosophically or more directly about the socioeconomic problematic is consonant with other patented subtexts: his denial that he was a philosopher himself; his affirmation that Nietzsche was among the last philosophers, if not simply the last; and his thesis that *modern* as opposed to *pre*modern political philosophy is no longer produced by more or less secretive gentlemen for members of present society but only by more or less secretive specialists for the future. If *post*modernity has lost a sense of the future in its fascination with the way the present plays and replays the past, and if postmodernism nevertheless remains committed to a democratizing project of some kind, then Nietzsche is doubly no friend of the postmodern and postcontemporary.[110] In other respects, reasonably enough, Nietzsche was prepared to take it or leave it, depending on current exigencies. According to another argument by Strauss, in his programmatic essay "What Is Political Philosophy" (1945–1955), properly modern political philosophers — "from Machiavelli to Nietzsche" — are attempting what "no earlier philosopher" had ever considered doing: namely, "guaranteeing the posthumous success of his teaching by developing a specific strategy and tactics for this purpose."[111] Uncannily enough, Strauss is absolutely right, for this is exactly what Nietzsche — an admirer of Machiavelli in *Beyond Good and Evil* and elsewhere for "stylistic" reasons, among others — attempted to do: namely, "guarantee his posthumous success." But, for Strauss, the result of Nietzsche's attempted preemptive strike was that modern men have been brought to their point of maximum politico-philosophical crisis, to their abject inability to face their own political responsibility. Turning to face Nietzsche directly, Strauss writes: "He used much of his unsurpassable and inexhaustible power of passionate and fascinating speech for making his readers loathe, not only socialism and communism, but conservatism, nationalism and democracy as well. After having taken upon himself this great political responsibility, he could not show his readers a way toward political responsibility. He left them no choice except that between irresponsible indifference to politics and irresponsible political options. He thus prepared a regime which, as long as it lasted, made discredited democracy look again like the golden age."[112] But a golden age is precisely what democracy is not, for Strauss or for any (other) Nietzschean. Liberal democracy can be variously defined: for example, as Winston Churchill's "the worst form of government, except for any other," or, as Nietzsche and Strauss might hope, "the fascoid-liberal with a human face." In any event it requires the will and resolve necessary to preserve what is "best" and "most civilized" about intellectual elitism, social hierarchy, and the economic division of labor. Which includes the supposedly irreducible, even salutary opposition between the "Noble" and the "Base" but does so, somehow, without allowing it to turn explicitly fascist or national socialist — *not necessarily* Fascist or National Socialist — as it has in the recent past. In *Thoughts on Machiavelli* (1953–1958), Strauss tells his readers: "The United States of America may be said to be the only country in the world which was founded in explicit opposition to Machiavellian principles," and is now "the bulwark of freedom."[113] Capitalism is not mentioned—a symptomatic silence. But Strauss also wants to steel these same readers to something else. He tells them that not only Tom Paine but Machiavelli would insist that, like ancient Rome, the United States of America, too, was instaurated by an act of murder: that is, "the fate of the Red Indians" (p. 14). Read between the lines, then, the *real* thesis of *Thoughts on Machiavelli* is not its exoterically stated one that "Machiavelli was a teacher of evil" (p. 9). Rather, it is the esoterically stated thesis that *Machiavelli is evil because he exposed to those out of the know what should remain only for those in the know.* It should go without saying that Strauss *shares* Nietzsche's fascoid-liberal criticism of "not only socialism and communism, but conservatism, nationalism and democracy as well." So Strauss's praise of Nietzsche's language must be ironic, exoteric. On pragmatic grounds, this language has sometimes turned out to be, and can remain, counterproductive in achieving the order of rank both men cherish. And certainly Nietzsche, like the Machiavelli he admired, should never have come as dangerously close as he did to exposing esotericism to view—even though most "socialists and communists" have seemed cheerfully oblivious to this fact, the wool firmly over the eyes of these would-be wolves in sheep's clothing.

Certainly many "leftist" intellectuals today—including "postmoderns"—*do* seem to "loathe, not only socialism and communism, but conservatism, nationalism and democracy as well." In this negative, prophylactic way, at least, Nietzsche's rhetoric has turned out to be remarkably effective. The "hearts and the minds" of many of "the best and the brightest" have in fact been diverted from other possible lines of thought and march. But Nietzsche, as a yea-sayer, not just a nay-sayer, had much grander ambitions than this. "Loathing," recalling Strauss's word, and "hatred," recalling Spinoza's, are relatively Noble virtues for Nietzsche, and they certainly beat calling something "evil," which is the term of "slave morality." But loathing per se is often counterproductive and unrealistic for producing the desired social effects. Nietzsche did loathe many socialists and communists, such as they were—and *not* always for the wrong reasons. But loathing is not always the best way to hold them in perpetual check; or—better yet—to get them to blunder and take themselves out of the game or resign; or—best of all—to recruit the most intelligent and active for one's own side. As a professed fan of Spinoza—and as a proto-Freudian—Nietzsche might have known that hatred and love are locked in a most mysterious embrace, and that, in the words of *The Ethics,* "If we conceive that anyone loves, desires, or hates anything which we ourselves love, desire, or hate, we shall thereupon regard the thing in question with more steadfast love, &c. On the contrary, if we think that anyone shrinks from something that we love, we shall undergo vacillation of soul."[114] Today we inhabit a world, an age of *particularly* vacillating souls; and for this situation Nietzsche, whom so many of us admire or at least read and reread, was not without responsibility. But nor, still in his terms and esoterically, was Nietzsche *irresponsible* — merely *dangerous* for many. As for being *accountable* exoterically and in our terms — that is yet another matter.

"We" — some of us — thus must probe deeper in Nietzsche's own view of the illocutionary strategy and tactics — his "unsurpassable and inexhaustible power of passionate and fascinating speech" — that are to be deployed and employed in his project of proleptic cultural, social, and personal transformation. To some extent this proleptic probe must remain theoretical and abstract, irrespective of what the empirical effects might be on specific readers, dead or living. For it is difficult — if not impossible — to say exactly what this effect is, by Nietzsche's design and by the very nature of the game being played and the war being waged. Especially in the notebooks used to plot *Thus Spoke Zarathustra* and *Beyond Good and Evil,* Nietzsche developed his own peculiar version of Channel 4's "dialectic," beyond any traditional dialectic in its form and intent.

One page in his notebooks may be as close to an explicit exposure of the "dialectic" of Nietzsche/anism as one can come and shows why the common attempt to present Nietzsche as a radically un- or antidialectical thinker is so misguided.[115] In this important matter, Deleuze has long been part of the problem rather than its solution.[116] Under one of his many headings entitled "Will to Power" — after having just completed *Thus Spoke Zarathustra* and before beginning to publish "retroactively" the *exoteric* philosophy behind it — Nietzsche outlines the following three-step argument: First ("thesis"), he notes the necessity for the existence of "a great man, who feels justified in sacrificing people like a field commander sacrifices people, not in the service of an 'idea' but because he wants to rule" (*KGW* 8/1:37). This is presumably a matter of *relatively* esoteric wisdom; at least it never made it into *Beyond Good and Evil* with quite this brutality. Second ("antithesis"), he notes that today, with technological advances and with the modern socio-economic division of labor—if and when it is properly maintained—"ever less physical strength is required: by being clever one can let other people work, man is becoming *more powerful* and *more intellectual*" (*KGW* 8/1:37). Finally ("synthesis"), this "captain without an army who had to recruit only by means of books," as Strauss would say, drew from this opposition—that is, between the *rulers* and the *workers* required to support them—a specific lesson about how to speak and to write books that are theoretically open to all who can read. From his assumptions about military and economic reality, Nietzsche came to the consequences for illocutionary tactics and strategies, and continued: "This is the reason why today it is necessary, at times, to speak crudely and to act crudely [grob]. Something fine and covert is no longer understood, not even by those who are related to us. That which one does not *speak about loudly*, even scream, *simply does not exist:* pain, renunciation, burden, resolute duty and the great overcoming—No one sees or smells anything of them . . . " (*KGW* 8/1:37). What Is to Be Done? No doubt about it: "The time is right for a palace revolution / But where I live the game to play is compromise solution / Well, what can a poor boy do? / 'Cept to sing for a rock and roll band. . . . "[117] Unlike Mick Jagger and Keith Richards, Nietzsche wasn't a rocker, really, let alone a cyberpunk rocker. Poor Nietzsche's world would remain one of compromise solution for a long time, perhaps forever. A classical philologist, deep thinker, fascoid-liberal revolutionary, and brilliant rhetorician, the "band" and "street" for this fighting man was pen, paper, typewriter, printing press, written and silently read books. His musical taste, informed initially by the European romantics, then by Wagner and the latter's great rival Brahms, ended up on the side of Georges Bizet's *Carmen* (1875)—which does qualify as protopunk.[118] But this merely historical or existential accident, having much to do with available job opportunities, certainly did not prevent Nietzsche, who was jobless but no slacker, from preparing a "language" or "music" that might occupy both popular culture and the cybermatrix, someday. He developed not only a "musical semiotic" but a "musical politics"—one far more politically specific and rhetorically canny than is currently known.[119] What Nietzsche could and did do was write books like *Beyond Good and Evil*, his first post-preface to his great popular hit-to-be, *Thus Spoke Zarathustra*.

However the public face of *Beyond Good and Evil* might appear to anyone, the esoteric intent was crystal clear in Nietzsche's mind, in the mind of this prototypical "good European." He wrote in 1885 to himself:

> *These Good Europeans* that we are: What distinguishes us from the Men of the Fatherland? First, we are atheists and immoralists, but for the time being [*zunächst*] we support the religions and morals of the herd instinct: for these prepare a type of human that must one day fall into our hands, that must *desire* our hands. Beyond Good and Evil, but we demand the unconditional maintenance of the herd morality. We hold in reserve many types of philosophy that need to be taught: Under some conditions the pessimistic type, as hammer; a European Buddhism might perhaps be indispensable. We probably support the development and maturing of democratic institutions: They enhance weakness of the will: We see in "Socialism" a goad that in the face of comfort——Position toward nations or peoples [Völkern]. Our preferences; we pay attention to the results of interbreeding. . . . By possessing a *disciplina voluntatis*, we are in advance of our fellow men. All strength applied to *the development of will power*, an art that allows us to wear masks, an art of understanding *beyond* affects (also to think a "supra-European" manner on occasion).[120]

That Nietzsche wears illocutionary masks is hardly at issue. What is at issue is the kinds of masks he adapts as the occasion demands, the fact that he intended these masks to look like one thing and yet have another effect entirely, and the more or less unconscious effect — "beyond affect" — of his masks on "readers."

It is unfortunate in this regard that Oswald Spengler's tip has not been followed up. Nietzsche, wrote the author of *The Decline of the West* in 1924, "lived, felt, and thought with his ear. After all, he was hardly able to use his eyes. His prose is heard, nearly sung, not 'written.' The vowels and cadences are more important than the metaphors."[121] And this "ear" of Nietzsche will reappear with Derrida. For Nietzsche's early mentor Schopenhauer, and in his train Wagner, music is no mere representation or expression of human consciousness but nothing less than a "*copy of the will itself [Abbild des Willens selbst]*," and hence the ultimate simulacrum of the world in its full complexity.[122] Said more precisely than Spengler, music also has a proleptic semiotic, social, economic, and political function. In the words of Jacques Attali's *Noise: The Political Economy of Music* (1977): "Music is prophecy. Its styles and economic organization are ahead of the rest of society because it explores, much faster than material reality can, the entire range of possibilities in a given code. It makes audible the new world that will gradually become visible, that will impose itself and regulate the order of things; it is not only the image of things, but the transcending of the everyday, the herald of the future."[123]

Reading Nietzsche's resulting "musical" works, his esoteric semiotics, take the advice of professional musicians. For example, Lou Reed: "Don't believe half of what you see and none of what you hear."[124] Or, better yet, U2: "Don't believe what you hear, / Don't believe what you see, / If you just close your eyes, / You can feel the enemy. . . . What are we going to do now it's all been said? / No new ideas in the house, / And every book has been read."[125] And these days Nietzsche is in effect the *only* book many people read and think they need, figuratively or even literally. Make no mistake: his esoteric as well as exoteric influence is still growing; its aspirations are for international domination. For Nietzsche has perfected what Jean-Jacques Rousseau described as "the first language": "Instead of arguments, it would have aphorisms. It would persuade without convincing, and would represent without reasoning. It would resemble Chinese in certain respects, Greek and Arabic in others."[126]

So it is that in Nietzsche the reader is circling around and around in what some might regard as a properly hermeneutic circle: from published to unpublished thoughts and, more authentically, from Nietzsche's texts to their interpretation, from Nietzsche to us, and back again. But this constant circling through the matrix of Bataille-&-Nietzsche-owned-and-operated Channel 3 is not *quite* the only possibility open. A merely hermeneutic, interpretive response is certainly not the main effect that Nietzsche's peculiar view of causality either was intended to have or is actually having on people. This effect—its structure and structuring efficacy—may not be knowable entirely, and Nietzsche thought or hoped that it could not be. He might have been positively *encouraged* in this hope by Althusser's notion that "the structure is immanent in its effects, a cause immanent in its effects in the Spinozist sense of the term, [and] that *the whole existence of the struc-*

ture consists of its effects, in short that the structure, which is merely a specific combination of its peculiar elements, is nothing outside its effects."[127] But at least, in Nietzsche's case, the intent behind this structure, which he was consciously suppressing from exoteric view and which so many Nietzscheans are unwilling or unable to ferret out or track down—this informing cause *might* or even *can* be known. In Nietzsche's own words, it will entail something "horrific" and "terrible" for most people.

With the possibility of grasping the informing cause of Nietzsche's corps/e in mind, recall Negri's warning question about what happens when *"natura naturata* [mode and effect] wins a total hegemony over *natura naturans* [substance and cause]": "What could be the work of the devil if not this?"[128] Metaphors of demonization aside, it seems that, to get at this question and this properly Nietzschean intention through Nietzsche himself, we need to get beyond him. To *get* after him, we have to *go* after him. Maybe we will remain trapped, after all, in a dialectical spiral or hermeneutic circle—one that always leads nowhere fast but with the illusion of getting far at least slowly. In other words, pretty much like cyberfiction and cyberspace. But if this is so, then maybe we can track Nietzsche down here, and fight it out with him on technocultural turf we *may* know better than he. What, then, are the best critical and philosophical tools at our disposal beyond interpretation? Where can we look for philosophical and critical help? — One would hope to a leading philosopher of our own age.

After Derrida

Jacques Derrida's intensive reading of Nietzsche and attack on "interpretation" is a good index of which Channels are currently available in both "Theory" and Nietzsche/anism. As important in this regard as Derrida's well-known monograph on Nietzsche, *Spurs: Nietzsche's Styles* (1972; 1978),[129] is his lesser-known *Otobiographies: The Teaching of Nietzsche and the Politics of the Proper Name* (1976; 1982).[130] For the latter text attempts to engage Nietzsche's political thinking and legacy explicitly. Both texts exemplify Derrida's painstaking care with linguistic nuance, and both share certain conceptual, methodological, and ideological problems that grant less radical access to Nietzsche than is supposed by Derrida or his own readers, some of whom come to a critical, philosophically informed reading of Nietzsche only through Derridian mediation. Because these problems are rather more evident in *Spurs*, it is necessary to begin with it before turning to *Otobiographies*. And it is *Spurs*—in/famous because it broaches "the question of woman"—that has defined much of what is taken to be not merely the Derridian position with regard to Nietzsche but the entire poststructuralist methodology *grosso modo*.

Five basic problems with *Spurs* need to be registered. First, the likelihood that Nietzsche was bisexual or gay complicates, even obviates, Derrida's a priori insertion of "Nietzsche"—or rather, in Derrida's terms, the articulations of "woman" with "style" (stylus, spur, spoor, phallus, trace, *différance*) and with "veiling," and then of "veiling" with "sailing" (based on an exploitation of the French homonym *le/la voile*)—into an exclusively heterosexual problematic.

Second, as several critics have pointed out, Derrida operates with some embarrassingly a priori assumptions about what the category of "woman" means and what living women "are"—both generally and in Nietzsche.[131]

Third, philologically and philosophically embarrassing for Derrida's argument/performance in *Spurs* is that his articulation of "woman" and "veiling" misses the point that the philologist Nietzsche was *already* consciously playing with a fairly well-known—albeit problematic— "etymology" of the derogatory German word for women: *Weib*. Standard dictionaries trace this term via the Brothers Grimm to the Germanic/Indo-European root and English cognate **wibal*ueip:* "veil" and "veiled bride," "to conceal" and "to hide"—and otherwise "to make esoteric." In other words, something "in 'woman'" was being intentionally hidden from view by Nietzsche that Derrida, for all his otherwise extraordinary linguistic acumen, seems unable to grasp.

Fourth, there is the notorious case of the missing umbrella, which Derrida brandishes in *Spurs* to bully off the field the claim of any mere "interpretation" to have located a "single meaning" in the Nietzschean "text"—a text that is imagined instead to be the exemplary instance of always already deferred difference, or *différance*. But Nietzsche's "umbrella" has a much simpler plausible explanation—as *causa materialis, formalis,* and *finalis,* even perhaps as *causa efficiens.* Occam's razor— combined with a simple vacation anecdote—turns out to provide a somewhat sharper instrument than poststructuralism to pry open Nietzsche's referent and intention in writing in quotation marks: "'I have forgotten my umbrella.'" This was written sometime in 1881, in a notebook used while on walks high in the mountains near Sils Maria, the "birthplace" of Zarathustra, of the thought of Eternal Recurrence of the Same, and of much else besides. Old Theodor Adorno and Herbert Marcuse, on a sort of pilgrimage to Sils in 1966, met there a much older man, a Herr Zuan, who vividly recounted that he and other village children used surreptitiously to fill Nietzsche's loosely furled umbrella, needed to shield his hypersensitive eyes from the blinding Alpine sun, with small rocks when he walked past—taking great delight when the philosopher opened the umbrella and the stones pelted down on his unprotected head. Nietzsche then would storm after the kids, transforming the now useless tool into an effective weapon.[132] Of course, *no* anecdote could ever *fully* explain the existence of this snippet of text in Nietzsche's notebook, and the existence of the quotation marks in which it is embedded still retain at least some of their mystery—indeed this is one of Derrida's points. Nevertheless, this mystery arguably has little or nothing to do with textual multivalency or indeterminacy, or at least not only this. Barthes once remarked that explicit quotation, every use of quotation marks, "destroys multivalence," specifically multivalence grasped as "a transgression of ownership."[133] Yet ownership—of his "one intent"—is presumably just what Nietzsche preferred to conceal within his discourse—its structural causality—for its maximum perlocutionary force.

A poststructuralist—perhaps Derrida himself—might wish to play around further with the French word for "quotation marks": *guillemets.* It derives from "Guillaume," "William," or "Wilhelm"—as in the normally suppressed middle term in the proper name "Friedrich Wilhelm Nietzsche." Nietzsche was named after the patron of his father, the monarch Friedrich Wilhelm of Prussia (1795–1861; king of Prussia, 1840–1861), who died insane in office. Nietzsche himself abandoned his middle name early in life—leaving it bracketed, under erasure—in part because of the unpleasant memories of the king's fate, dating from when Nietzsche was in boarding school. After his own breakdown during the first days of 1889, Nietzsche *restored* his middle name, once again signing off epistles: Friedrich Wilhelm Nietzsche.[134] "Wilhelm" derives from Teutonic roots: *wil-helm,* meaning "will helmet," "resolute helmet," "helmet of resolve." "Helmet of the Will to Power," so to speak. Which is also to say: exoterically concealed and protected esoteric Will. So it is as if Nietzsche's insane, ineffectual military and aristocratic namesake had to be suppressed within his own "proper name," only in order to resurface as "scare quotes" prophylactically helmeting—fascistically armoring—even the most innocuous and fragmentary of his remarks, allowing the exoteric to guard the esoteric militant resolve behind each and every one of them. And so on. . . . The point here, however, is that if one is going to play with Nietzsche's words, to fuck with him, then why not go all the way? In some cultures—notably trickster cultures and Nietzsche's culture—proper names are *consciously* withheld for strategic reasons. In such cultures "A proper name (or constellation of names) evokes a connection to community, place (in time and space), and universe—all of which create and narrate a vital sense of self that struggles against indeterminacy"[135]—in Nietzsche's case with the intent to preserve the afterlife of his corpse as combat corps. For Derrida, by contrast, the "name" or "politics of signature" transcribed as "Nietzsche" marks the irreducibly indeterminate *différance* between on the one hand what Heidegger posited as "the unity and uniqueness of Nietzsche's thinking, which, as a fulfilled unity, is itself in a fair way to being the culmination of occidental metaphysics," and on the other the possibility that "Nietzsche is not at all a thinker of beings" but rather the thinker of an entirely new and other, nonbinary and nonmetaphysical relationship to life and death, or, more precisely, "life-death."[136] For Derrida this relationship must remain nameless; it must be named as corps/e.

As Derrida acknowledges, the quotation marks around the umbrella snippet may refer to an overheard conversation among bourgeois fellow travelers and sojourners in the hotel restaurant in Sils, though this does not account for why he recorded it. Or perhaps Nietzsche was citing Nietzsche to remind himself not to forget his desperately needed umbrella. Perhaps something else entirely is going on here—something to do, say, with psychosexual vulnerability, which Derrida would also not necessarily deny. But the more important thesis with regard to Derrida's argument/performance is twofold: first, that "Nietzsche's 'umbrella'" may have a simpler *and* more intentional referent than poststructuralism can theorize or interpret; and, second, that Derrida's influential claim that Nietzsche's written work "in its entirety" cannot be reduced to a single interpretation or intention turns out to be more complex and problematic than even Derrida assumes. More political than "the politics of signature."

Fifth and finally, *Spurs* does not undertake to attack, except coyly, the political dimensions of Nietzsche's "text" — the snippet about the umbrella but also more generally. Nor do most subsequent responses to Derrida. For Derrida's most sustained attempt to get after Nietzsche/anism politically, one must turn to *Otobiographies: The Teaching of Nietzsche and the Politics of the Proper Name*, also known as *The Ear of the Other*.[137]

Within the field of contemporary "leftist" theory, the most coherent, rigorous, self-critical, and influential analysis/performance of continental, post-Nietzschean and post-Heideggerian philosophy remains the Derridian strain of poststructuralism, though its uncompromising rigor makes it more "popular," or at least talked about, than actually practiced. Yet even it fails to take adequate account of the esoteric dimension either of intellectual history generally or of Nietzscheanism in specific.

Derrida *does* recognize the existence of the esoteric tradition in philosophical writing, though not so much in a *political* or *illocutionary* sense.[138] He *does* sometimes point to a kind of "secret" in philosophical writing that he quite properly refuses to reduce to any simply form/content distinction. Thus, in a characteristically scintillating argument pitting Heidegger against Meyer Schapiro on the problem of "truth in art," Derrida says that he is not interested in any mere "correspondence," in most senses of the word, between these two thinkers or the traditions of thought represented by each. But, Derrida adds: "— I would be interested nevertheless in a secret correspondence, obviously: obviously secret, crypted in the ether of evidence and of truth, too evident because the cipher in this case remains secret precisely because it is not concealed."[139] This is a most fruitful and only apparently paradoxical suggestion. Derrida intimates the existence, somewhere, of a potentially verifiable code — one that is imagined to be invisible precisely *because* it is *so* manifest, evident, and obvious. This intimation points to the existence of Channel 4, yet it has *not* been sufficiently developed by Derrida as a way of grasping either philosophy and art or the political philosophy and illocutionary practice of his own two greatest precursors, Nietzsche and Heidegger. This failure or reluctance is part of Bataille's legacy and due also to Derrida's virtually a priori suspicion of categories of thought related to intentionality and authorship. This he shares with most discourses on the contemporary bourgeois marketplace: from hermeneutics to structuralism, from poststructuralism to new historicism, from deconstruction to post-Marxism and cultural studies. Yet to throw the category of conscious intention out with the bathwater of free play eventually risks prematurely foreclosing the capacity to have intentions of one's own and to have them taken seriously by others — and hence ever to act in purposeful ways collectively. In which case Nietzsche just smiles.

Intentions are of course exceedingly complex things, philosophically speaking. As not only Derrida has shown, in his brilliant critiques of *"vouloir-dire"* structures, but also Donald Davidson has argued, intentions cannot be reduced to rational-deliberative and forensic processes, involving as they do all manner of "[w]ants, desires, principles, prejudices, felt duties, and obligations" as well as judgments[140] — not to say ideologies. But to the extent that intentions also may involve deception and sub-rosa manipulation — as they in fact do in the case of Nietzsche and Nietzscheanism — most merely philosophical notions about intentions — rational-deliberative or otherwise — become exceedingly difficult to grasp and interpret, even to *see* in the first instance or last. At a paradigmatic and precedent-setting moment in early legal debates about the place of intention in law and the interpretation of law, English Star Chamber judges ruled in 1633 that a writer tried for sedition cannot appeal to his intentions or "heart" to excuse the possibility that his writings might be read to have seditious effect. "Itt is said, hee had noe ill intencion, noe ill harte, but hee maye bee ill interpreted. This must not be allowed him in excuse, for he should not have written any thinge that would bear [that] construccion, for hee doth not accompanye his booke, to make his intencion knowne to all that reades it."[141] Put in terms of the corps/e, this means that any writer, including Nietzsche, can be held responsible for sedition by simple virtue of the fact of having written a corpus that exceeds and outlives his or her physical corpse, thereby producing a more or less unwitting, potentially seditious corps that cannot be controlled by the living or physically present writer. What remains unclear to this day, however, is: Seditious in what way? against whom? by what means? to what effect? How might Nietzsche have inscribed the problem of proleptic intention and interpretation into his own writing?

If "the politics" of Nietzsche's "teaching" is to be taken really se-

ESOTERIC SEMIOTICS

riously, as Derrida rightly says it must, then it might appear necessary, at some point, to have to "interpret" his texts, if not his "intentions." But in Nietzsche's case, paradoxically enough, "interpretations" are not so much impossible — exoterically they are eminently possible — as counterproductive — precisely the wrong way to read and respond to the esoteric dimension of what he published. To that extent, Derrida would be right to be suspicious of "interpretation," though he is so in a different context. Nietzsche's "intention" remains a problem, however, until more is known about what it is and how it works — including to produce and program its own "deconstruction."

Nietzsche's preferred term for "interpretation" is *Einverleibung* ("incorporation," "incarnation," or "embodiment"), and strictly speaking one cannot *interpret* something that one already always *totally is*. If one simply assumes — with Hegel, following Kant — that *transcendental self-reflection* dialectically posits *otherness* as *opposed* to identification, and thus both require synthesis of a nonidentificatory kind, then — as Fichte and Schelling fretted[142] — major problems occur when identification is too quickly lost in the dialectical shuffle. But the contemporary version of this problem is that working within this problematic you can't *grasp* Nietzschean Channel 4, only *look at* it. Channel 3 as viewed even through Bataille's eyes has suggested that conventional or unconventional hermeneutic procedures are inadequate to grasp Nietzsche's corps/e, in so far as we are dealing with a type of in-fluenza that always already in-forms the interpreter monistically to such an extent that there is nothing "out there" *or* "in here" *to* interpret, only *be*. Derrida's point of attack on the problem of interpretation as it relates to Nietzsche and Nietzschean "politics" is rather different, more conventional *and* influential.

Otobiographies argues/enacts the antihermeneutic, Channel 2 proposition that "interpretations are not *hermeneutical* or *exegetical readings*, but rather *performative interventions* in the *political rewriting* of the *text* and of its *destination*."[143] Each emphasized concept is significant. This Derridian move is not unprecedented with regard to Nietzsche. Years earlier, at the international conference at Royaumont on Nietzsche in 1964, Michel Foucault argued that "Nietzsche's semiology" and "hermeneutics" were "two ferocious enemies." Since for Foucault, and supposedly Nietzsche, every *interpretandum* is always already *interpretans*, it follows that there is nothing — also no "sign" — just lounging about

"out there" to be interpreted "in here," but rather a more or less elaborate *mise-en-abîme* of prior interpretations of interpretations, and so
forth.[144] This position was also remarkably "Heideggerian," which in
the French context means also "Nietzschean." As early as *Being and
Time* (1927), Heidegger had argued with precision both that there is
nothing "behind," "beneath," or "beyond" existential phenomena and
yet also that these phenomena are never empirically or positivistically
"given." Rather, they have to be elicited by, with, and from fundamental phenomenology. To be sure — though this is a lesser-known aspect
of *Being and Time* — Heidegger also mysteriously notes that while
some "cover ups" are "accidental," some are "necessary":[145] that is,
exo/esoteric.

As salutary as Derrida's or Foucault's "Heideggero-Nietzschean"
position may be as a "semiotic" criticism of much that passes today for
"interpretation" and "hermeneutics," we are really only tuned somewhere in or between old Channels 2 and 3, as owned and operated by
Bataille. Channel 1 — the channel not only of "facts" but of "intentions" — is of distant memory at best. But so, too, is the possibility of
consciously detectable interference *from* it. Derrida is appropriately
wary of what he calls *mal d'archives:* the disease or curse (*le mal*) of
having to use inadequate archives of all kinds — in Derrida's case particularly the psychoanalytic — to uncover evil (*le mal*) and thus the
archives du mal.[146] But he does not apply this principle to Nietzsche. In
short, we are still not tuned to *Nietzsche's* Channel 4. Indeed, compared
to Bataille's attempt to confront the problem of Nietzsche's own "politics" and its imagined misappropriation by the Right, Derrida's newer
program seems oddly out of focus — by turns too complicated and not
complicated enough, even politically and rhetorically naïve.

For the aesthetics, politics, prophecy of Nietzsche's Channel 4, "writing" and "reading," "rewriting" and "rereading," have two sides: an
"interpretive" or "political" face (Channel 2) as well as their "philological" or "exegetical" face (Channel 1). When Derrida defines — or
rather replaces — "interpretations" by saying that they "are not hermeneutical or exegetical readings, but rather performative interventions in
the political rewriting of the text and of its destination," then categories
that Nietzsche held distinct begin to get muddled. Allowing apparently
"free" movement from the one channel to the other, Nietzsche's confidence trick *allows* for the consciousness that what he is saying is at times

uncertain and undecidable, and hence encourages perspectivism, relativism, or pluralism. But what this same movement *disallows* is anything but the subconscious incorporation of *one* basic message that will be politically and socially effective in inverse proportion to what he regards as a "slave's" capacity to perceive it. Channel 3's function in this case is to give off the appearance, the *méconnaissance,* that the two channels can be synthesized, so as to leave them behind. Since, like most Nietzscheans in the tradition of Bataille and Deleuze, Derrida mistrusts Hegelian synthesis, his tendency is to avoid Channel 3 entirely. So he prefers to channel surf: between Channel 1 in the one direction, as exemplified by his remarkably close textual analyses; and Channel 2 on the other, as registered in his salvos against "hermeneutical or exegetical reading," in the sheer pleasure taken in disregarding what Nietzsche intended for the sake of the "text," and in the *apparently* free ability to "rewrite" that "text" into Derrida's own philosophical and political agenda whenever he sees fit.

The "exegetical" dismissed by Derrida, even as he practices exegesis of another kind, is important to keep alive conceptually and to use *against* Nietzsche, because he himself programmed it with such philological — which, in European jargon, means also *scientific* — precision, in his attempt to prefigure and predetermine future incorporations of his social vision.[147] The relations and tensions between any "medium" and its "message" are too complex to be reduced to Derrida's surprisingly *binary* opposition between "performative intervention" or "political rewriting" versus "hermeneutical or exegetical reading." For all its self-reflexivity in *theoretical* matters, Derrida's *methodology* can be surprisingly undertheorized, at least in the case of Nietzsche. As a critique of a *type* of hermeneutics Derrida's binary opposition is unobjectionable; but the poststructuralist *alternative* as exemplified by Derrida's Nietzsche is inadequate. To be sure, Derrida is considerably more philologically "objective" than is de Man, whose readings and translations of Nietzsche can be shrewdly willful. But Derrida's *version* of philological rigor often shades into philosophical wordplays that are projected subjectivistically onto, rather than being elicited objectivistically from, a Nietzschean text that is thus never allowed its *full* — and most *dangerous* — say. As night falls, Derrida stands holding the umbrella over Nietzsche's head, protecting him if not from himself then from others.

Derrida's alternative to the "hermeneutic" Channel 3 is not a new

Channel 4, let alone Nietzsche's. It is more a hypermodern version of a subjectivistic Channel 2 that does assume the existence of an objectivistic Channel 1 but, at its occasional worst, no longer knows how to watch it for more than a minute or so, an advertisement or two. And this is all the distraction that Nietzsche needs to create a corps/e. Derrida's antihermeneutical, antidialectical "option" between "exegesis" and "intervention" runs the unacceptable risk of not knowing what Nietzsche intended to do, and *therefore* of buying into Nietzsche's own way of handling what he calls in *On the Genealogy of Morals* "the origin of a thing and its use." Derrida's methodological approach to Nietzsche betrays a binary simplicity obviously out of synch with Derrida's own laudable *political intentions* in his rewriting of Nietzsche *and* with his profound *philosophical critique* elsewhere in his œuvre of binary oppositions. That Derrida pulls up short of applying this critique to *Nietzsche* reveals that he is a member of the corps/e, a Nietzschoid. So it is, then, that Nietzsche's own intention remains the *skandalon* for poststructuralism and for Left-Nietzsche/anism generally: that is, a *material* as well as *ethical* stumbling block that one keeps tripping over, never cleanly clearing.

Now it should go without saying that the re/construction of any intention is never a *sufficient* critical act in and of itself; but it is *necessary* to make this attempt if accounts are ever going to be settled with Nietzsche's esoterically transmitted and incorporated effects. Symptomatic in this regard is the obsessive recurrence of poststructuralism to the concept of "play" (*Spiel, jeu*) — as if a term often provided *by* Nietzsche for *exoteric* delectation could ever really deconstruct or combat the deepest and most lethal aspects of his writing, including its appropriation by national socialists and fascists. While Derrida is rarely associated with Marcuse, to say the least, these two Nietzschoids are remarkably similar in orientation in their commitment to an ostensibly "Nietzschean" concept of "play."[148]

Yet what rightly worries Derrida in *Otobiographies* much more than hermeneutics when reading Nietzsche is the paradigm of reading or listening based on the logocentric authority of a human *voice* speaking directly, without apparent spatiotemporal mediation, into the *ear* of another person who remains more or less passive. Thus do masters speak to students. What is thus transmitted or "taught" is a "proper name" that can turn out to be decidedly *improper.* This, then, is the problematic of the "teaching of the proper name" and "the ear of the other." According to Derrida, however, such an authoritarian "pedagogic" model is not only—unfortunately—*represented* in some of Nietzsche's early writing but also—especially—*deconstructed* by Nietzsche's later work. This privileging the mature texts over the youthful is not adequately problematized and would be contested by Nietzsche's notion of Eternal Recurrence of the Same. This autodeconstruction is shown most notably, for Derrida, by Zarathustra's synecdochic vision in *Thus Spoke Zarathustra* of *fragmented* humanity as a human ear walking without head or body. This is what Zarathustra calls "the inverse cripple."[149]

This dismembered, fragmented body and body politic, with its modern division of labor, was familiar to Rousseau, Schiller, Hegel, and Hölderlin. But it was Hölderlin's epistolary novel *Hyperion* (1799) that served as Nietzsche's most proximate source. In Hyperion's penultimate letter to his friend Bellarmin (the "good German") he writes: "It is a hard word, and yet I say it anyway, because it is the truth. I can imagine to myself no people that is more fragmented [zerrißner] than the German. You see manual laborers, but no human beings, thinkers, but no human beings—Is it not a battle field [wie ein Schlachtfeld], where hands and arms and all manner of limbs [Glieder] lie dismembered [zerstückelt] and under one another, while the shed blood of life trickles away into the sand?"[150] The German socialist Arnold Ruge read this passage in 1843 and was deeply moved. Lamenting what he perceived to be the continuing, total absence of any sign of revolutionary ferment among the Germans, their dominant mood one of servility and submission to despotism still a half century after Hölderlin, he copied out the text and sent it to his friend Karl Marx. Marx was not entirely impressed, calling it and Ruge's accompanying letter a "fine elegy, a funeral song that sucks the breath away," but adding that for the purposes at hand "there is absolutely nothing political about it."[151] The times were indeed problematic: 1843 was three years after Friedrich Wilhelm IV had ascended the throne of Prussia and a year before his namesake Friedrich Wilhelm Nietzsche would be born. But the communist Marx was intent to find signs of revolution where the socialist Ruge could not. As he had written Ruge just two months earlier, there were many fissures in Friedrich Wilhelm's "comedy of despotism" and "ship of fools."[152] Various stripes of European socialists, democrats, and fascists have been less critically disposed to Hölderlin's famous image of fragmentation, absorbing it as gospel and as irrevocable fact. The same passage made an even more powerful impression on Nietzsche. Like Marx, however, he was more concerned to *do* something about the fragmentation, undertaking to "rewrite it politically," albeit for his own purposes. These purposes Marx would have grasped and combated in a way that leftists under Nietzsche's sway apparently cannot.

Nietzsche incorporated Hyperion's diatribe against modernity at an axial moment near the end of the second part of *Thus Spoke Zarathustra,* in Zarathustra's speech "On Deliverance" ("Von der Erlösung"). This text was to be crucial also to Heidegger as the central exhibit in his deconstruction of "revenge" (*Rache*) in Nietzsche.[153] Derrida mentions neither Hölderlin nor Heidegger in this context; rather, Nietzsche's text allows him to weave his thread through an intricate labyrinth with at least three major parts: (1) the theme and structure of philosophic and linguistic fragmentation; (2) the active-passive duplicity concealed in the pedagogy of listening suggested by the image of the ear, actually one of several severed organs mentioned by Zarathustra; and (3) the question of whether the name of the text's author, "Nietzsche," understood biographically or autobiographically, is responsible for his "teachings" and its often terrific and horrific consequences. But before reading Derrida, if possible, read Nietzsche.

In conversation with the hunchback, one of his most important interlocutors, Zarathustra comes the closest so far in the text to representing the constitutive concept of the entire book, its unrepresentable thought of Eternal Recurrence of the Same. Zarathustra has resisted, in part, because if this doctrine is to have its desired perlocutionary force it has to be incorporated sub rosa at the right time, at the appropriate social conjuncture, in the right persons. Zarathustra first tells the hunchback that on the bridge from man to Superman he has witnessed among other things a peculiar kind of cripple: "an ear the size of a man" on a tiny stalk of body. After describing this singular ear in detail, "On Deliverance" continues:

> When Zarathustra had spoken thus to the hunchback and to them whose mouth-piece and intercessor he was, he turned with deep displeasure to his disciples and said:

"Truly, my friends, I traffic among men as among the fragments and limbs of men!

This is to my sight the most terrible — that I find men shattered and scattered as over a field of battle and of slaughter [Schlacht- und Schlächterfeld].

And when my sight flees from the present to the past, it finds always the same: fragments and limbs and gruesome randomness — but no men!

The present and the past on earth — ah, my friends, that is my greatest burden; and I would not know how to live, were I not a seer of that which must come.

A seer, a willer, a creator, a future itself and a bridge to the future — and ah, at the same time yet a cripple on this bridge: all that is Zarathustra.

And often even you ask yourselves: 'Who is Zarathustra for us? How should he enjoin us?' And, just like me, you gave yourselves questions as an answer.

Is he a Promiser? A Fulfiller? A Conqueror? Or an Inheritor? An Autumn? Or a plowshare? A Doctor? Or a Convalescent?

Is he a Poet? Or an Honest Man? A Liberator? Or an Oppressor? A Good Man? Or an Evil Man?

I traffic among men as the fragments of the future: that future that I see.

And all that is my expression and my aspiration — that I bring together and express what is fragment and riddle and gruesome randomness.

And how would I bear it to be a man if man were not also a poet and a riddle solver and the deliverer of randomness!

To deliver the past and to recreate all 'it was' into a 'so I wanted it to be!' — that would be what I would call deliverance!"[154]

This passage from *Thus Spoke Zarathustra* is cited at length less to highlight the degree of interface with Hölderlin's *Hyperion* than to contextualize Nietzsche's appropriation of it in order to grasp its connection to what Zarathustra means by "deliverance." What Nietzsche does in terms of political ideology is to deflect Hölderlin's "Swabian Jacobin" sentiments toward a cosmopolitan Right, transforming them in the process for posterity. Nietzsche thought a great deal of his own text, reciting from it in *Ecce Homo* in an aura of mystery.[155] Yet at the same time, the passage remains remarkably concrete. Its uncanniness is partly due to Nietzsche's reference to specific limbs of the body — not only the monstrous ear, but also the "mouth-piece": that is, the foregrounding of the medium through which messages, including "On Deliverance," are delivered.

Metonymies tend willy-nilly to convey a certain "realism-" or "reality-effect" in relation to metaphoric uses of language.[156] And metaphors and metonymies, Nietzsche noted in private, are the twin phalanxes of "syntax" (a Greek root of which is "to draw up an army for battle") — his "mobile army of metaphors and metonymies."[157] This was how Nietzsche had secretly defined the warfare of "truth and lie in the extramoral sense." He referred to this key principle, originally minted in 1873, only once in public: over ten years later and then merely in passing as "an essay I have kept secret."[158] Thus he alerted a few readers to the existence of a text about which he would say nothing more to others. The consequences of such illocutionary warfare are potentially exceptionally "cruel" whenever the need arises, as can be seen reading not even between the lines another passage about "ears" later in *Thus Spoke Zarathustra*:

> Oh my brothers, am I cruel? But it is I who says: What falls ought to be given an extra push!
>
> Everything of today that falls, that declines: now, who would want to stop that! But in my case, I *want* to give it an extra push!
>
> Do you know the lust that rolls stones into precipitous depths? These people of today: just look at them, how they roll into my depths!
>
> A prelude am I of better players, Oh my brothers! A precedent! *Act* on my precedent!
>
> And whom you do not teach to fly, teach him for me — *to fall faster!*
>
> I love the brave: but it is not enough to be a broadsword — one has to know *whom* to see and hit!
>
> And often there is more bravery when a man holds himself back and passes by: *so* that he can save himself for a more worthy enemy.
>
> I ought to have only enemies that can be hated, but none that are despised: Thou shalt be proud of thine enemy. Thus taught I, already Once before.
>
> The more worthy enemy, Oh my brothers, you should save for yourselves: that is why you have to pass much by —
>
> — especially past the rabble that shouts in your ear about the people and nations [Volk und Völkern].
>
> Keep your eye pure from their Pro and Con! There is much justice and injustice: he who sees it becomes angry.
>
> Looking down and striking hard — that becomes one and the same thing: so go away into the forests and let your sword rest!

Go *your* ways! And let the people and peoples go theirs! — Dark ways, verily, and not even illuminated by the summer lightning flash of a single hope!

. . . Oh blessed distant time when a people said: "I want to be *master* over peoples!"

For, my brothers: the best shall rule, the best also *wants* to rule! And wherever the teaching is otherwise, there the best is absent![159]

Thus would Nietzsche-Zarathustra have *us* "pass by" less the current "rabble that shouts in your ear about the people and nations" — that is, nationalists of all kinds: including national socialists *and* "socialists in one country" — than a "worthier enemy" of the future: a properly *communist* enemy who — under Nietzsche's "prophetic" influence — has yet to materialize. Nietzsche's intent was to have Hyperion's disembodied, disincorporated image reincorporated and reembodied by a body politic in which fragmentation, in the form of division of labor and of ruler and ruled, would be reinscribed beneath the level of conscious ability to do anything about it. As Nietzsche-Zarathustra says in the same speech: "*Wer Ohren hat, der höre!* [Let him who has ears hear!]"[160] At such Scriptural moments, Right-Nietzscheans prick up their ears, and the Nietzschoid corps/e is stone deaf.

It should go without saying that Derrida *intends* his deconstruction of the Nietzschean "ear" as committed antifascism. And *Otobiographies* is based to a remarkable extent on the question of what Nietzsche himself would think about national socialism, or at least on what the "proper name 'Nietzsche'" qua "text" would think as rewritten by Derrida. For Derrida this "proper name" and its "authorizing signature" would never have underwritten fully developed national socialism, indeed would have attempted to deconstruct and combat it. Derrida is undoubtedly right about Nietzsche's response to actually existing German Nazis; but Italian Fascisti would be more difficult nuts to crack with Derrida's method. Nonetheless, as Derrida also rightly acknowledges, things are not entirely so straightforward or politically correct in Nietzsche's textual politics.

Derrida shows that in several of Nietzsche's early texts, but in particular his attacks on the German education system in the Basel lecture series "On the Future of Our Institutions of Higher Learning" (1872),

Nietzsche was playing with fire — taking enormous risks with the future by insisting on the need for strong leaders, *Führer*. But, for Derrida, Nietzsche rectified or problematized his earlier positions in later books, most notably *Thus Spoke Zarathustra* and *Ecce Homo*. The "umbrella" in *Spurs* thus reappears as the "ear" in *Octobiographies* — each serving an isomorphic revisionist function. And Derrida later adapts a similar tack in his apologias for the fascist moment in the young de Man and middle Heidegger. In Derrida's view, in these books of his maturity Nietzsche effectively deconstructs such key authoritarian structures as "the State," "the Leader," and "the Father." Indeed, this moment in Nietzsche's text is held to be exemplary for post/modernity.

"The name of Nietzsche is perhaps today, for us, in the Occident, the name of he who was the only one — along with Kierkegaard perhaps in another way, and perhaps again Freud — to treat philosophy and life, science and the philosophy of life *with his name, in his name*. The only one perhaps to have put in play his name — *his names* — and his biographies. With nearly all the risks that this entails: for 'him,' for 'them,' for his lives, his names and their future, the political future singularly of what he bequeathed to sign [l'avenir politique singulièrement de ce qu'il a laissé signer]."[161] At the end of the day — surviving the phenomenological reductions provided by Derrida's self-consciously reiterated "perhaps," and his further hedging of bets with a strategically placed "nearly" — Nietzsche is for Derrida *the* hero of *otobiography*. Which is to say that Nietzsche is *the* problematizer both of the authoritarian mouth that speaks and of the uncritical receptor ear (Greek: *ous, otos*) that passively listens, harkens, is impregnated aurally. But this high honor Derrida himself must pay for by not settling accounts with Nietzsche's esoteric semiotics. Derrida claims that Nietzsche has trouble "signing his name," in the extended political sense of authorizing a specific political cause, that he "defers" signing. But Derrida fails to ask *why* Nietzsche did so. What *exactly* was, and is, to be signed by Nietzsche's corps/e? Are all Nietzsche's cards really on the table of his text for us to read and rewrite? Derrida forgets his own question in *Spurs* about Nietzsche's "umbrella": What if *every* text Nietzsche "signed" himself or left us "to sign" was no less a part of an eso/exoteric strategy than everything else he made public, including the most violent-, fascist-, and authoritarian-"*sounding*" rantings. These rantings Derrida does not ignore, exactly; but nor does he mention or deconstruct the most draconian of them, especially those in Nietzsche's notebooks. Appeals to texts published or intended for publication such as *Thus Spoke Zarathustra* and *Ecce Homo* beg the question of esoteric manipulation. Derrida can always "recontextualize," as Rorty says, the rantings he does see, turning against them supposedly finer and nobler Nietzschean philosophemes. The notion of "Nietzschean play" particularly symptomatizes a curious lack of radicality in Derrida's perhaps antihermeneutic but only *nominally* "political" reading of Nietzsche's politics.

Even in *Otobiographies* Derrida has not gotten past that origin-ary moment of Theory in 1966 when in Baltimore he had torn himself and contemporary philosophy and literary criticism away from structuralism to poststructuralism: rejecting the — bad — nostalgia for meaning in Rousseau and Lévi-Strauss, embracing — good — Heideggerian and above all *Nietzschean* affirmation of semiotic free play. "Turned toward presence — lost or impossible — of the absent origin," Derrida had said, "the structuralist thematic of ruptured immediacy is therefore the sad side — *negative,* nostalgic, guilty, Rousseauist aspect of the thinking of play and the play of thinking [la pensée du jeu], whose other side would be Nietzschean affirmation, the joyous affirmation of a world of signs without fault, without truth, without origin, and opened up to active interpretation. *This affirmation then determines the* noncenter *otherwise than as the loss of center.* And it plays without security. For it is a *sure* play: that which is limited to the *substitution* of pieces that are *given and existing, present.* In absolute chance, affirmation surrenders itself [se livre] also to *genetic* indetermination, to the *seminal* adventure of the trace."[162]

This instaurative act of poststructuralism is fascinating for its own enormously seductive ludic — not to say phallic — energy. As a description of what *Nietzsche* — or Heidegger — was about, it is *ludicrous.* Occluded already in 1966 is the possibility, if not the fact, that all through Nietzsche's "play" something sinister is transpiring all along the textual surface, between the lines and words. As in the case of the umbrella a few years later, Derrida — often accused of being *too* playful — is not nearly playful *enough.* In the coming years, most notably in *Otobiographies,* Derrida speaks brilliantly of Nietzsche's exoteric web of "authorizations" and "signatures" as modalities of "play." Concomitantly, he has been silent about Nietzsche's esoteric intentions, strategies, and tactics. Nietzsche, for his part, had written the following remark in

1883 about his design in writing *Thus Spoke Zarathustra:* "To play the great play—to stake the existence of humanity, in order perhaps to attain something higher than the survival of the race."[163] What on earth might this "something," this *x,* be? And at whose expense?

In *Otobiographies,* Derrida makes his own another of Nietzsche's paradigms of appropriation, one more obscure than the figure of "play" and applied by Nietzsche to himself in quasi-analytic fashion. It is Nietzsche's "biographical" remark in *Ecce Homo: How One Becomes What One Is* that he is "already dead as my father, while as my mother, I am still living and becoming old."[164] The characteristically intricate "rewriting" of this passage in *Otobiographies* involves what Derrida calls "the *dynamis* of the borderline between the 'work' and the 'life,' the system and the subject of the system."[165] Derrida is then quick to link the Nietzschean Father to the State: "the otograph of the State" is its authoritarian Leader-Principle, what the Nazis called *Führerprinzip.* But Derrida makes it seem as if *for Nietzsche* all States are pretty much the same, which is simply untrue. He also misreads the relatively simple—and sexist—equations Nietzsche makes in *Ecce Homo* between "death = father" and "life = mother." Informed as he is by the today commonplace distinction between an "actual" life and its "textual" mediations, Derrida argues: "It is certainly not wrong to say that Nietzsche speaks of his father and mother as 'real,' but he speaks of them 'in *Rätselform*': symbolically, by way of an enigma. . . . "[166] So far so good, but what then is the point of the enigma beyond continuous deconstruction of future "political" misreadings of this text? It would seem that, in terms of Nietzsche's own esoteric semiotics, "father" stands for the original intention of a *corpus* fated to die, to become *corpse;* "mother" stands for the subsequent reception of that text, its afterlife as *corps;* and "sister" stands for the problem of this corps/e's always being in danger of being deflected from the original intent, and to anticipate and control all responses as much as possible.

Intentions aside, Derrida oddly remains in a hermeneutically circular relation to Nietzsche's writing and Nietzschean politics. This circling is betrayed in wordplays that *incorporate* Nietzsche's own more or less *exoteric* self-understanding. For instance, Derrida writes telegraphstyle: "*Ecce Homo:* 'In order to understand anything at all of my *Zarathustra,* one must perhaps be similarly conditioned as I am—with one foot beyond life.' A foot, and going beyond the opposition between life and/or death, a single step ['—avec un pied *au-delà* de la vie.' Un pied, et *par-delà* l'opposition entre la vie ou le mort, un seul pas]."[167] This way of oscillating so swiftly from text to commentary and back that the difference is elided can be an appropriate, effective way to "inworm" Nietzsche's system. But Derrida's worm is unable to penetrate far enough to virus the matrix.[168] Sooner or later, Derrida submits to Nietzsche's unquestioned higher authority. Nietzsche remains a kind of *Führer.* He ends up oscillating from life to death and back as corps/e. To be sure, as noted by his translator, Derrida puns with French *pas audelà*, a rebus. It means simultaneously: *"step(s)* beyond" and *"not* beyond" (p. 19 n. 1). *Only* in this punning way can Derrida manage to keep alive a certain ludic ambivalence—an ambivalence which, tautologically and hermeneutically, always already is imagined to inform Nietzsche's own text. Not only can the interpreter not know the text better than the author, as hermeneutics would claim, but the interpreter *tends* to become the text without grasping the *difference.* Surely, Derrida *intends* to be philosophically vigilant and politically anti-authoritarian. But it is necessary to "step" beyond ambivalent wordplaying, beyond what Derrida calls the Nietzschean texts' "contradicting duplicity" (p. 15/60) and their "unrepresentable scene" (p. 16/63). Derrida knows better than most the distinction between a "scene" that is *in principle* sublimely unrepresent*able* and one that is *thus far* unrepresent*ed*. But in the case of Nietzsche he does not adequately draw this distinction—on which hinges the difference between the Sublime and the sub-liminal. It is on such bare-bones distinctions that Nietzschean esotericism preys and feeds. A weird Prometheus and vulture at once, Nietzsche gnaws on his own corpse and corps.

Symptomatic of the corps/e, Derrida combines philological rigor with hyperbolic claims: "Nietzsche died as always before his name and therefore it is *not a question* of *knowing* what *he* would have thought, wanted, or done. . . . [T]he effects or structure of a text are not *reducible* to its 'truth,' to the intended meaning of its presumed author, or even its supposedly unique and identifiable signatory" (p. 29/pp. 93–94). "Reducible" begs interesting and robust questions. It is crucial to keep open the *question* of Nietzsche's intention, the *possibility* of grasping and settling accounts with it. To re/construct a truth *ex hypothesi* is not necessarily to *reduce* everything to it; and not to concern oneself at some level with other people's intentions is to suggest that one's own are equally nonexistent or irrelevant. When it comes time for Derrida to ask what he regards as *the* "political" question—"Has the 'great' Nietzschean politics misfired or is it, rather, still to come in the wake of a seismic convulsion of which National Socialism or fascism will turn out to have been mere episodes?" (p. 31/99)—it is terribly unclear whether Derrida's text "itself" (or he "himself"—if "he" still meaningfully exists in this textual world) can exist without *some* assumptions about what Nietzsche *"wanted"* "Nietzschean politics" to be, and how it might operate *"without knowing."*

In the end, Derrida's textual-political rewriting fluctuates not between the three main channels of interpretation but between two simple antinomies: *either* gestures of anarchism incorporating Nietzsche's *Thus Spoke Zarathustra*—"*The* State: here we have the *main* defendant indicted in this trial" (p. 33/104)—*or* a duly helpless indecisionism that is totally un-Nietzschean—"We are not, I believe, bound to decide" (p. 32/101). With this last, defeatist remark, "we" are transfixed before a sadomasochistic "choice": *either* terrorism—ultraleftist or ultrarightist—*or* reflux from the Left into right-wing yuppiedom. As a glance at how Nietzsche conceived the exoteric-esoteric distinction reveals, in the Nietzschean world "we" are not *supposed* to "decide" anything that really matters: namely, the breaking of humanity in half.

Derrida suggests that there can and will "always" be "a Nietzscheanism of the right and a Nietzscheanism of the left" (p. 32/102), but apparently without our being able even to *ask* whether this "undecidability" might have been *preprogrammed* in Nietzsche's own texts for some more specific "political" reason. Derrida himself is not uninterested in this question, he just doesn't follow through in the case of Nietzsche. Writing about one of Nietzsche's more protofascist-sounding remarks, Derrida insists that he does "not aim to 'clear' its 'author' and neutralize or defuse either what might be troublesome in it for democratic pedagogy or 'leftist' politics, or what served as 'language' for the most sinister rallying cries of National Socialism" (p. 23/81). But neutralization or defusing is exactly what Derrida helps accomplish, in spite of his attempt to elaborate: "On the contrary, the greatest indecency is *de rigeur* in this place. One may even wonder why it is not enough to say: 'Nietzsche did not think that,' 'he did not want that,' or 'he would have surely vomited this,' that there is falsification of the legacy and an interpretive mystification going on here. One

ESOTERIC SEMIOTICS

may wonder how and why what is so naïvely called a falsification was possible (one can't falsify just anything), how and why the 'same' words and the 'same' statements — if they are indeed the same — might several times be made to serve certain meanings and certain contexts that are said to be different, even incompatible. One may wonder why the only teaching institutions or the only beginning of a teaching institution that ever succeeded in taking as its model the teaching of Nietzsche on teaching will have been a Nazi one" (pp. 23–24/81–82). Derrida even asserts: "There is nothing absolutely contingent about the fact that the only political regimen to have *effectively* brandished his name as a major and official banner was Nazi" (p. 31/98). All this may seem to be close to an argument of *Nietzsche's Corps/e,* but it is not.

In his political rereadings of Nietzsche's and Heidegger's relationships to national socialism, Derrida does what many lesser philosophers and literary critics do, mentioning or using the work of no social historian of the period, even though his analyses depend on many historical presuppositions (Channel 1), some of which are not only problematic but downright false. *Pace* Derrida, it was not the Nazis but Italian fascists who most openly and unproblematically embraced Nietzsche as their own. In fact, a quite large range of opinions about Nietzsche was not only allowed but actively encouraged throughout the Third Reich. Indeed, "Nietzsche" was one of a very small number of topics about which one could "agree to disagree" publicly, in lectures and in print. In this sense, "Nietzsche" was precisely how Nazi hegemony worked, but *not* because his name was "brandished" only in a positive, affirmative manner. Rival Nazi Party members from Alfred Baeumler to Alfred Rosenberg to Martin Heidegger openly and vigorously contested the right to represent Nietzsche. And other Nazis debated not merely how but *whether* his thought was proto- or indeed fully Nazi. Indeed, many thought it was *anti*-Nazi, and said so freely.[169] By *inflating* Nietzsche's alleged use and/or abuse by German national socialism, and by suggesting that it is not *wholly* wrong to *conflate* the two, Derrida renders it impossible to grasp the complexity of Nietzsche's actual influence on Nazism *and fascism* and the complexity of *liberal democratic complicity with fascism* of all types — which is what Derrida also thinks that he is interrogating in *Otobiographies.* His view of *Heidegger's* relationship to national socialism is — or rather has become — comparatively complex. Here Derrida recognizes very clearly

that national socialism was an exceedingly heterogeneous phenomenon and that we can never assume that we are free from what he rightly
calls "Nazisms" (in the plural), that we can yet presume to "think"
them, even with Heidegger's more or less unwitting aid.[170] Derrida's
view of the problem of *Nietzsche* and Nazisms is not correspondingly
complex and lucid. At times appearing to take seriously the question
of Nietzsche's intentions and responsibility — or rather what Derrida
rightly calls, though only in scare quotes, Nietzsche's " 'programming
machine' " (*machine programmatrice*) — he ends up by dismissing the
problems of intentionality and responsibility as basically irrevelant to
the task he insists is "not only decipherment but also transformation —
that is, a practical rewriting according to a theory-practice relationship
which, if possible, would no longer be part of the program" (p. 30/
pp. 95–96). Derrida's project of political rewriting may be all well and
good for some purposes, but carrying it off in the case of Nietzsche
requires paying much closer attention to what Nietzsche's "programming machine" is esoterically, not just exoterically.

Derrida and his readers have not *worked through* Nietzsche hermeneutically *or* antihermeneutically and so continually *act him out* as
corps/e. And this holds just as true for the otherwise very different and
rival poststructuralism of Foucault, to whom Nietzschean new history
and cultural studies appeal. Foucault was at least as hostile to mere
"interpretation" as is Derrida — though less interested in advancing a
new kind of philosophical close reading — and also passed too quickly
from concern about what Nietzsche *meant* in order to try to make *use* of
him, as if these two channels were totally incommensurate. In Foucault's own words in 1975:

> Nowadays I prefer to remain silent about Nietzsche. When I was teaching
> philosophy I often used to lecture on Nietzsche, but I wouldn't do that any
> more today. If I wanted to be pretentious, I would use "the genealogy of
> morals" as the general title of what I am doing. It was Nietzsche who spec-
> ified the power relation as the general focus, shall we say, of philosophical
> discourse — whereas for Marx it was the production relation. Nietzsche is
> the philosopher of power, a philosopher who managed to think of power
> without having to confine himself within a political theory in order to do so.
> Nietzsche's contemporary presence is increasingly important. But I am tired
> of people studying him only to produce the same kind of commentaries that

are written on Hegel or Mallarmé. For myself, I prefer to utilize the writers I like. The only valid tribute to thought such as Nietzsche's is precisely to use it, to deform it, to make it groan and protest. And if commentators then say that I am being faithful or unfaithful to Nietzsche, that is of absolutely no interest.[171]

Foucault, too, was very happy with Channel 2, very happy to be Nietz-schoid corps/e.

For Derrida, the philosopher's proper relationship to others is inscribed by incorporation, death, and mourning — a problematic that, he says, "has only a limited affinity with that of Heidegger."[172] Nonetheless, this problematic is properly Nietzschean albeit, in Derrida's case, appears to be so in unwitting ways. Derrida defines "mourning as the attempt, always doomed to fail (thus a constitutive failure, precisely), to incorporate, interiorize, introject, subjectivize the other in me. Even before the death of the other, the inscription in me of her or his mortality constitutes me. I mourn therefore I am, I am — dead with the death of the other, my relation to myself is first of all plunged into mourning, a mourning that is moreover impossible. This is also what I call ex-appropriation, appropriation caught in a double bind: I must and I must not take the other into myself; mourning is an unfaithful fidelity if it succeeds in interiorizing the other ideally in me, that is, in not respecting his or her infinite exteriority" (p. 321). The problem is that Derrida's suitably complex ethic of ex-appropriative consumption was radically betrayed in advance by Nietzsche, who proleptically programmed his corpus to handicap, manipulate, and incorporate a duped corps, disrespecting any truly independent integrity it might otherwise possess.

"Political rewriting" or "utilization" of Nietzsche has meant re/enacting *part* of his own program. Paying "tribute" is always risky business. The "aporia" reached with poststructuralism recalls Bataille's Channel 3 and the likelihood that no program between Channels 1 and 3 is ever going to be radical enough to get after or beyond Nietzsche — or even to *see* or *hear* him except in programmed ways. *This* is a question of responsibility — not so much *Derrida's* or *Foucault's* responsibility — that's their affair and that of their often unwished-for oto-acolytes — but rather *Nietzsche's* responsibility and that of the *rest* of us. To get *after* Nietzsche means being *after* poststructuralism, at least as it has been incorporated as the corps/e. In other terms, poststructuralism has hardly arrived at a vantage point where it might say: "Nietzsche may be the master key and its affirmation, but we're not turning him either."[173]

Postscript: *Mondo 2000* — the neo-'60s' richly sponsored magazine of cyberspace, cybervid, cybermusic, cyberdrugs, and "esoterrorism" — has produced a quasi-tongue-in-cheek — any obvious difference between seriousness and irony has long been effaced in such discourse — "Manifesto of Art Damage." "Art Damage" is defined as "Camp with a Ph.D., attitude with brains and a wink. . . . Part sampling, part burlesque, Art Damage could not *exist* until now. It took a particular convergence of forces before it could even appear: the global village, marketing research, media sophistication, and the Borgesian Library of All Time and Space." The manifesto then warns: "But there is *good* Art Damage and *bad* Art Damage — and there are people who wouldn't recognize ironic distance at two feet." According to the manifesto, Nietzsche is "Good Art Damage," Derrida is "Bad Art Damage," and God is "Not Art Damage."[174] Leaving God out of this one, *Mondo 2000* may be on to something when comparing Derrida to Nietzsche, and not necessarily to the former's discredit. But — irony and all kidding aside, if that's still possible — this version of Nietzschean cyberpunk, too, has Nietzsche's esoteric semiotics exactly half right and half wrong: right exoterically, wrong esoterically.

After Klossowski

Nietzsche developed a theory and practice of semiotics earlier than Ferdinand de Saussure, from whom structuralism and poststructuralism evolved affirmatively or critically. Yet the most suggestive attempt after Bataille to get after Nietzsche's semiotic was made not by poststructuralists but by Pierre Klossowski, who influenced them. Already in the late 1930s, Klossowski was sending out probes into the Nietzschean matrix — probes whose information has still been inadequately processed, even if they did not extend far enough, in part because Nietzsche himself was hidden aboard. Think of Ridley Scott's 1979 *Alien*. By 1957 Klossowski intimated the existence of something like a Nietzschean esoteric semiotics in his essay "Nietzsche, Polytheism and

Parody."[175] One of Klossowski's central ideas is that Nietzschean "parody" is linked to a question of "polytheism," and both are linked to the question of "naming" and other types of "origin" — whether Orphic, Adamic, or performative speech-act. This quasi-theological problematic can be clarified with reference to existentialism.

As Søren Kierkegaard remarked, *polynymity* is intimately related to *pseudonymity* and to forms of *censorship*, both externally and internally imposed. Kierkegaard tried — "ironically" or "existentially" — to confront the responsibility involved in the resulting choices for writing. "In a legal and in a literary sense, the responsibility is mine," Kierkegaard wrote, "but, easily understood dialectically, it is I who have *occasioned* the audibility of the production in the world of actuality, which of course cannot become involved with poetically actual authors and therefore altogether consistently and with absolute legal and literary right looks to me."[176] But the problem in reading Kierkegaard is immediate: Can *this* profession be taken at face value, existentially, or is it itself ironic? Is it itself manipulated by an esoteric theory and practice of naming and signing? As Adorno put it: "No writer is more cunning in his choice of words than Kierkegaard or aims at concealing more through his language than he who inexhaustibly denounced himself as a 'spy in a higher service,' part of the secret police, a dialectical seducer. There is no way to meet up with him in the fox kennel of infinitely reflected interiority other than to take him at his word; he is to be caught in the traps set by his own hand."[177] In effect, Klossowski operated more lucidly than most Nietzscheans within this "Kierkegaardian" labyrinth.

Klossowski was fascinated that even a superficial reading of Nietzsche's work encounters an apparently willful, arbitrary substitution of more or less proper names of humans, demigods, and gods. "Socrates" comes to mean "Christ" and vice versa; "Dionysus" begins to look like "Apollo" or "Goethe"; "Wagner" and "Bismarck" morph into one another. Nietzsche even says that the most often-used names in his writing, notably "Schopenhauer" and "Wagner" — that is, "philosophy" and "cultural politics" — are to be read as surrogates for *himself*.[178] This suggestion of a closed economy of proper names *as signs* in Nietzsche was taken up first, and in some ways most radically, by Klossowski among all Nietzscheans. In "Nietzsche, Polytheism and Parody," Klossowski argues that the substitution of im/proper names — to the point

of total interchangeability and carnivalesque saturnalia — is not without pattern or design. Rather, it indicates that a supposedly "schizoid"
Nietzsche may have worked out a remarkably conscious and coherent
theory of heterogeneous, multiple selves — a possibility with deep semiotic, illocutionary, and political implications. In this system — in
principle, if not always fact — *any* im/proper name in history can be
substituted for *any* other, *including* Nietzsche's own, as he himself suggested. Three questions immediately arise from Klossowski's argument, though he did not raise them himself in this form: first, whether
this nominal interchangeability could be "democratizing" in effect, if
not intent, as radical polytheism tends to be; second and alternatively,
whether there is a crucial contradiction precisely here between Nietzsche's original elitist intent and its effect on Nietzscheans; and, finally, whether Nietzsche is consciously concealing something — some
"Name" or "rigid designator" — behind, beyond, or between the lines
and words of an only *nominal* interchangeability. In short: How
does a semiotics in which signs are *totally* interchangeable and arbitrary — *simulacra without original* — square with the — *origin-ary* — desire always to *differentiate* society into hierarchically arranged castes or
classes?

These questions touch again on the likelihood that for Nietzsche
what is always already logically prior to any statement is the exoteric-
esoteric distinction. Klossowski did not pursue this problematic in its
full complexity for reasons that remain unclear but that arguably include the preservation of his version of esotericism.[179] This is also why
Leo Strauss pulls up short when reading and writing "Nietzsche," but
also why it is not appropriate to compare Strauss to Derrida, since the
latter is not similarly committed to esotericism.[180] Klossowski preferred instead to say that what might be called a "nominal semiotic" is
somehow *liberating*. This semiotic would be nominal both in Klossowski's sense that it is a semiotic of *names;* but also because for this
very reason it is not quite the *esoteric semiotics* Nietzsche had in mind,
since that is not *reducible* to names — involving as it does "musical"
strategies beneath the level of cognition. With regard, then, to Klossowski's claim for liberation, the typically unasked question is always:
Liberating for whom? For the many "names" in Nietzsche's works tend
to be far more rigid as designators than they appear.

Klossowski was also one of the first to propose a theory of the "simulacrum" (*le simulacre*) later developed especially by Jean Baudrillard. Manuel De Landa, in his book on technowarfare, explains that historically and theologically "simulacrum" is more "than a fancy term for a propaganda campaign." Rather, "it refers to the many ways in which a heterogeneous system of symbols (literary images of hell and heaven, stucco angels and cherubs, special theatrical effects) may become essential elements in strategies of social domination. After the Council of Trent (1545 – 1563), the pope and his paramilitary army decided to codify into images the main passages of the Bible, to impose an unambiguous interpretation on them and to marshal their 'correct meanings' in people's minds. Instead of merely serving to rally people for a particular cause, images were to be imposed on the population at large (including the Jesuits themselves) as a new kind of 'spiritual currency.' Simulacra may be classified into three categories according to the technology used to create images and symbols: the counterfeit, the replica and the simulation."[181] In Baudrillard's own words, "There is a strict correlation between the mental obedience of the Jesuits (*'perinde ac cadaver'*) and the demiurgic ambition to exorcise the natural substance of a thing in order to substitute a synthetic one. Just like a man submitting his will to his organization, things take on the ideal functionality of the cadaver. All technology, all technocracy are incipiently there: the presumption of an ideal counterfeit of the world, expressed in the invention of a universal substance and of a universal amalgam of substances. Reunify the scattered world (after the Reformation) under the aegis of a homogeneous doctrine, universalize the world under a single word (from New Spain to Japan: the Missions), constitute a political elite *of the state,* with an identically centralized strategy: these are the objectives of the Jesuits. In order to accomplish this, you need to create effective simulacra. . . . "[182] Baudrillard's depiction of the Jesuits is far closer to what Nietzsche was really about than a Baudrillard or a Klossowski ever say. Nietzsche was fascinated by the Jesuits and their way with corps/es, and he was a master of simulacra in a multiple sense.

Zarathustra seems to demand that we continually ask of ourselves the basic "existentialist" question: "Are you authentic? Or only an actor [Schauspieler]? A destroying simulacrum? Or the thing simulated, destroyed? [Ein Vertreter? oder das Vertretene selbst?] Perhaps in the end you are only a destroying simulacrum of an actor. . . . "[183] Before yet again celebrating Nietzsche as the first and/or most radical semiotician, however, note that German *vertreten* means "to represent" or "defend" as in parliament, senate, or court of law, as well as "to substitute for" and "to make a copy of." But *vertreten* also means "to block access" and, taken literally, even means "to trample underfoot." So it is that *Nietzsche's* simulacrum can both occlude and destroy.

According to Klossowski's approach to Nietzsche's semiotic, Eternal Recurrence of the Same means that there has never been "a first time" or an "original" of anything. Rather, as a mode of the Sublime, it tends to *terminate* discussion of all *terms* — "concepts," but also the two ultimate "limit conditions" of birth and death. Following Bataille, Klossowski argues that in the Eternal Recurrence of the Same there cannot be an "end of history," nor any "ultimate doctrine." This includes the doctrine of Eternal Recurrence of the Same *itself*, since the very possibility of doctrines is precisely what is being "parodied." Nor, philologically or hermeneutically speaking, is there any "authentic" version of "texts" — which Klossowski calls "pastiches." Even though history does not "end" with Nietzsche, it sort of "stops" in that maximal compression of spatial logic and linguistic time that is parodic pastiche. Also eliminated in this Nietzschean hegemony is any real distinction between the pre-, the post-, and the contemporary. Rorty's suggestion that the term "postmodernity" be replaced by "post-Nietzschean" was prefigured by Klossowski.

The more abstract and depoliticized aspects of Klossowski's discussion of proper names in Nietzsche has fed into several other currents of contemporary thought. It prompted Deleuze and Guattari's "schizoid" reading of Nietzschean "naming" or "name-effectivity" in the context of post-Oedipal neocapitalism, as well as Derrida's theory of de/authorizing "signatures" and "the politics of proper names"; and it anticipated Foucault's more famous "Nietzschean" critique of authorship in "What Is an Author?" (1969).[184] And Klossowski had begun to put a conceptual handle on Nietzsche's otherwise slippery way of conjoining the epistemological problem of decentered Truth with the theological problem of the death of the monotheistic and patriarchal Name-of-Names: God. Finally, Klossowski's way of reading Nietzsche as "parodic pastiche" foreshadowed several German posthermeneutic, French poststructuralist, and North American deconstructivist theories, as well as North Atlantic pragmatism à la Rorty — indeed, virtually any embrace of "play" as "Nietzschean affirmation."[185]

At stake in Klossowski's argument is a dominant view of history and historicity, since an assumption of "relativism" and "historicism," extending back at least to Ranke, is that history is a series of more or less discrete periods, each one of which "as it really was" is "equidistant" to a monotheistic God. Nietzsche's "parodic" and "polytheistic" substitutions of all proper names seem not merely to disrupt periodization as a concept but to render history itself simply irrelevant. But Nietzsche's original version of all this has more complex ramifications than Klossowski seems able to get after. Like historicism and neohistoricism alike, Nietzsche does *affirm* relativism — at least exoterically — and yet he simultaneously *denies* the theological assumptions upon which historicism is based. Another way Klossowski accesses this conundrum is to turn attention away from Nietzsche's themes to his mode of textual production, though here, too, he pulls up short. Klossowski developed a prototype of the poststructuralist notion that there is "nothing outside the text." He rewrote Nietzsche's compressed history of philosophy — the aphorism in *Twilight of the Idols* entitled "How the 'Real World' Finally Became a Fable" — to read: "there is nothing outside the tale" or "myth,"[186] thus forging a conceptual hinge between Nietzsche and Derrida. But Klossowski's view of history and textuality is not quite up to the duplicity behind Nietzsche's neo-Renaissance way of telling history *as if* it were *nothing more* than the story, tale, fable, myth, or text of great names and leaders.

In "The Use and Disadvantage of History for Life" (1874), what Nietzsche terms "monumental history" enjoyed a certain privilege not quite shared by its "critical" and "antiquarian" cousins, though he is always prepared to mix 'n' match these three major modes of thinking and use history as the situation demands.[187] What is often overlooked, however, is how this famous essay concludes by conjuring up a proleptic vision of "the downfall of an entire decorative culture." Nietzsche has paved the path to this conclusion by alluding to himself as an "architect of the future," by speaking affirmatively of the "hygiene of life," by embracing the Platonic doctrines of the need for "necessary lies" and for a working class or caste to service genuine, as opposed to merely decorative, culture, and by railing against universal literacy, specifically as it might be accessible to workers — making *this* argument written in logographic necessity inaccessible to them.

Once again, Klossowski does not follow up on the most radical implications of Nietzsche's esoteric semiotics, which ends up sounding like an exoteric warrant for self-perpetuating self-deconstruction rather than an elaborate illocutionary project for social transformation. Finally, Klossowski's project of philological re/construction is sacrificed by valorizing what Klossowski calls "the supreme image": namely, a supposedly "Nietzschean laughter" imagined to be radically *open-ended* and *intransitive* but nonetheless also, somehow, *liberating* in a self-creative world freed from God, Truth, Father, and any other *Name*. But French *nom*, as Lacan noted, sounds like *non:* both "name" and "no," as in "le *nom* du père" in the Symbolic Order's simultaneous interdiction and socialization of the human *infans*. And along with the exit of *the name* (*le nom*), in the Bataillean-Klossowskian way of reading and rewriting Nietzsche, enters *a ban* (*un non*) on grasping Nietzsche's intentions as the virtual or actual origin of his corps. In short: an-archism.

What also is "forgotten" in such ostensibly emancipatory paradigms is that Nietzsche theorized and talked a lot about "laughter" but, all kidding aside, had little existential sense of humor.[188] His often excruciating physical pain notwithstanding, all kidding and compassion again aside, his project was too serious, too bizarre, too potentially lethal. Not only was Nietzsche a masked man, a dancer, an *alazon,* an *eiron,* a grifter, a confidence man, and a trickster coyote who sometimes fools himself—for therein precisely lies his seductive charm.[189] He certainly *was* all of these "names," but he was also something else besides in Channel 4.

Now, Klossowski is arguably one of Nietzsche's *most* insightful readers—alongside Bataille, Heidegger, Strauss, and a handful of others. All such claims must be taken with a large grain of salt, however. The very notion of a Pantheon of "Nietzsche's most insightful readers" is itself infected by Nietzschean elitism, which insists that *everything* be divided up according to "order of rank." Not only are there *many* insightful readers of Nietzsche, but in a sense everyone is *equally* insightful, *everyone* being to some extent a philosopher, as Gramsci put it. Alternatively, if Nietzsche/anism is working at its *maximum* level of structural causality, Nietzsche's effect would be distributed *throughout* society as its absent cause. It would then be *unnecessary* to read Nietzsche. If Nietzsche were read *nonetheless*—for some comparatively contingent reason or other—his readers would still be divided up, as they are now, in two basic groups: (1) those few who think, rightly or wrongly, that they know more about Nietzsche than others, and so must struggle to maintain that advantage; and (2) those many who think, rightly or wrongly, that they know less, and so must struggle to know more. But it would amount to the same thing; for everyone would know *almost* equally little about the most esoteric dimension of his most exoterically transmitted signs. But mere recognition of this possibility — this actual-virtuality — provides a tiny window of opportunity to see through Nietzsche/anism. It is *this* window that Klossowski — alongside Bataille, Heidegger, and Strauss — closes, even as he suggests its existence.

Klossowski had a keen sense not only of the "parodic" aspect of Nietzsche's project but its underlying *seriousness*, and there are several indications in other writings that he did not fully believe that Nietzschean "parody," "polytheism," and theory of "proper names" was to be taken *only* at face value or as liberatory, at least not for all people. This second, underlying tendency of Klossowski's approach to Nietzsche tends to be overlooked.[190] To be sure, this neglect is partly due to the fact that Klossowski himself continually pulled up short of revealing the more sinister levels of the Nietzschean semiotic that he had glimpsed. This reticence indicates that Klossowski was not a "weak" or "gentle" Nietzschean but rather "strong" and "tough."[191] In other words, he was a reasonably conscious member of the corps/e.

Not by chance, Klossowski had begun to develop his theory of the *circulus vitiosus* in the late 1930s in the company of Bataille and other French and German intellectuals as part of the attempt of the Collège de Sociologie to analyze the reasons behind the spread and fascination of fascism and national socialism. Under the pretext of talking about the relationship between the Marquis de Sade and the French Revolution, Klossowski pitted against the image of the vicious circle, linked to Nietzsche's Eternal Recurrence of the Same, his own notion of "permanent insurrection" (*l'insurrection permanente*). Klossowski's point of departure was de Sade's notorious thesis that "a nation that has thrown off its monarchical yoke can only maintain itself by crimes, since it is already in crime."[192] The precise "Nietzschean" implications of this thesis in the year 1939 — or any other — are not exactly pellucid, having rather different resonance in a democracy than under the fascist boot. Interest in comparing de Sade and Nietzsche in conditions of fascoid modernity was part of a more general European tendency. A few years later, in *Dialectic of Enlightenment* (1944), Adorno and Horkheimer would also analyze de Sade and Nietzsche together as major critics of the Enlightenment about which they were all so ambivalent. But the German critical theorists come to the idiotic conclusion that Nietzsche's attack on "compassion" (*Mitleid*) somehow "redeemed the unshakable confidence in man that is constantly betrayed by every form of assurance that seeks only to console."[193] While valid perhaps as a politico-philosophical stance in its own right, this claim has *nothing* to do with Nietzsche's own position — *except* as it is exhibited exoterically for public consumption.

Over the ensuing years, Klossowski explicitly brought his theory of the vicious circle together with the problem of secrets and secret societies. Yet here again Klossowskian ambivalence was at work — this time in oscillatory motion between a comparatively objective, critical *description* of fascism and a comparatively subjective, less critical *prescription* of some sort of Nietzschean elite to be the remedy for virtually all ills of modernity. The "Circle" of Stefan George as a complex *deconstructor and/or precursor* of Nazism lurked in the background for Klossowski, as it did for the Collège de Sociologie generally. The early 1970s found Klossowski advancing the bold suggestion that Nietzsche's doctrine of Eternal Recurrence of the Same must be grasped not only *politically* in some vague sense but as a form of specific *conspiracy* — though not in any common sense of either term. Klossowski stated flatly: "The conspiracy of Nietzsche can be conceived only to the extent that it might be conducted by some secret community, imperceptible and unseizable [*insaissable*], the action of which can wage war [*sévir*] under any sort of regime."[194] But just here Klossowski abruptly cut his line of inquiry. This potentially very deep — if, for him, anarchistic or libertarian[195] — insight *should* have cut a decisive caesura into the reception of Nietzsche. Certainly a smart and receptive audience was firmly in place. For Klossowski delivered this suggestion publicly in a short talk entitled "Circulus vitiosus" at the conference "Nietzsche Today?" Convened at Cerisy-La-Salle in July 1972, this event was groundbreaking in the twentieth-century reception of Nietzsche. In attendance were major French and German intellectuals of several generations and ideological persuasions — all of them more or less "Nietzschean" by self-definition. Listeners at Klossowski's talk included Deleuze, Derrida, Eugen Fink (the Heideggerian philosopher and theoretician of play), Sarah Kofman, Philippe Lacoue-Labarthe, Karl Löwith, Jean-François Lyotard, Jean-Luc Nancy, and Bernard Pautrat. They delivered what were to become in many cases seminal papers on Nietzsche. But, for all intents and purposes, Klossowski's hint about the esoteric, political, and conspiratorial dimension of Nietzsche's semiotics was ignored, quickly displaced in France and Germany — and later even more in North America — by an ultimately less complex and exoteric notion of "play" that Klossowski himself had also anticipated earlier. His passing allusion to political conspiracy and a possible link to Nietzsche's illocutionary practice and perlocutionary effect was roundly ignored. Thus ignored, too, was the understated link in Nietzsche between the "vicious circle" of the *philosophical* concept of Eternal Recurrence of the Same and the potential for vicious *actions* on the part of a secret political circle.

In his major work, *Nietzsche et le cercle vicieux* (Nietzsche and the vicious circle, 1969), Klossowski had made the paradoxical suggestion that the name "Nietzsche" — or rather the *text* called *The Gay Science* — was "the fruit of the greatest solitude imaginable, [and yet he/it] speaks essentially to those spirits who themselves will know how to recover this solitude."[196] Here Klossowski developed an argument that he had begun in the 1950s about *The Gay Science* — the crucial transition leading from Nietzsche's supposed flirtation with "positivism" to *Thus Spoke Zarathustra.* In Klossowski's argument, Nietzsche's "nobleness" qua "solipsism" remained at the root of his attitude toward textual production and reception.[197] From Klossowski's consistent perspective over four decades, Nietzsche's esoteric semiotics logically *should* have constituted *the* central problem for reading Nietzsche. But Klossowski repressed or suppressed it by his own brand of hagiography, all too common throughout the Nietzsche Industry, whereby Nietzsche represents "the greatest solitude imaginable." Nevertheless, in his scandalously untranslated *Nietzsche et le cercle vicieux,* Klossowski developed his concept of Nietzsche's "pulsatile semiology" (*sémiologie pulsionnelle*).[198] It makes a major — potential — contribution toward grasping Nietzsche's esoteric semiotics.

The term "pulsatile semiology" was derived conceptually from Bataille but used with significantly greater precision by Klossowski. It describes the way in Nietzsche that a more or less "conscious semiology" was radically "abbreviated" and eventually came to *appear* "authentically spontaneous."[199] But rather than pressing on to ask, as he *sporadically* did from the 1930s on, whether this properly Nietzschean semiotic might also have a quite concrete, consciously articulated esoteric doctrine and political conspiracy within Nietzsche's illocutions, at the end of his book Klossowski once again uncannily folds Nietzsche's semiotic back into a more traditionally intransitive, self-sufficient act — a relapse once again into "parodic" or "polytheistic" thinking.[200] What was effectively buried by this move, this time decisively for twentieth-century Nietzscheanism, was the question of more sinister kinds of coherence and incoherence indwelling Nietzsche's project. Klossowski was eminently candid about the fact that Nietzsche's version of the "vicious circle" entailed the necessity for mechanisms of "selection" that might have horrific *social* consequences,[201] but what these are to be, and how Nietzsche wanted to implement them beyond thematizing in a *pulsatile semiology* — this Klossowski did not say, indeed preferred to lead this question back into questions of "pathology" — but basically only *Nietzsche's* pathology.[202] When Klossowski puns on the term *corps,* he comes close to linking pulsatile semiology not only to Nietzsche's theory of the existential Self qua physical body under the sign of the vicious circle, but to an embodied, potentially vicious *military* corps — but just here is where Klossowski always hesitates to say more.[203] The "new," "French," and "leftist" Nietzsche has never really broken out of this Klossowskian aporia, this exitless labyrinth. Klossowski was courageous to begin the probe of Nietzsche's esoteric semiotics, though he himself seems to have gotten too close for comfort. Whenever this un/canny moment occurs in Nietzsche/anism, it is necessary to return to Nietzsche.

Nietzsche Again

In *On the Genealogy of Morals: A Polemic* (1887) — after *Beyond Good and Evil* the second of his two major "retrospective prefaces" to *Thus Spoke Zarathustra* — Nietzsche spoke explicitly of "signs" to anticipate not only Klossowski's "pulsatile semiotic" but the "ghost semiotic" informing the consensual hallucination of postcontemporary cyberspace. Nietzsche generated his semiotic argument not out of a purely theoretical fascination, but out of his pragmatic "genealogical" analysis — in the exact center of his book: part 2, aphorism 12 — of what he called "the cause of the origin of a thing and its eventual utility."[204] *On the Geneal-ogy of Morals* has been dubbed "the Bible of the neostructuralist theory of power,"[205] and whether or not they allude to this aphorism explicitly, its argument undergirds the thought of Nietzscheans of nearly all ideological persuasions. Aphorism 2:12 is worth citing at length especially because it can be used to produce a properly Nietzschean account of the lethal embodiment of Nietzsche's corps/e — not least in contemporary technoculture. Large chunks of this oft-cited text will be given first, but with its seldom-cited last sentence withheld for a moment.

Nietzsche begins:

> The cause of the origin of a thing and its eventual utility, its actual employ-ment and place in a system of purposes, lie worlds apart. Whatever exists, having somehow come into being, is again and again reinterpreted to new ends, taken over, transformed, and redirected by some power superior to it; all events . . . are a subduing, a becoming master, and all subduing and becoming master involves a fresh interpretation, an adaptation by which any previous "meaning" and "purpose" are necessarily obscured, even obliter-ated. No matter how well one has understood the utility of any physiological organ (or legal institution, social custom, political usage, form in art or religious cult [or, one might interpolate, in a philosophy]), this means nothing regarding its origins. . . . Yet purposes and utilities are themselves only signs [Anzeichen] that a Will to Power has become master of some-thing less powerful and imposed upon it the character of a function; and the entire history of a "thing" and organ as custom can in this way be a contin-uous sign-chain [*Zeichen-Kette*] of ever new interpretations and adaptations the causes of which do not even have to be related to one another but, on the contrary, in some cases succeed and alternate with one another in purely chance fashion. The "evolution" of a thing, custom, organ is therefore by no means its *progressus* toward a goal, even less a logical *progressus* by the shortest route and with the smallest expenditure of force — but rather a succession of more or less profound, more or less mutually independent processes of subduing, plus the resistances they encounter, the attempts at transforma-tion for the purpose of defense and reaction, and the results of successful counteractions. The form is fluid, but the "meaning" even more so. (*KGW* 6/2:329–331)

In our current postmodernist climate, all this sounds familiar, even *natural*. In addition to Benjaminian, Foucauldian, Deleuzian, Baudrillardian, new historical, and cultural studies types of argument, it sounds like a pretext for one or more of the following: cohabitation with *"différance"* (Derrida), "the differend" (Lyotard), and "unlimited semiosis" (Eco); or, alternatively, open season on "master narratives" (Lyotard), "performative felicity" (Austin), and "restricted fusion of horizons" (Gadamer). But what stands out in Nietzsche's influential argument is not only its apparent extremism but its equally extreme reluctance to specify exactly what is meant by terms such as "superior power" — which always lurk about, more or less visibly, in the background.

In Nietzsche's expressed *exoteric* view, the origin and the use — think also of him and his reception — are said to be "worlds apart"; use means "nothing" vis-à-vis origins; "purpose and utilities are themselves *only* signs"; the apparent development of "all" conceivable phenomena through their *"entire* history" — from biological organs equally up through individual subjectivities all the way to social institutions — is "by *no* means" to be understood teleologically, and certainly *not* as "progress"; new interpretations are *never* necessarily related to their originary objects, authors, or historical moments — randomly and robustly alternating as they do among themselves "in a *purely* chance fashion," governed *only* by an abstract (not to say metaphysically hypostatized) "Will to Power." Now, all this too sounds familiar to "us" — not merely as specifically "Nietzschean" but as the more or less homogenized fare peddled as *common sense* at intellectual and pop-cult marketplaces, where Nietzsche appears as a founding father in a world supposedly absent of fathers. What is too typically ignored in the postmodernist mind-set, however, is any *specific* interest and profit Nietzsche might have chosen to draw from his argument. And this interest and profit have only exoterically to do with the much ballyhooed "perspectivism," "relativism," "pluralism," "aestheticism," or "Dionysiac play," all of which — lo and behold! — are always already "inscribed" or "figured" in Nietzsche's texts. For Nietzsche's part, however, as Zarathustra is forever fond of putting it, the fundamental question is *"Wozu?* [So what? To what end?]"

The postmetaphysical — more or less Heideggerian — response to such passages focuses on its perspectivism, which is held to be a good thing, though unfortunately contaminated occasionally in Nietzsche by residues of metaphysical grounding as in Will to Power, which is held to be bad. Lyotard's position in *The Inhuman* (1988) is symptomatic of this dominant reading and could easily be about aphorism 2:12.

> Nietzsche tries to emancipate thought, the way of thinking, from what he calls metaphysics, i.e. from that principle, prevalent from Plato to Schopenhauer, which states that the only thing is for humans to discover the ground which will allow them to speak in accordance with the true and to act in accordance with the good or the just. The central theme of Nietzsche's thought is that there is no "accordance with," because there is nothing that is a primary or originary principle, a *Grund,* as the Idea of the Good was for Plato or, for Leibniz, the principle of sufficient reason. Every discourse, including that of science or philosophy, is only a perspective, a *Weltanschauung.* But just at that point Nietzsche *succumbs* to the temptation to designate what grounds the perspectivizations, and calls it the will to power. His philosophy thus reiterates the metaphysical process, and even obstinately accomplishes its essence, for the metaphysics of will with which he concludes his enquiry is the very metaphysics harboured by all the philosophical systems of modern Western thought, as Heidegger shows. The fact that Nietzsche's writing repeats the same *error or fault* in spite of itself is a sign for reflection of what a rewriting could be that escaped, as far as possible, the repetition of what it rewrites.[206]

The political stakes for Lyotard are high, for he begins *The Inhuman* by saying that Nietzsche was "taken hostage by fascist mythology" (p. 1)—a formulation that begs several embarrassing questions. With all the respect otherwise due Lyotard, this particular framework is politically naïve and philosophical nonsense—at least it is in terms of what Nietzsche *intended* and *if* intention still matters. If Channel 1 is wholly irrelevant, then we are of course "free" in Channel 2 to appropriate Nietzsche as a perhaps misguided but basically well-meaning anarchist or libertarian or perspectivist or whatever else we may "choose." The question to ask is whether we might ask *why* it might have been that Nietzsche would have "succumbed" to such an elemental "mistake" or "fault." And is not Nietzsche's "perspectivism" simply an epistemological name or sign for Will to Power? Who is really "taken hostage"? Could not Nietzsche's "mistakes" or "faults" be willed strategies or tactics that are often—wittingly or unwittingly—obfuscated by Nietzsche/anism?

Althusser's terse characterization in "The Transformation of Philosophy" (1976) of contemporary Nietzscheanism's account of the history of philosophy "in terms of the will to power . . . somewhat in Nietzsche's manner" remains apt.[207] "At a given moment," Althusser paraphrases Nietzsche, "there existed men motivated by *ressentiment* who, wounded by the world, set about dominating it through thought—in short, making themselves masters of the world, conceiving it exclusively through their own thought. The philosophers were precisely these specialists in the violence of the concept, of *Begriff,* of appropriation, who asserted their power by subjecting to the law of Truth all the social practices of men, who became sadder and sadder and lived on in the night" (pp. 250–251). Althusser is precisely critical, if only by implication, of Nietzsche/anism. He continues: "We know that such a perspective is not foreign to some of our contemporaries who, naturally enough, discover in philosophy the archetype of power, the model of all power. They themselves write the equation knowledge = power and, in the style of modern and cultivated anarchists, affirm: violence, tyranny, state despotism are Plato's fault—just as they used to say a while back that the Revolution was Rousseau's fault. The best way to respond to them is to go further than they do and introduce the scandalous fracture of practice into the very heart of philosophy. This is where Marx's influence is perhaps most profoundly felt" (p. 251). The more restricted task here is to combat Nietzsche/anism's doctrine or sign of Will to Power by introducing into its heart the "scandalous fracture" between the practice of Nietzscheanism and Nietzsche's own illocutionary practice.

Here, in any case, is the commonly withheld continuation, the punch line, of aphorism 2:12 of *On the Genealogy of Morals,* the final ellipsis being Nietzsche's:

> The magnitude of an "advance" can even be *measured* by the mass of things or people that had to be sacrificed to the prosperity of a single *stronger* species of man—now, that *would* be an advance. . . . (*KGW* 6/2:331)

Assume *ex hypothesi* that Nietzsche's precipitate willingness to abandon "perspectivism"—and its equivalents—is not due to a relapse into "metaphysical grounding"—which is for him always a strategy anyhow—but occurs rather on behalf of an unabashed and potentially very violent elitism and motored by a single political will that is never quite stated except in the guise of perspectivism and by ellipsis. Assume also that this intent is not merely a significant impulse in his thinking *inter alia* but, as we saw him putting it earlier himself, its *"one* intention." Can we really "deconstruct" it textually? The preceding bulk of aphorism 2:12 already was informed by a very muscular and armored discursive formation that functionally delimits the potential for really unlimited semiosis. It is only the longer passage that readers really *see* — and then immediately proceed to ignore the punch line. Or they *do* see the punch line, too, but choose not to *believe* that Nietzsche really meant it. Or they think that one can have the argument without the punch line, that there is no necessary relation of structural causality between them. Or, if the perlocutionary effect is working *maximally,* readers begin even to *desire* the social implications — but only secretly, subconsciously, abjectly, and sadomasochistically, perhaps against their own best conscious interests. Then Nietzsche and his readers can have it both ways: readers read and do not see, see and do not read. And, in the event, some version or combination of these possibilities is what typically happens among Nietzscheans.

Now assume that Nietzsche's pragmatic demand for "sacrifice" is near his *own* thinking's "origin." Imagine further that blindness *to* this potentially murderous moment has been embodied by virtually all the supposedly "fresh interpretations" of his work — from their various inceptions onward. As visible in the aphorism on esotericism in *Beyond Good and Evil,* Nietzsche does not fully discuss his intent, nor should he in his terms. Rather, he lets the cat out of the bag *and* the mice don't see it coming. In a different context, Paul Cantor has explained this principle succinctly in Straussian terms: "As difficult as this task may sound, the great factor working in favor of the would-be esoteric writer is the tendency of the conventional reader to assimilate whatever he reads to what he already believes. If he sees a familiar belief stated in a work, he will want to attribute that belief to the writer, especially if the belief is stated prominently and more than once. If, on the other hand, he encounters a passage that contradicts his familiar beliefs [and/or, it is crucial to add, reinforces the deepest, least conscious, most scandalous of these beliefs], he will tend not to notice it, or at least not make much of it, especially if the passage is not clearly expressed or does not feature prominently in the overall argument or appears only once (or any combination of these factors)."[208] In short, something can be deconstructed and yet still *believed* in a Channel inaccessible to deconstruction.

It seems the punch line to Nietzsche's aphorism 2:12 of *On the Genealogy of Morals* is not really there to be "interpreted" in the first place. Rather, it is un/cannily in/visible. The general principle involved here is a very old one. As formulated in the seventeenth century by William Congreve:

> No mask like open truth to cover lies,
> As to go naked is the best disguise.[209]

It is necessary to return to this problematic of invisibility *as* visibility from several angles as it applies to Nietzsche: namely, the fact that readers seem literally unable to register certain passages in the Nietzschean text, which they can and do look at but do not really see or observe. Another way of conceptualizing this problematic is the point of view of production, with the help of Emily Dickinson's radically punning lines:

> Tell all the Truth but tell it slant —
> Success in Circuit lies . . . [210]

. . . where, however, in the case of Nietzsche/anism, the Truth is socially horrific, and the underlying — and lying — Circuit not only that of rhetoric and hermeneutics but also, today, of fiber-electronic media.

Nietzsche's esoteric semiotics is a version of "The Emperor's New Clothes," one of the most profound of fairy tales. More precisely, it is a mode of *production*. It is related to Freudian and Lacanian notions of how "perversity" and the "symptom" *work*, to Žižek's analysis of how "ideology" *works*, and to Althusser's thesis about the way structural causality *works* in capitalist economics. Althusser, Freud, Lacan, and Žižek all take as axiomatic the famous joke with the punch line: "Why are you telling me that you are going to Cracow and not to Lemberg, when you're really going to Cracow?"[211] Thanks to the metaphysical tradition and its equivalents, we are so obsessed with, so fixated in, the "perverse" a priori belief that the Truth or the Real *must* be concealed that we are incapable of recognizing Them if or when They are displayed naked before us. Caught up in the asymmetrical, paranoid pathology of this self-fulfilling prophecy, we automatically assume Truth (writ large and singular) to be a lie, yet remain forever ambivalent about whether lies might nevertheless contain truths (writ small and plural) and truths lies. If this problematic has become common currency in theoretical quarters, it is thanks to Nietzsche's "Jewish joke," which is always on his corps/e.

Too much intellectual leftism is predicated on the assumption that if anyone it is Nietzsche who stands *outside* esoteric semiotics. He, at least, told the truth that there is no Truth (*Wahrheit*) save radical honesty (*Wahrhaftigkeit*) about that fact, and so forth ad nauseam. Nietzsche/anism's version of the truth-that-is-invisible-because-it-is-visible mechanism in *Beyond Good and Evil* is graphically illustrated by the fact that the Marxist Terry Eagleton, in his book *Walter Benjamin or Towards a Revolutionary Criticism* (1981), cites only the first part of aphorism 2:12 but—symptomatically for Western Marxism—overlooks the punch line. Nietzsche's culminating thesis—"The magnitude of an 'advance' can even be *measured* by the mass of things or people that had to be sacrificed to the prosperity of a single *stronger* species of man—now, that *would* be an advance . . . "—has been taken seriously and literally only by the *Right*, from Nietzsche's earliest reception on, beginning around 1895.[212] Eagleton—who can be critical of Nietzsche's ideological thematic on other occasions[213]—argues that Nietzsche's aphorism gives "revolutionary criticism" two basic things: First, it provides "a full-blown presentation" of the positive pole of Marx's discourse—namely, a certain "structuralist" tendency—the negative pole of which is represented by residual traces in Marxian discursive practice of "the presence of an organicism at odds with the 'structural' analysis." In short, the Nietzschean text provides a welcome therapeutic supplement to Marxism. Second, Eagleton argues that in effect Nietzsche, without knowing Marx, "presses Marx's transitional formulations to a boldly affirmative point." But not affirmative in a wholly unproblematic way for Eagleton. Not only was this Nietzschean pressure "not lost on Walter Benjamin"—in some respects the quintessential Western Marxist—but already, according to Eagleton, aphorism 2:12 of *On the Genealogy of Morals* "could well provide an epigraph to Benjamin's views of cultural revolution, his antihistoricist insistence on the ruptures, recyclings and re-insertions that underlie the bland ideology of 'cultural history.'" Recall also Foucault's even more influential position that "the general title of what I am doing" is "the genealogy of morals," along with his repeatedly expressed unconcern about what

Nietzsche's own intentions were. Of course, Eagleton is not unaware of the dangers faced both by Benjamin and by Marxists today who flirt with Nietzsche. Eagleton continues: "But Nietzsche's standpoint is equally ideological: by spurning all continuity as metaphysical, he threatens to subvert much of what Benjamin designates by 'tradition.' If Marx wishes to sublate the 'earlier meaning,' Nietzsche desires to suppress it. Benjamin's writings are in a crucial sense post-Nietzschean, unthinkable without that astonishing iconoclasm; yet he knew also that there are traditions of political struggle, 'earlier meanings' that, if only they could be remembered, would blow Nietzsche's own astonishing iconoclasm into the historical rubble he had himself created."[214]

On the one hand, then, it is possible that Eagleton does not need to *cite* the punch line of aphorism 2:12, for he seems to have paraphrased the gist of it well enough. On the other hand, by *not* actually citing the punch line and, more important, by not analyzing Nietzsche's own, original way of preparing it by means of a long illocution that is, in point of fact, absolutely fundamental not merely for Benjamin but for Western Marxism and poststructuralism alike, and, finally, by remaining generally fixated at the level of ideology-criticism when reading Nietzsche — by means of all these moves Eagleton ends up unable to grasp the incorporating power of Nietzsche's "astonishing iconoclasm." Yet it was just this iconoclasm, it seems, that is *both* the catalyst of Benjaminian criticism — which indeed, for Eagleton, is "unthinkable" without it — *and yet also,* by means of some mysterious alchemical conversion, a way of "blowing up" this same iconoclasm. In other words, Eagleton's argument cannot grasp the reasons for Nietzsche's enormous positive influence on exemplary leftist intellectuals, including Benjamin and himself; nor can this argument explain the surely not unrelated phenomenon that, by and large — with a few notable exceptions, including Eagleton among the vanguard — Benjamin's own effect on the Left has tended to be depoliticizing in any sphere beyond institutional politics and academia. Uncanny it is that the Left has chosen to build an entire Benjamin Industry or Videodrome out of the rubble of an already substantially Nietzsche/anized literary criticism. For Benjamin himself (*pace* Eagleton), like his Frankfurt School friends and most of his readers today, *also* spared Nietzsche his most hyperacute, hypercritical eye. The claim that Benjamin is really post-Nietzschean is wishful thinking; and with this claim collapses yet another attempt to produce a really "revolutionary criticism" by the Left. Not acknowledging that Nietzsche did maintain a form of metaphysics beyond the type imagined by Heidegger — namely, a properly Nietzschean metaphysics as esoteric semiotics — runs the unacceptable risk of being once again incorporated by and into Nietzsche's corps/e.

What also really ought to cease — for the sake of variety if nothing else — is the tedious practice, as has been reiterated recently by Andrew Benjamin, of fetishizing Nietzsche's idea that the history of philosophy is essentially one of "anoriginal conflict,"[215] but at the same time of simply ignoring this idea's specific gravity and application. Whenever Nietzsche published such remarks as "Plato versus Homer: this is the whole, the authentic antagonism," he did so because, as he also says, a major "symptom of declining life" today is the paucity of battle — an enervation registered very specifically by "equal rights for women" and "international courts instead of war."[216] Yet, in *Art, Mimesis and the Avant-Garde: Aspects of a Philosophy of Difference* (1991), Andrew Benjamin cites only the first point of the aphorism, ignoring the second and thus himself is incorporated by it.

Such incorporation is one reason to *accept* Eve Kosofsky Sedgwick's self-consciously "wild" suggestion in *Epistemology of the Closet* — a title and slogan applicable to Nietzsche less as "gay man" than as an esoteric political thinker — that Nietzsche made a certain "wager with his culture." But it is equally important to *reject* Sedgwick's fantasy that Nietzsche's wager was "disastrously mistaken" if this entails the so easy a priori assumption that he did not know exactly what he was doing and wagering. Sedgwick defines and paraphrases Nietzsche's "wager" as one in which "the progress he had painfully made in wrestling the explicit bases of his thought inch by inch away from the gravely magnetic axis of good/evil could be most durably guaranteed by battening them to the apparently alternative, scientifically guaranteed axis of health/illness or vitality/morbidity. (Whoever does not agree with me on this point I consider *infected*)."[217] Sedgwick is quite right that this conception contained "genocidal potential." She is very wrong that Nietzsche was, as she puts it, "completely blindsided" by the activation of this thought by certain "cultural developments." In *this* aspect of quarterbacking, at any rate, Nietzsche knew *exactly* what he was doing and ought to be held responsible, accountable for it.

This is not to argue, however, that Nietzsche should be held accountable for the *specific* appropriations of his work, say, in two world wars or by fascists today. In his own terms *any* specific appropriation of his work is epiphenomenal to his concealed intent, his "one horrific thought." Rather it is to argue that Nietzsche must be held accountable for *concealing* that "one horrific thought." Read between the lines, American poet Hart Crane was unintentionally on to something during the worst of World War I. In "The Case Against Nietzsche" (1918), Crane exclaimed: "Nietzsche, Zeppelins, and poisoned-gas go ill together. But Great Indra! One may envy Nietzsche a little; think of being so illusive, so mercurial, as to be first swallowed whole, then coughed up, and still remain a mystery!"[218]

According to Stanley Rosen, in the most explicit account to date of Nietzsche's esotericism, Nietzsche is radically *honest*. Read properly, he exposes pretty much all he had to say about his esotericism, which is "the bluntest version of modern Enlightenment."[219] This argument has Nietzsche almost exactly backwards. Rosen tends—or pretends—to take Nietzsche at his word with regard to this honesty. "Nietzsche's constant insistence upon his honesty is not inconsistent with this advice [i.e., 'the moment we understand that we are inhabiting a lie, we must forget or be destroyed']: honesty compels Nietzsche to reveal his esoteric teaching, to expose it to public view, and thus to transform it into an exoteric teaching. Nietzsche mitigates this risk by coating the bitter medicine of honesty with the sugar of creativity" (p. 199). Roughly, for Rosen, Nietzsche's exoteric teaching consists in "the recommendation to return to the cruel creativity of the Renaissance city-state or to the *polis* of Homeric—more generally: pre-Socratic—Greece. Cruelty is linked with creativity" (p. 196). By contrast, Nietzsche's esoteric teaching follows another logic: "Since what the traditional philosophers call Being or nature is in fact chaos, there is no eternal impediment to human creativity, or more bluntly put, to the will to power" (p. 197). In a sense, then, although Rosen would not put it this way, Nietzsche's esoteric teaching—which ironically returns "to precisely the doctrine for which he criticizes Platonism and Christianity: it empties human existence of intrinsic value" (p. 198)—*deconstructs* his more blood-chilling, exoteric adhesion to Machiavellian *virtù* by transforming creativity into an ontology available in principle to everyone. But this conclusion *seems* at once remarkably conventional and overly academic—intestine to the perennial conflict between "the ancients and the moderns." What this conclusion *cannot* account for is what the neo-Straussian Rosen himself says it must: namely, the scandalously warm embrace the elitist Nietzsche has received from Left-Nietzscheans, for surely they have been reading him exoterically, not esoterically. What this conclusion *does* serve, however, is to throw Left-Nietzschoids further off the scent of Nietzsche's esoteric semiotics, domesticating it for their philosophical delectation. Things seem to stand rather differently with regard to what Nietzsche himself had in mind for his corps/e. He was able, even while exposing his "exoteric" *political* teaching, to "coat" its "bitterness" with the "sugar" of philosophy and rhetoric—thus preserving "creativity" especially for those modern and postmodern men to come who would thereby *think* themselves to be "democratic" and not "cruel," but who could become unwittingly cruel and undemocratic. And it is for this, in part, that Nietzsche must be held responsible and accountable.

If there are precious few models of appropriation left today to get *after* the kind of intentionality required to determine responsibility and accountability, this is not the least result of Nietzsche's programming. When locked in Channel 3, Nietzscheanism is always a circular, hermeneutic, interpretive, dialectical process that does not allow his—or our—responsibility even to be theorized, let alone practiced. From this virtually hegemonic perspective—as expressed by a Marxist student of the appropriation of Heinrich von Kleist's dramas under national socialism—any notion of a "'guilty' collaboration" by texts "is *fundamentally external* to their subsequent political appropriation."[220] From such unprincipled and relativistic points of view, Nietzsche's esoteric semiotics will remain forever invisible. Nor is it any improvement to say, with de Man, that during the Nazi period "certain figures of the German past [were interpreted] along racist lines," adding: "Goethe, Hölderlin, Kleist, and Nietzsche were most frequently *distorted* in this fashion. These attempts were *often ludicrous,* but *sometimes effective enough* to demand *vigorous reaction.* Some of these trends still exist *today, but* are no longer left unchallenged. It should be clear to anyone who follows the German critical writing that . . . the *poets themselves,* in their own works, provide a *very adequate* defense against such misrepresentations."[221] The most charitable thing to be said about this way of surfing between Channels 1, 2, and 3 is that it itself is "ludicrous" and certainly anything *but* "a very adequate defense" to view the Channel 4 that is Nietzsche's corps/e. Finally, it must be said—in light of the pro-

Nazi journalism of the young de Man—that the ease with which de Man's own work can be "defended very adequately" against certain forms of "Nietzscheanism" is in doubt today, just as there is little doubt about his personal failure in the 1940s "vigorously to react" *against* national socialist racism and subsequent silence about this failure. It should also be noted, however, that de Man's complex works ought *not* to be simply dismissed on these grounds by the ad hominem attacks all too prevalent today. It is certainly possible, including on the Left, to defend aspects of de Manian theories and readings—thinking here not of Derrida's rather convoluted apologia for his late friend but of the reasoned arguments of Michael Sprinker and Fredric Jameson, among others.[222] It is possible to hold with equal conviction, however, that the view *of Nietzsche* held by de Man and his closest followers is fundamentally wrong and obscurantist. Nietzsche was of far greater influence than de Man, as de Man was among the first to admit. In any case, his esoteric semiotics cannot be as easily deconstructed *or* exonerated.

Nor are "de Man" and "Derrida" as easily separable in the matter of Nietzsche as some followers imagine. To visualize their relationship— that is, their hegemonic "agreement to disagree" on the relatively minor, exoteric Nietzsche so as to conceal the more major and esoteric— see Mark Tansey's *Derrida Queries De Man* (1990) (plate 2).[223] Re-envisioning Sidney Paget's last illustration in *The Strand* magazine for Arthur Conan Doyle's "The Adventure of the Final Problem" (1893), it depicts the mortal combat between Sherlock Holmes (Derrida?) and Moriarty (de Man?) on quintessentially Nietzschean and Zarathustrian turf: the thin strip of trail above Reichenbach Falls in Switzerland.[224] Here, the complementary opposites Moriarty and Holmes might both have plunged to death, locked in lethal "hermeneutic," "dialectical," "dialogic," "deconstructive" embrace. Now in Tansey's painting—as throughout his explicitly postmodernist œuvre— the represented geophysical site is inscribed by or made out of a written corpus. The textual—prepostliterate—base of this palimpsest undoubtedly belongs to Nietzsche. It is suitably ambiguous whether the two leading contemporary or postcontemporary Left-Nietzschoids—which is really Moriarty, which Holmes?—are "playfully" dancing, waltzing together in the "Zarathustrian" manner over the abyss, or whether one or both is about to die or be murdered in the monochrome blue dawn/twilight. Sir Arthur eventually had to bring Holmes back to life, by massive popular and commercial demand. Since Nietzsche served as a model for the characterization of *both* the Supercriminal Moriarty—responsible for all crimes but virtually invisible and accountable for none—*and* the Supersleuth Holmes,[225] Tansey leaves us to wonder exactly whose Nietzschean corpse today is really resurrected by public demand, whose corps it actually, imperceptibly informs right now.

Postscript.

> His career has been an extraordinary one. He is a man of good birth and excellent education. . . . He won a . . . Chair at one of our smaller universities and had, to all appearance, a most brilliant career before him. But . . . a criminal strain ran in his blood, which, instead of being modified, was increased and rendered infinitely more dangerous by his extraordinary powers. Dark rumours gathered around him in the University town, and eventually he was compelled to resign his Chair and to . . . set up as an Army coach. So much is known to the world, but what I am telling you now is what I have myself discovered. . . . For years past I have continually been conscious of some power behind the malefactor, some deep organizing power which forever stands in the way of the law, and which throws its shield over the wrong doer. . . . He is the Napoleon of Crime. . . . He is the organizer of half that is evil and of nearly all that is undetected in this great city. He is a genius, a philosopher. . . . He has a brain of the first order. He sits motionless, like a spider in the centre of its web, but that web has a thousand radiations, and he knows well every quiver of each one of them. He does little himself. He only plans. But his agents are numerous and splendidly organized. . . . The agent may be caught. . . . But the central power which uses the agent is never caught—never so much as suspected. . . . , the Professor was fenced round with safeguards so cunningly devised that . . . it seemed impossible to get evidence which would convict. . . . I had at last met an antagonist who was my intellectual equal.[226]

And equals in Nietzsche's corps/e are his actually and virtually indistinguishable victims.

Esoterrorism: The Process of Weeding Out

> Only the true philosopher is an audacious animal and talks to himself as did Turenne: "Carcasse, tu trembles? Tu tremblerais bien davantage, si tu savais où je te mène."[227]

> It was well said of a certain German book that *"es lässt sich nicht lesen"* — it does not permit itself to be read. There are some secrets which do not permit themselves to be told. . . . Now and then, alas, the conscience of man takes up a burthen so heavy in horror that it can be thrown down only into the grave. And thus the essence of all crime is undivulged.[228]

> . . . that's just what the world needs — more literate exterminators. . . .[229]

This last voice drifts over from the Interzone where "Nothing is true, everything is permitted" — the epigraph of David Cronenberg's film about William S. Burroughs. This slogan is a basic ethical or ethnological problematic of Cronenberg's œuvre and that of Burroughs, especially the latter's trilogy *Cities of the Red Night* (1981), *The Place of Dead Roads* (1983), and *The Western Lands* (1987). "Nothing is true, everything is permitted" has been "the first line in the canon of the secret tradition, a nihilist catchphrase, an entry into negation, a utopianism, a shibboleth."[230] It sounds quintessentially "Nietzschean," though Burroughs happens to turn not to Nietzsche but to premodern Near Eastern thought — as did Nietzsche. The slogan is attributed to Hassan i Sabbah II, Old Man of the Mountain, the twelfth-century leader of the cult of Ismailians in what is now Iran — also the home of Zoroaster-Zarathustra. Hassan i Sabbah's assassins are said by Burroughs to have killed "at a distance" by means of what he calls "organic communication" because, unlike telepathy, "the whole organism is involved."[231] This is related to what Cronenberg means by "scanning." In *Scanners* (1981), telepathy is not mind reading. Rather, it is the direct linking of two nerve systems separated by space; what it links are not only brains to hearts but brains and hearts to computer matrixes, with potentially murderous intent. This is no Cartesian, metaphysical, or binary interpersonal world but deformed neo-Spinozist monism, in which a representative dialogue between two biologically related but mortal enemies is: "'I'm one of you?' 'You're one of me?' 'Yes.'"[232]

"Organic communication" and "scanning" are precise ways of describing what Nietzsche had in mind with his illocutionary warfare — which, following Spinoza, he thought of as *actio in distans*. Guy Debord refers in his 1978 film *In girum* — his history of the Situationist

International—to the slogan "Nothing is true, everything is permitted" as coming from Hassan i Sabbah II's gnostic disciple, Rashid al-Din Sinan, another Old Man of the Mountain and leader of the Assassins, the millenarian terrorists of the Levant.[233] According to Debord, Rashid al-Din Sinan "surrendered only in his final hour, it is said, and then only to the most faithful of his fanatical followers"— clearly a figure for Debord himself. Burroughs's basic *political* problematic, also derived from Hassan i Sabbah, is that *"paradise actually exists and that it can be reached."*[234] Whereas for Burroughs—alongside Cronenberg and Debord—this notion can entail a project of radical democracy, for Nietzsche it entails an equally radical elitism. For his part, Nietzsche preferred to frame the slogan "Nothing is true, everything is permitted" in scare quotes: " 'Nichts ist wahr: Alles ist erlaubt' "; for him this was just one of the many "prejudices of the age."[235] In other words, it was a hypothesis—something to make *use* of, whether it was true or not, for his own mode of communication, scanning, assassination.

In Stuart Gordon's film *Re-Animator* (1985), a scientist develops a serum that can revitalize animal and human victims after he has killed them. Their personalities are altered in the process, rendering his revived corps of corpses violent. By contrast, Nietzsche's process of reanimation was hardly so crude; his corps is not necessarily violent in appearance, only in effect.

The esoterrorist process of weeding out for Nietzsche is embedded in a characteristically complex matrix of ideas and illocutionary experiments to implement them. This matrix includes calculations and prejudices involving the necessity for a social formation ultimately based on male domination, on various types of "breeding," and on a political economy of slavery and its modern equivalents. Thus, the people who had to be "weeded out" included potential mothers and all forces in opposition to slavery. Nietzsche's affirmation of euthanasia, paradoxical for a "life philosopher," was not illogical in his terms. Rather, it emerged out of hard-headed historical and scientific calculations: including about the *social* as well as cultural drift of the late nineteenth century, its political economy and differences between men and women, his self-described "Jesuitical" ideas and writing at this particular historical conjuncture, and his teaching of Eternal Recurrence of the Same with regard to its transformative social function. Here special philological techniques are required to grasp Nietzsche's process of weeding out.

Now, most readers of Nietzsche's published and unpublished writings — not especially attentive readers, necessarily — quickly come upon certain phrases that they *look at but do not see*. These phrases tend to involve Nietzsche's affirmation of human slavery and its modern equivalents by any means necessary. At stake are processes of distinguishing workers from nonworkers, those in the know from those not in the know, those who will survive from those who will not, those who must be weeded out and those who will do the weeding.

These passages — whether published in *Beyond Good and Evil* and *Thus Spoke Zarathustra* or unpublished in a notebook — might appear to involve something that a reader does not *desire* to see and then *represses*. Were this the case, these passages would be read not in the primary field of vision but peripherally, much as the "dream work" snares an overlooked detail from waking life into the dream, investing it with visual power in inverse proportion to the dreamer's ability to recall and analyze it after reawakening. Yet notions derived from conventional psychoanalysis, including "desire" and "repression," are alternatively too complex or not complex enough to grasp the peculiar "ocular" — read also: occulted — nature of Nietzsche's corpus. In his case, readers do not see something precisely *when* they are looking at it directly. They also do not really *hear* when Nietzsche *speaks* — his esoteric paradigm is as much "Wagnerian" as visual. Here a term on the margins of Freudian psychoanalysis is helpful. Adapted, then discarded by Freud himself before being resuscitated by Jacques Lacan, the term is "scotomization" — from Greek *skotos:* darkness. As often happens in Greek, the term has a referent that is both material — as in the architectural term "scotia": the sunken molding at the base of a pillar that casts a strong definitional shadow — and moral, for it is out of darkness that unseen danger and aggression often come. Ornament as crime. In "Aggressivity in Psychoanalysis" (1948), Lacan remarks: "The theoretical difficulties encountered by Freud seem to me in fact to derive from the mirage of objectification, inherited from classical psychology, constituted by the idea of the *perception/consciousness* system, in which Freud seems suddenly to fail to recognize the existence of everything that the ego neglects, scotomizes, misconstrues in the sensations that make it react to reality, everything that it ignores, exhausts, and binds in the significations that it receives from language: a surprising *méconnaissance* on the part of the man who succeeded by the power of his dialectic in forcing back the limits of the unconscious."[236] *Repression* implies that readers of Nietzsche unwittingly deny some unpleasant aspect of his thought access to their consciousness — for example, his misogyny or elitism — through some deficiency in *themselves*. Which is something that might then be expected to resurface in unruly, disruptive ways beneath their sensorium *but* which might also be clarified and expunged by Enlightenment or psychoanalysis. This interpretive paradigm is too easy — too "humanist" in Althusser's sense and too "moral-liberal" in Gramsci's — to grasp Nietzsche's Channel 4. By contrast, *scotomization* — though Lacan would not put it this way — refers to a physical blind spot *intended* by Nietzsche — a textual blind spot produced at the center of the visual-textual field whenever something potentially very dangerous to the reader is at stake — most notably, willing subservience as slaves under the illusion of being "free." Out of sight, out of mind. Unlike what is merely repressed, however, it does not need to return. Once is enough. Once Nietzsche has scotomized you, that's pretty much it — at least in his theory. At this point, Nietzsche's "text" is inaccessible, as he himself would say, to "explanation" or "clarification" (*Erklärung*), and the resulting corps/e begins to morph into the un/canny world of cyberpunks and cyborgs — into techno-Nietzsche/anism.

Textual scotomization is not a matter of "clarification," then, but of "text." And of "reading." Nietzsche defined "lack of philology" as occurring when "one continually confuses the clarification with the text — and what a 'clarification'!"[237] Thus he could use the common lack of philology to his advantage, anticipating it in the way he wrote. In the process of writing *Beyond Good and Evil* Nietzsche rejects "clarification" for "interpretation" or "unpacking" (*Auslegung*), and this also has to be calculated into his illocutionary and perlocutionary strategies. "Unpacking, *not* clarification. There are no conditions of fact, everything is fluid, ungraspable, in retreat; what is most enduring are still our opinions — in most cases a new unpacking on top of an old unpacking that has become incomprehensible, that is now itself only sign [Zeichen]."[238] *Therefore*, it is logical to conclude, signs are needed that are not too easy to unpack and that nonetheless form opinions.

The modernist Nietzsche was also likely guided by the premodern Epicurean materialist doctrine, as expressed by Lucretius, that "nothing is harder than to separate the *facts* as revealed from the questionable *interpretations* promptly imposed on them by the mind."[239] Alternatively, paraphrasing Althusser, one might say that if the truth of Nietzsche/anism cannot be read in its manifest discourse, it is because the text of Nietzsche is not a text in which a voice (the Logos) speaks but the inaudible and illegible notion of the effects of a structure of structures.[240] But not *totally* inaudible and illegible in the case of Nietzsche's corps/e. Naked may be a most effective form of disguise, but it is not always the best. Because of the darkest, most potentially criminal and, as he said, "terrible" or "horrific" nature of the secrets he had penetrated, Nietzsche tried to write books that, appropriating Edgar Allan Poe's phrase, do not permit themselves to be seen fully when looked at — though Nietzsche's relative success in doing so need not prevent us from attempting to tell their story better than it has been told. This story is not a matter of form and rhetoric — that is, locution, illocution, perlocution — in a merely abstract way. It is also meant to be *dangerous* for most of humanity, and it may be just that.

For Nietzsche, always at ultimate stake was a single underlying *social* — that is, political *and* economic — agenda. It was never to be made *fully* visible to all readers but rather scotomized. This principle is behind his published dictum in 1887, couched in a metaphoric of reading and unpacking texts, that "One does not only want to be understood when one writes, but rather just as precisely also *not* understood."[241] A year or so earlier, in private, he put the matter explicitly in terms of vision — more specifically as the problem of looking at something we cannot see, but not just any old thing. In late 1885 or early 1886, he wrote to himself: " — we cannot bear the sight anymore, *therefore* we abolish slavery[.]"[242] And *nowhere* in Nietzsche's notebooks does he do anything but enthusiastically affirm the necessity of slavery and its modern cognates. So his fundamental task was to make the *sight* of slavery — along with the basic mechanisms for maintaining it, violent and nonviolent alike — in/visible and bearable even as we look at them. Nietzsche's texts are thus informed by "anamorphosis" in the Lacanian sense: that is, the reader is intended to disavow having read precisely what is made most legible. The Nietzschean text consists of "detours and obstacles" — "a trap for the gaze."[243] The Nietzschean

ESOTERIC SEMIOTICS

293

reader, snared in this "logic of disavowal," is thus in part a *masochistic* reader. Unlike in most masochistic "contracts" and "stagings," however, it is not true that here the "violence is never carried out, brought to its conclusion."[244] Rather, Nietzschean violence is rechanneled — made invisible in its scotomized and scotomizing visibility.

There is not merely a "politics," as is relatively well known, but also an *economics* in Nietzsche/anism. At concealed root, this political economy is ruthlessly antidemocratic; indeed its aspect is distinctly fascoid — not fascist or national socialist — or, better, "fascoid-liberal." Left-Nietzschoids, of whom there are many within and without the academy, tend to dismiss Nietzsche's elitism as just a contingent political stance. This cavalier mood must be particularly combated when it holds that at least Nietzsche's *texts* — as distinct from their author — are somehow invested with the power to "deconstruct" Nietzsche's own misogynist or imperialist "dross." No! If anything, it is the other way around: In Nietzsche it is the *political economy that is deep.* It provides a key to grasping Nietzsche's "rhetorical play," "question of style," and enormous effectivity in a world imagined to be definitively postcommunist. On the one hand the sometimes nasty "subject matter" or "content" of Nietzsche's "texts" certainly appears quite "legible."[245] This includes even the wild and crazy stuff, say, about the necessity for slavery, breeding, and euthanasia — all the stuff that smart Left-Nietzschoids rush to deconstruct, and good Right-Nietzscheans sometimes wish he had said less directly. On the other hand the same "text" must also be grasped as a "pretext" that Nietzsche employs in order to translate a still deeper politico-economic agenda "posttextually" into a more socially acceptable and realizable "context." Qua pretext, any content thus represented would, in theory at least, actually function to conceal both the text's textuality — that is, its mechanism of transmission — and its ideology — conscious as well as unconscious — by preventing most readers from focusing on what is being esoterically withheld from ear and eye. The Nietzschean text and its content *are* offered to view, and so are located in a sense "outside" ideology and textuality. Yet they are also designed to be invisible in their full pretextual intention and posttextual effectivity. The reader of Nietzsche is always dealing with an object that in the strong (Lacanian) sense remains *imaginary:* that is, an object only *apparently and partially* recognizable and controllable. So it is that the ideology, textuality, and deeper agenda of

Nietzsche's texts are at once revealed and concealed before our very eyes: *in/visibly*. What Althusser says of the mode of non/vision that informs *classical political economy* applies *precisely* to the way Nietzsche *wanted* to be read and has *been* read with regard to the esoterrorist process of weeding out. "What classical political economy does not see," Althusser stresses, "is not what it does not see, it is *what it sees;* it is not what it lacks, on the contrary, it is *what it does not lack;* it is not what it misses, on the contrary, it is *what it does not miss.* The oversight, then, is not to see what one sees, the oversight no longer concerns the object, but *the sight* itself. The oversight is an oversight that concerns *vision:* non-vision is therefore inside vision, it is a form of vision and hence has a necessary relationship with vision."[246] And if indeed "Nietzsche's position is the only one outside of communism," then it makes perfect sense to continue reading him in the manner of "classical economy."

A quasi-hieratic principle undergirds as much the words Nietzsche saw fit to publish, to produce, as it does those he chose not to publish, not to produce. But the latter contain particularly extreme remarks, and are closer to his deepest "one intention." In 1887–1888 he noted: "What I precisely do *not* ask is questions that have to do with 'saving' or 'freeing' people, but rather what type of man should be selected as higher, willed, and above all *bred.*"[247] Earlier, while composing *Thus Spoke Zarathustra,* he had noted: "First Basic Law: no consideration for numbers: the masses. The suffering and unhappy concern us little — only the first and most successful exemplars, so that they don't get short shrift out of consideration for the ill-bred ones (i.e., the masses)[.] *Destruction* of the ill-bred — to this aim one must emancipate oneself from previous morality."[248] It always follows that "Slavery is necessary."[249] But without the slaves — both as morally Base and as economic base — knowing *that* they have accepted slavery "willingly," even with a smile, as their eternally recurrent lot. Their destruction may be desirable and is always permissible "beyond good and evil."

Nietzsche's political economy did not hold any more truck with the financially wealthy than with the poor. While the point is then to promote "spiritual" rulers, this still means being supported by workers who, though not necessarily financially in bad shape, have absolutely no say in determining any significant aspect of their lives — or deaths. Nietzsche noted to himself: "Is it not a matter of indifference that the largest number of p[eople] live the longest length of time?"[250] "The decision. There will have to be countless sacrifices. An experiment."[251] Euthanasia followed from Nietzsche's analysis of his own historical conjuncture and from his disappointment with Schopenhauerian pessimism and Wagnerian cultural politics.[252] Which in turn necessitated the development of his own illocutionary politics: "The *deep infertility* of the 19th Century. I have met no one who could have contributed a really new Ideal. For the longest time, the character of German music led me astray with *hope*. A *stronger type,* in which our strengths are synthetically bound together [synthetisch gebunden] — my belief. Evidently Everything is *décadence*. One has to direct [leiten] this going-under [dies Zu-Grunde-gehen] so that it makes possible a new form of existence for the stronger."[253] Not only is euthanasia against the "decadent" in the cards, so are fascoid — as in the bound *fasces* — modes of leadership and directive based on strength and force.

Nietzsche did also publish some remarks supporting euthanasia *as a theme*.[254] But they were mild in comparison with his unpublished ones, which additionally involved the plotting of *rhetorical strategies for its social implementation* following the notion that "it is insufficient just to convey a teaching: one must still *forcefully transform* people so that they accept it!"[255] And this transformation can occur at any collective human cost. Perhaps Nietzsche's most succinct commandment concerning the ideal way, in his euthanasia, that elements of consent as well as coercion would be conjoined is this: "Thou shalt not kill till the animal has bowed its head."[256]

Nietzsche became fascinated no later than 1884 by the practice of medical vivisection, departing from the abhorrence shown by Schopenhauer.[257] Not only did Nietzsche affirm its employment on humans and other animals, he adapted the empirical procedure to his own illocutionary and esoterrorist project. As Nietzsche put it in his notebooks, both self-knowledge and knowledge generally begin with vivisection. "Vivisection — that is the point of departure! Many are now becoming conscious of the fact that it is going to hurt many beings *if knowledge is going to occur!* As if it has ever been different! And what pain!! Cowardly feeble rabble!"[258] What is more, Nietzsche intended to link vivisection — in the literal scientific and especially in the extended epistemological and illocutionary sense — to euthanasia. Vivisection was to be a "probe" or "test" (*eine Probe*): "he who does not survive does not belong to us. . . . "[259] This test is linked to what is for Nietzsche the absolute necessity for forms of human slavery and male dominance.

With regard to slavery, the proper Nietzschean is depicted with particular candor and precision by the narrator of Albert Camus's last published novel *La chutte* (*The Fall*, 1956): namely, the self-described "judge-penitent" and "Superman."[260] Camus himself was a Nietzschean, among other things, perhaps to the death. Legend has it: "Camus died early and romantically, a poet-philosopher in a car accident with a copy of Nietzsche's *Gay Science* on the seat beside him."[261] Wittingly or not, few works in any genre have gotten closer than *The Fall* to representing Nietzsche's more esoteric position on the necessity of slavery and on some of the ways to implement it under hostile, democratized conditions. What *The Fall* does not quite enable us to see is that for Nietzsche and the proper Nietzschean this implementation can require actually killing off the opposition by murder or causing self-inflicted death. For this esoterrorist aspect of Nietzsche/anism, Toni Morrison provides the better analysis in *Song of Solomon* (1977) with her depiction of the secret society, Seven Days. It retaliates tit-for-tat against killing blacks by killing whites, and its "secret is time."[262] "To take the right time, to last. Not to grow; that's dangerous because you might become known. They don't write their names in toilet stalls or brag to women. Time and silence. Those are their weapons, and they go on forever" (p. 155). However, Seven Days is "Nietzschean" at most formally, not ideologically. For its function is in principle properly *reactive:* that is, retribution against very specific acts of white violence. By contrast, Nietzsche—who was at times racialist but not essentially racist, and who had no particular animus against people of color—had in mind not mere reaction but proleptic initiatives against all possible opponents. Otherwise, *The Fall* is a landmark in the history of Nietzsche/anism, providing a far more dexterous grasp of Nietzsche's corps/e than most other analyses, including Camus's own "Nietzschean" fictions—notably his first novel *A Happy Death*—and his several philosophical depictions of Nietzsche, which are comparatively positive and mainly thematic in orientation.[263]

Camus's judge-penitent in *The Fall* confides: "Just between us, slavery, preferably with a smile, is inevitable then. But we must not admit it. Isn't it better that whoever cannot do without having slaves should call them free men? For the principle to begin with and, secondly, not to drive them to despair. We owe them that compensation, don't we? In that way, they will continue to smile and we shall maintain our good conscience."[264] Thus does the true Nietzschean, in this one's own words, "invite the good people to submit to authority and humbly to solicit the comforts of slavery, even if I have to present it as true freedom" (p. 46). From this perspective, — a descendent of Dostoyevsky's Grand Inquisitor, now transmitted through very special and exact techniques of persuasion — the Nietzschean is "well aware that slavery is not immediately realizable. It will be one of the blessings of the future, that's all. In the meantime, I must get along with the present and seek at least a provisional solution. Hence I had to find another means of extending judgment . . ." (p. 137). This expansive, proleptic means is illocutionary. For example: "I navigate skillfully, multiplying distinctions and digressions, too — in short I adapt my words to my listener and lead him to go me one better. I mingle what concerns me and what concerns others. I choose the features we have in common, the experiences we have endured together, the failings we share — good form, in other words, the man of the hour as he is rife in me and in others. With all that I construct a portrait which is the image of all and no one" (p. 139). But note also: with slavery as the esoteric meaning and intended consequence. In short, lacking access to more sophisticated media technologies, the true Nietzschean writes books, as the subtitle of *Thus Spoke Zarathustra* indicates: *For All and No Man* — which in this context really means something like "For a Few Esoterically but Also for the Rest Exoterically."

What all this has to do in Nietzsche's own mind with euthanasia, suicide, and the process of weeding out needs to be approached cautiously. Particularly when we recall Stanley Rosen's claims that "Nietzsche intends to accelerate the process of self-destruction intrinsic to modern 'progress,' " that "the more persons who can be convinced that they are modern progressives (or postmoderns), the quicker the explosion," and that Nietzsche has succeeded "in enlisting countless thousands in the ironical task of self-destruction."[265]

In his early, programmatic but unpublished essay "The Greek State" (1872), Nietzsche explicitly promoted not merely the modern version of his rigid designator "slavery" (*Sklaverei*), but the necessity for its "conscious or unconscious" acceptance *by* "slaves" or "workers" *in* their expropriated "surplus labor" (*Mehrarbeit*), *and* the concomitant necessity for an "esoteric writing" (*Geheimschrift*) appropriate to "the esoteric doctrine of the relation between the State and genius" (*Geheim-*

lehre vom Zusammenhang zwischen Staat und Genius).[266] This is *the* most important nexus in Nietzsche's œuvre.

Among other things, Nietzsche's phrases here give the lie to the common assumption that he was unfamiliar with the language and concepts of political economy, though his access to this world was heavily mediated by unexpected and concealed sources, as will be seen shortly. But these phrases give the lie also to postmodern liberal philosophers, notably Richard Rorty and John Rawls, who would enlist — explicitly or implicitly — *Nietzsche* to support their attack against what Rorty calls a "final vocabulary" and Rawls calls a "comprehensive doctrine" as being incompatible with a democratic body politic and public sphere.[267] Such arguments have *nothing* to do with Nietzsche's own position, his rigid designator, *except* at its exoteric levels. His doctrine held that slavery was *both* morally unobjectionable *and* absolutely prerequisite for great thinking and culture.

Of course, it might be objected that Nietzsche's view of the actual Greek State was itself *historically* conditioned. Too, Nietzsche's thought was sometimes willing to submit to new evidence coming from history and "science" (in the broad German sense of "systematic, falsifiable thought"), so he might have been willing to modify his view of the Greek State, allowing himself to be corrected by new evidence. In other words, "always historicize!" — even Nietzsche. The German point of view of Greece at his time prominently included the defense by humanist Wilhelm von Humboldt (1767–1835) of Hellenistic slavery as a necessary condition of "that liberal spirit which has not reappeared to a similar extent among any other people, that is to say the spiritual role of noble and great attitudes truly worthy of a free man."[268] This phrase is a linchpin in M. I. Finley's attempt in his *Ancient Slavery and Modern Ideology* (1979) to provide a historical-materialist account of what he insists was the indissoluble articulation of slavery and culture both in Athens and its uncritical defenders — much as Nietzsche had done but from the opposite ideological camp.[269] Today, however, the jury is out on the precise role of slavery in ancient Athens. Josiah Ober argues in *Mass and Elite in Democratic Athens* (1989): "In sum, while the importance of slavery to Athenian society and economy should not be underestimated, no direct, causal relationship between chattel slavery and social stability or democratic decision making is demonstrable in Athens."[270] At real issue, however, is not the historical question of the function of slavery in Greek society "as it really was," nor its relationship to the formation then of intellectual elites and of political and rhetorical culture. Rather, the point is twofold: First, Nietzsche *believed* that slavery had a necessary, direct, causal relationship with elites and high culture in Athens; and, second, he *affirmed* the necessity of this relationship — then *and* now equally. But even in historical terms it can be noted, still following Ober, that there was a deep gap in Athens between theory and practice. In terms of the relationship between democracy and *agón,* it seems that the spirit and letter of debate — of "communicative action" — was not always practiced in Athens, where elites ultimately doubted "the wisdom of the masses."[271] "Athenians of the fifth and fourth centuries B.C. believed in political equality, and their state organization reflected this basic principle. But all Athenians were not equal. Some citizens had superior abilities to communicate their ideas, were highly educated, possessed fortunes sufficient to free themselves from the necessity of laboring, belonged to noble clans, and were able to engage in a style of life inaccessible to most of their fellow citizens."[272] There is no doubt that slavery did exist, as well as the ideology and the rhetoric necessary to conceal it. In any case, the task of properly *Nietzschean* thought, as glimpsed perhaps most directly in "The Greek State," was to continue to suture this gap between political theory and esoteric practice, and to conceal the stitches in ways appropriate to conditions of modernity now, postmodernity to come. This is not to say that Nietzsche did not sometimes affirm slavery in *public,* in his *published* writings. He *often* did. But what he concealed even then was the *depth* of his commitment to it. For it only stands to reason that he would have followed in his *own* work what he held to be the necessary Greek triad: "slavery," "esoteric writing," "the esoteric doctrine of the relation between the State and genius." In one of his most succinct critiques of Kant's ethical system, Schopenhauer had remarked that "Reasonable and vicious are quite consistent with each other, in fact, only through their union are great and far-reaching crimes possible."[273] Whereas Schopenhauer waxed appalled at this possibility and immediately mollified it, Nietzsche strove to put it to work.

Nietzsche was well aware that rhetoric, as he himself emphasized, had been *"republican"* potentially, if not in principle. In the winter of 1872–1873 he taught his handful of University of Basel students that "rhetoric arises among a people who still live in mythic images and who have not yet experienced the unqualified need of historical accuracy: they would rather be persuaded than instructed. In addition, the *need* of men for forensic eloquence must have given rise to the evolution of the liberal art. Thus, it is an essentially *republican* art: one must be accustomed to tolerating the most unusual opinions and point of view and even taking a certain pleasure in their counterplay. . . . The education of the ancient man customarily culminates in rhetoric: it is the highest spiritual activity of the well-educated man — an odd notion for us!"[274] *Therefore* Nietzsche concluded, following the logic of his "reversal of all values," that a new rhetoric was needed to combat democracy under post/classical conditions.

In an early draft of "The Greek State" written in January 1871, Nietzsche had added to its basic notions — which contained a strong anti-Semitic undercurrent to boot — an explicitly misogynist agenda.[275] This section simply dropped away — symptomatic of his sensitivity about audience and ideal reader — when he presented "The Greek State" to Cosima Wagner as a gift for Christmas 1872. Anti-Semitism, at least of the "vulgar" sort, eventually evaporated out of most of Nietzsche's thinking. But throughout Nietzsche's written production a certain "sublime," "rigid designator" persisted, to which some access remains: for example, "A people or nation is a detour of nature to 5 or 6 great *men* [Ein Volk ist der Umweg der Natur zu 5, 6 grossen Männern]."[276] Nietzsche's theory not only of Will to Power but of historical and cultural development generally — most notably, always, the development of "genius" — was predicated on solipsistic, onanistic, masculinist, and misogynist assumptions. Arguably it is to Nietzsche's *credit* that he regarded these assumptions as based on verifiable scientific evidence — for hence they would also be falsifiable. Be this as it may, he wrote: "We remain always within ourselves. (As with wet dreams [Wie bei der Pollution])." Or: "The reabsorption of semen through the blood is the strongest nourishment and generates perhaps most of all the stimulus of power, the agitation of all powers for the overcoming of oppositions, and the thirst for contradiction and opposition. The feeling of power has until now risen highest [!] in abstinent priests and hermits (e.g., in the Brahmans)"; "The feeling of the passion of *submission* is perhaps *female* [*weiblich*]"; and "The Will *of* Power" (*Der Wille der Macht*) is forever underdeveloped in women because "the nourishment of the ovaries saps strength."[277] For Nietzsche, however, as *Thus Spoke Zarathustra* makes amply clear exoterically, women are primarily important to the extent that they can function as baby factories to produce to the Super- or Overman and his heralds. More esoterically speaking, however, actual biological birth is less significant to Nietzsche than the proleptic dissemination and pullulation of his corps/e. Hence, the more basic principle than mere sexualized biology for him is that "In all intercourse [Verkehr] of people what is central is *only* pregnancy."[278] Pregnancy in *all* possible meanings of the term — spiritual as well as zoological — of course, but always so as to favor men. In Nietzsche's scheme of things, men too can become pregnant when corpse becomes corps.

Nietzsche's masculinist-misogynist views are time-honored, of course, deeply fixated in European — and not only European — antiquity. But his version is not simple to evaluate, however much we deplore it. The fact that he assumed such views to be scientific might be taken either as a condemnation of science and scientism generally, as much as of Nietzsche, or as evidence that he would have changed his opinions about women in the face of better data, or as evidence that his critique of scientific paradigms was not nearly as radical as he and his followers like to think. In any case, Nietzsche's implication that women "sap strength" was archaic before it became modern. Aristotle had written in his *Generation of Animals*:

> There are some who think that the female contributes semen during coition because women sometimes derive pleasure from it comparable to that of the male and also produce a fluid secretion. This fluid, however, is not seminal; . . . the female, in fact, is female on account of an inability of a sort, *viz.*, it lacks the power to concoct semen out of the final state of the nourishment (this is either blood, or its counterpart in bloodless animals) because of the coldness of its nature. . . . No, what happens is what one would expect to happen. The male provides the "form" and the "principle of the movement," the female provides the body, in other words the material. . . . Thus, if the male is the active partner, the one which originates the movement, and the female *qua* female is the passive one, surely what the female contributes to the semen of the male will not be semen but material. And this is in fact what happens; for the natural substance of the menstrual fluid is to be classed as "prime matter." Taking, then, the widest formulation of each of these two opposites, *viz.*, regarding the male *qua* active and causing movement, and

the female *qua* passive and being set in movement, we see that the one thing which is formed is formed from them only in the sense in which a bedstead is formed from the carpenter and the wood, or a ball from the wax and the form.[279]

Millennia later, Nietzsche had not progressed one wit beyond this self-legitimating male fantasy. This was not exactly what Heidegger had in mind when he used to tell his students that they really ought to have studied Aristotle for years before even beginning to read Nietzsche, let alone grasping Will to Power. Nonetheless, Nietzsche's "Aristotelian" misogyny, as complex and self-deconstructive as it may be in *some* respects, remains at the *root* of his thinking.

For Nietzsche, misogyny made perfect sense in one crucial respect at least. His *writing* — not his actual penis lampooned by Wagner — *was* his phallus, his sexuality, his dissemination, his proleptic-prophetic procreation, his perlocutionary desire *and capacity* to incorporate everything, including everyday life. Understood in *this* context, Derrida's articulation of the *stylus* of Nietzsche's writing with the *phallus,* with *style,* and with the *spur/spoor/spore* of the *trace* turns out to be on the mark. Above all else, however, writing was Nietzsche's way of making war — "father of all things." Marie Hecht, the earliest known feminist critic of attempts to incorporate Nietzsche into feminism, was also near the mark when she wrote already in 1888–1889: "In truth, Nietzsche-anism in the world of women means giving up the demands of 'radical egalitarians.' For it reinforces yet again the biological role and, *in transfigured form,* reasserts male domination."[280] But it is the *illocutionary* complexity of this transfiguration that must be attacked more than the mere *theme.* Recall also that Nietzsche's view of the Self and his own "center" gives no support to celebrations of "the decentered subject" and its relatives. Rather, it was in his interest to keep the possibilities of the self-mastering and mastering male subject radically *open,* thus to make *use* of it as needed.

Nietzsche's acknowledgment in "The Greek State" about the necessity of esotericism for social cohesion and male genius remained his most enduring line of march, as well as his most explicit attempt to come to terms with the "inevitability" of slavery, to put it to work in combat against "socialism." The nexus of phallocentric thoughts here are as close as it may be possible to get to Nietzsche's rigid designator in the Kripkean sense — so rigid, in fact, that it is difficult to imagine how any moral scruple, including about matters of life and death, could get in its way. So enduring is this conceptual nexus that it is misleading to speak of anything like an "epistemological break" in Nietzsche's work, or of its clear periodization. To the extent that scientific thought requires the possibility of breaks, paradigm shifts, and self-reversals, Nietzsche cannot be lumped together with Freud or Marx. According to a time-honored tradition, however, Nietzsche's œuvre is divided up into three more or less distinct, more or less related periods, each having its "transition" texts: (1) an "early" period, including *The Birth of Tragedy* and the *Untimely Meditations,* when the budding classicist comes under the influence of Wagner and Schopenhauer and is active in German cultural politics; (2) a "middle" period of withdrawal, when he leaves academia for good, reacts against his prior intellectual formation, and enters into a more "positivistic," "critical," and even quasi-"democratic" phase, particularly in *Human, All-Too-Human;* and (3) a "late," "mature," "axial," or "creative" period, beginning with the last section of *The Gay Science* and continuing in *Thus Spoke Zarathustra* to the end in Turin. To be sure, this periodization is Nietzsche's own, and therefore suspect. For example, Zarathustra speaks of three basic phases or "transformations" of spiritual activity — "the camel" (beast of burden), "the lion" (beast of prey and revolt), and "the child" (playful creator) — and this quasi-Hegelian sequence is taken literally to apply to Nietzsche's "transformations" as well.

The *external* historical and ad hominem or psychological explanations for the supposedly distinct periods of Nietzsche's thought — in addition to its *internal* logic and pragmatic impetus — can be located in his relationship to his contemporaries, the specter of the Paris Commune after the defeat of France, the collapse of Nietzsche's career as a university professor, the re/unification and rapid industrialization and "socialization" of Germany under Prussian hegemony, and so forth. Ultimately, a full historical and sociological contextualization of Nietzsche's drift into esotericism would have to include his complex response to all the world events of which he was aware from his vantage point on the Swiss and Italian periphery of Germany, including events that affected him indirectly as his "geopolitical aesthetic." Nor are his sexuality and fluctuating, but increasingly miserable, health wholly irrelevant. But such external and internal "contextualization" in the end provides little more than yet another *description* of the overdetermined causes of Nietzsche's esotericism, and does not get *after* its philosophical and illocutionary taproot—which is what continues to feed his posthumous corps/e.

Particularly crucial in this regard remains Nietzsche's "break" with Wagner—germs of which were present, however, even in *The Birth of Tragedy* and the *Untimely Meditation* on "Richard Wagner in Bayreuth" (1876). This "break" eventually became irreversible: either by May 1877 in Sorrent, after what was to be his last personal encounter with Wagner, or by the end of that year, when he could have learned that Wagner was describing him behind his back as, among other things, an "onanist" and a "pederast." True or not, this assertion drove Nietzsche deeper into seclusion of all kinds, rhetorical as well as existential. By then it had also become clear to him that he could never return to teaching at a university due to the severity of his various—physiological primarily but also psychosomatic and psychological—ailments, which forced him to resign his post at Basel in May 1879. Henceforth, having lost any *institutional* base for his own cultural-political interventions, he was forced to come up with ever newer *illocutionary* models to incorporate readers no longer in the present but in the future—models post-Wagnerian in inspiration and elitist in ideological formation. Finally, the largely—though not entirely—indifferent response by his contemporaries to his writings, particularly to *Thus Spoke Zarathustra*, further led Nietzsche to experiment with ways of relating esoteric intent or cause to exoteric articulation and proleptic effect.

The persistence in Nietzsche of the ideas expressed in "The Greek State" of 1872 indicates that his political ideology and reflections about how to implement it remained remarkably unchanged over the course of his life. His later teaching of Eternal Recurrence of the Same reinforces the impression that his thinking could never be subject to substantial change or radical break, though his illocutionary strategies had been adjusted to respond to historical conjunctures, including Nietzsche's obsessive "predictions" about the future. Part of what this relative rigidity means is that—unlike Freud or Marx—Nietzsche was both theoretically and empirically impervious to the crises that come with such epistemological breaks as may distinguish, say, "the moment of 'ideology' and 'criticism'" from "the moment of 'science.'" Strictly speaking, ideologically speaking, there is no "mature" or "axial" Nietzsche for the same reason that there is also no "young" or "transitional" Nietzsche. Althusser once suggested that the "youth of a science is its prime of life; before this age it is old, its age the age of the preconceptions by which it lives, as a child does the preconceptions and hence the age of its parents."[281] In the case of more or less scientific thinkers like Freud and Marx, it may be necessary for readers to return to a certain "age" of their work, to find its "prime" break with its "preconceptions." On the one hand this principle might seem applicable to Nietzsche, given the staying power of "The Greek State," written when he was twenty-eight years old, since it was, in his own context, his first "scientific" work — at least for the themes it broached, though not yet for its illocution, which was perfected, in Nietzsche's view, only a decade later in *Thus Spoke Zarathustra*. On the other hand the very persistence in his work of the basic triad depicted in "The Greek State" — slavery plus esoteric writing plus social project — requires the opposite of any "epistemological break," and instead only a "Machiavellian" calculation of how to nurture and manipulate his corps/e under changing and often hostile circumstances. In the matter of fundamental politico-rhetorical convictions, there is no real difference between any *one* Nietzsche and a *prior* or *subsequent* incarnation. Modern or postmodern, precontemporary, postcontemporary, or just plain contemporary. Nonnegotiable and unchanging in Nietzsche remained interlocked demands: the social necessity for slavery *and* the secret tactics, strategies, and technologies required to realize it by whatever means necessary.

In 1881 — a full decade after "The Greek State" — Nietzsche wrote: "Slavery is to be seen everywhere, although this is not admitted: — we have to struggle to be everywhere, too, to know all conditions of slavery, in order to be able to represent all its views in the best possible way. This is the only way we can be master over slavery and make use of it. Our true essence [*Unser Wesen*] must remain concealed, just like the Jesuits who exercised dictatorship in the guise of *tools* and *functions*. What is our function, our mantle of slavery? Pedagogy? — Slavery should not be eradicated, it is necessary. Our task is to see to it that there will always be people *for whom* work is done, so that this gigantic mass of politico-commercial potential [diese große Masse von politisch-commerciellen Kräften] is not squandered. Even so that there will be *viewers* and *people who no longer play along in the game!*"[282] In short, anything *except* a Hands-On Imperative for viewers and players and, Nietzsche hoped, for most of *us*. Better couch potatoes at night and workers by day — thinking that they're at play, *we're* at play. In this sense reading Nietzsche or not reading him amounts to the same thing.

In the "Jesuitical" sense, Nietzsche's task was to *maintain* socialism, keeping it from becoming *communism*. In so doing he was "diplomatic." Gramsci noted not only that "The Society of Jesus is the last of the great religious orders," because its origins were "reactionary and authoritarian, its character repressive and 'diplomatic,' "[283] but also that it is immaterial whether a writer is "technically" Jesuit or not. Any writer is "Jesuit," in the extended Gramscian meaning, who declines, in principle or in practice, "to elaborate a modern 'humanism' able to reach right to the simplest and most uneducated classes," and who engages in conspiratorial, esoteric writing in this prophylactic project against the masses.[284] But Nietzsche's Jesuitism is exceptionally complex.

Even the most hostile things he said in public about "democracy" and the like were *exoteric posturing*. While working out the illocutionary strategy of *Thus Spoke Zarathustra,* he noted: "Zarathustra [is] happy about the fact that class war is *over,* and now there is finally time for a rank ordering of Individuals. Hatred against the democratic system of leveling is only *foreground:* in fact he [Zarathustra] is very happy that *this has come thus far.* Now he can finish his task. — "[285] But while Nietzsche thought of socialism as "inevitable,"[286] communism was not. Nietzsche was not as "mandarin" as he is commonly represented to be: that is, wholly ignorant about political economy.[287] For this reason, the orthodox Marxist objection — beginning at the end of the nineteenth century with Franz Mehring in Germany and Georgi Plekhanov in Russia — to all forms of "Nietzschean pseudoradicalism" that move only across the superstructure without ever descending into the economic structure is a paradigm far more applicable to *Left*-Nietzscheanism than to Right-Nietzscheanism *or* to Nietzsche himself.

In the early 1870s, not long after Nietzsche had been admitted into Wagner's inner family circle in Tribschen, Switzerland, he was entrusted by The Master with proofreading the essays from the latter's "Dresden" or "communist" period. So it was that Nietzsche encountered such texts as "The Revolution" (1849) and "Artistry of the Future: On the Principle of Communism" (1849) — both of which are riddled with positive albeit muddled allusions to Marx and Engels, including *The Communist Manifesto* (1848).[288] These unconscious caricatures of communism by Wagner were as close as Nietzsche came to communist literature, though he knew a bit more about socialism from reading secondary sources, journalism, Eugen Dühring, and Ferdinand Lassalle. The impression perhaps given by Adorno aside, Wagner enjoyed a quite good reception among large segments of the working class and socialist leaders during Nietzsche's lifetime and into the twentieth century, in part because of Wagner's revolutionary background as a self-described "communist" in 1848, in part because of the perception that his music dramas continued to retain elements of subversive, progressive ideology. This was the opinion not only in Germany and France but *messogiorno* Italy. For example, the first mainland socialist minister of note to visit Gramsci's Sardinia, Guido Podrecca in 1910, chose as his first lecture to socialist activists and proletarians in Cagliari the topic "The Revolutionary Thought of Richard Wagner."[289]

Now, in 1879 Nietzsche read with interest a German translation of the main work of the American political economist Henry Charles Carey (1793–1879), it being one of the main arguments in nineteenth-century political economy.[290] Nietzsche returned to read Carey, along with the infamous Dühring, in 1881, leading up to the composition of *Thus Spoke Zarathustra* (1883–1885).[291] Nietzsche remained interested in Carey because he recognized that Carey had influenced Dühring's work, which Nietzsche held in considerable contempt — as did Marx — on philosophical and stylistic grounds, but also — as Marx did not — for what Nietzsche regarded as its botched but otherwise admirable elitist aspect. In May 1887 Nietzsche wrote Gast that Dühring had "appropriated all essential *oeconomica*" from Carey.[292] But, as a notebook used in 1879 indicates, what Nietzsche himself *really* appropriated positively from Carey was the *economic* notion that competition, as Nietzsche paraphrased it, is at once "useful" and "fundamentally evil" — viewing this dual principle and its concealment — beyond good and evil, of course — as crucial to the maintenance of social order, "harmony," and "equilibrium."[293] In his aphorism "The Principle of Equilibrium" in the expanded version of *Human, All-Too-Human*, entitled *The Wanderer and His Shadow* (1880), Nietzsche concealed Carey's direct influence on his own argument that "robbers" and "authorities," "robbers" and "traders," are really two sides of the same coin, insofar as both serve in "dialectical" tandem to produce and legitimate socioeconomic "harmony."[294]

Unbeknownst to Nietzsche, but applicable to him, was Marx's earlier analysis of precisely this moment in nineteenth-century political
economy. The twin ideologically motivated illusions, first, that bourgeois capitalist relations of production are inherently "harmonious,"
and, second, that any "antagonisms" within its system of "free" competition are merely contingent and superficial, rather than structural, had
been exposed to light by Marx in volume 1 of *Capital* (1867), as well as
a decade earlier in the unfinished drafts of his *Grundrisse* (1857–1858).
In both works, Marx had made explicit reference to the work of Carey,
who exemplified for him not only the most recent American version
of this main current of capitalist self-legitimation — represented at the
time in France by Frédéric Bastiat's *Harmonies économiques* (1851),
which Nietzsche did not know — but also what happens to political-
economic thinking — indeed all thinking — when it fails to perceive the
fundamental contradiction between regional and global economies.[295]

Nietzsche's "thought" — Eternal Recurrence of the Same — is a *philosophical* version of the *political-economic* principle of "harmonization"
developed by Bastiat and Carey to legitimate bourgeois class rule. Eternal Recurrence of the Same turns out to produce its harmonization-
effect by means up to and including encouraging people to kill themselves or to murder. It must be noted first, however, that in Nietzsche's
thinking economic class is at most a contingent result of elitism,
though he has no more *principled* objection to class rule than he does to
any other manifestation of the Will to Power. Nietzsche was primarily
interested in intellectual and cultural castes, not economic classes in
the Marxist sense. And precisely this makes him attractive for post-
Marxists, and his patent elitism quite tasty, if invisible. The full complexity of Nietzsche's distinctive take on the political-economic cannot
be easily exposed to light, since his other primary concern was to conceal by "secret writing" the full mechanisms of social and philosophical
power. It is at *this* point that questions of "style" and "literature" become relevant for him. Had Nietzsche known Marx, he would have
directed much greater efforts against him than he had against Carey.
Marx, alas, would likely have ignored Nietzsche.

As for Nietzsche's way of reading literature, it was informed by remarkably specific considerations of political economy. This is visible in
over seventy pages of notes he took while reading Charles Baudelaire's
opus postumous in 1888, during his own last stage of creativity.[296] Nietzsche shared with Baudelaire, whom he had also read earlier, a complex

metaphoric of money, but not only that.[297] Christine Buci-Glucksmann has shown that many of the most infamous Baudelairean "figures" (or rather "signifying practices") — such as "the sterile woman," "the androgyne," "the lesbian," and especially "the prostitute" — were not only contradictory among themselves, for Baudelaire, but also intended by him to expose the multiple contradictions of capitalism as he knew them.[298] Nietzsche's reading notes indicate that he was as fascinated by this aspect of Baudelaire as were Walter Benjamin and Althusser years later.[299] In bourgeois and patriarchal ideology, the lesbian, androgyne, and prostitute are not *re/productive:* they re/produce neither children nor, insofar as they are social "parasites," surplus value, or corps/es. So it is, for instance, that "the prostitute" comes to embody or figure commodity production and fetishism, likewise the transformation of love by capital into an exchange value. As such, the prostitute both *is informed by* and *elicits* the fundamental nether experiences of alienation that shadow rationalizing and commercializing modernity: for example, boredom, melancholy, emptiness, spleen, vertigo, and more boredom. Other figures, however, such as "the lesbian" and "the androgyne," stand as points of ostensible resistance against precisely this objective commodification and its concomitant alienation effect. Along these lines, to employ James Jay Slawney's felicitous turn of phrase, Baudelaire had worked out an amazingly detailed and precise "materialist physiognomics of the somnambulistic society" of early capitalism.[300] Leaving his views of woman aside, Nietzsche himself had been groping toward a rudimentary analysis of capitalism all his mature life. He had been introduced to the theme of aesthetic resistance to "Americanism" — belief in progress; worship of money as a god; the commodification of art; the soon-to-be-Taylorized division of intellectual and manual labor that locked out the return of "Renaissance man" — when he had read intently Théophile Gautier's preface to *Les fleurs du mal* in 1885.[301]

Because he always circles back to the need for the esoteric dissemination of his philosophical and social agenda, Nietzsche is particularly pleased to find in Baudelaire's *opus postumous* echoes of his own theories: that is, "all true politics is essentially or inevitably Jesuit and revolutionary [Si tu étais jesuite et révolutionnaire, comme tout vrai politique doit l'être ou l'est fatalement]. . . . "[302] Nietzsche's last notebook excerpts from the *Œuvres posthumes* terminate as a dual-language reflection—part citation, part interpolation—on what he approvingly calls Baudelaire's "monstrous" or "hair-raising" (*Haarsträubend*) vision of what in *Thus Spoke Zarathustra* he had called "the last men." This speech by Zarathustra is considered today by neoconservatives and neoliberals alike to be Nietzsche's *decisive* attack not only against modernity but against all socialist and democratic attempts to forge something progressive out of modernity.[303] According to the final Baudelairean-Nietzschean pastiche, European politics has become so "Americanized" (*americaniziert*) that any effective "great politics" is in danger of being eliminated, if it has not been already. For Nietzsche, the "Party of Peace," of socialism, is in danger of triumphing over the "War Party," also called the "Spiritual" or "Intellectual Party." In his pastiche:

> The further development of humanity according to Baudelaire's idea. Not that we could again approach conditions in the wild, for example in the manner of the Jocose disorder of South American republics, where, gun in hand, one seeks one's sustenance amongst the ruins of our civilization. That would presuppose a certain vital energy. Technology is so Americanized, and progress will have so atrophied the spiritual Party in us, that Everything deranged [Alles Verrückte] that has been dreamt of by the socialists lags behind actual reality. No religion, no property; not even any more revolution. General collapse will not be revealed in political institutions (or *le progrès universel:* names don't matter much)[.] Is it necessary for me to add that the little bit of politics that remains will be debated laboriously in the embrace of general animality [se débattra péniblement dans les étreintes de l'animalité générale], and that, in order to keep themselves standing and to create a phantom of order, political governments will be forced to take their refuge in means that will make our contemporary humanity quake, *no matter how callous!* [qui feraient frissonner notre humanité actuelle, *pourtant si endurcie!*] (Hair-raising!).[304]

This last parenthetical insertion is—characteristically for the late Nietzsche—half-ironic, half *deadly* serious, since his discourse is now beyond the difference. He now immediately continues his passage as a running commentary on Baudelaire's apocalyptic vision of the end of bourgeois modernism. This age is said to culminate in abject debasement and degradation: "*avilissement.*" Nietzsche then starts up a new paragraph, which continues for a time with yet another dual-language vision of "the last man." Presently, however, when he has finally had enough of decadence, Nietzsche's tone abruptly changes. He abandons Baude-laire and his "dandy" with the familiar demand—in his own or Zara-thustrian voice—for "A little pure air!" And propelled by thin moun-tain air from "the pathos of distance" comes Nietzsche's spin back away from the Baudelairean problematic toward his own *"Tractatus politi-cus,"* his own plans for the "War Party" to be projected into any possible future, returning eternally.

It is important that Nietzsche usually restrained himself from *pub-lishing* his thoughts of an explicitly economic nature, particularly since many of his philosophical and cultural analyses *presuppose* arguments about the political economy. Whatever the full reason for this reticence may have been, its *effect* on his reception has been profound especially among Left-Nietzschoids generally, and not only of the "literary" per-suasion. Ignorance of Nietzsche's economic thinking—or rather the economic *dimension* of his one thought—leads to the a priori supposi-tion that Nietzsche's—exoteric—critique of power somehow *would* have included the capitalist mode of production, if only Nietzsche had not—supposedly—shared the common intellectualist, mandarin dis-dain for getting his hands dirty in the infrastructure. In point of fact, Nietzsche's hands *were* dirty.

A quite common and fundamental blunder in reading Nietzsche is to reduce his not infrequent use of the term "economics" to an imagined Freudian or Bataillean "psychodialectic" that is not merely of an exclu-sively heterosexual nature but one without any significant reference to political economy strictly conceived.[305] This position is grounded on the false assumption that Nietzsche was basically an exoteric thinker and writer, and so it makes perfect sense to suspend whatever judgment one might have about Nietzsche's also not infrequent affirmations of human slavery, reducing this affirmation to a silly choice that must obviously be rejected: either make light of Nietzsche's "self-glorifying sentimentality" or remark that this "oversensitivity is no justification for the adoption of a reactive stance."[306] This antinomy legitimates bail-ing out of reading Nietzsche seriously with the unintentionally positiv-istic claim that "our concern here is not to blame or to praise Nietzsche but rather to map the forces of his economy" (p. 85)—an "economy" that is always already bled dry of any real meaning or import.

The "leftist" misrecognition or ignorance of Nietzsche in this funda-mental matter makes particularly perfect sense sociologically and ideologically speaking. For one of the most impressive ways that capitalism and liberalism work hegemonically to win consent is to allow criticism of itself of *all* kinds — but *only* if these do not extend to actions taken against its economic base. Certainly, to say the very least, Nietzsche himself had no compelling reasons substantially to criticize the principle of raw power that lies at the taproot of the profit motive and surplus value; on the contrary, he had many compelling — esoterically concealed — reasons why this aspect of the Will to Power, too, ought to appear "natural" and "commonsensical." Additionally important is the political consideration that Nietzsche thought that the people he called "socialists" were at once potentially very powerful allies — viewed esoterically — and rivals — viewed exoterically — because, according to his analysis in unpublished notebooks, "Modern socialism intends to create the worldly counterpart to Jesuitism: *everybody* an absolute instrument. But the purpose, the goal has not been discovered till now."[307] The ultimate purpose and goal of history — according to Nietzsche's version of teleology and *causa finalis* — was the promotion of a few male geniuses, A Few Good Men, a few Contras to combat communism proleptically — even before the fact or possibility. *Prophetically.*

Nietzsche's *economic* thought — such as it is — is really quite straightforward and fully consistent with his aesthetics and politics. In the Nietzschean utopia of neo-aristocratic nobles, "Workers ought to learn to perceive like *soldiers.*" They will receive "subsistence but no wages." There will be "no relation between pay and output." In short: *To and from each according to his or her pre-established "type"* — a "type" (*Art*) determined by and for the ruling caste.[308] Because Nietzsche is commonly regarded as a Spinozist, it is important to contrast Spinoza's own definition of nobility (*generositas*), as "the desire by which every person endeavors according to the dictate of reason alone to help and join him- or herself in friendship with others," and Spinoza's absolute preference — in explicit opposition to monarchy and aristocracy — for democracy, "defined as a society which wields all its power as a whole."[309] But in light of the possibility that Nietzsche's position is the only one outside of communism, it is also important to contrast Marx's analysis in his *Critique of the Gotha Program* of the deep problems facing communist society "not as it has *developed* on its own foundations, but, on the contrary, just as it *emerges* from Capitalist society; which is thus in every respect, economically, morally and intellectually, still stamped with the birth marks of the old society from whose womb it emerges."

Only after noting that substantial "defects are inevitable in the first phase of communist society as it is when it has just emerged after prolonged birth pangs from capitalist society," did Marx append a rare vision of a communist future, along with the specific conditions required for its realization: "In a higher stage of communist society, after the enslaving subordination of the individual to the division of labor, and therewith also the antithesis between mental and physical labor, has vanished; after labor has become not only a means of life but life's prime want; after the productive forces have also increased with the all-round development of the individual, and all the springs of cooperative wealth flow more abundantly — only then can the narrow horizon of the bourgeois right be crossed in its entirety and society inscribe on its banner: From each according to his ability, to each according to his needs!"[310]

At just this non/synchronous moment — early May 1875 — Friedrich Nietzsche was vacationing in the Swiss Alps, nursing his health with homeopathic cures (always "fight fire with fire"), warning his friends against marriage (since women are "an inferior creation"), wondering what to give Wagner on his approaching birthday, working on his last *Untimely Meditations*[311] — and in general plotting new works on behalf of those men he would be calling "the future rulers of the earth."

Years later, in the autumn of 1883, Nietzsche was in a contemplative mood about the trajectory of his works. He returned to his textual "Jesuitism," refining his position somewhat. "Behind my first period grins the face of Jesuitism: I mean, the conscious holding-fast to illusion and its compulsory incorporation [zwangsweise Einverleibung] as *basis of Culture* [als *Basis der Cultur*]." After reflecting for a moment on the "Buddhist," world-denying component also inhabiting his "early period" — presumably from *The Birth of Tragedy* through at least the *Untimely Meditations* — Nietzsche continued his main line of thought, of march: "*NB! HISTORY OF THE HIGHER MAN.* The breeding of better people is monstrously more painful. *Ideal of the sacrifice necessary for it to be demonstrated with Zarathustra:* leaving his homeland, family, fatherland. . . . Every living thing reaches as far out around itself with its strength as it can and submits itself to the weaker one: in this way it has its enjoyment *per se*. The *increasing 'humanization'* in this tendency consists in the fact that one experiences ever more *finely* just *how difficult* it is to really *embody* the other: how crude damage does show our power over him, to be sure, but simultaneously *alienates* his will even more from us—thus makes him less conquerable."[312] In light of such remarks it is strange to hear intelligent Right-Nietzscheans—any Nietzscheans—claiming today that "Nietzsche is the first Platonic philosopher who knowingly refuses to cast his lot with the salutary lies. He refuses any form of Jesuitism."[313] And of course one way of "breeding" is "weeding."

If the more esoteric "grinning face" of Jesuitism was ever abandoned in Nietzsche's work—and it never was, really—Nietzsche's appreciation of the raison d'être of Jesuitism, its creation and maintenance of "order of rank," certainly was not abandoned. The "free spirit" was another word for the appropriate modern form of "Jesuit," and the free spirit's basic principle was: "War (but without powder!)."[314] In terms of aesthetics, what Nietzsche really admired was *one thing only:* "The work of art where it appears *without* artist, e.g., as *body,* as *organization* (Prussian officer *corps,* Jesuit *order*). To what extent the artist is only a preliminary stage. What does the 'subject' mean—?"[315] Rhetorical question. Answer: a potential slave worker or—failing that—a corpse. Full stop.

But this, too, is an *old* story. On coffins in the early Ptolemaic period of Egypt, circa 240 B.C.E., bound slaves and prisoners were depicted on the soles of the sandals of mummies to symbolize the ability of deceased rulers to overcome all opposition in the next, the future world. Souls on soles. It is in opposition to this age-old suffering that Rastafarians sing up against the Babylon of capitalism: "Downpresser Man: Where're You Goin' to Run to, Where're You Goin' to Hide?" This would not have been Nietzsche's song except as an invitation to learn to hide better, and he provides a very effective place of refuge.

Nietzsche did have a "hermeneutics," but not that of Bataille-Deleuze-Derrida-Foucault-Gadamer-Habermas-Klossowski-Ricoeur & Co. Whether it was eternally recurrent or just archaic, it can be called not only an esoteric semiotics but a "hermeneutic" or "rhetoric of euthanasia": *the process of weeding out.*

Coded written teachings such as Eternal Recurrence of the Same were android probes into the dark reaches of the past, present, and especially future: "the great test-probe" (*die große Probe*), Nietzsche called it. Namely: "Who can withstand the thought of Eternal Recurrence?—

Whosoever will be destroyed with the sentence 'there is no salvation' ought to die. I want *wars,* in which the vital and courageous *drive out* the others — you ought to expel them, shower them with every manner of contempt, or lock them up in insane asylums, drive them to despair, etc."[316] When all is said and done, a Nietzschean slogan such as "Eternal Recurrence of the Same" (or "Will to Power" or "Beyond Good and Evil" or whatever) is not an *ontological* fantasy on Nietzsche's part about how the world *is.* Rather, as his notebooks of 1884 scream to himself, before becoming illegible even to his best editors, it is a *pragmatic social* fantasy about how the world *ought to be, perhaps will be.* In his own words, Eternal Recurrence of the Same is a *"hammer"* in the hand of *the most powerful* human, ———."[317] And so Nietzsche's deepest, darkest desire was to write "An *evil* book, worse than Machiavelli and that mild-malicious, most subservient devil, Mephistopheles!"[318] If, as Leo Strauss wrote, Machiavelli was a teacher of evil, Nietzsche intended to be more evil still.

As is the case with virtually all of Nietzscheanism, not the Left but the Right has come closest to grasping the importance of eugenics and euthanasia for Nietzsche. While it is comparatively easy to deconstruct Nietzsche's remarks about *eugenics,* many of which he published, it is almost impossible to deconstruct his *enthusiasm* for euthanasia, on which he published far fewer remarks. Relatively progressive members of the early German women's movement, such as Helene Stöcker, began to approach this dimension of his thought, only to whitewash it away.[319] But Stöcker was influenced in this regard by figures much farther to the Right than herself, and who also saw this aspect of Nietzsche more clearly than she — including Stöcker's onetime lover, the pan-Germanic, Social Darwinian Nietzschean Alexander Tille. Tille (1866–1912) came under Nietzsche's influence in the 1890s and was one of the main conduits between him and the English-speaking world. He was an editor of the first English edition of Nietzsche's *Collected Works* and, most interestingly, was a director of the Organization of German Industrialists and then represented the German Employer's Association.[320] Thus Tille lends some credence to the claim — made by Mehring, Plekhanov, Tönnies, and most recently Arno Mayer[321] — that Nietzsche provided a significant intellectual buttress to prop up and legitimate the German Right at its shakier moments, not only the old landed aristocracy but also modern German industry, with Nietzscheanism as the ideological pivot between the two decisive forces. In his major work, *From Darwin to Nietzsche: A Book of Developmental Ethics* (1895), Tille used passages in Nietzsche, among other things, to defend the killing of socially "unproductive" people. Arguing as Social Darwinist *against* the democratic and egalitarian implications of Darwin's own thought and *with* Nietzsche on behalf of elites, Tille saw the Superman as the only authentic aim of world history.[322] Where Tille departed from his philosophical master was only in the fact that, for Tille, Nietzsche's "aristocratic radicalism" had to be brought up to technological and modernist speed, as it were. Most important, in terms of the political economy, Nietzschean eugenics and euthanasia now had to be put in the service not of the old landed aristocracy but of the "aristocracy of merit" combined with willing human wage labor.[323]

Tille's critical Nietzscheanism of euthanasia is closer to Nietzsche's own views and intentions than Left-Nietzschoids suppose. But what Tille failed to grasp, just like Left-Nietzschoids, is how euthanasia is not just a theme of Nietzsche's thinking — including the thought of Eternal Recurrence of the Same — but also a perlocutionary aim of his esoteric semiotics. The question of how *successful* this "hermeneutic of euthanasia" is also broached. With this esoterrorist problematic in mind, the relationship between Eternal Recurrence of the Same and the process of weeding out becomes more visible.

Eternal Recurrence of the Same is designed to be un/canny, its peculiar character overdetermined as a wound (Greek *trauma*) not only in temporality and history but in the body politic. In Nietzsche's hands the concept far outstrips in import Schopenhauer's vivid depiction of the man able to affirm life so much as to desire its "endless duration" (*endlose Dauer*) and "constant recurrence" (*immer neue Wiederkehr*).[324] Alphonso Lingis suggests that "the Nietzschean experience of eternity" is "not an eternity in extension, the endurance of a stagnant moment without past and without future, stretched out linearly without end, but an infinity in the present moment, an eternity in intensity. . . ."[325] In this respect, Nietzsche also appears as a follower of Spinoza — formally, not politically. Beyond the biographical fact that Nietzsche's own first encounter with his "thought" apparently had the force of an inarticulate traumatic experience, he subsequently intended this sublime trauma to be replicated in other people in such a way that while some might "work it through" in a psychoanalytic sense, most will "reenact it" in one form of intensive traumata or other. Eternal Recurrence of the Same is thus a mode of trauma as defined by Shoshana Felman and Dori Laub: that is, an event that has "no beginning, no ending, no before, no during and no after. This absence of categories that define it lends it a quality of 'otherness,' a salience, a timelessness and a ubiquity that puts it outside the range of associatively linked experiences, outside the range of comprehension, of recounting, and of mastery."[326] Felman and Laub are talking about the Holocaust. In comparing this terrible destruction and trauma with Nietzschean Eternal Recurrence of the Same the intent is not to trivialize the former but rather to attempt to get some purchase on the extreme importance assigned the latter by Nietzsche. There is nothing negative or pejorative per se about trauma; indeed, so far this description approximates Spinoza's definition of Mind operating at its highest, most noble level, reflecting on eternity and infinity. For here Mind lacks relationality to commonplace temporality and is equally "before" and "after" the existence of the physical Body qua distinct finite entity but with which it is also thus essentially identical.[327] Crucial to the specifically *Nietzschean* trauma of Eternal Recurrence of the Same is the problem of how to *respond* to this thought, which is inculcated slowly in *Thus Spoke Zarathustra* and never in its full aspect, even as the focus of attention inevitably shifts away from more or less accurate descriptions or relivings of the event "as it really was" or — rather more profoundly — "really will be" and toward the struggle for its current meanings, significations, uses, and incorporations. To this end, at stake in Nietzschean trauma are illocutions and perlocutions. Another thesis of Felman and Laub can be extrapolated to describe Nietzsche. Eternal Recurrence of the Same is not so much "a statement (any statement can but lag behind events), but a performative *engagement* between consciousness and history, a struggling act of readjustment between the integrative scope of words and the unintegrated impact of events."[328] As suggested by Freud about "traumatic neurosis," what was once apparently present goes into spatiotemporal limbo — between an Eden that never existed and a Heaven that will never come — becoming at once belated and anticipatory. It is both *here* and *not* here, no longer and not yet. But thus does the Sublime become subliminal. Freud himself noted: "It may happen that someone gets away, apparently unharmed, from the spot where he has suffered a shocking accident. . . . In the course of the following weeks, however, he develops a series of grave psychical and motor symptoms, which can be ascribed only to his shock or whatever else happened at the time of the accident," and which continue to work only beneath the surface of both personal *and* social consciousness — often during exceedingly long periods of "latency" — a lifetime in the case of individuals, millennia in that of society.[329] Eternal Recurrence of the Same was to have precisely such traumatic effect, to be precisely as difficult to unpack. Perhaps Freud's most stark definition of "the traumatic" is "any excitations from outside which are powerful enough to break through the protective shield."[330] And Nietzsche's corps/e has been particularly resilient to such external excitations, prophylactically ensconced as it is in Nietzsche's corpus. Especially after the "death" of communism.

Freud came to his ultimately horrifying vision of trauma by way of his reflections on the great limit conditions that are birth and death, both of which can be perceived as extremely violent acts. Freud had especially in mind on the one terminus death in the mechanized hell of the first global war, and on the other terminus the originary violence of archaic birth trauma as immortalized, or at least nominated, by Macduff's being "from his mother's womb untimely ripped."[331] We are reminded by Bataille that the "first" caesarean section, later performed on Gaius Julius *Caesar,* was what brought to life *another* of Nietzsche's hero-types, *Dionysus.*[332] Hence, Nietzsche's last signatures were not only "The Crucified One" but "Dionysus" and "Caesar." But deeper even than the trauma of death and birth, according to Burroughs, is *conception.*[333] For Nietzsche, lover of Caesar and Dionysus equally, the ultimate task of his most untimely and traumatic thought was not to *work through* this or any other wound or shock but to *use* Eternal Recurrence of the Same *to* shock, *to* wound, *to* kill, *to* give birth to his corps/e. In short, to *conceive:* that is, *to think and to beget* not only a corps but corpses — dead or undead.

During the writing of *Thus Spoke Zarathustra* — the text into which the principle of Eternal Recurrence of the Same was most effectively and covertly *embodied* not merely thematically but *rhetorically* — Nietzsche wrote to himself: "The doctrine of Eternal Recurrence as *hammer* in the hand of the *most powerful* people." And this "hammer" — musical and deformed socialist but also a bludgeon — had a very *specific* historical and social task. "The new Enlightenment — the old was on behalf of the democratic herd. The equalization of all. The new Enlightenment intends to show ruling natures the way — insofar as *everything is permitted* them that is not open to herd-beings."³³⁴ In this regard, Nietzsche was not *"post*-Enlightenment" or *"post*modern" — time or periodization hardly matters. In theological terms, the doctrine of Eternal Recurrence of the Same seems paradoxical because in one aspect it rejects any possible transcendence out of temporality and hence would seem to be quintessentially antitheological; in its other aspect, however, the doctrine itself seems predicated on transcendent experience and belief. The doctrine appears to be Nietzsche's version of Tertullian's *Credo, quia absurdum:* "I believe [in the Resurrection of Jesus] *because* it is absurd." In Nietzsche's case, however, the paradox can be resolved by assuming that he is ultimately interested in any *belief* not just for its theological and philosophical meanings but for what it can otherwise *do,* for its transformative social potential. "A belief like a guillotine, as heavy, as light" (Kafka, in 1920).³³⁵

In precisely this context it is important to grasp Nietzsche's lifelong interest in the Jesuits. At least by the mid-sixteenth century, the latter had begun to distinguish clearly between the secrets of nature and natural science (*arcana naturae*), divine secrets and theology (*arcana Dei*), and secrets of power and political theory (*arcana imperii*) — three "realms" that had previously worked in tandem, often in the same minds. As the struggle to maintain control over the secrets of nature was increasingly lost to natural science, to technology, and to the division of labor in all fields, and as Protestantism and Calvinism proved themselves to be powerful, often more powerful, adversaries on many fronts, the Jesuits conceded that in the modern epoch the realm of science was going to be essentially egalitarian and, in the words of historian Carlo Ginzburg, "open to all in principle, even artisans and peasants."³³⁶ Protestantism and Catholicism went their different ways, in theory, on the issue of control over divine secrets, *arcana Dei*. But, for the Jesuits, at least the realm of politics was still "forbidden to 'private citizens' attempting to penetrate the secrets of power" (p. 69). Think of Nietzsche's main cosmological principle — Eternal Recurrence of the Same — and especially of the political *use* he wanted to extract from it, when reading about esotericism and exotericism on the threshold of modernism and modernity. "Catholic censure of the helio-centric system has been judged," Ginzburg argues,

> depending on the circumstances, an act of blind intolerance or of stubborn pedantry. And yet we cannot exclude the possibility that it was also inspired by an obscure fear of the religious and political implications of the new cosmology. In the mid-seventeenth century, an Italian Jesuit, Cardinal Sforza Pallavicino, adapted a more flexible attitude towards scientific progress. He too alluded to the ancient analogy between the *arcana naturae* and the *arcana imperii*, the secrets of nature and the secrets of political power, but clearly opposed one to the other. It was possible to foretell the behavior of nature because natural laws were few, simple, and inviolable. But to predict the behavior of kings and princes was as reckless as attempting to foretell the inscrutable will of God. In the same spirit, the nobleman Virgilio Malvezzi, who was related to Sforza Pallavicino, wrote that "whoever adduces God as the reason to explain natural events is a poor philosopher, and he who does not adduce Him to explain political events is a poor Christian." (pp. 69–70)

Other historians have imaged the "culture of the baroque" as the first systematically hegemonic or "guided" society, indeed as the prototype of a mass culture more or less consciously using "rhetoric" to maintain political and economic control.[337]

For Nietzsche, *arcana naturae* — that is, Eternal Recurrence of the Same and aspects of Will to Power — and *arcana Dei* — that is, God Is Dead, or Never Existed — were comparatively exoteric doctrines, the latter more exoteric than the former, and both equally dangerous for their potentially leveling, democratizing implications. So what Nietzsche kept in "standing reserve," so to speak, were the deepest levels of his *arcana imperii*. When Nietzsche talked about Eternal Recurrence of the Same as a secret Jesuitical hammer "in the hands of the most power" he meant it: Greco-Renaissance elitism was to be kept alive and well forever, and his opponents will never quite grasp the fact, thinking him always on *their* and *our* side.

A key chapter in *Thus Spoke Zarathustra* is "The Convalescent," for it is here for the first time that Zarathustra makes public to his animals and other listeners a relatively coherent, though ultimately inarticulate, depiction of the doctrine of Eternal Recurrence of the Same.[338] In an unpublished notebook, however, Nietzsche reminded himself that behind this pivotal scene an entirely different — invisible and inaudible —

transformation was to take place both in Zarathustra and in some readers. He wrote: "With the *Convalescence* of Zarathustra, CAESAR stands there, unyielding, inexorable [unerbittlich], gracious [gütig] — the gap is destroyed between *being a creator, goodness, and wisdom.* Clarity, quiet, *no exaggerated yearning,* [but rather] happiness in *the instant that is appropriately applied and eternal!*"[339] But happiness for whom, in this new, explicitly imperial, world order? Intrigued in the late 1930s — another new age of empire — by Nietzsche's Eternal Recurrence of the Same, particularly in its relation to the modernist problem of boredom, Benjamin quipped: "The thought of Eternal Return emerged when the bourgeoisie no longer dared to look in the eye the impending development of the order of production it itself had set to work. The thought of Zarathustra and of Eternal Recurrence and the embroidered motto on the sofa pillow — 'Just a 15 Minute Quickie' — all belong together."[340] And today we think of Andy Warhol's "15 minutes," in which we "last men" are famous — kings and queens for a day. But when Benjamin — who was profoundly ambivalent about Eternal Recurrence because he, too, sought a nonteleological view of time and history, though in his case in opposition especially to *bourgeois* myths of progress — came to the remark in Nietzsche's notebooks about Zarathustra as Caesar he was startled.[341] If Eternal Recurrence of the Same is true, or believed to be true, then all is indeed permitted, even permissible. All current political actions, social hierarchies, patriarchies, and other power trips become legitimated, and the possibility of legitimation crisis in the halls and back rooms of power is eliminated. Any "critique of cynical reason" or of "knowledge-power" becomes not so much impossible as *irrelevant.* Benjamin suddenly glimpsed the connection in Nietzsche between the ancient idea of Eternal Recurrence and modernist boredom cum middle-class sensibility — and also national socialist aggression. But Benjamin mistakenly thought that this note showed that *Nietzsche himself* "*suspected*" the complicity of his teaching with imperialism."[342] Symptomatically for Western Marxism, Benjamin did not see that, like all Nietzsche's major publications, *Thus Spoke Zarathustra* had been intentionally programmed by Caesarism from its inception.

Supreme importance is ascribed to the thought of Eternal Recurrence of the Same by Nietzsche, who thus refers to it simply as "my thought." This status is reconferred in Heidegger's seminal thesis in

1936–1937 that "Thinking Being, Will to Power, as Eternal Recurrence, means thinking Being as Time." Heidegger immediately went on to distinguish himself from Nietzsche on the grounds that the latter ostensibly "thought this thought but did not think it as the *question* of Being and Time. Plato and Aristotle, too, thought this thought when they grasped Being as *ousía* [presence], but just as little as Nietzsche did they think it as a question."[343] In short, according to Heidegger, while Nietzsche definitively grasped the being of entities as Will to Power and hence technology, only Heidegger himself has grasped fully Being Itself as Time . . . and therefore as authentic history in its ongoing polemic with technocentrism. But metaphysics and rhetoric aside, Heidegger was in basic concord with Nietzsche in ideological and social matters.

In the German phrase for Eternal Recurrence of the Same, *Ewige Wiederkunft des Gleichen,* Nietzsche preferred the noun *die Kunft* to its synonym in the construction *die Wiederkehr.*[344] This is likely because *Kunft* derives from the common verb *kommen,* "to come," whereas *Kehr* derives from *kehren,* "to turn" — which implies mere mechanical, circular reiteration without adaptation to changing historical or political circumstances. Also *Wiederkehr* is weighted more to the past than the future, whereas what properly recurs for Nietzsche is also what is anticipated rhetorically, is prophecy. Dionysus is the demigod who *comes,* whose *being* is in his coming. Nietzsche's *Wiederkunft* indicates dynamic — retroactive, current, and proleptic — praxis. As Kafka noted, "Beyond a certain point there is no return. This point has to be reached."[345] Or, as phrased by Lou Reed, "this is the time" precisely because "there is no time" and vice versa.[346]

Klossowski once suggested that Nietzsche seems to have reckoned with the curious fact that, sooner or later, his readers *forget* about the doctrine and its full implications.[347] *Something* about it does seem occulted from view. But why? And what is this *it*? For Nietzsche, something *comes* not only from the past but also out of the *future* into the present, and then flows multidirectionally backward and outward yet again. To draw the political and economic consequence immediately, "slavery" and "nobility" must always stay the same in immobile essence, yet must also always come again and again and once again — differently only as the situation demands.[348] But Eternal Recurrence of the Same is impossible to "define" *stricto sensu,* if the very act of definition requires some sort of spatiotemporal distance from the object in question. In terms of the doctrine's philosophical definition at least, what recurs definitionally always tends to be something different with each attempt to pin it down, as Deleuze has noted in detail.[349] And in this case, by Nietzsche's scotomizing design, no such distance exists. Related to scotomization but better able to capture its lethal aspect, and hence to bridge the space between Nietzsche's esoteric semiotics and esoterrorist process of weeding out, is the figure of Medusa.

In an important paper entitled "Nietzsche médusé" (medused Nietzsche) delivered in 1972 at the conference "Nietzsche Today?", Bernard Pautrat shed light, but not quite enough, on the darker rules of Nietzsche's game.[350] Pautrat began under the sign of Bataille and Klossowski by pointing out that Nietzsche's problem was less in talking *about* a doctrine called Eternal Recurrence of the Same than in talking always already *within it* and *by means of it*. "Because time is not linear, it admits of neither before nor after: if everything returns eternally, then the future is already a past, necessarily, and the present is then at the same time a past *and* a future" (p. 16). The consequences of this problematic for any *semiotic* are severe. In this view, signs too could exist only within a field of extreme spatiotemporal compression and conflation. Pautrat argued that Nietzsche's doctrine cannot be fully represented *in* any Nietzschean text nor even *as* the text—not even *Thus Spoke Zarathustra*. Rather, to use Althusserian terms, the doctrine is the text's symptomatic silence, its determinant absence. For his part, Pautrat was pushing Klossowski's notion of Nietzsche's pulsatile semiology harder in terms of the relationship of sign and representation to effect. Speaking of the sign "Eternal Recurrence of the Same," Pautrat concluded: "So it is that the sign itself has vanished: a blind spot, one no longer sees it. This does not necessarily mean that one does not see its trace, its vestige on the sand of the text [le sable du texte], but in the end it is no longer there, literally [en propre]" (pp. 12–13). But what, if any, is the scotomizing sign *function*—the *de-signs*—of such more or less scotomized or medused signs? Pautrat seemed to recognize for a split second that Nietzsche's point was to build into his text not only the *theme,* say, of the Medusa but also something—*mirabile dictu et visu*—that *literally* "cannot be looked at, under the penalty of being immediately *medused,* petrified, congealed, hardened unto death" (p. 13). Pautrat also recognized that the ultimate effect of this medusing sign or

NIETZSCHE'S CORPS/E

nonsign would be "to harden the world into mortal combat: this is therefore also the effect of the thought of eternal return" (p. 13). But what Pautrat did not specify is the precise nature or purpose of Nietzsche's "mortal combat."

Nietzsche explicitly referred to the thought of Eternal Recurrence of the Same as "a Medusa's head." He recorded this image in the winter of 1884–1885, while working on the last part of *Thus Spoke Zarathustra* and planning up to six more parts. He wrote to himself: "In Zarathustra 4: the great thought as *Medusa's head:* all features of the cosmos become immobile, a frozen death struggle [Todeskampf]."[351] When Benjamin read and copied out a slightly different version of this notebook entry, he — symptomatically for the "leftist" reception of Nietzsche — overlooked the fact that Nietzsche was giving himself instructions not merely about how to describe "Medusa" but about how to *write* Medusa.[352] Pautrat, to his credit, goes beyond Benjamin in this regard, though he seems unaware that Benjamin had worked with the same passages. For Nietzsche himself, "Medusa" was an illocutionary principle, the desired perlocutionary effect of which was to exert lethal petrifaction on some readers, who would be medused, immobilized, rendered impotent. In general his task was to separate the men from the boys, both from women, and generally divide readers into two basic groups: those few empowered ones who are "in the know," and those many disempowered ones who are "out of the know." "It really must be stressed that it is precisely the first elements, the most elementary things, which are the first to be forgotten. . . . The first element is that there really do exist rulers and ruled, leaders and led. The entire science and art of politics are based on this primordial, and (given certain general conditions) irreducible fact. . . . In the formation of leaders, one premise is fundamental: is it the intention that there should always be rulers and ruled, or is the objective to create the conditions in which this division is no longer necessary?"[353] *Here* is where Nietzsche and communism part company, for he *wanted* there always to be leaders and led, *and* wrote accordingly. "The Nightwanderer's Song," the penultimate chapter of the last completed part of *Thus Spoke Zarathustra,* was designed — by means of its intentionally hypnotic, multiply repeated lines and glosses ("O Man, beware . . . ," etc.) — *as* "Medusa's head."[354] Whether it actually has this effect on empirical readers is one thing, but verbal and musical repetitiveness — the basic subliminal advertising technique — was explicitly intended by Nietzsche *as* a verbal equivalent of the thought of Eternal Recurrence of the Same, *as* the freezing, castrating, killing head of the Medusa.[355]

With this singular esoterrorist locutionary, illocutionary, and perlocutionary act, Nietzsche also linked up his magnum opus with the experience he had described in his earliest major writings, including *The Birth of Tragedy Out of the Spirit of Music,* as "Dionysian": namely, the absolute "synthesis" and actual fusion of the "poet, the actor, and the viewer" and also, as he put it now in the 1880s, "the creator, the lover, the destroyer."[356] Certain technological developments would have to occur before cyberpunk could fear and/or desire exactly the same effect — with similar possibilities of success.

Returning to Pautrat, it is as if *even* he "forgets" the fundamental element of Nietzsche's medusing doctrine. Scotomized, he looks quickly away from the supposedly "most" literal and pragmatic aspect of Nietzsche's semiotic, looks away from the supposedly "most" lethal combat, looks away from what Pautrat ends up — in the manner of Klossowski or Derrida — calling Nietzsche's "game." As is so often the case in Nietzscheanism, it is for Pautrat, too, a "senseless game" (*jeu insensé*), with a nod toward psychoanalysis and the psychoanalytic Medusa, but no longer toward Nietzsche's esoteric semiotics or process of weeding out. In this instant of looking away, Pautrat is corps/ed.

He is not alone. For Deleuze and Foucault as well, Eternal Recurrence of the Same is also ultimately only "an *empty sign,* a passageway to be crossed, the formless voice of the abyss whose approach is indissociably both happiness and disgust, disgust."[357] The etymological recollection that *ciphers* are simultaneously *nullities* as well as *signs* is fundamental to Lacan's early essay on the mirror stage, which concludes: "In the recourse of subject to subject that we preserve, psychoanalysis may accompany the patient to the ecstatic limit of the '*Thou art that,*' in which is revealed to him the *cipher* of his mortal destiny, but it is not in our mere power as practitioners to bring him to the moment where the real journey begins."[358] From Nietzsche's point of view, however, such trips are in principle never to be made available to just anyone. Death trips, for the "all-too-many."

Pautrat's psychoanalytic terms are problematic for getting at Nietzsche's own ideas in several respects. Hélène Cixous in her 1976 essay "The Laugh of the Medusa" insisted that it not be "forgotten" that Medusa in mythology and in psychoanalysis is a *woman,* and that throughout the history of philosophy, as throughout all history, woman has been reduced "to the place of seduction: she appears as the one who is taken for; the bait in person, all veils unfurled, the one who doesn't give but who gives only in order to (take)."[359] Cixous added elliptically: "Woman is obviously not that woman Nietzsche dreamed of who gives only in order to. Who else could ever think of the gift as a gift-that-takes. Who else but a man, precisely the one who would like to take everything" (p. 259). But Cixous's perspective, effective as it is as a critique of many masculinist and heterosexist views of Nietzsche, does not get us closer to the complex but abject perniciousness of Nietzsche's own view, or to the medusing violence that covertly underwrites his esoteric semiotics and estoterrorism.

As is indicated by the subtitle Pautrat's book *Versions of the Sun: Figures and System of Nietzsche* (1971), it is indeed crucial to distinguish the *plural figures* of Nietzsche's writing, including his doctrine of Eternal Recurrence of the Same, from his *singular system.*[360] But it is even more crucial to take a step further in terms of political philosophy. For Nietzsche, plural figures are effects of a semiotic of *difference* and *exoterics,* whereas the singular system is an effect of a semiotic of *repetition* and *esoterics.* The *system* recurs eternally as "the same," while it is the *figures* that recur in the mode of difference, under different historical and social conditions. Two millennia ago, Sun Tzu summed up the essential tactical and strategic problem as part of his general dictum that "to win without fighting is best": "victory in war is not repetitious, but adapts its form endlessly."[361] In Nietzsche's case, therefore, when one speaks of "semiotics" or "signs" we are reminded that there *are* no signs but only "sign functions," or what Julia Kristeva calls *une practique significante:* a signifying practice that dialectically authorizes *and/or* interdicts specific meanings, specific actions. Kristeva defines "signifying practice" as "the constitution and the countervailing of a sign system [la constitution et la traversée d'un système de signes]. Constituting a sign system calls for the identity of a speaking subject within a social framework, which this subject recognizes as a support for that identity. Countervailing the sign system is accomplished by the subject undergoing a violent process that challenges the social institutions with which the subject had previously identified, and it thus coincides with times of rupture, renewal, or revolution in society."[362] Applying Kristevan terminology, the intended function of Nietzsche's indeed revolutionary practice of signification—as multiple, dynamic, disruptive *figures* and as a singular, stable, totalizing *system*—was to construct and empower fascoid-liberal forms of subject identity, to destroy or manipulate any form that might resist them.

Regarding the relationship of Nietzsche's "thought," Eternal Recurrence of the Same, to his semiotic system, what is crucial to acknowledge is the practical, strategic, and tactical concern behind all the apparent abstraction. Thus, Nietzsche wrote in a notebook used in 1882–1883: "The thought is only a sign, just as the word is only a sign for the thought."[363] This *aperçu* might be read as yet another example of Nietzsche's commitment either to what a semiotician might call "unlimited semiosis" or to what a psychoanalyst might view as the unlimited and abysmal chain of signification without origin in the *mise-en-abîme* of semantic undecidability. Yet, properly unpacked, Nietzsche's point is not merely the trivial formal one that words are signs for thoughts and that thoughts are signs for words—with the upshot that all these terms mutually deconstruct one another. What he is implying, rather, is that such relationships are transitive—"the word is only a sign *for* the thought"—and that "*the* thought," Eternal Recurrence of the Same, is not something in which he *believes* as some religious revelation or existential experience *outside* this semiotic. *Even* Eternal Recurrence of the Same is "only a sign." What he does not say here, however, is what this thought is a sign *for* in addition to being imbricated in this formal semiotic structure, what it is as *signifying practice*. This is not to say that Nietzsche does not attribute a quasi-religious aura to Eternal Recurrence of the Same; but then it is, in Spinozist terms, a "theologico-*political*" aura. Nietzsche also makes it amply clear that he did not *find* his thought ready-made, ontologically. Rather, he *produced* it. "Immortal is the moment in which I engendered the Recurrence. For the sake of this moment, I *endure* the Recurrence."[364] And for him whatever is produced or engendered has *use*.

All of Nietzsche's major outlines for the various parts of *Thus Spoke Zarathustra* stress what this practical aspect will be: namely, as he put it in a notebook used in 1884, "the production or education [Erziehung] of the future *rulers.*" These are to be selected according to two basic criteria: First, there is the ability to withstand not the *fact* of Eternal Recurrence of the Same but the *thought*. Like "Will"—or Will to Power and the Superman — Eternal Recurrence of the Same is a polemic hypothesis, a "poetic invention" (*eine Erdichtung*). Second, there is the willingness of those who are not able to withstand it to kill themselves or, if need be, to be killed. Each main section of *Thus Spoke Zarathustra* was designed to inculcate a different aspect of this ultimate mission.[365] Each aspect was a mode of one substance, as it were, one process of weeding out.

Eternal Recurrence of the Same may therefore seem *post* theological, *post* ontological, *post* historical; but, if you prefer, it is equally *pre* theological, *pre* ontological, *pre* historical, and so on.[366] If you can't be born or give birth, you can be reborn and give birth again; if you can't die or kill, you can *re* die and *re* kill. You are disoriented, lose your bearings in the sublime matrix — expected things become different, unexpected things remain the same. Reason becomes just one software package among others, and crashes. Synapses are momentarily opened, vulnerable, penetrable, and primed for incorporation. . . .

Klossowski once remarked that there are two basic types of assassins or murderers. The first, the more petty human type, is one who might "yield to the temptation to commit homicide — and to whom one could say: 'you've already murdered, you've done it once before, try not to do it again' — such a man would understand nothing of Eternal Return. But a murderer who would murder in such a way that he would also want Eternal Return — that would perhaps be another kind of murderer."[367] But the Nietzschean Klossowski waffled on whether Nietzsche was this second kind or higher murderer — *precisely* the kind Nietzsche thought himself to be.

And if "we" do not literally commit suicide when reading Nietzsche's corpus, and he obviously could not *count* on people to blow out their brains, even if some have done so after reading him, then the "suicide" will have to take more metaphoric, nuanced, intricate, and subterranean forms — esoterrorist forms more socially productive for "those in the know." In dealing with his opponents, euthanasia and war are Nietzsche's *second* choice, he said. The *first* is *suicide*. "I do not speak to you as to a people [Volk]," Nietzsche-Zarathustra says; "For it, the *ultimate* is to despise and destroy itself; the second highest is to despise and destroy one another."[368] If overt coercion and domination are impossible, inappropriate, or ineffective — as indeed they are in many situations — then noncoercive coercion and hegemony will have to work in tandem with them. At least this, apparently, was *Nietzsche's intention*. Whether he was *successful* or not is an even more serious problem — especially since in Nietzsche's world, by esoteric definition and design, virtually no one could ever know for sure whether s/he had fully incorporated a properly Nietzschean thought or not. Nonetheless, surety aside, what is at stake is a more or less surreptitious — both unconscious and musical — process of weeding out. That this process was absolutely crucial to Nietzsche *ought* to be clear enough, legible enough. In private he screamed it out:

> *Ruling humanity with the goal of overcoming it[.] Overcoming through teachings on which humanity perishes [zu Grunde geht].* EXCEPT FOR THOSE WHO CAN SURVIVE THESE TEACHINGS.[369]

And:

> The "Truth," the "destruction of illusions," "also of moral illusion" — is the GREATEST MEANS of the OVERPOWERING of humanity (its SELF-DESTRUCTION!)[370]

Two remarks help update and map the process of weeding out as we enter the postcontemporary. The first is about Nietzsche's onetime friend and hero Richard Wagner, originator of *Gesamtkunstwerk*, the Artwork of the Future, and anticipator of hypertext, virtual reality, and cyberspace.[371] This remark comes from the despiser of popular culture, the Left-Nietzschoid Theodor Adorno. The second remark comes from the Right-Nietzschean Greg Ginn of the rock band Black Flag, originator of the term "the process of weeding out."

Adorno:

> The unconscious, which Wagner learned about from Schopenhauer, has already become ideology for him: the task of music is to warm up the alienated and reified relations of men and make them sound *as if they were still human*. This technological hostility to consciousness is the very foundation of the music drama. It combines the arts in order to produce an intoxicating brew.[372]

And Ginn:

> The revolution will probably be televised. But I don't have a T.V. and I'm not gonna watch. With talk of rating records and increased censorship it may

be getting difficult for some to speak their minds. Black Flag already has enough problems with censorship coming from the business sector. Some record companies have refused to stock and/or display certain Black Flag records because of objectionable cover art and/or lyrical content. Now, with additional government involvement, the "crunch" is on. Hope does not lie in the fact that fortunately these straight pigs show little ability in decoding intuitive data. For example, even though this record may communicate certain feelings, emotions, and ideas to some, I have faith that cop-types with their strictly linear minds and stick-to-the-rules mentality don't have the ability to decipher the intuitive contents of this record. Of course, there may be a problem in that much of the public, most of whom comply with the whole idea of hiring the pigs in the first place, seem equally unable to intuitively feel and listen to music. Still here it is, "The Process of Weeding Out."[373]

The process of weeding out is not only a matter of the articulations that exist between high philosophy or the negative dialectic and technoculture, but in the current theory and practice of warfare. G. Gordon Liddy — he of Watergate and other fame — not only often cites Nietzsche in interviews and public lectures, he also sports a mustache that makes him uncannily like Nietzsche in appearance. No doubt he is part of his corps/e. Or compare the remarks of the Right-Nietzschean Lieutenant Colonel Oliver North, then at the National Security Council, to those of the more Left-Nietzschoid Paul Virilio. First Virilio: "There is no more need for an armed *body* to attack civilians, so long as the latter have been properly trained to turn on their radios or plug in their television sets. No need for solid, laboriously-moved bodies when their spectral image can be projected anywhere at all in an instant. From now on, military assault is shapeless in time and space, absolutely vaporous. And the populations' orgiastic participation is no more than the irrational support of a *techno-logistical supra-nationality,* the final stage of delocalization, and thus of servitude."[374] But "delocalization" is a buzzword not only in the rhizomic, speed-is-war world of post-Oedipal capitalism, not only in the Hacker's Ethic, but also at West Point, Annapolis, and the Pentagon.[375] It is small secret in Washington that Nietzschean principles, through the mediation of Straussians, exert considerable effect on government officials right up to the presidency.[376] Lastly, hear out Ollie North: "There is great deceit [and] deception practiced in the conduct of covert operations. . . . They are at essence a lie."[377] In other words: "Truth and Lie in the Extramoral Sense" — televised or not, and always sooner "imag-inary" or "musical" than linguistic or philological.[378] But, for all that, no less lethally *real.* Perhaps this is also what Althusser saw when he noted (in 1985, a year of desperate personal crisis): "hallucinations are also facts."[379] And Althusser would not have entirely disagreed with Lionel S. Johns, adjunct-director of the Office of Technology Assessment of the U.S. Senate: "In politics, unlike physics, perceptions are facts."[380] Politically speaking, Althusser may also have been implying that, while communism itself is a hallucination in some respects, for reasons good as well as bad, what is commonly perceived to be the global hegemony of capitalism, too, can be perceived as a hallucination in the future, as it was in the past. And, with this perception, it is possible to Act Up against capitalism and Nietzsche on behalf of a properly communist spirit.

As for Nietzsche himself, he theorized and deployed what he called the "Machiavellian" attempt to exert "posthumous authority" by means of "musical style" and "festival art." Crucial to Nietzsche, from his early twenties on, was the project of using language to create a certain "mood" (*Stimmung*), a notion with a venerable philosophical and musical tradition but one associated in particular for him with various forms of struggle and combat.[381] *Thus Spoke Zarathustra* was never intended by Nietzsche as either "philosophy" or "art" to be merely "read," but rather as a vehicle to create a certain invisible, barely audible mood and also as an instance of what he called the "higher art" of "festivals." Similarly, the "social wars" Nietzsche hoped such "festivals" would promote were to be one way his present doctrines would be "incorporated" and "embodied" (*einverleibt*) in and by the future qua *arcana imperii.*[382] And incorporation and embodiment always come to sound suspiciously like principles of *biology,* of *zoology.* So perhaps it's time, as Nietzsche himself liked to say, for a few "remarks for donkeys." It is true enough: Nietzsche's work cannot be *reduced* to either its Social Darwinian or its esoteric components *simply.* Although, speaking frankly, maybe it *ought* to be thus reduced, since he himself entertained this thought often, and at least then it might become *more* visible. It is true enough: *Theoretically,* one need not accept *all* of a body of thought to make positive, even progressive use of the *rest* of it. Although one *might* first wish to know better what the original body of thought looked like. It is true enough: Neither Nietzsche nor his spokesman Zarathustra ever claims actually to *be*, say, the Superman, although this disclaimer really has less to do with any more or less sophisticated — "noble" — theory of alterity or the Other than with remarkably grubby pragmatic and suasive — "base" — concerns. It is true enough: Most — *not all* — of the many authoritative-, fascist-, and violent-sounding claims in Nietzsche's work *can* be undercut or deconstructed by other, equally explicit but more self-effacing, critical, and even emancipatory statements in the same text. Although, to repeat the basic question: Emancipatory for whom? Some readers will think immediately of the leitmotifs that extend from the burial of the tightrope dancer to Zarathustra's Last Supper with the Last Men, since this trajectory describes the doctrine of the peripatetic teacher who always must abandon his mobilized pupils or readers at the very moment they think they have found him. And one may indeed eventually arrive at Deleuze and Guattari's "nomadic" theorist and practitioner of postmodern warfare: the corps/e without organs.[383] Because violence lies at the root of Nietzsche's process of weeding out, and because Deleuze and Guattari are among the Left-Nietzschoids who have thought most about violence generally, their point of view requires an especially hard look.

A notable problem with Deleuze and Guattari's dual theory of "deterritorialization" and of the nomadic *corps sans organes* is that it seems to describe equally well the mechanisms *of* capitalism and capitalist aggression but also more or less effective combat *against* them. But there is no doubt that Nietzsche — "the only position outside of communism" — wanted to be exactly what Deleuze and Guattari claim for him: namely, a "war machine." They argue in *A Thousand Plateaus* (1980), the second volume of *Capitalism and Schizophrenia*, that in addition to the two basic forms of state — what Gramsci calls "coercion" and "consent" — there is a *third* term that is external to both, yet without dialectical synthesis. Appearances to the contrary: the coercive aspect of the state only appears to have the war machine under its control; just as the consent form only appears not to require the war machine. The two perennial forms of the state give off the further appearance of encompassing all significant actual and possible forms of life. As such, they together constitute what can variously be called a "problematic," a "difference-engine," "unacknowledged consensus," "virtual reality," and so forth. For their part, Deleuze and Guattari refer to this statist matrix as an "interiority" against which the war machine functions as "exteriority," illustrating the latter with brief but brilliant analyses of the work of Heinrich von Kleist and Nietzsche. But the problems come precisely when Deleuze and Guattari begin to use *Nietzsche* — both as a main *source* of their thesis about the war machine and as one of its primary *illustrations*. They argue, for example: "To place a thought in an immediate relation with the outside, with the forces of the outside, in short to make thought a war machine, is a strange undertaking whose precise procedures can be studied in Nietzsche (the aphorism, for example, is very different from the maxim, for a maxim, in the republic of letters, is like an organic State act or sovereign judgment, whereas an aphorism always awaits its meaning from a new external force, a final force that must conquer or subjugate it, utilize it)."[384] The problem with this argument is not the standard one often leveled against *Capitalism and Schizophrenia,* indeed against much current theory: namely, that it is unclear where the authors themselves stand in this matter, in terms of whether the rhizomic milieu of exteriority and the war machine exemplified, say, by Kleist's dramas or Nietzsche's aphorisms are "a good thing" or "a bad thing," a "repressive thing" or a "liberatory thing." After all, Deleuze and Guattari explicitly take as one of their basic starting points a "Nietzschean" — and, for that matter, Spinozist — position "beyond good and evil." One might well wish to attack this position on any number of grounds. But it is quite disingenuous to do so in the guise of moral indignation alone, if one cannot morally ground one's *own* position of attack. And precisely this grounding is difficult — if not actually impossible or moot — in the wake of Nietzsche.

But this grounding is difficult or impossible in Nietzsche's own terms *only* as he is grasped *conventionally,* which is to say *exoterically.* And the problem with their argument, on which much of their own hope for war against the oppressive state apparatus depends, is that Deleuze and Guattari grasp Nietzsche conventionally and exoterically. On the one hand their take on the war machine can give extraordinary insight into Nietzschean/ism; on the other it is not the Nietzsche *they* think they are seeing. Put differently: With regard to Nietzsche's in/visible corps/e, Deleuze and Guattari give the wrong answer to the right questions, and the right answer to the wrong questions. For, in spite of his aphoristic style, in spite of his often very powerful attacks on the state in general and the post-1870 German state in specific, Nietzsche *was* committed to an esoteric conception of the state as a dual, remarkably traditional and premodern mechanism of consent and coercion. Call this conception "The Greek State," as in Nietzsche's eponymous early essay. On the other hand, leaving the matter of Nietzsche's esoteric intentions aside, the main *question* of Deleuze and Guattari about the war machine *precisely* describes Nietzsche's original esoteric intent: namely, to produce his corps/e as a part of everyday life, including as spectacular technoculture. Deleuze and Guattari refer to "a system of relays and plug-ins, extrinsic linkages belonging to the war machine" (p. 356). "Could it be," they then ask about the machine, "that it displays to the utmost its irreducibility, that it scatters into thinking, loving, dying, or creating machines that have at their disposal vital or revolutionary powers capable of challenging the conquering State? Is the war machine already overtaken, condemned, appropriated as part of the same process whereby it takes on new forms, undergoes a metamorphosis, affirms its irreducibility and exteriority, and deploys that milieu of pure exteriority that the occidental man of the State, or the occidental thinker, continually reduces to the something other than itself?" (p. 356). The simplest answer to this complex set of questions (*pace* Deleuze and Guattari) is that this "man of the State" is both *Nietzsche* — more or less consciously — and his *corps/e* — more or less unconsciously. Being — theoretically, if not actually — *everywhere* in intent and agency, Nietzsche's territory cannot be deterritorialized without a counterintent and counteragency *greater* than it. To be sure, this perspective does require some sort of ethical and/or political decision: to wit, that Nietzsche's corps/e to date has been "a bad thing," not "a good thing."

Certainly there is nothing — necessarily or essentially — good or bad about either territorialization or deterritorialization. Reading the great North Vietnamese military strategists, such as Truong Son, and having experienced part of the war firsthand, a critic points out that in the kind of warfare theorized and practiced by the Viet Cong there was "a fluidity of combinative intensities which allows at once for the most primitive and the most advanced methods of warfare."[385] Was Truong Son a Nietzschean? Perhaps. But if he was a communist in Gramsci's terms, then his *intention* with regard to the division between leaders and led was "to create the conditions in which this division is no longer necessary." Is it possible, then, to be both communist and Nietzschean? Emphatically not—and not only because communism is ostensibly dead.

The principle of "fluidity of combinative intensities" is a lesson long known to *capitalism* too, and few forces in history have been better at "deterritorialization" than it. Nietzsche's own way with illocutionary combat would be much less interesting or influential were he not prepared to go with the flow of history, to take on different psychoplasmic avatars. This is not to say that these avatars, too, are—necessarily or essentially—good or bad. It is to say that we often have to decide whether or not they are, and also whether or not Nietzsche can be held accountable for them.

Nietzsche says in his unpublished notebooks that doctrines like "even" the Superman, Eternal Recurrence of the Same, Will to Power, and so on are neither essential concepts nor mere metaphors but eminently *practical* tools and weapons: winnowing strategies to produce and steel, as Nietzsche says, those "who will survive them," those who are not "destroyed."[386] If, as Elaine Scarry has argued, "the goal of the torturer is to make the one, the body, emphatically and crushingly *present* by destroying it, and to make the other, the voice, *absent* by destroying it,"[387] then Nietzsche was a supreme torturer—whose goal, however, was not simply to destroy the body and voice of his corps but rather to make them sing a "new song" *as if* they were alive and free. God is dead, all is permitted . . . and business as usual. Nietzsche thinks: "Get ready for the future: It is murder."[388]

Someday we may say with Ernst Bloch (in 1932) that "No Nietzsche was required in Germany to allow antitheses such as blood versus spirit, wantonness versus morality, intoxication versus reason to become a conspiracy against civilization."[389] But that day has not arrived. We must still ask: What if Nietzsche were not sufficient, certainly, but nonetheless necessary and complicitous even now in continuing to legitimate and instaurate certain *kinds* of fascism that we do not fully understand, cannot fully grasp? Similarly, Bataille wrote (in 1929–1930) that "It is not the masters who need a [Nietzschean] morality: exploiters are not going to seek their values in unbalanced philosophy. When their values are given to them immediately by the economic conditions of exploitation, American bankers dispense with *Will to Power.*"[390] Perhaps this, too, will turn out to be true . . . someday.

Deleuze and Guattari, Bloch and Bataille are themselves of Nietzsche's corps/e, each in his own way, and thus not *always* the most reliable of witnesses or comrades. With respect to Bloch's version of Nietzscheanism, Hans Günther, a rival communist and student of Lukács, was right to point out two basic problems with Bloch's argument: first, that Nietzsche's problem was how to construct and defend a social formation not merely *against* the masses but with their unwitting *assistance;* and, second, that Bloch failed to grasp that just those "intoxicated and irrational" aspects of Nietzsche that Bloch wanted to appropriate were exactly what prevents us "from drawing truly revolutionary consequences."[391] But then, if Nietzsche had his wish, *all* more or less Nietzschoid "leftists" are always going to be more part of the problem than the solution.

The basic paradox remains, the paradox that Left-Nietzscheanism exists at all. How could it overlook — read and yet not read — Nietzsche's persistent attacks, in print as well as in notebooks, against his mortal enemy, variously described as "Christians," "Platonists," "the masses," "newspaper readers," "beer drinkers," "cigar smokers," "women," "Wagnerians," "decadents," "anarchists" — but most especially as "socialists" and all other "preachers of equality"? To turn the question around: How was Nietzsche able to calculate that he could enlist precisely these people to his cause, against their own best interests? In the fall of 1883, Nietzsche wrote: "The eudaemonic, social ideals lead people *backwards* — but these same ideals — objectionable as they may be in terms of intellectual honesty — may lead to a very useful *species of worker* — they will produce the *ideal slave of the future* — the lower class *that must not be lacking!*"[392] And that must not *know* what it is *really* lacking. In other words, don't kill every opponent. The future would be much simpler were it *only* murder.

Nietzsche was arguably the greatest *fascoid-liberal* philosopher. As important, he seems to have been remarkably effective in pulling the wool over the eyes of what he himself called the "lower" or "working class" or, if you insist, "caste" — including many of its representatives and leaders, even some would-be wolves in sheep's clothing: over the eyes, then over the bodies and, if need be, over the corpses. At least three related questions remain: What historical and ideological conditions permitted Nietzsche even to imagine this process of weeding out to be feasible? Has he really succeeded as the esoterrorist he would have liked to be? Can we ever really know for sure in our postcontemporary, still Nietzschean condition?

Consider, finally, the current flipped-out, postleftist cynicism that traces its genealogy explicitly to Nietzsche. In the 1980 film *Maledetti Vi Amerò* (you damned bastards, I will love you), the young, coke-snorting, suicidal leftist named Ricardo is confronted by the impossible choice facing many of his — my — generation. It is the choice between terrorism and what in Italy is called the "transformation" (*trasformismo*) or "reflux" (*riflusso*) to yuppiedom. This antinomy produces in Ricardo the following variant of *P.C. à la Nietzsche:* "Eroticism is left-wing, but pornography is right-wing. Even penetration is right-wing, whereas foreplay is left-wing. Heterosexuality is right-wing, whereas homosexuality has a deep transgressive value and thus is left-wing. Moroccan and Afghan hash, pot, and mushrooms are left-wing, but amphetamines, coke, and heroin are right-wing. *Nietzsche has been reevaluated and is now left-wing, whereas Marx is right-wing.*"[393] Ricardo inserts a pistol into his mouth and blows out his brains.

4 Trasformismo

from Gramsci to Dick, or, The Spectacular Technoculture of Everyday Life

Preliminaries

The effect of Nietzsche is a transformation, for the melody of
his vision did not end even with his death. . . . [1]

Because the bourgeoisie is triumphing, it is transforming
both the workers and the ex-colonial peasants into bourgeois.
In short, through neocapitalism the bourgeoisie is
becoming the human condition.[2]

. . . though it is impossible to govern the mind as completely as
the tongue, nevertheless minds are, to a certain extent, under
the control of the sovereign, for he can in many ways bring
about that the greatest part of his subjects should follow his
wishes in their beliefs, their loves, and their hates. Though such
emotions do not arise at the express command of the sovereign
they often result (as experience shows) from the authority of his
power, and from his direction; in other words, in virtue of his
right; we may, therefore, without doing violence to our understanding, conceive men who follow the instigation of their
sovereign in their beliefs, their loves, their hates, their
contempt, and all other emotions whatsoever.[3]

It may be anachronistic to attribute to Nietzsche any serious thoughts —
neutral, negative, or positive — about current technoculture — the tendency to fuse culture, in both the broad and narrow sense, with digital
information technologies — and hence about his afterlife as techno-
Nietzschean/ism. Nevertheless, as a rule of thumb, it is worse to under-
estimate than to overestimate Nietzsche, whose influence would *be*

much less had he *anticipated* less. He did take the pulse of the mass — or as he called it, "philistine" — culture of his own, early capitalist time; and he would have extrapolated the basic principles governing this criticism to take some measure of modern and postmodern spectacularization. The continued success of Nietzsche/anism will depend on its ability to transform individuals and collectivities according to Nietzsche's directives but under everyday conditions of postmodernity wherever they might be found.

Not having exposure or access to radio, film, video, HDTV, or even telephones and phonographs, let alone cyberspace, and having barely discovered the typewriter, Nietzsche was aware of technoculture in at least two crucial protoforms: the Wagnerian *Gesamtkunstwerk* . . . and the newspaper. He criticized "the music drama of the future" not in principle but in kind: Wagner had betrayed its politico-philosophical, world-historical mission by selling out to such epiphenomenal and counterproductive aberrations as anti-Semitism, Christianity, and the Germans. Presumably Nietzsche would have had the same reservations about the future of Virtual Reality technologies, including e-mail, the global web, and so forth. Thus Nietzsche was led to produce his own "total work of art," one much smaller in apparent scale but, it has turned out, in impact having much transformative power: his written corpus. By contrast, his objection that the great *alternative* kind of writing and thinking in his time — that is, that produced in and by the newspaper — was *necessarily democratizing* may appear rather less prescient.[4] Critics of the newspaper on the Right, Center, and Left — including Karl Kraus, Georg Simmel, and Walter Benjamin — have tended to conclude that its power is anything but democratic, having rendered the newspaper reader "increasingly unable to assimilate the data of the world around him by way of experience"; that "the linguistic usage of newspapers [has] paralyzed the imagination of their readers"; that "the principles of journalistic information (freshness of the news, brevity, comprehensibility, and, above all, lack of connection between the individual news items)" — that all this only serves "to isolate what happens from the realm in which it could affect the experience of the reader."[5] In short, and giving the critique a more leftist spin, the newspaper prevents the formations of a geopolitical consciousness of the kind necessary to produce authentic communism, and with which Nietzsche is in competition. But all "experiential" criticisms of the newspaper or e-mail, which would imagine themselves to be Nietzschean, can appeal only to Nietzsche's many *exoteric* attacks on newsprint. From his *esoteric* perspective, all such baneful effects are actively *desired* by him for a huge slice of humanity, in order to increase the mechanisms of social and intellectual hierarchization. And this exo/ esoteric problematic can be expected to carry over *mutatis mutandis* into his proleptic critique of more current forms of mass-cultural spectacle and technoculture.

In this regard, Nietzsche's imagination already as a teenager was remarkably prescient. He dreamt of technologies of dissemination. The eighteen-year-old schoolboy wrote: "It is deathly still in the room — the one sound is the pen scratching across the paper — for I love to think by writing, given that the machine that could imprint our thoughts into some material without their being spoken or written has yet to be invented. In front of me is an inkwell in which I can drown the sorrows of my black heart, a pair of scissors to accustom me to the idea of slitting my throat, manuscripts with which I can wipe myself, and a chamber pot."[6] This passage from 1862 defines the outlines of Nietzsche's subsequent project: that is, to take advantage of the limited technology of writing to work on the "material" of the human race until ever more advanced techniques of subliminal and subcutaneous "imprint" can be found. And Nietzsche was to have remarkable success in sublimating and transforming the scatological, masochistic, suicidal aspect of his juvenile project into a fully mature and more social process of weeding out.

The most accurate signposts leading to a properly communist grasp of the interrelationship between Nietzsche and popular, mass, and/or junk culture were staked out by Gramsci, following his neo-Leninist dictum that "the philosophy of an age is not the philosophy of this or that philosoper, of this or that group of intellectuals, of this or that broad section of the popular masses. It is a combination of all these elements."[7] In Gramsci's definition, "popular" writings are neither "composed by the people for the people" nor are they "composed for the people but not by the people"; rather, these are writings "which the people adopt because they conform to their way of thinking and feeling."[8] For Gramsci, "the people" is not necessarily "a homogeneous cultural collectivity"; rather, it consists of "numerous and variously combined cultural stratifications which, in their pure form, cannot always be identified within specific historical popular collectivities" (p. 195). It is along these lines that the design and influence of Nietzsche's writings must be grasped. His stratified — apparently heterogeneous — corps reads and incorporates his corpus as if this corps had composed it, and thereby unwittingly composes and conforms itself. Like Lenin, Gramsci did not himself read Nietzsche in any depth. But both, at rather different historical conjunctures, had no choice except to confront the ever growing phenomenon of Nietzscheanism as "popular" phenomenon.

For his part, Lenin knew of Nietzsche through several secondary accounts — Russian, German, French, Italian, and English — though claims about the extent to which Lenin read him firsthand are exaggerated, and certainly he never read him as is required: viscerally.[9] Lenin's *Materialism and Empirio-Criticism* (1908), written during his exile in Switzerland, was an at least indirect attack on "Nietzschean" ideas, to the extent that one of its main targets, the work of the physicist and socialist Ernst Mach, had come under Nietzschean influence. Nietzsche's "perspectivism" was translated by empirio-critical Austro-Marxism into a form of epistemological and scientific relativism by several leading European intellectuals, including natural scientists. Lenin, as if anticipating postmodern leftist Nietzscheanism, rightly feared the consequences this translation would have not only on heuristic notions of scientific truth but also on the problem of mobilizing concerted political action against a class enemy that was always already "Nietzscheanized." *Materialism* can be read as Lenin's desperate, ultimately unsuccessful attempt to stave off the ongoing transformation of intellectuals from the Left to the Right of the ideological spectrum of Nietzsche/anism, and hence as a preliminary critique of the epistemological aporias of poststructuralism, deconstruction, new historicism, and cultural studies. For his part, Gramsci's concerns with Nietzscheanism, viewed through the bars of his fascist prison in the late 1920s and 1930s, were as political as Lenin's but less epistemological and more cultural. And they were marked by ambivalence. For Gramsci, Nietzscheanism was symptomatic of a deep contradiction that informs all traditional intellectuals sooner or later: that is, between thoughts and words, words and actions. Of particular concern to him was the way this contradiction empowers and legitimates the transformation of intellectuals from the Left to the Right, without their being *aware* of this drift. But another implication of Gramsci's take on Nietzsche points away from unconscious manipulation to a failure of *conscious will*. Both pro- and anti-Nietzscheanism, as historical and sociological phenomena, were for Gramsci issues less of psychological or moral hypocrisy, less of theory, than of what he called "style." "The problem," Gramsci wrote in his reflections on "History and Anti-History," "is precisely that of seeing things historically. That all those Nietzschean charlatans in verbal revolt against all that exists, against conventionality, etc., should have ended up by accepting it after all, and have thus made certain attitudes seem quite unserious, may well be the case, but it is not necessary to let oneself be guided in one's own judgments by charlatans. In opposition to fashionable titanism, to a taste for wishful thinking and abstraction, one must draw attention to a need for 'sobriety' in words and in external attitudes, precisely so that there should be more strength in one's character and concrete will. But this is a question of style, not 'theory.'"[10] The terms of Gramsci's preliminary analysis of Nietzscheanism echo the analysis by Marx and Engels in *The German Ideology* (first published 1932) of the "philosophic charlatanry" and radical-phrase-mongering-with-conservative-effect of the Young Hegelians.[11] But it was Gramsci who first provided the basic communist tools for an analysis of Nietzscheanism as the contemporary form of philosophical hegemony, replacing Hegelianism in this social function, notwithstanding the widespread assumption today that Nietzsche broke radically with Hegel and dialectical thought.[12]

From a Gramscian perspective, what is at ultimate stake in Nietzsche/anism is a question of ideologico-political *transformation,* sometimes imaged by Gramsci as a process of *psychological* but at other times as *physiological* and *mental* incorporation. That is, the overall and specific effect of Nietzsche on European intellectuals can be described the way Gramsci described Benedetto Croce's effect on Italian intellectuals in the late 1920s and early 1930s: namely, as "the largest amount of 'gastric juices' needed for the digestive process," by which leftists are eventually "conformed" to the problematic of the Right.[13]

Croce went in his own lifetime from being sympathetic to Marxism to a liberal supporter of Mussolini to finally a liberal critic of fascism. In short, Gramsci touted Croce as the prototypical fascoid-liberal in Italy, if not Europe. Today, this distinction is held, more or less globally, by

Nietzsche. "Liberalism," Charles Taylor remarks rather wistfully, "is also a fighting creed."[14] With an Argus eye on Nietzsche's corps/e, add: "That's just the Hell of it!" It is important to stress in just this regard that Nietzsche was not merely "liberal" but also a *"democratic* philosopher" — *albeit in the Gramscian sense.* Which is to say that Nietzsche, in his contemporary "gastric" function, "is a philosopher convinced that his personality [i.e., corpse] is not limited to himself as a physical individual [i.e., corpus] but is an active social relationship of modification of the cultural environment [i.e., corps]. When the 'thinker' is content with his own thought, when he is 'subjectively,' that is abstractly, free, that is when he nowadays becomes a joke."[15] But Nietzsche's corps/e is many things before it is a joke.

We arrive at a major polemic-hypothesis *and* at an apparently insoluble methodological problem. The extent to which the recruiting project of Nietzsche's esoteric semiotics and process of weeding out can be said to be *successful* must be measured not only theoretically and hypothetically but also historically, even "physically": that is, in the number and quality of actual readers who, pushed more or less unwittingly and "democratically" from the Left to the Right, have been actually incorporated and transformed into Nietzsche's corps/e. But it is impossible to take the full measure of this process in any convincing empirical way, especially given that one of its defining features is subliminality. What can be done, however, is to look for possible *traces* of Nietzschean transformation while considering the actual-virtuality that, with Nietzscheanism as with neocapitalism, Nietzsche's rigid designator, his self-described *"one* intent" or "center," has finally, more or less reluctantly, come home to roost.

> It is the throw of one sense, that with
> The shovel grasps the wheat,
> And throws swinging toward clarity it over the threshing-floor.
> A horrific thing. Dust falls.
> But grain comes to the end.[16]

The horrific history of Nietzscheanism runs parallel to, and intersects with, more general tendencies of ideological and social transformation. This transformation occurs both in individuals, such as Mach and Adler (and Jean Bourdeau even earlier), and more collectively. In 1893 the publicist and popular philosopher Ludwig Stein intimated that "even" inner circles of the socialist movement had been infiltrated by Nietzscheanism.[17] The author of the first analysis of Nietzsche that was both Marxist and critical, namely, the German dramatist Paul Ernst in 1890, was soon squarely in the Nietzschean camp, and pushed to the Right to boot.[18] From the late nineteenth century on, the transformative power of the corps/e has grown exponentially, technoculturally, techno-Nietzschoculturally.

Gramsci's rather sanguine assumption that one could do a simple end run around Nietzscheanism with an Enlightenment feint of the head here, a muscular swivel of the hips there, was tempered by his recognition that Nietzscheanism had taken firm root not merely among intellectuals of the academic or urban persuasion but also deep within the everyday life of popular and mass culture. Today, the technocultural form taken by Nietzsche's corps/e — its more or less "imag-inary" claim for global postcontemporary hegemony — is related to what is being called "the reconfigured eye" of digital image manipulation and synthesis. "The burgeoning ubiquity of pixel-traffic paraphernalia — of sophisticated, mass-produced devices for production, transformation, accumulation, retrieval, distribution, and consumption of arrays of intensity values — signals that digital imaging technology is being mobilized in the games of signification and implicated in the conterminous, intertwined relationships of power and division of labor that construct postindustrial subjectivity. The uses of digital imaging technology are becoming broadly institutionalized, and reciprocally, that technology is restructuring institutions, social practices, and the formation of belief. A worldwide network of digital imaging systems is swiftly, silently constituting itself as the decentered subject's reconfigured eye."[19] Gramsci had only limited access even to film and radio. Nonetheless, he, like Marx and Lenin, did appreciate the hegemonic function of theater, opera, music, and all forms of literature. Which enabled Gramsci to make a fruitful suggestion that has still to be adequately explored, to the effect that Nietzsche's notion of the Superman had significant predecessors in French serial novels both "high" and "low": in Honoré de Balzac's Rastignac but also in Alexandre Dumas's heroes Athos and Joseph Balsamo.[20] Gramsci went further, however, with the disturbing suggestion that what he called the "popular origin of the 'super-man'" was, so to speak, a phenomenon of Nietzscheanism even *without*

Nietzsche.[21] In other words, Nietzscheanism does not seem to require Nietzsche for its inception or effectivity. This version of structural causality would have delighted Nietzsche, indeed was anticipated by him, and it certainly ought to give Nietzscheans pause — especially under conditions in which neocapitalist global culture has taken on significantly more pervasive and spectacular forms.

It is certainly debatable how effective Gramscian interventions can be in and against technoculture.[22] But at least Gramsci's fundamental *questions* point toward a better grasp of techno-Nietzsche/anism: "Every time one comes upon some admirer of Nietzsche, it is worth asking himself and trying to find out if his 'superman' ideas, opposed to conventional morality, are of genuine Nietzschean origin. In other words, are they the result of a mental elaboration located in the sphere of 'high culture' or do they have much more modest origins?"[23] However, the problem with grasping current Nietzsche/anism from a communist perspective — assuming that there still is one — remains not only that neither Lenin nor Gramsci ever took — or had — the time to read Nietzsche, it is that communism, in all its enthusiasm for "electrification," needs to find a balance between the technophiliac and technophobic if it will grasp Nietzsche/an technoculture. To this end, Gramsci's insight that transformative influence does not necessarily run along expected paths is intriguing but needs developing.

A great literary Nietzschean of the Right, Jorge Luis Borges, once imagined that Franz Kafka influenced Charles Dickens, claiming that "the fact is that every writer *creates* his own precursors."[24] At one level, this bon mot boils down to the obvious observation that Kafka influenced Dickens in the *consumerist* sense that after reading the former it is no longer possible to read the latter from a non-Kafkaesque perspective. The initially surrealist-sounding claim becomes more plausible in this regard when one takes into account a certain socioeconomic base of history. Both Dickens and Kafka were responding to different but related stages and situations of bureaucratic, technological, and economic modernism — with the one writer nearer the historical inception of the modern form, in England, and the other on its later geopolitical periphery. Rather more interesting, however, is the Borgesian fantasy that influence can be projected *literally* back into the past, as well as merely into the present and future. That Nietzsche entertained this possibility for his own work — and the doctrine of Eternal Recurrence of the Same *authorizes* it — indicates that he himself would have accepted the retroactive influence of contemporary technoculture on him. That an effect might in a sense precede its cause is not necessarily mystical, being an important paradox of both modern logic and psychoanalysis.[25] Nor is the thesis that one might "predict the past," and its concomitant that one might "remember the future," wholly far-fetched, since in historiography, if not history, what "is" retroactively determines what "was." The problematic, tropical reversal of cause and effect is active in the technocultural imaginary both of "First World" and of "Third." Chris. Marker could be speaking of Nietzsche's corps/e: "Such was the aim of the experiments — projecting emissaries into time, in order to summon the past and the future to the aid of the present."[26] And, in a masterpiece of Latin American "magical realism," Gabriel García Márquez images similar crosstemporal, chiasmic reversals.[27] But in what sense exactly has the everyday life of current technoculture influenced Nietzsche? If structural causality is to be taken seriously, literally, as a way of grasping Nietzsche's corps/e today, then this question is not quite as weird as it otherwise sounds.

Whether or not postmodern everyday life "is really Nietzschean" or "influenced Nietzsche" — whatever either claim might mean — clearly the conception and analysis of that life, as it is advanced by Foucault and those under his influence, is profoundly Nietzschean in orientation. This is exemplified in a remark made by Foucault in a 1977 interview translated as "Sexuality of History," the more demanding original title of which was "Les rapports de pouvoir passent à l'intérieure des corps." Foucault implied that the most axial knowledge-power relations occur when they insinuate themselves into the interior of the corps/e. The resulting sites exist only obscurely within the microsocial: "Between every point of a social body, between a man and a woman, between members of a family, between a master and a pupil, between everyone who knows and everyone who does not, there exist relations of power which are not purely and simply a projection of the sovereign's great power over the individual, they are rather the concrete, changing soil in which the sovereign's power is grounded, the conditions which make it possible for it to function."[28] For "sovereign" can be substituted the polymorphously perverse power relation that is the neocapitalist spectacle but also the "Nietzsche" who provided Foucault with the tools to analyze the incorporation of power rela-

tions. If Nietzsche has succeeded in significantly handicapping his subsequent reception subconsciously — and he has — then his anticipating
this response — as he did — is also confirmed by the everyday occur-
rence that his readers tend to think that it is *they* who have discovered
Nietzsche for the first time, *really* for the first time. This misrecognition
does seem to characterize most "first" encounters with Nietzsche, especially among male adolescents in the psychoplasmic brood that is his
corps/e. In this sense, perhaps, it is "we" who "influence" Nietzsche —
but only because he programmed "us" from the first in this way. But if
"Nietzsche" is "us" in these postmodern days as techno-Nietzsche/
anism, then "he" must also be the technocultural real of "TV" and its
equivalents — for that is a good part of who "we" are. Put differently:
Nietzsche is Horace Pinker.

When, in Wes Craven's junk-cult film *Shocker* (1989), the serial killer
Horace Pinker (Mitch Pileggi) passes into the electric circuit of the city
in which he has just been executed by electrocution, he gains the quasi-
posthumous capacity to appear and disappear *interactively* with and
within television.[29] This informing, televisual interactivity has two
modes. Pinker can emerge from actual TV *sets* to kill and reenter them
to escape. But also, channel surfing at will, he can interact with the
programs on TV. This transformative capacity impacts not merely re-
runs of old and current movies — where he can talk with the characters
and change the plots — but also documentary movies and live video
coverage of current events around the globe, including wars and revolutions — the implication being that he can alter History Itself. Fast-
forward but also fast-reverse. It must be stressed, however, that Nietzsche is Horace Pinker and that Horace Pinker is Nietzsche's corps/e
not in terms of *theme* or *content:* that is, a particularly heinous and
implausible murderer. This would be "Nietzscheanism" of only the
most crude, obvious, *and* most easily detectable sort, though Nietzsche
certainly has no objections to murder in principle. This would be the
form of "Nietzscheanism" that not merely the "moral majority" would
reject but likely any sane person. Rather, the esoterrorist Nietzsche
is the merely terrorist Horace Pinker in the *structure* of the spectacular technoculture of everyday life — which is to say in his effectivity as
an instance of structural causality. If Nietzsche actually had access to
Horace Pinker's technological expertise — that is, as a TV repairman
with preternatural electronic genius, not necessarily as a natural born

killer—and he *had* at least this desire—then he would hardly need to kill so brutally. Instead, his effectivity would lie in his capacity to influence visual and aural images that appear in the mass media—and hence in history—without viewer/auditors being aware of his presence. *Shocker* received predictably negative reviews on the Left when it was released. An exception occurred in the pages of the then *People's Daily World* (Communist Party, USA), a newspaper not usually distinguished by complexity of response to junk culture, among other things. Yet the film was grasped here as a complex allegory for late capitalism, and this was one of the rare moments when *organized* communism has come very close—albeit implicitly and unknowingly—to insight into the deep structure of Nietzsche's corps/e under technocultural conditions.

None of this is to suggest that Nietzsche himself would have *liked* all the influence that he has come to exert proleptically on the everyday life of technoculture, and it retroactively on him. Reaganomics would give him as little satisfaction as Newt Gingrich's Virtual America and Contract with America; and G. Gordon Liddy and Rush Limbaugh would surely disgust him. For in many *personal* respects Nietzsche was an exceptionally kind-hearted man. Yet another "word for donkeys"! Otherwise the Left might not read him at all. On the *contrary*, Nietzsche would almost certainly judge that this reciprocal influence is often miserably botched in terms of his *positive, creative* intentions. But just as certainly he would judge that this influence has been remarkably successful *negatively, prophylactically.* For his corps/e has a powerful way of anticipating and preventing genuinely communist—or other—*options* both to Nietzsche/anism and to the predatory "blond beast" that is neocapitalism. In 1994, the hundred-and-fiftieth anniversary of Nietzsche's birth, the jury was still out even on the existence, never mind the success, of what he called his "War Party" and "spiritual" or "intellectual party" that he had pitted to the death against the "Party of Peace" and "socialism."[30] If Nietzsche were to take pleasure in the existence of Left-Nietzscheanism, and of the fate of actually existing socialism, it would be *only* if both have made it impossible for a more proper Left to think and do *other* things than it does, think *alternative* thoughts to what it thinks, build communism. Beyond this essentially prophylactic, privative, and negative effectivity, Nietzsche would have a much harder time seeing *fully positive* incorporations of his teaching around the world. But, then, in certain circumstances, under the sign of Eternal Recurrence of the Same, "There ain't no success like failure . . . ," to cite part of a phrase by Bob Dylan. And, to rephrase a remark by a historian of "posthistory," under postindustrial conditions the masters do not necessarily remain masters, but the slaves still remain slaves.[31] "All over the world, the left is fighting rear-guard actions, staging holding operations, trying to gain time to rally people around a new vision. That seems a defensive and not very exalted task. Yet, if we fail, we really find ourselves in *le temps des assassins.*"[32] *Le temps de Nietzsche.*

The argument here is *not* that it is necessary to find out for the first time what Nietzsche "really meant" and then decide if it might still be appropriated. At least some of what Nietzsche "really meant" — including some of his most hair-raising, inflammatory, and murderous rantings — has been fairly well known, at least to some people, for a long time. In *this* respect there is passing little esoteric about him. But what these same people typically have not grasped is that the overall design and effect of Nietzsche/anism is to push them more or less gradually from the ideological Left to the Right, transforming leftists without their being aware of it — by means of a corpus of writing ensuring that his corpse lives on as corps. Such transformation or conversion has a technical name in social and intellectual history, in Italian *trasformismo.* But before applying it to Nietzsche/anism — in some ways its greatest exemplum — further historical preliminaries are required in order to make clearer what is and is not at stake.

Much of what Nietzsche "really meant" has not been unknown merely to some "high-priced men," to apply Frederick Winslow Taylor's term to professional philosophers and critics.[33] Elements of a *proletarian* appropriation of Nietzsche were manifested already in the 1890s. A sociological study conducted in 1897 and published in 1900 on the books owned and read by Leipzig workers suggests that Nietzsche's books were better represented in Germany than those of socialists such as Ferdinand Lassalle and August Bebel, not to mention Marx and Engels.[34] Even earlier, by 1892, leaders on the Left, notably the young Kurt Eisner, were warning that Nietzsche was becoming more seductive to workers than Marx, whose ideas and rhetoric appeared stodgy and old-fashioned in comparison with the racier Nietzsche.[35]

But, if sociologist Adolf Levenstein is to be believed, this proletarian reading formation was actually quite *critical* of Nietzsche, at least by the eve of World War I. In other words, much of what Nietzsche "really meant" was intimated by *working-class* readers.[36] In 1912 Levenstein polled various types of laborers as to their reading habits in general and their knowledge of Nietzsche in specific. He published the results of this survey twice: once in 1912 and again in 1919 immediately after the war. Entitled *Friedrich Nietzsche in the Judgment of the Working Class,* this is a remarkable text that has been symptomatically ignored by middle-class Left-Nietzscheans. To be sure, Levenstein's reconstruction of working-class reading formations is problematic by current sociological standards; indeed some of his correspondents sound suspiciously like Levenstein himself talking.[37] Nonetheless, his book represents a very early *possible* response to Nietzsche by a class deeply mistrusted by Nietzsche. And the stakes with this ignored virtual-actuality are — or at least *were* — very high, especially in Germany. Consider the thesis of a historian of national socialism, Rainer Stollmann, about the movement's "aesthetic" roots, though he does not factor Nietzsche into his account. Stollmann does not deny that the Nazis cynically manipulated the masses — in Nietzschean fashion, as it were — but shifts the responsibility for that manipulation onto the — Nietzscheanized — middle classes. Referring to the overdetermined crisis mentality of Weimar, including the devastating effects of the Great Depression, he argues: "The 'deception' and 'manipulation' of the masses which was certainly practiced by the ruling clique of the Nazi Party functioned only because the 'old' and 'new' middle levels of society were more disposed toward self-deception than the industrial workers. The crisis pauperized them, threatened them with bankruptcy, and turned them materially and socially into proletarians — which from a financial point of view they quite often had already been. The theoretical differences between them and the proletariat — namely morality, religion, family, customs, ideals — were asserted all the more strongly for reasons of compensation. Since petit bourgeois economy or small scale production is without perspective, it denounces any material interest at all as 'greed,' 'egotism,' 'selfishness,' etc."[38] The sociological function of Nietzsche's corps/e was to provide a version of "aesthetic" compensation that would make the deep class and personal egotism of the bourgeoisie housebroken, *salonfähig.* But so it is also that the economic conditions for the return of fascism are ever present in Nietzsche/anism as a primary agent of middle-class self-deception. It is in this context that the question of how the pretechnocultural proletariat might read — did read — Nietzsche takes on significance. The implications — philosophical and perhaps political — of this possibility are alive today in a perspicacious remark by Balibar: "in fact there are only supermen where there are also subhumans, who are themselves split up into several categories: on the one hand foreigners, slaves, colonials, and workers, constituted into a special 'race' in the imaginary of industrial societies, and on the other hand, precisely, women, equally liable, from antiquity to the present day, of being perceived as a 'race' opposed to that of men, and who have always been particularly forbidden from acting as a 'mass.' "[39]

Thus Spoke Zarathustra was known firsthand to Levenstein's — mostly male — workers in 1914–1919, including in the trenches of "the war to end all wars." It seems that not only the German officer corps carried *Faust,* the Bible, and *Thus Spoke Zarathustra* in its backpack. When this famous claim originated is unclear, and would not have displeased Nietzsche. When Elisabeth Förster-Nietzsche petitioned German President Paul von Hindenburg for a pension in 1926, she stressed the ethical and pedagogic attributes of her brother's œuvre, adding: "His major work *Thus Spoke Zarathustra* was the book which — together with the Bible and Goethe's *Faust* — was taken most often to the front by German soldiers."[40] Förster-Nietzsche's petition was signed by such notables as Nobel laureate Rudolf Eucken, Count Harry Keßler, Oswald Spengler, and Hans Vaihinger. But Levenstein's workers knew Nietzsche in other contexts as well. Many of the responses to the sociologist's questionnaire were conventionally uncritical, but the critical ones advanced an almost unique grasp of Nietzsche that remains relevant under postmodern conditions. One anonymous worker put the whole matter with a precision anticipating Balibar: "Nietzsche has only contempt and disgust for the herd-man; but he forgets something: the herd can exist without the Superman, but the latter can't exist without the herd."[41] But, as important, this response did not preclude these same "workers who read history," as Brecht would say, from imagining that they might activate his hostile writings for working-class ends — *someday.* In 1910, Heinrich Mann had taken a superficially similar position with regard to Nietzsche, as had some earlier socialist commenta-

352

tors dating back to the past century: that is, that a "democratic reversal" of Nietzsche's neo-aristocratism was possible, even desirable in Germany; but Mann's argument was opaque and indecisive compared to the blunt response of the workers represented by Levenstein.[42] They also experimented with substituting "proletariat" for "Superman" when reading *Thus Spoke Zarathustra* — a most interesting exercise indeed.

Needless to say, however, there is nothing *necessarily* progressive about this demand, in effect, to *collectivize* the Nietzschean Superman. It all depends on what *kind* of collectivity is involved. Nietzsche himself had certain collectives in mind, far beyond the exoteric claims of extreme individualism. The particular demand of Levenstein's workers not only had been shared earlier with Russian socialist "God-Builders," such as Maxim Gorky and Anatoly Vasilyevich Lunacharsky, but also would be shared later with various national socialists and their apologists.[43] Another of Levenstein's anonymous workers concluded: "On the basis of democratic solidarity, on the basis of a Socialist means of production that would prevent the exploitation of people, on the basis of the greatest possible freedom of individuals. . . . — This is, seen from my working-class point of view, the 'meaning of the earth' proclaimed by Zarathustra, and that will bring happiness to all people. *That's* how I'd *like* to approach Nietzsche." Indeed, this may be the *only* way to approach him from the Left, *if* it is still possible to do so. The worker circa 1912 continued: "For the person who can look further into the distance, the way goes through socialism to the possibility of individuality in Nietzsche"[44] — not from Nietzsche to socialism. But this opportunity was missed then and appears irretrievable today. Thanks, in good measure, to Nietzsche.

It is also decisively not the case that what Nietzsche "really meant" is to be found only in his *un*published notebooks. To be sure, these are fully available in German and more recently French, Italian, and Japanese, but not in, say, English or Afrikaans, Arabic, Bengali, Czech, Chinese, Dutch, Esperanto, Finnish, Flemish, Hebrew, Hindi, Hungarian, Icelandic, Korean, Norwegian, Polish, Portuguese, Russian, Spanish, Swahili, Swedish, Thai, Ukrainian, Urdu, Vietnamese, Yiddish — in all of which languages Nietzsche's published, more exoteric writings have long been available. Nietzsche was not being megalomaniac but geopolitically coy (read: proleptic and prophetic) when, nearing the end in late 1888, he extended his global claws to write Ruggero Bonghi: "I now have my readers everywhere, exclusively *select* intellects . . . in Vienna, in St. Petersburg, in Stockholm, in Paris, in New York — I don't have them in Germany."[45] His correspondent, Bonghi (1826–1895), was an important liberal politician and historian of the French Revolution. He had shown great interest in promoting Nietzsche "officially" in southern Europe; indeed, he was the first significant member of the Italian intelligentsia to do so. As it also happens, Bonghi's writing provided a conduit for Gramsci in prison for factual information about several historical topics, though not Nietzsche.[46] Which may be the closest Nietzsche and Gramsci ever came — ever *can* come — to having a mutual "friend." But the point is that Nietzsche's occasional but consistent rantings against democracy are also sufficiently represented in the books Nietzsche himself *published*.

What normally distinguishes Nietzsche's published from unpublished works is less the *content* of his doctrines and the *violence* of their expression — including his expressed desire to eliminate or silence his many enemies, real and imagined — than intimations about how to *implement* his doctrines subliminally — to begin processes of transformation beneath the surface of our consciousness, even skins. "The problem is: how can you randomize your strategy, yet move purposefully toward your goal?"[47] This Philip K. Dickian question is one of the most characteristic problems of Nietzschean rhetoric and politics. Dick was influenced by Nietzsche and by a theory and practice developed for use in games, business, and warfare called "minimax": "Good strategy requires the use of the principle of 'minimax,' that is, a policy in which a range of possible high and low gains is adopted on the assumption that one might be found out. But to avoid being found out one obscures the specific pattern of play by randomizing the strategy with chance plays. . . ."[48] *Nietzsche* is minimax but not any one "content" he ever recorded in print.

Finally, the point of *Nietzsche's Corps/e* is not even that inadequate *attention* has been given to the nasty passages in Nietzsche — the passages from aesthetics to politics to prophecy and back again, from published books to unpublished notebooks. Attention has been called *repeatedly* to these passages by reasonably clear and distinct voices on the Left, the Center, and the Right — from even before Nietzsche's death to the present time. The point of Nietzsche's esoteric semiotic and process of weeding out is that, when reading the nasty passages in Nietzsche, *we do not really see them*. And this is quite *literally* true: *virtually* literally true, as it were. This, then, is what is most un/canny of all about Nietzsche's corps/e.

We *look at* the "crazy" stuff in the corpus of this dead man. We *read* it, may even *interpret* or *deconstruct* it. But we don't ever *see* it completely — *especially* when we *think* we do. Part of this mechanism is confirmed repeatedly by almost everything produced by workers in the Nietzsche Industry. The really crazy stuff just does not register, does not compute. Nevertheless, for this very reason, it sinks in and goes to work. And — sooner or later, gradually or suddenly — the Nietzschean corps is formed: the new flesh, the new organ, the new body, the brood, the avatar. For we tend to " 'see' only what has become distant enough to take on the aura of universality."[49]

Walter Benjamin's theory of the "dialectical image" spoke mysteriously of "the point," "site," or "passage" (*Stelle*) in every "true work of art" through which the viewer "sees" or "blasts" *through* the work into the Real.[50] Apparently Benjamin meant such remarks literally, at least as possibility; and the Nietzsche who claimed to be "not a man but dynamite" would have appreciated what Benjamin was talking about, having helped program him to say it. According to Benjaminian definition, Nietzsche's corpus, almost in its entirety, would qualify as a "true work of art" — but only in terms of an aesthetic-prophetic-politics for the benefit of a very few men, not for the rest of us. To "us" — after the death of socialism the scare quotes are especially obligatory — Nietzsche says: *"In order to act, you have to believe errors; and you will still act according to these errors after you have seen through them as errors."*[51] This was close to Nietzsche's deep principle of individual and collective transformation, and he had also hit upon a key principle of consumer capitalism generally, one of the most powerful mechanisms of transformation ever known. According to a central thesis of Horkheimer and Adorno, "The triumph of advertising in the culture industry is that consumers feel compelled to buy and use its products even though they see through them."[52] For his part, Nietzsche is not primarily interested in exposing this principle to view in Enlightenment fashion, even though he just did in part of his German corps/e; he is much more interested in putting it to work for his own anti-Enlightenment, esoteric, and darker ends.

It is also uncanny to compare Nietzsche's principle of believing-and-acting-in-error to a central thesis in Deleuze and Guattari's *Capitalism and Schizophrenia,* a text that "claims its descent from Nietzsche."[53] Here, a good "schizoid Nietzsche" and "schizoanalysis" is pitted against a bad "psychologist as modern priest." The latter position is rejected by Deleuze and Guattari because it "reterritorializes" the properly deterritorialized, molecular, nomadic Nietzschean subject: weaving it back into the molar artifice of capitalist territories and beliefs that recode and regulate all production but especially the production of the increasingly capitalist, capitalized social subject. But note the terms in which Deleuze and Guattari mount their antihermeneutic, antipsychoanalytic attack against the psychoanalyst-priest and all that "he" stands for in "his" many normalizing functions. According to Deleuze and Guattari, "there is no unconscious material, so that schizoanalysis has nothing to interpret. There are only resistances, and then machines, desiring machines." "To be sure, it is not psychoanalysis that makes us believe: Oedipus and castration are demanded, then demanded again, and these demands come from elsewhere and from deeper down." "But psychoanalysis did find the following means, and fills the following function: *to ensure that beliefs survive, even after they have been repudiated! And to instill a belief in something into those who no longer believe in anything,* . . . reconstituting a private territory for them, a private *Urstaat,* a private capital (the dream as capital, Freud said . . .). That is why, inversely, schizoanalysis must devote itself with all its strength to the necessary destructions. Destroying beliefs and representations, theatrical scenes. And, when engaged in this task, no activity will be too malevolent."[54] Whatever one thinks of schizoanalysis it ought not appeal to *Nietzsche* for support as the authors of *Anti-Oedipus* continually do. As Nietzsche's principle of believing-and-acting-in-error makes clear enough, what Deleuze and Guattari describe as the position of the bad psychoanalyst was precisely *Nietzsche's* position. *In their own terms* Nietzsche was not a schiz or schizoanalyst but Oedipal, reterritorializing, paranoid, molar, organic, totalitarian, statist, capitalist. . . . So it is that ignorance of Nietzsche's esoteric semiotic takes its toll on a major current on the Left, folding it back into his corps/e.

For Nietzsche, all "noble" and "base" lies are told on behalf of some people at the expense of others. This a version of the neo-Kantian "Philosophy of 'As If,'" as further developed by Octave Mannoni to analyze the psychosocial structure of *Je sais bien, mais quand même:* "I know very well [that it is not true], but nonetheless [I still believe it, and act accordingly]."[55] In much the same spirit, Foucault made the general point about post-May '68 that "the intellectual discovered that the masses no longer need him to gain knowledge: they *know* perfectly well, without illusion; they know far better than he and they are certainly capable of expressing themselves. But there exists a system of power which blocks, prohibits, and invalidates this discourse and this knowledge, a power not only found in the manifest authority of censorship, but one that profoundly and subtly penetrates an entire societal network. Intellectuals are themselves agents of this system of power — the idea of their responsibility for 'consciousness' and discourse forms part of the system."[56] Nietzsche's *personal* view of " '68" is irrelevant until one has grasped the fact that he would have affirmed the *structure* that Foucault has identified with Nietzsche's help. Finally, if this structure of Nietzsche/anism is the structure of global commodity capitalism, then this gives considerable weight to the proposition that "Nietzsche's position is the only one outside of communism."

The epitaph to all schizoanalyses of the subject in Nietzsche's name has been provided by Žižek's remarks that "the elated 'deconstructionist' logomachy focused on 'essentialism' and 'fixed identities' ultimately fights a straw man. Far from containing any kind of subversive potentials, the dispersed, plural, constructed subject hailed by postmodern theory (the subject prone to particular, inconsistent modes of enjoyment, etc.) simply designates *the form of subjectivity that corresponds to late capitalism.* Perhaps the time has come to resuscitate the Marxian insight that Capital is the ultimate power of 'deterritorialization' which undermines every fixed social identity. . . . "[57] But for his part Žižek wants to call the philosophical basis of late capitalism "Spinozist," pitting himself explicitly with Kant and Hegel against "Spinozism, or, the ideology of late capitalism."[58] He concludes: "The only true dilemma today is whether or not the late-capitalist Spinozism is our ultimate horizon: is all that seems to resist this Spinozism mere 'remainders of the past,' simply limited, 'passive' knowledge, unable to contemplate the Capital-Substance *sub specie aeternitatis,* as a self-sufficient machinery, or can we effectively call this Spinozism into question" (p. 219). Yet it is much more precise, terminologically and ideologically speaking, to substitute for Žižek's "Spinozism" the term "Nietzsche/anism."

The Nietzschean "Self," circa 1886 and 1996, is illuminated, up to a point, by a central early thesis of Lacan about the "mirror stage" to the effect that our anticipations of the future are linked to the past, our recollections of the past to the future. According to Lacan, the earliest and/or latest anticipation and/or recollection we can ever have—or more precisely: our projective and/or retroactive fantasy backward and forward to the misrecognition of the mirror stage—is not of wholeness or unity but of "fragilization" in general and of the "fragmented body" (*le corps morcelé*) most specifically. It is with regard to this kind of corpus or corpse, then, that Lacan spoke of love as "always having to undo again, or sever" the "knot of imag-inary servitude": this being our "mortal destiny's *cipher*"[59]—in the dual sense of both "zero" and "sign." But, *pace* some Left-Lacanians, Nietzsche did not love all people, all Selves the same, and he reserved a very hard "center" for himself, though not for all his corps/e. In her *Tales of Love* (1983), Julia Kristeva theorizes the existence of an interior "idealism" that predates and prefigures the Oedipal and that lives on after it has come under more or less decisive attack. The resulting amorous manifestations or "histories of love" include the protocyborg "fantasy of an androgyne before sexualization," but are then socially determined or reconditioned so as to deny access to alternative possibilities of subject-formation. The new logic of Self becomes: "All appearances 'mean,' therefore the Self is sacred."[60] But this principle, *pace* Kristeva, comes close to *Nietzsche's* esoteric notion of Self and *amor fati*—which he was interested not in deconstructing but in putting to divisive social work, to esoterrorism.

In the brave new world of the future, it seems, the Self is something that can be Taylorized and programmed at will, according to the dictates of the Will to Power, in the guise of virtually any avatar. Compare the exploded and reconstituted technoself of Gibson's *Count Zero* (1986):

It took the Dutchman and his team three months to put Turner together again. They cloned a square meter of skin for him, grew it on slabs of collagen and shark-cartilage polysaccharides. They bought eyes and genitals on the open market. The eyes were green. He spent most of those three months in a ROM-generated simstim construct of an idealized New England boyhood of the previous century. The Dutchman's visits were gray dawn dreams, nightmares that faded as the sky lightened beyond his second-floor bedroom window. You could smell the lilacs, late at night. He read Conan Doyle [read: Nietzsche] by the light of a sixty-watt bulb behind a parchment shade printed with clipper ships. He masturbated in the smell of clean cotton sheets and thought about cheerleaders. The Dutchman opened a door in his back brain and came strolling in to ask questions, but in the morning his mother called him down to Wheaties, eggs and bacon, coffee with milk and sugar.[60]

Whereupon, in this tale of love, keyboard cowboy Turner sets out into the matrix to get his revenge. Where in this world is Nietzsche? In techno-Nietzsche/anism he is arguably *everywhere.*

So is Nietzsche's principle that "In order to act, you have to believe errors; and you will still act according to these errors after you have seen through them as errors." Nietzsche would have to adjust very little of his esoteric semiotics to insinuate himself into not only cyberspace but the rest of everyday life. As Žižek suggests, it is *normal* for the subjects of ideological systems to be perfectly aware that exoteric, public claims about what is, say, "freedom," "justice," "equality," "prosperity," "democracy," and so on, are politically manipulated terms that — whether under "Liberal Capitalism" or "Actually Existing Socialism" — amount to real freedom, justice, and prosperity only for an elite few. And yet the deeper point is that these same people carry on *as if* this very ideology applied equally to them.[62] Nietzsche would savor such mechanisms of "conscious illusion" — after all, he helped invent them.[63]

Of course, it is not reasonable to expect people to dwell on things they feel they cannot radically change; just as it is not reasonable to expect them to cut their own throats, ideological or fleshy. As political scientists and critics of postmodern technoculture have noted, much of the public in the "First World" — and not only here — has abandoned the perception of the world and of everyday life in terms of an exclusive "Left-Center-Right" "continuum" or "choice." Instead, this modernist "political" perception has been significantly supplanted by a dual perspective or "frame" that is part *economic,* part *pragmatic.* On the one hand basic social difference is still grasped as being between "the 'haves' and the 'have-nots'"; on the other hand social issues are now grasped only as being between "'those where I can exert some influence' and 'those where I cannot.'"[64] This "dual perspective" (the term was Gramsci's and before him Machiavelli's) could yet be salutary for rejuvenated communism — it ought to be capable of working just such fissures and differences between ideology and economics. But nothing can help a leftism always already infliltrated by a *Nietzschean* denial of difference between the Left, the Center, and the Right: that is, a denial of political difference that is *exoteric,* and that ends up tilting social and economic difference always toward the Right, as part of its basic process of surreptitious transformation.

Baudrillard has remarked that in the current society of the spectacle among the traditional distinctions obliterated are between "watching TV" and "being watched by TV," and with them vanishes the possibility of living and thinking *"as if TV wasn't there."*[65] With Nietzsche/anism, the entire Enlightenment project would indeed seem to explode or implode into the thin air of the "aesthetics" currently called cyberspace. And, to the extent that communism has always involved not only the building of "a new social formation" but also "a new form of organization of matter,"[66] and hence of techno-human interface, it is particularly exigent that it — as the only position outside of Nietzscheanism — come to terms with all the current transformations of mechanic technoculture in a way that shuns the false antinomy between merely personal, privatizing prostheses in its one aspect, and the total obliteration of the individual in collective machines in its other. So it is necessary to cut the ground out from under Nietzsche's seminal exoteric claim, beginning in *The Birth of Tragedy,* that life is "justified" *only* as an "aesthetic" or "artistic phenomenon."[67] The meaning of this remark is misunderstood, trivialized, and depoliticized when grasped as a philosophical argument promoting "life as literature" or "thinking on stage."[68] Nietzsche, at least, was refreshingly candid — mostly in his unpublished notebooks, it is true — about just *whose* "life" and "stage" he had in mind and for *whose* benefit his "aesthetic philosophy" existed. For him, *his corpus must be instrumentalized, harnessed for war.* He reminded himself: "Philosophy [is] *not for the people,* and therefore *not the basis of a culture,* therefore only *the tool of a culture* [also nur *Werkzeug einer Kultur*]."[69] For this reason, socialist polemicist and critic Franz Mehring (1846–1919), Nietzsche's contemporary and a friend of Engels, was quite right to warn throughout the 1890s that the Left should never "aestheticize away the fact that Nietzsche combated proletarian class struggle from the same elevated circles of thought as did the next best stockbroker or the next best reptile."[70] Nietzsche's personal view of stockbrokers and reptiles aside, this is *not* the exaggeration it likely sounds to refined academic ears today.

Key for Nietzschean aesthetics as it bears on postmodernity is a simple maxim he underlined in 1881: *"Reduction of morality to aesthetics!!!"*[71] An awful lot of socioeconomic baggage comes along with his peculiar "aesthetic" reductionism, including the following tripartite "utopian" scheme: (1) the institutionalization of *suicide* as public festival; (2) the rigorous, institutionalized separation of *sexual pleasure* from marriage, since "a population of workers needs good whorehouses"; and (3) the "absolute necessity" that "the wise acquire for themselves the monopoly of the *money-market* [das Monopol des *Geldmarktes*], so as to direct it "amorally" and "aesthetically" with their more or less concealed "life-style and aims."[72] Exclusively for the elite, the potential geniuses, was reserved the neo-Grecian pleasures of "free individuals": namely, in Nietzsche's own words, those males who are to relearn "the art of coitus" with young boys (*Knabenliebe*) as a cure for "effeminization," and who will support abortion — but less as a right of individuals than as a social duty for the sake of breeding that men, not women, will determine. And this entire agenda is naturally based for him socially and economically on "slavery," including the right to kill dissenters.[73]

In *Minima Moralia* (1951), Adorno suggested that both the main proponent of "the bourgeois doctrine of violence" (Nietzsche) and the latter's "main adversary" (Marx) shared a common "lie": namely, that art or culture "creates the illusion of a society worthy of man which does not exist; that it conceals the material conditions upon which all human works rise, and that, comforting and lulling, it serves to keep alive the bad economic determination of existence." But, Adorno quickly added, "precisely this notion, like all expostulation about lies, has a suspicious tendency to become itself ideology."[74] Yet this depends, one might think, on the *kind* of art and on what one can *make* of it. Adorno tended to turn "Art" into a hypostatized, personified category, and to this extent followed Nietzsche's — exoteric — lead much more than Marx's. According to Adorno's neo-Kantian attack against the instrumentalization of art, taking a position that makes it impossible to understand Nietzsche esoterically, since instrumentalization of both philosophy and art was always part of what he had in mind: "The closer the mode of production of artifacts comes to material mass-production, the more naively it provokes that fatal question [namely: 'What's it for?']. Works of art, however, try to silence it. 'Perfection,' as Nietzsche put it [in *Human, All-too-Human*], must not have become, that is, it should not appear made. Yet the more consequentially it distances itself, through perfection, from making, the more fragile its own mode of existence necessarily becomes: the endless pains to eradicate the traces of its own making, injure works of art and condemn them to be fragmentary."[75] So it is, however, that the very influential "critical theory" version of Western Marxism became collaboratory: not so much with a nostalgic, antiproductivist "aestheticism" — for Adorno's was a relentlessly ironic and itself "fragmentary" view of art through a particularly sharp negative-dialectical prism — but nonetheless with the ideological and political transformation, via a very uncritically assimilated Nietzsche, of post/modern intellectuals from the Center and Left to the Right.[76] In the end, Adorno was corps/ed.

So what about Nietzsche's success or failure technoculturally in his own terms? Was Nietzsche comparatively victorious or vanquished in his project actually to transform mankind, to instaurate a new order of rank, to produce a caste or corps of "artist-warriors" on the backs of more or less willing slaves? According to the late Allan Bloom in the chapter of *The Closing of the American Mind* (1987) entitled "The Nietzscheanization of the Left and Vice Versa": "The continuing effort of the mutant breed of Marxists has been to derationalize Marx and to turn Nietzsche into a leftist. Nietzsche's colossal political failure is attested to by the fact that the Right, which was his only hope that his teaching would have its proper effect, has utterly disappeared, and he himself was tainted by its ugly last gasp, while today virtually every Nietzschean, as well as Heideggerian, is a leftist."[77] Now, these are very peculiar, blundering ideas, and likely intentionally duplicitous. "It is a rule of common prudence to 'believe' that all these blunders are intentional and in each case to raise the question as to what the blunder might be meant to signify."[78] Would not the fact that "*virtually* every Nietzschean" is "a leftist" be a remarkable triumph for the Right? *Especially* for any properly Nietzschean Right of the Bloomian stamp that is itself nothing if not elitist? And has the Right — even as defined by Bloom himself "in its only serious meaning": namely, as "the party op-

posed to equality (not economic equality but equality of rights)"[79]—
"*utterly* disappeared"? Even Rush Limbaugh doesn't believe that. As
for Nietzsche, he was not in favor of economic equality—*except* if it
produces the appearance of social "harmony" à la Carey and Bastiat,
except as it allows for the *intellectual* inequality defended by Bloom &
Co. Which is certainly not to say that Nietzsche would have any personal use for either poverty or Allan Bloom. Besides, there is surely
enough economic inequality in the world to satisfy almost any Right-
Nietzschean. Is Nietzsche's brand of "active nihilism"—or even his
supposedly "momentary lapses" in favor of genocide, breeding, and the
like—wholly "noncontagious," as "leftists" such as Habermas and
Rorty have *also* thought? Nietzsche *intended* his corps/e to abandon
any radical democratic and anticapitalist—that is, authentically communist—project. Bloom is right about only one thing, however, and it
is important: Western Marxists have indeed derationalized Marx and
turned Nietzsche into a leftist—but that's quite a *victory* for Nietzsche
and his corps/e.

Thinking of the World War II and cold war period, Lukács argued in
the 1950s that "it is not good enough to say that the intellectual and
artistic level of Schopenhauer and Nietzsche is immeasurably higher
than the coarse and contradictory demagogy of Hitler and Rosenberg.
For if a person educated in philosophy and literature is able to follow
epistemologically the nuances of Nietzsche's reworking of Schopenhauer, and to appreciate with aesthetic and psychological sensitivity the
nuances of his critique of decadence, and yet still believes in the Zarathustra myth, the myth of the Superman and 'eternal recurrence,' this is
at bottom harder to fathom than the despairing belief of a poorly
educated working youth—someone who was never or only temporarily a member of a party and was left out in the cold after finishing his apprenticeship—that Hitler would realize 'German socialism.'"[80] There
is still much truth in Lukács's perspective. But what is additionally at
issue today with Nietzsche/anism is not *only*, as it was for Lukács, the
global working class, the political clout of which has diminished significantly under conditions of postmodernity, nor even its enervation by
the mass media and other less polite techniques of persuasion. *Also* at
issue is the influence exerted on the traditional working class and on the
new social worker by the entire Society of the Spectacle—defined by
the late Debord, in part, as "the autocratic reign of the mass market

economy," "the activities of the world's owners." Has a spectacular Nietzscheanism, which is isomorphic with the Society of the Spectacle, *"integrated"* itself into reality to the same extent as it was describing it, and . . . was reconstructing it as it was describing it"?[81] If Nietzsche was really a prophet, if he was really a political aesthetician or aesthetic politician of the first rank and relevance, then he must at least, at bare minimum, have proleptically tele-vised or fore-seen *"letzte Menschen"*: that is, "last" or "ultimate" or "posthuman" men and women *like us.*

Not assuming that any of these theses or problems can be adequately formulated or proven, there are two fundamental ways of making the issue of Nietzsche's relative success and failure more precise — historically, politically, and in terms of their current relevance — without falling into the trap of the kind of class-collaboratory hermeneutics and synthesizing "dialectics" that seeks unity where there ought to be none and celebrates "dialogue" and the "dialogic" where there is only always already consensus and monologue. One way is to produce a *historical framework* (*Gestell,* Heidegger might say) within which to locate Nietzsche and Nietzscheanism. But history is worse than worthless if it is not, in Manfredo Tafuri's phrase, "the continuous contestation of the present" — a site in which to seek alternatives to the present and for the future. On the proper relationship between past and present, Gramsci noted that "the present is a *criticism* of the past, besides [and because of] 'surpassing' it. But should the past be discarded for this reason? What should be discarded is that which the present has 'intrinsically' criticized and that part of ourselves which corresponds to it. What does this mean? That we must have an exact consciousness of this real criticism and express it not only theoretically, but *politically.* In other words, we must stick closer to the present, which we ourselves have helped create, while conscious of the past and its continuation (and revival)."[82] So, in addition to the *historical-critical* approach to Nietzsche's current success and failure, we must be alive to all manifestations of the most "intrinsic" forms of Nietzsche/anism as it has in-formed and trans-formed not only the more or less distant past but also the *contemporary and postcontemporary.* Which also means the spectacular technoculture of everyday life. "Contrary to the whole rationalist tradition, which requires only a straight, true idea in order to correct a bent, false idea, Marxism considers that ideas have a historical existence only in so far as they are taken up and *incorporated* in the materiality of social relations."[83] The success or failure of Nietzsche depends on his ability to continue to *transform* opponents into his corps/e.

Trasformismo

Trasformismo (transformism) is the best tool with which to grasp Nietzsche's corps/e, particularly the existence of Left-Nietzscheanism. Its basic meaning is historical transformation from one political or ideological position to another, but particularly from the Left to Center and then Right. As developed by Gramsci, *trasformismo* is related to other concepts equally germane: for example, the intimate relationship between *liberalism* and *fascism* as two modes of "passive revolution" or "revolution-restoration"; the key role of *intellectuals*—both by academic training and social-directive function—as points of articulation between ruling groups and ruled; and the thesis that high philosophy is inscribed by everyday life and common sense—which is never entirely good sense—and vice versa—the way common sense and everyday life are inscribed by philosophy or, as Gramsci hoped, the communism he called "philosophy of praxis."

Trasformismo has been succinctly defined by its leading conservative historian as "the desertion of liberals to the right" and as governments that "talk left and act right."[84] Or, as Régis Debray once famously quipped, "revolutions revolutionize counter-revolutions." A *trasformista* is a quick-change artist. One contributing cause/effect of *trasformismo* is that bourgeois political parties, such as the current Democratic and Republican Parties in the United States, tend to represent only oscillatory social groupings around a single unmolested core of dominant economic interest, rather than representing more fundamental class differences and antagonisms. Such parties typically share a static procapitalist ideology, while giving off the appearance of dynamically "debating" and "opposing" one another, thus suppressing and precluding radical alternatives to capitalism. This includes the violent production, in effect, of "terrorists" who are then immediately figured as "radical evil."

In "The Violence of Liberal Democracy" (1993), Žižek calls the new type of insurgency—for example, the Khmer Rouge in Southeast Asia and Sendero Luminoso in South America—an "infinite judgment" (Kant) and "creative sublimation" (Hegel) vis-à-vis both late capitalism and its externalized and/or internalized "other," which is fundamentalist nationalism.[85] The latter's judgment against late capitalism is not infinite and absolute, to speak Kantian and Hegelese, but merely finite and relative, since it remains deeply embedded in a capitalist economic matrix. In this global situation, Žižek argues, liberal democracy and capitalism meet in the new insurgency the absolute limits of their old claim to be "universal." The globe is bifurcated into a liberal-democratic "inside," where "we" are, and a fundamentalist-nationalist "outside," where "they" are. This radical "scissure" is an effect, in part, of an absence: that is, "the 'socialist' bloc," as representative of "the true 'third way,' a desperate attempt at modernization outside the constraints of capitalism" (p. 92) — a scissure filled by the "infinite judgment" and "zero point" of the new insurgency (p. 93). As for what remains of the old "third way," the bloody breakup of socialism (e.g., ex-Yugoslavia) — here we are looking, according to Žižek, not into the past but the future, including of late capitalism. In the words again of Leonard Cohen, "Get ready for the future: It is murder." If this is so, then Nietzsche's corps/e has a novel global configuration and constituency to work with and on, but one of transformative power relations with which Nietzsche was quite at home *in principle.*

As defined by Mao, liberalism in particular is a synonym for *trasformismo:* "People who are liberals look upon the principle of Marxism as abstract dogma. They approve of Marxism, but are not prepared to practice it or to practice it in full; they are not prepared to replace their liberalism by Marxism. These people have their Marxism, but they have their liberalism as well — they talk Marxism but practice liberalism; they apply Marxism to others but liberalism to themselves. They have both goods in stock and find a use for each. This is how the minds of certain people work."[86] More generally, as Althusser liked to quip, *trasformismo* is the idealist way people have of believing that the world is coming round to their position — when in fact they are merely coming round to the world's. The problem remains that when it is working most efficiently *trasformismo* is not perceptible as such to those who are *being* transformed.

As is the case with the hegemony of which it is one facet, *trasformismo* involves a form of unacknowledged consensus or problematic that allows only certain questions to be raised — irrespective of any answer — and disallows the rest. Since the claim that an unacknowledged consensus or problematic exists always presupposes the existence or possibility of an observation point outside it, the epistemological and ontological status of such claims must remain hypothetical, heuristic, proleptic. The appearance can be given off, for example, that a substantive debate between "Right-Nietzscheans" and "Left-Nietzschoids" is taking place; but in fact this very debate conceals a more general drift from and against the Left to and on behalf of the Right. In anthropological terms, Nietzschean *trasformismo* is intimately related to carnival and other rituals to the extent that they conform to the basic principle that the "supreme ruse of power is to allow itself to be contested ritually in order to consolidate itself more effectively."[87] Which is not to say that such "symbolic" — as opposed to "actual" — contestation is in principle without *any* political efficacy either for the Left or the Right, depending on the conjunctures in which it occurs.

The liberal-Nietzschean variant of carnivalesque ritual arises in significant measure because of leftist ignorance of, or unconcern with, a scientific, philological reconstruction of how Nietzsche intended to say and do what he said he was going to do. In Althusserian terms, Nietzschean *trasformismo* helps overdetermine a more general and ubiquitous affirmation by intellectuals of the proposition that reading, viewing, and listening are inscribed by a more or less "Manichaean conflict between 'liberty' and 'oppression,' a mythical contest whose enabling concept is the striving individual for whom liberty exists only as a predatory meritocracy — a zero-sum struggle for power — and for whom oppression is defined as any interference with the right of 'talented' elites to exploit the 'mediocre' masses."[88] The irony here is that this supposedly Nietzschean — or Foucauldian-Nietzschean — view of the world turns out to be also that of "the professional middle class, and . . . embraced enthusiastically by both its liberal and conservative factions, each as unwilling to call into question the assumptions on which rest their class freedom from proletarianization and their class power over the working class."[89] Nietzschean *trasformismo* provides a necessary — albeit insufficient — condition of *just* this unwillingness. And it confirms Nietzsche as a supreme fascoid-liberal thinker and writer, perhaps the greatest possible one: in short, as "the only position outside of communism" — not an untimely man, but a man for all times.

Originally developed to analyze nineteenth- and early twentieth-century Italy, Gramsci's argument about *trasformismo* does *not* entirely explain why Nietzsche has found such a generally positive reception on the Left—a reception, it seems reasonably clear, that Nietzsche would have really savored only for its privative, negative effect of preventing leftist intellectuals from doing other things, thinking alternative thoughts, often with the *appearance* of maximum "leftist" radicality. But *trasformismo* at least *helps grasp* the "paradox" of Left-Nietzscheanism as a specific historical event and tendency.

Following Gramsci's lead, it is necessary to do to Nietzsche what Gramsci did to Croce and Marx to Hegel.[90] The achronological series Hegel-Croce-Nietzsche *itself* registers the process of *trasformismo* from Left to Right. This is to say that it is necessary to "recontextualize" Nietzsche within the ongoing *trasformismo* of intellectuals from the Left to the Right, in dynamic relation to the perennial crisis of liberalism and its own oscillatory, reciprocal relation to various manifestations of fascism. But it is not in relation to national socialism, necessarily, which is why so much *German*-oriented theory and criticism is counterproductive in getting after Nietzsche and Nietzscheanism. This is not the least reason why departments of German and German studies are conceptually bankrupt, having outlived any more profound raison d'être they might have had or have.

Trasformismo both is made possible by and contributes to the recurrent inability of liberalism to solve the inherent, constitutive, Jekyll-and-Hyde contradiction in all capitalism between the nominal affirmation of free trade and other freedoms — some of them genuine — on the one hand, and the periodic necessity — not only but especially at times of domestic and foreign economic crisis and/or war — for state intervention on the other. At stake here, too, is the fact that "democracy" means different things in First World countries than elsewhere.[91] These profound contradictions are also expressed in what *for liberalism* is a set of insoluble contradictions: between capitalism and democracy; between freedom and equality; between the rights of middle-class property owners and of their employees; between capitalists and others; between the international drive of capital and attempts to contain it nationally by means of different national-popular agendas; and so forth. Consequently, the problem to be faced politically and globally is threefold: (1) that fascism "solves" such crises — for a time, for some people — better or more efficiently than does liberal democracy; (2) that no fascist regime has yet come apart from internal pressures alone, though the fascist move or drive to imperialist aggression — in the impossible attempt to solve what are *for capital* ultimately insoluble economic, political, and cultural contradictions — has so far in history led to being crushed by *more* liberal democracies, with the help of existing socialism; and (3) that liberal intellectuals, often of good will, more or less unwittingly collaborate in the process of politico-historical transformation, up to and including its fascist deformation. In Gramsci's terms "fascoid-liberalism" is a basic mode of "passive revolution" or "revolution-restoration": that is, it can give off the *modal appearance* of radical political and cultural change, yet the economic-corporative *constitutive structure* of capitalism remains intact, enabling the reconstruction of liberalism after the superstructural "aberrations" have been "definitively" defeated. Which happened in Europe with Christian Democratic and Christian Socialist Parties after World War II because, in Gramscian terms, "fascism as a form of state totalitarianism" concealed "a new form of reformism linked to state capitalism."[92] And vice versa: state capitalism harbors the basic ingredients of fascism. A similar argument can be applied *mutatis mutandis* to the development and demise of "Actually Existing Socialism," among other reasons, because it, too, retains capitalist elements. *Nietzschean* elements.

In terms of philosophy, we have seen Gramsci noting that "all those Nietzschean charlatans in verbal revolt against all that exists, against conventionality, etc., should have ended up by accepting it after all." But now it is just as important to ask: Were and are Nietzscheans *only* charlatans? Clearly not. For then the task of combating them would be *much* easier. In that case Enlightenment *would* be effective, Reason *would* be effective, logical argument *would* be effective, straightforward discourse *would* be effective. But they no longer are. If Nietzsche did not *really sound* liberating, playful, funny, beautiful, sublime, deconstructive, loving, and so on, he would not be half as fascinating, half as dangerous, half as entertaining today — all around the globe, perhaps until the end of the world.[93]

To see and grasp Nietzsche with Gramsci's help as a *fascoid-liberal revolutionary* is to *begin* to resolve the paradox — the *apparent* contradiction — of the existence of *Left*-Nietzscheanism — in the face of Nietzsche's own published contempt for democracy, feminism, socialism, and the like, including his ambivalence toward the in fact dubious brand of European and German liberalism he encountered in the 1870s and 1880s. It is also to begin to grasp the concomitant existence of *Right*-Nietzscheanism, in the face of Nietzsche's own published affirmation of free spirits, cosmopolitanism, and the like. Liberal androids and fascoids can find/produce *exactly the same* support in his published works — *not* in two or more different *aspects or passages* of his works, which can then be set one against another, so as to deconstruct themselves. Such deconstruction has proven to be altogether too easy — because it *seems* so hard to do. On the contrary, however, both ideologies and groups in fact find/produce Nietzsche's support in *the same passages in the same published works. As* his corps, they find/produce Nietzsche's corpse, again and again and again. Thus might his corps/e actually become "the only position outside of communism." What is to be done? The ball is in the court of communism, when it exists.

Listening to Félix Guattari and Toni Negri — "communists like us," like the author of *Nietzsche's Corps/e* — it is possible to imagine that the ongoing events in Eastern Europe and the former USSR show that revolution is still possible; that actually existing, bureaucratic, command-economy socialism is discredited; that such socialism was tragicomically "locked in a competition with the rhythm of its own development and with that of the capitalist countries"; that socialism "did not commit itself to overcoming the capitalist system and the system of wage labor, but instead became a [sometimes criminal and murderous] social-economic alternative of capitalism"; that socialism was "nothing other than one of the forms taken by capitalist management of the economy and power, whereas communism is [or must be] an absolutely radical political and economic democracy and an inspiration to freedom"; *and* that — precisely for all these reasons — it is *communism* that remains "the minimum essential program" of humankind, a radical possibility of liberation from the slavery of coerced work, and the "free organization of cooperation in production."[94]

Already for Althusser, and arguably Marx and Lenin before him, *"there is no socialist mode of production,"* insofar as "social formations in the transition period called Socialism are based not on a single, Socialist mode of production (stamped perhaps with the birth marks of the old, capitalist society), but on a *contradictory combination of two modes of production, the capitalist and communist.*"[95]

Nietzsche didn't personally *like* socialism *or* capitalism, either, though he was very willing to *use* socialism *and* capitalism to produce some form or other — some other form — of "slavery." If need be, Nietzsche *could* make his peace with liberal democracy or "even" socialism and fascism, if likely not with most of national socialism. He — his corps/e — could not and *cannot* make peace with real communism, if and when communism ever . . . exists. Fascoid-liberals never can.

For transformed intellectuals not to realize or see even the *possibility* — the actual-virtuality — of real communism is a main effect of what Gramsci — describing Croce's influence on Italian intellectuals in the 1920s and the fatal weakening of their resistance to, if not actual acceptance of, fascism — would likely call, in his particularly apt turn of phrase, Nietzschean philosophy's "gastric juices": that is, its way of digesting, absorbing, incorporating, transforming intellectuals of the Left to the Right, its way of conforming potentially oppositional forces by means of their own consent, *as if* by their own conscious or subconscious will. The critical problem nowadays is that of promoting alternatives to both capitalism *and* socialism. This entails, in part, the ability *aprioristically* to see alternatives to the increasingly total, global *pax americana/pax japonica* and capitalist New World Order at the very moment of its most intimate internal decay. This includes the systemic, institutionalized criminalization of race and poverty in the United States, for instance — all of which Nietzsche might have lamented, though for radically wrong reasons. His *in*-formative *trans*-formations exist not only outside people in technoculture but also deep inside people, which can be theorized as the most basic power of *trasformismo* — from Hegel, to Croce, to Nietzsche, and beyond.[96]

Trasformismo can never be a sign of Nietzsche's "failure," but only of the fact that, under the circumstances, his esoteric semiotics has had at least "weak" success. Finding and producing alternatives is not only a problem of direct action — though this is a huge problem — but also a problem of imag-ination, of the sociopolitical imaginary, of vision. The problem is to learn to *see* what Nietzsche and Nietzscheanism have made in/visible. But if capitalism is "a world-historical force whose ultimate development is a global mode of production," and if — for this reason among others — "socialism in one country" must always fail eventually, and if "the possibility of communism presupposes the development of capitalism as a global system whose class structure is truly international and homogeneous,"[97] then perhaps the time has now come to see and grasp Nietzsche's corps/e for the first time. Certainly both the *threat to* and *opportunity for* radical — communist — democracy of the most anti-Nietzschean sort has never been greater, since "With respect to democracy, the collapse of socialism's inhuman face is simply the obverse of the collapse of capitalism with a human face: either democracy means democratic control over the means of production and the process of accumulation, or it means nothing at all."[98] *Nietzsche* was aware of, or intuited, *trasformismo* as a powerful historical motor. It only stands to reason that he would have attempted to *use* it — along with all other historical contingencies — to his advantage. After all, this was a man who considered his body to be a seismograph. So sensitive it was not only to earthquakes but also to the most minute changes in weather that he mused to friends about putting his body on display at the International Exhibition in Paris, making a few needed bucks on the side. Certainly it also stands to reason that such a body would be sensitive, at the very least, to shifts in mere intellectual climate. Some people apparently *do* need Weathermen to tell them which way the wind blows.

Technoculture/Everyday Life

Readers who turn to Nietzsche's corpse qua corpus to grasp the problem of the articulation of aesthetics, politics, and prophecy must particularly resist the tendency to ignore their (our) own "national-popular" culture and its Nietzscheanism. High philosophy today morphs into mass or junk culture, indeed strives to exist *only* in this form. On the other hand, cultural studies as the current "discipline" purporting to deal with this situation will remain counterproductive to the extent that it remains definable as "junk culture minus philosophy" or, to be more precise, when the philosophy it thinks it has to legitimate itself remains Nietzschean, remains part of the corps/e.

The Situationist International used to insist that not only was God dead but also — along with Him, Her, or It — aesthetics and the arts, the political and politics as we have traditionally known them: both "high" and "low," both far above quotidian life and deeply, invisibly informing it. It was in this context that the term "corpse" came to situationist life. One of the leaflets passed out at the University of

Strasbourg in the spring of 1966 — the first of the great student uprisings of the period — was entitled "*De la misère étudiant* [on the poverty of student life]." Written by situationist Mustapha Khayati, one of its slogans read: "In any era when art is dead the student is the most avid consumer of its corpse." Two years later, the following clarification appeared on the walls around the Sorbonne, reappearing three years later in René Viénet's détourned kung-fu film *Can Dialectics Break Bricks?:* "People who talk about revolution and class struggle without referring explicitly to everyday life, without understanding what is subversive about love and positive about the refusal of constraints, have corpses in their mouths."[99] And as late as 1988 there came another update: "Since art is dead, it has . . . increasingly become easy to disguise police as artists."[100] Including, one might wish, *Nietzsche,* particularly in the multiple forms *his* corpse takes today. How — in this looking-glass situation where little is as it seems — might one begin to look for national-popular manifestations of Nietzsche's corps/e *hic et nunc:* that is, in the postmodern, postcontemporary condition, in the spectacular technoculture of everyday life?

After the "defeat" of communism Nietzsche/anism itself is undergoing *trasformismo:* from a mode of overt insurrection and struggle into a system of security and foresight in a technocultural situation in which "the doctrine of security is founded on . . . the saturation of time and space by speed, making *daily life* the last theater of operations, the ultimate scene of strategic foresight."[101] In that event the search for Nietzsche's corps/e must continue to take place not in terms of "Nietzschean" themes — either explicit or implicit — but rather of more or less occluded signs embedded in an everyday life that is ever more mediated and saturated by spectacular technoculture and by traces of the properly Nietzschean intent to exert proleptic, esoteric, subliminal effect, traces of his *actio in distans.* The terrain on which this search must be conducted is not familiar to scholars trained only to read, let alone to read only Nietzsche.

One of the determining features of the fascoid-liberal axis, according to Gramsci, is the failure of "traditional" intellectuals like Croce to link up with something like a national-popular attitude. They tend, as Marx and Engels liked to say, to ignore the need "to 'leave philosophy aside' . . . to leap out of it and devote oneself like an ordinary person to the study of actuality. . . . "[102] And what is it about North American —

or almost any national—intellectuals that they (we) are so schizoid about which region of the globe to live in and/or study? For white male—but not only white male—North Americans, Europe has traditionally been a main site of sadomasochistic attraction; for Europeans it has traditionally been the other way around, with other sites qualifying as well. Alternatively, many American intellectuals (an old story), having backed away more or less gradually from their Euro-centered academic training and "the canon," now suddenly veer "multiculturally" toward their "own"—or some "other"—previously repressed "popular culture," living now only to "decipher" its "natural language," "to make a formal method of the shiny pleasures they'd known in their Europe-shadowed childhoods—an Aristotelianism of bubble gum wrappers and detergent jingles."[103] Surely, the truth must lie not merely somewhere in between these false alternatives but in some alternative unforeseen by both, and by "multiculturalism," "interdisciplinarity," "cultural studies"—and all other shibboleths warding off serious thought.[104] It is likely, however, that many of these same intellectuals will eventually turn away once more from their own (junk) cultures (our culture), to seek themselves once again in distant times, on foreign soil, on other capes.[105] For its part, junk culture often has a more appropriately dialectical view of such "choices" than does high-culture and its critics.[106] But Gramsci's worry was that all such intellectual "turns" from one *terra deserta, terra incognita* to the other and back again are hardly ever undertaken—for bad reasons as well as good—in order to search for genuinely international—let alone communist—alternatives to capitalist business as usual. The not uncommon antinomy is debilitating: *either* ignore the national-popular completely and search too soon for cosmopolitan alternatives, which remain cultural only; *or* plunge into the national-popular and never extricate oneself from it. The one search—the cultural version of "Socialism in one country"—never leaves home to encounter an alternative other; whereas the other search—the cultural version of "permanent revolution" without any base of operations—is continually landing on other people's shores, only to find that they themselves have abandoned them—having set off for the New World, the Brave New World, the New World Order. "Happy is it to practice the Yoga of Renouncing-One's-Own-Land,"[107] perhaps. But the more peculiar problem, at least for genuine communism, is that almost anywhere one goes these days—home or abroad, high culture or low—some more or less "traditional," more or less "cyborg" version of Nietzsche's corps/e is ready and waiting.

Nietzsche/anism threatens to be globally hegemonic in the sense of becoming a system or formant of thought having lost its sense of "traumatic origin": that is, Nietzsche's corpse and corpus as traumatic origin of the corps. As explained by Zizek's analysis of the current resurgence of radical nationalism and anti-internationalism, "A system reaches its equilibrium, i.e., establishes itself as a synchronous totality, when—in Hegelese—it 'posits' its external presuppositions as its inherent moments and thus obliterates the traces of its traumatic origins."[108]

Increasingly global, but as yet unequally distributed, technoculture makes some very attractive promises. So does the global neocapitalism that produces it, otherwise neither would be half as seductive as they are. But so far, by and large, these are deeply ambivalent promises, as we currently slam-dance between technophilia and technophobia: as if technology were somehow only *outside* humans, so that they might accept or reject it, rather than already, at least partially, *in* them as posthumans.[109]

Not incidentally, the young Hegel, at the time in accord with the poet Hölderlin's ideas, developed his today must mistrusted, even despised "master narrative"—or, as he himself preferred to call it, "dialectical tragedy in the realm of the ethical"—from a remarkably similar concern about the relationship between technophobia and technophilia, such as they then were. As Hegel put it, the perennial responsibility of humanity is to grasp, appropriate, and "sublate" what for him was the logical contradiction between two basic and "necessarily connected phenomena": namely, as paraphrased by Lukács, "the indissoluble bond between *progress*" on the one hand, and on the other "*the debasement of mankind,*" whose "fragmentation" by the modern division of labor was informed by "the *purchase* of progress at the *cost* of that debasement."[110] And this is precisely the philosophical, economic, and political point where Marx and Engels joined the fray—not to produce some master narrative of their own, necessarily or primarily, but rather to supply theoretical tools and weapons to the base in their struggle against the debasing masters. If Nietzsche were really a cyborg today, were really operating as an avatar in the cyberspatial matrix, then he would of course take sides in this updated perennial struggle: not necessarily on the side of the *actually* existing masters — but who are they exactly? — for this he never did wholeheartedly, but certainly, from everything we know here and now about him, on the side of the *principle* of (male) masters against the (male and female) slaves.

"Hegelian" master narratives and "our" more or less appropriate mistrust of them aside, one promising technocultural possibility is being held out by what Trinh T. Minh-ha and Donna J. Haraway are calling "inappropriate/d others" or "coyote nature" and "cyborgs."[111] As Haraway has posed the problem in "The Actors Are Cyborg, Nature Is Coyote, and the Geography Is Elsewhere" (1991): "If feminists and allied cultural radicals are going to have any chance to set the terms for the politics of technoscience . . . we must transform the despised metaphors of both organic and technological vision to foreground specific positioning, multiple mediation, partial perspective, and therefore a possible allegory for antiracist feminist scientific and political knowledge."[112] Note, however, that an essential part of this formulation sounds exactly like what is commonly perceived as "Nietzschean": namely, an apparently radical commitment to "perspectivism" as an ostensibly progressive force. Yet, we may now imagine, precisely this is *not* Nietzsche's commitment, or is so only esoterically. This quibble may seem to be of small consequence, since Haraway herself does not appeal to Nietzsche to make this particular argument, which is decidedly progressive and democratic in intent, in ways that Nietzsche's is not — esoterically *or* exoterically. Nonetheless, this terminological convergence, however momentary, ought to send up a red flag of warning for any cyborg project that would be at once "scientific" and "political" in liberatory ways. Haraway continues to outline her ambitions and timely project, working toward the cyborg, by introducing the notion of "coyote nature." Defining her "possible allegory for antiracist feminist scientific and political knowledge," she writes: "Nature emerges from this exercise as 'coyote.' This potent trickster can show us that historically specific human relations with 'nature' must somehow — linguistically, scientifically, ethically, politically, technologically, and epistemologically — be imagined as genuinely social and actively relational. And yet, the partners in this lively social relation remain inhomogeneous. Curiously, as for people before us in Western discourses, efforts to come to terms with the nonrepresentability, historical contingency, artifactuality, and yet spontaneity, necessity, fragility, and stunning profusions of 'nature' can help us refigure the kinds of person we might be. We need a concept of agency that opens up possibilities for figuring relationality within social worlds where actors fit oddly, at best into previous *taxa* of the human, the natural, or the constructed" (p. 21). Again, there seems much to recommend this explicitly post-Aristotelian logic. But the question, also again, is whether it remains implicitly *Nietzschean* as well. Nietzsche seems to have always already occupied this terrain. For few figures in the high canon of European thought come more to mind as candidates for "coyote" status, what with his alleged love of masks, "spontaneous" linguistic games, and historical "contingencies." Yet this apparent love, too, is only exoteric, concealing more rigid designators, more sinister agendas. The properly cyborg promise of celebrating difference only after having obliterated all *enslaving* differences between men and women (wo/men), straights and queers, people of color and whites, religious freaks and atheists, manual and mental workers, and so on — this entire project may therefore hang in a certain Nietzschean balance. Certainly Haraway's "cyborg" and Trinh's "inappropriate/d other" will always be at Nietzschean risk, especially if, still citing Haraway, "To be inappropriate/d is not to fit in the *taxon,* to be dislocated from the available maps specifying kinds of actors, not to be originally fixed by difference" (p. 23) — if and when this terrain, too, is always already staked out by Nietzsche. Of the cyborg project, Haraway is reasonably careful to say — via a wild punning with her own name, but making very precise what she means by "we" — that, "from perspectives in the ripped-open belly of the monster called history . . . we cannot name and possess this thing we cannot not desire. This is the spiritual and political meaning of poststructuralism/postmodernism for me. 'We,' in these discursive worlds, have no routes to connection other than through the radical dis-membering and dis-placing of our names and our bodies. We have no choice but to move through a harrowed [!] and harrowing [!] artifactualism to elsewhere. Emerging from this process are excessive and dislocated figures that can never ground what used to be called 'a fully human community.' That community turned out to belong only to the masters" (p. 25). Masters, one must add, who live on nowhere more complexly than as Nietzsche's corps/e.

Cyberpunks may be quick to point out, in post-Spinozist fashion, that today the cyberspatial matrix *is* "the Other," *is* "metaphysics," *is*

"God"; but also that this apparently totalitarian system does not (yet) exclude the possibility of inworming it, virusing it, opening it up to democratic uses. But what must be made as clear as possible in this actual or virtual world is that the description of "She [or better: S/he], the Inappropriate/d Other" as a humanoid moving about "with always at least two/four gestures: that of affirming 'I am like you' while pointing insistently to the difference; and that of reminding 'I am different' while unsettling every definition of otherness arrived at"[113] — that this description, also commonly understood today as "Nietzschean," is *anything but* positive or progressive in Nietzsche's *own* protocyborg terms: Overman, Superman, or Hyperman by name.

The technologically foreseeable "end" of ancient differences — including, in the last instance, divisions of labor — need not necessarily be only "parodic," as Debord seemed to think in his updated thesis on the Society of the Spectacle. As he rightly warned, however, *to date* this project has relentlessly tended to be parodic in the increasingly integrated and global Society of the Spectacle, whose "highest ambition" "is still to turn secret agents into revolutionaries, and revolutionaries into secret agents."[114] Which defines, fairly exactly, one aspect of techno-Nietzsche/an *trasformismo*. Nonetheless, "cybernetic capitalism" is not (or not yet) as total as is imagined (and likely secretly desired) by many (more or less Nietzschean) versions of "leftist" economism and technological determinism (à la *Virilio*) — a *self-fulfilling* determinism with which Marx would have had no patience.[115]

Nietzsche would have *relished* the current "leftist" presentation of the basic technosocial options available to "us" as being only two in number: "Athens without Slaves . . . or Slaves without Athens?"[116] As has been pointed out, navigating between the technophilia of "silicon positivists" and the technophobia of "technological determinists," the formulation "'slaves without Athens' . . . is actually the inverse of . . . 'Athens without slaves.'"[117] For Nietzsche, Athens and slavery were simply indivisible, the one a code term for the other, so that either terminological option was fine with him. Precisely *this* "choice" he could program and handicap with comparative ease. To repeat, if Nietzsche was such a great prophet, and is so important globally today, then the very least he must have foreseen is cyberspace and cyborgs: Nietzschoids. How, then, would Nietzsche and Nietzscheanism have preempted the apparent challenge to "order of rank" that is promised to and by inappropriate/d others? And what, finally, does Nietzsche's corps/e look like in the postcontemporary everyday of junk culture, cyberspace, and science fiction?

"Science fiction" (SF) as medium and as concept exists at a crucial interface between "high" and "low" culture, between past and present everyday life and future technologies of transformation. Haraway notes the radical ambivalence of science fiction in terms applicable also to global Nietzsche/anism. "SF is inherently 'impure' — a major source of its lure to inappropriate/d others, for whom the 'economy of the same' and its injunction to purity, textual or otherwise, rouses well-founded historical suspicions. But the 'impurities' of SF are hardly utopian; they are deeply troubling as well as promising. SF is an imperialist genre, in which the 'star wars' heroes riding into battle on armored dinosaurs cohabit the universe with the fantastic figures of First World feminist and multicultural imaginations."[118]

Slogans such as "science fiction" thus refer here less to some literary or filmic genre somewhere on the peripheries and interstices of various literary "cultures" than to a theoretical problem of the articulation of science and fiction, history and historiography, philosophy and junk culture. As such, "science fiction" is a variant of Nietzsche's great exo/ esoteric slogan: "Eternal Recurrence of the Same [but only in order to maintain social difference]!" According to the Left-Nietzschoid Michel De Certeau, also theorizing the articulation between "science" and "fiction": "This combination may be what constitutes the essence of the historical: a return of the past in the present discourse. In broader terms, this mixture (science and fiction) obscures the neat dichotomy that established modern historiography as a relation between a 'present' and a 'past' distinct from each other, one being the producer of the discourse and the other being what is represented by it, one the 'subject,' the other the 'object' of a certain knowledge. This object, presumed to be exterior to the work of the laboratory, in fact determines its operations from within."[119] Similarly, a slogan like "cyberspace" means not merely a technology but also something like "The ability of the human mind to create a world created only by the human mind, which is the world inside the computer matrix,"[120] but with the "as-if" illusion of interactive control of primary reality as well. *Just like Nietzsche/anism.*

Greil Marcus has suggested, too optimistically perhaps, that one of the foundational left-modernist critiques of mass culture—Adorno's *high-cultural, philosophical, and above all Nietzschoid* negative dialectic— has ended up as the paraphernalia of actually existing *punks,* as what might be called their corps/e: "As Adorno's prepared corpses, more consciously prepared than he could have imagined, they exploded with proofs of vitality—that is, they said what they meant."[121] But if post-contemporary punks and cyberpunks *are* Adorno, this does not bode well, necessarily. For the vitality of both is seriously threatened by *Nietzschean* incorporations and transformations. On the other hand there are signs that even if the spectacularization of everyday life were to become global, even if the Real were to become merely virtual—and maybe it always already is—there would still be trouble—and hence potential crashes, breakdown, and *struggle*—in the cyberspace that Laurie Anderson has dubbed "The Puppet Motel":

> And all the puppets in this digital jail
> They're runnin' around in a frenzy
> In search of the Holy Grail.
> They're havin' virtual sex.
> They're eatin' virtual food.
> No wonder these puppets
> Are always in a lousy mood.
> So if you think we live in a modern world
> Where everything is clean and swell
> Take a walk on the B side of town
> Down by the Puppet Motel
> Take a whiff. Burning Plastic.[122]

Were Nietzsche to hear Virilio calling "*daily life* the last theater of operations" in global military strategy today, he would want a piece of the action. Political scientist and media analyst Arthur Kroker is not entirely off the mark when he suggests that "Writing one hundred years after Nietzsche, at the end of the twentieth and not the nineteenth century, Virilio *is* the truth of Nietzsche's prophecy. Indeed, it might even be suggested that *The Will to Power* and *Pure War* are the beginning-and-end-points of the twentieth century."[123] More specifically: "the exterminatory nihilism of Nietzsche's 'will to power' is replaced by

Virilio's 'dromacracy'; Nietzsche's 'ascetic priests who work to alter the direction of *ressentiment*' anticipate Virilio's 'warrior priests'; Nietzsche's 'maggot man' is substituted by Virilio's description of the parasited body as a 'metabolic vehicle'; Nietzsche's 'nowhere' of the 'noonday sun,' populated by those living in a postcatastrophe time after the 'wiping clean of the horizon,' grounds Virilio's image of the endlessly circulating body of the social mass drifting in perfect polar inertia between past and future; and, finally, Nietzsche's power as an empty 'perspectival simulacra' is the metaphysical basis, the 'grammatical error,' for Virilio's theorization of virtual power as a 'sight machine'" (pp. 28–29). But there are two significant and related *differences* between Virilio and Nietzsche. The first is a matter of historical and ethico-political analysis, in that Virilio argues that Nietzschean Will to Power in "First World" nations is actually a thing of the *past* in "dromospheric terms": that is, in terms of the problem of "pure war," which has replaced already old-fashioned "total war" in that it obliterates distinctions between offense and defense. Virilio elaborates: "The will-to-power of industrial nations who, at the turn of the century, practiced the techniques of total war, has now been replaced by the theoretical operation of a totally involuntary war, on the part of post-industrial nations investing increasingly in informatics, automation, and cybernetics. In these societies, the use of human labor-force and the direct responsibility of people has been displaced by the powers of 'anticipated' and 'deferred' substitution, the power of the system of auto-directed armaments, self-programmed detection networks, and automotic respondents who lead humanity to the confinement of a hopeless waiting."[124] Visible between the lines of Virilio's patented nihilistic eschatology—which is either therapeutic *or* a lethal self-fulfilling prophecy, depending on your point of view—is that Virilio sometimes appears horrified by what he calls "the fatal construction of the *automation of the declaration of war*"[125] and the concomitant geopolitical disappearance of human responsibility. Nietzsche, by contrast, exoterically deconstructed the notions of responsibility and accountability, apparently dissolving them with Eternal Recurrence of the Same and Will to Power; though he maintained a belief in his *own* responsibility and accountability esoterically. The second difference, and it is equally decisive, is that Virilio still desperately holds on to a modicum of modernist *critique* of postmodern military tactics, strategies, and technologies, whereas Nietzsche basically would have been impatient with mere critique, moving quickly to *appropriate* them for his own *use,* at least conceptually and rhetorically, as metaphors and techniques of persuasion to preserve power for elites over corpses—"now that the living outnumber the dead."[126]

Because of such differences it is important to illuminate, monitor, and combat any trace of Nietzscheanism that informs the most radical of the cyberpunk hackers—those who might actually crack The Code, virus The System, break The Ice around The Base, and generally Set Information Free. The hacker is typically suspended between two postures: on the one hand the "gradual and willing accommodation of the machine, the system, the parent organism"; on the other "the root of street cool, . . . the knowing posture that implied connection, invisible lines up to hidden levels of influence."[127] Nietzsche's corps/e thrives in such tense environments.

Consider now the following claim by a leading cyberpunk wirehead hacker, Michael Synergy. Among other things, he has hinted that he is responsible for the second greatest crash in Wall Street history. In an interview Synergy has said:

> This is all about personal empowerment. . . . Because of the way that computers are networked, I'm as powerful as a government agency. I'd say I have about as much power as a group in the Defense Department here. . . . In a couple of years I'll be much more powerful than they are because they're still stuck in local mode. One of the things about computer viruses is that I can go beyond boundaries. Things about networks I can go beyond. One of the things I learned a long time ago is the old rule of thumb: distance means nothing to a computer hacker, 'phone freak, whatever. For anyone using a computer, 'phone line, fax (who knows?): distance doesn't mean anything anymore. I can be anywhere I want. And one of the other things I found out about computer viruses is that it's a beautiful lever: "Give me a lever and I shall move the earth." A computer virus is a way of building a little AI [Artificial Intelligence] of me that can go out and copy itself millions of times, and do whatever it has to. One of the things I was asked recently was: "Sure, you can take down the banking system. But would you really?" I've told people before and I'll tell people again: If I think it's necessary, I will. One of the reasons I said that is that someone asked me: "What happens if

we get a fascist government here in the States — would you be willing to take it down?" The more they get computerized, the more powerful I get, the more willing I will be to do that.[128]

Not only in the cyberspace matrix but in some contemporary evolutionary theory, too, genetic material is said to be transported in viruses from one species to another. An enthusiastic reader of the scientific and quasi-scientific literature of his time, Nietzsche would immediately attempt to integrate such notions into his own proleptic illocutionary practice.[129] Our current genetic and virus theories — conducted for the time being primarily on plants, not humans and other animals — suggest that viral genes can "sabotage themselves."[130] When certain viral genes are incorporated into certain objects that are commonly destroyed by these same genes — the procedure is a standard technique of discerning gene function — it turns out that this incorporation can make the object in question resistant to the virus. It may be that the presence of the gene already in the DNA of the object interferes with the capacity of the virus to pullulate, hence its inability to inworm the object and destroy it. Presumably Nietzsche — given not only his deep interest in the hard sciences but also the extent of his current influence on nearly every field except the hard sciences — would have grasped the theory behind *any* scientific hypothesis or advance. Today, "language" is not, as Burroughs is fond of saying, "a virus from outer space," but a virus from Fred Nietzsche.

In any case, it is necessary to demand of the psychoplasmic, counteresoterrorist Synergy's claim: Is it only Nietzschean megalomania and Left-Nietzscheanism as usual, business as usual? For "distance" also takes on new meaning, to say the least, when Eternal Recurrence of the Same is understood as a principle of rhetorico-political manipulation, with the aim of returning the Same basic set of hierarchical doctrines but in the guise of ever renewed Otherness. Is Synergy just another corps/e, albeit in techno-Nietzschoid drag? Or is he talking about something *radically* democratic and communal — in principled opposition to true Nietzsche/anism and beyond it? At least he implies that in the world of cyberspace and the cyberpunk hacker meaning and intentionality and responsibility still exist; though, if some programmers have their way, someday such things will exist only in brains in vats. The prognosis on the ability of cyberpunk hackers *actually* to crack the most sophisticated codes of the Information Age is undecided, to say the least, as Space Ship Earth gravitates toward a society not of "architectural" discipline à la the Nietzschean Foucault but of electronic control à la the Nietzschean Deleuze.

Deleuze argues in his "Postscript on Control Societies" (1990) that the modern *disciplinary societies* of the eighteenth and nineteenth centuries, as analyzed by Foucault, and which replaced the premodern *societies of sovereignty,* are themselves being supplanted today by postmodern *societies of control.* So it is that societies based — successively — on taxation and then on the organization of production by spaces of enclosure — womb to family to school to factory to barracks to prison to hospital to tomb — are fast becoming, under conditions of neocapitalism, societies controlled and modulated technoculturally.[131] The situation is ambivꞵent, cuts two ways. In the one direction certain signs indicate that the potential of individuals and groups of cyberpunks to encrypt their own codes may be as great as that of more or less Nietzsche/anized governments, businesses, police forces, and militaries.[132] In the other, as Andrew Ross has argued in a sobering assessment of the liberatory claims of hackers, this promise "is related, first of all, to the author's local *intention or motivation,* whether psychic or fully social, whether wrought out of a mood of vengeance, a show of bravado or technical expertise, a commitment to a political act, or in anticipation of the profits that often accrue from the victims' need to buy an antidote from the author."[133] In other words: *De te fabula narratur.*

At the end of *Nietzsche's corps/e, two* analytic conditions must be met. If, *first,* it is possible to locate the Nietzschean corps/e — or at least some of its members — here and now in technocultural everyday life, and, *second,* if it is possible to detect Nietzsche's in/direct influence on this life — or it on him — then it is also possible, finally, to attain the vantage point — an Archimedean point — from which to see, grasp, and begin to settle accounts with Nietzsche's original corpse, corpus, and corps in their full historical intent, extent, and power. And all this in a situation in which we must continually ask the Spinozist question: "Is global Difference the same today as global Identity?"[134] Indeed, these two conditions, constitutive of the postcontemporary and contemporary alike, *must* be met, if we are no longer to "suffer from the dead as well as the living," and if this "dead man" is to cease "seizing the living."[135] Remarkably, these conditions *can* be met.

In fact they *are* met, *mirabile dictu,* in the published and unpublished work of Philip K. Dick. Dick was America's most prolific, and arguably greatest, "science fiction" writer: the inspiration for the now classic New Bad Future films *Blade Runner* and *Total Recall* and who knows what else besides.[136] Of the several properly Nietzschean themes, structures, and loops in Dick, among the most serious involve the construction of systems of technophobic-technophiliac "paranoia" that do not quite occlude or obviate the real world of political economy, including subliminal and liminal levels of power and social "order of rank."[137] On what the Nietzschean "order of rank" might look like in the new bad future — not to say in some parts of the world right now — see *Clans of the Alphane Moon* (1964), in which different social functions are divided up by psychopathological type — *exoterically* without any grounding term, and so deconstructable, but with the *esoteric* grounding term being concealed thematically *and* formally.[138] And so it is in Nietzsche's corps/e, too, that "The text imposes its own understanding and shapes the reader's evasions."[139]

But now think back over the entire, long, *virtually* interminable extent of Nietzsche's corps/e, as *Nietzsche's Corps/e* begins to conclude with a pastiche of two passages from Dick's posthumously published notebooks or "auto-exegesis" entitled *In Pursuit of Valis.* First, however, it is important to note that Dick (1926–1982) was an avid, astute, untutored reader of both Heidegger and Nietzsche, though the question of direct influence is not the main point. In a letter to Claudia Bush (July 16, 1974), Dick wrote, "I had planned to call my next book, THUS SPOKE ZOROASTER, but I guess I had better not." Also not unreasonably, he was convinced that the categories of *Dasein* in *Being and Time* were "based" on Gnosticism and German mysticism, such as that of Jakob Boehme. One of Dick's last main protagonists, Bishop Tim Archer, "gets into Heidegger & *Dasein.*"[140] Leaving Nietzsche aside for the moment, the hypertextual link, so to speak, between Dick and Heidegger was "predicted" — or at least made plausible implicitly — by Marshall McLuhan already in *The Gutenberg Galaxy: The Making of Typographic Man* (1962), in that remarkably prescient section entitled "Heidegger Surf-Boards Along on the Electronic Wave as Triumphantly as Descartes Rode the Mechanical Wave." McLuhan, circling close to one of his central early theses, argued: "The alphabet and kindred gimmicks have long served man as a *subliminal* source of philosophical and religious assumptions. Certainly Martin Heidegger would seem to be on better ground [than the metaphysical tradition] in using the totality of language itself as philosophical datum. For there, at least in non-literate periods, will be the ratio among all the senses. . . . "[141] But McLuhan—unlike most McLuhanites *or* cyberspatial Heideggerians and Nietzscheans—still possessed the good sense to add a caveat: "An enthusiasm for Heidegger's excellent linguistics could easily stem from naïve immersion in the metaphysical organicism of our electronic milieu. . . . There is nothing good or bad about print *but the unconsciousness of the effect of any force is a disaster,* especially a force that we have made ourselves" (p. 66; emphasis added). This untutored reading of Heidegger is not entirely off the mark. Near the end of an interview filmed for television, conducted months before his death in 1976, Heidegger reaches across his desk and opens up a notebook from which he reads the following remark that he attributes to Heinrich von Kleist: " 'I stand back before one who is not yet here [da ist], and bow before his spirit a century in advance.' "[142] Presumably, reading the Nietzschean Heidegger, *we* are to follow suit, incorporating the proleptic *Führerprinzip,* transforming ourselves accordingly. Finally, in the same television interview, Heidegger uses a surprising analogy to illustrate the claim that authentic thinking is a matter of only a few people "directly," of the many only "indirectly."[143] Only a tiny handful of people in the entire world, he says, know how television actually works— these being the *media-tors*—even as everyone else merely uses television and is used by it—literally: the *media-ted.* Presumably, this thesis would be true a fortiori of all post-Nietzschean thinking. For his part, Dick—who sometimes had good reason to believe he was an android—resisted better than almost anyone becoming fully Heidegerized. *Nietzschized* is always a slightly different matter. And so it was in the agonized case of Dick.

The first passage to be cited from Dick's auto-exegesis—and the terrible "ironies" provided by mental illness, drug addiction, and their pain aside—provides one of the most succinct and brilliant descriptions extant of the *properly* Nietzschean articulation of aesthetics, politics, prophecy: that is, the desire to write proleptically so as to have the maximum possible and subcutaneous effect in the future, after the death of one's material body, under the sign of the slogan, as Nietzsche himself put it in 1882, "*sub specie trecentorum annorum* [under the aspect of three hundred years]."[144] "To be ignited in 300 years—that is my desire for fame."[145] Elsewhere, Nietzsche spoke in Social Darwinian terms of millennia and had his own version of a millennial Reich: "The age of experiments [Experimente]! The claims of Darwin are to be tested—through experimentations [Versuche]! As is the evolution of higher organisms out of the lowest. Experimentations [Versuche] must be conducted for millennia! Raise apes into men!"[146] Whatever one may think of *Dick's* ideological position in these matters, his insights into the nature of *Nietzsche/anism* and *Nietzsche's corps/e* rival the greatest insights anyone has ever had. When reading Dick's following remarks put on Peter Tosh singing: "400 years, 400 years, 400 years, O, O / I And it's the same, the same philosophy, / I said it's 400 years, 400 years, 400 years, / Look how long, O, O— / The people, my people, they still can't see. . . . / Come on, come on, let's make a move. . . ."[147]

Dick wrote in 1975 for his eyes only:

My very recent book dream, the masterpiece novel gummed into the ency-clopedia—it refers to such as the above novel [*Flow My Tears, the Policeman Said*] *cum* covert message, as well as [my novel] UBIK, etc. I'm beginning to think this most recent dream did not carry the message: *Write* such a book. But rather: You *did* write such books (with the gospel reassembled from trashy bits, as [Stanislaw] Lem put it).[148] (So as to get past the Soviet Marxist materialist censors.) "There are other sheep whom I must bring in," as Christ said. This dream told me not what to do but explained to me what I have been doing. I, so fashionable to Marxists both in the West & East—I unknown even to myself, carrying the gospel to them in a form acceptable to them. I wonder, now that (3-74) [Dick's quasi-schizophrenic, quasi-mystical revelation in March 1974] it was explained to me, if I could do it, now being self-conscious and deliberate and doing it myself per se; maybe my work is done, successfully. I was finally told what I had done: the sheep in wolf's clothing, so to speak. [. . .] Maybe now I can rest. It's interesting— you can flatout outfront tell a Marxist that my work is theological in nature [. . .] and it doesn't register, as if I never said it. "He doesn't comprehend his own work," as one of them said. Not only can't they see it unaided, they

can't see it aided. Yet I am positive that on some level (right hem[isphere])
they are absorbing it; ah yes: subliminally!! I think this is why so many of my
dreams—plus my intuitions themselves about my 3-74 experience—contained elements pertaining to the USSR. Paranoiacally, I had it backward;
they weren't influencing my thoughts, but I theirs (via my stories, novels,
speeches, letters, oral discourse!!). Lord—I think when they see the cross I
wear, or read theological elements—find them in my writing, they think I
am "one of them," but adding these as a sort of disguise to fit into capitalist
Christian Western society; my golly, they have it backward, but it's layer
under layer; the *bottom* which (spreading the gospel to the Soviets) was
unknown even to me. Until it was revealed to me in 3-74. Probably the most
severe assault delivered in my work is against materialism as such, in my
probing into the illusory nature of apparent reality . . . but surely this is a
prime assault against the Enemy, against Marxism as one form of it.[149]

Thus spake, in our own Night of the Living Dead, the eternally re-
turning, eternally returning as "different," corpse of Friedrich Wilhelm
Nietzsche—in 1975, dictating into the notebooks of Philip Kendred
Dick.

We might indeed conclude that the esoteric project at issue for Dick
was itself intended as some sort of Christian or Gnostic Gospel. At least
one passage in the New Testament—and probably every significant
religious book—complicates this thesis: namely, Mark 4:11–12. As
depicted by Frank Kermode in *The Genesis of Secrecy* (1979), when asked
by his disciples what the Parable of the Sower meant, Jesus replied,
"that they, his elect, know the mystery of the kingdom and do not need
to be addressed in parables, but those outside are addressed only thus,
'*so that* seeing they may see and not perceive, and hearing they may hear
but not understand, *lest* at any time they should turn, and their sins
be forgiven them.'"[150] This biblical passage and principle—both described by Albert Schweitzer as "repellent"—are fully in accord with
Dick's and Nietzsche's esoteric semiotic or Channel 4. Alternatively
put: *The Bible, too, is Nietzsche/an.*

Leaving biblical esotericism aside, however, consider the following
note, produced around 1978. Dick wrote:

Lem & the party experts saw correctly that in my writing I was handing over
weapons (secrets) of power to the disenfranchised of the capitalist west;

their appraisal of me is correct. Over & over in my books (1) power is studied; (2) who has it; & (3) how those denied it manage to get it. Although not appearing left wing my training is really Fascistic — not "Fascistic" as Marxist rhetoric defines it but as Mussolini defined it: in terms of the deed & the will, with reality de-ontologized, reduced to mere stuff on which the will acts in terms of deed. Since few living people correctly understand (genuine) Fascism, my ideology has never been pejoratively stigmatized by the left, but those to whom I appeal are in essence the core-bulk of latent masses, the fascist mob. I speak of & for the irrational & the anti-rational, a kind of dynamic nihilism in which values are generated as mere tactics. Thus my real idol is Hitler, who starting out totally disenfranchised rose to total power while scorning *wealth* (aristocracy) plutocracy to the end. My real enemy is plutocracy; I've done my (Fascistic homework. [. . .] My fascistic premise is: "There is not truth. We *make* truth; what we (first) believe *becomes* objectively true. Objective truth depends on what we believe, not the other way around." This is the essence of the Fascist epistemology, the perception of truth as ideology imposed on reality — mind over matter.[151]

As earlier reference to Mussolini's own words has made sufficiently clear, Dick was quite precise *formally* — "irony" and/or "insanity" aside — in describing his own "epistemology" as "fascistic." "Nietzschean," in this case, would mean actually and virtually the same thing. The precise political *content* of such messages ("Hitler," "plutocracy," etc.) is symptomatically far less important than their exoteric *medium* of incorporation, and their proleptic esoteric intent: namely, to destroy, disarm, recruit, or otherwise *transform* any (virtual) Left for the sake of an (actual) Right.

Such *exactly* — to terminate abruptly — is the current everyday state of Nietzsche's spectacular, technocultural corps/e: his aesthetic corpus; the core of his political thought; and their joint prophetic production of the Nietzschean corps.

The tradition of thought extending from Spinoza to Althusser and beyond holds that "stating propositions without premises" means "falling short of philosophy."[152] In that case, Nietzsche was not merely a great philosopher but perhaps the most daring philosopher of the technofuture — while keeping to himself his most secret premises and conclusions. In 1880 he published this aphorism:

Premises of the Machine Age. — The press, the machine, the railway, the telegraph are premises whose thousand-year conclusion no one yet has dared draw.[153]

And so it is also with Nietzsche's writing, proleptically designed accordingly.

It is often more difficult to change how people think than how they otherwise live, and today people tend to think as more or less manipulated Nietzsche/ans. But if Nietzsche/anism is then a cognitive and lived form of universalism — alongside racism, nationalism, and sexism — this is not necessarily reason to despair. What is to be done? Communists can give an answer that is "at least negative."[154] I do not think that we can effectively face Nietzsche's corps/e with the abstract motto of universality. The corps/e has always already occupied this place. So the struggle is *inside this place,* to transform universalism, not to abandon it — I never said that — for this would amount to surrendering without combat.

Epilogue

Too Much Nietzsche

TOO MUCH NIETZSCHE?

When your students start showing signs of Sturm und Drang, it's a good idea to have cable TV in your residence halls. Because it's more than just entertainment. It's a real escape from school pressure.

It's never been easier to provide such a wide selection of popular entertainment as Showtime, The Movie Channel and MTV. As a leader in cable TV on campus, Viacom Networks College Group will help you create the ideal programming line-up. We'll also provide free consultation to help you choose the most cost-effective way to deliver it.

While, unlike Nietzsche, cable TV may not be part of a classical curriculum, it certainly offers an entertaining view of our popular zeitgeist.

Become cable literate. Join the growing number of schools that recognize the value of cable TV on campus.

CALL (212) 708–1351[1]

Here TV stands, presumably, for Terminal Velocity as well as TeleVision: where the distinction between TV and "the classical" Nietzsche is always already obviated; where Nietzsche *is* cable TV, including "public access" HDTV, and *is* the chronicle of higher — and lower — education. And, if there's too much of anything, just flush it . . . out of sight being out of mind.

The Toilet Was Full of Nietzsche

Inside the restroom, Jonny splashed rusty water onto his face. The room stank of human waste, and the paper-towel dispenser was empty. On the floor he found half a copy of *Twilight of the Gods*. The toilet was full of

Nietzsche. Jonny dried his hands with the few remaining pages. The water made him feel a little better. However, the comedown from the speed had left him jumpy and nervous.[2]

Maybe the still-speeding Jonny had mistaken Nietzsche for Wagner. An easy enough mistake to make in the space where gods and idols are the same, same as you. "Some Shit Never Changes" — cyberpunk slogan. Then again, some does. "Shit Happens" — not unlike Heidegger's Being. But when you've flushed it, where does Nietzsche go. . . ?

Nietzsche in Dormancy

A Nietzsche lies dormant in every writer, and this is doubtless why a writer lay dormant in Nietzsche.[3]

Thus wrote Louis Althusser during the first of his confinements in prison. So how will the repressed-suppressed, the dormant return in the postcontemporary future. . . ?

Caput Mortuum, *or,* The Industrialists of the Corps/e

What Marx and Engels said of Hegel's Absolute Spirit and Its fate must today be said of the dead heads and industrialists of Nietzsche/anism.

Certainly it is an interesting event we are dealing with: the putrescence of the absolute spirit. When the last spark of its life had failed, the various components of the *caput mortuum* began to decompose, entered into new combinations and formed new substances. The industrialists of philosophy, who till then had lived on the exploitation of the absolute spirit, now seized upon the new combinations. Each with all possible zeal set about retailing his apportioned share. This was bound to give rise to competition. . . . [4]

Mao III

She sees his right hand is shaky. She repositions the camera and resumes shooting.

He puts down the glass and looks into the camera.

He says, "Mao believed in the process of thought reform. It is possible to make history by changing the basic nature of a people. When did he realize this? Was it at the height of his power? Or when he was a guerrilla leader, at the beginning, with a small army of vagrants and outcasts, concealed in the mountains? You must tell me if you think I'm totally mad."

She leans across the table and takes his picture.

He says, "Mao regarded armed struggle as the final and greatest action of human consciousness. It is the final drama and the final test. And if many thousands die in the struggle? Mao said death can be light as a feather or heavy as a mountain. You die for the people and the nation, your death is massive and intense. Die for the oppressors, die working for the exploiters and manipulators, die selfish and vain and you float away like a feather of the smallest bird."

She moves toward the end of the roll.

He looks at the camera and says, "Be completely honest. I want to hear you say it, so I'll finally know. Living in this filth and stink. Talking to these children every day, all the time, over and over. But I believe every word, you know. This room is the first minute of the new nation. Now tell me what you think."

The interpreter drinks and wipes his mouth with a napkin.

"He is saying very simple. There is a longing for Mao that will sweep the world."

Eloquent macho bullshit. But she says nothing because what can she say. She runs through the roll, leaving a single exposure.[5]

But is not — in all such contemporary texts, not excluding *Nietzsche's Corps/e* — "Mao" or "Marx," "Engels," "Trotsky," "Luxemburg," and, yes, even "Lenin," "Gramsci," "Althusser" — really, always already, to-day, just another name, signature, or name-effect for the incorporated signifier "Nietzsche"? *Not yet* . . .

On the Dead Burying Their Dead

The real Nietzsche — lover of the "aristocratic" that he was — once, in his *Gay Science,* bestowed upon himself a title: Prinz Vogelfrei (Prince Free-as-a-Bird). The term refers not only to any Unbearable Lightness of Being, any really noble or free thinking. For it is also a legal slogan designating a criminal, a jail bird. So far beyond the law and commonweal, so heinous s/he is that it is permissible to shoot her/him on sight. If you can ever get the target in your sights and the gun is loaded. And the possibility or likelihood that you *can't* may remind even us postmoderns of Hegel's great caveats about the difference between the public and philosophers; about the way high philosophy enters into junk culture, especially as both are conflated in "Avant-Pop"; about the difficulties of burying the dead always; and about the potentially belated effects — for better or worse — of all human activities. Some of us will be more encouraged than others by Hegel in the case of a book called *Nietzsche's Corps/e* and, more important, Nietzsche's corps/e . . .

> . . . the public must often be distinguished from those who pose as its representatives and spokesmen. In many respects the attitude of the public is quite different from, even contrary to, that of its spokesmen. Whereas the public is inclined good-naturedly to blame itself when a philosophical work does not appeal to it, these others, certain of their own competence, put all the blame on the author. The effect of such a work on the public is more noiseless than the action of these dead men when they bury their dead. The general level of insight now is altogether more educated, its curiosity more awake, and its judgment more swiftly reached, so that the feet of those who will carry you out are already at the door. But from this we must often distinguish the more gradual effect which corrects, too, contemptuous censure, and gives some writers an audience only after a time, while others after a time have no audience left.[6]

Nietzsche's Last Words

Straightforward case of self-defense. As dead Nietzsche spirals down to heavy earth — if he does — "like a feather of the smallest bird" — perhaps — we postcontemporaries can still recall that "cause" (*aíton, aítia*) for the premodern Greeks meant also "culpability," "responsibility," "accountability." The ball is in y/our court. Only then let Nietzsche — his *corps/e* — have a last word, a last slogan, *and* a last communist — Marxist - Leninist - Trotskyist - Maoist - Gramscian - Althusserian — exposure:

Wie leicht nimmt man die Last einer Entschuldig[ung] auf sich, so lange man nichts zu verantworten hat.

ABER ICH BIN VERANTWORTLICH.

How lightly one takes the burden of an ex[cuse] upon oneself, so long as one has to be responsible for nothing.

BUT I AM ACCOUNTABLE.[7]

The Last Word

"On s'engage et puis . . . on voit." Rendered freely this means: "First engage in a serious battle and then see what happens."[8]

Notes

1   Nietzsche, The Only Position as Adversary

1. Georges Bataille, *The Accursed Share: An Essay on General Economy*, vols. 2: *The History of Eroticism* [1950–1951] and 3: *Sovereignty* [1950–1954], trans. Robert Hurley (New York: Zone Books, 1991), 373 (*Sovereignty*), translation modified. *La part maudite, Œuvres complètes,* ed. Denis Hollier et al. (Paris: Gallimard, 1970–1988), 8:405. "La position de Nietzsche est la seule en dehors du communisme." Actually, Bataille supplies a footnote that retreats a step from this stark assertion.

2. Richard Rorty, "Introduction: Pragmatism and Post-Nietzschean Philosophy," in *Philosophical Papers*, vol. 2: *Essays on Heidegger and Others* (Cambridge: Cambridge University Press, 1991), pp. 1–6.

3. Fredric Jameson, *The Geopolitical Aesthetic: Cinema and Space in the World System* (Bloomington and Indianapolis: Indiana University Press and London: BFI, 1992), pp. 4–5.

4. Ibid., p. 31.

5. Ibid., p. 82.

6. Slavoj Žižek, *Tarrying with the Negative: Kant, Hegel, and the Critique of Ideology* (Durham: Duke University Press, 1993), p. 218.

7. See Antonio Negri, *The Savage Anomaly: The Power of Spinoza's Metaphysics and Politics* [1981], trans. Michael Hardt (Minneapolis and Oxford: University of Minnesota Press, 1991). For an important communist counterbalance to Negri's reading of Spinoza, see Étienne Balibar, "Spinoza, the Anti-Orwell: The Fear of the Masses" [1985], in *Masses, Classes, Ideas: Studies on Politics and Philosophy Before and After Marx,* trans. James Swenson (New York and London: Routledge, 1994), pp. 3–37. Although they share a communist approach, Balibar is more cautious than Negri in assigning immediately liberatory value to Spinoza's notion of *multitudo,* preferring to stress instead the "experimental" nature and "aporetic" structure of Spinoza's analysis of "the fear of the masses" in the double sense of the genetic metaphor: namely, the masses' fear of power, and power's fear of them, about which Spinoza himself remained radically and productively ambivalent. Part of the difference between Negri and Balibar can be explained by the supposition that Spinoza

employed an exo/esoteric mode of writing, and by the constitutive reluctance of communist analysis to engage this problematic.

8. See, for example, Gilles Deleuze and Félix Guattari, *Capitalism and Schizophrenia*, vol. 2: *A Thousand Plateaus* [1980], trans. Brian Massumi (Minneapolis: University of Minnesota Press, 1987), pp. 123–125, 256–261, and 507, and *What Is Philosophy?* [1991], trans. Hugh Tomlinson and Graham Burchell (New York: Columbia University Press, 1994), p. 49; and Deleuze's two books on Spinoza. For a more conventional view of Spinoza and Nietzsche, see Yirmiyahu Yovel, *Spinoza and Other Heretics*, vol. 1: *The Marrano of Reason*, and vol. 2: *The Adventures of Immanence* (Princeton: Princeton University Press, 1989), esp. 2:104–135. The jury on the depth of Nietzsche's relationship to Spinoza is still out; for contrasting points of view see two monographs: Robert Snel, *Het hermetisch universum: Nietzsches verhouding tot Spinoza en de moderne ontologie* [1987] (Delft: Uitgeverij Eburon, 1989); and R. Henrad, *Nietzsche en Spinoza: Vreeme verwanten* [1987] (Delft: Uitgeverij Eburon, 1989). The most extensive scholarly account remains William S. Wurzer, "Nietzsche und Spinoza" (Diss., University of Freiburg, 1974; Meisenheim am Glan: Heim Verlag, 1975).

9. Michael Hardt and Antonio Negri, *Labor of Dionysus: A Critique of the State-Form* (Minneapolis: University of Minnesota Press, 1994), p. 17.

10. Louis Althusser, "Philosophie et marxisme: Entretiens avec Fernanda Navarro (1984–1987)," in *Sur la philosophie*, ed. Olivier Corpet (Paris: Gallimard, 1994), pp. 13–79; here p. 59; ellipsis in original. After around 1980, roughly speaking, Althusser seems to have changed his mind about Nietzsche (and Heidegger), who is mentioned in his earliest philosophical and political writings only in a perfunctory, commonplace way, and only in his last writings as a legitimate, materialist contributor to what he begins calling "aleatory materialism." Contrast his obligatory asides about Nietzsche in "L'internationale des bons sentiments" (1946), "Du contenu dans la pensée de G. W. F. Hegel" (1947), and even as late as "Marx dans ses limites" (1978) with his more complex and positive remarks in "Le courant souterrain du matérialisme de la rencontre" (1982) and especially "Portait de philosophie matérialiste" (1986), all in his *Écrits philosophiques et politiques*, vol. 1, ed. François Matheron (Paris: Stock/IMEC, 1994; *Édition posthume d'œuvres de Louis Althusser*, vol. 4/1), pp. 35–57 (here p. 35), 59–238 (here pp. 76, 199, 239, and 241), 357–524 (here p. 467), 539–579 (here pp. 561 and 569), and 581–582 (here p. 582), respectively. (On Althusser's shift to a more positive valorization of Heidegger in much the same regard, see "Le courant souterrain," pp. 539–543, 547, 550–551, and 562–564.)

11. The Left certainly has no monopoly over the notion that the "end" of communism is coterminous with the demise of bourgeois "democracy"—following the cynical logic that the latter *without opposition ceases to have any reason to exist*. Indeed, this thesis is far more prevalent and influential on the Right, being shared by "Straussians" as different as Allan Bloom and Francis Fukuyama. See Peter Levine,

Nietzsche and the Modern Crisis of the Humanities (Albany: State University of New York Press, 1995), pp. 260–261 n. 5. Compare also the claim once made by Benito Mussolini: "Here the problem arises: but how do you manage to do without an opposition? . . . Opposition is not necessary to the functioning of a healthy political régime. Opposition is stupid, superfluous in a totalitarian régime like the Fascist régime. Opposition is useful in easy times, academic times, as was the case before the war, when there were discussions in the Assembly about if, how and when socialism would be achieved, and indeed a whole debate about this — though this was clearly not serious, despite the men who took part in it. But *we* have the opposition within ourselves, dear sirs, we are not old nags who need a touch of the spur. We keep a strict check on ourselves . . ." (Benito Mussolini, speech of May 26, 1927; as cited in *Selections from the Prison Notebooks of Antonio Gramsci,* ed. and trans. Quintin Hoare and Geoffrey Nowell Smith [New York: International Publishers, 1971], p. 254 n. 56).

12. The Mekons, "Funeral," *The Curse of the Mekons,* © 1991 Blast First/Mute Records, Ltd., BFFP 80 C. "Your dead are buried ours are reborn / you clean up the ashes we light the fire / they're queuing up to dance on socialism's grave / this funeral is for the wrong corpse / This is my testimony a dinosaur's confession / how can something really be dead when it hasn't even happened / democracy is an alibi the peaceful country an ordered cemetery / what you call a sane man is now an impotent man / this funeral is for the wrong corpse / This is my testimony a dinosaur's confession / how can something really be dead when it hasn't even happened / smart bombs replace the dumb bombs we can aim right into someone's kitchen / hard rice sprays from the cooking pot into the eye's delicate jelly / when the natural order gets unruly the cost of living starts going up / Coo what a scorcher! are you ashamed of your bum? / this funeral is for the wrong corpse." The Mekons, originally out of Leeds, trace their genealogy in uneven development to punk rock's heyday in 1976–1977 around the Sex Pistols. Depending on how one hears it, "Funeral" either confirms or puts the lie to the perception that "The present-day Mekons are like any casualties of a defeated revolution — nervous, on good terms with oblivion, filled with rage and guilt" (Greil Marcus, "The Return of King Arthur" [1986], in *Rantors & Crowd Pleasers: Punk in Pop Music 1977–92* [New York: Doubleday, 1993], pp. 331–337; here p. 331). And Marcus, too, *likes* the Mekons.

13. Contemporaneous and independent philosophical support for The Mekons' questioning "the death of socialism" is provided by a former student of Althusser, communist philosopher Alain Badiou. See his *D'un désastre obscur (Droit, État, Politique)* (Paris: Éditions de l'aube/Monde en cours, 1991). Jacques Derrida, too, has resisted rejoicing at the funeral. See his *Spectres de Marx: L'état de la dette, le travail du deuil et la nouvelle internationale* (Paris: Éditions Galilée, 1993). This study in "hauntology" is dedicated to the assassinated South African communist Chris Hani. The tripartite subtitle of Derrida's hauntology refers to the desolate state (and

State) of the "postsocialist" world, to the resulting work of mourning (in the psychoanalytic sense), and to the *nouvelle Internationale* that is in the process of formation in response to both. Resisting the common perception that he himself was ever non- or anti-Marxist, Derrida now asks: "Who can say either 'I am Marxist' or 'I am not Marxist'?" — adding, however, that his thought, like deconstruction generally, is simply inconceivable except as a critical appreciation of Marxism: that is, its "specter" or "spirit," in the sense of *esprit* and *fantôme*. For an important critique, however, see Aijaz Ahmad, "Reconciling Derrida: Spectres of Marx and Deconstructive Politics," *New Left Review* 208 (1994), 88–106. In 1993–1994, Deleuze began writing a book on "the greatness of Marx." Visual artists, even in the First World, are also protesting the alleged death. See, for example, the passionate and precise statement by artist and photographer Claude Caroly, which accompanies his exhibit "Tournée 1991 Paris-Berlin-Prague": "Oui bien sûr, je montre Berlin, Dresde, Prague, sans indulgence, avec sévérité et vous pourriez en déduire que je décris l'éroulement du Communisme, une métaphore en somme. Erreur. Je crois au communisme. Mais de quoi parle-t-on alors? Il s'agit simplement de mon angoisse face à une victoire et une défaite, face à la projection simpliste du monde, face à ce mal universel dont on veut nous faire croire que c'est celui des autres. Ne me demandez pas si ce travail témoigne de mes certitudes, il ne témoigne que de mon désarroi. . . ." Note finally that even nearly a half century ago one of Beckett's personae, when confronted by an orator speaking elliptically and telegraphically of "Union . . . brothers . . . Marx . . . capital . . . bread and butter . . . love," remarked that "It was all Greek to me" but also that the orator called *him* a *"living corpse"* for not listening to what was being said (Samuel Beckett, "The End," trans. Richard Seaver and the author, in *Stories & Texts for Nothing* [*Nouvelles et textes pour rien,* 1958] [New York: Grove Press, 1967], pp. 47–72; here p. 66; emphasis added). Communists and communism have *always* been "dead," it seems — and for that no less alive.

14. See Mike Davis, *City of Quartz: Excavating the Future in Los Angeles,* photographs by Robert Morrow (London and New York: Verso, 1990).

15. Linton Kwesi Johnson, "Di Good Life," *Tings an' Times,* © 1991 Shanachie Records Corp., 43084. This future-oriented project contrasts with today's rather lugubrious "Gothic Marxism," which seems able to keep living on only by feeding off the past. Cf. Margaret Cohen, *Profane Illumination: Walter Benjamin and the Paris of the Surrealist Revolution* (Berkeley, Los Angeles, and London: University of California Press, 1993), pp. 11–12.

16. Gregory Elliott, "Analysis Terminated, Analysis Interminable: The Case of Louis Althusser," in *Althusser: A Critical Reader,* ed. Gregory Elliott (Oxford and Cambridge, Mass.: Blackwell, 1994), pp. 177–202; here p. 196.

17. Atif Khan, "On the Philosophy of Louis Althusser," unpublished manuscript, Cornell University, 1995.

18. See *The Last Bolshevik* (Chris. Marker, France, 1993).

19. Ernesto Laclau, *New Reflections on the Revolution of Our Time* (London and New York: Verso, 1990), p. 183; emphasis added. This book often reads like a remarkably old, left-liberal reflection on revolution's imagined impossibility. Similarly benign views of Nietzsche are ubiquitous in post-Marxism, particularly when they are of Foucauldian — which is also to say Nietzschean — persuasion. See, for example, Michelle Barrett, *The Politics of Truth: From Marx to Foucault* (Stanford: Stanford University Press, 1991).

20. Laclau, *New Reflections on the Revolution of Our Time,* p. 112; emphasis added. Not only "Nietzsche" is explicitly enlisted in this project but also "Heidegger," "Wittgenstein," and — small surprise — "pragmatism."

21. See Jameson, *The Seeds of Time* [1991] (New York: Columbia University Press, 1994).

22. See V. I. Lenin, *The State and Revolution: The Marxist Theory of the State and the Tasks of the Proletariat in the Revolution* [1917–1918], *Collected Works,* various translators (Moscow: Progress Publishers, 1972), 25:385–497; here esp. 475–479.

23. Generally speaking, when the term "ideology" occurs in this book it means not a problem of false consciousness (Marx), which notoriously entails impossible access to true consciousness, but rather a set of material interests in conflict with others (Lenin). Thus defined, ideology is more even than "a 'representation' of the Imaginary relationship of individuals to their Real conditions of existence" — a relationship that no social transformation can eradicate but only modify because in this sense "ideology has no history" (Althusser, "Ideology and Ideological State Apparatuses [Notes towards an Investigation]" [1969–1970], in *Lenin and Philosophy and Other Essays,* trans. Ben Brewster [New York and London: Monthly Review Press, 1971], pp. 127–186; here pp. 159 and 162). For ideology is also a *relay* between people and the *element* in which all possible human relationships transpire in struggle and in peace: "In class society ideology is the relay whereby, and the element in which, the relation between people and their conditions of existence is settled to the profit of the ruling class. In a classless society ideology is the relay whereby, and the element in which, the relationship between people and their conditions of existence is lived to the profit of all people" (Althusser, "Marxism and Humanism" [1965], in *For Marx* [1965], trans. Ben Brewster [New York: Vintage, 1969], pp. 219–247; here pp. 235–236).

24. Karl Marx, *Critique of the Gotha Program* [1875], in *The Marx-Engels Reader,* 2d ed., ed. Robert C. Tucker (New York: W. W. Norton & Company, Inc., 1978), pp. 525–541; here p. 531.

25. Regarding what William Haver calls the *"impossibility* of psychoanalytic 'working through'" and the *"refusal* to mourn" — which is not the refusal to grieve — see Takenishi Hiroko, "The Rite," in *The Crazy Iris and Other Stories of the Atomic Aftermath,* ed. Kenzaburo Oe (New York: Grove Press, 1985), pp. 169–200; Ota Yoko, *City of Corpses* [1945], in *Hiroshima: Three Witnesses,* ed. and trans. Richard H. Minear (Princeton: Princeton University Press, 1990), pp. 143–273; David Woj-

narowicz, *Close to the Knives: A Memoir of Disintegration* (New York: Vintage, 1991); and the analysis of this problematic in William Haver, "A World of Corpses: From Hiroshima and Nagasaki to AIDS," forthcoming article. Finally, on the refusal to work as a political and economic tactic, think less of contemporary slacker culture than of the essays collected in *Autonomia: Post-Political Politics,* ed. Sylvère Lotringer and Christian Marazzi, special issue of *Semiotext(e)* 3:3 (1980).

26. William S. Burroughs, *Cities of the Red Night* (New York: Holt, Rinehart and Winston, 1981), p. 157.

27. Avital Ronell, "Our Narcotic Modernity," in *Rethinking Technologies,* ed. Verena Andermatt Conley (Minneapolis and London: University of Minnesota Press, 1993), pp. 59–73; here p. 62. On drugs in a related but nonmetaphoric sense, see Burroughs, appendix [1956] to his *Naked Lunch* [1959] (New York: Grove Weidenfeld, 1991), pp. 215–232.

28. Ronell, "Namely, Eckermann," in *Looking After Nietzsche,* ed. Laurence A. Rickels (Albany: State University of New York Press, 1990), pp. 233–257; here p. 233. Reprinted in Ronell, *Finitude's Score: Essays for the Millennium* (Lincoln and London: University of Nebraska Press, 1994), pp. 159–181.

29. See Kurt Breysig, "Gedenkrede an Friedrich Nietzsches Bahre," *Die Zukunft* 32 (September 8, 1900), 413–414. Actually, Breysig did find Nietzsche comparable — most favorably at that — only to Jesus, Buddha, and Zoroaster among all other figures in history. Breysig was an associate of the Stefan George Circle.

30. Žižek paraphrasing Jameson in "Introduction: The Spectre of Ideology," in *Mapping Ideology,* ed. Slavoj Žižek (London and New York: Verso, 1994), pp. 1–33; here p. 1.

31. Althusser, "The Object of *Capital,*" in Louis Althusser and Étienne Balibar, *Reading Capital* [*Lire le Capital,* 1965, 2d ed. 1968], trans. Ben Brewster (London: NLB, 1970), pp. 71–198; here p. 184.

32. Crime & the City Solution (Bronwyn Adams, Simon Bonney, Chrislo Haas, Alexander Hacke, Mick Harvey, Thomas Stern), "The Adversary," as recorded on *Music from the Motion Picture Soundtrack of Until the End of the World, A Film by Wim Wenders,* © 1991 Warner Bros. Records Inc., 9 26707–4.

33. Nick Cave & The Bad Seeds, "City of Refuge," *Tender Prey,* © 1988/92 Mute Records, Ltd., 9 61059–4.

34. See Jameson, *Postmodernism, or, The Cultural Logic of Late Capitalism* (Durham: Duke University Press, 1991), pp. 67–129, and *The Geopolitical Aesthetic,* pp. 22–35.

35. Albert Kalthoff, *Zarathustrapredigten: Reden über die sittliche Lebensauffassung Friedrich Nietzsches* (Leipzig: Eugen Diederichs, 1904), p. 4. The author of these "Zarathustra Sermons," Pastor Kalthoff, was a leader-member of a remarkably extensive German Protestant movement that had begun by the 1890s to "synthesize" Christianity and Nietzsche and, in Kalthoff's case, Marx as well. Thinking that he had proved definitively by his philological research that the historical Jesus did not

exist, Kalthoff held to the belief that the Early Church had nonetheless produced "the widest communist manifesto that was ever framed." Adding gleaned notions of Marx and Nietzsche into this pot, Kalthoff brewed what has been called the first "Theology of Hope," even "Liberation Theology." See James Bentley, *Between Marx and Christ: The Dialogue in German-Speaking Europe 1870–1970* (London: NLB, 1982), esp. pp. 37–41 and 57–59.

36. See Friedrich Nietzsche, *Werke,* ed. Fritz Koegel (Leipzig: C. G. Naumann, 1899), 12:5–130, which assembles his remarks from the summer of 1881 on "The Incorporation of the Basic Errors," "The Incorporation of the Passions," "The Incorporation of Knowledge (The Passion of Cognition)," "The Individual as Experiment," and "The New Weight of Gravity."

37. Franco Bolelli as cited in Maurizio Viano, *A Certain Realism: Making Use of Pasolini's Film Theory and Practice* (Berkeley, Los Angeles, London: University of California Press, 1993), p. 18.

38. Jonathan Crary and Sanford Kwinter, Foreword to *Incorporations,* ed. Jonathan Crary and Sanford Kwinter (New York: Zone Books, 1992), pp. 12–15; here p. 12.

39. See Maggie Kilgour, "Metaphors and Incorporation," in *From Communion to Cannibalism: An Anatomy of Metaphors of Incorporation,* ed. Maggie Kilgour (Princeton: Princeton University Press, 1990), pp. 3–19.

40. Chris Rodley, ed., *Cronenberg on Cronenberg* [1992], 2d, expanded ed. (London and Boston: Faber and Faber, 1993), p. 29.

41. The "economic-corporate" is a keyterm in Antonio Gramsci's attempt in "The Modern Prince" (1931–1934) to describe and change social "relations of force." Extrapolated from the Leninist concept of "trade-union consciousness," it constitutes the narrow (i.e., necessary but insufficient) mode of particular economic consciousness that communists must make more universal politically, culturally, and hegemonically. It is an index of the critical moment when "the development and expansion of the particular group are conceived of, and presented, as being the motor force of a universal expansion, of a development of all the 'national' energies. In other words, the dominant group is co-ordinated concretely with the general interests of the subordinate groups, and the life of the state is conceived of as a continuous process of formation and superseding of unstable equilibria (on the juridical plane) between the interests of the fundamental group and those of the subordinate groups — equilibria in which the interests of the dominant group prevail, but only up to a certain point, i.e. stopping short of narrowly economic-corporate interest" (*Selections from the Prison Notebooks of Antonio Gramsci,* p. 182). In Gramsci's analysis, fascism and liberalism are particularly skillful in exploiting the economic-corporative moment; indeed, this is a major source of their power, individually and *en bloc.* See his "Some Aspects of the Southern Question" [1926], in *Selections from Political Writings (1921–1926),* ed. and trans. Quintin Hoare (New York: International Publishers, 1978), pp. 441–462. It is not commonly recognized

in the English-speaking world how concerned Gramsci was with questions of economy — a concern that becomes evident as more of his prison writings become accessible. See his *Further Selections from the Prison Notebooks,* ed. and trans. Derek Boothman (Minneapolis: University of Minnesota Press, 1995), pp. 161–277.

42. Antonin Artaud, *The Theater and Its Double* [1938], trans. Mary Caroline Richards (New York: Grove Press, 1958), p. 8.

43. See Elaine Scarry, *The Body in Pain: The Making of the World* (Oxford and New York: Oxford University Press, 1985).

44. See Georg Wilhelm Friedrich Hegel, *Vorlesungen über die Geschichte der Philosophie* [various versions from 1805 to 1830; first published by K. L. Michelet in 1833–1836], *Werke in zwanzig Bänden,* ed. Eva Moldenhauer and Karl Markus Michel (Frankfurt am Main: Suhrkamp Verlag, 1971), 18:441–516; here 514. For a translation, see Hegel, *Lectures on the History of Philosophy,* ed. and trans. E. S. Haldane, 3 vols. (London: Routledge and Kegan Paul, 1955; rpt. of the 1892–1896 ed.), 1:384–448.

45. Hegel, *Vorlesungen über die Philosophie der Geschichte* [various versions from 1822 to 1831; first edited and published by E. Gans in 1837], *Werke in zwanzig Bänden,* 12:329–330. For a translation, see Hegel, *Lectures on the Philosophy of History,* trans. J. Sibree (New York: The Colonial Press, 1899), pp. 269–270.

46. Bryan S. Turner, *The Body and Society: Explorations in Social Theory* (Oxford: Basil Blackwell, 1984), p. 251. To be sure, Turner is not wrong to accuse both Marxism and structuralism of having neglected the human body; and his concept of individuality is more complex than *simply* "bourgeois: "The body is at once the most solid, the most elusive, illusory, concrete, metaphysical, ever present and ever distant thing — a site, an instrument, an environment" (p. 8).

47. Hegel, *Vorlesungen über die Geschichte der Philosophie,* in *Werke,* 1:515.

48. For a related — but also very different — version of Nietzsche's relationship to Socrates, see Werner Dannhauser, *Nietzsche's View of Socrates* (Ithaca: Cornell University Press, 1974).

49. According to Plato's narrative, Socrates only *seemed* to assert that he had never taught an esoteric doctrine, adding, "if anyone asserts that he has ever learned or heard from me privately anything which was not open to everyone else, you may be quite sure that he is not telling the truth" (*Apology,* 33b). And Socrates claimed never to have participated in any "secret societies," or other such activities in Athens (36b). On the other hand, after the jury had decided the death penalty, he predicted rather ominously that his accusers would discover after his death that they "will have more critics, whom up till now I have *restrained without your knowing it;* and being younger they will be harsher on you and will cause you more annoyance" than he himself has done (39c–d; emphasis added). It seems, therefore, that Socrates had withheld *at least one thing* from public scrutiny after all. This contradiction may be resolved only by assuming that the ultimate Socratic irony consists in the fact that Socratism had already inculcated itself into the jury, such that it was condemning

itself by condemning him, indeed that it was condemning the Athenian state to its demise. Thus, by claiming that no one had "ever *learned* or *heard*" from him "privately anything which was not open to everyone else," Socrates did not strictly exclude the transmission of knowledge by *other* than rational or audible means, which is after all *part* of his teaching in the first place. For a translation, see Plato, *Socrates' Defense (Apology)*, trans. Hugh Tredennick, in *The Collected Dialogues of Plato, Including the Letters,* ed. Edith Hamilton and Huntington Cairns, 2d, corrected ed. (Princeton: Princeton University Press, 1963), pp. 3–26. Many contemporary philosophers, political theorists, and rhetoricians deny that Plato's dialectic, as imputed to Socrates, was as logical or dialogic as it might appear. To them the Socratic method sooner resembles an interested interrogation than a genuine dialogue, and Plato may well have had ulterior, antidemocratic motives behind his unfair representations of opponents, including the Sophists. It remains to be seen what Nietzsche's position was in this regard.

50. Martin Heidegger, *Nietzsches metaphysische Grundstellung im abendländischen Denken: Die Ewige Wiederkehr des Gleichen* [Freiburg summer semester 1937], ed. Marion Heinz, *Gesamtausgabe* (Frankfurt am Main: Vittorio Klostermann, 1986), 2/47:79–80; emphasis added. This seminar was republished — ostensibly verbatim — in *Nietzsche,* 2 vols. (Pfullingen: Günther Neske, 1961), 1:255–472; here 331–332. It was originally given at the University of Freiburg in 1937, years after Heidegger supposedly had given up his commitment to Nazism. In most cases it is important — as is almost never done — to compare and contrast the *1961* version of Heidegger's ostensible "confrontation" with national socialism in his Nietzsche lectures with the *original* seminars of the late 1930s and early 1940s. But in the case of this passage Heidegger made only minor stylistic changes.

51. Michel de Certeau, *The Practice of Everyday Life* [*Arts de faire,* 1974], trans. Steven Rendall (Berkeley, Los Angeles, London: University of California Press, 1988), p. 149.

52. Think of Andres Serrano's exquisitely composed photographs of human corpses that are alive with overdetermined — part precise, part obscure — iconographic and psychological power: for example, in the series *Morgue* (1992) and *Object of Desire* (1992).

53. Benedict de Spinoza, *The Ethics* [completed 1675, published 1678], in *On the Improvement of the Understanding, The Ethics, Correspondence,* trans. with an introduction by R. H. M. Elwes (New York: Dover Publications, Inc., 1955; rpt. of the 1883 ed.), pp. 43–271; here p. 216 [part 4, prop. 39, note].

54. Nietzsche, "Nachgelassene Fragmente, Juli-August 1882," in *Kritische Gesamtausgabe, Werke,* ed. Giorgio Colli and Mazzino Montinari (Berlin and New York: Walter de Gruyter, 1967ff), 7/1:7. This edition will be cited as *KGW,* with appropriate section, volume, and page numbers. Nietzsche's notebooks, which he did not intend for publication, are referred to in the *KGW* as his "Nachgelassene Fragmente" (posthumous fragments); they will be abbreviated as "NF," followed

by the date of composition assigned by the editors. The *KGW* is the most authoritative edition of Nietzsche's work but does not include his early writings. The earliest of these—though still not including his later philological work and lectures at the University of Basel—have been reprinted from an unfinished edition undertaken in 1933–1940 as *Frühe Schriften*, 5 vols., ed. Hans Joachim Mette (Munich: C. H. Beck, 1994), with the editorial and critical apparatus remaining inadequate.

55. Nietzsche, "NF, Sommer-Herbst 1882"; *KGW* 7/1:57; emphasis added.

56. Nietzsche, "NF, Herbst 1883"; *KGW* 7/1:533, 627.

57. Also see Stanley Corngold, *The Fate of the Self: German Writers and French Theory* (New York: Columbia University Press, 1986), pp. 95–128. The Nietzschean self is strikingly similar or parallel to the "poetic self" described by Corngold: that is, a self that "cannot be known in advance of its articulation; it can come to life only for a reader. But it is not produced *ab ovo* by that reader. It is present to him as the being which intended by an act of writing to be present to the future of that act" (p. ix).

58. Spinoza, *Short Treatise on God, Man, and His Well-Being* [c. 1662], in *The Collected Works of Spinoza*, ed. and trans. Edwin Curley, 2d, corrected ed. (Princeton: Princeton University Press, 1988), 1:53–156; here 75 [first dialogue, para. 8].

59. Gilles Deleuze, *Spinoza: Practical Philosophy* [1970], trans. Robert Hurley (San Francisco: City Lights Books, 1988), p. 13.

60. Arthur Schopenhauer, *The World as Will and Representation* [1819 and 1844], trans. E. F. J. Payne (Indian Hills, Colo.: The Falcon's Wing Press, 1958), 1:5; *Sämtliche Werke*, ed. Julius Frauenstädt and Arthur Hübscher (Wiesbaden: F. A. Brockhaus, 1965), 2:6 [first bk., ch. 2].

61. Ludwig Wittgenstein, *Tractatus Logico-Philosophicus* [1921], dual-language ed., with an introduction by Bertrand Russell (London and New York: Routledge, 1992), p. 150/151 [prop. 5.632].

62. Balibar, "Spinoza, the Anti-Orwell," in *Masses, Classes, Ideas*, p. 12.

63. Negri, *The Savage Anomaly*, p. xix.

64. As the liberal political philosopher Norbeto Bobbio has pointed out, following the lead of Joseph Schumpeter, elitism in the abstract is not necessarily a problem. Not only do elites remain "even" in representative democracies, but there are many kinds of elites, not all of which necessarily block democratic participation. Rather the problem is the specific ways that some elites attempt to impose their will on society and to what ultimate ends they do so. See Norbeto Bobbio, *The Future of Democracy: A Defense of the Rules of the Game*, ed. Richard Bellamy, trans. Roger Griffin (Minneapolis: University of Minnesota Press, 1987), pp. 31–33. And some elites, notably the Gramscian and Leninist Communist Party, are designed to eliminate elitism eventually.

65. Nietzsche, *Werke*, 12:215. "Alle Wesen nur Vorübungen in der Vereinigung (Einverleibung) von Gegensätzen."

66. Nietzsche, "NF, Juli-August 1882"; *KGW* 7/1:34–35; here 35. This collection was intended as a gift for his then close friend Lou Andreas-Salomé (1861–1937)— hence the "our" in the aphorism.

67. "In bourgeois society, living labor is but a means to increase accumulated labor. In Communist society, accumulated labor is but a means to widen, to enrich, to promote the existence of the laborer. In bourgeois society, therefore, the past dominates the present; in Communist society, the present dominates the past. In bourgeois society capital is independent and has individuality, while the living person is dependent and has no individuality. And the abolition of this state of things is called by the bourgeois abolition of individuality and freedom! And rightly so. The abolition of bourgeois individuality, bourgeois independence, and bourgeois freedom is undoubtedly aimed at" (Marx and Frederick Engels, "Manifesto of the Communist Party" [1848], in *Collected Works*, various translators [New York: International Publishers, 1976ff], 6:477–519; here 499).

68. Marx, *Grundrisse: Foundations of the Critique of Political Economy* [1857–1858, first published 1939], trans. with a foreword by Martin Nicolaus (New York: Vintage Books, 1973), p. 361.

69. Burroughs, *Cities of the Red Night*, p. 13.

70. HDTV allows not only particularly sharp images but the possibility of technohuman, digital interface of the kind required today for the newest and most powerful technologies. "American industry, many economists say, will stand or fall with high-definition television. Economists and business consultants have registered their belief in the importance of HDTV for American economic interests. Economic well-being depends on how soon American industry can produce [and/or afford, one ought to add] these flat-screen displays for home video, for other countries are competing for the video market. The importance of the state-of-the-art interface goes beyond economic competition and includes national defense. The U.S. military depends on the latest video displays. . . . A nanosecond delay or a slight distortion in visual information can spell disaster" (Michael Heim, *The Metaphysics of Virtual Reality* [New York and Oxford: Oxford University Press, 1993], p. 76). On HDTV and its implications, see further Jean-Luc Renaud, "Toward Higher Definition Television," in *Future Visions: New Technologies of the Screen,* ed. Philip Hayward and Tana Wollen (London: BFI, 1993), pp. 46–71.

71. See Victor Tausk, "The Influence Machine" [1919], trans. Dorian Feigenbaum, in *Incorporations,* pp. 542–569; and Theodor W. Adorno, "Television and the Patterns of Mass Culture" [first published 1954 in English as "How to Look at Television"], in *Mass Communications,* ed. Wilbur Schramm (Urbana: University of Illinois Press, 1960), pp. 594–612; here p. 602. Adorno is paraphrasing a central thesis of Lowenthal.

72. Davis, *City of Quartz,* p. 12. On the contribution of a "Southern-Californized" Nietzsche to the right-wing inception of Los Angeles in the minds and actions of such men as General Harrison Gray Otis and Willard Huntington Wright, and on the more recent "Nietzschean porno-mythology of motorcycle gangs and hotrodders," see pp. 28 and 66. See further Davis, *Beyond Blade Runner: Urban Control and the Ecology of Fear* (Westfield, N.J.: Open Magazine Pamphlet Series, 1992). Finally, for an analysis of what can be called "Nietzschean architecture," see Kazys Varnelis,

"The Spectacle of the Innocent Eye: Vision, Cynical Reason, and the Discipline of Architecture in Postwar America" (Diss., Cornell University, 1994).

73. Davis, *City of Quartz,* p. 21.

74. Ibid., p. 25.

75. Jonathan Crary, "Critical Reflections," *Artforum* (February 1994), 59 and 103; here 59.

76. Negri, *Marx Beyond Marx: Lessons on the "Grundrisse"* [1978–1979], ed. Jim Fleming, trans. Harry Cleaver, Michael Ryan, and Maurizio Viano, 2d ed. (London: Pluto Press; New York: Autonomedia, 1991), pp. 100–101.

77. Jameson, *The Geopolitical Aesthetic,* p. 25.

78. Alex Callinicos, "What Is Living and What Is Dead in the Philosophy of Althusser" [1988], in *The Althusserian Legacy,* ed. E. Ann Kaplan and Michael Sprinker (London and New York: Verso, 1993), pp. 39–49; here p. 48. Whereas Callinicos folds Althusserian Marxism into this problematic, this book attempts to liberate it.

79. The neo-Heideggerian popularizer Michael Heim — dubbed by his publisher "the philosopher of cyberspace" — writes on virtual reality "in the hope that my beloved *philosophia* will awaken from her slumber and once again radiate brightly and move beautifully as she has in past centuries and in my dreams" (Heim, *The Metaphysics of Virtual Reality,* p. xviii). As if high philosophy (sexism and self-promotion aside) could be extracted — as a *homogeneous* whole, as it ostensibly *originally* was — like "the rational kernel within the mystical shell"!

80. Nietzsche's most extensive diatribe against the nascent culture industry is in his seldom-read first "untimely meditation" on David Friedrich Strauss. See Nietzsche, *Unzeitgemässe Betrachtungen, Erstes Stück: David Strauss der Bekenner und der Schriftsteller* [1873]; *KGW* 3/1:153–238 [Untimely Meditations: David Strauss, the Confessor and the Writer].

81. See Daniel Bell, *The Coming of Post-Industrial Society: A Venture in Social Forecasting* (New York: Basic Books, 1973).

82. Ernest Mandel, *Late Capitalism* [1972], rev. ed. (London: NLB, 1975), p. 387. A spokesman for the United Secretariat of the Fourth International (USec), the late Mandel's claim to represent the legacy of Trotsky is disputed by other factions of the Fourth International, such as the Spartacist League (SL) and the International Communist League (ICI).

83. Davis, "Urban Renaissance and the Spirit of Postmodernism" [1985], in *Postmodernism and Its Discontents: Theories, Practices,* ed. E. Ann Kaplan (London and New York: Verso, 1988), pp. 79–87; here pp. 81 and 82–83. Obviously the attempt to locate the incept date of postmodernism and to attempt to map it onto the general development of capitalism is at stake as well: the '60s? the mid-'70s? Here Davis disagrees with Jameson, for example, or rather with the latter's appeal to Mandel. But as soon as "postmodernism" is grasped not as a problem of history but as a way of producing and receiving artifacts "hermeneutically," the issue of its

precise social "birth" and "death" becomes relatively moot. And this is exactly what has happened in the case of Nietzsche, who is all too easy to read as if he were a postmodern writer.

84. Davis, *Prisoners of the American Dream: Politics and Economy in the History of the U.S. Working Class* (London: Verso, 1986), p. 233.

85. Althusser, "Contradiction and Overdetermination: Notes for an Investigation" [1962; 1965], *For Marx*, pp. 87–128; here p. 113.

86. Deleuze and Guattari, *What Is Philosophy?* p. 21.

87. Actually, a more useful definition of "essentialism" than that commonly employed in cultural and literary studies comes from the history of science: namely, the conflation of *words* and *things*. Entailed then is the "rejection of the attitude of attributing importance to *words and their meaning (or their 'true' meaning)*," or at least *undue* attention (Karl Popper, *Unended Quest: An Intellectual Autobiography* [Glasgow: William Collins Sons & Co./Fontana, 1976], p. 17). As Spinoza had noted, "we may never, while we are concerned with inquiries into actual things, draw any conclusions from abstractions; we shall be extremely careful not to confound that which is only in the understanding with that which is the thing itself" (Spinoza, *On the Improvement of the Understanding* [1661, unfinished], in *On the Improvement of the Understanding, The Ethics, Correspondence*, pp. 1–41; here 34).

88. Henri Lefebvre, *The Production of Space* [1974], trans. Donald Nicholson-Smith (Oxford and Cambridge, Mass.: Basil Blackwell, 1991), p. 285; emphasis added.

89. To repeat, *Nietzsche's Corps/e also* can qualify as a commodity, for it is what *identifies-produces* Nietzsche/anism.

90. Deleuze and Guattari, *What Is Philosophy?* p. 5. This "Nietzschean" definition has accompanied Deleuze throughout his career; compare the following remark made in the late 1960s: "A philosophy's power is measured by the concepts it creates, or whose meaning it alters, concepts that impose a new set of divisions on things and actions. It sometimes happens that those concepts are called forth at a certain time, charged with a collective meaning corresponding to the requirements of a given period, and discovered, created or recreated by several authors at once" (Deleuze, *Expressionism in Philosophy: Spinoza* [*Spinoza et la problème de l'expression*, 1968], trans. Martin Joughin [New York: Zone Books, 1990], p. 321).

91. Nietzsche, "NF, April-Juni 1885"; *KGW* 7/3:207.

92. Deleuze and Guattari, *What Is Philosophy?* p. 17.

93. Balibar, "Althusser's Object," *Social Text* 39 (Summer 1994), 157–188; here 157. Communists must not back down from confronting Lenin's assertion in 1917 that "the theory of the class struggle was created *not* by Marx, *but* by the bourgeoisie *before* Marx, and, generally speaking, it is *acceptable* to the bourgeoisie. Those who recognize *only* the class struggle are not yet Marxist; they may be found to be still within the bounds of bourgeois thinking and bourgeois politics. To confine Marxism to the theory of the class struggle means curtailing Marxism, distorting it,

reducing it to something acceptable to the bourgeoisie. Only he is a Marxist who *extends* the recognition of the class struggle to the recognition of the *dictatorship of the proletariat*. This is what constitutes the most profound distinction between the Marxist and the ordinary petty (as well as big) bourgeois. This is the touchstone on which the *real* understanding and recognition of Marxism should be tested" (Lenin, *The State and Revolution*, in *Collected Works*, 25:416–417). John Ehrenberg takes this passage as his point of departure to argue that, properly understood, the dictatorship of the proletariat is at the *core* of communism and that in theory (though not as it has been generally practiced) it "still describes the democratic and revolutionary politics" of what remains the "only alternative" to capitalism, for the latter "has not undergone some sort of miraculous transformation over the last decade or so; its contradictions and driving forces are the same as they were when Marx, Engels, and Lenin were still alive" (John Ehrenberg, *The Dictatorship of the Proletariat: Marxism's Theory of Socialist Democracy* [New York and London: Routledge, 1992], pp. 4 and 188). But, while these contradictions and driving forces may be the same in essence, the forms they take are certainly different, and Lenin would be among the last communists to refuse to adjust to and test them. Nonetheless, the dictatorship of the proletariat remains "the ideal of the masses learning to govern themselves by the actual practice of governing themselves," this being the only notion "that keeps alive the possibility that humanity might raise itself above the level of bestiality" (Robert Paul Resch, *Althusser and the Renewal of Marxist Social Theory* [Berkeley, Los Angeles, Oxford: University of California Press, 1992], p. 32). See further, Balibar, *On the Dictatorship of the Proletariat* [1976], trans. Grahame Lock, afterword by Louis Althusser (London: New Left Books, 1977); and Nicos Poulantzas, *State, Power, Socialism* [1977], trans. Patrick Camiller (London: New Left Books, 1978). As Resch notes, these books represent the two "nuanced positions within the Althusserian camp" on the elimination by the USSR in 1976 of the official slogan "dictatorship of the proletariat"—Balibar's being more Leninist, Poulantzas's more Gramscian (p. 366).

94. See Henri Bergson, *La pensée et le mouvant* (Paris: Presses Universitaires de France, 1934); and Gilles Deleuze, "La conception de la différence chez Bergson," *Les études bergsoniennes* 4 (1956), 77–112, *Bergsonism* [1966], trans. Hugh Tomlinson and Barbara Habberjam (New York: Zone Books, 1988), *The Fold: Leibniz and the Baroque* [1988], foreword and translation by Tom Conley (Minneapolis: University of Minnesota Press, 1993), pp. 104–106, and *Expressionism in Philosophy*, pp. 88–89. See further the clear (if uncritical) exposition of Deleuze's critique of Bergson in Michael Hardt, *Gilles Deleuze: An Apprenticeship in Philosophy* (Minneapolis and London: University of Minnesota Press, 1993), ch. 1: "Bergsonian Ontology: The Positive Movement of Being," esp. pp. 16–18.

95. Deleuze, *Bergsonism*, p. 96; see further Hardt, *Gilles Deleuze*, p. 17.

96. See Althusser, "The Object of *Capital*," in *Reading Capital*, p. 198.

97. Readers curious about that strange subject known as the "author"—including

her/his motivation in writing about something s/he not merely does not like, but hates — may be interested in a central proposition of Spinozist ethics that "If a man has begun to hate an object of his love, so that love is thoroughly destroyed, he will, causes being equal, regard it with more hatred than if he had never loved it, and his hatred will be in proportion to the strength of his former love," and the proposition that "Joy arising from the fact that anything we hate is destroyed, or suffers other injury, is never unaccompanied by a certain pain in us." Another matter entirely, however, is Spinoza's concomitant proposition that "Hatred which is completely vanquished by love passes into love: and love is thereupon greater than if hatred had not preceded it." Of such a love, the author has no knowledge in the case of Nietzsche/anism — less because of any personal inadequacy, possibly, than because of the constitutive duplicity of the phenomenon here in radical dispute. See Spinoza, *The Ethics,* pp. 155, 160, and 159 [part 3, props. 38, 47, and 44]. Readers even more curious are advised that, yes, the author remains in 1995–1996 and since "the '60s" — in spite of often severe reservations (with several Maoist and Trotskyist "deviations") — a communist, indeed a member of the CPUSA. While he criticizes aspects of his own book severely as yet another way in which, alas, "reading has become the appropriate form of politics," he agrees also with Aijaz Ahmad about the significance of the Gramscian phrase "community of praxis": namely, "if you do not explicitly partake of the life of identifiable communities of individuals as they actually struggle in their lives, your criticism may have keenness of intelligence and observation but it is also likely to have that Orwellian lovelessness that comes, inevitably, from having 'floated upwards' and from 'rooting yourself in yourself.'" Academic discourse being one form of community, no matter how limited. See "Blindness in Literary and Cultural Studies" [interview with Aijaz Ahmad by Shuchi Kapila], *The Bookpress* 3:3 (April 1993), 12–13; here 13; and Ahmad, *In Theory: Classes, Nations, Literatures* (London and New York: Verso, 1992), esp. pp. 169–175. Finally, a word about the trope of "speaking as a . . . ": for example, "speaking as a communist . . . " or "as a Nietzschean. . . . " On the one hand it is sometimes important to label one's position as clearly as possible, so as not to give the impression of having attained a position of objectivity and neutrality that one does not in fact possess, but also as an act of solidarity with some people against others. On the other hand one thereby risks buying into mass-mediatized images of what this label means, and, as Barbara Johnson puts it, of "treating as *known* the very predicate I was trying to discover" (Barbara Johnson, "Lesbian Spectacles: Reading *Sula, Passing, Thelma and Louise,* and *The Accused,*" in *Media Spectacles,* ed. Marjorie Garber, Jann Matlock, and Rebecca L. Walkowitz [New York and London: Routledge, 1993], pp. 160–166; here p. 160). See further Nancy K. Miller, *Getting Personal* (New York and London: Routledge, 1991).

98. This is not to defend all types of "materialist monism"; see Althusser, "On the Materialist Dialectic: On the Unevenness of Origins" [1963], in *For Marx,* pp. 161– 218; here pp. 201–202. Nor is this to suggest that Nietzsche/anism cannot be

described by classical metaphysics — virtually anything can. In the Platonic tradition generally, it is deemed logically necessary to "elucidate the essential nature and characteristics" of something "before describing its effects" (Plato, *Symposium*, 201d–202). Aristotle might call Nietzsche/anism a "substance," in the technical sense of something that at once *underlies* ("Nietzsche") and *undergoes* ("Nietzsche-anism") change, both *retains its identity* and yet (a move denied later by Descartes) is capable of *admitting or emitting contrary qualities*. See Aristotle, *Cat.* 4a 19–21 and 2b 29. As Deleuze suggests, Spinoza's notion of causality was anti-Cartesian, not anti-Aristotelian (Deleuze, *Expressionism in Philosophy*, p. 157). Speaking Hegelese metaphysics, one might say that it is as Nietzscheanism that Nietzsche "survives his own supersession," and that their relationship, qua Nietzche/anism, would be one of "dialectical negation" or *Aufhebung*. But such metaphysical "definitions" remain paradoxical and — as metaphysical systems tend to do — provide little more than yet another *description* of phenomena that thus remain *ungrasped*. For his part, Spinoza would likely not have considered Nietzsche to be an "uncreated substance" (e.g., God and Nature) — although Nietzsche has been treated this way, at least implicitly, by many Nietzscheans. But Spinoza makes it conceptually possible to think of substance as having more than one attribute, indeed an infinite number. This is in contrast to Descartes, who did hold that substances can have only one attribute, and which would reduce Nietzsche/anism only to the question of what Nietzsche "really meant." Whether *Nietzsche's Corps/e* can ultimately evade such metaphysical snares is obviously open to doubt.

99. A recent book in English on the phenomenon of "Nietzscheanism" is symptomatic of this general problem, informed as it is by several methodological, ideological, and theoretical prejudices and confusions. "Nietzscheans" are defined as "*simply* those who regarded themselves as significantly influenced by Nietzsche and sought to give this influence some concrete or institutional expression"; and it is further assumed that it is "*clear* that Nietzsche was not identical with *any* of the political appropriations made in his name." The author of these assertions — which in fact are anything but simple and clear — then feels himself under surprisingly little obligation to read Nietzsche himself — and almost never his notebooks, with the occasional exception of the so-called *Will to Power* — nor to ask how Nietzsche might have attempted rhetorically to control his subsequent "legacy." This refusal is particularly strange because Nietzsche remains for this author the "*central* inspiration" for Nietzscheanism, in spite of the self-evident fact that "there were always other forces and influences at work" in its formation (Steven E. Aschheim, *The Nietzsche Legacy in Germany 1890–1990* [Berkeley, Los Angeles, Oxford: University of California Press, 1992], pp. 13, 14, and 15; emphases added). In addition to his own extensive archival research into the reception of Nietzsche, Aschheim gets appropriate mileage out of such standard research tools for analyzing this reception as Richard Frank Krummel's *Nietzsche und der deutsche Geist*, 2 vols. (Berlin and New York: Walter de Gruyter, 1974 and 1983). Krummel's massive — though hardly com-

prehensive and not always accurate — book is part of an extensive literature, mostly in German, documenting and analyzing various aspects of the reception of Nietzsche, and Aschheim has made conscientious use of much of it. Though, to repeat, his own knowledge of *Nietzsche* does not extend much beyond standard references and clichés. So his book is predictably rich in interesting and useful detail, especially for readers with no access to German accounts. Aschheim claims to be sociologically neutral and abstentionist. For example, he refuses to ask — let alone answer — "what Nietzsche 'really' meant," even though he admits, at the end of his book, that "to argue for the centrality of interested, mediated appropriations does not, of course, render irrelevant the role of the Nietzschean text in this process" (p. 316). But this claim of neutrality is belied, among other things, by Aschheim's own distinctly ideological positions: for example, unreflected historicism. Aschheim cites a remark made by Eric Vögelin in 1944 to the effect that, while one ought not deny "the horror passages" in Nietzsche's writing, "their existence should not be an incentive either to whitewash or to condemn Nietzsche, but rather to explore the structure of his thought which produced them." But, just as one obviously ought never "whitewash" any complex phenomenon, so too one ought never give up in advance the possibility that — after its structure has been grasped as firmly as possible — the same phenomenon may well be worthy of being "condemned" (Eric Vögelin, "Nietzsche, the Crisis and the War," *Journal of Politics* 6:1 (February 1944), 201; as cited in Aschheim, *The Nietzsche Legacy in Germany*, p. 318).

100. Deleuze and Guattari, *A Thousand Plateaus*, p. 403.

101. Warren Montag, "Spinoza and Althusser Against Hermeneutics: Interpretation or Intervention" [1988], in *The Althusserian Legacy*, pp. 51–58; here p. 53. (Montag is paraphrasing Spinoza's *Theologico-Political Treatise*, esp. ch. 7.) For a general study of the Marxist tradition's view of Spinoza, see Rainer Bieling, "Spinoza im Urteil von Marx und Engels: Die Bedeutung der Spinoza-Rezeption Hegels und Feuerbachs für die Marx-Engelssche Interpretation" (Diss., Freie Universität Berlin, 1979). And, for an approach to Althusser's Spinozism that is more skeptical than Montag's, placing it in the context of French intellectual history, see Peter Dews, "Althusser, Structuralism, and the French Epistemological Tradition," in *Althusser: A Critical Reader*, pp. 104–141.

102. Montag, "Spinoza and Althusser Against Hermeneutics," in *The Althusserian Legacy*, p. 52.

103. Spinoza, *A Theologico-Political Treatise* [1670], in *A Theologico-Political Treatise and a Political Treatise*, trans. R. H. M. Elwes (New York: Dover Publications, 1951; rpt. 1883 ed.), pp. 1–278; here, p. 5 [preface]. See further Žižek, *Tarrying with the Negative*, p. 235 — where Žižek, following Étienne De La Boétie's notion of *servitude voluntaire*, makes much the same point, notwithstanding his own imagined anti-Spinozism.

104. Pierre Bourdieu, *L'ontologie politique de Martin Heidegger* (Paris: Les éditions de minuit, 1988), p. 102. Compare too Bourdieu's brilliant, untranslatable turn of

phrase describing Heidegger's apologia for his Nazi past: "De fait, rien n'est renié, tour est re-denié" (p. 115). In other words: Heidegger could deny any element of his exoteric political ontology, without at the same time denying his esoteric one — the latter being fascoid at root.

105. Spinoza, *A Theologico-Political Treatise*, p. 112 [ch. 7].

106. Žižek, *The Sublime Object of Ideology* (London and New York: Verso, 1989), p. 43.

107. Marvin Minsky, *The Society of Mind* [1985], illustrations by Juliana Lee (New York: Simon & Schuster/Touchstone, 1988), p. 78. For an imaginative account of the "first" such engine, see William Gibson and Bruce Sterling, *The Difference Engine* (New York: Bantam Books, 1991).

108. Minsky, *The Society of Mind*, p. 78; emphasis added.

109. Nietzsche, "NF, Juli-August 1882"; *KGW* 7/1:13.

110. See, for example, William Gibson, *Neuromancer* (New York: Ace Books, 1984), pp. 5 and 51, and *Count Zero* (New York: Ace Books, 1987), pp. 38–39.

111. Althusser, *L'avenir dure longtemps* [1985], in *L'avenir dure longtemps* [*suivi de*] *Les faits,* ed. Olivier Corpet and Yann Moulier Boutang (Paris: Stock/IMEC, 1992; *Édition posthume d'œuvres de Louis Althusser,* vol. 1: *Textes autobiographiques*), pp. 7–279; here p. 74. "Je tiens en effet tout au long de ces associations de souvenirs à m'en tenir strictement aux faits: mais les hallucinations sont aussi des faits."

112. Burroughs, *Blade Runner, a Movie* [1979] (Berkeley: Blue Wind Press, 1990), [p. 6].

113. This saying is commonly attributed to Pythagoras. See, for example, Apuleius, *De Magia,* XLIII, 50 (ed. Helm). It is important to add, however, that Pythagoras is traditionally thought to have been one of the earliest practitioners of esoteric writing, and hence it was in his best interest to make it *appear* that any conscious response to a text was possible, precisely so as to promote the subconscious incorporation of distasteful messages. See Jean-Jacques Rousseau, "Observations by Jean-Jacques Rousseau on the Answer to His Discourse [*Discourse on the Sciences and Arts of 1750*]," in *The First and Second Discourses and Essay on the Origin of Languages,* trans. Victor Gourevitch (New York: Harper & Row, Publishers, 1986), pp. 41–42. On Pythagorean esotericism also see, earlier than Rousseau, the extraordinary work of John Toland, *Tetradymus* (London: J. Brotherton and W. Meadows, 1720), pp. 61–100, esp. pp. 65–66 and 72–73.

114. Jameson, *Postmodernism, or, The Cultural Logic of Late Capitalism,* p. xxi.

115. The notion of "proleptic handicapping" (German *Vorgabe*) includes the sense meant in various sports, games, horse racing, and so on. It was one of several productive interventions in the 1970s by significant East German literary critics and theorists (Naumann, Träger, Schlenstedt, Weimann) in their attempt to grasp the ways that texts maintain at least weak control over their subsequent appropriation, and to oppose the aestheticizing and subjectifying tendencies of West German "reception" theory (Wolfgang Iser, Hans Robert Jauß). See, most notably, Manfred

Naumann, "Literatur und Leser," *Weimarer Beiträge* 16:5 (1970), 92–116, "Literary Production and Reception," *New Literary History* 8:1 (1976), 107–126, and "Das Dilemma der 'Rezeptionsästhetik,'" *poetica* 8:3/4 (1976), 451–466; Claus Träger, "Zur Kritik der bürgerlichen Literaturwissenschaft: Methodologischer Kreislauf um die unbewältigte Geschichte (Teil I)," *Weimarer Beiträge* 18:2 (1972), 10–42, and "Zur Kritik der bürgerlichen Literaturwissenschaft (Teil II)," *Weimarer Beiträge* 18:3 (1972), 10–36; *Gesellschaft — Literatur — Lesen: Literaturrezeption in theoretischer Sicht*, ed. Manfred Naumann et al. (Weimar and Berlin: Aufbau-Verlag, 1973); Robert Weimann, "'Rezeptionsgeschichte' und die Krisis der Literaturgeschichte: Zur Kritik einer neuen Strömung in der bürgerlichen Literaturwissenschaft," *Weimarer Beiträge* 19:8 (1973), 5–33 [trans. Charles Spencer as "'Reception Aesthetics' and the Crisis of Literary Theory," *CLIO* 5:1 (1975), 3–33]; and Dieter Schlenstedt, *Wirkungsästhetische Analysen: Poetologie und Prosa in der neueren DDR-Literatur* (Berlin, GDR: Akademie-Verlag, 1975).

116. Leo Strauss, "Persecution and the Art of Writing" [1941] in *Persecution and the Art of Writing* [1952] (Chicago and London: The University of Chicago Press, 1988), pp. 22–37; here p. 24. Strauss and his disciples have never quite applied this principle to Nietzsche — in spite or, more likely, because of the supreme importance he has in the Straussian system.

117. Strauss, *Thoughts on Machiavelli* [1958] (Chicago and London: The University of Chicago Press, 1978), p. 13. This book remains the best introduction to how to read Nietzsche.

118. Robert Darnton, "Censorship, a Comparative View: France, 1789 — East Germany, 1989," *Representations* 49 (Winter 1995), 40–60; here 58.

119. An offshoot of liberal pluralism — weaving its uncertain, rearguard way between Leo Strauss and Jacques Derrida — represents only a partial exception, although it does recognize the problem of esotericism in Nietzsche as theme. Cf. Levine, *Nietzsche and the Modern Crisis of the Humanities,* esp. pp. 125–135.

120. Laurence Lampert, *Nietzsche and Modern Times: A Study of Bacon, Descartes, and Nietzsche* (New Haven and London: Yale University Press, 1993), pp. 276–277. See further pp. 306–310, where Lampert applies esoteric criteria to Nietzsche most explicitly (read: exoterically). But see also Lampert, *Nietzsche's Teaching: An Interpretation of "Thus Spoke Zarathustra"* (New Haven and London: Yale University Press, 1986), where for unstated reasons the esoteric problematic is *not* applied to Nietzsche's purported masterpiece, and *Leo Strauss and Nietzsche* (Chicago: University of Chicago Press, 1996), where it is..

121. See, for example, Philippe Lacoue-Labarthe, *The Subject of Philosophy* [*La sujet de la philosophie (Typographies I)*, 1979], ed. Thomas Trezise, trans. Thomas Trezise et al. (Minneapolis: University of Minnesota Press, 1993), p. 15. As is most of his work, this is a very exact and exacting study of Nietzsche (among others) in terms of the mutual imbrication of "literature" and "philosophy," which Lacoue-Labarthe sees as foundational for all serious thought and writing. As such, *The*

Subject of Philosophy's extensive and intensive take on Nietzsche, quite brilliant in its own terms, certainly ought not to be *reduced* to the criticism that it fails to see the esoteric problematic explicitly enough. Nonetheless, this book remains *symptomatic* of a more general blindness among Left-Nietzscheans — in spite and because of the fact that Lacoue-Labarthe is one of the brightest and most self/critical members of the corps/e.

122. Jean Genet, *Un captif amoureux* (Paris: Gallimard, 1986), pp. 10–11.

123. Althusser, "Reply to John Lewis" [1972–1973], in *Essays in Self-Criticism,* trans. Grahame Lock (London: NLB, 1976), pp. 33–99; here p. 78.

124. James Baldwin, "If Black English Isn't a Language, Then Tell Me What Is?" [1979], in *The Price of the Ticket: Collected Nonfiction 1948–1985* (New York: St. Martin's/Marek, 1985), pp. 649–652; here p. 651; also cited and discussed in Nora M. Alter, "Chester Himes: Black Guns and Words," in *Alteratives,* ed. Warren Motte and Gerald Prince (Lexington, Kentucky: French Forum, Publishers, 1993), pp. 11–24. The latter essay is an analysis of how a politically committed author's turn to fictional genres can be a dual-index: first, not of a "break" with an explicitly political agenda but rather a "channel" for other related kinds; and, second, the substantial — personal, literary, and social — risks when various forms of mediation between "fact" and "fiction" break down, as they almost always do eventually. This dual problematic bears fundamentally on the phenomena of Nietzsche and Nietzscheanism.

125. Balibar, "Spinoza, the Anti-Orwell," in *Masses, Classes, Ideas,* p. 33.

126. Friedrich Schlegel, "Über die Unverständlichkeit" [1800], in *Kritische Schriften,* ed. Wolfdietrich Rasch (Munich: Carl Hanser Verlag, 1964), pp. 530–542; here p. 538. Ostensibly written as a response to the complaint that the *Athenäum* — the most significant journal of early romanticism — was incomprehensible, Schlegel was in fact speaking of the problem of incomprehensibility at much higher levels of theoretical and practical interest. If Nietzsche is to be regarded as either "romantic" or "postromantic," it ought to be primarily in the terms of this quotation from Schlegel; all other terms more commonly used are mere literary history.

127. Today Althusserianism, or rather what is left of it, is under siege on several fronts for various reasons, including by Marxists or former Marxists; see, for example, *Althusser: A Critical Reader* (1994). In addition to the recent vigorous direct defense of Althusserianism by Resch in *Althusser and the Renewal of Marxist Social Theory,* less directly by various works of Žižek, and more critically by the essays collected in *The Althusserian Legacy* (1993), see also the less consequential essays in the special issue of *Studies in Twentieth Century Literature* 18:1 (Winter 1994), "The Legacy of Althusser," ed. Philip Goldstein.

128. See further David Macey, "Thinking with Borrowed Concepts: Althusser and Lacan," in *Althusser: A Critical Reader,* pp. 142–158; here p. 146.

129. This juxtaposition of Althusser and Heidegger is in no way intended to be comprehensive with regard to the philosophical question of causality, nor does it adequately represent the variety of positions available today in philosophy or in the

natural and social sciences. For a major depiction and original theory of causation there, but not in continental philosophy or the human sciences, see Richard W. Miller, *Fact and Method: Explanation, Confirmation and Reality in the Natural and the Social Sciences* (Princeton: Princeton University Press, 1987), esp. chs. 2 and 4. Also from within the Anglo-Saxon problematic see *Causation*, ed. Ernest Sosa and Michael Tooley (Oxford: Oxford University Press, 1993). Nevertheless, the Althusserian and Heideggerian positions—though they are not always clear, sometimes are self-contradictory, and may even be simply untrue or debilitating in serious ways—do represent two of the most directly relevant and opposing theories in the human sciences or humanities generally, most notably in continental philosophy and literary theory, and specifically for grasping Nietzsche/anism.

At the same time, it is important to note that, in France, Althusser has been understood to have been profoundly, albeit indirectly influenced *by* Heidegger. This assumption requires clarification. As his *L'avenir dure longtemps* makes quite clear, Althusser certainly respected Heidegger as a philosopher. Derrida, interviewed about his relationship to Althusser, has claimed that his friend "was always fascinated" with Heidegger "without having ever given any public sign of this fascination." Although Derrida remarks "I don't believe Althusser ever read Heidegger well," nonetheless Althusser was supposedly one of many French intellectuals "impregnated" by Heidegger—which leads Derrida to make the following blanket claim and demand: "For Althusser, if I may be allowed to say it in such a brutal way, Heidegger is *the great unavoidable thinker of this century*. Both the great adversary and also a sort of essential ally or virtual recourse (Althusser's entire work should be read following this indication)." This hyperbolic assertion needs to be taken with a large grain of salt, however, and begins to sound rather dubious—not to say wildly self-serving and self-descriptive—the moment Derrida intimates that he himself was Althusser's main—even sole—direct source of information about Heidegger ("Politics and Friendship: An Interview with Jacques Derrida" [1989, with Michael Sprinker], trans. Robert Harvey, in *The Althusserian Legacy,* pp. 183–231; here pp. 189–191). On the other hand Derrida suggests, in his genuinely moving eulogy to Althusser, that he has in turn incorporated Althusser into himself—as the latter's corps/e, so to speak. See Derrida, "Text Read at Louis Althusser's Funeral" [1990], in *The Althusserian Legacy,* pp. 241–245. For his part, Althusser valued less Heidegger than he did Derrida; indeed, the latter is for him "a giant" among all contemporary philosophers. See Althusser, *L'avenir dure longtemps,* in *L'avenir dure longtemps* [*suivi de*] *Les faits,* pp. 170 and 174.

Nonetheless it must be said that what Derrida and his interviewer both ignore in the interview "Politics and Friendship" is that Althusser *did* mention Heidegger in public. Indeed, a significant pattern of references spans Althusser's publishing career, and it is quite critical. As early as his 1964 essay, "Freud and Lacan," Althusser had remarked on the purely *strategic* reasons for Jacques Lacan's appropriation of Heidegger, who remained, however, a thinker "completely foreign to his scientific undertaking." A year later, in the first section of *Reading Capital,* Althusser implied that Heidegger remained trapped in the classical epistemological problematic of idealism in a way *less* "conscious and honest" than his great predecessor Edmund Husserl. In "Lenin and Philosophy" written in 1968—still before the question of Heidegger's relationship to Nazism was widely or adequately raised—Althusser pitted Lenin's notion of "partisanship in philosophy" against the trajectory of Western philosophy from Plato to Heidegger, noting of the latter that "in some of his writings, the history of philosophy" has been "dominated" by a "contradiction": namely, as he emphasized, *"the theoretical denegation of its own practice, and enormous theoretical efforts to register this denegation in consistent discourses."* And, eight years down the road, in his relatively late essay, "The Transformation of Philosophy," Althusser reformulated this critique by asserting, "All philosophies with which we are familiar, from Plato to Husserl, Wittgenstein and Heidegger, have been produced as 'philosophies' and have themselves furnished the proofs of their philosophical existence by means of rational theoretical systems that generate discourses, treatises, and other systematic writings which can be isolated and identified as 'philosophy' in the history of culture," and thus "convey the knowledge of an object of their own"—the precise problematic that Althusser attempted to analyze and contest by means of his reflection on the oxymoronic notion of "Marxist philosophy" as being more properly grasped as a "transformation *of* philosophy," in both senses implied by this genitive construction. See Althusser, "Freud and Lacan" [1964, corrected 1969] and "Lenin and Philosophy" [1968–1969], both in *Lenin and Philosophy and Other Essays,* pp. 195–219 and 23–70; here pp. 203 and 64, respectively; "From *Capital* to Marx's Philosophy" [1965], in *Reading Capital,* pp. 11–69; here p. 53; and "The Transformation of Philosophy" [1976], in the collection *Philosophy and the Spontaneous Philosophy of the Scientists & Other Essays,* ed. with an introduction by Gregory Elliott, trans. Ben Brewster, James H. Kavanagh, Thomas E. Lewis, Grahame Lock, and Warren Montag (London and New York: Verso, 1990), pp. 241–265; here p. 242.

　　In any case, Derrida's oddly ill-informed depiction of the relationship of Althusser to Heidegger elides its *differentia specifica.* For a more balanced view, see Callinicos, "What Is Living and What Is Dead in the Philosophy of Althusser," in *The Althusserian Legacy.* Callinicos argues that parts of Althusser's work (especially the first section of *Reading Capital*) do indeed evidence infection by what Callinicos, borrowing a phrase from the neoliberal political philosophers Luc Ferry and Alain Renaut, refers to as the ubiquitous "Nietzscheo-Heideggerian register" that dominated French intellectual life in the early 1970s. While admitting that fundamental aporias of Althusser's work can indeed be traced to this register, Callinicos goes on to distill what he calls Althusser's "enduring strengths"—including nothing less than "the critique of Hegelian Marxism, the conceptual clarification of historical materialism, and the elaboration of a realist philosophy of science"—all of which are dead set against Nietzsche and Heidegger, not to mention, with regard to the last two examples at least, Derrida. Cf. Luc Ferry and Alain Renaut, *La pensée 68* (Paris: Gallimard, 1985), pp. 113–114.

130. See Schopenhauer, *Über die vierfache Wurzel des Satzes vom zureichenden Grunde* [1813], ed. Michael Landmann and Elfriede Tielsch (Hamburg: Verlag von Felix Meiner, 1970).

131. See, for example, Aristotle, *Metaphysics*, 1013a–1014a; *Physics*, II, 194b–195a; and *Posterior Analytics*, II, 94a. See further Spinoza, *On the Improvement of the Understanding*, in *On the Improvement of the Understanding, The Ethics, Correspondence*, pp. 35–36.

132. See Aristotle, *Physics*, II, 197a–198a; also see Plato, *Laws*, X, 889c, where chance is identified with mere physical necessity.

133. See, for example, Aristotle, *Eth. Nich.*, 1112a.

134. Hélène Cixous, *La ville parjure ou Le réveil des érinyes* (n.p.: Théatre du Soleil, 1994), p. 126.

135. See Heidegger, "Die Frage nach der Technik" [1953], *Vorträge und Aufsätze* (Pfullingen: Günther Neske, 1954), 1:5–36. For a translation see *The Question Concerning Technology: Heidegger's Critique of the Modern Age*, trans. William Lovitt (New York: Harper & Row, Publishers, 1977). The vexed question of the philological, philosophical, or historical "accuracy" of Heidegger's representation of pre-Socratic thinking—or anything else—appears to be less resolvable than all the different camps involved in this debate would like and is of no concern here.

136. Félix Guattari, "Machinic Heterogenesis," in *Rethinking Technologies*, pp. 13–27; here p. 13; see further his *Chaosmose* (Paris: Éditions Galilée, 1992).

137. In spite of his abhorrence for voluntarism, Althusser held, for example, that in practice "It is often sufficient that a simple individual take an initiative for the atmosphere to be changed" (Althusser, *Les faits* [1976], in *L'avenir dure longtemps* [*suivi de*] *Les faits*, pp. 281–356; here p. 310). Indeed, this might be said to be one half of Althusser's formative experience in a German prisoner of war camp from 1940–1945; the other half, however, was his encounter in the same camp with communism as a lived experience, before it came to him as a theory (see p. 313). Finally, note that in *L'avenir dure longtemps*, Althusser avers that his "belated" reading of Heidegger's *Letter on Humanism* (1947) "influenced my arguments concerning *theoretical* antihumanism in Marx" (p. 176).

138. So it is that in many quarters today Althusser's alleged productivism is deeply suspect, whereas Heidegger's apparent commitment to "deep ecology" is uncritically lauded. But this dual response overlooks the fact that Althusser took one of his main points of epistemological departure from Spinoza's notion of "immanent causation," which entails a principled refusal—superficially very much like Heidegger's—to accept any vulgar distinction between a Creator God and "His" Creation; *natura naturans* and *natura naturata;* artificer and artifact; and, by extension, *any* producer and produced, not merely Nietzsche and Nietzscheanism. For a clear introduction to Spinoza's position on causation, see Stuart Hampshire, *Spinoza*

(Harmondsworth: Penguin Books, 1951), pp. 40–55. For the broader philosophical context of Spinoza's position, see Harry Austryn Wolfson, *The Philosophy of Spinoza: Unfolding the Latent Process of His Reasoning* (Cambridge, Mass.: Harvard University Press, 1934), 1:296–330; and R. S. Woolhouse, *Descartes, Spinoza, Leibniz: The Concept of Substance in Seventeenth-Century Metaphysics* (London and New York: Routledge, 1993), esp. ch. 7: "Causation, Occasionalism and Force." One thing that distinguishes Spinoza and Althusser together from Heidegger on the matter of causation has been suggested by Nicolas Tertulian in a different context. It is that the "purely theoretical aspects of scientific process and search for truth beyond any immediate finality (tangible 'results') are completely obscured by Heidegger's reasoning. He treats the principle of causality itself as a simple projection of the utilitarian apprehension of the world and deprives it thus of any real ontological import. Here, he adapts the neopositivist prejudices on the subject without noticing that he's doing so" (Tertulian, "The History of Being and Political Revolution: Reflections on a Posthumous Work of Heidegger," in *The Heidegger Case: On Philosophy and Politics,* ed. Tom Rockmore and Joseph Margolis [Philadelphia: Temple University Press, 1992], pp. 208–227; here p. 212). Another significant reason why Althusser ought not to be conflated with Heidegger (or Nietzsche) is that Spinoza "seems to have attached no importance to aesthetic experience in his scheme of human development and happiness; and this is only one symptom of his general detachment from Greek . . . influences" (Hampshire, *Spinoza,* p. 29). Finally, Heidegger's — and Nietzsche's — notion of Being was infected by a profound commitment to social and natural hierarchy against which the ontology of Spinoza — and, following him, Althusser — was radically opposed. "The conception of being in Spinoza is . . . an overdetermined conception, outside of every possible analogy or metaphor. It is the conception of a powerful being, which knows no hierarchies, which knows only its own constitutive force" (Negri, *The Savage Anomaly,* p. 5). A recent example of the thorough muddling of Spinozist, Nietzschean, Heideggerian, and even Althusserian positions is provided both between the lines and explicitly throughout the book of a leading apologist for deconstruction, Christopher Norris, *Spinoza & the Origins of Modern Critical Theory* (London and Cambridge, Mass.: Basil Blackwell, 1991).

139. For supplemental and/or alternative discussions of Althusser's account of causality see Callinicos, *Althusser's Marxism* (London: Pluto Press, 1976), pp. 39–52; Jameson, *The Political Unconscious: Narrative as a Socially Symbolic Act* (Ithaca: Cornell University Press, 1981), pp. 35–43; Elliott, *Althusser: The Detour of Theory* (London and New York: Verso, 1987), pp. 177–185; and particularly Resch, *Althusser and the Renewal of Marxist Social Theory,* ch. 1. It must be said, however, that Resch's way of citing from Althusser is sometimes philologically erratic, insufficiently critical, and overly depoliticizing. For these reasons Elliott's meticulous book provides an important corrective — before the fact, as it were — to Resch's. Whatever its ultimate liabilities might be, Althusser's tripartite notion of causality is far more

precise a tool than that produced elsewhere on the Left, including by the Frankfurt School and its compatriots. Walter Benjamin's presentation of Marxist causality in the theoretical section of his magnum opus is particularly confused, for instance (Walter Benjamin, *Das Passagen-Werk* [1927–1940, published posthumously], ed. Rolf Tiedemann [Frankfurt am Main: Suhrkamp Verlag, 1982], 1:573–574 [section N: "Erkenntnistheoretisches, Theorie des Fortschritts"]). For a—not entirely felicitous—translation of this section of "The Arcades Project," see *The Philosophical Forum* 15:1–2 (Fall-Winter 1983–1984). In a manner typical for the Western Marxist treatment of the topic, Benjamin's use—not mention—of the categories of expressive, transitive, and structural causality conflates them. The real problem, however, lies less with Benjamin himself, who has interesting things to say about virtually every topic he touches, than with the fact that reading him is as close as too many intellectuals come to Marxism.

140. The assignation of proper names of philosophers to the various types of causality is necessary but also relative and problematic, as is even the attribution of what Deleuze and Guattari call "name-effects" or "conceptual personae." To the extent that these types are not only intended to be *descriptions* of their work but also ways of *interpreting* it, not only ways of *consuming* but also ways of *re/producing* it, and although, say, Descartes may be a "transitive causalist," Kant an "expressive causalist," and Spinoza a "structural causalist"—*in comparison with other thinkers or one another*—it is also possible and necessary to think of all three types of causality as ways of *reading* Descartes, Kant, and Spinoza, or their equivalents. And Deleuze reads Leibniz very differently than does Althusser, so that "expressionism" in Leibniz for Deleuze approximates what Althusser means by structural causality. Thus, according to the dialectic of intellectual consumption-production, one can—and perhaps, if the stakes are made clear, one should—read Kant, or at least significant aspects of his work, *as* a "transitive" and/or "structural causalist," Descartes—for example, in respect to his view of substance as having only one attribute—*as* an "expressive causalist," and so forth.

141. Althusser, "The Object of *Capital,*" in *Reading Capital,* p. 186–187.

142. Althusser, "'On the Young Marx': Theoretical Questions" [1960], in *For Marx,* pp. 49–86; here p. 56.

143. Evry Schatzman, "La cosmologie: Physique nouvelle ou classique?" *La recherche* 91 (1978); as cited in Paul Virilio, *The Lost Dimension* [*L'espace critique,* 1984], trans. Daniel Moshenberg (New York: Semiotext[e], 1991), p. 44.

144. Althusser, "'On the Young Marx,'" in *For Marx,* p. 56.

145. "Ideology," in this context, is understood not as an epistemological problem (say of truth versus falsity) but rather functionally: namely, a type of unacknowledged subject-centricity that is in actuality "governed by 'interests' beyond the necessity of knowledge alone" (Althusser, "The Object of *Capital,*" in *Reading Capital,* p. 141). To the consternation of some fans and to the delight of his many foes, Althusser's own position on whether ideology ought to be understood epistemolog-

ically, functionally, or politically took a significant turn around 1967; but this matter is of no concern here.

146. Althusser, " 'On the Young Marx,' " in *For Marx*, p. 57.

147. The discussion, entitled "Gespräch über Nietzsche," took place in Frankfurt am Main, June 1950. Horkheimer was the moderator, but took active part in the discussion with the invited guests, Adorno and Gadamer. The program was rebroadcast on Hessische Rundfunk, September 19, 1991.

148. For a discussion of Heidegger's use of this trope in the context of German political thought, see Hans Sluga, *Heidegger's Crisis: Philosophy and Politics in Nazi Germany* (Cambridge, Mass. and London: Harvard University Press, 1993), pp. 79–81.

149. Adorno, "Trying to Understand *Endgame*" ["Versuch, das Endspiel zu verstehen," 1961], in *Notes to Literature*, ed. Rolf Tiedemann, trans. Shierry Weber Nicholsen (New York: Columbia University Press, 1991), 1:241–275; here 259, translation modified. See *Noten zur Literatur I*, ed. Rolf Tiedemann (Frankfurt am Main: Suhrkamp Verlag, 1974), p. 303.

150. Among Walter Kaufmann's many writings about Nietzsche, see primarily *Nietzsche: Philosopher, Psychologist, Antichrist* [1950], 4th ed. (Princeton: Princeton University Press, 1974).

151. Žižek, *The Sublime Object of Ideology*, p. 30.

152. Spinoza, *On the Improvement of the Understanding*, in *On the Improvement of the Understanding, The Ethics, Correspondence*, pp. 33–34; see further Deleuze, *Expressionism in Philosophy*, p. 156, from which the above paraphrase is derived. As put by Deleuze, it follows that "Spinoza does not believe in the sufficiency of clarity and distinctness, because he doesn't believe there is any satisfactory way of proceeding from the knowledge of an effect to a knowledge of its cause" (Deleuze, *Expressionism in Philosophy: Spinoza*, p. 157).

153. *Selections from the Prison Notebooks of Antonio Gramsci*, p. 178.

154. Althusser, "The Object of *Capital*," in *Reading Capital*, p. 188.

155. Balibar, preface to *Masses, Classes, Ideas*, pp. vii–xxiii; here p. xx; see further, in the same book, "In Search of the Proletariat: The Notion of Class in Marx" [1984], pp. 125–149.

156. Marx to Joseph Weydemeyer, March 5, 1852; in Marx and Engels, *Collected Works*, 39:60–66; here 62. Actually, this is the first of what Marx stresses, in this very important document, as his three basic contributions to history: the other two being recognition of the necessity at one "phase" for "the *dictatorship of the proletariat*" and the thesis that "this dictatorship itself constitutes no more than a transition to the *abolition of all classes* and to a *classless society*" (pp. 62 and 65).

157. Nietzsche, "NF, Herbst 1887"; *KGW* 8/2:77; last two emphases added.

158. Ibid.

159. Althusser, "The Object of *Capital*," in *Reading Capital*, pp. 188–189 and 193.

160. Spinoza, *The Ethics*, p. 62 [part 1, prop. 18]. "Deus est omnium rerum causa immanens, non vero transiens."

161. Deleuze, *Expressionism in Philosophy: Spinoza,* p. 16; emphasis added.

162. Nietzsche, "NF, Sommer-Herbst 1884"; *KGW* 7/2:157. "Coordination statt *Ursache und Wirkung.*"

163. Althusser, "The Object of *Capital,"* in *Reading Capital,* p. 193.

164. Althusser, "Cremonini, Painter of Abstraction" [1966], in *Lenin and Philosophy,* pp. 229–242; here p. 237.

165. *Selections from the Prison Notebooks of Antonio Gramsci,* p. 149.

166. For the theory behind this assertion, see Balibar, "On the Basic Concepts of Historical Materialism," in *Reading Capital,* pp. 199–308; here esp. p. 291.

167. In terms of specific political implications, structural causality ought to be severely criticized, modified, even rejected, if it were to lead inevitably to the conceptual antinomy between what Elliott has called "abrupt discontinuity or seamless continuity," and if the only practical option then available is "condemning subjects to the eternal tyranny of ideological delusion." See Elliott, *Althusser: The Detour of Theory,* pp. 137 and 179.

168. Nietzsche, "NF, Sommer-Herbst 1884"; *KGW* 7/2:182.

169. Lucien Goldmann, *The Philosophy of the Enlightenment: The Christian Burgess and the Enlightenment* [*Der christliche Bürger und die Aufklärung,* 1968], trans. Henry Maas (Cambridge, Mass.: The MIT Press, 1973), p. 18; for a more extensive analysis of this fundamental contradiction of the Enlightenment tradition and of capitalism, see further his *Mensch, Gemeinschaft und Welt in der Philosophie Immanuel Kants* (Zurich: Europa Verlag, 1946).

170. See Marx, *The Eighteenth Brumaire of Louis Bonaparte* [1852], and "Preface [to the second edition of *The Eighteenth Brumaire of Louis Bonaparte*]" [1869], in Marx and Engels, *Collected Works,* 11:99–197, and 21:56–58; here 57.

171. The terms in quotation marks are from Davis, *City of Quartz,* p. 83. Actually, in analyzing the power base of the "city of the future," Davis strikes a judicious balance between conspiracy theory and structural analysis; see esp. ch. 2: "Power Lines." This balance is characteristic of the best work today on urban planning and its failures; see, for example, Martha Rosler, "Fragments of a Metropolitan Viewpoint," in *If You Lived Here: The City in Art, Theory, and Social Activism,* ed. Brian Wallis (Seattle: Bay Press, 1991), pp. 15–43.

172. *Selections from the Prison Notebooks of Antonio Gramsci,* p. 234.

173. Beckett, *Endgame* (New York: Grove Press, 1958), p. 30.

174. Cixous, *La ville parjure ou Le réveil des érinyes,* p. 16.

175. Sigmund Freud, *Civilization and Its Discontents* [1929–1930], trans. and ed. James Strachey, introduction by Peter Gay (New York and London: W. W. Norton and Company, 1989), p. 15.

176. Max Horkheimer and Theodor W. Adorno, *Dialectic of Enlightenment* [written 1944, published 1947], trans. John Cumming (New York: The Seabury Press, 1969), p. 234.

177. See J. G. Ballard, *The Atrocity Exhibition* [1967–1969], rev. and expanded ed. (San Francisco: Re/Search Publications, 1990), pp. 19–37.

178. Corngold, *Franz Kafka: The Necessity of Form* (Ithaca and London: Cornell University Press, 1988), p. 312.

179. Jean-Luc Nancy, "Corpus" [1990], *The Birth of Presence,* trans. Werner Hamacher and David E. Wellbery (Stanford: Stanford University Press, 1993), pp. 189–207; here p. 198.

180. Nietzsche, *Also sprach Zarathustra: Ein Buch für Alle und Keinen* [1883–1885]; *KGW* 6/1:44 [part 1: "On Reading and Writing"].

181. On these two rival Christian traditions, see Jonathan Bishop, *Some Bodies: The Eucharist and Its Implications* (Macon, Ga.: Mercer University Press, 1993).

182. See his last letters (dated December 31, 1888–January 4, 1889), in Nietzsche, *Kritische Gesamtausgabe, Briefwechsel,* ed. Giorgio Colli and Mazzino Montinari (Berlin and New York: Walter de Gruyter, 1975ff), 3/5:567–579; hereafter cited as *KGB,* with appropriate volume, section, and page numbers.

183. Žižek, *Tarrying with the Negative,* p. 202.

184. Ibid., p. 208. To be sure, Žižek appeals to Lacan in order to reject Spinozism — indeed, to reject what Žižek calls "Spinozism, or, the ideology of late capitalism" (pp. 216–219). But this particular appeal to Lacan is tendentious. It is true, as Žižek notes (p. 216), that Lacan, at the very end of his *Seminar XI* (1964), did indeed very sharply polemicize, on behalf of Kantian moral responsibility, against what he imagined to be Spinozism's "serene, exceptional detachment from human desire." Žižek fails to note, however, that Lacan seems to have taken directly from Spinoza a much more fundamental definition: that is, of "the Real" as "that which always returns to its place." Earlier in *Seminar XI,* for example, Lacan had said of the Freudian term *Wiederholen* (repeating): "If I wished to make a Spinozian formula concerning what is at issue, I would say — *cogitatio adequata semper vitat eandem rem.* An adequate thought, *qua* thought, at the level at which we are, always avoids — if only to find itself again later in everything — the same thing. Here, the real is that which always comes back to the same place — to the place where the subject in so far as he thinks, where the *res cogitans,* does not meet it" (Jacques Lacan, *The Four Fundamental Concepts of Psycho-Analysis* [1964, published 1973], ed. Jacques-Alain Miller, trans. Alan Sheridan [New York and London: W. W. Norton, 1981], pp. 275–276 and 49). Ironically enough, Žižek's way of dealing with Spinoza, and part of Lacan's, can be traced to Marx. In the words of Spinozist and communist philosopher Balibar, "Marx read Spinoza closely; but by way of an astonishing quid pro quo, inscribed within the tradition of the *Aufklärung,* and in his struggle against romantic pantheism, he has only seen in Spinoza an apology for rationalism and democracy" (Balibar, "The Vacillation of Ideology," in *Marxism and the Interpretation of Culture,* ed. Cary Nelson and Lawrence Grossberg [Urbana and Chicago: University of Illinois Press, 1988], pp. 159–209; here p. 204 n. 6). However, Žižek's view of Spinoza is more directly derived from that of the today liberal-minded Laclau, who also saddles Spinoza and — unlike Žižek — Althusser with the charge of having promoted "a closed system of the structure." See Laclau, "Metaphor and

Social Antagonisms," in *Marxism and the Interpretation of Culture*, pp. 249–258; here p. 253. Žižek's view of Althusser has always been more complex and positive; see, for example, *Tarrying with the Negative*, pp. 139–140.

185. Georg Lukács, *The Destruction of Reason* [1952], trans. Peter Palmer (Atlantic Highlands, N.J.: Humanities Press, 1981), p. 374.

186. Virilio, *The Lost Dimension*, p. 17. Virilio does not identify the author, if any, of this "new scientific definition of surface."

187. This matter can be parsed in other ways, of course. If, for example, as Roland Barthes proposed in his thesis about "a lover's discourse," any body subjected to the gaze of loving desire is transformed, by a more or less covert act of analysis and dissection, into a fragmented but fetishized corpse ("as if the mechanized cause of my desire were in the adverse body"), then it is certainly possible that Nietzsche, too, as an adverse body will always be fetishized over and over again by any corps that gazes upon him, desirous to know him and his works — even by the explicitly adversarial, nonloving gaze of this book. Nonetheless, this risk of unwilling, reverse fetishization is worth taking. Cf. Roland Barthes, *A Lover's Discourse: Fragments* [*Fragments d'un discours amoureux*, 1977], trans. Richard Howard (New York: Hill and Wang, 1978), p. 71.

188. Nietzsche, "NF, November 1882–February 1883"; *KGW* 7/1:195.

189. *Wittgenstein* (Derek Jarman, UK, 1993). See further *Wittgenstein: The Terry Eagleton Script, The Derek Jarman Film* (London: BFI, 1993), pp. 86 and 70.

190. From an article by Gramsci in *La Città Futura*, 1917; as cited in Giuseppe Fiori, *Antonio Gramsci: Life of a Revolutionary* [1965], trans. Tom Nairn (London: New Left Books, 1970), p. 107.

191. Althusser, *L'avenir dure longtemps*, in *L'avenir dure longtemps* [*suivi de*] *Les faits*, p. 165.

192. Leonard Cohen, "First We Take Manhattan," *I'm Your Man*, © 1988 CBS Records Inc., CK 44191. "First we take Manhattan, then we take Berlin."

193. Heidegger, *Was heißt Denken?* [written 1951–1952, published 1954] (Tübingen: Max Niemeyer, 1984), p. 49. For a translation, see *What Is Called Thinking?* trans. with an introduction by J. Glenn Gray (New York: Harper & Row, Publishers, 1968).

194. On this distinction, see *Selections from the Prison Notebooks of Antonio Gramsci*, pp. 229–239. For an update, see Manuel De Landa, *War in the Age of Intelligent Machines* (New York: Zone Books, 1991); and for the failure of all binary models to grasp the Nietzschean "war machine" that ultimately eludes them, see Deleuze and Guattari, *A Thousand Plateaus*, pp. 351–423. From the perspective of the war machine, "battle and nonbattle are the double object of war, according to a criterion that does not coincide with the offensive and the defensive, nor even with war proper and guerrilla warfare" (p. 416).

195. For a reflection — by a Jesuit scholar working both against and in the tradition in question — both on the "adversativeness" that has dominated much recorded

history, with a particular critique of *masculinist* definitions of life and society as combat, including in academia, and on possible alternatives, see Walter J. Ong, S.J., *Fighting for Life: Contest, Sexuality, and Consciousness* (Ithaca and London: Cornell University Press, 1981). But the most common and effective forms of warfare do not necessarily *appear* as fighting, contest, or violence but rather are indirect, and women can be as adversative and bellicose as men. The research of the sociolinguist Deborah Tannen, presented in her best-seller *You Just Don't Understand*, suggests (though not consistently and with little terminological or theoretical precision) that it is not the absence or presence of struggle that distinguishes the ways of living and communicating of women and men (i.e., that men—either genetically or by social conditioning—are irrevocably committed to ideologies and practices of struggle whereas women are not) but rather that (in North American society at least) struggle is precisely what men and women have in common, though in different modalities. In Tannen's view, for men "life . . . is a contest, a struggle to preserve independence and avoid failure," for women "life . . . is community, a struggle to preserve intimacy and avoid isolation" (Tannen, *You Just Don't Understand: Women and Men in Conversation* [New York: Ballantine Books, 1990], p. 25; see also ch. 6: "Community and Contest: Styles in Conflict." Needless to say, the categories of "men" and "women" used here would need to be de-essentialized, as Tannen insufficiently recognizes, for she pays scant attention to other historical periods and social formations or to issues of nonheterosexuality. But what is particularly important is that Tannen is depicting two basic types of military, economic, and political struggle—be they ultimately gendered or not—that are both time-honored and Nietzschean: "war of position" and "war of maneuver"; "high-intensity conflict" and "low-intensity conflict"; "hot war" and "cold war"; "coercion" and "hegemony," "hangman" and "priest," and so on.

196. Althusser, "Is It Simple to Be a Marxist in Philosophy?" [1975], in *Philosophy and the Spontaneous Philosophy of the Scientists*, pp. 203–240; here p. 205. Kant's remark is in the preface to the first edition of his *Critique of Pure Reason* (1781).

197. Althusser, *Les faits*, in *L'avenir dure longtemps* [*suivi de*] *Les faits*, p. 353. Althusser's esoteric term for this eclectic supplement to Marx was "aleatory materialism" (*le matérialisme aléatoire*). See his *Sur la philosophie*, pp. 34–44. In his version of the battlefield of philosophy, Althusser eventually found himself caught up in what he called the apparently irreducible "difference" between on the one hand the necessary *isolation and solitude* of the philosopher, "who must limit himself to putting forward theses without ever being able to verify them himself," and on the other the *responsibility* entailed by his thesis, in his "Response to John Lewis," that "a Communist is never alone." He then suggested, as a critique of Marx, that "the entire difference is certainly there, but one can grasp it if *every* philosopher effectively seeks to 'change the world'"; but then Althusser added his crucial rider: "which he cannot do alone without a genuinely free and democratic communist organization, having close ties with its grass roots and beyond them with other popular mass move-

ments" (Althusser, *L'avenir dure longtemps,* in *L'avenir dure longtemps* [*suivi de*] *Les faits,* p. 165).

198. Ibid., p. 234.

199. Wittgenstein, *Philosophische Untersuchungen/Philosophical Investigations* [written 1945 and 1947–1949, published 1953], dual-language ed., trans. G. E. M. Anscombe (Oxford: Basil Blackwell, 1968), p. 47/47e.

200. Ibid., p. 48/48e. Note that in this system it would, however, be a mistake to equate "picture" with the words "image" or "idea." "An image [Vorstellung] is not a picture, but a picture can correspond to it [kann ihr entsprechen]" (p. 101/101e).

201. See, for example, Gerhard Hilbert, *Moderne Willensziele* (Leipzig: A. Deichert, 1911), p. 19.

202. Parmenides, Fr. 2; Empedocles, Fr. 17; Heraclitus, Fr. 53.

203. Heraclitus, Fr. 125. See further Kathleen Freeman, *The Pre-Socratic Philosophers: A Companion to Diels, "Fragmente der Vorsokratiker,"* 2d ed. (Cambridge, Mass.: Harvard University Press, 1959), pp. 105 and 129; and W. K. C. Guthrie, *A History of Greek Philosophy,* vol. 1: *The Earlier Presocratics and the Pythagoreans* (Cambridge: Cambridge University Press, 1962), p. 449.

204. Heidegger wrote; "The *pólemos* named here [i.e., in Heraclitus's Fr. 53] is a conflict [Streit] raging prior to everything divine and human, it is no war [Krieg] in the human manner. As thought by Heraclitus, battle [Kampf] in the first instance allowed the realm of being to pull away [auseinandertreten] into opposites, allowed position and order and rank to relate in being. In such pulling-away [Auseinandertreten], cleavages, intervals, distances, and points of articulation are opened up. In setting-apart [Aus-einander-setzung] cosmos comes to be. (Setting-apart neither separates nor much less does it destroy unity. It constitutes unity, is collection [*lógos*]. *Pólemos* and *lógos* are the same thing)" (Heidegger, *Einführung in die Metaphysik* [Freiburg summer semester 1935, published 1953], ed. Petra Jaeger, *in Gesamtausgabe* [Frankfurt am Main: Vittorio Klostermann, 1983], 2/40:66). For another translation, see *An Introduction to Metaphysics,* trans. Ralph Manheim (Garden City, New York: Anchor Books, 1961), p. 51.

205. Heidegger, *Einführung in die Metaphysik,* p. 66. Also see "The Origin of the Work of Art" [1935], trans. with an introduction by Albert Hofstadter (New York: Harper & Row, Publishers, 1971), pp. 17–87; here pp. 61–62, where one "way in which truth occurs is in the act that founds a State." See further his "Die Selbstbehauptung der deutschen Universität" [1933] and "Das Rektorat 1933/34" [1945], both in *Die Selbstbehauptung der deutschen Universität (Rede, gehalten bei der feierlichen Übernahme des Rektorats der Universität Freiburg i. Br. am 27.5. 1933)* [*und*] *Das Rektorat 1933/34,* ed. Hermann Heidegger (Frankfurt am Main: Vittorio Klostermann, 1983), esp. pp. 18–19 and 28–29. For translations of the last two texts, see the (important but ultimately very obscurantist) anthology *Martin Heidegger and National Socialism: Questions and Answers* [1988], ed. Günther Neske and Emil Ket-

tering, trans. Lisa Harries and Joachim Neugroschel (New York: Paragon House, 1990).

206. Heidegger, *Parmenides* [Freiburg winter semester 1942–1943], ed. Manfred S. Frings, *Gesamtausgabe* (Frankfurt am Main: Vittorio Klostermann, 1982), 2/54:134 and 74. See further his *Heraklit* [Freiburg summer semester 1943 and summer semester 1944], ed. Manfred S. Frings, *Gesamtausgabe* (Frankfurt am Main: Vittorio Klostermann, 1979), 2/55:186–204, and again "Die Frage nach der Technik," translated in *The Question Concerning Technology*.

207. Lacan, for example, reduced *alétheia* to an erotic, rather than esoteric, problematic, noting "that when we are attentive to the manner in which Martin Heidegger discovers for us the play of truth in the word *alétheia*, we only find again a secret in which truth has always initiated its lovers, and from which they believe that it is in what truth hides that it offers itself to them *most truly*" (Lacan, "Le séminaire sur 'La lettre volée'" [1956], in *Écrits I* [Paris: Éditions du Seuil, 1966], pp. 19–75; here p. 31). For a translation, see "Seminar on the Purloined Letter," trans. Jeffrey Mehlman, *Yale French Studies* 48 (1972), 39–72; special issue on *French Freud: Structural Studies in Psychoanalysis*.

208. Heidegger, *Heraklit*, *Gesamtausgabe*, 2/55:139.

209. Stanley Rosen, *The Question of Being: A Reversal of Heidegger* (New Haven and London: Yale University Press, 1993), p. xiv.

210. On the transformation of "aesthetics" — under conditions specific to technological, socioeconomic, and political modernity — from a theory of the senses into the ideology of beauty, see Terry Eagleton, *The Ideology of the Aesthetic* (Oxford and Cambridge, Mass.: Blackwell, 1990), and Susan Buck-Morss, "Aesthetics and Anaesthetics: Walter Benjamin's Artwork Essay Reconsidered," *October* 62 (Fall 1992), 3–41. Though momentous, this transformation is not irreversible, as seems to be indicated nowadays by developments of the technologies of cyberspace and virtual reality; but nor was it irreversible already for Nietzsche in theory if not also in fact.

211. See, for example, Heidegger, *Beiträge zur Philosophie (Vom Ereignis)* [1936–1938], ed. Friedrich-Wilhelm von Hermann, *Gesamtausgabe* (Frankfurt am Main: Vittorio Klostermann, 1989), 3/65:31 and 395–401. Whether this explicitly esoteric work, and not the earlier and more exoteric *Being and Time* (1927), constitutes Heidegger's magnum opus has become a hot topic of debate among Heideggerians. See further his relatively esoteric seminar *Grundfragen der Philosophie: Ausgewählte "Probleme" der "Logik"* [Freiburg winter semester 1937–1938], ed. Friedrich-Wilhelm von Hermann, *Gesamtausgabe* (Frankfurt am Main: Vittorio Klostermann, 1984), 2/45.

212. See, for example, Nietzsche, "Die dionysische Weltanschauung" [the Dionysian worldview, 1870], "Ueber das Pathos der Wahrheit" [on the pathos of truth, 1872], "Homer's Wettkampf" [Homer's contest, 1872], "Die Philosophie im tragischen Zeitalter der Griechen" [philosophy in the tragic age of the Greeks, 1873], and "NF, Sommer 1875"; *KGW* 3/2:43–69, 249–257, 277–286, and 293–366; and 4/1:173–203, respectively. These texts from the NF have been translated as "The

Struggle between Science and Wisdom," in *Philosophy and Truth: Selections from Nietzsche's Notebooks of the Early 1870s* [1979], ed. and trans. Daniel Breazeale (Atlantic Highlands, N.J., and London: Humanities Press International, Inc., 1991).

213. Nietzsche, *Also sprach Zarathustra; KGW* 6/1:45 [part 1: "On Reading and Writing"]. "Muthig, unbekümmert, spöttisch, gewaltthätig — so will uns die Weisheit: sie ist ein Weib und liebt immer nur einen Kriegsmann."

214. See Nietzsche, *Zur Genealogie der Moral: Eine Streitschrift* [1887]; *KGW* 6/2:257-430. Book 3 — "What Is the Meaning of Our Ascetic Ideals?" — also begins with the motto just cited from *Thus Spoke Zarathustra.*

215. On Brecht's notion of "crude thinking" as a crucial component of properly dialectical thought, see Walter Benjamin, "Brechts Dreigroschenroman" [1935], in *Gesammelte Schriften,* ed. Rolf Tiedemann and Hermann Schweppenhäuser (Frankfurt am Main: Suhrkamp Verlag, 1980), 9:440–449; here esp. 445–447. For a translation, see Benjamin, *Reflections: Essays, Aphorisms, Autobiographical Writings,* ed. with an introduction by Peter Demetz, trans. Edmund Jephcott (New York and London: Harcourt, Brace, Jovanovich, 1978). See further Ernst Bloch, Georg Lukács, Bertolt Brecht, Walter Benjamin, and Theodor Adorno, *Aesthetics and Politics,* afterword by Fredric Jameson, translation editor Ronald Taylor (London: NLB, 1977), pp. 60–109. Jameson notes that Marxist *plumpes Denken* stands not on its own but rather in supplemental relationship to "the intellectual positions that it corrects — the overcomplicated Hegelianism or philosophic Marxism for which it substitutes some hard truths and plain language" (Jameson, "Criticism in History" [1976], in *The Ideologies of Theory: Essays 1971–1986,* vol. 1: *Situations of Theory,* foreword by Neil Larsen [Minneapolis: University of Minnesota Press, 1988], pp. 119–136; here p. 119). Finally, for a defense of the necessity for a certain "strategic crudeness" to show that the circular "subtle description" or *ludic pomo* of much current cultural theory can be complicit with the global logic of wage labor and capital, see Mas'ud Zavarzadeh, *Seeing Films Politically* (Albany: State University of New York Press, 1991); also Michael Parenti, *Make-Believe Media: The Politics of Entertainment* (New York: St. Martin's Press, 1992).

216. Gramsci, "In principe era il sesso" [1917], in *Opere di Antonio Gramsci,* ed. Felice Platone (Turin: Einaudi, 1947–1972), 6:337.

217. Nietzsche, "NF, Winter 1884"; *KGW* 7/2:80.

218. Ibid., 7/2:81.

219. Montag, "Spinoza and Althusser Against Hermeneutics," in *The Althusserian Legacy,* p. 52; emphasis added.

220. See Herman Melville, "The River," appendix A of *The Confidence-Man: His Masquerade* [1857], ed. with an introduction and notes by Stephen Matterson (Harmondsworth: Penguin Books, 1990), pp. 341–343.

221. For a reflection on the problem of having and narrating alternative lives, see Stanley Corngold and Irene Giersing, *Borrowed Lives* (Albany: State University of New York Press, 1991).

222. Franz Kafka, "The Truth about Sancho Panza" [1917], in *Dearest Father: Stories and Other Writings*, trans. Ernst Kaiser and Eithne Wilkins (New York: Schocken Books, 1954), pp. 69–70.

223. Paul A. Cantor, "Leo Strauss and Contemporary Hermeneutics," in *Leo Strauss's Thought: Toward a Critical Engagement*, ed. Alan Udoff (Boulder and London: Lynne Rienner Publishers, 1991), pp. 267–314; here p. 277.

224. See Plato, *Phaedrus*, 275d9–275e5 and 264b7–c5, and Leo Strauss, *The City and Man* [1962, first published 1964] (Chicago and London: The University of Chicago Press, 1977), pp. 52–62.

225. For a comparison in this context of Plato to Nietzsche as esoteric writers, see Stanley Rosen, "Suspicion, Deception, Concealment," in *Arion* [3d ser.] 1:2 (1991), 112–127.

226. Arnold Schoenberg as cited in Kyle Gann's obituary for John Cage in *The Village Voice* (October 13, 1992).

227. Jameson, *The Geopolitical Aesthetic*, p. 3. See further his "Cognitive Mapping," in *Marxism and the Interpretation of Culture*, pp. 347–357.

228. Donna J. Haraway, "A Cyborg Manifesto: Science, Technology, and Socialist-Feminism in the Late Twentieth Century" [1983–1985], in *Simians, Cyborgs, and Women: The Reinvention of Nature* (New York: Routledge, 1991), pp. 149–181; here p. 149.

229. Jean Baudrillard, *Forget Baudrillard* [interview with Sylvère Lotringer], in *Forget Foucault & Forget Baudrillard*, trans. Nicole Dufresne, Phil Beitchman, Lee Hildreth, and Mark Polizzotti (New York: Semiotext[e] Foreign Agents Series, 1987), pp. 65–137; here p. 68. Baudrillard himself submits, however, to a certain premature cynicism — the old-fashioned, time-honored celebration of Nietzsche/anism as "thrilling" even while recognizing that it is "a world where the name of the game remains secret" (p. 71). And if, as Baudrillard also proposes, the Society of the Spectacle circa 1968 has today passed without trace at the end of the twentieth century into the Cynical Society, the Society of Ceremony, then the triumph of Nietzsche/anism — botched ceremony or not — would indeed be total. Cf. his *The Ecstasy of Communication* [*L'Autre par lui-même*, 1987], trans. Bernard and Caroline Schutze, ed. Sylvère Lotringer (New York: Semiotext[e] Foreign Agents Series, 1988), pp. 103–104.

230. Barthes, *S/Z* [1970], trans. Richard Miller, preface by Richard Howard (New York: Hill and Wang, 1974), p. 53.

231. Žižek, *Looking Awry: An Introduction to Jacques Lacan through Popular Culture* (Cambridge, Mass., and London: The MIT Press, 1991), p. 23.

232. Althusser, "The 'Piccolo Teatro': Bertolazzi and Brecht (Notes on a Materialist Theatre)" [1962], in *For Marx*, pp. 129–151; here p. 143.

233. Althusser to Fernanda Navarro, October 11, 1984; in the "Correspondance" in *Sur la philosophie*, pp. 81–137; here pp. 114–115.

234. Kirk Rising Ireland, "Anglers, Satyr-Gods, and 'Divine Lizards': Comedy in Excess" (Diss., Cornell University, 1994), 46–47.

235. V. N. Vološinov, *Marxism and the Philosophy of Language* [1929–1930], trans. Ladislav Matejka and I. R. Titunik (New York and London: Seminar Press, 1973), p. 23. If, as is possible, the author of this book was the Nietzschean Mikhail Bakhtin, then it is arguable that he himself did not take this remark at face value but used it not only to placate Stalinist censors but also in his effort, as a closet neo- or even ultraconservative, to attack both vulgar Marxism and Marxism. As can be learned from Leo Strauss, it is standard practice under censorship systems to place orthodox remarks at the beginning and end of books, placing the heterodox in the middle. But, in this case at least, this practice does not mean that the orthodox remark is necessarily untrue, the heterodox true.

236. Michel Serres, *La naissance de la physique dans le texte de Lucrèce: Fleuvres et turbulences* (Paris: Les éditions de minuit, 1977), p. 29; also Deleuze and Guattari, *A Thousand Plateaus*, p. 367.

237. "What actually distinguishes the concept of the *problematic* [*problematique*] from subjectivist concepts of an idealist interpretation of the development of ideologies is that it brings out within the thought *the objective internal reference system of its particular* themes, the system of *questions* commanding the *answers* given by the ideology. If the meaning of an ideology's answers is to be understood at this internal level it must first be asked *the question of its questions*. But this problematic is *itself an answer*, no longer to its own internal questions—problems—but to *the objective problems posed* for ideology *by its time*" (Althusser, "'On the Young Marx,'" in *For Marx*, p. 67 n. 30).

238. Negri, *The Savage Anomaly*, p. 11.

239. Should the reader again prefer a sharper statement of ideological—as opposed to merely methodological—purpose, here it is. This book tries to be an argument for and a performance of the untimely/timely relevance today of *real* communism. With this end in mind, it is written in the spirit of Toni Negri and other "communists like us." Like him and them, it attempts to combine "old-fashioned" philological and scholarly work—known at least as well to Marx, Engels, Lenin, Rosa Luxemburg, Trotsky, Mao, and Gramsci as to Nietzsche or any of us—with a certain, equally "passé" and "intransigent" insistence on keeping alive some basic political and economic themes of "orthodox communism"—though not of much "actually existing socialism" or even "Marxism." This book is not *Marxist* so much as *communist*. From the Althusserian perspective, "Marxism had [and has] an original meaning (a 'problematic' of its own) *only* if it was [and is] a theory of and for the communist tendency. The criterion for accepting or rejecting any 'Marxist' thesis was [and is] always the same, be it presented as an 'epistemological' or a 'philosophical' criterion: namely whether it made [and makes] a communist *politics* intelligible, implementable, or not" (Balibar, "The Non-Contemporaneity of Althusser" [1988], in *The Althusserian Legacy*, pp. 1–16; here p. 4).

240. Marx and Engels, *The German Ideology: Critique of Modern German Philosophy According to Its Representatives, Feuerbach, B. Bauer and Stirner, and of German Socialism According to Its Various Prophets* [1845–1846, published 1932], in *Collected Works*,

5:19–539; here 49. Compare also the remark of Alex Trocchi about definition: "Revolt is understandably unpopular. As soon as it is defined it has provoked the measures for its containment. The prudent man will avoid the definition which is in effect his death sentence" (Trocchi, "Invisible Insurrection of a Million Minds" [1966]; as cited in Jon Savage, *England's Dreaming: Anarchy, Sex Pistols, Punk Rock and Beyond* [New York: St. Martin's Press, 1992], p. 371).

241. Félix Guattari and Toni Negri, *Communists Like Us: New Spaces of Liberty, New Lines of Alliance* [1985], with a "Postscript, 1990" by Toni Negri, trans. Michael Ryan et al. (New York: Semiotext[e] Foreign Agents Series, 1990), p. 10. It should be unnecessary to add: "The project: to rescue 'communism' from its own disrepute. Once invoked as the liberation of work through mankind's collective creation, communism has instead stifled humanity. We who see in communism both collective and individual possibilities must reverse that regimentation of thought and desire which terminates the individual" (p. 7).

242. Ibid., p. 10.

243. See William Butler Yeats, "The Second Coming" [1920], in *Selected Poems and Three Plays of William Butler Yeats,* ed. M. L. Rosenthal, 3d rev. ed. (New York: Collier Books, 1986), pp. 89–90; here p. 89.

244. Guattari and Negri, *Communists Like Us,* pp. 16–17.

245. Compare, too, Trotsky's important answer to a very common question: "does not an excess of solidarity, as the Nietzscheans fear, threaten to degenerate man into a sentimental, passive, herd animal? Not at all. The powerful force of competition which, in bourgeois society, has the character of market competition, will not disappear in a socialist society, but, to use the language of psychoanalysis, will be sublimated, that is, will assume a higher and more fertile form. There will be the struggle for one's opinion, for one's project, for one's taste. In the measure in which political struggles will be eliminated — and in a society where there will be no classes, there will be no such struggles — the liberated passions will be channelized into technique, into construction which also includes art. Art then will become more general, will mature, will become tempered, and will become the most perfect method of the progressive building of life in every field. It will not be merely 'pretty' without relation to anything else" (Leon Trotsky, *Literature and Revolution* [1922–1923], excerpted in his *On Literature and Art,* ed. Paul N. Siegel [New York: Pathfinder Press, Inc., 1970], pp. 29–62; here pp. 60–61).

246. Nonetheless worth reading is the accompanying cover story written by *Der Spiegel*'s editor in chief and entitled "A Nietzsche for Green and Alternative Politics?" See Rudolf Augstein, "Ein Nietzsche für Grüne und Alternative?" *Der Spiegel* 35:24 (June 8, 1981), 156–184. The original illustration of *Denker Nietzsche, Täter Hitler* (1981) was the work of Michael Mathias Prechtl (born 1926) and is reproduced in the catalogue *Für F. N.: Nietzsche in der bildenden Kunst der letzten dreißig Jahre* (Weimar: Stiftung Weimarer Klassik, 1994), p. 103.

247. Reproduced in *Für F. N.: Nietzsche in der bildenden Kunst der letzten dreißig*

Jahre, fig. 5; see further, in the same catalogue, Hansdieter Erbsmehl, "'Schatten über Europa': Nietzsche in Werken von Max Ernst und Joseph Beuys," pp. 19–25; esp. pp. 22–24.

248. See Nietzsche, *Ecce homo: Wie man wird, was man ist* [1888]; *KGW* 6/3: 335 ["Thus Spoke Zarathustra," 1]. For a historical — nonphilosophical — discussion of Nietzsche's political views, see Peter Bergmann, *Nietzsche, "the last antipolitical German"* (Bloomington and Indianapolis: Indiana University Press, 1987); for a philosophical — ahistorical — discussion of Nietzsche's critique of liberalism, see Mark Warren, *Nietzsche's Political Thought* (Cambridge, Mass., and London: The MIT Press, 1988), esp. pp. 152–158. But both books downplay or explain away the fascoid aspect of Nietzsche's thought, and neither takes into account its esoteric aspect.

249. The phrases in quotation marks are from Mao Tse-Tung, *Talks at the Yenan Forum on Literature and Art* [May 2, 1942], trans. anon. (Peking: Foreign Languages Press, 1967), p. 9. Compare Spinoza's central early thesis: "we may never, while we are concerned with inquiries into actual things, draw any conclusion from abstractions; we shall be extremely careful not to confound that which is only in the understanding with that which is in things [*in res*]. The best basis for drawing a conclusion will be either some particular affirmative essence, or a true and legitimate definition" (Spinoza, *On the Improvement of the Understanding*, in *On the Improvement of the Understanding, The Ethics, Correspondence*, p. 34 [section 13], translation modified).

250. Jeffrey Mehlman, *Walter Benjamin for Children: An Essay on His Radio Years* (Chicago and London: The University of Chicago Press, 1993), p. 42. Mehlman relates the story of the seventeenth-century Sabbati Zevi, who headed a messianic Jewish revival only to be forced by the Turkish sultanate to convert to Islam, "thus leaving the masses who had rallied to his call with the excruciating dilemma of how to absorb the paradox of an apostate messiah." The "solution" was "voluntary Marranoism," or rather the Sabbatian doctrine that "it was the task of the Messiah to descend into evil in order to defeat it from within" (p. 42). Mehlman suggests that this premodern version of virusing the matrix was built upon a paradox: on the one hand (citing Scholem), "the legacy of Sabbatian antinomianism" was centered around a "commandment to be fulfilled by means of a transgression [*mitzvah haba'ah ba-averah*]'"; on the other (paraphrasing Bataille), "'Transgression is not the negation of a prohibition [*interdit*], but its completion'" (p. 66). See further Gershom Scholem, *Major Trends in Jewish Mysticism* (New York: Schocken, 1941), p. 99; *Sabbatai Zevi: The Mystical Messiah*, trans. R. J. Z. Werblowsky (Princeton: Princeton University Press, 1973); and Bataille, *L'érotisme, édition illustrée* (Paris: Les éditions du minuit, 1957), p. 70. Actually, Bataille says something rather different: "Au delà de l'interdit nous devons maintenant envisager la transgression."

251. Judith Butler, *Bodies that Matter: On the Discursive Limits of Sex* (New York and London: Routledge, 1993), p. 241.

252. See Samuel Rosenberg, *Naked Is the Best Disguise: The Death & Resurrection of Sherlock Holmes* (Indianapolis and New York: The Bobbs-Merrill Company, 1974).

253. In the German Democratic Republic, for example, "In the 1950s and 1960s . . . it was dangerous to own works by authors like Freud and Nietzsche. But such books circulated through networks of trusted friends. A friend would appear with a volume and give you a time limit, often two days, to read it. You would shut yourself up in a safe place and pore over the text, day and night. The effect was overwhelming: 'It cut into you like a knife' . . . " (Darnton, "Censorship, a Comparative View," 56). Nietzsche would have savored this effect, corresponding as it would to something like an ideal reading situation for his work, in which the critical capacity is at a minimum vis-à-vis the text and vis-à-vis the surrounding social environment is at a maximum.

254. Althusser, "Contradiction and Overdetermination," in *For Marx*, p. 116.

255. For the now classic analysis (the argument dating to 1983–1984) of the articulation in postmodernism of pastiche and the schizoid, see Jameson, *Postmodernism, or, The Cultural Logic of Late Capitalism*, pp. 16–31. Compare further a remark of Deleuze on what might be called the *ethics*, as well as the aesthetics, of creating philosophical concepts: "some concepts must be indicated by an extraordinary and sometimes even barbarous or shocking word, whereas others make do with an ordinary, everyday word that is filled with harmonics so distant that it risks being imperceptible to a nonphilosophical ear. Some concepts call for archaisms, and others for neologisms, shot through with almost crazy etymological exercises" (Deleuze and Claire Parnet, *Dialogues*, trans. Hugh Tomlinson and Barbara Habberjam [Minneapolis: University of Minnesota Press, 1987], p. 17).

256. Himself admitting exceptions, Adorno is right to argue for the use of dashes (*Gedankenstriche:* thought-strokes) against parentheses (*Klammer:* clamps). "The test of a writer's sensitivity in punctuating is the way he handles parenthetical material. The cautious writer will tend to place that material between dashes and not in round brackets, for brackets take the parenthesis completely out of the sentence, creating enclaves, as it were, whereas nothing in good prose should be unnecessary to the overall structure. By admitting such superfluousness, brackets implicitly renounce the claim to the integrity of the linguistic form and capitulate to pedantic philistinism. Dashes, in contrast, which block off the parenthetical material from the flow of the sentence without shutting it up in a prison, capture both connection and detachment" (Adorno, "Punctuation Marks" [1956], in *Notes to Literature*, 1:91–97; here 95).

257. Heim, *The Metaphysics of Virtual Reality*, pp. 30–35. "Like fractal structures, a text can turn back on itself linguistically, and hypertext shows the turns, the links, the recurring motifs, and the playful self-references" (p. 9).

258. Gramsci, *Prison Notebooks;* as cited in Joseph A. Buttigieg, introduction to Gramsci, *Prison Notebooks*, ed. with introduction by Joseph A. Buttigieg, trans. Joseph A. Buttigieg and Antonio Callari (New York: Columbia University Press, 1992), 1:1–64; here 59–60 [notebooks 7 § 6 and 11 § 27]. See further Buttigieg,

"Philology and Politics: Returning to the Text of Antonio Gramsci's *Prison Note-books*," *boundary 2* 21:2 (Summer 1994), 98–138.

259. See, for example, Nietzsche, "NF, Frühjahr 1888"; *KGW* 8/1:250: "*Lack of philology*: one constantly confuses the explanation [Erklärung] with the text—and what an 'explanation!'" As will be seen later, Nietzsche moves to replace "explanation" in this thesis with the, for him, more positive term "interpretation," which is pitted against "facts." Nonetheless, he will remain dedicated to the proposition not only that the "text" exists but also that it has a very specific, albeit esoteric political task. For Nietzsche has self-interested reasons for diverting "explanation" away from his own texts and this project.

260. Gramsci, "Culture and Class Struggle" [1918], in *Selections from Cultural Writings*, ed. David Forgacs and Geoffrey Nowell Smith, trans. William Boelhower (Cambridge, Mass.: Harvard University Press, 1985), pp. 31–37; here p. 32.

261. See Negri, *The Savage Anomaly*, pp. 98–108 ("Philology and Tactics").

262. Montag, "Spinoza and Althusser Against Hermeneutics," in *The Althusserian Legacy*, p. 55.

263. Cf. Nietzsche, "Versuch einer Selbstkritik" [1886], in *Die Geburt der Tragödie. Oder: Griechenthum und Pessimismus* [expanded ed. 1886]; *KGW* 3/1:5–16 ["Attempt at a Self-Criticism"]; and *Ecce homo*; *KGW* 6/1:307–313 ["The Birth of Tragedy"].

264. Nietzsche, "NF, Herbst 1881"; *KGW* 5/2:513.

265. See Rosalyn Diprose, "Nietzsche and the Pathos of Distance," in *Nietzsche, Feminism and Political Theory*, ed. Paul Patton (London and New York: Routledge, 1993), pp. 1–26.

266. Althusser, "From *Capital* to Marx's Philosophy," in *Reading Capital*, p. 16.

267. Montag, "Spinoza and Althusser Against Hermeneutics," in *The Althusserian Legacy*, p. 55.

268. See Thomas Hobbes, *Leviathan or the Matter, Forme and Power of a Commonwealth Ecclesiasticall and Civil* [1651], ed. with an introduction by Michael Oakeshott (Oxford: Basil Blackwell, 1955), pp. 246–255.

269. Montag, "Spinoza and Althusser Against Hermeneutics," in *The Althusserian Legacy*, p. 56.

270. Ibid. As Montag goes on to show, Althusser's development of Spinoza's materialist way of reading was part of a multifront intervention directed not only against the idealist tendencies of hermeneutics and structuralism but also against the ostensible "materialism" of deconstruction.

271. Bataille, *Theory of Religion* [1948, first published 1974], trans. Robert Hurley (New York: Zone Books, 1992), p. 9. *Théorie de la religion; Œuvres complètes*, 7:281–361; here 285.

272. Hegel, *Phenomenology of Spirit* [1807], trans. A. V. Miller, with an analysis and foreword by J. N. Findlay (Oxford: Oxford University Press, 1979), pp. 2–3 [preface § 3]; emphasis added.

273. Ibid., p. 39 [preface § 64].

274. Émile Zola, preface [1877] to *L'Assommoir* [1872], trans. Leonard Tancock (Harmondsworth: Penguin Books, 1970), pp. 21–22; here p. 21.

275. Peter Szondi, *Theory of the Modern Drama* [1956], trans. Michael Hays (Minneapolis: University of Minnesota Press, 1987), p. 96.

276. Deleuze and Guattari, *A Thousand Plateaus*, p. 356. Actually, the authors are speaking about Kleist, but in this regard "Kleist" and "Nietzsche" are for them virtually convertible terms.

277. Ibid., p. 377.

278. Eve Kosofsky Sedgwick, *Epistemology of the Closet* (Berkeley and Los Angeles: University of California Press, 1990), p. 165.

279. Derrida, "Force et signification" [1963], in *Écriture et différence* (Paris: Éditions du Seuil, 1967), pp. 9–49; here p. 11. For a translation, see *Writing and Difference*, trans. Alan Bass (Chicago: The University of Chicago Press, 1978). In this early essay, Derrida identifies the capacity to "comprehend force from within itself" with "creativity" in order to suggest, first, that literary criticism remains structuralist "in every age, in its essence and destiny," and, second, that philosophy and criticism be reoriented to provide an immanent critique of force.

280. Contrast Frederick Engels, *Ludwig Feuerbach and the End of Classical German Philosophy* [1886] (Peking: Foreign Languages Press, 1976), pp. 40–41, with Althusser's definitive critique in "Contradiction and Overdetermination," in *For Marx*, esp. pp. 93–94.

281. Peter Sloterdijk, *Critique of Cynical Reason* [1983], trans. Michael Eldred, foreword by Andreas Huyssen (Minneapolis: University of Minnesota Press, 1987), p. xxix.

282. For an analysis of the modernist obsession with the human body as prosthetic armoring, as ambivalent response to the inwardness enforced by modernity, and as symptomatic of the death drive, see Hal Foster, *Compulsive Beauty* (Cambridge, Mass., and London: The MIT Press, 1993) and ongoing work.

283. See Max Horkheimer, "Materialism and Morality" [1933], in *Between Philosophy and Social Science: Selected Early Writings*, ed. G. Frederick Hunter, trans. G. Frederick Hunter et al. (Cambridge, Mass., and London: The MIT Press, 1993), pp. 15–47.

284. Nietzsche, *Die fröhliche Wissenschaft* ("*la gaya scienza*") [1st ed. 1882]; *KGW* 5/2:80 [aphorism 38]; emphasis added.

285. Bataille, "Propositions" [1937], *Visions of Excess: Selected Writings, 1927–1939*, ed. with an introduction by Allan Stoekl, trans. Allan Stoekl, with Carl R. Lovitt and Donald M. Leslie Jr. (Minneapolis: University of Minnesota Press, 1985), pp. 197–201; here p. 197. *Œuvres complètes*, 1:467–473; here 467.

286. See J. L. Austin, *How to Do Things with Words* [1962], 2d ed., ed. J. O. Urmson and Marina Sbisà (Cambridge, Mass.: Harvard University Press, 1975), pp. 94–120 and 145–146; see further "Performative Utterances," *Philosophical Papers* [1961], 2d ed., ed. J. O. Urmson and G. J. Warnock (Oxford: Oxford University

Press, 1970), pp. 233–252. According to Austin in *How to Do Things with Words,* it is necessary to distinguish between different types of perlocutionary act or effect — which are *not* conventional, as opposed to illocutionary ones, which are — in terms of whether and how the speaker's or writer's "design, intention, or purpose" is fulfilled or unfulfilled. For instance, the speaker or writer may perform an act "in the nomenclature of which reference is made either . . . only obliquely, or even . . . not at all, to the performance of the locutionary or illocutionary act" (p. 101). And the fact that the object person does not *mention* a term or doctrine does not necessarily mean that s/he is not *using* it or being used *by* it. In other words, the listener or reader may well not be conscious of the full design, intention, or purpose behind a locution, illocution, and perlocution. Interestingly, major critics of Austin as different from one another as John Searle and Derrida have failed to take up fully the rather more sinister implications of Austin's work. Turning to the problem of analyzing this problematic, Austin also noted that with the descriptive or "constative" utterance "we abstract from the illocutionary (let alone the perlocutionary) aspects of the speech act, and we concentrate on the locutionary: moreover, we use an oversimplified notion of correspondence with the facts — over-simplified because essentially it brings in the illocutionary aspect"; whereas, "with the performative utterance, we attend as much as possible to the illocutionary force of the utterance, and abstract from the dimension of correspondence with facts" (pp. 145–146). But this means that the very capacity to distinguish the constative from the performative is relative, contingent, and overdetermined by other factors. And it is particularly difficult if not impossible to distinguish them, when the distinction is always already blurred by design — as it is in exemplary fashion in Nietzsche's discursive practice.

In Brechtian terminology, performatives would count as "social gests": that is, not mere "gesticulations" — though they involve this — but rather condensed ways of "conveying particular attitudes" so that "conclusions can be drawn about the social circumstances." See Brecht, "On Gestic Music" [c. 1934], in *Brecht on Theatre: The Development of an Aesthetic,* ed. and trans. John Willett (New York: Hill and Wang; London: Methuen, 1964), pp. 104–106.

287. Bill Nichols, *Representing Reality: Issues and Concepts in Documentary* (Bloomington and Indianapolis: Indiana University Press, 1991), p. 234.

288. Valery Podoroga, "Evnukh dushi (Pozitsii chteniia i mir Platonova)," *Voprosy filosofii* 3 (1989), 21–26; translated and expanded as "The Eunuch of the Soul: Positions of Reading and the World of Platonov," *South Atlantic Quarterly* 90:2 (Spring 1991), 357–408; here 391–392.

289. Althusser, "From *Capital* to Marx's Philosophy," in *Reading Capital,* p. 46.

290. Colin MacCabe, preface to Jameson, *The Geopolitical Aesthetic,* pp. ix–xvi; here pp. xii–xiii.

291. See Georg Förster, *Machtwille und Machinewelt: Deutung unser Zeit* (Potsdam: Alfred Protte, 1930), p. 67. For Förster, the Nietzschean Superman could be realized under conditions of modernity not in terms of any — effeminate — "self-

referential" thought but only in the—masculinist—"iron world of technology" (p. 78). This techno-Nietzschean problematic had been anticipated internationally, however, by Nietzscheans such as Ernst Jünger, Filippo Marinetti, and Wyndham Lewis, among many others.

292. Nietzsche, "NF, Herbst 1885–Herbst 1886"; *KGW* 8/1:98.

293. Nietzsche, *Jenseits von Gut und Böse: Vorspiel einer Philosophie der Zukunft* [1886]; *KGW* 6/2:92 [part 4, aphorism 108]; ellipsis in original. An apogee in literary criticism of this supposedly "Nietzschean" principle (affirmatively grasped now as a matter of "textual pluralism") was reached in 1970 by Barthes in *S/Z*; see, for example, p. 5, where he appeals explicitly to Nietzsche for his methodology. This was a seminal moment in contemporary literary criticism, for it demonstrated that a text commonly understood as "modernist" could be transformed into what was in effect "postmodern." North American literary-theoretical "deconstruction" also developed, notably in the work of Paul de Man, out of Nietzsche's alleged views of interpretation. While de Manian deconstruction does often appear poised to acknowledge (though it actually does so far too coyly) the darker aspects of Nietzsche's political ideology, sometimes termed the "Dionysian," nonetheless its general drift is to "deconstruct" (i.e., to expose the linguistic mechanisms of the supposedly irreducible, "allegorical" tension in both rigorous philosophical and rigorous literary language between referentiality and figurality, constatation and performance, rhetoric and eloquence, literature and philosophy) this "Dionysian" with the aid of a "rigorously" critical or "Apollinian" moment that either *textually* already "undermines" the former moment or can be *made* to "undermine" it by an act of "reading," as opposed to the more contingent and subsequent act of interpretation. In this system, "allegory" means "repetitive of a potential confusion between figural and referential statement"; it opposes the category "historical," which here means only "revelatory of a teleological meaning." But precisely this deconstructive move— which was to a large extent anticipated by a more or less intentional "misreading" of Nietzsche—ends up leaving the full complexity and efficacy of Nietzsche's politico-rhetorical project of exploitation *remarkably intact,* in the guise of what de Man hyperbolically and obscurantistically dubs an "allegory of errors [that] is the very model of philosophical rigor" (Paul de Man, "Rhetoric of Tropes [Nietzsche]" [1974], in *Allegories of Reading: Figural Language in Rousseau, Nietzsche, Rilke, and Proust* [New Haven and London: Yale University Press, 1979], pp. 103–118; here pp. 116–118). The most consistently interesting development of de Manian "allegory" has been that of Jameson—who, however, follows Walter Benjamin's pathbreaking discussion of allegory rather more closely than he does de Man's, though the latter, too, was influenced by Benjamin in this regard.

294. Nietzsche, "NF, Herbst 1885–Herbst 1886"; *KGW* 8/1:152.

295. For an example of a savvy reader doing just this, see Samuel Weber, *Institutions and Interpretation,* afterword by Wlad Godzich (Minneapolis: University of Minnesota Press, 1987), pp. 4–6.

296. For a major Althusserian-Marxist defense of postdialectical thought in this sense, and of its premodern, Spinozist antecedents, see Pierre Macherey, *Hegel ou Spinoza* (Paris: Presses Universitaires de France, 1979), and *Avec Spinoza: Études sur la doctrine et l'histoire du spinozisme* (Paris: Presses Universitaires de France, 1992); for an alternative Althusserian approach that nonetheless stresses certain dialectical tendencies in Spinoza's political philosophy, see the work of Balibar, including *Spinoza et la politique* (Paris: Presses Universitaires de France, 1985); see further André Tosel, *Spinoza et le crépuscule de la servitude: Essai sur le Traité théologico-politique* (Paris: Auber, 1984). Central to orthodox Marxism, including especially the properly Leninist tradition, is the principle, as expressed by philosophical materialist and textual critic Sebastiano Timpanaro, that "contradictions are described in terms of conflicts between forces, not in terms of the identity of opposites; and the Hegelian 'trichotomies' are regarded as idealist rubbish, 'which it would be absurd to confuse with materialist dialectics'" (Sebastiano Timpanaro, "Karl Korsch and Lenin's Philosophy," in *On Materialism* [1973], trans. Lawrence Garner [London: NLB, 1975], pp. 221–254; here p. 252). Timpanaro cites here from Lenin, "Karl Marx" [1914–1915], in *Collected Works*, 21:43–97. For yet another relevant perspective on the dialectic as real opposition, not synthesis or mere contradiction, see Lucio Colletti, "Marxism and the Dialectic" [1974], trans. John Matthews, *New Left Review* 93 (September–October 1975), 3–29. Alternatively, for a spirited rejection of the notion that Hegelian thought, or German Idealism generally, promotes synthesis in any facile sense, see Žižek, *Tarrying with the Negative*. But the dialectic is certainly to be rejected whenever, as Negri notes, it is "the form in which bourgeois ideology is always presented to us in all its variants—even in those of the purely negative dialectics of crisis and war" (Negri, *The Savage Anomaly*, p. 20).

297. Althusser, "Ideology and Ideological State Apparatuses," in *Lenin and Philosophy*, p. 174. A number of critics have—rightly—pointed out that in general the mechanism of interpellation, first proposed in 1970, is more contradictory and less necessarily debilitating or supportive of a functionalist status quo than Althusser implies; see perhaps most notably Michel Pêcheux, *Language, Semantics and Ideology* [*Les vérités de La Palice*, 1975] (New York: St. Martin's Press, 1982); Göran Therborn, *The Ideology of Power and the Power of Ideology* (London: Verso, 1980); and Žižek, *The Metastases of Enjoyment: Six Essays on Woman and Causality* (London and New York: Verso, 1994), pp. 57–62. This important theoretical debate notwithstanding, however, *Nietzschean* interpellation has remained a remarkably homogeneous historical phenomenon.

298. See Deleuze, *Spinoza: Practical Philosophy*, pp. 92–93; Althusser and Balibar, *Reading Capital*, pp. 16–17, 102–107, and 187–189; Althusser, "Elements of Self-Criticism" [1974], in *Essays in Self-Criticism*, pp. 101–161; here pp. 132–141; and "Is It Simple to Be a Marxist in Philosophy?" in *Philosophy and the Spontaneous Philosophy of the Scientists*, here esp. pp. 216 and 224–228; and Negri, *The Savage Anomaly*, passim. See further Resch, *Althusser and the Renewal of Marxist Social Theory*, pp. 42–

49 and 57–60, and Montag, "Spinoza and Althusser Against Hermeneutics," in *The Althusserian Legacy*. However, in the interests of critiquing excessively Eurocentric modes of thought, it is important to add that Spinozism has no monopoly on the complex view of nature as at once natured and naturing. For example, the important eighteenth-century Japanese philosopher, physician, and social critic, Ando Shoeki (1703–1762), responded to the ways that Taoism and Buddhism were being appropriated to legitimate the feudal state by elaborating a rigorous and intricate idea of nature with ideographs such as *shizen* (roughly: "self-nature") and *gosei* (roughly: "the nature of mutual determination" or "the naturing of interactive processes") on behalf of an explicitly liberatory project. While Ando was well aware of certain trends in Dutch thought, and thus may have been indirectly influenced by Spinozism, it is quite unlikely that he knew Spinoza's work directly. For an edited translation of some of Ando's works with a useful introduction, see Toshinobu Yasunaga, *Ando Shoeki: Social and Ecological Philosopher in Eighteenth-Century Japan* (New York and Tokyo: Weatherhill, 1992). It is unfortunate, however, that today in much Japanese philosophy Ando's work is commonly assimilated not to Spinoza and Althusser but to Heidegger and Nietzsche.

299. Negri, *The Savage Anomaly*, p. 129.

300. Balibar, "The Non-Contemporaneity of Althusser," in *The Althusserian Legacy*, pp. 12–13.

301. Pier Paolo Pasolini, "Un intervento rimandato" [1948], in *Dialogo con Pasolini: Scritti 1957–1984* (Rome: Rinascita, 1985), p. 109.

302. The view of Gramsci presented here is in solidarity with Ahmad's observation that most of his readers today simply refuse "to acknowledge the full import of the fact that Gramsci was a communist militant" (Ahmad, *In Theory: Classes, Nations, Literatures*, p. 218).

303. See again Guattari and Negri, *Communists Like Us*, and — another important document of twenty-first-century thought — *Autonomia: Post-Political Politics*. Contrast the gist of Heidegger's argument in "Die Zeit des Weltbildes" [1938], in *Holzwege*, pp. 73–110, translated as "The Age of the World Picture," in *The Question Concerning Technology: Heidegger's Critique of the Modern Age*.

304. *Selections from the Prison Notebooks of Antonio Gramsci*, p. 405.

305. This remark is meant quasi-ironically. A recent article by two classicists intimates that at least *their* philology and knowledge of Greek is superior to Nietzsche's and to that of the rest of us. See Anton Bierl and William M. Calder III, "Friedrich Nietzsche: 'Abriss der Geschichte der Beredsamkeit'; A New Edition," *Nietzsche-Studien* 21 (1992), 363–389. These authors conclude with "the welcome truth that by November 1872 traditional historical philological scholarship bored Friedrich Nietzsche. *Incipit tragoedia*" (389). Indeed!

306. Cornelius Castoriadis, "Social Transformation and Cultural Creation" [1978], in *Political and Social Writings*, vol. 3: *Recommencing the Revolution: From Socialism to the Autonomous Society*, trans. and ed. David Ames Curtis (Minneapolis

and London: University of Minnesota Press, 1993), pp. 300–313; here p. 305. The former communist Castoriadis is very fond of this turn of phrase, without following his own advice. It also occurs automatically, for example, in "The 'End of Philosophy'" [1986–1990] and "The Crisis of Culture and the State" [1986–1987], both in his *Philosophy, Politics, Autonomy,* ed. David Ames Curtis (New York and Oxford: Oxford University Press, 1991), pp. 13–32 and 219–242, respectively.

307 Althusser, "From *Capital* to Marx's Philosophy," in *Reading Capital,* pp. 15–16; translation modified.

308. Althusser, "Freud and Lacan," in *Lenin and Philosophy,* p. 196.

309. See Derrida, "Text Read at Louis Althusser's Funeral," in *The Althusserian Legacy,* p. 244.

310. See Althusser, *L'avenir dure longtemps* (1985) and also *Les faits* (1976), in *L'avenir dure longtemps* [*suivi de*] *Les faits.* These texts — quite different in tone and both unfinished — were written before and after Althusser fatally strangled his wife Hélène Rytman in 1980. He died in October, 1990.

311. See his *Journal de captivité: Stalag XA 1940–1945, Carnets — Correspondances — Textes,* ed. Olivier Corpet and Yann Moulier Boutang (Paris: Stock/IMEC, 1992; *Édition posthume d'œuvres de Louis Althusser,* vol. 2: *Journal et textes de captivité*).

312. Yann Moulier Boutang, *Louis Althusser: Une biographie,* vol. 1: *La formation du mythe (1918–1956)* (Paris: Bernard Grasset, 1992), p. 213.

313. See Althusser to Lacan, December 10, 1963; "Correspondance avec Jacques Lacan 1963–1969," in his *Écrits sur la psychanalyse: Freud et Lacan,* ed. Oliver Corpet and François Matheron (Paris: Stock/IMEC, 1993; *Édition posthume d'œuvres de Louis Althusser,* vol. 3: *Écrits sur la psychanalyze*), pp. 267–305; here pp. 286–298.

314. See Althusser's letters to Navarro in 1984–1985, in *Sur la philosophie,* esp. pp. 108, 116, and 120.

315. The extensive — more or less post-Lacanian — literature on the Dora case includes Steven Marcus, "Freud and Dora: Story, History, Case History," in *Representations: Essays on Literature and History* (New York: Random House, 1975), pp. 247–310; Suzanne Gearhart, "The Scene of Psychoanalysis: The Unanswered Questions of Dora," *Diacritics* (March 1979), 114–126; Toril Moi, "Representation of Patriarchy: Sexuality and Epistemology in Freud's Dora," *Feminist Review* 9 (Autumn 1981), 60–74; *A Fine Romance: Freud and Dora,* ed. Neil Hertz, special issue of *Diacritics* (Spring 1983); *In Dora's Case: Freud-Hysteria-Feminism,* ed. Charles Bernheimer and Clair Kahane (New York: Columbia University Press, 1985); and Jerry Aline Flieger, "Entertaining the Ménage à Trois: Psychoanalysis, Feminism, and Literature," in *Feminism and Psychoanalysis,* ed. Richard Feldstein and Judith Roof (Ithaca and London: Cornell University Press, 1989), pp. 185–208.

316. Frank J. Sulloway, *Freud, Biologist of the Mind: Beyond the Psychoanalytic Legend* (New York: Basic Books, 1979), pp. 482–483. See further Ernest Jones, *The Life and Work of Sigmund Freud,* 3 vols. (New York: Basic Books and London: Hogarth Press, 1953–1957), vol. 2: *Years of Maturity, 1901–1919,* pp. 152–153; vol. 3:

The Last Phase, 1919–1939, p. 135; and *Free Associations: Memories of a Psycho-Analyst* (New York: Basic Books and London: Hogarth Press, 1959), pp. 227–228.

317. Spinoza, Marx, Lenin, Trotsky, Mao, Gramsci, Althusser, and cyberpunk hackers all work esoterically *to some extent,* but this is necessitated mainly by practical constraints and cautions.

318. "To live in a glass house is a revolutionary virtue par excellence. It is also an intoxication, a moral exhibitionism that we badly need. Discretion concerning one's own existence, once an aristocratic virtue, has become more and more an affair of petit-bourgeois parvenus" (Benjamin, "Surrealism" [1929], in *Reflections,* pp. 177–192; here p. 180). Benjamin was inspired by an experience in Moscow: at a hotel, Tibetan lamas, who had come to discuss the relation of religion and the revolution, habitually left their doors open. This vision of a completely transparent, and self-transparent, society was explicitly anticipated by Rousseau.

319. Miller, "Social and Political Theory: Class, State, Revolution," in *The Cambridge Companion to Marx,* ed. Terrell Carver (Cambridge: Cambridge University Press, 1991), pp. 54–105; here p. 75.

320. See, for example, Gramsci, *Selections from Cultural Writings,* p. 126, especially the section of the prison notebooks with the heading "Father Bresciani's Progeny" (pp. 301–341) where Gramsci is particularly keen to reject the novelist Antonio Bresciani's presentation of the Revolution of 1848 as having been, in the words of Gramsci's editors, "entirely the work of fanatical conspirators and secret societies, while at the same time expropriating revolutionary language to the cause of reaction" (p. 298).

321. Jameson, *The Geopolitical Aesthetic,* pp. 9 and 22.

322. On attempts — beginning already at the end of the nineteenth century and lasting until now — of the political "Left" in Germany to synthesize Marx and Nietzsche, indeed to replace the former with the latter, see Aschheim, *The Nietzsche Legacy in Germany,* ch. 6: "Nietzschean Socialism: Left and Right," esp. pp. 164–192.

323. The influence of Nietzsche on Freud has long been a topic of discussion and conjecture. See, for example, Ronald Lehrer, *Nietzsche's Presence in Freud's Life and Thought: On the Origins of a Psychology of Dynamic Unconscious Mental Functioning* (Albany: State University of New York Press, 1995). The best general framework may have been provided by Timpanaro, however, although even he concedes too much to Nietzsche. He argues that psychoanalysis is irrevocably informed by an internal, core contradiction: namely, as "a doctrine that never entirely abandoned certain materialist principles, *and* a metaphysical and even mythological construction." In this respect, Timpanaro continues:

It is no accident that he [Freud] was to acknowledge Nietzsche and later Schopenhauer as the thinkers who were most akin to him, his "precursors" — even if he always scrupulously insisted that he had arrived at conclusions similar to theirs before he had read their works, and by purely scientific means. For its part, the literature of European decadence could scarcely have found so much inspiration in psychoanalysis, if this had really been a doctrine of materialist enlightenment. Students of Freud, especially those who — with the best intentions — have argued for the materialist and enlightened nature of his work, do not seem to have paid sufficient attention to this paradox. It is certainly true that if we liberate the genuine Nietzsche from ultra-irrationalist and even pre-fascist interpretations of his work, we find a potent critic — even if an "internal" critic — of the hypocrisy and false moralism of the bourgeois Christian ethic; and in his vitalism there are undoubtedly materialist and hedonistic elements. But the aphoristic and contradictory character of Nietzsche's thought is such that it can instill materialism only in someone who has already become a materialist by another route (and not merely by pragmatic adaptation in a particular discipline). Certain of Nietzsche's professions are also genuinely enlightened . . . [Timpanaro is thinking of aphorism 197 in *Day Break*]. But this is an enlightenment that is nearly entirely consumed in a polemic against a certain type of romanticism, and therewith remains within the limits of an exasperated aristocratism. In the case of Schopenhauer — whose influence is in any case essentially restricted to Freud's late work — there is no need even for the niceties of distinction that Nietzsche allows us to make. (Timpanaro, *The Freudian Slip: Psychoanalysis and Textual Criticism* [1974], trans. Kate Soper [London: NLB, 1976], pp. 184–186)

Nietzsche himself was neither "ultra-irrationalist" nor "prefascist," as these terms are commonly understood, but tendencies at least as sinister are absolutely fundamental both to his thought and to his influence — neither of which, in any event, is as "distinct" from the other as Timpanaro implies.

324. *Minutes of the Vienna Psychoanalytic Society,* ed. Herman Nunberg and Ernst Federn, trans. M. Nunberg (New York: International Universities Press, Inc., 1962), I (1906–1908):358 [April 1, 1908].

325. Eagleton, *Ideology: An Introduction* (London and New York: Verso, 1991), p. 126.

326. *Uccellacci e uccellini* (Pier Paolo Pasolini, Italy, 1966). This film is one of the major statements (by a rare non- or anti-Nietzschean) about "the death of ideology," "the death of communism," and other deaths as well. The Crow's last words before his death: "Once upon a time, there was the beautiful color red. . . . Oh, middle class, you've identified the whole world with yourself. This identification means the end of the world; but the end of the world will also be your end." See also Pasolini's filmbook *Uccellacci e uccellini* (Milan: Garzanti, 1966), p. 59. Here, he wrote of Totò and Ninetto: "They perform an act of cannibalism, called communion by Catholics: namely, they swallow the body of Togliatti (or of Marxists) and incorporate it; after they incorporate it, they carry it on down the road, so that even though you don't know where the road is going, it's obvious that they have incorporated Marxism." The Crow is an allegorical figure not only for "Left-wing intellectuals in the era before Togliatti's death," for Palmiro Togliatti (the then recently

deceased leader of the Italian Communist Party and comrade of Gramsci) and for Marxism *tout court* but also, according to Pasolini, an allegory for himself and other First-World left-bourgeois intellectuals like him, at the time, as the film puts it, when "it is the sunset of great hopes, the age of Brecht and [Roberto] Rossellini is over, while the workers advance in the sunset." Nonetheless, Pasolini also described the film as having been made "by a Marxist, from the inside, totally unwilling to believe that Marxism is ended." Finally, the Crow says: "Don't weep for the end of what I believe in, because surely someone else will come to take up the red banner, carrying it forwards; I weep only for myself." See further Marc Gervais, *Pier Paolo Pasolini* (Paris: Seghers, 1975), pp. 142–143; Barth David Schwartz, *Pasolini Requiem* (New York: Pantheon Books, 1992), pp. 483–491; and Viano, *A Certain Realism*, pp. 146–160.

327. Pasolini as cited in Viano, *A Certain Realism*, p. 17.

328. Pasolini, "Perchè quella di Edipo è una storia," introduction to the filmbook of his *Edipo re* (Milan: Garzanti, 1967), p. 14.

329. Viano's *A Certain Realism* is a good book about Pasolini but is wholly mistaken both in its depiction of Nietzsche and hence in its attempt to bring a Nietzschean perspective to bear on the filmmaker and poet.

330. In addition to the writings of Walter Benjamin and Ernst Bloch (both of whom remained rather more ambivalent about Nietzsche than others associated with critical theory), see most notably Horkheimer and Adorno, *Dialectic of Enlightenment* [written 1944, published 1947], and Herbert Marcuse's many works, beginning with *Eros and Civilization: A Philosophical Inquiry into Freud* [delivered as lectures 1950–1951, published 1955], 2d ed. (New York: Vintage Books, 1961). Particularly Left-Nietzschoid is Marcuse's *An Essay on Liberation* (Boston: Beacon Press, 1969). This ideological drift is particularly unfortunate because in this text Marcuse, more perhaps than any other member or associate of the Frankfurt School, began to grasp power as an eso/exoteric problematic. He follows Freud to argue that the "power of society in shaping the whole experience, the whole metabolism between the organism and its environment," ought not to be reduced to ideology — the reason being that the proper site of ideology is beneath the threshold of consciousness and in "patterns of behavior" (p. 11). In other words, social power can be esoteric, though Marcuse failed to read his philosophical mentor Nietzsche accordingly. Already of Nietzschean inspiration, however, was the underlying concept behind the seminal *Dialectic of Enlightenment*, as Horkheimer's drafts and contributions make particularly clear. For two different takes on the extensive, basically affirmative and uncritical Frankfurt School appropriation of Nietzsche, see Reinhart Mauer, "Nietzsche und die kritische Theorie," *Nietzsche-Studien* 10/11 (1981–1982), 34–58 (followed by a discussion, 59–79); and José Guilherme Merquior, *Western Marxism* (London: Paladin, 1986). Whereas Merquior critiques Western Marxism and the Frankfurt School specifically after having reduced it to Nietzscheanism (which he dislikes), Mauer argues that the Frankfurt School did not under-

stand Nietzsche (whom he likes) at his ostensibly most radically demystifying root because its own lingering traces of positive, affirmative dialectic would have thereby been exposed and called on the carpet.

331. See Paul Ricoeur, *Freud and Philosophy: An Essay on Interpretation* [The Terry Lectures, Yale University, 1961], trans. Denis Savage (New Haven and London: Yale University Press, 1970), pp. 20–36 (ch. 2: "The Conflict of Interpretations"). Later Ricoeur proposed, in the same basic vein but more interestingly, that "Heideggerian deconstruction must now take on Nietzschean genealogy, Freudian psychoanalysis, the Marxist critique of ideology, that is, the weapons of the hermeneutics of suspicion. Armed in this way, the critique is capable of unmasking the *unthought* conjunction of *hidden* metaphysics and *worn-out* metaphor" (Ricoeur, *The Rule of Metaphor: Multi-Disciplinary Studies of the Creation of Meaning in Language* [1975], trans. Robert Czerny, with Kathleen McLaughlin and John Costello, S.J. [Toronto and Buffalo: University of Toronto Press, 1977], p. 285). The typical problem with all such Ricoeurian formulations, however, is that they ignore the possibility that thinkers — such as Nietzsche and Heidegger — consciously concealed their full intentions in their "metaphors" so as to have maximum subconscious effect. Be this as it may, Peter Dews has rightly noted in a different context that "the force of the thought of Marx, Freud and Nietzsche can scarcely be sidestepped by the elementary move of pointing out the self-undermining character of the determinism supposedly implied by the 'hermeneutics of suspicion,' by countering genealogy with simple asseverations of the autonomy of textual meaning . . . " (Dews, *Logics of Disintegration: Post-structuralist Thought and the Claims of Critical Theory* [London and New York: Verso, 1987], p. xiv). Actually, Dews is complaining less about Ricoeur directly than about a derivative thesis of Renaut and Ferry in *La pensée 68.*

332. Hans-Georg Gadamer, "The Philosophical Foundations of the Twentieth Century" [1962], in *Philosophical Hermeneutics,* trans. and ed. by David E. Linge (Berkeley, Los Angeles, London: University of California Press, 1976), pp. 107–129; here p. 116.

333. Far more fruitful — potentially — is Gadamer's claim that interpretation after Marx, Nietzsche, and Freud involves what he calls *hintergehen,* which (as the translator points out) does not merely denote "to go behind" something (including so as to get at a deeper level "behind the surface of what is meant," "behind the subjectivity of the act of meaning," as Gadamer puts it) but also connotes "to deceive" and "to double cross." See Gadamer, "The Philosophical Foundations of the Twentieth Century," in *Philosophical Hermeneutics,* p. 117. However, the fundamental problem in the case of Nietzsche — to an extent untrue of Freud and Marx — is that the principle of *hintergehen* was consciously and successfully employed as a technique of — esoteric — textual *production,* and not merely of — exoteric — textual interpretation as is assumed by consumption-oriented philosophical hermeneutics *and* by its various rivals in the current intellectual marketplace.

334. See Deleuze, *Nietzsche et la philosophie* (Paris: Presses Universitaires de France, 1962), esp. pp. 169–189. For the too tardy translation of this seminal book, see *Nietzsche and Philosophy,* trans. Hugh Tomlinson (New York: Columbia University Press, 1983).

335. There are severe problems with Deleuze's basic thesis, and with *Nietzsche et la philosophie* generally, for grasping Nietzsche/anism. A recent commentator on Deleuze's early work has unwittingly implied that it lacks any notion of the exo/esoteric distinction. In direct opposition to Heidegger, for example, Deleuze "limits us to a strictly immanent and materialist ontological discourse that refuses any deep or hidden foundation of being. There is nothing veiled or negative about Deleuze's being; it is fully expressed in the world. Being, in this sense, is superficial, positive, and full" (Hardt, *Gilles Deleuze,* p. xiii). While this (neo-Spinozist) approach to ontology may well make for good philosophy and politics of its own kind, it can lead only to a superficial grasp of Heidegger and of Nietzsche; and (*pace* Hardt and Deleuze himself) it is "Nietzschean" in name only, only exoterically.

336. See Dews, *Logics of Disintegration,* p. 2. As he acknowledges, Dews is here following an argument advanced already in 1969 by Paolo Caruso, *Conversazioni con Claude Lévi-Strauss, Michel Foucault, Jacques Lacan* (Milan: U. Mursia, 1969), p. 117.

337. Dews's book is one of the first major attempts from a leftist perspective to articulate German critical theory and French poststructuralism. It can also be read as a tacit but sustained confrontation with Nietzscheanism. See Dews, *Logics of Disintegration,* esp. pp. 157–177 and 197–219. Unfortunately, however, Dews himself breaks no new ground on the latter front, in part because he appears not to know Nietzsche's own work independently of the Nietzschean thinkers he wishes to critique. Thus the "dilemma" Dews finds "at the heart of Nietzsche's thought" (p. 179), and which resurfaces as "the fundamental inconsistency" of "Nietzschean pluralism" (p. 218), represents a superficial, exoteric epistemological problem that is removable (and removable only) by settling accounts with the more esoteric, rhetorical, and political dimension of Nietzsche's intent.

338. See Jean Hyppolite, "The Structure of Philosophic Language According to the 'Preface' to Hegel's *Phenomenology of Mind* " [1966], in *The Structuralist Controversy: The Languages of Criticism and the Science of Man,* ed. Richard Macksey and Eugenio Donato (Baltimore and London: The Johns Hopkins University Press, 1972), pp. 157–169; here p. 157.

339. De Man, "Temporality in Hölderlin's 'Wie wenn am Feiertage . . .'" [Gauss Lecture, Princeton University, 1967; announced as "The Problem of Aesthetic Totality in Hölderlin"], in *Romanticism and Contemporary Criticism: The Gauss Seminars and Other Papers,* ed. E. S. Burt, Kevin Newmark, and Andrzej Warminski (Baltimore and London: The Johns Hopkins University Press, 1993), pp. 50–73; here p. 51. This essay is representative of what is most valuable in de Manian deconstruction.

340. Michel Foucault, "Structuralism and Post-Structuralism" [interview with

Gerard Raulet, 1983], trans. Jeremy Harding, *Telos* 55 (Spring 1983), 195–211; here 199. Foucault was first deeply impressed by Nietzsche in 1953, having discovered the *Untimely Meditations* while on vacation in Italy, though "like any good *normalien* he had in fact read Nietzsche years before" (James Miller, *The Passion of Michel Foucault* (New York: Simon & Schuster, 1993), pp. 66–67). This was a turning point in Foucault's life.

341. See Foucault, "Nietzsche, Freud, Marx," in *Nietzsche* [Colloque Philosophique International de Royaumont, July 4–8, 1964] (Paris: Les éditions de minuit, 1967), pp. 183–192 (followed by a discussion, pp. 193–200). See further *The Order of Things: An Archaeology of the Human Sciences* [*Les mots et les choses*, 1966], trans. anon. (New York: Random House, 1970), where Foucault writes: "The first book of *Das Kapital* is an exegesis of 'value'; all Nietzsche is an exegesis of a few Greek words; Freud, the exegesis of all those unspoken phrases that support and at the same time undermine our apparent discourse, our fantasies, our dreams, our bodies. Philology, as the analysis of what is said in the depths of discourse, has become the modern form of criticism" (p. 298); and *The Archaeology of Knowledge* [1969], in his *The Archaeology of Knowledge & The Discourse on Language*, trans. A. M. Sheridan Smith (New York: Harper Colophon Books, 1976), where Foucault speaks of the work of Marx, Freud, and Nietzsche as the three major modern "decenterings" of the subject (pp. 13–14). For a too uncritical account of Foucault's Nietzscheanism, see Michael Mahon, *Foucault's Nietzschean Genealogy: Truth, Power, and the Subject: 1961–1975* (Albany: State University of New York Press, 1992). And for an important — unfortunately not very influential — attempt by one of Althusser's students to rescue the early Foucault, himself a student of Althusser, from his Nietzschean tendencies, see Dominique Lecourt, *Marxism and Epistemology: Bachelard, Canguilhem and Foucault* [1969–1972], trans. Ben Brewster (London: NLB, 1975), pp. 187–213.

342. Foucault, "Politics and Ethics: An Interview" [with Paul Rabinow, Charles Taylor, Martin Jay, Richard Rorty, and Leo Lowenthal, 1983], trans. Catherine Porter, in *The Foucault Reader*, ed. Paul Rabinow (New York: Pantheon Books, 1984), pp. 373–380; here p. 374.

343. Jürgen Habermas, *Knowledge and Human Interests* [1968], trans. Jeremy J. Shapiro (Boston: Beacon Press, 1971), p. 299; see further esp. chs. 2 (Marx), 10 (Freud), and 12 (Nietzsche). Habermas's overall project may be viewed as the tripartite attempt to establish the authority of self-critical Reason as philosophically and socially prior to the epistemological skepticism, and consequent ideological irrationalism (1) of Nietzsche himself, as exemplary post-Enlightenment thinker; (2) of French postmodern Nietzscheanism; and (3) of powerful Nietzschean tendencies of the Frankfurt School. See Habermas, "The Entwinement of Myth and Enlightenment: Re-Reading *Dialectic of Enlightenment*," *New German Critique* 26 (Spring–Summer 1982), 13–30, and *The Philosophical Discourse of Modernity: Twelve Lectures* [1985], trans. Frederick Lawrence (Cambridge, Mass.: The MIT Press,

1987). Like all of critical theory, however, Habermas has never grasped Nietzsche except thematically and exoterically, never in terms of illocutionary "cause" and perlocutionary "effect."

344. This is the philosophical, methodological, historiographical, and ideological *core* of Sloterdijk's *Critique of Cynical Reason;* see pp. 195–213.

345. Habermas, "Zu Nietzsches Erkenntnistheorie (ein Nachwort)" [1968], in *Kultur und Kritik: Verstreute Aufsätze* (Frankfurt am Main: Suhrkamp Verlag, 1973), pp. 239–263.

346. Habermas, "Conservative Politics, Work, Socialism and Utopia Today" [interview with Hans-Ulrich Reck, 1983], trans. Peter Dews, in *Autonomy and Solidarity: Interviews,* ed. with an introduction by Peter Dews (London: Verso, 1986), pp. 131–147; here p. 132.

347. See André Glucksmann, *The Master Thinkers* [1977], trans. Brian Pearce (New York: Harper & Row, Publishers, 1980), esp. pp. 207–236 (Marx), 237–263 (Nietzsche), and the brief nods to Freud on 167 and 259.

348. See Bernard-Henri Lévy, *Barbarism with a Human Face* [1977], trans. George Holoch (New York: Harper & Row, Publishers, 1979).

349. See Hans Küng, *Does God Exist?: An Answer for Today* [1978], trans. Edward Quinn (New York: Doubleday & Company, Inc., 1980), pp. 217–261 (Marx), 262–339 (Freud), and 341–424 (Nietzsche). Küng uses the nexus to define the agenda of Catholic metaphysics, ontology, and theology in the following manner: "If today 'metaphysics' is understood as a human 'projection' (Feuerbach), an ideological 'superstructure' (Marx), an ideal 'afterworld' (Nietzsche), an unreal 'wishful world' (Freud), or even if 'metaphysics' is understood simply as 'true reality' in the sense of Plato's world of ideas, set apart from present reality, all of which must be at the expense of this reality of ours, then we are not pursuing metaphysics. If, however, 'metaphysics' means that the purely empirical cannot be sustained from its own resources and must be surpassed in an approach to a meta-empirical that does not lie behind, beyond, above, outside this reality, but — so to speak — constitutes the inner aspect of present reality, then we are pursuing 'metaphysics' or — a word that may be preferred in order to avoid misunderstanding — *ontology* ('theory of being'). What is important is to understand the thing properly; we need not trouble about the word" (pp. 550–551).

350. Cf. J. P. Stern, *Friedrich Nietzsche* [1978] (Harmondsworth: Penguin Books, 1979), pp. 17–32 (ch. 1: "Nietzsche in Company").

351. Callinicos, "What Is Living and What Is Dead in the Philosophy of Althusser," in *The Althusserian Legacy,* p. 41.

352. Edward W. Said, *Culture and Imperialism* (New York: Alfred A. Knopf, 1993), p. 269.

353. See Ahmad, *In Theory: Classes, Nations, Literatures,* esp. ch. 5: "*Orientalism* and After: Ambivalence and Metropolitan Location in the Work of Edward Said."

354. For the most recent book on the nexus along these lines see Jeremy Barris,

God and Plastic Surgery: Marx, Nietzsche, Freud and the Obvious, a Book (New York: Autonomedia, 1990).

355. For this argument see Balibar, "On the Basic Concepts of Historical Materialism," in *Reading Capital,* esp. pp. 201–208.

356. Also reproduced in *Mark Tansey: Visions and Revisions,* with an introductory essay by Arthur C. Danto, notes and comments by Mark Tansey, ed. Christopher Sweet (New York: Harry N. Abrams, Inc., 1992), p. 98.

357. Arthur C. Danto, "Mark Tansey: The Picture Within the Picture," in *Mark Tansey: Visions and Revisions,* pp. 7–29; here p. 15.

358. Mark Tansey, "Notes and Comments" [interview with Christopher Sweet, 1991], in *Mark Tansey: Visions and Revisions,* pp. 127–135; here p. 127.

359. Baudrillard, *Cool Memories 1980–1985* (Paris: Éditions Galilée, 1987), p. 278.

360. Actually, Baudrillard's own point is rather different. In one of several more nihilist moods in *Cool Memories,* he is intent to distinguish "the Nietzschean, Marxo-Freudian Age" as a *past* historical period: namely, as part of an age of "hard ideologies and radical philosophies," as opposed to our *current* "soft" and "spoilt" age, which is characterized by "altruism, conviviality, international charity, and the individual bleeding heart," by "emotional outpourings, solidarity, cosmopolitan emotiveness, and multi-media pathos" — all of which, Baudrillard claims, was "harshly condemned by the Nietzschean, Marxo-Freudian age." The point here is that Nietzsche, at least, was prepared to go either way: toward the "hard" or the "soft" as history demands. And thus it is also that we still have Nietzscheans who are "soft" and ones who are "hard," as Baudrillard believes himself to be, and no longer Freudian or Marxist. Not fortuitously in this regard, Tansey has grouped Baudrillard with Barthes and Derrida in his extraordinary revision of Paul Cézanne's *Mont Sainte-Victoire* (1987); Derrida and Barthes then reappear grouped with Lacan and Jean-François Lyotard in another update of Cézanne's *The Bathers* (1989). See *Mark Tansey: Visions and Revisions,* pp. 86–87 and 91, respectively.

361. See Steven Best and Douglas Kellner, *Postmodern Theory: Critical Investigations* (New York: The Guilford Press, 1991), pp. 126–128. Exemplary of this axial "turn" in Baudrillard's thought is his essay "On Nihilism" [1980], *On the Beach* 6 (Spring 1984), 38–39.

362. Ian Forbes, "Marx and Nietzsche: The Individual in History," in *Nietzsche and Modern German Thought,* ed. Keith Ansell-Pearson (London and New York: Routledge, 1991), pp. 143–164; here p. 163.

363. For his great early period, see Wilhelm Reich, *SEX-POL: Essays, 1929–1934,* ed. Lee Baxandall, introduction by Bertell Ollman, trans. Anna Bostock et al. (New York: Random House, 1966).

364. Ronald Bogue, *Deleuze and Guattari* (London and New York: Routledge, 1989), p. 83. See further Deleuze and Guattari, *Capitalism and Schizophrenia,* vol. 1: *Anti-Oedipus* [1972], trans. Robert Hurley, Mark Seem, and Helen R. Lane (New York: The Viking Press, 1977).

365. Derrida, "Structure, Sign and Play in the Discourse of the Human Sciences" [1966], in *Writing and Difference*, pp. 278–293; here p. 292.

366. See Derrida, "White Metaphor: Metaphor in the Text of Philosophy" [1971] and "Qual Quelle: Valéry's Sources" [1971], both in *Margins of Philosophy* [1972], trans. with additional notes by Alan Bass (Chicago: The University of Chicago Press, 1982), pp. 207–271 and 273–306, respectively. One of his more "Nietzschean" accounts of Freud is "Speculations — On Freud," trans. Ian McLeod, *Oxford Literary Review* 3:2 (1978), 78–97. Derrida's two monographs on Nietzsche focus on "the question of style" and on "otobiography" and date from 1972 and 1982, respectively.

367. For Derrida's extended reflection on Marx as "specter" (playing on the double translation of German *Geist* into French: *esprit* and *fantôme*), by way of a forceful comparison with the ghost in Shakespeare's *Hamlet*, see again *Spectres de Marx*.

368. Žižek, *Looking Awry*, pp. 141–142. It is important to add, however, that Žižek's remark occurs in the context of a quite valid criticism of Habermas's attempt to distinguish modernity from postmodernity.

369. For a typical example of how deeply Nietzschean political philosophy — alongside its great progeny, Heideggerian political ontology — has penetrated into contemporary cultural studies, "even" of a supposedly "leftist" stamp, see Iain Chambers, *Migrancy, Culture, Identity* (London and New York: Routledge, 1994), or Paul Gilroy, *The Black Atlantic: Modernity and Double Consciousness* (Cambridge, Mass.: Harvard University Press, 1993). This is not to say that the specific analyses in these books are necessarily invalid, only that all uncritical, direct and indirect, appeals to Nietzsche and to Heidegger must be ruthlessly scrutinized. For instance, many of the worst theoretical and analytic excesses in the recent work of Homi K. Bhabha appear to be underwritten by Nietzsche. If the question of intention remains relevant, particularly illicit is the use of Heidegger and Nietzsche to serve as the philosophical base of radically liberatory projects. The latter may not *need* a philosophical base, but *if* they do appeal to one, it ought not to be Nietzsche or Heidegger, unless their exo/esoteric problematic were acknowledged. To date, cultural studies must be defined as "junk culture without philosophy."

370. Laclau, *New Reflections on the Revolution of Our Time*, pp. 32–33. Laclau provides this important illustration: "The word 'man' differentiates the latter from 'woman' but is also shared with 'human being' which is the condition shared by both men and women. What is peculiar to the second term is thus reduced to the function of accident, as opposed to the essentiality of the first."

371. Burroughs, *Cities of the Red Night*, p. 114.

372. Karl von Clausewitz as cited in Guy Debord's autobiography *Panegyric*, vol. 1 [1989], trans. James Brook (London and New York: Verso, 1991), p. 3.

373. Sun Tzu, *The Art of War* [c. 400 B.C.E.], trans. Thomas Cleary (Boston and London: Shambhala Publications, 1988), p. 172.

374. Lenin, *Materialism and Empirio-Criticism* [1908], in *Collected Works*, 14:343; emphasis altered. This book can be read as an indirect attack on "Nietzschean" ideas, as will be seen later.

375. For an introduction to the philosophical and political similarities and differences between the perspectives of Leninism, Gramscianism, Althusserianism, *operaismo*, and *movimento autonomo*, all of which are properly critical of Western Marxism and the Frankfurt School, see Yann Moulier, introduction, trans. Philippa Hurd, to Negri, *The Politics of Subversion: A Manifesto for the Twenty-First Century*, trans. James Newell (Oxford and Cambridge, Mass.: Polity Press/Basil Blackwell, 1989), pp. 1–44.

376. We can only build communism out of the material created by capitalism, out of that refined apparatus which has been molded under bourgeois conditions which — as far as concerns the human material in the apparatus — is therefore inevitably imbued with the bourgeois mentality. That is what makes the building of communist society difficult, but it is also a guarantee that it can and will be built. In fact, what distinguishes Marxism from the old, utopian socialism is that the latter wanted to build the new society not from the human material produced by bloodstained, sordid, rapacious, shopkeeping capitalism, but from very virtuous men and women reared in special hothouses and cucumber frames. Everyone now sees that this absurd idea really is absurd and everyone has discarded it, but not everyone is willing or able to give thought to the opposite doctrine of Marxism and to think out how communism can (and should) be built from the mass of human material which has been corrupted by hundreds and thousands of years of slavery, serfdom, capitalism, by small individual enterprise, and by the war of every man against his neighbor to obtain a place in the market, or a higher price for his product of his labor (Lenin, "A Little Picture in Illustration of Big Problems" [1918–1919, published 1926 in *Pravda*], in *Collected Works*, 28:386–389; here 388)

On respect for traditions of thought rivaling Marxism and the need to study them carefully, see especially one of Lenin's last philosophical testaments, "On the Significance of Militant Materialism" [1922], in *Collected Works*, 33:227–236.

377. Aschheim, *The Nietzsche Legacy in Germany*, p. 192.

378. "Capitalism will *never* be completely and *exhaustively* studied in *all* the manifestations of its predatory nature, and in all the most minute ramifications of its historical development and national features. Scholars (and especially the pedants) will never stop arguing over details. It would be ridiculous to give up the socialist struggle against capitalism and to desist from opposing, on such grounds, those who have betrayed that struggle" (Lenin, "The Collapse of the Second International" [1915], in *Collected Works*, 21:205–259; here 212).

379. Althusser, *Les faits*, in *L'avenir dure longtemps* [*suivi de*] *Les faits*, p. 313.

380. Althusser to Fernanda Navarro, July 30, 1984, in *Sur la philosophie*, pp. 107–109; here p. 109.

NOTES TO PAGES 116–117

381. Front 242 (Daniel B and P. Codenys), "The Rhythm of Time," *Tyranny for You,* © 1991 Epic/Sony Music Entertainment Inc., ET 46998.

382. Will Friedwald [jacket note], *Cab Calloway: Best of the Big Bands,* © 1990 CBS Records, Inc., CT 45336.

383. Adorno, *Aesthetische Theorie* [1969], ed. Gretel Adorno and Rolf Tiedemann (Frankfurt am Main: Suhrkamp Verlag, 1970), p. 273.

384. René Viénet, *Enragés et situationnistes dans le mouvement des occupations* (Paris: Gallimard, 1968), p. 17; emphasis altered.

385. Karl Ferdinand Gutzkow; as cited in *Wörterbuch der deutschen Sprache,* ed. Daniel Sanders, 3 vols. (Leipzig: Otto Wigand, 1860), 1:729; and as discussed by Sigmund Freud, "The 'Uncanny'" [1919], *Art and Literature,* ed. Albert Dickson (Harmondsworth: Penguin Books, 1985; The Pelican Freud Library, vol. 14), pp. 335–376. Also Anthony Vidler, *The Architectural Uncanny: Essays in the Modern Unhomely* (Cambridge, Mass., and London: The MIT Press, 1992), pp. 17–44.

386. Friedrich Wilhelm Joseph Schelling; as cited in *Wörterbuch der deutschen Sprache,* 1:729; emphasis added. On the centrality for Freud of Schelling's phrase, though still not on its most canny political implications in terms of the exo/esoteric distinction, see further Cixous, "Fiction and Its Phantoms: A Reading of Freud's *Das Unheimliche,*" *New Literary History* 7 (Spring 1976), 525–548; and Vidler, *The Architectural Uncanny,* p. 26.

387. Early on, the Situationist International described its project as the "embodiment" of "the supersession of both the Bolshevik Central Committee (supersession of the mass party) and of the Nietzschean project (supersession of the intelligentsia)" (Raoul Vaneigem, "Basic Banalities [II]" [1962], in *Situationist International Anthology,* ed. and trans. Ken Knabb [Berkeley: Bureau of Public Secrets, 1981], pp. 118–133; here p. 132).

388. Nietzsche, *Ecce homo; KGW* 6/3:363 ["Why I Am a Destiny," 1].

389. Raymond Williams, *Marxism and Literature* (Oxford: Oxford University Press, 1977), p. 110.

390. Partly as backlash against the active repression and passive repression of Nietzscheanism in the former German Democratic Republic, since 1989 Nietzsche and the Nietzsche Archive have quickly returned as key players in cultural politics in Eastern and united Germany — as they had been before 1945. The so-called Stiftung Weimarer Klassik (the Weimar Classicism Foundation) runs the Nietzsche Museum and publishes books related to Nietzsche (e.g., *Für F. N.: Nietzsche in der bildenden Kunst der letzten dreißig Jahre*). The foundation also offered an elaborate three-year program on Nietzsche, predictably entitled "Entdecken & Verraten" (discovery and betrayal). In addition to periodic celebrations (e.g., Nietzsche's 150th birthday on October 15, 1994) and various "workshops," this program included an interwoven series of fifteen major events: "Students in Conversation about Friedrich Nietzsche" (held on seven occasions from February 1994 to October 1995); "From Röcken to Basel: How One Does Not Become What One Is Not"

(October 15–17, 1993); "Untimely Bayreuth: Beyond Schopenhauer and Wagner" (February 18–20, 1994); "Late Enlightenment: Nietzsche's Free Spiritualism" (May 20–22, 1994); "Zarathustra's Utopian Missive" (September 23–25, 1994); "Nietzsche in the Cosmopolis: The French Nietzsche" (December 9–11, 1994); "The Eternal Recurrence" (March 17–19, 1995); "The Will to Power" (June 16–18, 1995); and "Nietzsche's Arrival in Weimar" (October 20–22, 1995). More to come. The sessions and collateral events go from morning to night. Speakers are almost invariably from Germany or Austria and Switzerland. The standard conference fee is 50 DM, which does not include excursions, musical events, meals, housing; this fee is halved to 25 DM for "students, unemployed, and those in the military and civil service."

391. For a criticism of this book, before the fact, for its Eurocentric bias, see Ahmad, *In Theory: Classes, Nations, Literatures*. However, Ahmad is simply wrong to depict as "Nietzschean" the "idea that no true representation is possible because all human communications always distort the facts" (p. 193). This is true at most of Nietzsche's exoteric epistemological stance and not true at all of his deeper political and rhetorical position. Nietzsche's way of communicating leaves esoteric facts to do their work unmolested.

392. Davis, *City of Quartz*, p. 310. For the already classic analysis of terms such as "flexible accumulation" to articulate political economy and cultural production, and as a way of criticizing the understanding of postmodernism as representing a radical break with Fordist modernism, see David Harvey, *The Condition of Postmodernity: An Inquiry into the Origins of Cultural Change* (Oxford: Basil Blackwell, 1989).

393. U2 (Bono, The Edge, Adam Clayton, Larry Mullen Jr.), "Hawkmoon," *Rattle and Hum*, © 1988 Island Records, Ltd., 422–842–299–4.

394. Both have occurred quite literally in Nietzsche's case. For a relatively recent "psychological" attempt to equate Nietzscheanism with Satanism, see Samuel J. Warner, *The Urge to Mass Destruction* (New York and London: Grune and Stratton, 1957). This is an old current in the reception of his work, however, which became especially prominent during World War I, when Nietzsche was canonized in Germany, demonized by the Allies, and again thereafter. See Aschheim, *The Nietzsche Legacy in Germany*, pp. 134–136 and 299–300. The immediate postwar moment in Nietzsche's reception as demonization was represented not only by Thomas Mann's well-known *Doktor Faustus* (1947) but by various today unknown self-described "Christian" commentators as well as by Friedrich Meinecke in *The German Catastrophe: Reflections and Recollections* [1946], trans. Sidney B. Fay (Boston: Beacon Press, 1963), where the alleged covenant between Nietzsche and Nazism was explicitly called "demonic" (p. 24).

395. Robert G. L. Waite, *The Psychopathic God: Adolf Hitler* [1977] (New York: Da Capo Press, 1993), p. xvii.

396. "Information wants to be free" is "the Hacker's Ethic." See Steven Levy, *Hackers* (New York: Doubleday & Co., Inc., 1984), pp. 39–49.

397. See Foucault, "Final Interview" [with Gilles Barbedette and André Scala, 1984], trans. Thomas Levin and Isabelle Lorenz, *Raritan* 5:1 (Summer 1985), 1–13; here 9.

398. Ernesto Che Guevara, *Guerrilla Warfare* [1960], authorized trans. J. P. Morray, with an introduction and case studies by Brian Loveman and Thomas M. Davies Jr. (Lincoln and London: The University of Nebraska Press, 1985), p. 69.

399. Deleuze, "Letter to a Harsh Critic" [1973], *Negotiations, 1972–1990,* trans. Martin Joughin (New York: Columbia University Press, 1995), pp. 3–12; here pp. 6 and 184 n. 4.

2 Channeling beyond Interpretation

1. Lenin, "On Slogans" [1917], in *Collected Works,* 25:185–192; here 185.

2. Ernst Bloch, "Der Impuls Nietzsche," in *Erbschaft dieser Zeit* [1935], expanded ed. (Frankfurt am Main: Suhrkamp Verlag, 1962), pp. 358–366; here p. 359; emphasis added.

3. See Marc Sautet, *Nietzsche et la Commune* (Paris: Le Sycamore, 1981).

4. Kristin Ross, *The Emergence of Social Space: Rimbaud and the Paris Commune,* foreword by Terry Eagleton (Minneapolis: University of Minnesota Press, 1988), p. 150.

5. See especially the extraordinary fragment "coauthored" by Hegel, Schelling, and Hölderlin, the so-called "Oldest System-Program of German Idealism" [c. 1796], in Friedrich Hölderlin, *Sämtliche Werke,* ed. Friedrich Beißner (Stuttgart: Verlag W. Kohlhammer, 1961; Große Stuttgarter Ausgabe), 4:297–299. Extant in Hegel's handwriting, the text was apparently dictated by Schelling with Hölderlin's prompting at significant junctures.

6. Nietzsche, "NF, November 1882–Februar 1883"; *KGW* 7/1:185.

7. Nietzsche, "NF, Frühjahr 1884"; *KGW* 7/2:103.

8. For the now classic view of the mass media as part ecstatic, part anxious human prosthesis, see H. Marshall McLuhan, *Understanding Media: The Extensions of Man* (New York: McGraw-Hill, 1964); for the equally classic counterview a few years later of the mass media as a hyperreification of human sociality within the matrix of commodity capitalism, on which the mass media depend, see Debord, *La société du spectacle* (Paris: Buchet-Chastel, 1967). On these two takes on modernity, finding a common — though to some extent itself contradictory — source in the work of Walter Benjamin, see Hal Foster, "Postmodernism in Parallax," *October* 63 (Winter 1993), 3–20, esp. 16–19. Virilio, who notes that Greek *esthesis* meant "unmeasured," updates McLuhan to attend to some geospatial, geotemporal, geophysical implications of the postmodern sea change in aesthetic theory and practice: "Instead of operating in the space of a constructed social fabric, the intersecting and connecting grid of highway and service systems now occurs in the sequences of an imperceptible organization of time in which the man/machine interface replaces the façades

of buildings as the surfaces of property allotments" (Virilio, *The Lost Dimension,* pp. 13–14 and 36). After all, as the Spinozist Althusser remarked, "the pair of notions *person/thing* is at the root of every bourgeois ideology" (Althusser, "Reply to John Lewis," in *Essays in Self-Criticism,* p. 51).

9. McLuhan, *Understanding Media,* p. 11.

10. Baudrillard, *The Ecstasy of Communication,* p. 53; see further *Forget Foucault* [1977], in his *Forget Foucault & Forget Baudrillard,* pp. 7–64; esp. pp. 31–36.

11. Haraway, "A Cyborg Manifesto," in *Simians, Cyborgs, and Women,* p. 150.

12. See Alice Jardine, "Of Bodies and Technologies," in *Discussions in Contemporary Culture,* vol. 1, ed. Hal Foster (Seattle: The Bay Press, 1987), pp. 151–158.

13. For a preliminary attempt, see Daniel W. Conway, "*Das Weib an sich:* The Slave Revolt in Epistemology," in *Nietzsche, Feminism and Political Theory,* pp. 110–129.

14. This and the following definition of psychoplasmics is derived from David Cronenberg's 1979 film *The Brood.* Note also that an elaborate political discourse circulating around the word and concept "brood" (German *Brut,* French *couvée,* Spanish *cría,* Italian *covata*) was ubiquitous in northern and southern Europe throughout the 1970s—used not only negatively by the state and mass media to stigmatize "terrorist" groups such as the Red Army Faction (RAF), but also as positive self-descriptions by the groups themselves, though not necessarily their "sympathizers." See Matthew T. Grant, "Critical Intellectuals and the New Media: Bernward Vesper, Ulrike Meinhof, the Frankfurt School, and the Red Army Faction" (Diss., Cornell University, 1993). The Right has no monopoly on broods.

15. Spinoza, *The Ethics,* p. 87 [part 2, prop. 7, note].

16. See A. J. Greimas, *Sémantique structurale* (Paris: Larousse, 1966), pp. 172–191. Translated as *Structural Semiotics: An Attempt at a Method,* trans. Danielle McDowell, Ronald Schleifer, and Alan Velie (Lincoln and London: University of Nebraska Press, 1983). Over the years, Jameson has used narrative semiotics to analyze what he calls "the political unconscious"; see, for example, his *The Political Unconscious,* esp. pp. 46–49, 121–127, and 166–168. More recently, Jameson has linked the capacity of the actant to appear in different guises to the postmodern sense of paranoia and conspiracy in the face of total global systems such as neo-capitalism; see his *The Geopolitical Aesthetic,* pp. 33–34.

17. Neal Stephenson, *Snow Crash* (New York: A Bantam Spectra Book, 1992), p. 33.

18. Virilio, *The Lost Dimension,* p. 113.

19. Thin White Rope (Matthew Abourezk, Roger Kunkel, Guy Kyser, Steve Siegrist, John von Feldt), "Whirling Dervish," *Sack Full of Silver,* © 1990 Frontier Records, 01866-34638-4.

20. Front Line Assembly (Bill Leeb, Rhys Fulber), *TACTICAL Neural Implant,* © 1992 Third Mind Records, TMC 9188.

21. See *Total Recall* (Paul Verhoeven, USA/Holland, 1990) and the short story on

which it is loosely based: Philip K. Dick, "We Can Remember It for You Wholesale" [1965–1966], in *The Collected Stories of Philip K. Dick*, vol. 2: *We Can Remember It for You Wholesale*, introduction by Norman Spinrad (New York: A Citadel Twilight Book, Carol Publishing Group, 1990), pp. 35–52.

22. K. Michael Hays, *Modernism and the Posthumanist Subject: The Architecture of Hannes Meyer and Ludwig Hilberseimer* (Cambridge, Mass. and London: The MIT Press, 1992), p. 221.

23. Virilio, *The Lost Dimension*, p. 115.

24. Jean-Pierre Changeux, *L'homme neuronal* (Paris: Fayard, 1983); as cited in Virilio, *The Lost Dimension*, p. 114.

25. For the first analysis of this technology and its broader epistemological, social, and political implications, see William J. Mitchell, *The Reconfigured Eye: Visual Truth in the Post-Photographic Era* (Cambridge, Mass. and London: The MIT Press, 1993).

26. The following discussion of Videodrome is derived from *Videodrome* (David Cronenberg, Canada, 1983). For analyses of *Videodrome* see Jameson, *The Geopolitical Aesthetic*, pp. 11–35; Steven Shaviro, *The Cinematic Body* (Minneapolis and London: University of Minnesota Press, 1993), pp. 138–144; and Serge Grünberg, *David Cronenberg* (Paris: Cahiers du Cinéma/Collection "Auteurs," 1992).

27. In *Rabid* (David Cronenberg, Canada, 1976–1977).

28. The Mekons, "Charlie Cake Park," *Honky Tonkin'*, © 1987 Twin Tone Records/ Rough Trade Inc., TTR 87113–2.

29. Virilio, *The Lost Dimension*, p. 22. Actually, "Videodrome" is not part of Virilio's vocabulary.

30. Ibid. Contrast the modernist *velo*drome, beloved by Brecht, made of concrete, the site of multiday bicycle races.

31. These two remarks are from Cronenberg's *Videodrome*.

32. Maurice Blanchot, "Everyday Speech" [1959], in *Everyday Life*, ed. Alice Kaplan and Kristin Ross, special issue of *Yale French Studies* 73 (1987), 12–20; here 13.

33. Jameson, *The Geopolitical Aesthetic*, p. 23; see further "The Existence of Italy," in *Signatures of the Visible* (New York and London: Routledge, 1992), pp. 155–229; here esp. pp. 118–120.

34. See Lenin, *What Is to Be Done?: Burning Questions of Our Movement* [1901–1902], *Collected Works*, 5:347–529; here 418; and *Selections from the Prison Notebooks of Antonio Gramsci*, pp. 132 and 158.

35. *The Silence of the Lambs* (Jonatha Demme, USA, 1991).

36. Nietzsche, *Also sprach Zarathustra: Ein Buch für Alle und Keinen* [1883–1885]; *KGW* 6/1:185 [part 2, "The Stillest Hour"].

37. In "minor literature" (*la littérature mineure*), "There is nothing that is major or revolutionary except the minor." According to Deleuze and Guattari, Kafka is a chief practitioner of a minor literature on the Left. Despising as he did "all language of masters . . . Kafka's fascination for servants and employees" and common lan-

guage ostensibly has the intent, if not also the actual effect, of inworming and undermining all the major institutions of power (Deleuze and Guattari, *Kafka: Toward a Minor Literature* [1975], trans. Dona Polan, foreword by Réda Bensmaïa [Minneapolis: University of Minnesota Press, 1986], p. 26). In other words, Kafka would be a major early practitioner of what Italian post-Marxists today are calling "weak thought." But Nietzsche's own way with minor literature is proof that it can — not to say will always — be mobilized on behalf of newer sites of fascoid-liberal power that are ever more difficult to resist and combat. In this respect, Kafka might be viewed as an exemplary fighter *against* Nietzsche's corps/e, notwithstanding the fact that he, too, was for a time a reader of Nietzsche.

38. The German title, *Jenseits von Gut und Böse: Vorspiel einer Philosophie der Zukunft*, plays aggressively both with Richard Wagner's slogan of the "music of the future" (*Zukunftsmusik*) and with the classical philologist Ulrich von Wilamowitz-Möllendorff's parodic ridicule of Nietzsche's first book *The Birth of Tragedy Out of the Spirit of Music* (1872) as "philology of the future" (*Zukunftsphilologie*). Erwin Rohde — himself a philologist and Nietzsche's close friend at the time — in turn ridiculed Wilamowitz-Möllendorff's detailed and hostile criticisms as *Afterphilologie*, meaning not only post- or pseudo-philology but also an ass-backwards philology of anality for assholes, "anal-philology" (German *After-:* "anus," "backwards," "second-hand," "fake" — with the homophobic and/or homosexual associations being rather more closeted than open). For the main documents of this confrontation see *Der Streit um Nietzsches "Geburt der Tragödie": Die Schriften von E. Rohde, R. Wagner, U. v. Wilamowitz-Möllendorff*, ed. with an introduction by Karlfried Gründer (Hildesheim: Olms Verlagsbuchhandlung, 1969).

39. Nietzsche, "NF, Frühjahr 1884"; *KGW* 7/2:46.

40. Agnes Heller, *A Theory of History* (London: Routledge and Kegan Paul, 1982), p. 201.

41. Lacan, *The Four Fundamental Concepts of Psycho-Analysis,* p. 23.

42. Adorno, *In Search of Wagner* [written 1937–1938; first published 1952], trans. Rodney Livingstone (London: NLB, 1981), p. 35. Adorno also has in mind the Brechtian notion of the "social gest" or "musical gest" as the most concentrated perceptible form of intersubjective and social behavior.

43. Thomas Mann, notes on "The New Generation" [1910]; as cited in T. J. Reed, *Thomas Mann: The Uses of Tradition* (Oxford: Oxford University Press, 1974), pp. 136–138.

44. Don DeLillo, *Mao II* (New York: Penguin Books, 1992), p. 85.

45. For the best introduction to political ontology in the following sense, see Bourdieu, *L'ontologie politique de Martin Heidegger,* esp. pp. 13 and 57–58. But while Bourdieu has done the most to promote the centrality of political ontology for understanding Heidegger, he has not grasped all its ramifications. His commitment to a neo-Hegelian, neo-Panofskyan concept of what he calls the "philosophical field" makes it too difficult to articulate the specific, strategic aspects of Heidegger's think-

ing and writing. Nor does he provide adequately close readings of his textual evidence. The tendency of Bourdieu's sociological presuppositions is always to dissolve individual passions and interests into typically unconscious structures. For better or worse, Bourdieu can differentiate thinkers only according to various levels of more or less "euphemistic" discourse, rather than also of conscious intentions, ambitions, and rhetorical strategies (see, e.g., pp. 51 and 98).

46. To be more precise, one ought to replace the too static concept "ontology" in this definition by the German *seinsgeschichtlich* (meaning something like: "the way Being becomes or reveals itself exoterically as authentic, esoteric history"), since this, approximately, is Heidegger's own explicit recommendation. But the simpler term "political ontology" is accurate enough — provided its dynamic, changing, historically charged aspects are kept in mind. See Heidegger, *Beiträge zur Philosophie (Vom Ereignis); Gesamtausgabe, 3/65:103.*

47. *"The Last [Das Letzte]* is that which not only needs the longest pre-paration or van-guardism [Vor-läuferschaft], but rather itself *is* this, not the stopping, but rather the deepest beginning that extends the farthest and has the hardest time getting itself back. The Last withdraws itself thus from all calculation and must thus be able to bear the burden of the crudest and most common misinterpretation. How could it otherwise remain the one that passes? If we already grasp 'death' so little in its extremity, how do we want, then, to be prepared for the rare hint of the last God [dem seltenen Wink des letzten Gottes]?" (Heidegger, *Beiträge zur Philosophie [Vom Ereignis]*; *Gesamtausgabe, 3/65:405*).

48. Ibid., 3/65:421–422. For Heidegger's most extensive discussion of Nietzsche and Hölderlin qua nexus, written in 1937–1938, at the same time he was working on his *Beiträge*, see *Grundfragen der Philosophie; Gesamtausgabe, 2/45:124–136.* For useful preliminary attempts to reveal the political stakes behind Heidegger's reading of Hölderlin, see Otto Pöggeler, "Heideggers politisches Selbstverständnis," and especially Annemarie Gethmann-Siefert, "Heidegger und Hölderlin: Die Überforderung des 'Dichters in dürftiger Zeit,'" both in *Heidegger und die praktische Philosophie,* ed. Annemarie Gethmann-Siefert and Otto Pöggeler (Frankfurt am Main: Suhrkamp Verlag, 1988), pp. 17–63 and 191–227, respectively.

49. The teenage Nietzsche, too, had admired Hölderlin, keeping up a certain dialogue with him over the years until his breakdown in 1889, by which time, however, he had turned violently against him. But *nowhere* has Hölderlin — or *any* other writer — been elevated to the extremities imaged by Heidegger.

50. See Manfred Frank, *Der kommende Gott: Vorlesungen über die Neue Mythologie, I. Teil* (Frankfurt am Main: Suhrkamp Verlag, 1982).

51. See further Louis Harmand, *Société et économie de la république romaine* (Paris: Librarie Armand Colin, 1976), esp. pp. 57–61.

52. See Epicurus, in Diogenes Laertius, *Lives,* X:31; Lucretius, *De rerum nat.,* IV:437–501; and *Stoicorum veterum fragmenta* (ed. Hans von Arnim), I:143, II:836 and 879.

53. Nietzsche, "NF, November 1887–März 1888"; *KGW* 8/2:358. " . . . das Christenthum paßt sich an das schon bestehende überall eingewachsene *Anti-Heidenthums* an, an die Culte, welche von Epicur bekämpft worden sind . . . genauer, an die *Religionen der niederen Masse der Frauen, der Sklaven, der NICHT-VORNEHMEN Stände.*" Note: Nietzsche had intricate ways of emphasizing certain words over others, of building up hierarchical registers of concepts, of using ellipses, and so forth; his logo- and phonocentric graphology is often difficult to transcribe accurately. There are many references to Epicurean philosophy throughout Nietzsche's writing. For an earlier but typical exoteric version, see *The Gay Science* (1882), aphorism 45; and for his placement of Epicurus among the elite in his pantheon, alongside "Montaigne, Goethe and Spinoza, Plato and Rousseau, Pascal and Schopenhauer," see *Human, All-Too-Human II, Part One: Mixed Opinions and Maxims* (1879), aphorism 408. Some of these references to Epicurus are explicitly epistemological in nature, but the cited passage is indicative of what most interested Nietzsche ultimately. Finally, with regard to Nietzsche's "Roman" tendency, note that Adorno was *exactly right* to claim that "in every one of Nietzsche's periods there resounds the millennial echo of rhetorical voices in the Roman Senate"; but Adorno was *dead wrong* to add immediately: "—but without the actor's denial of play acting" (Adorno, *Minima Moralia: Reflections from Damaged Life* [1951], trans. E. F. N. Jephcott [London: NLB, 1974], p. 154).

54. Althusser, "Freud and Lacan," in *Lenin and Philosophy,* p. 203; emphasis added.

55. Strauss, *Thoughts on Machiavelli,* p. 154.

56. On Nietzsche's sexuality, contrast Luce Irigaray, *Marine Lover of Friedrich Nietzsche* [1980], trans. Gillian C. Gill (New York: Columbia University Press, 1991), with Joachim Köhler, *Zarathustras Geheimnis: Friedrich Nietzsche und seine verschlüsselte Botschaft* (Nördlingen: Greno, 1989). Irigaray uses Nietzsche's textual production and the problematic of gender in effect to deconstruct one another by means of figures and images of fluidity and the sea. Köhler argues—not unconvincingly, if via largely circumstantial evidence—that Nietzsche "was homosexual" and that *Thus Spoke Zarathustra* in particular is an esoteric celebration of gay male liberation.

57. Nietzsche, "NF, November-Februar 1883"; *KGW* 7/1:187. "Der Entschluß. Unzählige *Opfer* muß es geben."

58. Spinoza, *A Theologico-Political Treatise,* p. 27 (ch. 2).

59. Gramsci's group of *Ordine Nuovo* socialists adapted this slogan around 1919 from the French scholar, writer, musicologist, and later antifascist Romain Rolland (1866–1944). It sustained Gramsci in prison. See, for example, *Selections from the Prison Notebooks of Antonio Gramsci,* p. 175. "Pessimism" is meant in the philosophical sense of the radically nontranscendent, atheistic, materialist worldview that Gramsci tended to call "historicism."

60. Gramsci, "Il cieco Tiresia" [*Avanti!* (Turin ed.), April 18, 1918], in *Sotto la Mole, 1916–1920* (Turin: Einaudi, 1960), pp. 392–393. See further *The Divine Comedy*

of Dante Alighieri, with translation and comment by John D. Sinclair (New York: Oxford University Press, 1939), pp. 132–143. For insight into the complexity of Gramsci's interest in Dante see Frank Rosengarten, "Gramsci's 'Little Discovery': Gramsci's Interpretation of Canto X of Dante's *Inferno*," *boundary* 2 14:3 (Spring 1986), 71–90; and Paul Bové, "Dante, Gramsci, and Cultural Criticism," *Rethinking Marxism* 4:1 (Spring 1991), 74–86. Some of Gramsci's reflections on Canto X are translated in *Selections from Cultural Writings*, pp. 150–163. See further Gramsci to Tania Schucht, September 30, 1931, in his *Letters from Prison*, ed. Frank Rosengarten, trans. Raymond Rosenthal, 2 vols. (New York: Columbia University Press, 1994), 2:73–77. Because Gramsci's confrontation with Dante is his most extensive analysis of how to read another's writing, it also provides the best instruction on how to read Gramsci himself—following the rule of thumb: "As one reads, one writes."

61. See Dante Germino, *Antonio Gramsci: Architect of a New Politics* (Baton Rouge and London: Louisiana University Press, 1990), p. 242. To be sure, Dante scholars and students of Gramsci alike have noted that the cogency of this reading of Canto X of the *Inferno* is open to considerable dispute qua literary-historical exercise. At issue, in part, in the words of the *dantista* Natalino Sapegno, is whether "the condition that Farinata describes, of a knowledge limited to future things and incapable of perceiving them when they approach and become present" is "shared by all the damned" in Dante, or is only "characteristic of the Epicureans alone, with whom it would acquire a more evident function of *contrappasso* [roughly, 'retributive justice'], striking them in the essence of their sin, which was precisely to believe only in the present and to reject the sense of the eternal" (Dante Alighieri, *La Divina Commedia*, vol. 1: *L'Inferno*, ed. with commentary by Natalino Sapegno, 11th ed. [Florence: La Nuova Italia, 1978], p. 118 [commentary on line 102]); also cited and discussed by Rosengarten, "Gramsci's 'Little Discovery,'" 76.

62. Gramsci, *Selections from Cultural Writings*, pp. 152 and 153.

63. Ibid., p. 162. For the original, see Gramsci, *Quaderni del cacere*, ed. Valentino Gerratana (Turin: Einaudi, 1975), 1:527.

64. Ibid.

65. Virilio, *Popular Defense & Ecological Struggles* [1978], trans. Mark Polizzotti (New York: Semiotext[e] Foreign Agents Series, 1990), p. 87.

66. *Selections from the Prison Notebooks of Antonio Gramsci*, pp. 170–171.

67. See *AMOK: Sourcebook of the Extremes of Information in Print*, Fourth Dispatch, ed. Stuart Swezey and Brian King (N.C., Ore.: The Subterranean Company, n.d. [c. 1989]), pp. 349–351. Alongside Bataille, Nietzsche is the only person to have an entire section devoted to him in this self-described "post-industrial" catalogue of texts and videos. The categories, in order, are: Control, Exotica, Mayhemayhem, Natas, Neuropolitics, Orgone, Parallax, Pulps, R & D, Scratch 'n' Sniff, Sensory Deprivation, Sleaze, Tactics, Bataille, and Nietzsche. At least in AMOK, therefore, it is Bataille himself, not communism, who appears to be "the only position"—or at least the only proper name—"outside of Nietzsche."

68. On early Nietzsche cults and commodities, see Jürgen Krause, *"Märtyrer" und "Prophet": Studien zum Nietzsche-Kult in der bildenden Kunst der Jahrhundertwende* (Berlin and New York: Walter de Gruyter, 1984).

69. Bataille, *The Accursed Share*, vols. 2 and 3:97 (*The History of Eroticism*). *Œuvres complètes*, 7:85.

70. Pablo Neruda, "Para lavar a un niño" [to wash a child, 1962], in *A New Decade* (*Poems: 1958–1967*) [dual-language ed.], ed. with an introduction by Ben Belitt, trans. Ben Belitt and Alastair Reid (New York: Grove Press, 1969), pp. 144–145. "Oh vigilancia clara / Oh dulce alevosía! / Oh tierna guerra!"

71. Giacomo Leopardi, "La ginestra o il fiore del deserto" [the broom or the desert flower, 1836], in *A Leopardi Reader* [dual-language ed.], ed. and trans. Ottavio M. Casale (Urbana, Chicago, and London: University of Illinois Press, 1981), pp. 205–213 and 262–269; here pp. 207 and 263. "Qui mira e qui ti specchia, / Secol superbo e sciocco, / Che il calle insino allora / Dal risorto pensier segnato innanti / Abbandonasti, e volti addietro i passi, / Del ritornar ti vanti, / E procedere il chiami."

72. Strauss, *Thoughts on Machiavelli*, p. 12.

73. Marx and Engels, *The German Ideology*, in *Collected Works*, 5:28–29. This thesis is a main source of Althusser's notion of "problematic": "It could not be better said that it is not answers which make philosophy but the *questions* posed by the philosophy, and that it is *in the question* itself, that is, *in the way it reflects that object* (and not in the object itself) that ideological mystification (or on the contrary an authentic relationship with the object) should be sought" (Althusser, " 'On the Young Marx,' " in *For Marx*, p. 66 n. 29).

74. R.E.M. (Bill Berry, Peter Buck, Mike Mills, Michael Stipe), "King of Birds," as recorded on *Number 5 Document*, © 1993 IRS Records/EMI Records, Ltd., 0–7777–13200–2–6.

75. See Ferdinand Tönnies, *Der Nietzsche-Kultus: Eine Kritik* (Leipzig: O. R. Reisland, 1897).

76. For an alternative account of "Right-" and "Left-"Nietzscheans produced in this book, see Levine, *Nietzsche and the Modern Crisis of the Humanities* (1995), esp. ch. 8: "Nietzsche Today." Levine takes his point of departure from Strauss's thesis that Nietzsche brings modern thought to its unavoidable, decisive crossroads: "To avert the danger to life, Nietzsche could choose one of two ways: he could insist on the strictly esoteric character of the theoretical analysis of life—that is, restore the Platonic notion of the noble delusion—or else he could deny the possibility of theory proper and so conceive of thought as essentially subservient to, or dependent on, life or fate. If not Nietzsche himself, at any rate his successors adapted the second alternative" (Strauss, *Natural Right and History* [1950], 7th printing [Chicago and London: The University of Chicago Press, 1971], p. 26; also partially cited by Levine, p. 162). In Levine's analysis, however, Strauss's last remark is not to be taken at face value. "Nietzsche's postmodern followers have 'adapted the second alterna-

tive,' and have become unabashed prophets of the end of morality and metaphysics. But Nietzsche and Strauss follow the former path, keeping the full 'truth' of nihilism a secret" (p. 162). In other words, Strauss and followers such as Allan Bloom, exactly like Nietzsche, are "esoteric nihilists," whereas Derrida—representative for Levine of "Left-"Nietzscheanism—develops only Nietzsche's exoterically intended message. Levine's own position, then, is to develop a more properly "postmodern"—that is, nonmetaphysical, pragmatic, and explicitly "humanist historicism"—which would avoid the allegedly still metaphysical pitfalls of Nietzschean, Straussian, *and* Derridian *"Weltanschauung* historicism." Which is to say a more or less unwitting commitment, appearances to the contrary, to "the theory that each person belongs to a single delimited culture" (p. 187). Superficially similar to certain arguments in this book, Levine's account is troubled by his reluctance to move past a philosophical and cultural problematic into more political terrains. Symptomatically, ideology is *terra incognita* to him. Levine's failure is overdetermined, and hardly his alone. Although he is very good at bringing out aspects of the esoteric *thematic* of Nietzsche and Strauss—he is less knowledgeable about Derrida—Levine does not wonder how esotericism might be *implemented* as an illocutionary strategy. Moreover, he tacks onto his analysis of Nietzsche and Nietzscheanism his own rather feeble "postmodern" plea for liberal pluralism in the humanities. At the very end of his book, this plea uncritically and without comment incorporates a similar-sounding one from Nietzsche that, according to Levine's own prior argument, would have been designed by Nietzsche as exoterically manipulative. Symptomatic, too, is Levine's choice of "Right-" and "Left-"Nietzscheans for analysis. By picking for his "Right-"Nietzschean Leo Strauss—rather than, say, Stanley Rosen—Levine already carves out a less than radical space for depicting or opposing Straussianism. Rosen, as will be shown presently, is even more complex and elusive than is Strauss himself in terms of damage control against insight into Nietzsche's own illocutionary strategies *and* their unwitting perlocutionary effect on the Left. By the same token, picking Derrida as his "Left-"Nietzschean allows Levine not to consider, say, Richard Rorty's take on Nietzsche and Nietzscheanism. For to have confronted Rorty—or Ernesto Laclau—would have required Levine to admit that *both* his supposedly specific "democratic" and "pragmatic" critique of Nietzsche *and* his concomitant overall program for postmodern humanism are already firmly in place in Rorty's work. By contrast, none of Levine's own cultural heroes (e.g., Isaiah Berlin, Clifford Geertz, John Rawls) has developed an explicit analysis of Nietzsche; Habermas represents only a partial exception here, since Levine does not mention Habermas's critique of Nietzsche, and since Habermas's basic project is not radically different from Levine's. Because he has come to terms with Nietzsche/an esotericism primarily as a—philosophical and cultural—theme, rather than also as a—political—strategy of subcutaneous influence, Levine can insist that Nietzsche's antidemocratic *Weltanschauung* was at once *"wrong"*—and hence correctable by Levine's rational argument—and—unlike Levine—*"unable* to get an adequate conceptual grip on what it meant to be a humanist" in this, the age of the "Last Man" (p. 213) — two claims that suddenly and very conveniently ignore the fact that Levine has already admitted that Nietzsche's project is esoteric. Finally, Levine announces the raison d'être of his book to be this: "to use my alternative paradigm to provide a new theoretical understanding of the modern humanities — and also to vindicate the life of the modern humanist, Nietzsche's Last Man" (p. xxi). This desire may be all well and good, but Levine is far from having pulled it off, not only for the aforementioned reasons but because he believes that "Nietzsche's worst nightmare is a herd which has seen all its morals dethroned but is unable to say a new 'Yes'" (p. 159) — in other words, Nietzsche's *worst nightmare* would be Levine's *Nietzsche and the Modern Crisis of the Humanities*. Nice work if you can get it, but rather too reassuring, not to say megalomaniac and therefore . . . "Nietzschean."

77. On Tönnies, his simultaneous critique of and adherence to Nietzscheanism, and on the Nietzschean and "irrationalist" orientation of German sociology generally, see Arthur Mitzman, *Sociology and Estrangement: Three Sociologists of Imperial Germany* (New York: Knopf/Random House, 1973); Jürgen Zander, "Ferdinand Tönnies und Friedrich Nietzsche," in *Ankunft bei Tönnies: Soziologische Beiträge zum 125. Geburtstag von Ferdinand Tönnies*, ed. Lars Clausen and Franz Urban Pappi (Kiel: W. Mühlau, 1981), pp. 185–227; Wolf Lepenies, *Between Literature and Science: The Rise of Sociology* [*Die drei Kulturen*, 1985], trans. R. J. Hollingdale (Cambridge: Cambridge University Press, 1988); Harry Liebersohn, *Fate and Utopia in German Sociology, 1870–1923* (Cambridge, Mass. and London: The MIT Press, 1988); and Aschheim, *The Nietzsche Legacy in Germany*, pp. 39–41. Zander and Liebersohn in particular show that Tönnie's very influential binary opposition between *Gesellschaft* and *Gemeinschaft* was profoundly indebted to what he regarded as the "communitarian" or *Gemeinschaft* impulse of the Dionysian as depicted by Nietzsche in *The Birth of Tragedy*.

78. See Wilhelm Carl Becker, *Der Nietzschekultus: Ein Kapitel aus der Geschichte der Verirrungen des menschlichen Geistes* (Leipzig: Richard Lipinski, 1908). While it is unlikely that Nietzsche would have *personally* approved of German genocide against entire tribes in southeast Africa — carried out under the leadership of Hermann Göring's father and documented by Eugen Fischer, later head of the Nazi Institute of Racial Hygiene and Heidegger's friend — his notion of Will to Power makes it impossible to find *logical* reasons to oppose such policies, let alone expansionist power grabs generally.

79. Ahmad, *In Theory: Classes, Nations, Literatures*, p. 222.

80. Althusser, *Les faits*, in *L'avenir dure longtemps* [*suivi de*] *Les faits*, pp. 351–352.

81. On early "Left"-Nietzscheans, see: William J. McGrath, *Dionysian Art and Populist Politics in Austria* (New Haven: Yale University Press, 1974); *Intellectuals and the Future in the Hapsburg Monarchy 1890–1914*, ed. Laszlo Peter and Robert B. Pynsent (London and New York: Macmillan, 1988); R. Hinton Thomas, *Nietzsche in German Politics and Society 1890–1918* (Manchester: Manchester University Press,

1983); Joelle Phillipi, "Das Nietzsche-Bild in der deutschen Zeitschriftenpresse der Jahrhundertwende" (Diss., University of the Saarland, 1970); Ernst Behler, "Zur frühen sozialistischen Rezeption Nietzsches in Deutschland," and Vivetta Vivarelli, "Das Nietzsche-Bild in der Presse der deutschen Sozialdemokratie um die Jahrhundertwende," both in *Nietzsche-Studien* 13 (1984), 503–520 and 521–569, respectively; Krause, *"Märtyrer" und "Prophet": Studien zum Nietzsche-Kult in der bildenden Kunst der Jahrhundertwende;* Bergmann, *Nietzsche, "the Last Antipolitical German";* Seth Taylor, *Left-Wing Nietzscheans: The Politics of German Expressionism, 1910–1920* (New York and Berlin: Walter de Gruyter, 1990); Aschheim, *The Nietzsche Legacy in Germany,* ch. 2: "Germany and the Battle over Nietzsche, 1890–1914," ch. 3: "The Not-So-Discrete Nietzscheanism of the Avant-Garde," and ch. 6: "Nietzschean Socialism: Left and Right"; and Sautet, *Nietzsche et la Commune.* One of the best introductions to Nietzsche in historical context remains Richard Hamann and Jost Hermand, *Epochen deutscher Kultur von 1870 bis zur Gegenwart,* vol. 2: *Gründerzeit* (Berlin, GDR: Akademie-Verlag, 1965), esp. pp. 24–202. In some respects, Hermand's sociological placement of Nietzsche in historical context has not been superseded; thus, it opens up the possibility for more speculative approaches to Nietzsche and Nietzscheanism.

82. See J[ean] Bourdeau, "Nietzsche socialiste malgré lui" [feuilleton], *Journal des Débats politiques et littéraires,* September 2, 1902.

83. See Nietzsche's correspondence about and to Bourdeau for mid- to late December, 1888 in *KGB* 3/5:529–531, 537, 539, 546, 548, 557, 559–561, 564, 566, and 568–569.

84. For recent takes on "Nietzsche and feminism," see the very uneven anthologies *Nietzsche, Feminism and Political Theory,* and *Nietzsche and the Feminine,* ed. Peter J. Burgard (Charlottesville and London: University Press of Virginia, 1994). A substantial problem with both collections of essays is that the authors do not address *at all* the problematic of Nietzsche's eso/exotericism, so that they all take his supposedly "contradictory" statements, in this case about "women," at face value, in spite of varying degrees of theoretical sophistication and appearances sometimes to the contrary. Another problem is that the authors do not *adequately* address Nietzsche's view of *men,* including a distinctly homoerotic, homosocial, and homosexual problematic. And the occasional references in *Nietzsche and the Feminine* are insufficient and undertheorized. Today, the work on Nietzsche by Irigaray is arguably the most significant in terms of both philosophy and feminism. Developing critically a famous argument of Derrida in *Spurs: Nietzsche's Styles* (1978), Irigaray has gone farthest to argue that women — not "Woman" — should *affirm* the dissembling veil that Nietzsche attributed to them: that is, the veil that both conceals and reveals patriarchal Truth, indeed virtually *all* forms of essentialism. Whatever validity this current tendency of feminism may have in other respects, and it may be considerable, it is philologically and philosophically *mistaken* to appeal to *Nietzsche* for any help in such projects. See especially Irigaray's 1980 *Marine Lover of Friedrich Nietz-*

sche. It must also be said that Irigaray's own brand of Nietzscheanism, symptomatically for these times, is virtually *pre*-Marxist. For a Marxist-feminist critique of her work see Toril Moi, *Sexual/Textual Politics: Feminist Literary Theory* (London and New York: Methuen, 1985), esp. pp. 127–149; though other more or less "Nietzschean" feminists are implicated as well.

85. See the annotated bibliography by Peter Pütz, *Friedrich Nietzsche* [1967], 2d, rev. and expanded ed. (Stuttgart: J. B. Metzlersche Verlagsbuchhandlung, 1975; Realien zur Literatur, 62), pp. 67–89.

86. See Heide Schlüpmann, "Zur Frage der Nietzsche-Rezeption in der Frauenbewegung gestern und heute" [1986], in *Nietzsche heute: Die Rezeption seines Werkes nach 1968,* ed. Sigrid Bauschinger, Susan L. Cocalis, and Sara Lennox (Bern and Stuttgart: Francke Verlag, 1988), pp. 177–193.

87. See, for example, Helene Stöcker, "Friedrich Nietzsche und die Frauen," *Das Magazin für Literatur* 67 (1898), 128–132 and 153–158, and *Die Liebe und die Frauen* (Minden in Westfallen: J. C. C. Bruns, 1906).

88. Stöcker, "Nietzsche" [c. 1935?], unpublished manuscript, Swarthmore College Peace Collection, 21; cited in Schlüpmann, "Zur Frage der Nietzsche-Rezeption in der Frauenbewegung gestern und heute," in *Nietzsche heute*, p. 177. Schlüpmann also discusses at length the many positive references to Nietzsche in one of Stöcker's main works, *Die Liebe und die Frauen* (1905–1906). On Stöcker, see further Ascheim, *The Nietzsche Legacy in Germany*, pp. 88–92, 125, and 166. For the standard English treatment of early German feminism see Richard J. Evans, *The Feminist Movement in Germany 1894–1933* (London and Beverly Hills, Sage, 1976), though Nietzscheanism is insufficiently addressed.

89. Schlüpmann, "Zur Frage der Nietzsche-Rezeption," in *Nietzsche heute*, p. 179.

90. Alfred Rosenberg, *Der Mythos des 20. Jahrhunderts: Eine Wertung der seelische-geistigen Gestaltenkräfte unserer Zeit* [1930] (Munich: Hoheneichen-Verlag, 1936), p. 523; emphasis added. Actually, this best-seller was seldom read and never taken seriously by Hitler's innermost circle, where it was ridiculed as "Rosenberg's metaphysical belch." For the first important critique of Rosenberg's Nietzsche, see Bataille, "Nietzsche and the Fascists" [1937], in *Visions of Excess*, pp. 182–196; here p. 188. *Œuvres complètes*, 1:447–465. See further Manfred Frank, "*Der Mythos des 20. Jahrhunderts* (Alfred Rosenberg, Alfred Baeumler)," in *Gott im Exil: Vorlesungen über die neue Mythologie, II. Teil* (Frankfurt am Main: Suhrkamp Verlag, 1988), pp. 105–130.

91. "In his name, the contamination of the race by blacks and Syrians progressed, whereas he himself strictly submitted to the characteristic discipline of our race. Nietzsche fell into the dreams of colored gigolos, which is worse than falling into the hands of a gang of thieves" (Rosenberg, *Der Mythos des 20. Jahrhunderts*, p. 523).

92. For two representative recent attempts to articulate Marx and Nietzsche positively see Nancy S. Love, *Marx, Nietzsche, and Modernity* (New York: Columbia University Press, 1986); and David B. Myers, *Marx and Nietzsche: The Reminiscences*

and *Transcripts of a Nineteenth-Century Journalist* (Lanham: University Press of America, 1986). The former is a sober, critical work of political history and theory, the latter an imaginary "encounter" between Marx and Nietzsche; the former is also much more hard-headed with regard to the unsettling elements of Nietzsche's social philosophy, but the cumulative effect of both books is to overlook its most problematic aspects.

93. See Ernst Nolte, "Marx und Nietzsche im Sozialismus des jungen Mussolini," *Historische Zeitschrift* 191:2 (October 1960), 249–335, and *Three Faces of Fascism: Action Française, Italian Fascism, National Socialism* [1963], trans. Leila Vennewitz (New York: A Mentor Book, 1969), esp. pp. 218–219 and 246. More recently, as part of his now explicitly "revisionist" agenda, Nolte reduces virtually all of twentieth-century German — indeed European — history to a murderous "civil war" between "Marxist annihilation" and "Nietzschean annihilation." See Nolte, *Nietzsche und der Nietzscheanismus* (Frankfurt am Main: Propyläen Verlag, 1990), pp. 10, 193, and 265. This is not to say that all German conservatives are united in this negative view of Nietzsche. Their very positive political appropriation is represented today by the quite influential Karl Heinz Bohrer. See, for example, "Why We Are Not a Nation — And Why We Should Become One," *New German Critique* 52 (Winter 1991), 72–83; here esp. 82–83; *Nach der Natur: Über Politik und Ästhetik* (Munich: Hanser Verlag, 1988); *Die Kritik der Romantik: Der Verdacht der Philosophie gegen die literarische Moderne* (Frankfurt am Main: Suhrkamp Verlag, 1989); and "Die Ästhetik am Ausgang ihrer Unmündigkeit," *Merkur* 500 (October/November 1990), 851–865. On Nietzsche and German national socialism, see Arno Münzer, *Nietzsche et le Nazisme* (Paris: Éditions Kimé, 1995). Finally, on certain protofascist tendencies in Nietzsche's own work and its early fascist reception, see Bernhard H. F. Taureck, *Nietzsche und der Faschismus: Eine Studie über Nietzsches politische Philosophie und ihre Folgen* (Hamburg: Junius, 1989), esp. pp. 25–26 and 97–101. Taureck rightly articulates Nietzsche's political philosophy with the ideology not of German national socialism but of Italian fascism, without simply conflating — as Nolte has come to do — Marxism, Nietzscheanism, and fascism.

94. See Kwame Nkrumah, *Handbook of Revolutionary Warfare: A Guide to the Armed Phase of the African Revolution* (New York: International Publishers, 1969), p. 13.

95. Strauss, "Liberal Education and Responsibility" [1962], *Liberalism Ancient and Modern* [1968], with a new foreword by Allan Bloom (Ithaca and London: Cornell University Press, 1989), pp. 9–25; here p. 24.

96. See Lukács, *The Destruction of Reason*, esp. pp. 202–203 and 309–399. This book was hugely influential on the reception of Nietzsche both in the Soviet Union and in Eastern Europe, even when Lukács the man was officially *persona non grata* for political reasons. See, for example, S. F. Oduev, *Auf den Spuren Zarathustras: Der Einfluß Nietzsches auf die bürgerliche deutsche Philosophie* [1971], trans. Günter Rieske (Berlin, GDR: Akademie-Verlag, 1977); and the many works on Nietzsche of Heinz Malorny, including "Friedrich Nietzsche gegen den klassischen bürgerlichen Hu-

manismus," in *Philosophie und Humanismus: Beiträge zum Menschenbild der deutschen Klassik* (Weimar: Böhlau Verlag, 1978), pp. 220–234. While *Nietzsche's Corps/e* happens to be in considerable *philosophical* agreement with these authors about Nietzsche, their *philological* approach to his texts was never substantially different from that of "bourgeois" scholarship, and their *politico-normative* approach to the scholarship of others tended to be Stalinist. It may also be noteworthy — after all, there are no coincidences if the doctrine of Eternal Recurrence of the Same holds true — that the last publication of the philosophy division of the East German Academy of Sciences, a book entitled *Modernity-Nietzsche-Postmodernity*, was a desperate last-ditch effort to provide Marxian resistance to what had long been too hot a topic. See *Moderne-Nietzsche-Postmoderne*, ed. Manfred Buhr (Berlin: Akademie-Verlag, 1990).

97. Adorno, *Minima Moralia*, p. 188. The other such philosophy for Adorno is that of Henri Bergson.

98. Rosen, "Nietzsche's Revolution" [1987], in *The Ancients and the Moderns: Rethinking Modernity* (New Haven and London: Yale University Press, 1989), pp. 189–208; here p. 189. Also see his important *The Mask of Enlightenment: Nietzsche's "Zarathustra"* (Cambridge: Cambridge University Press, 1995), esp. pp. 137–138 and 235–250.

99. See Maxim Gorky, *My Universities* [1923], trans. Ronald Wilks (Harmondsworth: Penguin, 1979), pp. 40–41. This book was a particular favorite of Lenin's.

100. See Hans-Joachim Becker, *Die frühe Nietzsche-Rezeption in Japan (1893–1903): Ein Beitrag zur Individualismusproblematik im Modernisierungsprozeß* (Wiesbaden: Otto Harrassowitz, 1983), pp. 107–109.

101. There have been at least two major waves of "Nietzsche fever" in mainland China: the first from 1915 to 1920, during the so-called May Fourth New Cultural Movement (e.g., in the work of intellectuals such as Chen Duziu, Hu Shi, Liang Qichao, and Lu Xun, and in the fiction of Mao Dun, Mu Shiying, and Xie Bingxin), and the second in the 1980s, as part of the general "culture fever" (e.g., the philosophers Chen Guying and Zhou Guopind and the novelist Liu Xiaobo).

102. On Nietzsche's impact in Japan, see *Nietzsche and Asian Thought,* ed. Graham Parkes (Chicago and London: The University of Chicago Press, 1991); and the much superior, earlier book by Becker, *Die frühe Nietzsche-Rezeption in Japan (1893–1903)*. By far the most extensive and insightful treatment in English of "Nietzsche in China" is Carlos Rojas, "Nietzsche and the Body Politic: Culture and Subjectivity in Twentieth Century China" (senior honors thesis, Cornell University, 1995). On Nietzsche in Russia, see the very uneven anthology *Nietzsche in Russia,* ed. Bernice Glatzer Rosenthal (Princeton: Princeton University Press, 1986). For two different accounts of Nietzsche and southern Europe see Udo Ruckser, *Nietzsche in der Hispania: Ein Beitrag zur Hispanischer Kultur- und Geistesgeschichte* (Bern and Munich: Francke Verlag, 1962); and *Nietzsche in Italy,* ed. Thomas Harrison (Saratoga, Calif.: Anima Libri, 1988). The former represents traditional scholarship to the point of inducing sleep, the latter is adventurous to the point of losing all contact

with Nietzsche and what a cyberpunk might call "primary reality," the world lurking outside the matrix. For a straightforward account of Nietzsche's influence in contemporary Italy see Giangiorgio Pasqualotto, *Nietzsche e la cultura contemporanea* (Venice: Arsenale cooperativa editrice, 1982). On France, see Louis Pinto, *Les neveux de Zarathoustra: La réception de Nietzsche en France* (Paris: Éditions du Seuil, 1995), and Alan D. Schrift, *Nietzsche's French Legacy: A Genealogy of Poststructuralism* (New York and London: Routledge, 1995). On Australia, see Noel Macainsh, *Nietzsche in Australia: A Literary Inquiry into a Nationalist Ideology* (Munich: Verlag für Dokumentation und Werbung, 1975). On Eastern Europe, see Ernst Behler, "Nietzsche in der marxistischen Kritik Osteuropas," *Nietzsche-Studien* 10/11 (1981–1982), 80–96. On the East German reception, see Denis M. Sweet, "Friedrich Nietzsche in the GDR: A Problematic Reception," *Studies in GDR Culture and Society* 4 (1984), 227–241, and "Nietzsche Criticized: The GDR Takes a Second Look," *Studies in GDR Culture and Society* 7 (1987), 141–153. One of the most significant debates about Nietzsche in any country occurred at the 10th Writers' Congress of the German Democratic Republic in November 1987, and in articles written by Heinz Pepperle, Wolfgang Harich, Stephan Hermlin, among others, which were published in the GDR journal *Sinn und Form* from 1986 to 1988. On the specific problem of Heideggerian Nietzscheanism in the former USSR and today, see Geoff Waite, "Politicheskaya ontologiya" [political ontology], trans. E. V. Oznobkinoi and E. V. Petrovskoya, in *Philosophiya Martina Heideggera i sovremennoste* (Martin Heidegger's philosophy and the present), ed. N. V. Motroshilova et al. (Moscow: "Nauka," 1991), pp. 188–214. This is the first collection of essays published on Heidegger in the USSR; the other contributors are W. Anz, V. V. Bibikhin, H. Brunkhorst, F.-W. von Hermann, V. Hösle, V. I. Molchanov, N. V. Motroshilova, J.-L. Nancy, V. A. Podoroga, O. Pöggeler, and R. Rorty. On Nietzsche in North America, see *Nietzsche in American Thought and Literature*, ed. Manfred Pütz (Columbia, S.C.: Camden House, Inc., 1995).

103. The first album of Will to Power (Bob Rosenberg, Suzi Carr, Dr. J), *Will to Power,* © 1988 CBS Records, Inc., ET 40940, has as its jacket-cover slogan: "'A strong life masters its environment . . . whatever does not destroy me makes me stronger, life remains . . . WILL TO POWER!' – Nietzsche"; and has among its cuts "Zarathustra," "Freebird Medley (Free Baby)," and "Anti-Social." Other current "Nietzschean" bands are far less naïve, well-meaning, and benign. In one recent song, the German skinhead band out of Stuttgart with the "Nietzschean" name Neue Werte (new values) instructs Germans how to deal with the nearly two-million-strong "Turkish" population: "Kill their children, rape their women. . . . " Alfred Rosenberg salutes from his grave.

104. Rosen, "Nietzsche's Revolution," pp. 189–190.

105. Rorty, "De Man and the American Cultural Left" [1989], in *Philosophical Papers,* vol. 2: *Essays on Heidegger and Others* (Cambridge: Cambridge University Press, 1991), pp. 129–139; here p. 137.

106. Rorty, "Introduction: Pragmatism and Post-Nietzschean Philosophy," in *Essays on Heidegger and Others*, p. 1.

107. Rorty, "Philosophy as Science, as Metaphor, and as Politics" [1986–1989], in *Essays on Heidegger and Others*, pp. 9–26; here esp. p. 19.

108. Rorty, *Contingency, Irony, and Solidarity* [based on lectures delivered 1986–1987] (Cambridge: Cambridge University Press, 1989).

109. Ibid., pp. 119–120.

110. Jean-François Lyotard, *Discours, Figure* (Paris: Éditions Klincksieck, 1971), p. 283.

111. Rosalind Krauss, "The Im/pulse to See," in *Vision and Visuality*, ed. Hal Foster (Seattle: Bay Press, 1988), pp. 51–75; here p. 66.

112. François Laruelle, *Nietzsche contre Heidegger: Thèses pour une politique nietzschéene* (Paris: Payot, 1977), p. 9. This remains the most extensive attempt in political philosophy to distinguish Nietzsche from Heidegger at the expense of the latter, on behalf of the former.

113. LAIBACH: *A Film from Slovenia* (Daniel Landin, A TV Slovenia/Mute Film Production, 1993). This film is part documentary, part critical analysis provided by Žižek, part music video, part advertisement. On Laibach, see further Žižek, *The Metastases of Enjoyment*, pp. 71–72 and 208.

114. But, in addition to Žižek's take on the film in the film, Laibach confirms Balibar's neo-Spinozist analysis that today "borders, boundaries or limits are no longer mainly (or apparently) on the *fringes* of every political 'community,' they are located *everywhere* (just as the 'peripheries' of the world economy are more and more in its 'center'). It is, therefore, a world in which the *projective mechanisms* of identification or (imaginary) recognition of the 'human' and the 'infra-human' (perhaps even the 'superhuman,' since there is no stable 'measure' of humanness in this respect, or better said, the 'mismeasure' is the actual rule), which classical psychoanalysis described mainly at the *individual* level (although they are in reality profoundly *transindividual*) become direct stakes and objects of politics" (Balibar, preface to *Masses, Classes, Ideas*, pp. xix–xx; on the Spinozist origins of this argument, see pp. 27–28 and 34–35).

115. For a rare glimpse at Heidegger's view of the relationship between esotericism and political ontology see his *Beiträge zur Philosophie (Vom Ereignis); Gesamtausgabe*, 3/65:3 and 61–62; and *Grundfragen der Philosophie; Gesamtausgabe*, 2/45:191–223.

116. Tom Rockmore, *On Heidegger's Nazism and Philosophy* (Berkeley, Los Angeles, Oxford: University of California Press, 1992), p. 16.

117. See, for example, Jeffrey Herf, *Reactionary Modernism, Technology, Culture, and Politics in Weimar and the Third Reich* (Cambridge: Cambridge University Press, 1984).

118. Josef Goebbels, speech of February 17, 1939; as cited in Herf, *Reactionary Modernism*, p. 196.

119. Compare and contrast, for example, Reiner Schürmann, *Heidegger on Being and Acting: From Principles to Anarchy* [*Le principe d'anarchie: Heidegger et la question de l'agir,* 1982], trans. Christine-Marie Gros, in collaboration with the author (Bloomington: Indiana University Press, 1987), with Gianni Vattimo, *The End of Modernity: Nihilism and Hermeneutics in Postmodern Culture* [1985], trans. with an introduction by Jon R. Snyder (Baltimore: The Johns Hopkins University Press, 1991). See further their contributions to the anthology *The Problem of Technology in the Western Tradition,* ed. Arthur M. Melzer, Jerry Weinberger, and M. Richard Zinmann (Ithaca and London: Cornell University Press, 1993), ch. 8: Schürmann, "Technicity, Topology, Tragedy: Heidegger on 'That Which Saves' in the Global Reach," and ch. 9: Vattimo, "Postmodernity, Technology, Ontology."

120. See especially Vattimo's major attempt in the early 1970s to produce a Nietzsche for the Left: *Il soggetto e la maschera: Nietzsche e il problema della liberazione* (Milan: Bompiani, 1974), which is being translated into English by Bruno Bosteels.

121. For example, the full political-ontological dimension of Heidegger's famous 1936 talk in Rome on "Hölderlin and the Essence of Poetry" remains obscure because we do not have access to Heidegger's companion lecture on "Europe and German Philosophy," which he delivered six days later in Rome at the Kaiser Wilhelm Institut. Karl Löwith, who was present at the Hölderlin talk and who sensed what was politically at stake, cannot help us here. As a Jew he was not invited or allowed to attend the Nietzsche event at the national socialist think tank. Heidegger himself conceived the two lectures as necessary pendants to one another. See Hugo Ott, *Martin Heidegger: Unterwegs zu seiner Biographie* (Frankfurt am Main and New York: Campus Verlag, 1988), pp. 132–137 and 251–253. On the larger context of Heidegger's invitation to Rome and on Heidegger's subsequent misrepresentation of it, see Victor Farías, *Heidegger und der Nationalsozialismus,* trans. Klaus Laermann, with an introduction by Jürgen Habermas (Frankfurt am Main: S. Fischer, 1989), pp. 311–317.

122. On Heidegger and national socialism, see especially Alexander Schwan, *Politische Philosophie im Denken Heideggers* [1965], 2d, expanded ed. (Opladen: Westdeutscher Verlag, 1989); Ott, *Martin Heidegger,* along with his numerous articles on the subject; the anthology *Heidegger und die praktische Philosophie;* and, especially important, Dieter Thomä, *Die Zeit des Selbst und die Zeit danach: Zur Kritik der Textgeschichte Martin Heideggers 1910–1976* (Frankfurt am Main: Suhrkamp Verlag, 1990). For useful but ultimately not very incisive recent attempts to relate Heidegger's relationship with technology and national socialism to the influence of Nietzsche among others, see (in addition to the contextual depiction in Herf's *Reactionary Modernism*) Silvio Vietta, *Heideggers Kritik am Nationalsozialismus und an die Technik* (Tübingen: Max Niemeyer, 1989); Michael E. Zimmerman, *Heidegger's Confrontation with Modernity: Technology, Politics, Art* (Bloomington and Indianapolis: Indiana University Press, 1990); Richard Wolin, *The Politics of Being: The Political Thought of Martin Heidegger* (New York: Columbia University Press,

1990); Rockmore, *On Heidegger's Nazism and Philosophy*, pp. 204–243; and some of the essays in *The Heidegger Case: On Philosophy and Politics*. Vietta's book is, knowingly or not, an apologia for Heidegger's Nazism, whereas Zimmerman, Wolin, and Rockmore think they are more critical. But all share an inadequate appreciation of Heidegger's and Nietzsche's *esotericism* and *rhetoric,* and so remain locked in a merely *thematic* problematic. Of all these, Rockmore goes farthest in tackling the problem of concealment and unconcealment but not as an illocutionary practice of subliminal communication. On Heidegger's strategic attempt to backdate his critique of technology, as part of his attempt to cover up his quite early personal commitment to the Nazi Party, see Hans Ebeling, "Das Ereignis des Führers: Heideggers Antwort," in *Martin Heidegger: Innen- und Außenansichten,* ed. Forum für Philosophie Bad Homburg (Frankfurt am Main: Suhrkamp Verlag, 1989), pp. 33–57. Heidegger's backdating and its political motivations are egregiously whitewashed both by his readers who use him simply to *oppose* technoculture *and* by those who wish to use him simply to *cooperate* with it. For an example of the latter see Heim, *The Metaphysics of Virtual Reality,* esp. p. 54. For an example of the former, see the works of Hubert L. Dreyfus, which are as hopelessly confused as is Heim with regard to Heidegger's political agenda and illocutionary technique. See Dreyfus, *What Computers Can't Do: A Critique of Artificial Reason* [1979], rev. ed. (Cambridge, Mass.: The MIT Press, 1992), *Mind over Machine: The Power of Human Intuition and Expertise in the Era of the Computer,* with Stuart E. Dreyfus and Tom Athanasion (New York: The Free Press, 1985), and *Being-in-the-World: A Commentary on Heidegger's "Being and Time," Division I* (Cambridge, Mass.: The MIT Press, 1990).

123. Rorty, *Contingency, Irony, and Solidarity,* p. 20; emphasis added.

124. Ibid., pp. 53–54.

125. Ansell-Pearson, *An Introduction to Nietzsche as Political Thinker,* p. 170. Similarly deficient is the author's objection to a book by William Connolly—in which Nietzsche is discussed in terms of "radical liberalism"—on the grounds that "there is something risible about the attempt to enlist Nietzsche's thinking to the cause of a postmodern liberalism" (p. 178). For Connolly is exactly like Ansell-Pearson in that both begin and end with the assumption that Nietzsche did not have a unified political stand, stance, or theory but rather what is hallucinated as "a diverse set of ethical and political possibilities." Cf. William E. Connolly, *Political Theory and Modernity* (Oxford: Basil Blackwell, 1988), p. 140, to *An Introduction to Nietzsche as Political Thinker,* pp. 1 and 199.

126. Ansell-Pearson, *An Introduction to Nietzsche as Political Thinker,* p. 171.

127. Kirk Rising Ireland, "Fish Hooks, Nostrils, and Nietzsche," unpublished manuscript, p. 5. See further his "Anglers, Satyr-Gods, and 'Divine Lizards': Comedy in Excess."

128. Northrop Frye, *The Anatomy of Criticism: Four Essays* [1957] (Princeton: Princeton University Press, 1971), pp. 40–41.

129. Ireland, "Fish Hooks, Nostrils, and Nietzsche," pp. 5–6.

130. Rorty's notion of "irony" barely skims Nietzsche's surface. Appealing to Nietzsche, Hayden White argued that, "as the basis of a world view, irony tends to dissolve all belief in the possibility of positive social actions" (Hayden White, *Metahistory: The Historical Imagination in Nineteenth-Century Europe* [Baltimore: The Johns Hopkins University Press, 1973], p. 38). But if that were true, Nietzsche and his corps/e would have nothing to do with irony—except exoterically. Nor does it help matters to gloss White's argument by adding that "this kind of irony, the wit of the self-conscious mind, was itself put into question by the total ironism of Nietzsche—a 'world-historical irony,' as he called it, that even destroyed the pretensions to positivity of irony itself" (Vidler, *The Architectural Uncanny*, p. 192). This claim, still reading only the most exoteric level of Nietzsche's rhetoric, continues to obscure not merely the *core* content of his political philosophy but also his way of implementing it: that is, by forming his *corps*.

131. See, for example, *Glenngary Glen Ross* (James Foley, USA, 1992), based on the Broadway play by David Mamet. The pitch of real estate salesman Roma (Al Pacino) illustrates particularly well Ireland's theory of the eiron-alazon as a mode of properly Nietzschean confidence.

132. Althusser, "The 'Piccolo Teatro,'" in *For Marx*, p. 139 n. f; emphasis added.

133. Žižek, *The Metastases of Enjoyment*, p. 72.

134. Podoroga's position can be described as "postcontemporary" to the extent that it is comparable with Baudrillard's postpsychoanalytic thesis that "we have two existences, each one perfectly original and independent of the other (this is not psychological splitting). Any interpretation of the one by the other is impossible — this is why psychoanalysis is futile" (Baudrillard, *Cool Memories 1980–1985*, p. 146). But Podoroga, unlike Baudrillard, has lived and thought in, and through, a social formation claiming to be "communist," and unlike Baudrillard is thus careful to draw very exact, and exacting, distinctions between "we" and "you," "us" and "them." See Podoroga, "The Eunuch of the Soul," esp. 387–388.

135. For the classic account of the way visibility and invisibility are not only mutually imbricated in a single intellectual problematic but also as a matter of "embodiment" and "the flesh," see Maurice Merleau-Ponty, *The Visible and the Invisible* [posthumously published 1964], ed. Claude Lefort, trans. Alphonso Lingis (Evanston: Northwestern University Press, 1968). Merleau-Ponty argues, for example, that "it is not *I* who sees, not *he* who sees, because an anonymous visibility inhabits both of us, a vision in general, in virtue of that primordial property that belongs to the flesh, being here and now" (p. 142). On the way that the hegemony of images of vision in philosophy can go hand in hand with antiocularism, see Martin Jay, *Downcast Eyes: The Denigration of Vision in Twentieth-Century French Thought* (Berkeley, Los Angeles, London: University of California Press, 1993).

136. For relevant but less demanding views of Platonov than Podoroga's see the entry in *Handbook of Russian Literature*, ed. Victor Terras (New Haven and London: Yale University Press, 1985), pp. 341–342; and Thomas Seifrid, *Andrei Platonov:*

Uncertainties of Spirit (Cambridge: Cambridge University Press, 1992). On the great importance of Platonov for reflecting on the nexus utopia-modernism-death from the perspective of non-socialist realist, but communist, Second World culture, see Jameson's argument that *Chevengur* is "a text first read by the last surviving modernists in world culture, over whose shoulders we postmoderns are still in a position to peer," a text itself surviving "in the virtually universal débâcle of the modernist repertoire elsewhere . . ." (Jameson, *The Seeds of Time*, pp. 80 and 81).

137. Podoroga, "The Eunuch of the Soul," 362.

138. William Styron, *Darkness Visible: A Memoir of Madness* [1990] (New York: Vintage, 1992), p. 64.

139. Tracy B. Strong, *Friedrich Nietzsche and the Politics of Transfiguration* [1975], 2d, expanded ed. (Berkeley, Los Angeles, and London: University of California Press, 1988), p. 217, following the long train of Kaufmann's 1950 *Nietzsche: Philosopher, Psychologist, Antichrist*. Strong's occasionally interesting, more often erratic and unfocused work commences with the statement that it will "take at face value those claims in Nietzsche which appear the most histrionic and exasperating," yet tends not to do this. Never making clear enough what "transfiguration" has to do with political philosophy in general or Nietzsche's in particular, Strong remains too dependent on the apologetics of Kaufmann among others. Nor are these problems remedied by his more recent, particularly uneventful essay, "Nietzsche's Political Aesthetics," in *Nietzsche's New Seas: Explorations in Philosophy, Aesthetics, and Politics*, ed. Michael Allen Gillespie and Tracy B. Strong (Chicago and London: The University of Chicago Press, 1988), pp. 153–174.

Bruce Detwiler is right that there is in Strong's account "no sufficient explanation for Nietzsche's advocacy of war, slavery, or a long order of rank between classes and castes" (Detwiler, *Nietzsche and the Politics of Aristocratic Radicalism* [Chicago and London: The University of Chicago Press, 1990], p. 221 n. 23). But this remark is applicable to most of the Nietzsche Industry: Left, Right, and Center. Detwiler's book is the first systematic study in English to take Nietzsche's virulent antidemocratic animus more or less at its word. Unfortunately, Detwiler's account is innocent of a sufficiently coherent political, philosophical, or philological theory of its *own*, though it often does a good job of calling to task the readings of Nietzsche's politics produced by American commentators such as Kaufmann, Strong, and Mark Warren. The following comment sums up some of Detwiler's problems: "It is *not* my objective to *denigrate* the significance of Nietzsche's achievement, and I have *no* desire to *promote* Nietzschean politics, which, as I interpret them, are intriguing but odious. Nevertheless, there is something problematic about propounding Nietzschean ideas without exploring their ostensible political dimension. To the extent that Nietzsche's political views are *integral* with the rest of his thought—to the extent that they are made possible by it and in some ways even required by it (and I believe they are)—we stand guilty of both sanitizing and trivializing his contribution when we deliberately sweep under the rug its unsavory political implications"

(p. 5; emphasis added). This passage, too, is symptomatic of the Nietzsche Industry spearheaded by many people and institutions, including the international publication *Nietzsche-Studien*. Its underlying sense seems to be this: If Nietzsche's political views are *integral* with the rest of his thought — and they are, in Detwiler's view — and if these views are taken to be *odious* — and he thinks they are — then (*pace* Detwiler) *not* to have the wish to *denigrate* Nietzsche's achievement is *itself* nothing but a sanitization and trivialization of Nietzsche's "contribution" to whatever it is a contribution to. Detwiler attempts to explain what Nietzsche's "contribution" is exactly, by saying that "if one believes with [J. S.] Mill, as this writer does, in the value of even offensive challenges to one's beliefs, . . . then the proper response to Nietzsche's immoralism in the political sphere is to think it through" (p. 8). What, then, does Detwiler himself believe in, on what point does he stand to make his critique of Nietzsche's political thinking? Well, Detwiler believes in offensive challenges to his own beliefs. What beliefs exactly? Well, offensive challenges to them, and so on. This circular, if not also masochistic gesture, is hardly reassuring as a way of getting after or out of Nietzscheanism. Not a few of Detwiler's methodological and conceptual confusions — which time and again reveal Detwiler showing beyond much doubt that Nietzsche was a deeply protofascist thinker, and yet also denying the radical implications of this very demonstration — can be traced to the fact that, with the notable exceptions of Nietzsche's early essay "The Greek State" (1872) and the materials published by Nietzsche's sister as *The Will to Power*, Detwiler ignores virtually all of Nietzsche's unpublished notebooks and letters. Detwiler's attempt on pp. 14–16 to explain his principle of selecting published over unpublished work is particularly convoluted and no advance over Kaufmann's similar philological bias nearly a half-century ago. This is one reason — and he wrote his book under the partial guidance of a Straussian — that Detwiler does not entertain the possibility that Nietzsche was an esoteric thinker, and that perhaps he did not publish exactly what he could have said. On the one hand, then, *Nietzsche and the Politics of Aristocratic Radicalism* renders a valuable service to Anglo-American Nietzsche scholarship, though Detwiler seems ignorant of the most relevant German and French studies on his topic. He has convincingly uncovered some dominant patterns of Nietzsche's antidemocratic and protofascist political agenda. On the other hand, Detwiler can say only *what* Nietzsche's agenda looked like at the thematic level; his methodological and hermeneutic incoherency disallows the vitally important question of *how* Nietzsche intended to implement or disseminate this political project with, and as, writing. This failure becomes an issue especially at pp. 42–44, 65–66, 67, 130, 166, 169, and 188.

140. Rosen, "Remarks on Nietzsche's 'Platonism,'" in *The Quarrel Between Philosophy and Poetry: Studies in Ancient Thought* (New York and London: Routledge, 1988), pp. 183–203; here p. 189. The context of Rosen's claim is crucial to it. "An accurate account of the history of philosophy would . . . look something like this. There are three fundamental 'positions' or teachings: (1) the position of Plato and

Heidegger, or genuine Platonism, namely, the attempt to preserve the quarrel between poetry and philosophy in a third language that is the origin of both; (2)
'Platonism,' or the self-deluded attempt to replace poetry by a fundamentally mathematical philosophy which is actually itself poetry; (3) the teaching of Nietzsche, or
the self-conscious recognition that poetry is triumphant over philosophy. What is
today called 'postmodernism' is a version of the teaching of Nietzsche" (pp. 188–
189). For Rosen's most extensive development of this argument see *The Question of
Being*, esp. pp. 137–175. Whatever one may think of it for other—ideological—
reasons, Rosen's account of the "quarrel" in question is far more precise and valuable—both to grasp Nietzsche and generally—than is the account of a stridently
"postmodern" book that passes over Rosen in silence, even as it struggles to define
Nietzsche in similar terms. See Bernd Magnus, Stanley Stewart, and Jean-Pierre
Mileur, *Nietzsche's Case: Philosophy as/and Literature* (New York and London: Routledge, 1993 [actually 1992]). It is never made clear here what might really have been
at stake for Nietzsche politically—or even philosophically and poetically—in the
tendentious distinction between "philosophy" and "literature." Nor does this distinction matter very much to the authors, since these terms are imagined to refer
pretty much to the same thing anyway. Their more specific claim is that "the body of
Nietzsche's thought [is] *thoroughly* permeable and suturable, available to thoughtful
intervention, whether the means be marked 'literary' or 'philosophical'"; nonetheless, by a paradoxical and remarkably unconscious sleight of hand, the authors
claim in the same breath to have produced for and with Nietzsche not only "a kind
of suturing, even a kind of healing" but also "above all a kind of thinking that
has a *rigor* of its own—a rigor which, one hopes, has left mortis behind" (p. 255;
emphases added). A particularly pious hope in the case of this book, one might
add.

141. Rosen, "Remarks on Nietzsche's 'Platonism,'" in *The Quarrel Between Philosophy and Poetry*, p. 202.

142. See Shadia B. Drury, *The Political Ideas of Leo Strauss* (New York: St. Martin's
Press, 1988), esp. ch. 9: "Post-Modernity: Plato or Nietzsche?" and ch. 10: "Esoteri-
cism Betrayed." On Straussian Nietzscheanism, see further Levine, *Nietzsche and the
Modern Crisis of the Humanities*, pp. 152–167.

143. Rémi Brague, "Leo Strauss and Maimonides," in *Leo Strauss's Thought: Toward a Critical Engagement*, pp. 93–114; here pp. 104 and 105.

144. See, for example, for a useful introduction to this Straussian problematic in
relation to contemporary literary theory and criticism, Cantor, "Leo Strauss and
Contemporary Hermeneutics," in *Leo Strauss's Thought: Toward a Critical Engagement;* esp. p. 269. Because Cantor is silent about the likelihood that Strauss himself was an esoteric writer, and hence also a *Nietzschean* to one degree or another,
Strauss—bizarrely—is figured here as a wholly unproblematic, benevolent cham-
pion of liberal democracy and pluralism.

145. See Strauss, "Note on the Plan of Nietzsche's *Beyond Good and Evil*" [1973],

in *Studies in Platonic Political Philosophy*, with an introduction by Thomas L. Pangle (Chicago and London: The University of Chicago Press, 1983), pp. 174–191.

146. Strauss, *The City and Man*, p. 52.

147. Rosen, "Leo Strauss and the Quarrel Between the Ancients and the Moderns" [1986], in *Leo Strauss's Thought: Toward a Critical Engagement*, pp. 155–168; here p. 161.

148. Hampshire, *Spinoza*, p. 167.

149. Spinoza, *The Ethics*, p. 235 [part 4, prop. 72].

150. Rosen, "Remarks on Nietzsche's 'Platonism,'" p. 203.

151. Bataille, *Theory of Religion*, p. 59. *Œuvres complètes*, 7:316–317.

152. Spinoza, *The Ethics*, p. 234 [part 4, prop. 70].

153. Rosen, preface to *The Quarrel Between Philosophy and Poetry*, pp. vii–xiii; here p. vii.

154. Rosen, *Hermeneutics as Politics* (New York and Oxford: Oxford University Press, 1987), p. 193.

155. Nor can Rosen's arguments be found informing, for better or worse, the pages of *Revolutionary Worker*, the organ of the Maoist-inspired Revolutionary Communist Party, USA (RCPUSA). Its "Three Main Points": "(1) The whole system we now live under is based on exploitation—here and all over the world. It is completely worthless and no basic change for the better can come about until this system is overthrown. (2) Many different groups will protest and rebel against things this system does, and these protests and rebellions should be supported and strengthened. Yet it is only those with nothing to lose but their chains who can be the backbone of a struggle actually to overthrow this system and create a new system that will put an end to exploitation and help pave the way to a whole new world. (3) Such a revolutionary struggle is possible. There is a political Party that can lead in such a struggle, a political Party that speaks and acts for those with nothing to lose but their chains . . . " (*Revolutionary Worker* 787 [vol. 16:34], December 25, 1994).

156. DeLillo, *Mao II*, p. 141.

157. Warren, *Nietzsche's Political Thought*, p. 213.

158. See Lukács, "Nietzsche als Vorläufer der faschistischen Ästhetik" [written 1934, published 1935], in *Werke*, vol. 10: *Probleme der Ästhetik* (Neuwied am Rhein and Berlin: Luchterhand, 1969), pp. 307–339; esp. pp. 333–334.

159. Freud, *Group Psychology and the Analysis of the Ego* [1921], ed. and trans. James Strachey (New York: W. W. Norton & Co., 1952), p. 55; emphasis added.

160. Warren, *Nietzsche's Political Thought*, p. 209.

161. Ibid., p. xiv. Henning Ottmann, whose evaluation of Nietzsche's ideological position is in some ways similar to Warren's—though not as positively, or even at all, attuned to the problematic of postmodernism—provides a more solid reconstruction of the context and development of Nietzsche's political ideas in their own terms, something Warren does not necessarily set out to do. But Ottmann, too, has no clear sense of the distinction between Nietzsche's eso- and exoteric levels of

work, substituting instead a loose distinction between "truthfulness" and "masking" — and even then only in order to make the all-too-familiar claim that Nietzsche wrote for "those who can think for themselves," and so on. Cf. Ottmann, *Philosophie und Politik bei Nietzsche* (Berlin and New York: Walter de Gruyter, 1987). Nor do either Ottmann or Warren — who wrote independently of one another — delve with sufficient depth into Nietzsche's workbooks, and as a consequence they share the dual — more or less "postmodern" — defect of taking Nietzsche's philosophy too seriously as a positive — albeit more or less limited — contribution to contemporary political thought, and not seriously enough in its original revolutionary intent. This is not to say that the construction of that intent ought to be the only thing that matters; it is to say, however, that both Warren and Ottmann are symptomatic of most Nietzsche scholarship in that they base their own political notions to a significant degree on an intent that is never really scrutinized, and yet one that uncannily anticipates, prefigures, and informs their work, even at its most "critical" moments. For a somewhat more critical account of Nietzsche's political philosophy, but one that also passes over its esoteric dimension in silence, see Urs Marti, *"Der grosse Pöbel und Sklavenaufstand": Nietzsches Auseinandersetzung mit Revolution und Demokratie* (Stuttgart und Weimar: J. B. Metzler, 1993). Marti makes his point of departure the problem of how to appropriate under current postmodern conditions a body of thought, notably Nietzsche's, that emerged under modernism. But his "historical" formulation of Nietzscheanism ignores the possibility of esotericism, conceals the fact that Nietzsche was shrewder than to reduce his thought to historical and economic contingencies, and makes impossible an explanation of the massive influence of this thought precisely on postmoderns. Compare also Ansell-Pearson's *An Introduction to Nietzsche as Political Thinker,* where the esoteric is also wholly unknown territory, and where therefore Nietzsche must remain "ambiguous and paradoxical" (p. 1), "fundamentally ambiguous and double-natured" (p. 199). Ansell-Pearson's analysis on pp. 71–78 of Nietzsche's essay "The Greek State" is particularly deficient and certainly a retreat past Detwiler.

162. In 1984 Ofelia Schutte, in an unjustly overlooked book, made the argument, sensible enough on the surface, that "While Nietzsche has outlined various incentives for overturning the democratic influences of modern times and for instituting a 'purer' system of patriarchal domination under the banner of overcoming the 'evils' of 'effeminacy' and 'decadence,' it is up to us, not him, to make the choice as to what we want our political future and our moral values to be" (Schutte, *Beyond Nihilism: Nietzsche without Masks* [Chicago and London: The University of Chicago Press, 1984], p. 188). Sounds reasonable. But then why do "we" still need Nietzsche in the first place? For apparently, according to Schutte, "we" *do* need him, buying as some of "us" do into the notion of "a future . . . promised in Nietzsche's image of the child's 'sacred Yes' to life and in the symbol of the *Übermensch"* (p. 193). Henry Staten's imagined critique of Schutte's argument is no less free from her false assumption that Nietzsche in principle meant what he said about everything, was a

basically exoteric thinker and writer. See Henry Staten, *Nietzsche's Voice* (Ithaca and London: Cornell University Press, 1990), pp. 77–83.

163. See Nietzsche to Georg Brandes, December 2, 1887; *KGB* 3/5:205–207. Also see Brandes, "An Essay on Aristocratic Radicalism" [delivered as a lecture 1887], in *Friedrich Nietzsche* [*En Afhandlung om aristokratisk radikalisme*, 1889], trans. A. G. Chater (New York: The Macmillan Company, n.d.), pp. 3–56.

164. See, for example, Nietzsche, *Die fröhliche Wissenschaft* [1st ed. 1882]; *KGW* 5/2:75 [aphorism 29], and *Götzen-Dämmerung oder Wie man mit dem Hammer philosophiert* [written 1888, published 1889]; *KGW* 6/3:138 ["Skirmishes of an Untimely Man," aphorism 43].

165. Nietzsche, "NF, Frühjahr 1884"; *KGW* 7/2:99.

166. Georgi Plekhanov, *Art and Social Life* [1912], in *Selected Philosophical Works*, 2d, rev. ed., trans. K. M. Cook and A. Fineberg (Moscow: Progress Publishers, 1981), 5:630–687; here 664–665. In this and several other impressive works, Plekhanov provided the earliest and still most valid *sociological* approach to both Nietzsche and Nietzscheanism.

167. Rosen, "Nietzsche's Revolution," in *The Ancients and the Moderns*, pp. 190–193; emphasis added.

168. Pasolini, "Le ceneri di Gramsci" [the ashes of Gramsci, 1954], in *Poems* [dual-language ed.], ed. and trans. Norman MacAfee, with Luciano Martinengo, foreword by Enzo Siciliano (New York: Vintage Books, 1982), pp. 2–23; here pp. 12–13. " . . . Ma come io possiedo la storia, / essa mi possieda; ne solo illuminato: / ma a che serve la luce? / Non dico l'individuo. . . . "

169. Jean-Luc Nancy, "Exscription" [1977], trans. Katherine Lydon, in *On Bataille*, ed. Allan Stoekl, special issue of *Yale French Studies* 78 (1990), pp. 47–65; here pp. 47–48.

170. See Freud, *The Interpretation of Dreams* [1899–1900], trans. James Strachey (New York: Avon, 1965), p. 545. On the implications of this thesis for interpretation generally, see Mehlman, "Trimethylamin: Notes on Freud's Specimen Dream," *Diacritics* 6:1 (1976), 42–45, and *Walter Benjamin for Children*, p. 6.

171. Virilio, *The Lost Dimension*, p. 103.

172. Greimas's "semantic rectangle" or "elementary structure of signification" — even as developed by Jameson for Marxism as a way of problematizing all binary and merely "dialectical" paradigms — remains locked in Channel 3 as this book figures it. Jameson's "political unconscious" and the "conspiracy theory," both of which depend on the semantic rectangle, also pull up short of confronting the possibility and fact of consciously programmed subliminal reception. In *this* respect, what is to be said about the *structural* paradigms of Barthes and Althusser could also be said *mutatis mutandis* about those of Greimas and Jameson. Greimas's system suggests two basic ways the semantic rectangle is un/finished: either as "constitution": that is, so as to constitute an independent textual or semantic system with the supplement of a fourth term to the triangle of positive term, oppositional term, and

negative term; or as "transformation": that is, when the fourth term is not given, or given in an unexpected way, which then forces the uncompleted rectangle of signification to be propelled into yet another one, any resolution deferred indefinitely. In addition to Greimas, *Sémantique structurale,* see Greimas with François Rastier, "The Interaction of Semantic Constraints," *Yale French Studies* 41 (1968), 86–105. Finally, as Jameson puts it, "in actual practice, however, it frequently turns out that we are able to articulate a given concept in only three of the four available positions; the final one remains a cipher, or enigma for the mind" (Jameson, *The Prison-House of Language: A Critical Account of Structuralism and Russian Formalism* [Princeton: Princeton University Press, 1972], p. 166). Whatever spin one gives it, the semantic rectangle remains just that — a matter of a *meaning* accessible in principle to *conscious* perception. Wherever else its analytic powers may lie, and they are among the greatest in all linguistic and literary criticism, the rectangle has insufficient power to crack the code of Nietzsche's Channel 4.

173. Barthes, "The Third Meaning: Research Notes on Some Eisenstein Stills" [1970], in *A Barthes Reader,* ed. with an introduction by Susan Sontag (New York: Hill and Wang, 1982), pp. 317–333. A veritable "school" of cultural studies finds its theoretical and methodological warrant in this one essay.

174. Althusser, "On the Marxist Dialectic," in *For Marx,* p. 183.

175. Ibid., pp. 184–185.

176. "The theory of proper names should not be conceived of in terms of representation; it refers instead to the class of 'effects': effects that are not a mere dependence on causes, but the occupation of a domain, and the operation of a system of signs." This theory of name-effects was explicitly developed by Deleuze and Guattari out of a reading of Nietzsche's *Ecce Homo* (Deleuze and Guattari, *Anti-Oedipus,* p. 86; see also pp. 20–21, 63, 185–186, 343–345, and 367–368). See also, from a very different perspective, the account of naming given by Kripke. A distinction between proper names as "rigid designators" and "nonrigid or accidental designators" is considered in terms of the "tendency to demand purely qualitative descriptions of counterfactual situations," and of the concomitant "confusion of the epistemological and the metaphysical, between a priority and necessity" (Saul A. Kripke, *Naming and Necessity* [1972], 2d ed. [Cambridge, Mass.: Harvard University Press, 1980], pp. 48–49).

177. For the first and most enduring of Harold Bloom's analyses of literary epigonism see *The Anxiety of Influence: A Theory of Poetry* (London, Oxford, New York: Oxford University Press, 1973). A member of Nietzsche's corps/e, Bloom waffles uncontrollably on the question of whether his own great, admitted precursor, Nietzsche, *was* or was *not* beset by the anxiety or influence. From the perspective of structural causality, however, this question is moot.

178. See Umberto Eco, *Lector in fabula* (Milan: Bompiani, 1971), pp. 59–60.

179. Hyppolite, "The Structure of Philosophic Language According to the 'Preface' to Hegel's *Phenomenology of Mind,*" in *The Structuralist Controversy,* p. 167.

180. Myron E. Krueger, foreword to Heim, *The Metaphysics of Virtual Reality*, pp. vi–xi; here p. ix. Krueger is commonly called the primary "inventor" of VR technology.

181. Takayuki Tatsumi, "The Japanese Reflection of Mirrorshades," in *Storming the Reality Studio: A Casebook of Cyberpunk and Postmodern Science Fiction*, ed. Larry McCaffery (Durham and London: Duke University Press, 1991), pp. 366–373; here p. 372; emphasis added. But for William Gibson's most complex take to date on "Japan," see *Virtual Light* (New York: A Bantam Spectra Book, 1993).

182. Schopenhauer, *The World as Will and Representation*, 1:178; *Sämtliche Werke*, 2:210 [3d bk., ch. 34].

183. Althusser, "Is It Simple to Be a Marxist in Philosophy?" in *Philosophy and the Spontaneous Philosophy of the Scientists*, p. 227. In some respects Spinoza seems to part company with Althusser on this point.

184. Spinoza, *The Ethics*, p. 148 [part 3, prop. 27; proof]; emphasis added. Think again of the Nietzschean mind-body Videodromes and Interzones, dead zones, interfaces, psycho-somatic interchanges, telepathic metamorphoses, mutations, omnisexuality, bio-psycho-hardwiring, viral communications, psychoplasmic metaphysics, and implicit monism in Cronenberg's œuvre. Cronenberg himself avers that he is a "Cartesian," though his films struggle continually to overcome all forms of dualism. See, for example, *Cronenberg on Cronenberg*, p. 58.

185. Johann Gottlieb Fichte, "Darstellung der Wissenschaftslehre" [1801], in *Sämtliche Werke*, ed. J. H. Fichte (Berlin: Verlag Veit und Comp., 1845–1846), 2:19–20. See further Manfred Frank, *What Is Neostructuralism?* [1984], trans. Sabine Wilke and Richard Gray, foreword by Martin Schwab (Minneapolis: University of Minnesota Press, 1989), pp. 89–91.

186. Paul Auster, *The New York Trilogy*, vol. 1: *City of Glass* [1985] (New York: Penguin Books, 1987), pp. 15–16.

187. Debord, *La société du spectacle*, thesis 34.

188. Spinoza, *The Ethics*, p. 163 [part 3, prop. 51].

189. On Bataille's response to Heidegger, though she overlooks Heidegger's response to Bataille, see Rebecca Comay, "Gifts without Presents: Economies of 'Experience' in Bataille and Heidegger," in *On Bataille*, pp. 66–89.

190. Derrida, "De l'économie restreinte à l'économie générale: Un hegelianisme sans reserve" [1967], in *L'écriture et la différence* (Paris: Éditions du Seuil, 1967), pp. 369–407; here p. 369. For a translation see *Writing and Difference*.

191. See Bataille, "Nietzche in the Light of Marxism" [1951], in *Nietzsche's Return*, ed. James Leigh and Roger McKeon, special issue of *Semiotext(e)* 3:1 (1978), 114–119; here 116. Also see his *The Accursed Share*, vols. 2 and 3:367 (*Sovereignty*). *Œuvres complètes*, 8:401. For an account of Nietzsche and Bataille that differs from that of this book see Nick Land, *Thirst for Annihilation: Georges Bataille and Virulent Nihilism; an Essay in Atheistic Religion* (London and New York: Routledge, 1992).

192. Bataille, *Sur Nietzsche: Volonté de chance* [1944–1945]; *Œuvres complètes*, 6:17.

For a translation see, *On Nietzsche*, trans. Bruce Boone, introduction by Sylvère Lotringer (New York: Paragon House, 1992). Its title and main theme notwithstanding, this book is more a record of a stage of Bataille's spiritual odyssey during the German occupation and eve of liberation in terms of an imagined identification with Nietzsche, and less the conceptual confrontation with Nietzsche that occurs in many of his other works. On the relationship between Bataille's interpretation of Nietzsche and his cultural politics in the 1930s, see Jean-Michel Besnier, "Georges Bataille in the 1930s: A Politics of the Impossible," trans. Amy Reid, in *On Bataille*, pp. 169–180.

193. Lou Andreas-Salomé's *Friedrich Nietzsche in seinen Werken* (Friedrich Nietzsche in his works) was first published in 1894 (Vienna: C. Konegen). In it, "Salomé writes from within an implicit presumption of convergence. She inhabits Nietzsche's own words by quoting him in such a way and to such a degree that it is often difficult to discern where his ideas leave off and hers begin. . . . Nevertheless, writing is an act of separation and difference . . . " (Biddy Martin, *Woman and Modernity: The (Life)Styles of Lou Andreas-Salomé* [Ithaca and London: Cornell University Press, 1991], p. 94).

194. Bataille, "Nietzsche and the Fascists," in *Visions of Excess*, p. 194.

195. See further Jean-Joseph Goux, "General Economics and Postmodern Capitalism," trans. Kathryn Ascheim and Rhonda Garelick, in *On Bataille*, pp. 206–224.

196. In Kant's Third Critique, "The sublime is that in comparison with which everything else is small. . . . *The sublime is that, the mere ability to think which shows a faculty of the mind surpassing every standard of sense*" (Immanuel Kant, *Kritik der Urteilskraft* [1790], ed. Wilhelm Weischedel [Frankfurt am Main: Suhrkamp Verlag, 1974], p. 172; *Critique of Judgement*, trans. J. H. Bernard [New York: Hafner Press, 1974], p. 89). But, for Kant, every standard of sense is not every standard of mind, of Ideas. On the drift of post-Kantian, romantic, and postromantic thinking away from the assumption that the Sublime or Ideas were unsayable and into a problematic of re/presentation (*Darstellung*), and on the attendant philosophical and literary aporias of this assumption, see Philippe Lacoue-Labarthe and Jean-Luc Nancy, *The Literary Absolute: The Theory of Literature in German Romanticism* [1978], trans. Philip Barnard and Cheryl Lester (Albany: State University of New York Press, 1988); and Neil Hertz, *The End of the Line: Essays on Psychoanalysis and the Sublime* (New York: Columbia University Press, 1985). For a politically sharper, and less "Nietzschean," discussion of the problem of even talking about the Kantian Sublime, see Žižek's analysis of a decisive "paradox" here: namely, "the conversion of the impossibility of presentation into the presentation of impossibility" (Žižek, *For They Know Not What They Do: Enjoyment as a Political Factor* [London and New York: Verso, 1991], p. 144). Jean-François Lyotard has summarized the enormous ambition behind Kant's location of a feeling — or rather "enthusiasm" — that would both respond to something vital in human nature and yet would not require verification by comparison with any known or unknown empirical fact. Lyotard is par-

ticularly interested in the philosophical implications of what he calls the *différend,* a labile linguistic and conceptual moment in which an assertion that for one reason *must* be phrased for some other reason *cannot* be, or cannot *yet* be. And this notion, itself of a certain "Nietzschean" inspiration, comes close to how Nietzsche often used language. See Lyotard, *The Différend: Phrases in Dispute* [1983], trans. Georges Van Den Abbelle (Minneapolis: University of Minnesota Press, 1988), pp. 12–13. On the related Heideggerian notion of the "proximate," see Emil Kettering, *Nähe: Das Denken Martin Heideggers* (Pfullingen: Günther Neske, 1987); in this regard, Lyotard's *différend* reinvents a Heideggerian wheel. In *Kant's Critical Philosophy,* Deleuze argues that a point of the Kantian confrontation with the Sublime was to force the imagination, in Kant's own phrase, to "recoil upon itself," and thereby to learn that, in Deleuze's words, "it is reason which pushes [imagination] to the limit of its power, forcing it to admit that all its power is nothing *in comparison to an Idea"* (pp. 51–52; emphasis added). But it is also thus that the principle of comparability is recuperated by and for Idealism; in Deleuze's precise turn of phrase: "the Ideas of reason are speculatively indeterminate, practically determined" (p. 52). It should be unnecessary to add that, ideologically speaking, the Sublime is an open site, not necessarily owned by the Right, the Center, or the Left. On the possibility of mobilizing the theory of the sublime for Marxism, see Terry Eagleton, *The Ideology of the Aesthetic,* ch. 8: "The Marxist Sublime." But the properly Nietzschean question remains as how to use the Sublime as something subliminal.

197. A binary obverse of the Sublime is, roughly, what the non-Catholic theological tradition calls "Hell." It, too, strictly speaking — unlike the Catholic version — can be neither visualized nor described. Calvin grasped each and every word for Hell in the New Testament as "that which our senses are unable to comprehend" — much like the Kantian Sublime. Needless to say, the presumed actuality of Hell — or of the Sublime — hardly ceased to exist for merely linguistic reasons. See John Calvin, *Commentary on a Harmony of the Evangelists, Matthew, Mark, and Luke* [1555], trans. William Pringle (Edinburgh: The Calvin Translation Society, 1846), 3:182. What postmodernist commentators on Kant, on the Sublime generally, and on Nietzsche fail to note is its specifically Protestant — indeed *Calvinist* — inflection. Nietzsche had remarkably little to say about Calvin, though his fascination with determinism and fate — Eternal Recurrence of the Same, *amor fati* — bears remarkable similarities with predestination, *especially* since the latter so clearly has to do, as Max Weber showed, with mechanisms of social control. Nietzsche's reticence to talk about Calvin may even be a symptomatic silence.

198. See, for example, Wolfgang Kersting, "Politics, Freedom, and Order: Kant's Political Philosophy," and Eva Schaper, "Taste, Sublimity, and Genius: The Aesthetics of Nature and Art," both in *The Cambridge Companion to Kant,* ed. Paul Guyer (Cambridge: Cambridge University Press, 1992), pp. 342–366 and 367–393, respectively.

199. Much nonsense has been written and assumed about the philosophical "in-

fluences" on Nietzsche, as if he were a professional philosopher or informed critic of the institution. In fact he was not particularly well versed in the canon and was informed largely by secondary accounts, as anyone who has worked in his personal library in Weimar can testify. In spite of the fact that in 1868 he considered writing a doctoral dissertation "On the Ideology or Concept of the Organic in Kant," he did not know Kant beyond basic texts, any more than he knew Hegel, as was shown by Erich F. Podach in the 1930s. The most thoroughly read and annotated collected works in Nietzsche's private library were written not by academic philosophers but by Goethe, Schopenhauer, and Wagner. The neo-Kantian historian Friedrich Albert Lange (1828–1875) is an important exception, since Nietzsche learned much of what he knew about the history of philosophy from Lange's *History of Materialism and Critique of Its Present Significance*, which Nietzsche began devouring when it was published in 1866.

200. See Paul Ricoeur, *Le conflit des interpétations* (Paris: Éditions du Seuil, 1969), p. 55.

201. See Jameson, *The Prison-House of Language*, pp. 214–216.

202. The requirements for being a real "savage anomaly" are very severe: "Spinozian philosophy is an anomaly in its century and is savage to the eyes of the dominant culture. This is a tragedy of every philosophy, of every savage testimony of truth that is posed against time — against the present time and against the present reality. But the tragedy can open itself powerfully into the future" (Negri, *The Savage Anomaly*, p. 122). The view of Spinoza as a radical democratic, even protocommunist, is by no means uncontested, of course, and his own esotericism makes it difficult to decide. On the latter problem, see Yirmiyahu Yovel, *Spinoza and Other Heretics*, vol. 1: *The Marrano of Reason* (Princeton: Princeton University Press, 1989); and, though mysteriously, Leo Strauss, *Spinoza's Critique of Religion* [written 1925–1928, first published 1930] (New York: Schocken Books, 1982). The overall relevance of Spinoza's own ideas for contemporary political thought is equally ambiguous. On the one hand he took the position of many people in his authoritarian and intolerant age that no radically new political possibilities or alternatives could exist beyond those already assayed by history: that is, monarchy, aristocracy, and more or less liberal democracy. He wrote, for example, almost as a Hegelian before the fact, that "experience has revealed *all conceivable* sorts of commonwealth, which are consistent with men's living in unity, and likewise the means by which the multitude may be guided or kept within fixed bounds. So that I do not believe that we can by meditation discover in this matter *anything* not yet tried and ascertained, which shall be consistent with experience or practice" (Spinoza, *A Political Treatise* [1676], in *A Theologico-Political Treatise and a Political Treatise*, pp. 279–387; here p. 288 [ch. 1, § 3]; emphasis added). Spinoza's model of a — relatively — ideal social formation was certainly provided by mercantile Amsterdam; and generally absent from Spinoza's thinking was an adequate concept of history — though this is disputed by Macherey in *Avec Spinoza*, esp. pp. 111–140 ("Spinoza, la fin de l'histoire et

la ruse de la raison," 1986). On the other hand Spinoza was no conservative or ultra-conservative in the modern sense, either. Antiauthoritarianism in many guises—indeed as a certain "motor of history"—informs his *Political Treatise:* for example, in the fact that insurrection against authority, up to and including violent revolution, was considered not only legitimate but absolutely necessary—if and when such insurrection could ever be deemed "the lesser evil." Spinoza's political argument depends, in part, on the liberal assumption that people can be better swayed to your position by telling them that you offer them not the best or ideal solution to any problem but rather the least bad solution, for example, Winston Churchill's dictum that "Democracy is the worst form of government except for any other"; but the implications of this argument need not support liberal pluralism, which, as Spinoza also precisely anticipated, typically ends up as a cover for other, more covert forms of superstition and tyranny. On Spinoza and the Left, see further Friedrich Balke, "Die größte Lehre in Häresie: Über die Gegenwärtigkeit der Philosophie Spinozas," afterword to Pierre-François Moreau, *Spinoza: Versuch über die Anstößigkeit seines Denkens* [*Spinoza,* 1975], trans. Rolf Löper (Frankfurt am Main: Fischer Verlag, 1994), pp. 135–179.

203. Spinoza, *The Ethics,* pp. 43–271; here p. 174 [part 3, def. 4]; also compare part 3, prop. 52 and part 4, prop. 29. According to prop. 52: "An object which we have formerly seen in conjunction with others, and which we do not conceive to have any property that is not common to many, will not be regarded by us for so long, as an object which we conceive to have some property peculiar to itself." But on the one hand Spinoza regarded what he called Substance—or *Deus sive Natura,* God or Nature—as "that which is in itself, and is conceived through itself: in other words, that of which a conception can be formed independently of any other conception," and hence so absolutely unique as to be *beyond* comparability. On the other hand—since for him Substance is not something that can ever be fully grasped, and only conceptually approximated—comparison is not only possible but *required.* See Spinoza, *The Ethics,* pp. 45 and 263 [part 1, def. 1 and part 5, prop. 31 and note]. On Kant's own response to Spinozism, see George Di Giovanni, "The First Twenty Years of Critique: The Spinoza Connection," in *The Cambridge Companion to Kant,* pp. 417–448.

204. Negri, *The Savage Anomaly,* pp. 22 and 33.

Spinoza's reply [to neoscholasticism and Descartes] is clear: the very concept of possibility is negated, because every analogical conception of being is negated. Being is univocality. This univocal being cannot be translated into analogical being on the terrain of knowledge; but, still on the terrain of knowledge, neither is it possible to be univocal. In other words, the real analysis shows us a univocally determined being, which is tenable as such only on the ontological terrain and, therefore, in the adhesion to its totality. On the terrain of knowledge it is presented as equivocal being: It allows no possibility of homology. The tension that is released here, in part II [of *Metaphysical*

Reflections, 1633], can therefore be resolved only on the terrain of practice: of power (*potentia*), within the ontological determination as such. With one single move Spinoza destroys both the Scholastic representation of analogical being and the idealistic representation of univocality, both the NeoScholastic reformism of the image of Power (*potestas*) and the Cartesian and idealistic flight from the responsibility of transformation. (p. 43)

Note: This reading of Spinoza is superficially applicable to Heidegger's political ontology and Nietzsche's political philosophy, but only if one recognizes that Heidegger and Nietzsche had no intention of radicalizing and democratizing power (*potentia*) in the way suggested by Negri. Heidegger and Nietzsche may have been antischolastic and anti-Cartesian in terms of metaphysics, but were always esoterically committed to Power (*potestas*) as a principle of social cohesion — except, perhaps, in Heidegger's very last writings on "releasement" (*Gelassenheit*).

205. See Denis Hollier, "The Dualist Materialism of Georges Bataille" [1966], trans. Hilari Allred, in *On Bataille*, pp. 124–139.

206. Already in his first major work, the *Regulae* (1628–1629), while beginning by cautioning against *superficial* comparisons, Descartes argued that all human knowledge, save that derived from "simple and naked intuition of one single thing" — which was admitted to be basic but also philosophically uninteresting and scientifically useless — is the result of comparative operations (*per comparationem*). Indeed, in this — the first significant modern — account of rational methodology — still relatively unencumbered by Descartes's later and more overt metaphysical, theological, and conservative commitments — virtually the entire task of reason was put in the service of preparing for a type of comparison for which no assistance from "art" was said to be required or desired. Thus properly prepared, comparison was imagined to yield, by means of the now rigorous and pellucid "intuition of truth," that "light of nature" (*naturae lumine*) which could be said to define proleptically the vocation of the Enlighteners and their highest goal. In the *Regulae*, then, was instaurated a powerful comparative agenda that was to be in effect for several centuries to come. See René Descartes, *Regulae ad directionem ingenii* [written 1628–1629, published 1701], in *Œuvres de Descartes* [1897–1913], corrected ed., ed. Charles Adam and Paul Tannery (Paris: Librairie philosophique J. Vrin, 1966), 10:439–440 [rule 14].

But, as Spinoza seems to have intuited, Descartes — no more than Kant or any other Enlightener later — did not adequately radicalize or democratize his "comparative method," in terms of making as transparent as possible the particular theological and governmental — let alone, socioeconomic — constituencies he served. Spinoza himself put the matter rather differently, of course. From his perspective, as described by Stuart Hampshire, Descartes, beginning with his notions of Substance and Cause, "seemed to have stopped short in developing his own doctrines to their extreme logical conclusions, partly perhaps because he foresaw some at least of the uncomfortable moral and theological consequences which must ensue; he was a rationalist who not only remained undisturbed within the Catholic Church, but even provided the Church with new armour to protect its essential doctrines against the dangerous implications of the new mathematical physics and the new method in philosophy" (Hampshire, *Spinoza*, pp. 22–23).

Finally, it should be noted that Nietzsche's own insight into Spinoza and this entire problematic was for years handicapped by his greatest and most enduring philosophical predecessor, Schopenhauer. The latter's neo-Buddhist position on causal explanation, expressed already in his first important work, *On the Fourfold Root of the Principle of Sufficient Reason* (1813), vigorously rejected the thesis that Spinozism had achieved anything like a radical epistemological or ontological break with Cartesianism. Rather, Schopenhauer held — anticipating Heidegger, who never dealt with Schopenhauer in depth — that both systems were "ontotheological" (*ontotheologisch*), that "Spinoza's pantheism is really only the *realization* of Descartes's ontological proof," and that "if neoSpinozists (Schellingites, Hegelians, etc.), accustomed as they are to confuse words with thoughts, often indulge in solemn, pompous admiration of the *causa sui*, then I, for my part, see in *causa sui* only a *contradictio in adjecto* — a Before that is really an After, an impertinent command [ein freches Machtwort] to cut the infinite chain of causality" (Schopenhauer, *Über die vierfache Wurzel des Satzes vom zureichenden Grunde*, pp. 23 and 25).

207. See Benjamin, "Das Kunstwerk im Zeitalter seiner technischen Reproduzierbarkeit" [1935], in *Gesammelte Schriften*, 2:431–508. For the standard translation, see his *Illuminations*, ed. with an introduction by Hannah Arendt, trans. Harry Zohn (New York: Schocken Books, 1969).

208. Bataille, "The Notion of Expenditure" [1933], in *Visions of Excess*, pp. 116–129; here p. 117. *Œuvres complètes*, 1:302–320; here 303. See further Kant, "Beantwortung der Frage: Was ist Aufklärung?" [1783], *Was ist Aufklärung: Aufsätze zur Geschichte und Philosophie*, ed. Jürgen Zehbe (Göttingen: Vandenhoek & Ruprecht, 1967), pp. 55–61; here p. 55. "What Is Enlightenment?" in *The Enlightenment: A Comprehensive Anthology*, ed. with introductory notes by Peter Gay (New York: Simon & Schuster, Inc., 1973), pp. 383–389; here p. 384.

209. On potlatch and "the theme of the fateful gift, the present or possession that turns to poison," see Marcel Mauss, *The Gift: Forms and Functions of Exchange in Archaic Societies* [1925], trans. Ian Cunnison with an introduction by E. E. Evans-Pritchard (New York: W. W. Norton & Company, Inc., 1967), pp. 17–45 and 62. On the Socratic *pharmakon* as both "remedy," "poison," and "the movement, the locus, and the play (or production) of difference," see Derrida, "La pharmacie de Platon" [first version 1968], in *La dissémination* (Paris: Éditions du Seuil, 1972), pp. 69–197; esp. pp. 142–146. For a translation see *Dissemination*, trans. with an introduction and additional notes by Barbara Johnson (Chicago: The University of Chicago Press, 1981). Derrida has also explicitly analyzed potlatch in subsequent works, especially *Donner le temps* [1991], translated as *Given Time: 1. Counterfeit Money*, trans. Peggy Kamuf (Chicago and London: The University of Chicago Press, 1992).

210. Althusser, *L'avenir dure longtemps*, in *L'avenir dure longtemps* [*suivi de*] *Les faits*, p. 98.

211. Žižek, *Tarrying with the Negative*, p. 209; last emphasis added.

212. See Bataille, *The Accursed Share: An Essay on General Economy*, vol. 1: *Consumption* [1949], trans. Robert Hurley (New York: Zone Books, 1988), p. 71. *Œuvres complètes*, 7:73. "Sans doute le *potlatch* n'est-il pas réductible au désir de perdre, mais ce qu'il apporte au donateur n'est past l'inévitable surcrôit des dons de revanche, c'est le *rang* qu'il confère à celui qui a le dernier mot."

213. Nietzsche, "NF, Herbst 1883"; *KGW* 7/1:538.

214. Bourdieu, *Outline of a Theory of Practice* [1972], expanded ed., trans. Richard Nice (Cambridge: Cambridge University Press, 1977), p. 191.

215. These paraphrases of Burke's argument are from Vidler, *The Architectural Uncanny*, pp. 20–21. See further Edmund Burke, *A Philosophical Enquiry into the Origin of Our Ideas of the Sublime and the Beautiful* [1757], ed. with an introduction and notes by James T. Boulton (Notre Dame: University of Notre Dame Press, 1968), pp. 39–40.

216. Schopenhauer, *The World as Will and Representation*, 1:255; *Sämtliche Werke*, 2:301 [3d bk., ch. 51].

217. In Schopenhauer's system, tragedy is intimately related to the Sublime as "the dawning of the knowledge that the world and life can afford us no true satisfaction, and are therefore not worth our attachment to them" (Schopenhauer, *The World as Will and Representation*, 2:433–434; *Sämtliche Werke*, 3:495 [supplements to the 3d bk., ch. 37]).

218. Bataille, *Les larmes d'Eros* [1961]; *Œuvres complètes*, 10:573–639; here 577. Habermas depicts Bataille's project as the attempt to "carry out the radical critique of reason with the tools of theory," arguing that this project was decisively "undercut" by Bataille's commitment to irrationality (Habermas, *The Philosophical Discourse of Modernity*, p. 237). In light of Bataille's just-cited remark, however, Habermas's view of Bataille is insufficiently complex. Possessing prodigious gifts for critical paraphrase, Habermas has very little talent as a close reader.

219. Bataille, *Les larmes d'Eros*; *Œuvres complètes*, 10:609.

220. Lefebvre, *The Production of Space*, p. 289.

221. Sloterdijk, *Critique of Cynical Reason*, p. 77.

222. Deleuze, *Kant's Critical Philosophy: The Doctrine of the Faculties* [1963], trans. Hugh Tomlinson and Barbara Habberjam (Minneapolis: University of Minnesota Press, 1990), p. 64. For a current reading of Kant's and Nietzsche's ostensible views of "interpretation" (*Interpretation und Auslegung*) that is particularly locked without drift somewhere in the snow of Channel 3, see Werner Hamacher, "The Promise of Interpretation: Reflections on the Hermeneutical Imperative in Kant and Nietzsche," trans. Jane O. Newman and John H. Smith, in *Looking After Nietzsche*, pp. 19–47.

223. Bataille, *The Accursed Share*, vols. 2 and 3:368. (*Sovereignty*) *Œuvres complètes*, 8:402.

224. See Bataille, "The Notion of Expenditure," p. 118, and "Nietzsche and the Fascists," in *Visions of Excess,* pp. 194 and 187.

225. See Bataille, "Nietzschean Chronicle" [the continuation of "Nietzsche and the Fascists," 1937], in *Visions of Excess,* pp. 202–212, and the editor's note on p. 263.

226. Bataille, *Sur Nietzsche; Œuvres complètes,* 6:12–13.

227. Bataille, "Le labyrinthe" [1936]; *Œuvres complètes,* 1:433–441; here 436. Also see his *L'expérience intérieure* [1943]; *Œuvres complètes,* 5:7–189; here esp. 97–110. For a translation of the first text see "The Labyrinth," in *Visions of Excess,* pp. 171–177; for the second see *Inner Experience,* trans. with an introduction by Leslie Anne Boldt (Albany: State University of New York Press, 1988). See further Denis Hollier, *Against Architecture: The Writings of Georges Bataille* [*La prise de la Concorde,* 1974], trans. Betsy Wing (Cambridge, Mass.: The MIT Press, 1989), pp. 57–73; esp. pp. 71–73.

228. See, for example, Habermas, *The Philosophical Discourse of Modernity,* pp. 99–105 and 211–237.

229. See Alfred Baeumler, *Nietzsche, der Philosoph und Politiker* (Stuttgart: Reclam, 1931).

230. Bataille, "Nietzsche and the Fascists," in *Visions of Excess,* pp. 190–191; emphasis added.

231. The irreducibly pragmatic dimension and thrust of Nietzsche's thought was systematically discussed around the turn of the century by Hans Vaihinger, who was a leading neo-Kantian, first editor of the *Kant-Studien,* and founder of the so-called Philosophy of "As If." See Vaihinger, *Nietzsche als Philosoph* (Berlin: Reuther & Reichard, 1902), and "Nietzsche and His Doctrine of Conscious Illusion," ch. 3, § D of *The Philosophy of "As-If"* [begun 1876, published 1911], trans. C. K. Ogden from the 6th German ed. (New York: Harper & Row, Publishers and London: Routledge & Kegan Paul, Ltd., 1924), pp. 341–362. Symptomatically, Bataille knew of Vaihinger's work, as his frequent allusions to the notion of "as if" make clear, but did not make adequate use of it when reading Nietzsche. As will be seen later, Mussolini was positively influenced by Vaihinger, as well as by Nietzsche—which ought to give one additional pause. Finally, note that Vaihinger's English translator, Ogden, was also the main interpreter of Jeremy Bentham's *Handbook of Political Fallacies,* which Ogden considered the predecessor of the philosophy of "As If." See Ogden, *Bentham's Theory of Fictions* [1932] (Patterson, N.J.: Littlefield, Adams & Co., 1959). Thus Rorty's claim to have found a confluence of Anglo-Saxon and continental, post-Nietzschean currents of philosophy on pragmatic grounds was anticipated as early as 1902.

232. See, for example, Aristotle, *De An.,* I:403; *De Coelo,* II:291b–292a; *Eth. Eud.* VII:1235b and 1246a; *Eth. Nich.,* VII:1145b; *Meta.,* 982b, 995a32, and 996a; *Phys.* IV:217b; and *Top.,* VI:145b. Also see Plato, *Meno,* 80d; *Soph.,* 244a; and *Theaet.,* 210b–c. For the current "advanced" or "smart" usage, see nearly any text by a de Manian literary critic; for a much more precise and informed treatment, see Derrida, *Aporias* [1993], trans. Thomas Dutoit (Stanford: Stanford University Press, 1993).

233. See José Antonio Maravall, *Culture of the Baroque: Analysis of a Historical Structure* [1975; 1983], trans. Terry Cochran, foreword by Wlad Godzich and Nicholas Spadaccini (Minneapolis: University of Minnesota Press, 1986).

234. See Wilfried Barner, *Barokrhetorik: Untersuchungen zu ihren geschichtlichen Grundlagen* (Tübingen: Max Niemeyer, 1970). Nietzsche also admired certain Baroque artists: notably Nicolas Poussin (1594–1665), perhaps because he was a closeted libertine.

235. Maravall, *Culture of the Baroque,* p. 252; emphasis added.

236. Yovel, *Spinoza and Other Heretics,* vol. 1: *The Marrano of Reason,* p. 30. It must be said, however, that the second volume of Yovel's work, *The Adventures of Immanence* — which traces the legacy of Spinoza's thinking in Kant, Hegel, the Young Hegelians, Marx, Nietzsche, and Freud — is less comprehensively researched and ultimately less authoritative than the first volume. Yovel ignores the work of Deleuze and Negri, and treats Althusser's Spinozism only superficially; much more important, he does not adequately or systematically apply his initial, crucial distinction in Spinoza between exoteric and esoteric modes of expression to the latter's reception. For useful philosophical overviews of secret societies and the problems of secrecy and lying see Sissela Bok, *Secrets: On the Ethics of Concealment and Revelation* [1983], 2d, corrected ed. (New York: Vintage, 1989), especially pp. 45–58, and *Lying: Moral Choice in Public and Private Life* [1978] (New York: Vintage, 1989). Unfortunately Bok, too, does not deal at all with secrecy or lying as modes of illocutionary and perlocutionary rhetoric in literary or philosophical texts. All of Leo Strauss's work is interesting in this regard, even though he had reasons not to analyze Nietzsche radically in his own terms.

237. Lenin, "Party Organization and Party Literature" [1905], in *Collected Works,* 10:44–49; here 44. Compare Mao: "We Communists never conceal our political views" (Mao Tse-Tung, "On Coalition Government" [April 24, 1945], in *Quotations from Chairman Mao Tse-Tung* [Peking: Foreign Languages Press, 1966], p. 24). And: "The only way to settle questions of an ideological nature or controversial issues among the people is by the democratic method, the method of discussion, of criticism, or persuasion and education, and not by the method of coercion or repression" (Mao, "On the Correct Handling of Contradictions Among the People" [February 27, 1957], in *Five Essays on Philosophy* [Peking: Foreign Languages Press, 1977], pp. 79–133; here pp. 86–87). But theory and practice "even" for communists are too rarely one. It is Russian and Chinese Stalinists who have necessitated the production of some of the most sophisticated cultures of esoteric writing of the modern period. In the words of one Romanian practitioner: "Against history, we developed community through the use of a subtle and ambiguous language that could be heard in one way by the oppressor, in another by your friends. Our weapons of sabotage were ambiguity, humor, paradox, mystery, poetry, song and magic" (Andrei Codrescu, *The Disappearance of the Outside: A Manifesto for Escape* [New York: Addison-Wesley, 1990], pp. 33–39).

238. Negri, *The Politics of Subversion,* p. 125.

239. De Certeau, *The Practice of Everyday Life*, p. 197.

240. Negri, "Postscript, 1990," trans. Jared Becker, in Guattari and Negri, *Communists Like Us*, pp. 149–173; here pp. 172–173.

241. Marx, "Preface to the First German Edition" [1867] of his *Capital: A Critique of Political Economy* [1867–1887], ed. Frederick Engels, trans. Samuel Moore and Edward Aveling, 3 vols. (New York: International Publishers, 1967), 1:7–11; here p. 8.

242. *Clash Communiqué*, October 1985; also The Clash [jacket note], *Cut the Crap*, © 1985, Epic/CBS Records, Inc.

243. The Clash [jacket note], *White Riot/1977*, © 1977 Epic/CBS Records, Inc.

244. Nietzsche, *Morgenröthe: Gedanken über die moralischen Vorurtheile* [1881]; *KGW* 5/1:115 [part 2, aphorism 127]. It goes without saying that this slogan can be used by radical democrats as well as Nietzscheans. See, for example, South African writer Nadine Gordimer's essay, "Great Problems in the Street" [1963], in *The Essential Gesture: Writing, Politics and Places*, ed. and introduced by Stephen Clingman (Harmondsworth: Penguin Books, 1988), pp. 52–57. Gordimer alludes positively and innocently to Nietzsche's phrase on p. 54. But she concludes her essay in an entirely different and today appropriate register: "There is silence in the streets. The indifferent are left in peace. There is nothing to disturb them, now, but the detonations of saboteurs, and the hideous outbursts of secret society savagery" (p. 57). This attack on indifference is not really in solidarity with Nietzsche, however, but with the young Gramsci writing on the eve of the Bolshevik Revolution of 1917: "And so it is time to have done with the indifferent among us, the skeptics, the people who profit from the small good procured by the activity of a few, but who refuse to take responsibility for the great evil that is allowed to develop and come to pass because of their absence from the struggle" (Gramsci, "Indifference" [Turin ed. of *Avanti!*, August 26, 1916, unsigned], in *Selections from Political Writings [1910–1920], with additional texts by Bordiga and Tasca*, ed. Quintin Hoare, trans. John Mathews [New York: International Publishers, 1977], pp. 17–18; here p. 18).

245. For the classic notion that paranoia can be reduced to a defense mechanism against a subconsciously desired homosexual attack—which might be applicable to Nietzsche's sexuality—see Freud, "Psycho-Analytical Notes on an Autobiographical Account of a Case of Paranoia (Dementia Paranoides)" [1911], *Three Case Histories*, ed. Philip Rieff (New York: Collier Books, 1972), pp. 103–186. Mary Ann Doane has argued, however, that "there is a contradiction in Freud's formulation of the relationship between paranoia and homosexuality, because homosexuality presupposes a well-established and unquestionable subject/object relation. There is a sense in which the very idea of an object of desire is foreign to paranoia" (Doane, *The Desire to Desire* [Bloomington: Indiana University Press, 1986], pp. 129–130). In turn, Doane's position has been critiqued by Patricia White for failing to follow through on all implications of the sexuality at stake; see her "Female Spectator, Lesbian Specter: *The Haunting*," in *Sexuality & Space*, ed. Beatriz Colomina (Princeton: Princeton Papers on Architecture, 1992), pp. 131–161; esp. pp. 137–140: "Par-

anoia and Homosexuality." The philosophical problem is that Freud was too much part of Nietzsche's corps/e, too insufficiently Spinozist.

246. Foucault, *Mental Illness and Psychology* [1954], trans. Alan Sheridan (New York: Harper Colophon Books, 1976), p. 5. In this early text and later elsewhere, however, Foucault followed Bataille slavishly, systematically deinstrumentalizing Nietzsche's thinking, writing, and "madness," turning them all into manifestations of a "freedom" that mere psychology, indeed rational discourse in general, simply is powerless to grasp. For example, he concluded this book: "There is very good reason why psychology can never master madness; it is because psychology became possible in our world only when madness had already been mastered and excluded from the drama. And when, in lightning flashes and cries, it reappears, as in [Gérard de] Nerval or [Antonin] Artaud, Nietzsche or [Raymond] Roussel, it is psychology that remains silent, *speechless,* before this language that borrows the meaning of its own kind from that tragic split, from that freedom, that, for contemporary man, only the existence of 'psychologists' allows him to forget" (pp. 87–88). These phrases, alongside the same near mythologization of Nietzsche and his madness, reappear with obsessive insistence in Foucault's major books — revealing how much, like Bataille, Foucault was part of Nietzsche's corps/e. See, for example, *Madness and Civilization: A History of Insanity in the Age of Reason* [*Histoire de la folie,* 1961], trans. Richard Howard (New York: Random House, 1965), p. 278; *The Birth of the Clinic: An Archaeology of Medical Perception* [1963], trans. A. M. Sheridan Smith (New York: Pantheon Books, 1973), p. 197; *The Order of Things,* pp. 342 and 282–285; and *The Archaeology of Knowledge* and *The Discourse on Language* [1970], both in *The Archaeology of Knowledge & The Discourse on Language,* pp. 24 and 220, respectively.

247. Leo Bersani, "Pynchon, Paranoia, and Literature," *Representations* 25 (Winter 1989), 99–118; here 108–109. Because Nietzsche/anism taps successfully into mental and psychological processes that are apparently very deep and ancient, compare and contrast Philip K. Dick's insight: "Paranoia, in some respects, I think, is a modern-day development of an ancient, archaic sense that animals still have — quarry-type animals — that they're being watched. . . . I say paranoia is an atavistic sense. It's a lingering sense, that we had long ago, when we were — our ancestors were — very vulnerable to predators, and this sense tells them they're being watched. And they're being watched probably by something that's going to get them. . . . And often my characters have this feeling. But what really I've done is, I have atavised their society. That although it's set in the future, in many ways they're living — there is a retrogressive quality in their lives, you know? They're living like our ancestors did. I mean, the hardware is in the future, the scenery's in the future, but the situations are really from the past" (Dick in a 1974 interview, cited as the motto to *The Collected Stories of Philip K. Dick,* vol. 2: *We Can Remember It for You Wholesale*). From the tempting psychoanalytic perspective, Dick is simply projecting back into history, in this case the most archaic past, the scene of a constitutive moment of virtually all ego formation. For Lacan, for example, "paranoiac aliena-

NOTES TO PAGES 192–193

tion" always subtends the radical "fragmentation" of subjectivity in the imaginary, thus antedating the subsequent "assuaging" and "armoring" effects of subjectivity's symbolic construction as the subject of law and of language. See Lacan, "Le stade du miroir comme formateur de la fonction du Je, telle qu'elle est révélée dans l'expérience psychanalytique" [1949], in *Écrits I*, pp. 89–97. For a translation see *Écrits: A Selection*, trans. Alan Sheridan (New York: W. W. Norton & Company Inc., 1977). But Lacanian analysis does not quite explain the force of Dick's vision. Finally, in this context, listen to the *music* of paranoid corps/es, as produced by the great heavy metal band Black Sabbath, *Paranoid*, © 1971 Warner Bros., Records Inc., M5 3104; esp. "War Pigs," "Iron Man," "Electric Funeral," and the title cut "Paranoid" — this is nothing if not the contemporary birth of tragedy out of the spirit of music.

248. *The College of Sociology (1937–39)*, ed. Denis Hollier, trans. Betsy Wing (Minneapolis: University of Minnesota Press, 1988), p. 145. *Le Collège de Sociologie (1937–1939)*, ed. Denis Hollier (Paris: Gallimard, 1979).

249. Roger Caillois [with Bataille], "Brotherhoods, Orders, Secret Societies, Churches" [1938], in *The College of Sociology*, pp. 145–156; here p. 155.

250. Editor's note, *The College of Sociology*, p. 415 n. 3.

251. Caillois [with Bataille], "Brotherhoods, Orders, Secret Societies, Churches," in *The College of Sociology*, p. 151.

252. Editor's note, *The College of Sociology*, p. 415 n. 4. Also Bataille, *Œuvres complètes*, 1:645. Andler's biography is a landmark in the history of research on Nietzsche. Andler's balanced perspective was honed by his work on pan-Germanism and on what he called "German Socialist imperialism and expansionism." On these two aspects of Andler's lifework and their interrelationship, see Ernest Tonnelat, *Charles Andler: Sa vie et son œuvre* (Paris: Société d'Édition/Les Belles Lettres, 1937), pp. 167–282.

253. Charles Andler, *Nietzsche, sa vie et sa pensée*, 6 vols. (Paris: Éditions Bossard, 1920), 4:309.

3 Nietzsche's Esoteric Semiotics

1. Nietzsche, *Also sprach Zarathustra; KGW* 6/1:149 [part 2, "On the Land of Education"]. "Vollgeschrieben mit den Zeichen der Vergangenheit, und auch diese Zeichen überpinselt mit neuen Zeichen: also habt ihr euch gut versteckt vor allen Zeichendeutern!"

2. Baudrillard, *Simulations* [*Simulacres et simulation*, 1981], trans. Paul Foss, Paul Patton, and Philip Beitchman (New York: Semiotext[e] Foreign Agents Series, 1983), p. 88. On the influence of Nietzsche on Baudrillard's "political economy of the sign," see Lutz Niethammer, in collaboration with Dirk van Laak, *Posthistoire: Has History Come to an End?* [1989], trans. Patrick Camiller (London and New York: Verso, 1992), p. 141.

3. Strauss, "Persecution and the Art of Writing" [1941], in *Persecution and the Art of Writing* [1952] (Chicago and London: The University of Chicago Press, 1988), pp. 22–37; here p. 25.

4. Jane Siberry (with k. d. lang), "Calling All Angels," *When I Was a Boy*, © 1993 Reprise Records/Time Warner Company, 9–26824–4.

5. Eco, *Semiotics and the Philosophy of Language* [1984] (Bloomington: Indiana University Press, 1986), p. 14.

6. See Raoul Richter, "Friedrich Nietzsche und die Kultur unserer Zeit" [1906], in *Essays*, ed. Lina Richter (Leipzig: Verlag von Felix Meiner, 1913), p. 112. Richter was also author of "Nietzsches Stellung zu Entwicklungslehre und Rassentheorie" [1906], in *Essays*, pp. 137–177; this essay first appeared in the influential *Politisch-anthropologisch Monatsschrift* (political-anthropological monthly), then a major organ of racial anthropology. See further his *Friedrich Nietzsche, sein Leben und sein Werk* (Leipzig: Dürr, 1903) and *Nietzsche-Aufsätze* (Leipzig: Felix Meiner, 1917). Nowhere, however, did Richter make clear either the significance or the techniques of Nietzsche's esotericism. Richter was a racialist but not an anti-Semite. Basing himself on certain passages in Nietzsche, he held that the Superman of the future had to be bred to include not only German and Slavic but also Jewish features. See "Nietzsches Stellung zu Entwicklungslehre und Rassentheorie," pp. 172–174.

7. Already by 1900, the year of Nietzsche's death, members of the *völkisch* movement claimed—without much justification—that Nietzsche's attacks on the German *Volk* were only to be understood exoterically and strategically, not as what he really meant. See, for example, Wilhelm Schaner, "Friedrich Nietzsche," *Der Volkserzieher* 4:35 (September 2, 1900), 273; as cited in Aschheim, *The Nietzsche Legacy in Germany*, p. 120. The obviously self-serving nature of this claim concealed its deeper, unintentional insight into the structure of Nietzsche's exoteric-esoteric problematic. On the eve of the First World War, leaders of the right-wing German Youth Movement had established a three-stage dialectical process with which to approach Nietzsche: (1) he ought *not* to be read by recruits, since his message was too contradictory on its surface; (2) he was to be studied in *depth* for his esoteric message by older members, as the *only* important thinker really to combat the depraved state of European culture and political life; only then (3) could Nietzsche's life and work be dialectically *sublated*, since the Youth Movement itself would take up the sword where Nietzsche had let it fall, and since the entire age then would have incorporated his spirit. See, for example, Walter Hammer, *Nietzsche als Erzieher* (Leipzig: Verlag Hugo Vollrath, 1914); this book appeared before the war broke out and was enthusiastically greeted in the right-wing press. Hammer had also been an important theorist of vegetarianism and of the so-called Life-Reform Movement, and had written positively about Nietzsche in both contexts, beginning around 1909.

8. Nietzsche, "NF, Mai-Juli 1885"; *KGW* 7/3:263.

9. Friedrich Wilhelm Joseph Schelling, *Philosophische Briefe über Dogmatismus und Kriticismus* [1795], *Sämtliche Werke*, ed. Karl Friedrich August Schelling (Stuttgart

and Augsburg: J. G. Cotta'scher Verlag, 1856), 1/1:281–341; here 341. "Es ist ein Verbrechen an der Menschheit, Gründsätze zu verbergen, die allgemein mittheilbar sind. Aber die Natur selbst hat dieser Mittheilbarkeit Grenzen gesetzt; sie hat—für die *Würdigen* eine Philosophie aufbewahrt, die *durch sich selbst* zur *esoterischen* wird, weil sie nicht *gelernt,* nicht nachgebetet, nicht nachgeheuchelt, nicht auch von geheimen Feinden und Ausspähern nachgesprochen werden kann—ein Symbol für den Bund freier Geister, an dem sie sich alle erkennen, das sie nicht zu verbergen brauchen, und da doch, nur ihnen verständlich, für die andern ein ewiges Räthsel seyn wird." Contrast and compare to this proto-Nietzschean position Rousseau's earlier remark (c. 1749–1755), made before the French Revolution just as Schelling wrote after it: "any tongue with which one cannot make oneself understood to the people assembled is a slavish tongue. It is impossible for a people to remain free and speak that tongue" (Rousseau, *Essay on the Origin of Languages which Treats of Melody and Musical Imitation* [1749–1755], in Jean-Jacques Rousseau and Johann Gottfried Herder, *On the Origin of Language,* trans. with afterwords by John H. Morgan and Alexander Gode [Chicago and London: The University of Chicago Press, 1986], p. 73).

10. Bobbio, *The Future of Democracy,* p. 83.

11. See Heidegger, *Schelling, Vom Wesen der menschlichen Freiheit (1809)* [Freiburg summer semester, 1936], ed. Hildegard Feick, *Gesamtausgabe,* 2/42 (Frankfurt am Main: Vittorio Klostermann, 1988). For a translation see *Schelling's Treatise on the Essence of Freedom,* trans. Joan Stambaugh (Athens: Ohio University Press, 1985).

12. Hegel, *Lectures on the Philosophy of History,* pp. 237–238.

13. Deleuze, *Spinoza: Practical Philosophy,* p. 106; emphasis added.

14. Spinoza, *A Political Treatise,* in *A Theologico-Political Treatise and a Political Treatise,* pp. 295–296 [ch. 2, § 11]; emphasis added.

15. This, for example, is how "Nietzscheans" like Stefan George and his circle had used the term "esoteric" in their poetry and other writing, and how they understood Nietzsche's project. Along with Le Collège de Sociologie, with which it had some ties, the George Circle is among the "institutions" that have been most self-consciously "Nietzschean" in inspiration.

16. See Stanley Cavell, *The Claim of Reason: Wittgenstein, Skepticism, Morality, and Tragedy* (Oxford and New York: Oxford University Press, 1979), esp. the preface [1978], pp. xi–xxii.

17. See Arnold I. Davidson, "Questions Concerning Heidegger: Opening the Debate," *Critical Inquiry* 15:2 (Winter 1989), 407–426; here 409.

18. Rosen, "Nietzsche's Revolution," in *The Ancients and the Moderns,* p. 189.

19. Cavell, *The Claim of Reason,* p. xvii.

20. Ibid., p. xvi. This passage is also cited by Arnold Davidson in "Questions Concerning Heidegger," but Davidson then scurries past the problem of actually applying this argument to Heidegger, an attempt Cavell himself apparently has sanctioned but also not undertaken. (See Davidson's acknowledgment to Cavell at

the beginning of his essay.) Since 1978, Cavell has come to appreciate Heidegger, to say the least; whether the term "conversion" is too strong is not clear. For his attempt to deal with the question of Heidegger and Nazism see *Philosophical Passages: Wittgenstein, Emerson, Austin, Derrida* (Oxford and Cambridge, Mass.: Blackwell, 1995), pp. 12–41.

21. See *Selections from the Prison Notebooks of Antonio Gramsci*, p. 420.

22. Frank Kermode, *The Genesis of Secrecy: On the Interpretation of Narrative* (Cambridge, Mass., and London: Harvard University Press, 1979; The Charles Eliot Norton Lectures, 1977–1978), p. 58.

23. Ibid., p. 3.

24. Gramsci's most succinct formula for philosophical and political "democratic centralism," which includes what he meant by "dialectic," was "the critical pursuit of what is identical in seeming diversity of form and on the other hand of what is distinct and even opposed in apparent uniformity . . . " (*Selections from the Prison Notebooks of Antonio Gramsci*, p. 189). This was also Gramsci's way of relating to comrades. As described by a fellow communist militant: "If one was discussing a definite body of fact, Gramsci examined its various aspects, its various phases, its various relations with other facts, and its developments, until he saw it, and made others see it, in broad daylight. . . . If a discussion had no set theme, he willingly let himself be carried along by our questions . . . and in the course of the argument he himself raised new problems . . . " (Nicola Potenza, as cited in Paolo Spriano, *Antonio Gramsci and the Party: The Prison Years* [1977], trans. John Fraser [London: Lawrence and Wishart, 1979], pp. 100–101).

25. *Selections from the Prison Notebooks of Antonio Gramsci*, p. 326.

26. Perry Anderson, *Considerations on Western Marxism* [1976], augmented ed. (London: Verso, 1979), p. 67.

27. Gramsci to Tania Schucht, September 30, 1931, in *Letters from Prison*, 2:77.

28. *Selections from the Prison Notebooks of Antonio Gramsci*, p. 423; translation slightly modified, in accord with the useful discussion of common sense in Thomas Nemeth, *Gramsci's Philosophy: A Critical Study* (Sussex: The Harvester Press and Atlantic Highlands, N.J.: The Humanities Press, 1980), pp. 75–83; here esp. p. 77.

29. *Selections from the Prison Notebooks of Antonio Gramsci*, p. 324.

30. Strauss, "The Literary Character of the *Guide for the Perplexed*," in *Persecution and the Art of Writing*, p. 66.

31. More precisely, this is Rosen's paraphrase of Alexandre Kojève's position. See Rosen, *Hermeneutics as Politics*, p. 110.

32. Kwame Nkrumah, *Handbook of Revolutionary Warfare* (London: Panaf Books, Ltd., 1968), p. 115.

33. See Astradur Eysteinsson, *The Concept of Modernism* (Ithaca and London: Cornell University Press, 1990).

34. Anderson, "Modernity and Revolution" [1983], in *Marxism and the Interpretation of Culture*, pp. 317–333; here esp. pp. 324–325.

35. Strauss, *Thoughts on Machiavelli*, p. 30.

36. Rosen, *Hermeneutics as Politics*, p. 123.

37. For example, Peter Berkowitz, *Nietzsche: The Ethics of an Immoralist* (Cambridge, Mass., and London: Harvard University Press, 1995) — which ends up reproducing, as positive solutions to imagined "contradictions" in Nietzsche's writing, virtually every exoteric cliché that Nietzsche wanted liberals to incorporate and believe.

38. Nietzsche, *Der Antichrist: Fluch auf das Christenthum* [1888]; *KGW* 6/3:188 [aphorism 23]; emphasis added.

39. See Michael Taussig, *Mimesis and Alterity: A Particular History of the Senses* (New York and London: Routledge, 1993), pp. 85–86.

40. Schopenhauer, *The World as Will and Representation*, 2:570–571; *Sämtliche Werke*, 3:654–655 [supplements to the 4th bk., ch. 45]. Schopenhauer has here in mind "the act of procreation" as "affirmation of the will-to-live," but the principle of the public secret has much broader implications both in his work and in Nietzsche's. Quite unlike his first philosophical mentor, however, Nietzsche did not denegrate the use of "codes" in aesthetics or in philosophical writing generally. Contrast, for example, Schopenhauer, *The World as Will and Representation*, 1:237–242; *Sämtliche Werke*, 2:279–286 [3d bk., ch. 50].

41. Nietzsche, *Morgenröthe; KGW* 5/1:279–280 [aphorism 457].

42. See, for example, Heidegger, "Der Wille zur Macht als Erkenntnis" [1939], in *Nietzsche* 1:473–658.

43. See Sarah Kofman, *Explosion I: De l' "Ecce Homo" de Nietzsche* (Paris: Éditions Galilée, 1992), and *Explosion II: Les enfants de Nietzsche* (Paris: Éditions Galilée, 1993).

44. Kofman, *Explosion I*, p. 41. See further Derrida, "Interpreting Signatures (Nietzsche/Heidegger): Two Questions" [1981], trans. Diane Michelfelder and Richard E. Palmer, in *Looking After Nietzsche*, pp. 1–17; and Lacoue-Labarthe, "Obliteration," trans. Thomas Trezise, *The Subject of Philosophy*, ed. Thomas Trezise (Minneapolis: University of Minnesota Press, 1993), pp. 57–98. For yet another analysis of Nietzsche's "names" in the same, basically uncritical Derridian vein, see Rodolphe Gasché, "*Ecce Homo* or the Written Body" [1976], trans. Judith Still, in *Looking After Nietzsche*, pp. 113–136.

45. Kofman, *Explosion*, p. 42.

46. Derrida, "Interpreting Signatures," in *Looking After Nietzsche*, pp. 1–2.

47. Kofman, *Explosion II*, p. 349–350.

48. Nietzsche to Heinrich Köselitz [Peter Gast], December 30; *KGB* 3/5:565–567; here 566.

49. Nietzsche to Jean Bourdeau, around December 17, 1888 [draft]; *KGB* 3/5:532–536; here 535.

50. Kofman, *Explosion I*, pp. 18 and 31.

51. Nietzsche to Malwida von Meysenbug, end of March 1884; *KGB* 3/1:489–490.

52. To date the most extensive treatment of Nietzsche in terms of a gay male problematic is Köhler, *Zarathustras Geheimnis*. But Köhler's is not really a theoretically or politically informed exercise in "queering the canon" in the positive sense; indeed there are several oddly homophobic moments in his work. The supposition that Nietzsche "was homosexual" — and that he was infected with syphilis not by a woman but by a man — has a long — if rather subterranean — history; it was explicitly discussed by Freud's circle in Vienna as early as 1908. Freud himself shied away from this hypothesis, for reasons that have never become clear; perhaps because of his own "unruly" nature. The most meticulous "medical biography" of Nietzsche — in terms both of his possible physical and mental illnesses and also, as important, of his limited awareness of them — does not address the question of Nietzsche's sexuality in any depth, though it does tend to side with Köhler's thesis that Nietzsche indeed "was gay," and that this may have had something to do with his concern with esoteric communication. See Pia Daniela Volz, *Nietzsche im Labyrinth seiner Krankheit: Eine medizinisch-biographische Untersuchung* (Würzburg: Königshausen & Neumann, 1990), esp. pp. 2, 20, 49–50, 59–60, and 193–194, with relevant endnotes. Nor is Köhler's hypothesis denied by the most extensive biography of Nietzsche attempted so far: Hermann Josef Schmidt's unfinished *Nietzsche absconditus oder Spuren lesen bei Nietzsche* (Berlin-Aschaffenburg: IBDK Verlag, 1991ff), of which four volumes have been published to date, following Nietzsche up to 1864; on Köhler, see Teil I/II: Kindheit, 40–41. This is a very quirky, self-published book. It oscillates more or less out of control between minute historical reconstruction, including some genuine discoveries, and the most rambling and impressionistic of interpretations.

From its inception, members of the Vienna Psychoanalytic Society held the position — not contradicted by Freud — that Nietzsche "had homosexual tendencies" or "was homosexual." According to some members of the society, this thesis was based on "reliable sources" who had known Nietzsche personally: likely the philosopher Paul Rée. Discussion of Nietzsche's homosexuality was to some extent also public, as is evident, for example, from a feuilleton that appeared in Vienna's prestigious *Neue Freie Press* around 1907. See again *Minutes of the Vienna Psychoanalytic Society*, vol. 1 (1906–1908):357–359 [April 1, 1908] and vol. 2 (1908–1910):29–32 [October 28, 1908]. For a rather different, and wholly unscientific, take on Nietzsche's sexuality see Barris, *God and Plastic Surgery: Marx, Nietzsche, Freud and the Obvious*. Barris pits a theory — and apparently a practice — of what he calls "the limp penis" with, and against, "The erect manhood of Marx's proletariat, proud to overcome; the rigid urgency of a Nietzsche; the competent penetration of a Freud, delaying the gratification of conclusion until the subject matter is ready to come to voice: all these have their place, their importance, and their distinguishable degrees and kinds of instructive and admirable achievement, of political, aesthetic and spiritual significance" (p. 204).

Actually, both the size and sexual preference of Nietzsche's penis have long been a matter of private and public controversy in the Nietzsche Industry—beginning already with its founder, Nietzsche himself. See Curt Paul Janz, "Die 'tödtliche Beleidigung': Ein Beitrag zur Wagner-Entfremdung Nietzsches," *Nietzsche-Studien* 4 (1975), 262–278. One of Nietzsche's personal physicians, Otto Eiser (1834–1897), confided the results of an examination of Nietzsche in late 1877 to Richard Wagner. (Eiser was a Wagnerian. A founder of the Frankfurt am Main Wagner Society, also in 1877 he published in *Bayreuther Blätter* a hagiographic "exegesis" of Wagner's *Ring of the Nibelungen.*) Based on this information, Wagner informed his inner circle, as Nietzsche discovered to his horror at a moment of overdetermined personal and philosophical crisis in his life, that Nietzsche's various somatic and psychological ailments were due to the "small size" of his penis, to "excessive onanism," and/or to "pederasty." Just when he learned of Eiser's incredible indiscretion is unclear, perhaps as early as 1877 and no later than 1882; in any event, Nietzsche was understandably hurt to the quick. This incident had considerable bearing not only on the nature of Nietzsche's break with Wagner but also on his subsequent analysis of the phenomenon of modernist "decadence," and most especially on his esotericism, since the incident occurred at the time of his "Zarathustra year." Janz's take on the issue has been contested, however. For further debate about Wagner's "mortal insult" and Nietzsche's reaction to it see Dieter Borchmeyer, "Wodurch hat Wagner Nietzsche tödlich beleidigt? Ein Replik auf Eugen Bisers Aufsatz 'Glaube und Mythos,'" *Philosophisches Jahrbuch* 92 (1985), 149–156; and Eugen Biser, "Der 'beleidigte' Nietzsche und der 'bekehrte' Wagner: Versuch einer Entzauberung," *Philosophisches Jahrbuch* 93 (1986), 175–180.

The question of whether or not Nietzsche "was gay" would be relevant only to the extent that this might have been one contributing factor, among others, in determining his profound commitment to esotericism.

53. Nietzsche to Malwida von Meysenbug; *KGB* 3/1:490.

54. Nietzsche to Elisabeth Förster-Nietzsche, mid-November, 1888 [draft]; *KGB* 3/5:473–474; here 474.

55. There is something crazy—literally—about the Sublime. Shoshana Felman once distinguished between *speaking* madness and speaking *of* madness as roughly equivalent to the difference between rhetoric and grammar. See Felman, *Writing and Madness* [*La folie et la chose littéraire,* 1978], trans. Martha Noel Evans and the author (Ithaca: Cornell University Press, 1985), pp. 12–13.

56. Richard Klein, *Cigarettes Are Sublime* (Durham and London: Duke University Press, 1993), p. xi.

57. Derrida, *Speech and Phenomenon and Other Essays on Husserl's Phenomenology* [1967], trans. David B. Allison (Evanston: Northwestern University Press, 1973), p. 54.

58. In addition to the work of Baudrillard, see, for example, the now classic philosophical discussion of simulacra as types of performative utterance in Derrida, "Signature Event Context" [1971], *Margins of Philosophy,* pp. 307–330. On the

simulacrum as re/presentational structure of a subrational "economy," see Lyotard, *Economie libidinale* (Paris: Les éditions de minuit, 1974), esp. pp. 57–115. On the simulacrum as "the power of the false and the false as power," see Deleuze, "Plato and the Simulacrum," trans. Rosalind Krauss, *October* 27 (Winter 1983), 45–56.

59. Fundamentally mistaken in this regard, for example, is Louis A. Sass, *Madness and Modernism: Insanity in the Light of Modern Art, Literature, and Thought* (New York: Basic Books, 1992), esp. pp. 150–154: "Verbal Concepts and Nietzschean Dualism." Sass, who ignores monist systems of thought—including Spinoza's—takes this "dualist" Nietzsche as "a kind of blueprint" for his entire book (p. 149); but the "profoundly ambivalent, perhaps even contradictory philosophical position" that Sass thus ascribes to Nietzsche (p. 150) is a function of Nietzsche's quite conscious commitment to esoteric rhetoric, and has nothing to do, unless of course ironically, with "schizophrenia" even in the extended sense that Sass has in mind, namely, as a primary mode of modernist hyperconsciousness alongside alienation from body and affect.

60. The late Tim Mason, a Marxist historian at Oxford, exposed the intricate dialectic between coercion and hegemony, political economy and ideology in the Nazi *Führerstaat;* and the very fact that Mason tended to downplay the specifically anti-Semitic and racist component of German national socialism makes his analysis all the more relevant for the study of fascism *and* Nietzscheanism, neither of which was essentialistically racist, though certainly racialist. See Mason, *Sozialpolitik im Dritten Reich: Arbeiterklasse und Volksgemeinschaft* (Opladen: Westdeutscher Verlag, 1977), and "Intention and Explanation: A Current Controversy about the Interpretation of National Socialism," in *Der "Führerstaat": Mythos und Realität; Studien zur Struktur und Politik des Dritten Reiches,* ed. Gerhard Hirschfeld and Lothar Kettenacker, introduction by Wolfgang J. Mommsen (Stuttgart: Klett-Cotta, 1981), pp. 21–42. To the extent that Nazism can be *reduced* to the *Führerprinzip*—and perhaps *only* to that extent . . . Nietzsche *can* be viewed as a Nazi.

61. Benito Mussolini and Alfredo de Marsico, cited in Amerigo Montemaggiore, *Dizionario della dottrina fascista* (Turin: G. B. Paravia & Co., 1934), pp. 369 and 371; from the entry on "Gerarchia"—the Italian word used to translate German *Rangordnung,* "order of rank."

62. Mussolini, "Relativismo e Fascismo" [*Il Popolo d'Italia* 279 (November 1921), 8], in *Opera omnia,* ed. Edoardo and Duilio Susmel (Florence: La Fireze, 1951–1963), 17:267–269; here 269.

63. It goes without saying that not *all* forms of relativism are fascist, even remotely. For a sophisticated historical treatment, and an original defense, of philosophical relativism that is not, see Joseph Margolis, *The Truth about Relativism* (Oxford and Cambridge, Mass.: Basil Blackwell, 1991). For a cogent argument against relativism that also does not link it to fascism see James F. Harris, *Against Relativism: A Philosophical Defense of Method* (La Salle, Ill.: Open Court, 1992).

64. Nietzsche to Paul Deussen, January 3, 1888; *KGB* 3/5:221–223; here 222;

emphasis added. Deussen (1845–1919) had been a friend of Nietzsche at university and had gone on to become a historian of Western and Eastern philosophy and scholar of the Indic Vedânta.

65. Nietzsche, "NF, Sommer 1886–Herbst 1887"; *KGW* 8/1:191.

66. This metaphor is owed to Balibar, "Spinoza, the Anti-Orwell," in *Masses, Classes, Ideas,* p. 33.

67. Nietzsche, "NF, Sommer 1886–Herbst 1887"; *KGW* 8/1:191.

68. See, for example, de Man's conceptually muddled, self-effacing claim:

> . . . I have a tendency to put upon texts an inherent authority, which is stronger, I think, than Derrida is willing to put on them. I assume, as a working hypothesis (as a working hypothesis, because I know better than that) that the text *knows* in an absolute way what it's doing. I know this is not the case, but it is a necessary working hypothesis that Rousseau knows at any given time what he is doing and as such there is no need to deconstruct Rousseau. In a complicated way, I would hold to that statement that "the text deconstructs itself, is self-deconstructive" rather than being deconstructed by a philosophical intervention from the outside of the text. The difference is that Derrida's text is so brilliant, so incisive, so strong that whatever happens in Derrida, it happens between him and his own text. He doesn't need Rousseau, he doesn't need anybody else; I do need them very badly because I never had an idea of my own, it was always through a text, through the critical examination of a text. . . . I am a philologist and not a philosopher: I guess there is a difference there. . . . I think that, on the other hand, it is of some interest to see how the two different approaches can occasionally coincide. . . . (Stefano Rosso, "An Interview with Paul de Man" [1983], in de Man, *The Resistance to Theory,* foreword by Wlad Godzich [Minneapolis: University of Minnesota Press, 1986], pp. 115–121; here p. 118)

Sometimes it is the text, sometimes the author that is said to "know" what it is doing — constraining the reader, including the reader of de Man, in limbo. A great precedent for de Man's maneuvres may be Kierkegaard, who also claimed to differentiate between "accidental" and "personal" authorship from "essential" and "productive" text. See Søren Kierkegaard, "A First and Last Explanation" [1846], *Concluding Unscientific Postscript to "Philosophical Fragments,"* in *Kierkegaard's Writings,* 12/1, ed. and trans. with introduction and notes by Howard V. Hong and Edna H. Hong (Princeton: Princeton University Press, 1992), pp. 625–630. But then Kierkegaard was a major esoteric writer, and so it is unclear by intention when he is to be taken literally, when figuratively. For more straightforward current philosophical struggles with the related problem of the connections, and lack thereof, between authorial and textual responsibility, see *The Political Responsibility of Intellectuals,* ed. Ian Maclean, Alan Montefiore, and Peter Winch (Cambridge: Cambridge University Press, 1990).

69. For his *Allegories of Reading,* de Man chose a splendid motto from Pascal: "Quand on lit trop vite ou trop doucement on n'entend rien. [When one reads

too fast or too leisurely, one hears (or understands) nothing.]" Nietzsche's was a rhetoric—a technology—of violent speed, as well as of leisure. Certainly "one hears nothing" of it if one "reads" him too slowly *or* too fast. But neither in the three essays on Nietzsche in *Allegories of Reading* nor elsewhere in his works does de Man *read* let alone *deconstruct* either *Nietzsche's esoteric intent*—which de Man does not and, in his own terms, cannot set out to do—or even—appearances to the contrary—*Nietzsche's illocutionary rhetoric.* Rather, he *constructs* a philologically arbitrary, depoliticized caricature of Nietzsche's—and perhaps de Man's own—*exoteric* philosophical and political desires. For a glimpse of at least the young de Man's political affiliation and phantasmagoria see his *Wartime Journalism 1939–1943,* ed. Werner Hamacher, Neil Hertz, Thomas Keenan (Lincoln and London: University of Nebraska Press, 1988). Debate still circles about whether the apparently pro-Nazi stance of the young de Man was later abandoned by him or whether it went deep underground in his writing, and some of his students deny that his early "journalism" was ever pro-Nazi in the first place. Unfortunately, the position taken on this vexed and still open question by the editors of this anthology is ultimately uncritical and obscurantist. For an ideologically conservative criticism of de Man and Nietzsche—though many aspects of it are objectionable—see Brian Vickers, *In Defense of Rhetoric,* 2d, corrected ed. (Cambridge: Cambridge University Press, 1990), pp. 453–471. Finally, note that de Man knew well the Straussian theory of exo/esoteric writing, as is revealed in passing in his analysis of dialogism in Mikhail Bakhtin—an analysis that seems to have a strong autobiographical undercurrent as well. It might follow logically that de Man would have coded exo/esotericism into his own writing. But the main point here is that he did not—perhaps for that very reason—use Straussian theory to read *Nietzsche's* writing. Cf. de Man, "Dialogue and Dialogism" [1981; 1983], in *The Resistance to Theory,* pp. 106–114; here pp. 107–108.

70. Gadamer, *Wahrheit und Methode: Grundzüge einer philosophischen Hermeneutik* [1960], 3d, expanded ed. (Tübingen: J. C. B. Mohr [Paul Siebeck], 1972), p. 510; and Ludwig Binswanger, *Grundformen und Erkenntnis menschlichen Daseins* [1962] (Munich and Basel: Ernst Reinhardt Verlag, 1964), pp. 218–219.

71. See Nietzsche, "NF, Sommer 1875"; *KGW* 4/1:195.

72. Kripke, *Naming and Necessity,* pp. 3–4 and 48. The rigid designator is comparable to Ferdinand de Saussure's notion of the "key-word," "anagram," "paragram," or "hypogram" as analyzed by Jean Starobinski and translated by de Man as "subtext or, better, infra-text." Saussure was fascinated by the possibility that "Latin poetry was structured by the coded dispersal (or dissemination) of an underlying word or proper name throughout the lines of verse" (de Man, "Hypogram and Inscription" [1981], in *The Resistance to Theory,* pp. 27–53; here pp. 36–37). Hypograms hover radically on the cusp between perceptibility and imperceptibility, as do rigid designators. But the Saussurean hypogram, at least as read by Starobinski and de Man, differs from the properly Nietzschean rigid designator in several respects. Although both are exo/esoteric by design, "The function of the textual elaboration

[of the hypogram]," according to de Man, "is not . . . to *state*" its "meaning (which would be devoid of all interest since there is nothing remarkable about the semantic kernel) but rather to hide it, as Saussure's key-word is hidden in the lines of verse, or rather, to disguise it into a system of variations or paragrams which have been overdetermined by codification in such a manner as to tantalize the reader into a self-rewarding process of discovery. . . . For although the hypogram behaves coyly enough, it will eventually be unveiled since this is, in fact, its *raison d'être:* the form is encoded in such a way as to reveal its own principle of determination" (p. 38). By instructive contrast: Nietzsche's esoteric semiotics is not coy in this sense; is not self-rewarding; is not semantically empty, transcendentally self-referential, or unremark-able; and perhaps cannot, in theory or in practice, be fully unveiled. By the same token, the purpose of textual elaboration in the case of Nietzsche's rigid designator precisely *should* be to expose its content and mode of incorporation to the maximum amount of light possible. Cf. further Jean Starobinski, *Words upon Words: The Ana-grams of Ferdinand de Saussure* [1971], trans. Olivia Emmet (New Haven: Yale University Press, 1979).

73. Spinoza, *The Ethics,* p. 68 [part 1, prop. 29].

74. Deleuze, *Spinoza: Practical Philosophy,* p. 92.

75. Nietzsche to Heinrich Köselitz [Peter Gast], September 2, 1884; *KGB* 3/1:524–526; here 525.

76. Giorgio Colli, "Nachwort," in Nietzsche, *Sämtliche Werke, Kritische Studien-ausgabe,* ed. Giorgio Colli and Mazzino Montinari (Berlin and New York: Walter de Gruyter and Munich: Deutscher Taschenbuch Verlag, 1980), 13:651–668; here 651–652. Hereafter cited as *KSA,* with appropriate volume and page numbers. Levine, in *Nietzsche and the Crisis of the Humanities* (1995), also points out the importance of this passage (pp. 129–130). More acutely than Colli, Levine notes its implications for Nietzsche's philosophy but also for its reception by the "Right" (Leo Strauss) and the "Left" (Derrida), since not only Will to Power but also Eternal Recurrence of the Same and the Superman (see also p. 126) are hereby exposed as mere "exoteric" teachings of a strategically withheld "esoteric doctrine." Nonetheless, Levine interprets the upshot for Nietzsche more culturally and philo-sophically than politically: for example, "to say 'yes' despite his knowledge of the abyss" (p. 130). In the end, Levine believes that "Nietzsche's exoteric program for cultural reform was explicitly antipluralist and antidemocratic, while his esoteric message was radically unpolitical" (p. 206) —a wholly incoherent distinction in Nietzsche's terms.

77. Nietzsche, *Götzen-Dämmerung; KGW* 6/3:39 ["Dicta and Arrows," § 36].

78. Boethius, *Philosophiae consolationis,* II, 74–77.

79. Nietzsche, Vorwort [1886] to *Menschliches, Allzumenschliches I: Ein Buch für freie Geister* [1878; 1886]; *KGW* 4/2:7–16; here 16 [preface, § 8].

80. For the medieval uses of these biblical maxims see, for example, Alan of the Isles (c. 1128–c. 1203), *A Compendium on the Art of Preaching,* and Humbert of

Romans (1198–1216), *Treatise on Preaching*, both in *Readings in Medieval Rhetoric*, ed. Joseph M. Miller, Michael H. Prosser, and Thomas W. Benson (Bloomington and London: Indiana University Press, 1973), pp. 228–239 (here pp. 235–236); and pp. 245–250 (here pp. 247–248), respectively.

81. Carlo Ginzburg, "Clues: Roots of an Evidential Paradigm" [1979], in *Clues, Myths, and the Historical Method* [1986], trans. John and Anne C. Tedeschi (Baltimore and London: The Johns Hopkins University Press, 1989), pp. 96–125; here p. 123.

82. Nietzsche, *Jenseits von Gut und Böse; KGW* 6/2:44–45 [part 2, aphorism 30].

83. "All oppressing classes stand in need of two social functions to safeguard their rule: the function of the hangman and the function of the priest. The hangman is required to quell the protests and the indignation of the oppressed; the priest is required to console the oppressed, to depict to them the prospects of their sufferings and sacrifices being mitigated (this is particularly easy to do without guaranteeing that these prospects will be 'achieved'), while preserving class rule, and thereby to reconcile them to class rule, win them away from revolutionary action, undermine their revolutionary spirit and destroy their revolutionary determination" (Lenin, "The Collapse of the Second International," in *Collected Works*, 21:231–232). For the modern concept of "hegemony" as part of the dialectic between overt coercion and tacit or noncoercive coercion, though often its Leninist taproot is repressed or suppressed, see, for example, Stuart Hall, Bob Lumley, and Gregor McLennan, "Politics and Ideology: Gramsci," in *On Ideology* (London: Hutchinson, 1978; Centre for Contemporary Cultural Studies, University of Birmingham), pp. 45–76; Joseph V. Femia, *Gramsci's Political Thought: Hegemony, Consciousness, and the Revolutionary Process* (Oxford: Clarendon Press, 1981); and Robert Bocock, *Hegemony* (London and New York: Tavistock Publications, 1986). The Leninist taproot is not suppressed in John Hoffman, *The Gramscian Challenge: Coercion and Consent in Marxist Political Theory* (Oxford and New York: Basil Blackwell, 1984).

84. For two non-Nietzschean explications of Hegel's position that are relevant here see Alexandre Kojève [Kojevenikov], *Introduction to the Reading of Hegel: Lectures on the Phenomenology of Spirit* [1933–1939], assembled by Raymond Queneau, ed. Allan Bloom, trans. James H. Nichols Jr. (New York and London: Basic Books, 1969), esp. chs. 2 and 3; and Genevieve Lloyd, "Masters, Slaves and Others," in *Radical Philosophy Reader*, ed. Roy Edgley and Richard Osborne (London: Verso, 1985), pp. 291–309, esp. pp. 292–299: "Hegel on Masters, Slaves and Women."

85. *Selections from the Prison Notebooks of Antonio Gramsci*, p. 235.

86. Ibid., pp. 134–135. This section of the notebooks, "The Modern Prince," was drafted in 1931–1932 and revised in this version in 1933–1934. In this matter, Gramsci desperately held on to a certain Enlightenment belief in rational progress. Even though "Machiavellianism has helped to improve the traditional political technique of the conservative ruling groups," and even though, by exposing its own techniques to view, "the philosophy of praxis" may do the same, nonetheless this

"should not disguise" the "essentially revolutionary character" of either Machia-vellianism or the philosophy of praxis. For Gramsci, this also "explains all anti-Machiavellianism, from that of the Jesuits to the pietistic anti-Machiavellianism of Pasquale Villari" (p. 136). Villari (1826–1917) had written a book on Machiavelli, *Niccolò Machiavelli e i suoi tempi* (1877–1882) and was a friend of Nietzsche's friend Malwida von Meysenbug. Nietzsche knew of Villari's work in German translation. Like Gramsci, he held his highly moralistic account of Machiavelli in contempt, though for exactly the opposite ideological reasons.

87. Ibid., p. 135.

88. See, for example, the claim by Rush Limbaugh — hyped by his publisher as "the most influential conservative spokesperson of our day," "America's #1 talk-show host," indeed "the most powerful man in America" — that not only "Liberalism" but *Gramsci* has "long ago captured the arts, the press, the entertainment industry, the universities, the schools, the libraries, the foundations, etc." (Rush Limbaugh, *See, I Told You So* [New York: Pocket Star Books, 1993], pp. 97–98).

89. See Mark Seltzer, *Bodies and Machines* (New York and London: Routledge, 1992), esp. pp. 95–96.

90. On Nietzsche's knowledge of the sciences in general and of physiology, in-cluding Fechner's work, and on his own pretension as a "natural philosopher," see Alwin Mittasch's widely neglected work *Friedrich Nietzsche als Naturphilosoph* (Stutt-gart: Alfred Kröner Verlag, 1952), and the equally neglected study by Karl Schlechta and Anni Anders, *Friedrich Nietzsche: Von den verborgenen Anfängen seines Philoso-phierens* (Stuttgart and Bad Cannstatt: Friedrich Frommann Verlag [Günther Holz-boog], 1962). For more recent attempts to breathe life into the theme of Nietzsche's articulation of "art" and "science," see, primarily, Helmut Pfotenhauer, *Die Kunst als Physiologie: Nietzsches ästhetische Theorie und literarische Produktion* (Stuttgart: J. B. Metzlersche Verlagsbuchhandlung, 1985); and, secondarily, *Kunst und Wissenschaft bei Nietzsche,* ed. Mihailo Djuric and Josef Simon (Würzburg: Königshausen & Neumann, 1986); and Babette E. Babich, *Nietzsche's Philosophy of Science: Reflecting Science on the Ground of Art and Life* (Albany: State University of New York Press, 1994). On the significance of early physiology for modernism and modernity, see Jonathan Crary, *Techniques of the Observer: On Vision and Modernity in the Nineteenth Century* (Cambridge, Mass., and London: The MIT Press, 1990). Nietzsche's proj-ect was more "phantasmagoric" than "stereoscopic," in the nineteenth-century sense outlined by Crary, though his own view of Nietzsche happens to be conventionally benevolent: because Nietzsche preferred to conceal rather than foreground the deepest levels of his rhetorical "machine" from public purview, keeping them *in camera* — in both meanings of the term.

91. Seltzer, *Bodies and Machines,* p. 95.

92. Ibid., pp. 95–96. On the link between sexuality and the machine in the context of German modernism, see Andreas Huyssen, *After the Great Divide: Modernism, Mass Culture, Postmodernism* (Bloomington: Indiana University Press, 1986). For a

necessarily speculative but, ideologically speaking, unnecessarily naïve reflection on Nietzsche's attitude toward technologies of writing, see Friedrich A. Kittler, *Discourse Networks 1800/1900* [1985], trans. Michael Metteer, with Chris Cullens, foreword by David E. Wellbery (Stanford: Stanford University Press, 1990), pp. 177–205: "Nietzsche: Incipit Tragoedia." In his otherwise important book, Kittler locates Nietzsche as the pivot point between two distinct discursive systems: idealism-romanticism and modernism. Yet he has no understanding of Nietzsche's complex position with regard to esoteric communication. Taking Zarathustra only at his exoteric word, Kittler writes: "Over the beginning of the literature of 1900 stands a curse. 'Whoever knows the reader will henceforth do nothing for the reader. Another century of readers — and the spirit itself will stink. That everyone may learn to read, in the long run corrupts not only writing but also thinking.' Zarathustra's curse strikes at the technological-material basis of the discourse network of 1800: universal alphabetization. Not content or message but the medium itself made the Spirit, the corpus composed of German poetry and German Idealism, into a stinking cadaver. The murderer of the letter met its own death" (p. 178). Kittler says nothing, however, about the cadavers Nietzsche himself planned to produce as corps/e. See further Nietzsche, *Also sprach Zarathustra; KGW* 6/1:44 [part 1, "On Reading and Writing"].

93. Claude Lévi-Strauss, "The Structural Study of Myth," in *Structural Anthropology* [1958], trans. Claire Jacobson and Brooke Grundfest Schoepf (Garden City, N.Y.: Anchor Books, 1967), pp. 202–238; here p. 212.

94. Nietzsche, *Ecce homo; KGW* 6/3:262 ["Why I Am So Wise," 1].

95. Buck-Morss, "Aesthetics and Anaesthetics," p. 10. See further Nietzsche, "NF, Frühjahr 1888"; *KGW* 8/3:149; and Heidegger, *Nietzsche: Der Wille zur Macht als Kunst* [Freiburg winter semester 1936–1937], ed. Bernd Heimbüchel, *Gesamtausgabe* (Frankfurt am Main: Vittorio Klostermann, 1985), 2/43:91–92. It must also be noted that "Male fantasies of androgyny are . . . strategies of totalization and ethical compensation" for underlying misogyny (Julie Ellison, *Delicate Subjects: Romanticism, Gender, and the Ethics of Understanding* [Ithaca and London: Cornell University Press, 1990], p. 19). Ellison is here paraphrasing the work of Carolyn G. Heilbrun, among others.

96. On the powerful masculinist bias of Machiavelli himself and to a lesser extent on Machiavellianism, though unfortunately not on Nietzsche, see Hanna Fenichel Pitkin, *Fortune Is a Woman: Gender and Politics in the Thought of Niccolò Machiavelli* (Berkeley, Los Angeles, London: University of California Press, 1984).

97. *Selections from the Prison Notebooks of Antonio Gramsci*, pp. 126–127. On Gramsci and Machiavelli, see Benedetto Fontana, *Hegemony and Power: On the Relation between Gramsci and Machiavelli* (Minneapolis: University of Minnesota Press, 1993).

98. Required might be a reading of Nietzsche's œuvre as painstaking as the one provided, say, by Stanley Fish on Milton. Fish argues that *Paradise Lost* is a text

about how readers come to be who they—ostensibly—are. See Stanley E. Fish, *Surprised by Sin: The Reader in Paradise Lost* [1967] (Berkeley, Los Angeles, London: University of California Press, 1971). In Nietzsche's case, however, such a reading would have to include the exposure and analysis of subconscious collective as well as merely individual embodiments.

99. Niccolò Machiavelli to Francesco Guicciardini, May 17, 1521, in *The Prince: A New Translation, Backgrounds, Interpretations, Peripherica*, trans. and ed. Robert M. Adams (New York: W. W. Norton & Company, 1977), pp. 133–135; here p. 135.

100. Sophocles, *Antigone*, trans. Elizabeth Wyckoff, in *Greek Tragedies*, ed. David Grene and Richmond Lattimore (Chicago and London: The University of Chicago Press, 1960), 1:177–227; here 187 [ll. 175–177].

101. Baltasar Gracián, *The Art of Worldly Wisdom: A Pocket Oracle* [*El Oráculo manual*, 1647], trans. Christopher Mauer (New York: Doubleday Currency, 1992), pp. 3, 54, and 73.

102. Francis Bacon, *The Essays* [1597 and 1625], ed. with an introduction by John Pitcher (Harmondsworth: Penguin, 1985), p. 76.

103. Ibid., p. 128. See further appendix 4: "Idols of the Mind" [from the *Novum organum*, 1620], pp. 277–285. In fact, Bacon was one of the great practitioners of esoteric writing, though arguably on behalf of a very different constituency than Nietzsche's. Cf. Cantor, "Leo Strauss and Contemporary Hermeneutics," in *Leo Strauss's Thought: Toward a Critical Engagement*, pp. 289–297; and Lampert, *Nietzsche and Modern Times*, pp. 15–141, 393, and 410.

104. See Schopenhauer, *Parerga und Paralipomena: Kleine philosophische Schriften* [1851], ed. Julius Frauenstädt, 7th ed. (Leipzig: F. A. Brockhaus, 1891), 2:258–260 ["Zur Rechtslehre und Politik," § 125].

105. Nietzsche, *Menschliches, Allzumenschliches I; KGW* 4/2:88–89 ["On the History of Moral Sensations," aphorism 93].

106. See Spinoza, *The Ethics*, in *On the Improvement of the Understanding, The Ethics, Correspondence*, pp. 212–215 [part 4, prop. 37], and *A Political Treatise*, in *A Theologico-Political Treatise and a Political Treatise*, pp. 292 and 294–295 [ch. 2, §§ 4 and 8].

107. See Schopenhauer, *Parerga und Paralipomena*, 2:260.

108. Saul Bellow, *Herzog* [1961] (New York: A Fawcett Crest Book, 1965), p. 389.

109. Strauss, "Note on the Plan of Nietzsche's *Beyond Good and Evil*," in *Studies in Platonic Political Philosophy*, p. 177.

110. A recent collection of essays on Nietzsche's relationship to postmodernism has the cumulative effect of egregiously misunderstanding him politically; see *Nietzsche as Postmodernist: Essays Pro and Contra*, ed. Clayton Koelb (Albany: State University of New York Press, 1990). The same must be said for the essays in *Exceedingly Nietzsche: Aspects of Contemporary Nietzsche-Interpretation*, ed. David Farrell Krell and David Wood (London and New York: Routledge, 1988). As for Strauss himself, he is not unconnected to at least one basic project of postmodernism: "virtual reality,"

at least in one of its preliminary manifestations, namely computer "outlining." The notion of post-Aristotelian outlining—a key to the hierarchical organization of thought—in elitist political philosophies, societies, and cyberspatial matrixes alike—was developed in close proximity to Strauss. "KAMAS (Knowledge and Mind Amplification System) was the first outliner on personal computers. A group of former philosophy professors wrote the program, seeing outlining as a vehicle for fostering a certain way of thinking. Compusophic Systems wanted to promote the educational philosophy of the Chicago school of the late 1940s and 1950s, which advocated the neoclassicism of Leo Strauss, Richard McKeon and Mortimer Adler. The group described KAMAS as the 'classic vehicle' for thinking, as it helps writers structure their thoughts in hierarchical levels" (Heim, *The Metaphysics of Virtual Reality*, pp. 47–48). And not thoughts only.

111. Strauss, "What Is Political Philosophy" [1954–1955], in *What Is Political Philosophy? and Other Studies* [1959] (Chicago and London: The University of Chicago Press, 1988), pp. 9–55; here p. 46. See further "The Three Waves of Modernity," in *Political Philosophy: Six Essays*, ed. with an introduction by Hilail Gildin (Indianapolis and New York: Bobbs-Merrill, 1975), pp. 81–98. For one of Strauss's most significant reflections on secret writing, though the example is Lessing, not Nietzsche, see his "Exoteric Teaching" [1939], *Interpretation* 14 (1986), 51–59, since reprinted in *The Rebirth of Classical Political Rationalism: An Introduction to the Thought of Leo Strauss*, selected and introduced by Thomas L. Pangle (Chicago and London: The University of Chicago Press, 1989), pp. 63–71. Unfortunately, Strauss's early work on one of the most important neo-Spinozists, Friedrich Heinrich Jacobi (1743–1819)—work that is assumed to contain not merely the future program of esoteric Straussian political philosophy but also its most unabashedly *Nietzschean* mode—has yet to see the light of day. Jacobi was the author of *On the Teaching of Spinoza in Letters to Mr. Moses Mendelssohn* (1785), a text of immense, and still not fully fathomed, significance for German and European intellectual history.

112. Strauss, "What Is Political Philosophy," in *What Is Political Philosophy?*, p. 46.

113. Strauss, *Thoughts on Machiavelli*, p. 13.

114. Spinoza, *The Ethics*, p. 151 [part 3, prop. 31].

115. Nietzsche, "NF, Herbst 1885–Frühjahr 1886"; *KGW* 8/1:37. There are a number of such reflections in Nietzsche's unpublished writings, including a passage he chose to strike from the second *Untimely Meditation: The Use and Misuse of History for Life* (1874), which made his intent behind speaking crudely on occasion all too clear. See the editors' philological apparatus in Nietzsche, *KSA* 14:68.

116. See once more Deleuze's depiction of Nietzsche as non- or antidialectical thinker in *Nietzsche et la philosophie*, pp. 169–189. Though here, too, Deleuze was anticipated by Bataille. See, for example, Bataille, *The Accursed Share*, vols. 2 and 3:368–371 (*Sovereignty*). *Œuvres complètes*, 8:402–404. Robert Paul Resch's analysis of the political impact on and of Deleuze's Nietzscheanism and related theory of what he calls "chaosmos" is worth noting in this regard.

Deleuze, following Nietzsche, sees a chaotic will to power as the ahistorical, ontological motor of history. To be sure, this chaosmos is always historically structured, but the principle of that structuration lies outside of history. For Deleuze, as for Nietzsche, history is merely one more (false) structure of meaning imposed on meaningless differences taking on a historical form. . . . Deleuze's problematic was a powerful influence on the French Left in the seventies, the decade Nietzsche replaced Marx as the central reference for French intellectuals. It seemed to provide a framework within which the ideals of May 1968 could survive the pessimism that attended their defeat. Indeed, that defeat could be rationalized by stressing the deficiencies of Marxism, which was ultimately held responsible for the failure of the revolution (Althusserian theory as a repressive and narrow rationalism; the reactionary nature of the French Communist Party, which lost the revolution by pursuing limited, traditional, self-interested tactics; and so on). Leaving aside (for the moment) the theoretical significance of the neo-Nietzschean dissidence, it is clear that its negative thrust cut two ways. It did attempt to provide a critical perspective against which domination could be measured, but it also exploited the extreme disappointment within the ranks of the Left after 1968 and contributed significantly to the general anti-Marxist fervor that swept Paris after 1975. Positively, it joined with poststructuralism to form the theoretical core of what became known in the United States as postmodernism. (Resch, *Althusser and the Renewal of Marxist Social Theory*, pp. 232–233)

This analysis of Deleuze may be basically correct, though Resch's polemic against much of the remainder of Deleuze's work—which is not reducible to Nietzscheanism—is misdirected and certainly counterproductive in intellectual coalition building. But what is especially curious is that Resch fully incorporates the Deleuzean interpretation of Nietzsche into his own criticism of Deleuze and of the anticommunist—at the very least anti-Althusserian—Left generally. Whatever else this move may accomplish, it effectively eliminates the possibility of ever theorizing "the theoretical significance of the neo-Nietzschean dissidence" in its full complexity and influence. Finally, it must be said that even a theorist as sharply—and to some extent justifiably—critical of Deleuze and Guattari as is Manfredo Tafuri—who aruges, for example, that their theory of the rhizome abdicates the painful but necessary requirement of "historical criticism" to "balance on the razor's edge that separates detachment and participation"—has incorporated into his work the very standard view of Nietzsche as critically progressive—which is the view of Deleuze and Guattari as well. See Tafuri, *The Sphere and the Labyrinth: Avant-Gardes and Architecture from Piranesi to the 1970s* [1980], trans. Pellegrino d'Acierno and Robert Connolly (Cambridge, Mass.: The MIT Press, 1990), pp. 4–11 and 291.

117. Mick Jagger and Keith Richards, "Street Fighting Man" [© 1968], *The Rolling Stones: Hot Rocks 1964–1971*, © London/Abkco Records, AC2T–04201.

118. On *Carmen* and Nietzsche, see Klein, *Cigarettes Are Sublime*, ch. 4: "The Devil in Carmen."

119. For instance, by Michael Allen Gillespie, "Nietzsche's Musical Politics," in *Nietzsche's New Seas: Explorations in Philosophy, Aesthetics, and Politics*, pp. 117–149. Quite early on in his reception, however, Nietzsche was commonly depicted as "musical." See, for example, Bernard Scharlitt, "Das musikalische Element in Friedrich Nietzsche," *Die Musik* 4 (1904), 108–112. Nietzsche has influenced many "classical" composers — not only the neoromantic Richard Strauss, as is well known, but also avant-garde Alban Berg. For a preliminary attempt to analyze Nietzsche's "media philosophy," see Rudolf Fietz, *Medienphilosophie: Musik, Sprache und Schrift bei Friedrich Nietzsche* (Würzburg: Königshausen & Neumann, 1992); on Nietzsche's "musical semiotics" see esp. pp. 82–91 and 130–144. More detailed on Nietzsche's own relation to music — though still missing the connection between his views and esoteric written communication — is Georges Liébert, *Nietzsche et la musique* (Paris: Presses Universitaires de France, 1995).

120. Nietzsche, "NF, Mai–Juli 1885"; *KGW* 7/3:234–235. The passage then concludes: "Preparation for becoming Masters of the Earth: The Legislators of the Future. At least out of our children. Basic attention to marriages."

121. Oswald Spengler, "Nietzsche und sein Jahrhundert" [1924], *Reden und Aufsätze*, ed. Hildegard Kornhardt (Munich: C. H. Beck'sche Verlagsbuchhandlung, 1938), pp. 110–124; here p. 112.

122. Schopenhauer, *The World as Will and Representation*, 1:257–259; *Sämtliche Werke*, 2:304.

123. Jacques Attali, *Noise: The Political Economy of Music* [1977], trans. Brian Massumi, foreword by Fredric Jameson, afterword by Susan McClary (Minneapolis: University of Minnesota Press, 1985), p. 11.

124. Lou Reed, "Last Great American Whale," *New York*, © 1989 Sire/Warner Bros. Records, Inc., 9–25829–4. Actually, Reed is referring to Americans — not Left-Nietzschoids — when he sings: "They say things are done for the majority / Don't believe half of what you see / and none of what you hear / It's a lot like what my painter friend Donald said to me: 'Stick a fork in their ass and turn them over, they're done.'"

125. U2 (Bono, The Edge, Adam Clayton, Larry Mullen Jr.), "Acrobat," *Achtung Baby*, © 1991 Island Records, Ltd., 314–510–347–4.

126. Rousseau, *Essay on the Origin of Languages*, p. 15.

127. See again Althusser, "The Object of *Capital*," in *Reading Capital*, pp. 188–189.

128. See again Negri, *The Savage Anomaly*, p. 129.

129. There exist several versions of this text. See, for example, Derrida, "La question du style," in *Nietzsche aujourd'hui?* [Colloque du Centre Culturel International de Cerisy-la-Salle, 1972], vol. 1: *Intensités* (Paris: Union Générale d'Éditions 10/18, 1973), pp. 235–287; and a dual-language edition of the expanded text, *Spurs: Nietzsche's Styles/Éperons: Les styles de Nietzsche* [1978], introduction by Stefano Agosti, trans. Barbara Harlow, drawings by François Loubrieu (Chicago and London: The University of Chicago Press, 1979).

130. Derrida, *Otobiographies: l'enseignement de Nietzsche et la politique du nom propre* [1976; 1982] (Paris: Éditions Galilée, 1984). In this text, Derrida puns briefly on the relationship between *corpus* and *corps* (p. 41). For a translation see *The Ear of the Other: Otobiography, Transference, Translation (Texts and Discussions with Jacques Derrida),* ed. Christie V. McDonald, trans. Avital Ronell and Peggy Kamuf (New York: Schocken Books, 1985), pp. 5–6. Another French philosophical position explicitly attacks the celebrations of the "death" of communism by articulating the notions of "corpse" and "corps"; see especially the concluding pages of Badiou, *D'un désastre obscur.*

131. See, for example, Mary Ann Doane, "Veiling over Desire: Close-ups of the Woman" [1989], in *Femmes Fatales: Feminism, Film Theory, Psychoanalysis* (New York and London: Routledge, 1991), pp. 44–75. For a critique specifically of *Spurs,* though in several respects less incisive than Doane's in *Femmes Fatales,* that struggles rather helplessly to remind Derridians of the "historical context" in which Nietzsche developed his ideas about women, and in particular of Nietzsche's "campaign against the values of egalitarianism," see Adrian Del Caro, "The Pseudoman in Nietzsche, or The Threat of the Neuter," *New German Critique* 50 (Spring/Summer 1990), 135–156; here 156. Del Caro, too, seems unaware of the homosexual component of Nietzsche's thought and is certainly unaware of the problematic of esotericism. With regard to Derrida's "woman," Julia Kristeva has justly argued that "If the feminine *is,*" then "it *exists* only through its relation to sense and signification, as their other, exceeder or transgressor — *says* itself, *thinks* (itself) and *writes* (itself) for the two sexes" (Kristeva, "Il n'y a pas de maître à langage," *Nouvelle revue de psychanalyze* 20 [Fall 1979], 119–140; here 134; also see "La femme, ce n'est jamais ça," *Tel quel* 59 [Fall 1974], 19–24). For Kristeva, following in the wake of Lacan, "*Woman as such* does not exist. . . . The problems of women have no interest except inasmuch as they bring to an impasse the most serious problems of our society: how to live not only without God, but without man?" (Kristeva, *About Chinese Women* [1974], trans. Anita Barrows [New York: Urizen Books and London: Boyars, 1977], p. 16). Judith Butler in *Gender Trouble: Feminism and the Subversion of Identity* (New York and London: Routledge, 1990) directly problematizes the question of whether gay as well as hetero-sexuality is primarily biological or sociocultural, though Butler does not know Nietzsche well. Donna Haraway suggests — also not with regard to Nietzsche — that the "refusal to become or to remain a 'gendered' man or woman . . . is an eminently political insistence on emerging from the nightmare of the all-too-real, imaginary narrative of sex and race" (Haraway, "'Gender' for a Marxist Dictionary: The Sexual Politics of a Word" [1987], *Simians, Cyborgs, and Women,* pp. 127–148; here p. 148).

132. See Adorno, "Aus Sils Maria," in *Ohne Leitbild: Parva aesthetica* (Frankfurt am Main: Suhrkamp Verlag, 1967), pp. 48–51. Adorno died three years later. For an account of Sils Maria as both historical travel goal for foreigners and as a complex allegory for Switzerland's own peculiar anxieties about modernity, see Iso Camartin,

Von Sils-Maria aus betrachtet: Ausblicke vom Dach Europas (Frankfurt am Main: Suhrkamp, 1991).

133. Barthes, *S/Z,* pp. 44–45.

134. See the facsimile of Nietzsche's postcard to his sister, Elisabeth Förster-Nietzsche, May 30, 1891, in Volz, *Nietzsche im Labyrinth seiner Krankheit,* p. 458.

135. Herta D. Wong, "Plains Indian Names and 'the Autobiographical Act'" [1992], in *Autobiography & Postmodernism,* ed. Kathleen Ashley, Leigh Gilmore, and Gerald Peters (Amherst: The University of Massachusetts Press, 1994), pp. 212–239; here p. 237.

136. Derrida, "Interpreting Signatures," in *Looking After Nietzsche,* p. 16.

137. For an analysis of the question of "Derrida and politics" that is rather more favorably disposed to Derrida and Nietzsche, see Dominick LaCapra, "Up against the Ear of the Other: Marx after Derrida," in *Soundings in Critical Theory* (Ithaca: Cornell University Press, 1989), pp 155–181. LaCapra provides a critical elaboration of Derrida's dictum that "il n'y a pas de hors-texte." Of course, there is nothing particularly scandalous or even remarkable about Derrida's claim about "texts" if one understands it to mean that they and their "readings" are always mediated by some sort of "con*text*" and "pre*text.*" The problem is that, as member of the corps/e, "even" Derrida has misunderstood the project of Nietzschean political thinking at its *esoteric* root.

138. See, for example, Derrida, "*Ousia* and *Gramme:* Note on a Note from *Being and Time*" [1968], in *Margins of Philosophy,* pp. 29–67. Derrida here links the exoteric to Aristotle's discussion of "ordinary" or "vulgar" time, and follows Heidegger to show that in effect there *is* no vulgar concept of time, in the — presumably more esoteric — sense that "The now is given simultaneously as that which is *no longer* and as that which is *not yet.* It is what is not, and is not what it is" (pp. 63 and 39). But this ontological problematic about time in relation to being does not require from Derrida an inquiry into esotericism as a question of political rhetoric. Nor, more surprisingly, does he deal with this question when he discusses the relation, in Nietzsche, between philosophy and metaphor. Cf. Derrida, "White Metaphor: Metaphor in the Text of Philosophy," in *Margins of Philosophy,* esp. pp. 216–219.

139. Derrida, *La vérité en peinture* (Paris: Flammarion, 1978), p. 309. "—Je m'intéresserais plutôt à une correspondance secrète, évidemment: évidement secrète, cryptée dans l'éther de l'évidence et de la vérité, trop évident parce que le chiffre en ce cas reste secret de n'être pas celé." This remark complicates the today standard notion — especially prevalent, it seems, among Germanists and would-be German leftists, none of whom has produced anything remotely as interesting on Nietzsche as has Derrida — that Derridian deconstruction is totally uninterested in "ideology-criticism" or in "exposing error" and as such is locked in its own self-perpetuating problematic. But it complicates also Gayatri Chakravorty Spivak's more or less approving assertion that "Derrida is interested in how truth is constructed rather than in exposing error. . . . Deconstruction can only speak in the language of the

thing it criticizes. So as Derrida says, it falls prey to its own critique, *in a certain way.* That makes it very different from ideology-critique . . . " (Spivak, *The Post-Colonial Critic: Interviews, Strategies, Dialogues,* ed. Sarah Harasym [New York and London: Routledge, 1990], p. 135). The real problem, as Spivak recognizes, hinges on who exactly is "constructing truth" or "crypting," and with what ideological motivations and consequences.

140. Donald Davidson, "Intending" [1974], in *Essays on Actions and Events,* corrected ed. (Oxford: Clarendon Press, 1989), pp. 83–102; here p. 102. For a relevant reflection on the connection between intention in literary semantics and criminal law see Annabel Patterson, "Intention," in *Critical Terms for Literary Study,* ed. Frank Lentricchia and Thomas McLaughlin (Chicago and London: The University of Chicago Press, 1990), pp. 135–146.

141. *Documents Relating to the Proceedings against William Prynne,* ed. S. R. Gardiner (New York: Johnson Reprint Corp., 1965: rep. of the original ed. of 1877); as cited in Patterson, "Intention," p. 135.

142. See Andrew Bowie, *Schelling and Modern European Philosophy: An Introduction* (London and New York: Routledge, 1993), esp. pp. 15–29, 55–90, and 127–177.

143. See Derrida, *Otobiographies,* pp. 101–102; *Ear of the Other,* p. 32. Derrida's methodological position is elaborated further in his uneventful "debate" with Hans-Georg Gadamer about reading and understanding as modalities of "Will to Power"—but the implications for reading Nietzsche remain basically unchanged, the lack of insight into Nietzschean esotericism as operative in Derrida as it is in Gadamer. See Derrida, "Guter Wille zur Macht (I): Drei Fragen an Hans-Georg Gadamer" and "Guter Wille zur Macht (II): Die Unterschriften interpretieren (Nietzsche/Heidegger)," both in *Text und Interpretation: Deutsch-französische Debatte mit Beiträgen von J. Derrida, Ph. Forget, M. Frank, H.-G. Gadamer, J. Greisch and F. Laruelle,* ed. Philippe Forget (Munich: Wilhelm Fink Verlag, 1984), pp. 56–58 and 62–77, respectively. The latter text has been translated in *Looking After Nietzsche.*

144. See Foucault, "Nietzsche, Freud, Marx," in *Nietzsche* [Colloque de Royaumont, 1964], esp. p. 192.

145. See Heidegger, *Sein und Zeit* [1927] (Tübingen: Max Niemeyer, 1972), pp. 34–39 [ch. 2, § 7 C]. For the later Heidegger, too, untruth is not at all privative, negative, or antithetical to truth; rather, concealment and untruth are of its very essence. See, for example, "On the Essence of Truth" [1930, published 1943] and "The End of Philosophy and the Task of Thinking" [1964], both in his *Basic Writings: From "Being and Time" (1927) to "The Task of Thinking" (1964),* ed., with general introduction and introductions to each selection by David Farrell Krell, various translators (New York: Harper & Row, Publishers, 1977), pp. 113–141 (here esp. p. 132) and 373–392 (here esp. p. 391), respectively. For an account of the influence of Heidegger and Nietzsche on Foucault as well as Derrida see Allan Megill, *Prophets of Extremity: Nietzsche, Heidegger, Foucault, Derrida* (Berkeley, Los Angeles, London: University of California Press, 1987).

146. Derrida, *Mal d'Archive: Une impression freudienne* (Paris: Éditions Galilée, 1995). In addition to the recalcitrant "archives" of the psyche encountered by psychoanalysis, Derrida has in mind the use and abuse of "facts" to prove or disprove the existence of the Holocaust and, though not explicitly, the construction of "dossiers" to "prove" the alleged complicity of Heidegger and de Man with Nazism (p. 1). His main primary texts include Yosef Hayim Yerushalmi, *Freud's Moses, Judaism Terminable and Interminable* (New Haven and London: Yale University Press, 1991), and several works by Freud himself.

147. For a compendium documenting Nietzsche's precise and peculiar relationship to "philology," see Eric Blondel, *Nietzsche: The Body and Culture, Philosophy as a Philological Genealogy* [1986], trans. Seán Hand (Stanford: Stanford University Press, 1991), even though Blondel symptomatically ignores the esoteric and explicitly political dimensions of Nietzsche's thinking and writing. See further Richard Roos, "Règles pour une lecture philologique de Nietzsche," in *Nietzsche aujourd'hui?* vol. 2: *Passion,* pp. 283–318.

148. See, for example, Marcuse, *Eros and Civilization,* esp. pp. 108–112. Of course, Derrida and Marcuse share a common pre-Nietzschean source for play in Kant — as mediated for Marcuse by Friedrich Schiller and for Derrida by Nietzsche himself, who had found his own sources in the pre-Socratics.

149. See Nietzsche, *Also sprach Zarathustra; KGW* 6/1:173–178 [part 2, "On Deliverance"].

150. Friedrich Hölderlin, *Hyperion* [1779], in *Sämtliche Werke,* ed. Friedrich Beißner (Stuttgart: Verlag W. Kohlhammer, 1943ff), 3:152. Nietzsche had read this passage in *Hyperion* no later than 1861. Hölderlin's sources for this image include Rousseau, *Discours sur les sciences et les arts* [1750], *Œuvres complètes,* ed. B. Gagnebin and M. Raymond (Paris: Bibliotèque de la Pléiade, 1964), 3:26.

151. Marx to Arnold Ruge, May 1843; letters from the *Deutsch-Französische Jahrbücher,* in Marx and Engels, *Collected Works,* 3:134.

152. Marx to Ruge, March 1843; letters from the *Deutsch-Französische Jahrbücher,* in Marx and Engels, *Collected Works,* 3:133–134.

153. See, for example, Heidegger, *Was heißt Denken?* esp. pp. 30–47.

154. Nietzsche, *Also sprach Zarathustra; KGW* 6/1:174–175 [part 2, "On Deliverance"].

155. See Nietzsche, *Ecce homo; KGW* 6/3:346 ["Thus Spoke Zarathustra," 8].

156. See Roman Jakobson, "Two Aspects of Language and Two Types of Aphasic Disturbances," in *Fundamentals of Language,* ed. Roman Jakobson and Morris Halle (The Hague: Mouton, 1956), pp. 69–96.

157. Nietzsche, "Ueber Wahrheit und Lüge im aussermoralischen Sinne" [1873]; *KGW* 3/2:375.

158. Nietzsche, Vorrede [1886] to *Menschliches, Allzumenschliches: Ein Buch für freie Geister. Zweiter Band; KGW* 4/3:3–11; here 4 [vol. 2, preface 1].

159. Nietzsche, *Also sprach Zarathustra; KGW* 6/1:257–259 [part 3, "On the Old and New Tablets," 20].

160. Ibid., 6/1:254 [part 3, "On the Old and New Tablets," 16].

161. Derrida, *Otobiographies,* p. 43; *Ear of the Other,* p. 6. This influential view of Nietzsche's "names" is not all that original — nor need it be — as a look at Klossowski's Nietzsche will show presently.

162. Derrida, "La structure, le signe et le jeu dans le discours des sciences humaines" [1966], in *L'écriture et la différence,* pp. 409–428; here p. 427. For a critical survey of the significance of "play," see Mihai Spariosu, *Dionysus Reborn: Play and the Aesthetic Dimension in Modern Philosophical and Scientific Discourse* (Ithaca: Cornell University Press, 1989). In his thinking about Nietzsche, Spariosu acknowledges the importance of the unpublished notebooks, but he tacks in the opposite direction. He uses "play" to deconstruct Nietzsche's published writings, whereas they are the comparatively exoteric expression of the former; and he thinks Nietzsche's "Dionysian play" is prerational yet postmodern and liberatory, whereas it is distinctly postrational and fascoid-liberal. But Spariosu is refreshingly candid about the seriousness of play — at least for some children: "unashamed pleasure in power and manipulation (e.g., in torturing, maiming, and killing insects and small animals; in getting their way with adults), immediacy of feeling, *insouciance* about 'moral' standards or the Other, lack of self-image or self-consciousness and therefore also of guilt . . . " (p. 97). Whether all this can be applied *mutatis mutandis* to Nietzsche's political philosophy and illocutionary strategies is an interesting question, though as Spariosu reminds us constantly this problem with play is a lot older and younger than just Nietzsche. Nonetheless, Spariosu himself cites Nietzsche as saying, "One would make a fit little boy stare if one asked him: 'Would you like to become virtuous?' — but he will open his eyes wide if asked: 'Would you like to become stronger than your friends?'" (p. 97 n. 53).

163. Nietzsche, "NF, Juni–Juli 1883"; *KGW* 7/1:386.

164. See again Nietzsche, *Ecce homo; KGW* 6/3:262 ["Why I Am so Wise," 1].

165. Derrida, *Otobiographies,* pp. 40–41; *Ear of the Other,* p. 5.

166. Ibid., p. 63; *Ear of the Other,* p. 16. For a better sense of what the "real" biographical pressures of his father, mother, and sister were on Nietzsche's *Ecce Homo,* see Mazzino Montinari's detailed account of the passages Elisabeth Förster-Nietzsche censored, in "Ein neuer Abschnitt in Nietzsches *Ecce homo*" [1972], *Nietzsche lesen* (Berlin and New York: Walter de Gruyter, 1982), pp. 120–168.

167. *Otobiographies,* p. 69. *Ear of the Other,* p. 19. Henceforth this text will be cited in parentheses: first the English, then the French edition.

168. For an early introduction to Derrida that makes effective use of the metaphor of "parasitic inworming" philosophical texts both to paraphrase Derrida's project and to criticize it politically and ideologically, see D. C. Wood, "An Introduction to Derrida" [1979], in *Radical Philosophy Reader,* pp. 18–42.

169. On the variety of responses to Nietzsche that existed all during the Third Reich, see the uneven but important thesis of Hans Langreder, "Die Auseinandersetzung mit Nietzsche im Dritten Reich" (Diss., University of Kiel, 1970). But see

also the earlier, published work of Konrad Algermissen, *Nietzsche und das Dritte Reich* (Celle: Verlag Joseph Giesel, 1947), even though Algermissen's own position was badly compromised by opportunism. At the inception of the Third Reich in 1933, Algermissen had written an extreme anticommunist book that was very much in the Nazified mood of the times. For a more recent and scholarly approach to the general conditions of philosophical discourse in the Third Reich see Thomas Laugstien, *Philosophieverhältnisse im deutschen Faschismus* (Hamburg: Argument-Sonderband, 1990). On Italian fascism and Nietzsche more specifically, see Taureck, *Nietzsche und der Faschismus*. See further Aschheim, *The Nietzsche Legacy in Germany*, esp. ch. 8: "Nietzsche in the Third Reich" and ch. 9: "National Socialism and the Nietzsche Debate." But the latter's own main thesis in this regard is fundamentally mistaken. When Aschheim finally comes to say what the relative degree of debate about Nietzsche among Nazis might *mean*, he stresses that "these scholarly presentations, the head-on criticisms, oppositional polemics, Aesopian deployments, indeed, the very employment of Nietzsche as a foil for coming to terms with national socialism *demonstrate the normative nature and the centrality of that thinker as definitive of the Nazi order.*" This is idealist nonsense on at least two levels: not only because no body of mere "thinking" could ever be "normative," "central," or "definitive," most especially not for an activist movement such as Nazism, but also because what the "debate" about Nietzsche in the Third Reich illustrates has far less to do with Nietzsche ultimately than with the operational complexity of hegemony. "Even" national socialism required — and requires — levels of consent posing as dissent. This is certainly not to deny the obvious, as put hesitantly by Aschheim: "in *some* meaningful way nazism was, *in part,* a frame of mind and . . . ideas (in their *most* general sense) were both central to its disposition as a historical project and to its subsequent comprehension" (p. 320; emphasis added), though how something that is "most general" can also be "central" demands clarification.

170. See, e.g., Derrida, "Heidegger, the Philosophers' Hell" [interview with Didier Eribon, 1987], *Points . . . : Interviews, 1974–1994,* ed. Elisabeth Weber, trans. Peggy Kamuf et al. (Stanford: Stanford University Press, 1995), pp. 181–190; here p. 186. Derrida is quite right that his many encounters with Heidegger over the years have always served to deconstruct from within certain gestures of closure in Heidegger's texts. Nonetheless, it is only comparatively recently, under the external pressure of disclosures by historians about the full extent and depth of Heidegger's commitment to national socialism, that the specifically political implications both of Heidegger's closure and of Derrida's deconstruction have become clear.

171. Foucault, "Prison Talk" ["Les jeux du pouvoir," interview with J.-J. Brochier, 1975], *Power/Knowledge: Selected Interviews and Other Writings 1972–1977,* ed. Colin Gordon, trans. Colin Gordon et al. (New York: Pantheon Books, 1980), pp. 37–55; here pp. 53–54.

172. Derrida, *"Istrice 2: Ick bünn all hier"* [interview with Maurizio Ferraris, 1990], in *Points . . . ,* pp. 300–326; here 321.

173. Ronell, *The Telephone Book: Technology-Schizophrenia-Electric Speech* (Lincoln and London: University of Nebraska Press, 1989), p. 135.

174. "Art Damage: The Manifesto" [editorial], *Mondo 2000* 6 (1992), 8–9.

175. See Pierre Klossowski, "Nietzsche, le polythéisme et la parodie" [1957], *Un si funeste désir* (Paris: Gallimard, 1963), pp. 185–228.

176. Kierkegaard, "A First and Last Explanation," *Concluding Unscientific Postscript*, p. 627.

177. Adorno, *Kierkegaard: Construction of the Aesthetic* [1933], trans., ed., and with a foreword by Robert Hullot-Kentor (Minneapolis: University of Minnesota Press, 1989), pp. 11–12.

178. See, for example, Nietzsche, *Der Fall Wagner: Ein Musikanten-Problem* [1888]; *KGW* 6/3:3–4 [foreword], and *Ecce homo; KGW* 6/3:316–321 ["Why I Write Such Good Books: The Untimely Meditations"].

179. Whether Klossowski thought of himself as a man of the Left, the Right, or something else is an ultimately related question but not particularly relevant — just as it was also not with regard to Bataille. Both are part of the corps/e.

180. For this reason the comparison of Strauss and Derrida as "Nietzscheans" by Levine is problematic in *Nietzsche and the Modern Crisis of the Humanities.*

181. De Landa, *War in the Age of Intelligent Machines*, p. 188.

182. Baudrillard, *Simulations*, pp. 88–89.

183. Nietzsche, *Götzen-Dämmerung; KGW* 6/3:59 ["Maxims and Arrows," aphorism 38].

184. See Foucault, "What Is an Author?" [1969], *Language, Counter-Memory, Practice: Selected Essays and Interviews*, ed. and with an introduction by Donald F. Bouchard, trans. Donald F. Bouchard and Sherry Simon (Ithaca: Cornell University Press, 1977), pp. 113–138.

185. For a recent attempt — too innocent of issues relating to political ideology — to describe the "ludic" quality of poststructuralist and posthermeneutic responses to Nietzsche, and to mediate between them, see Alan D. Schrift, *Nietzsche and the Problem of Interpretation: Between Hermeneutics and Deconstruction* (New York and London: Routledge, 1990).

186. Klossowski, "Nietzsche, le polythéisme et la parodie," in *Un si funeste désir*, p. 193. See further, Nietzsche, *Götzen-Dämmerung; KGW* 6/3:74–75 ["How the 'True World' Finally Became a Fable"].

187. See Nietzsche, *Unzeitgemässe Betrachtungen, Zweites Stück: Vom Nutzen und Nachtheil der Historie für das Leben* [1874]; *KGW* 3/1:239–330. Too, this essay ought to be read alongside the other three essays in this collection. "On the Use and Disadvantage of History for Life" deals with the historical and historiographical aspects of a tightly integrated *fourfold* problematic, the other sides of which are the mechanisms whereby high philosophy can be incorporated (Nietzsche's own relation to his master in "Schopenhauer as Educator"); the criticism of contemporary mass and popular culture ("David Friedrich Strauss as Confessor and Writer"); and

the possibilities and risks of an opposing cultural politics ("Richard Wagner in Bayreuth").

188. Nietzsche's nearly total lack of fun in any common sense of the term was recalled by Cosima Wagner — who was at least as deficient on this score — in a letter to Richard Strauss written after Nietzsche's death. See Cosima Wagner to Richard Strauss, letter of November 3, 1901, in *Cosima Wagner–Richard Strauss: Ein Briefwechsel*, ed. Franz Tenner, with Gabrielle Straus (Tutzing: H. Schneider, 1978), p. 245.

189. Which is to recall Ireland's important work on "comedy." In terms of personal lifestyle — excepting perhaps his occasional sexual exploits — Nietzsche was never himself a "Nietzschean" in common parlance: namely, an "immoralist" or a "confidence man" in the antibourgeois, antiworking-class, and quasi-aristocratic lifestyles of, say, André Gides' Michel, Thomas Mann's Felix Krull, or a Paul de Man. The fact that God is dead, and therefore all is *permitted,* did not mean for Nietzsche that all *should* be done. He was meticulous in maintaining his bourgeois cover, and did not leave, say, a trail of unpaid bills and distraught family and friends behind him. For the kind of master revolutionary Nietzsche was, the transformation of humankind is far too serious a matter to be compromised by any one man's foibles or "humors," including his own.

190. This is true, for example, of the account of both Klossowski and Nietzscheanism offered in the otherwise informative book by Vincent Descombes, *Modern French Philosophy* [*Le même et l'autre,* 1979], trans. L. Scott-Fox and J. M. Harding (Cambridge: Cambridge University Press, 1980). On Klossowski and Nietzsche, and for similarly blinded remarks about their relationship, see further Deleuze, *The Logic of Sense* [1969], trans. Mark Lester, with Charles Stivale, ed. Constantin V. Boundas (New York: Columbia University Press, 1990), pp. 280–301.

191. The distinction between "tough," "medium," and "gentle" Nietzscheans — all three of which did in fact represent significant strains of his own thought — goes back to Crane Brinton, *Nietzsche* [1941] (New York: Harper Torchbooks, 1965), esp. pp. 184–199, 221, and 231. Still readable after all these years, this book — written as part of the fight against Nazism — would have to be theoretically grounded and empirically updated, however, to account for many subsequent and more complex incarnations of Nietzsche's corps/e.

192. Klossowski, "Le Marquis de Sade et la Révolution" [1939], in *Le Collège de Sociologie,* pp. 369–393; here pp. 393 and 380. De Sade's seminal thesis had already provided the basis for Bataille's earlier essay "The Sacred Conspiracy" [1936], in *Visions of Excess,* pp. 178–81. *Œuvres complètes* 1:442–446.

193. Horkheimer and Adorno, "Juliette or Enlightenment and Morality," *Dialectic of Enlightenment,* pp. 81–119; here p. 119.

194. Klossowski, "Circulus vitiosus," in *Nietzsche aujourd'hui?* vol. 1: *Intensités,* pp. 91–103; here p. 94.

195. A basic problem for the communist tradition with regard to both anar-

chism — of the Left — and libertarianism — of the Right — is that both movements, which have many important criticisms of liberal democracy, attempt to "smash the State" immediately or prematurely, without the prerequisite social, political, cultural, and economic transformation, and so it is that they can be relatively easily contained by capitalism and/or totalitarian oppression.

196. Klossowski, *Nietzsche et le cercle vicieux* [1969], rev. and corrected ed. (Paris: Mercure de France, 1975), p. 47.

197. Klossowski, "Sur quelques thèmes fondamentaux de la 'Gaya Scienza' de Nietzsche" [1956], in *Un si funeste désir,* pp. 7–36; here p. 35.

198. See Klossowski, *Nietzsche et le cercle vicieux,* pp. 37–88.

199. Ibid., p. 81.

200. See, for example, Klossowski, *Nietzsche et le cercle vicieux,* esp. pp. 363–364 — his conclusion.

201. Ibid., pp. 177–249.

202. Ibid., pp. 179–193.

203. Ibid., p. 58.

204. See Nietzsche, *Zur Genealogie der Moral; KGW* 6/2:329–331 [part 2, aphorism 12]. The significance of placing key arguments in the exact centers of books — as opposed to the more obvious beginning or ending — was a major interpretive obsession and rhetorical practice of Leo Strauss. See John Finnis, "Aristotle, Aquinas, and Moral Absolutes," *Catholica* 12 (1990), 7–15. On this and on the significance of the central position of aphorism 12 in *On the Genealogy of Morals,* see Levine, *Nietzsche and the Modern Crisis of the Humanities,* pp. 162–163, 261 n. 8, and 263 n. 61.

205. Frank, *What Is Neostructuralism?* p. 181.

206. Lyotard, *The Inhuman: Reflections on Time* [1988], trans. Geoffrey Bennington and Rachel Bowlby (Stanford: Stanford University Press, 1991), pp. 28–29; emphases added.

207. See Althusser, "The Transformation of Philosophy," in *Philosophy and the Spontaneous Philosophy of the Scientists,* pp. 250–251. Althusser has in mind his own former student Foucault but especially the latter's students, the so-called "New Philosophers."

208. Cantor, "Leo Strauss and Contemporary Hermeneutics," in *Leo Strauss's Thought: Toward a Critical Engagement,* pp. 272–273. But Cantor distinctly fails to apply this principle to his own reading of Nietzsche; indeed, he whitewashes precisely aphorism 12 in *On the Genealogy of Morals.* See Cantor, "Friedrich Nietzsche: The Use and Abuse of Metaphor," in *Metaphor: Problems and Perspectives* (Brighton, Sussex: The Harvester Press; Atlantic Highlands, N.J.: Humanities Press, 1982), pp. 71–889; here esp. pp. 76–78.

209. William Congreve, *The Double Dealer* [1693], act V, scene 1.

210. Emily Dickinson, "Tell all the Truth . . ." [c. 1868, first published 1945], in *Final Harvest: Emily Dickinson's Poems,* ed. Thomas H. Johnson (Boston and Toronto: Little, Brown and Company, 1961), pp. 248–249; here p. 248.

211. See Žižek, *The Sublime Object of Ideology,* p. 197; although Žižek's gloss on the joke here is surprisingly ad hominem: "telling the truth represented a breach of the implicit code of deception which ruled their [the two interlocutors'] relationship: when one of them was going to Cracow, he was supposed to tell the lie that his destination was Lemberg, and vice versa."

212. See, notably, Alexander Tille, *Von Darwin bis Nietzsche: Ein Buch Entwicklungsethik* (Leipzig: C. G. Naumann, 1895), p. 235.

213. See, for example, Eagleton, *The Ideology of the Aesthetic,* ch. 9: "True Illusions: Friedrich Nietzsche."

214. Eagleton, *Walter Benjamin or Towards a Revolutionary Criticism* (London: Verso, 1981), p. 66; see also pp. 108 and 101. As he acknowledges, Eagleton's argument here is heavily influenced by Helmut Pfotenhauer, "Benjamin und Nietzsche," in *Walter Benjamin im Kontext,* ed. Burkhardt Lindner (Frankfurt am Main: Suhrkamp Verlag, 1978), pp. 100–126.

215. Andrew Benjamin, *Art, Mimesis and the Avant-Garde: Aspects of a Philosophy of Difference* (London and New York: Routledge, 1991), p. 29.

216. See Nietzsche, *Zur Genealogie der Moral; KGW* 6/2:420–423 [part 3, aphorism 25].

217. Sedgwick, *Epistemology of the Closet,* p. 178.

218. Hart Crane, "The Case Against Nietzsche," *The Pagan* 2/3 (April/May 1918), 34–35; here 35.

219. Rosen, "Nietzsche's Revolution," in *The Ancients and the Moderns,* p. 199.

220. Rolf Busch, *Imperialistische und faschistische Kleist-Rezeption 1890–1945: Eine Untersuchung* (Frankfurt am Main: Akademische Verlagsanstalt, 1974), p. 10; emphasis added.

221. De Man, "The Literature of Nihilism" [1966], in *Critical Writings, 1953–1978,* ed. Lindsay Waters (Minneapolis: University of Minnesota Press, 1989), pp. 161–170; here p. 163; emphasis added.

222. See Michael Sprinker, *Imaginary Relations: Aesthetics and Ideology in the Theory of Historical Materialism* (London and New York: Verso, 1987), esp. pp. 237–266; and Jameson, *Postmodernism, or, The Cultural Logic of Late Capitalism,* esp. pp. 219–259. See further Derrida, *Mémoires: For Paul de Man* (New York: Columbia University Press, 1986). Christopher Norris has noted similarities in the structure of Derrida's apologias for de Man in *Mémoires* and for Heidegger in *De l'ésprit: Heidegger et la question* (Paris: Galilée, 1987) — though Norris's own agenda is far more uncritically apologetic. Cf. Norris, *Paul de Man: Deconstruction and the Critique of Aesthetic Ideology* (New York and London: Routledge, 1988), pp. 193–198.

223. Reproduced in *Mark Tansey: Visions and Revisions,* p. 120.

224. See Sir Arthur Conan Doyle, "The Adventure of the Final Problem" [1893], in *The Illustrated Sherlock Holmes,* illustrated by Sidney Paget, with additional illustrations by George Hutchinson and Frank H. Townsend (New York: Clarkson N. Potter, Inc., 1984), pp. 314–327; here p. 314.

225. On Nietzsche's influence on Conan Doyle, see again the impressionistic and speculative but interesting account in Rosenberg, *Naked Is the Best Disguise: The Death & Resurrection of Sherlock Holmes,* esp. pp. 38, 42, 60, and 64–65.

226. Conan Doyle, "The Adventure of the Final Problem," pp. 316–317.

227. Nietzsche, "NF Sommer-Herbst 1884"; *KGW* 7/2:265. "Carcass, you're trembling? You'd tremble a lot more if you knew where I'm taking you" is a phrase attributed to the dominant field commander of the seventeenth century, Henri de la Tour d'Auvergne, Vicomte de Turenne (1611–1675), later buried in the Invalides by Napoleonic decree. Turenne's bon mot was a favorite of Nietzsche's. He used it as the epigraph of the new fifth book, "We Fearless Ones," of *The Gay Science* (1882) when the latter was reissued in 1887, after having also considered it as the epigraph for *Beyond Good and Evil* (1886). See Nietzsche, "NF, Herbst 1885–Herbst 1886"; *KGW* 8/1:84.

228. Edgar Allan Poe, "The Man of the Crowd" [1840; 1845], in *The Complete Works of Edgar Allan Poe,* ed. James A. Harrison, with textual notes by R. A. Stewart (New York: Crowell, 1902), 4:134–145; here 134.

229. *Naked Lunch* (David Cronenberg, Canada, 1991).

230. Greil Marcus: *Lipstick Traces: A Secret History of the Twentieth Century* (London: Secker & Warburg, 1989), p. 442. The slogan was first exploited in film culture by *Performance* (Donald Cammell and Nicholas Roeg, UK, 1970), forming its thematic and formal core. Two types of "performer" — rock musical and underworld (the term is British slang for "enforcer" or "hit man") — exchange identities and one is murdered by the other. James Fox as Chas Devlin is paired with The Rolling Stones' Mick Jagger as Turner, who reads the slogan aloud from a book about the original assassins.

231. See Burroughs, *Cities of the Red Night,* pp. xviii and 158–159, and *The Place of Dead Roads* (New York: Henry Holt and Company, 1983), pp. 169–173.

232. *Scanners* (Cronenberg, Canada, 1981).

233. See Debord, *In girum imus nocte et consumimur igni* [1978], in his *Œuvres cinématographiques complètes: 1952–1978* (Paris: Champ Libre, 1978), pp. 224–225. On the historical assassins, see Bernard Lewis's standard account, *The Assassins: A Radical Sect in Islam* [1967], 2d ed. (New York: Oxford University Press, 1987) — the likely source for both Burroughs and Debord.

234. See Burroughs, *Cities of the Red Night,* pp. xi–xv, and *The Place of Dead Roads,* pp. 171 and 173. For Burroughs's reflection on *himself* as Hassan i Sabbah see the final volume of the trilogy, *The Western Lands* (New York: Viking Penguin, 1987), pp. 191–210.

235. See Nietzsche, "NF, Sommer-Herbst 1884"; *KGW* 7/2:153. Nietzsche also puts the alternative phrase in scare quotes: "'Everything is false! Everything is permitted'" ("NF, Frühjahr 1884"; *KGW* 7/2:142). It is common to ignore the quotation marks, however; compare, for example, Rosen, "Nietzsche's Revolution," in *The Ancients and the Moderns,* p. 198.

236. Lacan, "Aggressively in Psychoanalysis" [1948], in *Ecrits: A Selection*, trans. Alan Sheridan (New York and London: W. W. Norton & Company, 1977), pp. 8–29; here p. 22.

237. Nietzsche, "NF, Frühjahr 1888"; *KGW* 8/3:250.

238. Nietzsche, "NF, Herbst 1885–Herbst 1886"; *KGW* 8/1:98.

239. Lucretius, *De rerum nat.,* IV:476; emphasis added.

240. "The truth of history cannot be read in its manifest discourse, because the text of history is not a text in which a voice (the Logos) speaks, but the inaudible and illegible notation of the effects of a structure of structures" (Althusser, "From *Capital* to Marx's Philosophy," in *Reading Capital,* p. 17). To repeat, it is certainly not the book *Nietzsche's Corps/e* that wishes to displace "history" by "Nietzsche," but rather Nietzsche/anism itself, Nietzsche's corps/e itself.

241. Nietzsche, *Die fröhliche Wissenchaft* [2d ed. 1887]; *KGW* 5/2:315 [aphorism 381].

242. Nietzsche, "NF, Herbst–Frühjahr 1886"; *KGW* 8/1:15.

243. See Lacan, *The Four Fundamental Concepts of Psycho-Analysis,* pp. 79–90, and *The Ethics of Psychoanalysis, 1959–1960,* trans. Dennis Porter (New York: W. W. Norton, 1992), p. 152.

244. Žižek, *The Metastases of Enjoyment,* p. 92.

245. The following model of "textuality" and "legibility" is derived from the visual theory developed by Jean-Louis Schefer, *Scénographie d'un tableau* (Paris: Éditions du Seuil, 1969).

246. Althusser, "From *Capital* to Marx's Philosophy," in *Reading Capital,* p. 21.

247. Nietzsche, "NF, November 1887–März 1888"; *KGW* 8/2:433.

248. Nietzsche, "NF, Frühjahr 1884"; *KGW* 7/2:71; emphasis added.

249. Ibid., 7/2:70.

250. Nietzsche, "NF, November 1882–Februar 1883"; *KGW* 7/1:169.

251. Ibid., 7/1:187.

252. For a discussion of Nietzsche's relationship to Wagner and Schopenhauer, see Liébert, *Nietzsche et la musique,* pp. 185–211, ch. 9: "'*Cave Musicam!*'" In Kofman's terminology, Schopenhauer and Wagner were two crucial "metaphors" for Nietzsche, in the complex sense of allowing him to "transport" himself backward and forward in time so as to become, in effect, himself always as if for the first time. See Kofman, *Explosion II,* pp. 131 and 158–174.

253. Nietzsche, "NF, Herbst 1883"; *KGW* 7/1:523.

254. For how euthanasia was to be incorporated, see, for example, his aphorism "Heilige Grausamkeit" (holy brutality) in *The Gay Science,* in which the killing of deformed infants is implied. See *Die fröhliche Wissenschaft* [1st ed. 1882]; *KGW* 5/2:106 [aphorism 73]. More controversially, this recommendation is expanded in *On the Genealogy of Morals* to include "decadents." See *Zur Genealogie der Moral; KGW* 6/2:383–385 [part 3, aphorism 13]. *Thus Spoke Zarathustra* is peppered with more or less implicit allusions to involuntary euthanasia and voluntary death.

255. Nietzsche, "NF, Herbst 1883"; *KGW* 7/1:545.

256. Nietzsche, "NF, November 1882–Februar 1883"; *KGW* 7/1:214. This principle was also incorporated into *Thus Spoke Zarathustra*.

257. See, for example, Schopenhauer, *On the Basis of Morality* [1841], trans. E. F. J. Payne (Indianapolis, New York, Kansas City: Bobbs-Merrill Company, Inc., 1965), p. 96.

258. Nietzsche, "NF, Frühjahr 1884"; *KGW* 7/2:133.

259. Ibid., 7/2:85.

260. See Albert Camus, *The Fall* [1956], trans. Justin O'Brien (New York: Vintage Books, 1963).

261. Arthur Kroker, *The Possessed Individual: Technology and the French Postmodern* (New York: St. Martin's Press, 1992), p. 8. Actually, this notion is itself a bit "romantic." A little Facel-Vega coupe split completely in two against a plane tree near Villeblevin on January 4, 1960 around 2:15 P.M. The driver, Michel Gallimard, along with two unnamed women had been blown out of the car on impact. Wedged between the back seats of the wreckage was Camus's corpse. But accounts of the remaining contents of the car vary, including about the books.

262. Toni Morrison, *Song of Solomon* (New York: Alfred A. Knopf, 1977), p. 155.

263. In Camus's major philosophical analysis of Nietzsche—the "Nietzsche and Nihilism" section of *L'homme révolté* (the rebel, 1951)—he does recognize that Nietzsche was a "strategic" thinker—positive as diagnostician, dangerous for his prescriptions—yet fails to ask how this strategy might have been worked out at the level of Nietzsche's *language*. This failure helps explain the basic contradictions in Camus's analysis of Nietzsche here: for example, on the one hand Camus says Nietzsche wrote only for the future, "never . . . except in terms of an apocalypse to come"; on the other "the fundamental difference" between Nietzsche and Marx is "that Nietzsche, in awaiting the superman, proposed to assent to what exists and Marx to what is to come." Camus then concludes his analysis by situating his "rebel" between and beyond anarchism, Nietzscheanism, and Marxist-Leninism. "Placed in the crucible of Nietzschean philosophy, rebellion, in the intoxication of freedom, ends in biological or historical Caesarism. The absolute negative had driven [Max] Stirner to deify crime simultaneously with the individual. But the absolute affirmation leads to universalizing murder and mankind simultaneously. Marxism-Leninism has really accepted the burden of Nietzsche's freewill by means of ignoring several Nietzschean virtues. The great rebel thus creates with his own hands, and for his own imprisonment, the implacable reign of necessity. Once he has escaped from God's prison, his first care was to construct the prison of history and of reason, thus putting the finishing touch to the camouflage and consecration of the nihilism whose conquest he claimed" (Camus, *The Rebel: An Essay on Man in Revolt* [1951], with a foreword by Sir Herbert Read, trans. Anthony Bower [New York: Vintage Books, 1956], pp. 65–80; here pp. 65–66 and 79–80). Thus, in contemporary terms, Camus's position reveals itself, ironically, as close to current German neoconserva-

tive and neoliberal interpretations of Nietzsche and nihilism: for example, Nolte, Bohrer et al.

264. Camus, *The Fall*, p. 28.

265. Rosen, "Nietzsche's Revolution," in *The Ancients and the Moderns*, pp. 190–192.

266. See Nietzsche, "Der griechische Staat" [1872]; *KGW* 3/2:258–271; here 261, 270, and 271.

267. See Rorty, *Contingency, Irony, and Solidarity;* and John Rawls, *Political Liberalism* (New York: Columbia University Press, 1993).

268. Wilhelm von Humboldt, *Gesammelte Schriften,* ed. Royal Prussian Academy of Sciences (Berlin: B. Behr, 1903–1936), 1:271.

269. See M. I. Finley, *Ancient Slavery and Modern Ideology* [1979] (Harmondsworth: Penguin, 1983), p. 57. Further compare and contrast the positions taken on Greek slavery and high culture by the Göttingen historian Arnold Heeren and by Frederick Engels, as cited by Finley on p. 12. For analysis of classist, racist, and politically conservative aspects of Humboldtian "Hellenomania," see Martin Bernal, *Black Athena: The Afroasiatic Roots of Classical Civilization,* vol. 1: *The Fabrication of Ancient Greece 1785–1985* (New Brunswick: Rutgers University Press, 1987), esp. pp. 281–316.

270. Josiah Ober, *Mass and Elite in Democratic Athens: Rhetoric, Ideology, and the Power of the People* (Princeton: Princeton University Press, 1989), p. 27.

271. See Ober, *Mass and Elite in Democratic Athens,* pp. 73–85, 187–199, and 297–299.

272. Ibid., p. 293.

273. Schopenhauer, *On the Basis of Morality,* p. 83.

274. Nietzsche, "Darstellung der antiken Rhetorik"/"Description of Ancient Rhetoric" [1872–1873], in *Friedrich Nietzsche on Rhetoric and Language* [dual-language ed. on facing pages], ed. and trans. with a critical introduction by Sander L. Gilman, Carole Blair, David J. Parent (New York and Oxford: Oxford University Press, 1989), pp. 2–206; here pp. 2 and 3.

275. See Nietzsche, "NF, Anfang 1871"; *KGW* 3/3:347–363; here esp. 363. If a recent anthology on the topic "Nietzsche and women" reaches any consensus, and whatever other interest the collected essays may have, it is that one need not be concerned with Nietzsche's unpublished work and that the entire topic can remain of thematic interest only; see *Nietzsche, Feminism and Political Theory.*

276. Nietzsche, "NF, Sommer–Herbst 1882"; *KGW* 7/1:105; emphasis added.

277. See Nietzsche Archive Manuscript M II 1 3 [18], and "NF, Herbst 1880"; *KGW* 5/1:537.

278. Nietzsche, "NF, Juli–August 1882"; *KGW* 7/1:28.

279. Aristotle, *Generation of Animals,* trans. A. L. Peck (Cambridge: Harvard University Press/Loeb Classical Library, 1943), 1:103, 109, and 113. See further Simone de Beauvoir, *The Second Sex* [1949], trans. H. M. Parshley (New York:

Bantam Books, 1961), esp. pp. 1–33: "The Data of Biology"; and *Not in God's Image: Women in History from the Greeks to the Victorians,* ed. Julia O'Faolain and Lauro Martines (New York: Harper & Row, Publishers, 1973), esp. pp. 117–126: "Biological and Medical Views."

280. Marie Hecht, "Friedrich Nietzsches Einfluß auf die Frauen," *Die Frau* 6:8 (1888–1889), 486–491; here 491; emphasis added.

281. Althusser, "Freud and Lacan," in *Lenin and Philosophy,* p. 200. Althusser's controversial application of the notion of epistemological break to Marx and Marxism was first developed in "'On the Young Marx'" (1960), in *For Marx;* it was subsequently criticized and modified by Althusser himself in his "Reply to John Lewis" (1972–1973) and "Elements of Self-Criticism" (1974), both in *Essays in Self-Criticism.*

282. Nietzsche, "NF, Frühjahr–Herbst 1881"; *KGW* 5/2:425; see further 381 and 388–390; and "NF, Herbst 1883"; *KGW* 7/1:553 and 635–636.

283. *Selections from the Prison Notebooks of Antonio Gramsci,* p. 332.

284. Gramsci, *Selections from Cultural Writings,* p. 211; see further the section here entitled "Father Bresciani's Progeny," pp. 301–341, including the editors' remarks, pp. 298–301. "Brescianism"—from the Jesuit priest and novelist Antonio Bresciani—was one of Gramsci's code terms for "Jesuitism."

285. Nietzsche, *Werke* (ed. Koegel), 12:325. "Zarathustra glücklich darüber, dass der Kampf der Stände *vorüber* ist, und jetzt endlich Zeit ist für seine Rangordnung der Individuen. Hass auf das demokratische Nivellirungs-System ist nur im *Vordergrund:* eigentlich ist er sehr froh, dass *dies so weit ist.* Nun kann er seine Aufgabe lösen. — "

286. On the inevitability of "socialism" for Nietzsche and related matters, see "NF, Ende 1880"; *KGW* 5/1:689; "NF, Frühjahr 1880 bis Frühjahr 1881"; *KGW* 5/1:753 and 764; "NF, Frühjahr–Herbst 1881"; *KGW* 5/2:343; "NF, Herbst 1881"; *KGW* 5/2:489.

287. For the classic account of the alleged ignorance of the economy on the part of German intellectuals—a thesis that ought not be applied to Nietzsche—see Fritz Ringer, *The Decline of the German Mandarins: The German Academic Community, 1890–1933* (Cambridge: Harvard University Press, 1969).

288. See Richard Wagner, "Die Revolution" [the revolution, 1849] and "Künstlertum der Zukunft: Zum Prinzip des Kommunismus" [artistry of the future: on the principle of communism, 1849], both in *Ausgewählte Schriften,* ed. Dietrich Mack, with an introduction by Ernst Bloch (Frankfurt am Main: Insel Verlag, 1974), pp. 114–122 and 123–137, respectively.

289. See Fiori, *Antonio Gramsci,* p. 63.

290. See Henry Charles Carey, *Lehrbuch der Volkswirthschaft und Sozialwissenschaft* [*Principles of Political Economy,* 1837], authorized German ed., trans. Karl Adler, 2d, rev. ed. (Vienna: Braumüller, 1870); and Nietzsche's letter to his editor Ernst Schmeitzner, June 8, 1879; *KGB* 2/5:417–418.

291. See Nietzsche to Heinrich Köselitz [Peter Gast], July 8, 1881; *KGB* 3/1:99–100.

292. See Nietzsche to Köselitz, May 20, 1887; *KGB* 3/5:78–80.

293. See Nietzsche, "NF, Juli 1879"; *KGW* 4/3:445.

294. Compare the published remarks in *Menschliches, Allzumenschliches II: Der Wanderer und sein Schatten* [Human, All-Too-Human, part 2: The Wanderer and His Shadow, 1880]; *KGW* 4/3:193–195 [aphorism 22] to the draft cited in the editors' notes, *KSA* 14:186, where the indebtedness to Carey is divulged.

295. See Marx, *Capital,* 1:533, 730, and 749, and esp. *Grundrisse: Foundations of the Critique of Political Economy* [1857–1858, first published 1939], trans. with a foreword by Martin Nicolaus (New York: Vintage Books, 1973), p. 886. On the importance of Marx's critique of the "harmonizers" Bastiat and Carey for the development of his own thought, see the incisive discussion by Negri, *Marx Beyond Marx,* pp. 53–55.

296. See Charles Baudelaire, *Œuvres posthumes et correspondances inédites, précédées d'une étude biographique,* ed. Eugène Crépit (Paris: Maison Quantin, 1887); and, for Nietzsche's extensive, complex gloss on this text when he discovered it in early 1888, see "NF, November 1887–März 1888"; esp. manuscript pages 11 [160]–11 [234]; *KGW* 8/2:317–334. For a preliminary description of Nietzsche's reading of Baudelaire's *Œuvres posthumes* see Karl Pestalozzi, "Nietzsches Baudelaire-Rezeption," *Nietzsche-Studien* 7 (1978), 158–178; esp. 166–171.

297. Unfortunately, the most systematic work to date on the nexus in intellectual history and literature between money, language, and thought deals with Nietzsche only in passing, and with Baudelaire not at all. See Mark Shell, *Money, Language, and Thought: Literary and Philosophic Economies from the Medieval to the Modern Era* [1982] (Baltimore and London: The Johns Hopkins University Press, 1993), esp. pp. 175–176.

298. See Christine Buci-Glucksmann, *La raison baroque, de Baudelaire à Benjamin* (Paris: Éditions Galilée, 1984), esp. part 2: "L'utopie du feminin."

299. See Walter Benjamin, *Das Passagen-Werk,* 1:301–489 [section J: "Baudelaire"] and 612–642 [section O: "Prostitution, Spiel"]; and Althusser to Fernanda Navarro, October 27, 1984; in *Sur la philosophie,* p. 117.

300. See James Jay Slawney, "The Phantom of Reason: Oneirocriticism from Baudelaire to Benjamin" (Diss., Cornell University, 1991), esp. 24–38.

301. See Gautier's introduction to Charles Baudelaire, *Les fleurs du mal, précédées d'une notice par Théophile Gautier, nouvelle édition* (Paris: Calmann Lévy, 1882), pp. 1–75; esp. pp. 48–50. Gautier (1811–1872) was himself an important poetic craftsman and precursor of the Parnassian school, and Baudelaire dedicated the first edition of *Les fleurs du mal* to him. His presentation of Baudelaire's life and works was positive albeit apologetic and generally would have reinforced Nietzsche's initial impression of both writers, alongside Poe—mentioned by Gautier—as major modern *décadents.* This was the copy of Baudelaire's magnum opus read by Nietz-

sche in Nizza, and is still in his library in Weimar. Nietzsche's command of French was insufficient to follow the complexities of Baudelaire's poetry beyond a certain thematic point — marked with red crayon in a few places, especially concluding stanzas — but he read Gautier with care.

302. Nietzsche, "NF, November 1887–März 1888"; *KGW* 8/2:325; ellipsis in original.

303. Compare, for example, the paradigmatic disagreements about Nietzsche and Marxism between Leo Strauss and Alexandre Kojève, as expressed in their private correspondence and in Strauss's analysis of Xenophone's *Hiero*. See Strauss, *On Tyranny*, rev. and expanded ed., including the Strauss-Kojève correspondence, ed. Victor Gourevitch and Michael S. Roth (New York: The Free Press, 1991), pp. 207–212 and 238–239.

304. Nietzsche, "NF, November 1887–März 1888"; *KGW* 8/2:333–334.

305. Most notably by Staten, *Nietzsche's Voice*, pp. 8–39 and 77–85. On "slave morality" as the irreducible base of Nietzsche's "social philosophy," see Karl Brose, *Sklavenmoral: Nietzsches Sozialphilosophie* (Bonn: Bouvier Verlag, 1990).

306. Staten, *Nietzsche's Voice*, p. 85.

307. Nietzsche, "NF, Frühjahr 1884"; *KGW* 7/2:76.

308. Nietzsche, "NF, Herbst 1887"; *KGW* 8/2:14.

309. Spinoza, *The Ethics*, p. 172 [part 3, prop. 59, note], translation modified, and *A Theologico-Political Treatise*, p. 203 [ch. 16]. According to Spinoza, people who "are governed by reason — that is, who seek what is useful to them in accordance with reason — desire for themselves nothing, which they do not also desire for the rest of mankind, and consequently, are just, faithful, and honorable in their conduct" (*The Ethics*, p. 202 [part 4, prop. 18, note]).

310. Marx, *Critique of the Gotha Program* [early May, 1875], in *The Marx-Engels Reader*, 2d ed., ed. Robert C. Tucker (New York: W. W. Norton & Company, Inc., 1978), pp. 525–541; here pp. 529–531.

311. See Nietzsche's letters for May, 1875; *KGB* 2/5:44–60.

312. Nietzsche, "NF, Herbst 1883"; *KGW* 7/1:533.

313. Lampert, *Nietzsche and Modern Times*, p. 293. The author bases this assertion, repeated several times, on a particularly limited selection and interpretation of Nietzsche's remarks about Jesuitism in his published and, to a lesser extent, unpublished writings.

314. Nietzsche, "NF, Herbst 1883"; *KGW* 7/1:541.

315. Nietzsche, "NF, Herbst 1885–Herbst 1886"; *KGW* 8/1:116–117; emphasis added. "Das Kunstwerk, wo es *ohne* Künstler erscheint z.B. als Leib, als Organization (preußisches Offiziercorps, Jesuitenorden). Inwiefern der Künstler eine Vorstufe ist. Was bedeutet das 'subject' —— ?"

316. Nietzsche, "NF, Frühjahr 1884"; *KGW* 7/2:81.

317. Nietzsche, "NF, Sommer-Herbst"; *KGW* 7/2:295. As always, the long dashes in the *KGW* and *KGB* indicate that the text is illegible to the editors.

318. Nietzsche, "NF, Sommer-Herbst"; *KGW* 7/2:239.

319. See Stöcker, "Zur Reform der sexuellen Ethik," editorial statement of the inaugural issue of *Mutterschutz: Zeitschrift zur Reform der sexuellen Ethik* 1:1 (1905). See further Aschheim, *The Nietzsche Legacy in Germany*, p. 92.

320. On Tille, see Alfred Kelly, *The Descent of Darwin: The Popularization of Darwinism in Germany, 1860–1914* (Chapel Hill: University of North Carolina Press, 1981), pp. 10–12; Hinton Thomas, *Nietzsche in German Politics and Society*, pp. 113–114; and Aschheim, *The Nietzsche Legacy in Germany*, pp. 89 n. 15 and 123–125. Among the other hats worn by Tille at one time or another were those of folklorist (the Faust legend), scholar of Icelandic sagas, historian of the German fascination with Christmas, and editor of the English edition of Nietzsche's works (1896). Tille also taught and lectured in Scotland and Italy, toting his Nietzschean baggage with him.

321. See Arno J. Mayer, *The Persistence of the Old Regime: Europe to the Great War* (New York: Pantheon, 1981).

322. The volume *Von Darwin bis Nietzsche* is peppered with Nietzsche's ideas, but see especially the last chapter, "Das neue Ideal," pp. 206–241. Tille's publisher, C. G. Naumann, had been one of Nietzsche's own presses. Naumann also brought out the work of Eugen Dühring—the nemesis not only of Nietzsche but of Marx and Engels.

323. See Tille, *Von Darwin bis Nietzsche*, esp. pp. 237–240. Aschheim is imprecise, however, to characterize Tille's racism as "rabid" (*The Nietzsche Legacy in Germany*, p. 123). In the racist climate of his time, Tille's enthusiasm for nationalism was comparatively temperate; his book ends with the claim that true nationalisms are in the service of humanity at large—a point he thinks was missed by Nietzsche himself. Aschheim is right, however, to suggest that Tille complicates the thesis that Nietzsche became a figure of "a new and radical right different from the traditionally conservative right" (p. 118) only after World War I, ostensibly having been largely hostile to Nietzsche originally.

324. Schopenhauer, *The World as Will and Representation*, 1:283–284; *Sämtliche Werke*, 2:334.

325. Alphonso Lingis, "The Will to Power," in *The New Nietzsche: Contemporary Styles of Interpretation*, ed. and introduced by David B. Allison (New York: Delta, 1977), pp. 37–63; here p. 60.

326. Shoshana Felman and Dori Laub, *Testimony: Crises of Witnessing in Literature, Psychoanalysis, and History* (New York and London: Routledge, 1992), p. 69. See further LaCapra, *Representing the Holocaust: History, Theory, Trauma* (Ithaca and London: Cornell University Press, 1991).

327. Spinoza, *The Ethics*, p. 264 [part 5, prop. 33, note].

328. Felman and Laub, *Testimony*, p. 114.

329. Freud, *Moses and Monotheism* [1937–1939], trans. Katherine Jones (New York: Vintage Books, 1967), p. 84; see further pp. 90–101.

330. Freud, *Beyond the Pleasure Principle* [1920], trans. James Strachey, introduction and notes by Gregory Zilboorg (New York: W. W. Norton & Co., 1961), p. 23.

331. On various forms and causes of trauma, including modern warfare, see Freud, *Beyond the Pleasure Principle*, pp. 6–8 and 23–29; on birth trauma and Macduff specifically, see his *Introductory Lectures on Psychoanalysis* [1917], trans. and ed. James Strachey (New York: W. W. Norton & Co., 1966), pp. 396–397 and 407. See further Shakespeare, *Macbeth*, act V, scene viii.

332. See Hollier, *Against Architecture*, pp. 138–170: "The Caesarean."

333. See again Burroughs, *Cities of the Red Night*, p. 157.

334. Nietzsche, "NF, Sommer-Herbst 1884"; *KGW* 7/2:295.

335. Franz Kafka, "Reflections on Sin, Suffering, Hope, and the True Way" [title given by Max Brod, 1920], in *Dearest Father*, p. 44 [nr. 87]. *Das erzählerische Werk*, vol. 1: *Erzählungen, Aphorismen, Brief an den Vater*, ed. Klaus Hermsdorf (Berlin, GDR: Rütten & Loening, 1983), p. 382. "Ein Glaube wie ein Fallbeil, so schwer, so leicht."

336. Ginzburg, "The High and the Low: The Theme of Forbidden Knowledge in the Sixteenth and Seventeenth Centuries" [1976], in *Clues, Myths, and the Historical Method*, pp. 60–76; here p. 69.

337. See again Maravall, *Culture of the Baroque: Analysis of a Historical Structure*, and Barner, *Barockrhetorik: Untersuchungen zu ihren geschichtlichen Grundlagen*.

338. See Nietzsche, *Also sprach Zarathustra*; *KGW* 6/1:266–273 [part 3, "The Convalescent," 1 and 2].

339. Nietzsche, "NF, Herbst 1883"; *KGW* 7/1:552.

340. Benjamin, *Das Passagen-Werk*, 1:175 [section D: "Die Langeweile, ewige Wiederkehr"]. Benjamin's quip about the pillow is related to Adorno's analysis in 1933 of the imbrication in Kierkegaard of existential pathos and bourgeois worldview; and Benjamin followed Karl Löwith's 1935 reading of Eternal Recurrence of the Same as a paradoxical "anti-Christian repetition of antiquity at the apex of modernity." But the link he saw between Zarathustra's idea of Eternal Recurrence of the Same and Caesarist imperialism was closer to Lukács's view of Nietzsche, also in the mid-1930s. Anticipations or parallels aside, Benjamin's attempt in his unfinished magnum opus to articulate Eternal Recurrence of the Same with such psychological and social phenomena as boredom and dreams, city and nature, rationalism and primitivism, enlightenment and myth, history and historicity, dandy and worker, leisure and labor, and so on is a major intellectual achievement, even in this very fragmentary and compressed form. In 1929–1930, Heidegger had also analyzed modernist boredom as a precondition for fascism and Nazism — which he, however, was then already warmly embracing. See the transcript of his course *Die Grundbegriffe der Metaphysik: Welt-Endlichkeit-Einsamkeit* [Freiburg winter semester 1929–1930], ed. Friedrich-Wilhelm von Hermann, *Gesamtausgabe* (Frankfurt am Main: Vittorio Klostermann, 1983), 2/29–30:111–116. A more depoliticized ver-

sion of the basic argument had appeared already in his *Being and Time* (1927). Thus does 1929–1930 mark the moment of Heidegger's irrevocable *philosophical* turn to national socialism—inspired, one might say, by the politics of boredom. His *political* turn had come even earlier.

341. Benjamin did not read the notebook itself but found the passage cited in Karl Löwith, *Nietzsches Philosophie der Ewigen Wiederkehr des Gleichen* (Berlin: Die Runde, 1935), p. 73; in the 2d ed. (Stuttgart: W. Kohlhammer, 1956), p. 77.

342. Benjamin, *Das Passagen-Werk*, 1:175 [section D: "Die Langeweile, ewige Wiederkehr"]; emphasis added.

343. Heidegger, *Nietzsche*, 1:28. Also see the original, slightly different version in *Nietzsche: Der Wille zur Macht als Kunst; Gesamtausgabe*, 2/43:22–23.

344. It is quite common in German to refer to Nietzsche's thought as *"Ewige Wiederkehr,"* but this was not his own preferred term.

345. Kafka, "Reflections on Sin, Suffering, Hope, and the True Way," in *Dearest Father*, p. 35 [nr. 5]. *Das erzählerische Werk*, 1:374. "Von einem gewissen Punkt an gibt es keine Rückkehr mehr. Dieser Punkt ist zu erreichen."

346. "This is no time for phony rhetoric / This is no time for political speech / This is a time for action / because the future's within reach / This is the time, This is the time, This is the time because There is no time / There is no time, There is no time, There is no time, There is no time" (Lou Reed, "There Is No Time," *New York*, © 1989 Sire/Warner Bros. Records, Inc., 9-25829-4).

347. Klossowski, "Oubli et anamnèse dans l'experiénce vécue de l'éternel retour du même," in *Nietzsche* [Colloque de Royaumont, 1964], pp. 227–235 (followed by a discussion, pp. 236–244). For a translation see *Nietzsche's Return*.

348. For reasons that are less clear—and the likely, additional reason of euphony aside—Nietzsche normally referred to what was to recur not as "the same" (*das Selbe*) but rather as "the equal" or "identical" (*das Gleiche*). Attempts, notably that of Löwith, to sort out this particular distinction are inconclusive. Löwith argued that the doctrine of Eternal Recurrence of the Same—to which he imprecisely refers as *Wiederkehr* rather than *Wiederkunft*—had a personal-existential as well as cosmological-historical aspect. He suggested that the term *das Selbe* refers to the former, *das Gleiche* to the latter; but since the doctrine requires both aspects, the two terms could be collapsed. See Löwith, *Nietzsches Philosophie der Ewigen Wiederkehr des Gleichen*, 2d ed., p. 161.

349. See Deleuze, *Différence et répétition* (Paris: Presses Universitaires de France, 1969), pp. 52–61 and 376–384.

350. See Bernard Pautrat, "Nietzsche médusé," in *Nietzsche aujourd'hui?* vol. 1: *Intensités*, pp. 9–30. For a translation, see *Looking After Nietzsche*.

351. Nietzsche, "NF, Winter 1884"; *KGW* 7/3:74. Also cited and discussed by Pautrat in "Nietzsche médusé." Another of Nietzsche's notes for *Thus Spoke Zarathustra* refers—in scare quotes to indicate esoteric circumspection—to *"'Medusa head.'* (c. 40 pages)" (Nietzsche, "NF, Winter 1884–85"; *KGW* 7/3:76–77). He

also planned a series of "Medusa-Hymns," which apparently were likewise never written. See the editors' notes in Nietzsche, *KSA* 14:711.

352. See Benjamin, *Das Passagen-Werk*, 1:173 [section D: "Die Langeweile, Ewige Wiederkehr"]. Benjamin was citing from the so-called Musarion edition of Nietzsche's works, published in the 1920s; here the editors misleadingly give "part two" instead of "part four"; but Benjamin was not paying really close attention anyway.

353. *Selections from the Prison Notebooks of Antonio Gramsci*, p. 144.

354. See Nietzsche, *Also sprach Zarathustra; KGW* 6/1:391–400 [part 4, "The Nightwanderer's Song"], and the editors' notes in Nietzsche, *KSA* 14:343.

355. See Nietzsche, "NF, Herbst 1884–Anfang 1885"; *KGW* 7/3:54.

356. Nietzsche, "NF, Winter 1884–85"; *KGW* 7/3:74. See further *Die Geburt der Tragödie aus dem Geiste der Musik* [1872]; *KGW* 3/1:26 and 43–44 [sections 2 and 5]; "Die dionysischen Weltanschauung" [the Dionysian worldview, 1870]; *KGW* 3/2:43–69; here 52 and 60; and "Die Geburt des tragischen Gedankens" [the birth of the tragic thought, 1870]; *KGW* 3/2:71–91; here 81 and 88.

357. Foucault, "Theatrum Philosophicum" [1970 review of Deleuze, *Différence et répétition* and *Logique du sens*], in *Language, Counter-Memory, Practice*, pp. 165–196; here p. 195.

358. Lacan, "Le stade du miroir," in *Écrits I*, p. 97; last emphasis added. For Lacan's later position on the cipher, explicitly in connection with the relation of political discourse and the Real, see his *Télévision* (Paris: Éditions du Seuil, 1974), p. 59. Lacan's conceptual orientation here is very Nietzschean, at least in structure though not in liberatory intent.

359. Cixous, "The Laugh of the Medusa" [1975–1976], trans. Keith Cohen and Paula Cohen, in *New French Feminisms: An Anthology*, ed. with introductions by Elaine Marks and Isabelle de Courtivron (New York: Schocken Books, 1981), pp. 245–264; here p. 259.

360. See Pautrat, *Versions du soleil: Figures et système de Nietzsche* (Paris: Éditions du Seuil, 1971).

361. Sun Tzu, *The Art of War*, p. 112.

362. Kristeva, "Practique signifiante et mode de production" [1973–1974], in Kristeva et al., *La traversée des signes* (Paris: Éditions du Seuil, 1975), pp. 11–30; here p. 11.

363. Nietzsche, "NF, November 1882–Februar 1883"; *KGW* 7/1:223. "Der Gedanke ist nur ein Zeichen, wie das Wort nur ein Zeichen für den Gedanken ist."

364. Nietzsche, "NF, November 1882–Februar 1883"; *KGW* 7/1:214.

365. See, for example, Nietzsche, "NF, Sommer-Herbst 1884"; *KGW* 7/2:280–282.

366. Further theological — and potentially heretical — implications of the ancient idea of Eternal Return — which is, however, not identical with Nietzschean Eternal Recurrence of the Same — have been known for a very long time, as Nietzsche was

at least partly aware. He apparently knew, for instance, that the early Helleno-Christian thinker Origen (185–253) had argued in his *De principiis* that if, as Aristotle had asserted, what lacks a beginning is incomprehensible, then our cosmos must have had a beginning; but this raises a new problem, if one follows the account of *Genesis* in the Jewish-Christian Bible. Origen was compelled to ask what God was doing before "He" created our cosmos. How did "He" avoid boredom? Origen's answer was that throughout eternity God is producing a series of other worlds that are not exact replicas of this one but very close. In short, "He" is repeating himself eternally — though always with a slight virtual difference, so as to avoid boredom. But this seems to indicate that God has little choice but to repeat "Himself" thus. In short, "He" is not all-powerful but "Himself" a servant to infinite time, much like the rest of us. See Richard Sorabji, *Time, Creation and the Continuum: Theories in Antiquity and the Early Middle Ages* (Ithaca: Cornell University Press, 1983), pp. 183–190, and Henry Chadwick, *Early Christian Thought and the Classical Tradition* (Oxford and New York: Oxford University Press, 1966), p. 118. On Nietzsche's knowledge of Origen, see Edgar Steiger, "Zarathustra auf der Schulbank und auf den Lehrstuhl," *Das literarische Echo* 17 (1915), 1349–1353. Finally, for the classic account of archaic notions of Eternal Return see Mircea Eliade, *The Myth of Eternal Return, or, Cosmos and History* [1949], trans. Willard R. Trask (Princeton: Princeton University Press, 1954). Compare the slogan of the situationists and of punk rock: "What are the politics of boredom?"

367. Klossowski, "Oubli et anamnèse," in *Nietzsche* [Colloque de Royaumont, 1964], p. 237.

368. Nietzsche, "NF, November 1882–Februar 1883"; *KGW* 7/1:126.

369. Nietzsche, "NF, Herbst 1883"; *KGW* 7/1:538. In light of remarks like this, it might not be *wholly* irresponsible to compare that of the Argentine General Iberico Saint-Jean (December 1976): "We'll begin by killing all the subversives, then their collaborators, their their sympathizers, then the indifferents, and finally the timid" (cited in Virilio, *Popular Defense & Ecological Struggles,* p. 74). Fascists have no monopoly on such behavior, alas, which has been indulged in at one time or another by members of all the world religions, by self-described "democrats," "communists," and so forth. But fascists, almost by definition, have a very special relationship not only to killing but to their own deaths. Often members of fascist military and political organizations not only produce corpses but also themselves are required to be what the Nazi SS termed *Kadavergehorsam:* "cadaver-obedient." This meant obedient to the death to the *Führer,* not merely in every fiber of one's being but also of one's corpse; the initiation oath to this effect was absolute, explicitly superseding any commitment, say, to spouse, progeny, friends, even fellow SS men and officers. A leading journal of the SS (the "black shirts") was titled *Das schwarze Korps* (the black corps), with its death's-head insignia.

370. Nietzsche, "NF, Herbst 1883"; *KGW* 7/1:539. Like all the passages being cited in this book in this regard, this one comes from the period when mental or

physical illness in the strict sense was not an issue, as it might have been, say, in late 1888, when Nietzsche continued to write similar things.

371. On Wagner as prophet of all this, see Heim, *The Metaphysics of Virtual Reality*, pp. 124–127.

372. Adorno, *In Search of Wagner*, p. 100; emphasis added.

373. Greg Ginn [jacket note], Black Flag (Greg Ginn, Kira, Bill Stevenson), *The Process of Weeding Out*, © 1985 SST Records, 087. There are no lyrics in the music on this album. Ginn, in spite of the apparently "progressive" nature of the remarks here, is an unpopular man for many musicians, in part because of his own capitalist-entrepreneurial activities. Actually, according to *Mondo 2000* — a leading magazine of cyberpunk — "the revolution *will* be televised" (Allen Hines, "Video Anarchism in America," *Mondo 2000* 6 (1992), 124–127). As noted by Greg Graffin of the left-wing neopunk rock band Bad Religion, TV is the dominant site of virtually *all* forms of mediation today: "Transfixed on the big blue screen / it's your window to the outside / a melancholy dream / a medium upon which you build reality / this episodic currency / that everybody needs . . ." (Bad Religion [Greg Graffin, Mr. Brett, Greg Hetson, Jay Bentley, Bobby Schayer], "Only Entertainment," *Generator*, © 1992 Epitaph Records, E–86416–4). On the other hand there is too much hype about the power of all media, including TV. While certainly not ignoring TV, the forces that be take a rather different tack: "The United States will never win a war fought daily in the U.S. media or on the floor of Congress" (Neil C. Livingstone, "Fighting Terrorism and 'Dirty Little Wars,' " in *Defense Planning for the 1980s*, ed. William Buckingham Jr. [Washington, D.C.: National Defense University Press, 1984], p. 188; cited in Michael T. Klare and Peter Kornbluh, "The New Interventionism: Low-Intensity Warfare in the 1980s and Beyond," in *Low-Intensity Warfare: Counterinsurgency, Proinsurgency, and Antiterrorism in the Eighties*, ed. Michael T. Klare and Peter Kornbluh [New York: Pantheon Books, 1988], pp. 3–20; here p. 18).

374. Virilio, *Popular Defense & Ecological Struggles*, pp. 71–72.

375. In addition to *Low-Intensity Warfare*, see Edward S. Herman, *The REAL Terror Network: Terrorism in Fact and Propaganda* (Boston: South End Press, 1982); Tom Barry, *Low Intensity Conflict* (Albuquerque: The Resource Center, 1986), with the ensuing series of *Updates on Low Intensity Conflict*, also published by the Resource Center; Nelson Blackstock, *Cointelpro: The FBI's Secret War on Political Freedom*, with an introduction by Noam Chomsky (New York: A Pathfinder Book/ Anchor Foundation, 1988); and Edward S. Herman and Gerry O'Sullivan, *The "Terrorism" Industry: The Experts and Institutions that Shape Our View of Terror* (New York: Pantheon Books, 1989). More recently, the doctrine of low-intensity conflict has been sublated as the major U.S. military strategy by constructive engagement — which includes the violent "surgical removal" of oppositional leaders — but both doctrines can be described as equally "Nietzschean."

376. For some sense of the "Nietzschean" influence on the White House see

Sidney Blumenthal's remarks about former Vice President Dan Quayle in "Dan's Big Plan," *Vanity Fair* (September 1992), 210–216 and 287–290; see further Kevin Sack, "Odd (and Successful) Couple: Vice President and Chief Aide," *The International Herald Tribune* (September 11, 1992), 3.

377. *Taking the Stand: The Testimony of Oliver L. North before the Joint House and Senate Select Committee on Iran and the Contras* (New York: Pocket Books, 1987), p. 12. Cited in Klare and Kornbluh, "The New Interventionism," p. 16.

378. For two useful translations and contextualizations of Nietzsche's famous — but commonly depoliticized — 1873 essay "On Truth and Lie in the Extramoral Sense," see *Philosophy and Truth: Selections from Nietzsche's Notebooks of the Early 1870s* (ed. Breazeale); and *Friedrich Nietzsche on Rhetoric and Language*. See further Heide Schlüpmann, *Friedrich Nietzsches ästhetische Opposition: Der Zusammenhang von Sprache, Natur und Kultur in seinen Schriften 1869–1876* (Stuttgart: J. B. Metzler, 1977).

379. See again Althusser, *L'avenir dure longtemps*, in *L'avenir dure longtemps* [*suivi de*] *Les faits*, p. 74.

380. Lionel S. Johns, as cited in Virilio, *The Lost Dimension*, p. 29.

381. For a philologically and conceptually precise outline and analysis of the importance of "mood" in Nietzsche, including passing mention of its combative aspect, see Corngold, "Nietzsche's Moods," *Studies in Romanticism* 29 (Spring 1990), 67–90.

382. See Nietzsche, *Jenseits von Gut und Böse; KGW* 6/2:43 ["The Free Spirit," aphorism 28]; "NF, Herbst 1880"; *KGW* 5/1:555; "NF, Frühjahr-Herbst 1881"; *KGW* 5/2:392, 395, and esp. 401–406; "NF, November 1882–Februar 1883"; *KGW* 7/1:185; "NF, April–Juni 1885"; *KGW* 7/3:174; and "NF, Herbst 1887"; *KGW* 8/1:185.

383. See Deleuze and Guattari, *A Thousand Plateaus: Capitalism and Schizophrenia* [1980], translation and foreword by Brian Massumi (Minneapolis: University of Minnesota Press, 1987), pp. 351–423; and Deleuze, "Pensée nomade," in *Nietzsche aujourd'hui?* vol. 1: *Intensités*, pp. 159–174. For a translation of the latter text, see *The New Nietzsche*.

384. Deleuze and Guattari, *A Thousand Plateaus*, pp. 376–377.

385. Herman Rapaport, "Vietnam: The Thousand Plateaus," in *The 60s Without Apology*, ed. Sohnya Sayres, Fredric Jameson, et al. (Minneapolis: University of Minnesota Press, 1984; special double issue of *Social Text* 3:3 and 4:1 [Spring–Summer 1984]), pp. 137–147; here p. 147 n. 8. See further *Vietnamese Studies*, vol. 20: *American Failure*, ed. Nguyên Khac Vien (Hanoi: North Vietnamese Government Publications, 1968); and Vo Nguyên Giap, *Écrits* (Hanoi: Éditions en langues étrangères, 1977).

386. Nietzsche, "NF, Frühjahr 1884"; *KGW* 7/2:81.

387. Scarry, *The Body in Pain*, p. 49.

388. Leonard Cohen, "The Future," *The Future*, © 1992 Leonard Cohen Stranger

Music, Inc. (BMI) and Sony Music Entertainment Inc./Columbia Records, CK 53226. This cut is also featured in Oliver Stone's brilliant film of techno-Nietzscheanism, *Natural Born Killers* (1994); *Natural Born Killers: A Soundtrack for an Oliver Stone Film*, © 1994 Warner Bros., Nothing/Interscope 92460-2.

389. Bloch, "Ungleichzeitigkeit und Pflicht zu ihrer Dialektik" [1932], in *Erbschaft dieser Zeit*, pp. 104–126; here p. 115.

390. Bataille, "'The Old Mole' and the Prefix *Sur* in the Words *Surhomme* and *Surrealist*" [c. 1929–1930, published 1968], in *Visions of Excess*, pp. 32–44; here p. 38. *Œuvres complètes*, 2:93–109.

391. See Hans Günther, *Der Herren eigner Geist: Ausgewählte Schriften* [first published as *Der Herren eigner Geist: Die Ideologie des Nationalsozialismus* (Moscow and Leningrad, 1935)] (Berlin and Weimar: Aufbau Verlag, 1981); here p. 290; also see his "Kritische Apologeten," *Internationale Literatur* [Moscow] 3 (1935), 103–105, and "Der Fall Nietzsche," *Unter dem Banner des Marxismus* 11 (1935), 542–556. Günther's analysis of Nietzsche is very important — not only historically but theoretically — and is unjustly neglected today.

392. Nietzsche, "NF, Herbst 1883"; *KGW* 7/1:549.

393. *Maledetti Vi Amerò* (Marco Tullio Giordana, Italy, 1980). For a discussion of the film, see Maurizio Viano, "The Left According to the Ashes of Gramsci," *Social Text* 18 (Winter 1987–1988), 51–60. The "Ashes of Gramsci" in Viano's title refers to Pasolini's great 1954 elegy, "Le ceneri di Gramsci," on the dynamics and contradictions of class betrayal. But "le ceneri di Gramsci" is also the phrase Ricardo uses for cocaine. And since coke, according to Ricardo himself, is right-wing, it serves as the material allegory, as it were, of the incorporating transformation (*trasformismo*) of the Left into the Right.

4 Trasformismo *from Gramsci to Dick, or, The Spectacular Technoculture of Everyday Life*

1. Spengler, "Nietzsche und sein Jahrhundert," p. 123. "Die Wirkung Nietzsches ist verwandelnd, weil die Melodie seines Schauens in ihm selbst nicht zu Ende kam."

2. Pasolini, "The PCI to the Young!! (Notes in Verse for a Prose Poem Followed by an 'Apology')" [1968], *Heretical Empiricism* [1972], ed. Louise K. Barnett, trans. Ben Lawton and Louise K. Barnett (Bloomington and Indianapolis: Indiana University Press, 1988), pp. 150–157; here p. 156.

3. Spinoza, *A Theologico-Political Treatise*, in *A Theologico-Political Treatise and A Political Treatise*, p. 216 [ch. 17].

4. Most notably and thoroughly in his *David Friedrich Strauss as Confessor and Writer* (1873), though attacking the newspaper remained a recurrent theme of his cultural criticism.

5. Benjamin, "Über einige Motive bei Baudelaire" [1939], *Gesammelte Schriften* 1/2:605–653; here 610–611. For a translation, see *Illuminations*.

6. Nietzsche, notebook fragment of 1862, in his *Werke und Briefe: Historisch-kritische Ausgabe,* ed. Karl Schlechta, Hans Joachim Mette et al. (Munich: Beck, 1933–1942), in *Werke,* 2:71. On Nietzsche's later encounter with the typewriter in 1882—he was the first philosopher to use one—though not on the more sinister dimensions of Nietzschean logographics, see Kittler, *Discourse Networks 1800/1900,* pp. 177–205; Kittler also cites this passage from the young Nietzsche.

7. *Selections from the Prison Notebooks of Antonio Gramsci,* p. 345. On the Leninist roots of Gramsci's political and cultural theory, see Hoffman, *The Gramscian Challenge,* esp. pp. 51–75, 145–158, and 175–190.

8. Gramsci, *Selections from Cultural Writings,* p. 195.

9. Cf. Aldo Venturelli, "Eine historische Peripetie von Nietzsches Denken: Lenin als Nietzsche-Leser?" *Nietzsche-Studien* 22 (1993), 320–330.

10. *Selections from the Prison Notebooks of Antonio Gramsci,* p. 369.

11. Marx and Engels, *The German Ideology,* in *Collected Works,* 5:28 and 30.

12. When Gramsci thought of the baneful effects of Nietzsche on leftist intellectuals he specifically had in mind not only certain members of his own party—for example, Amadeo Bordiga as "superman" representing force as opposed to hegemony—but also Mussolini, whose eventful transformation from the Left to Right was figured explicitly in the name of Nietzsche. After Gramsci, many Italian leftists underwent a more or less powerful "Nietzsche phase." Some of them even remained Marxists (unlike, e.g., Vattimo), perhaps most notably Galvano Della Volpe. See John Fraser, *An Introduction to the Thought of Galvano Della Volpe* (London: Lawrence and Wishart, 1977), esp. pp. 13–14, 19, 27, 47–48, 188, and 264–265. But this influence is nothing compared to the strength of the "Nietzschean phase" undergone by German and French leftists, including the young Lukács and virtually the entire Frankfurt School on one side of the Rhine, and on the other virtually all French intellectuals from Gide and Valéry to Malraux and Camus, Bataille and Klossowski, Deleuze and Guattari, Derrida and Foucault, Baudrillard and Virilio. In this context, Lenin, Gramsci, and Althusser are most welcome exceptions to a very powerful leftist and Nietzschean rule.

13. See Gramsci to Tania Schucht, June 6, 1932, in *Letters from Prison,* 2:179–182; here 182. Also see *Selections from the Prison Notebooks of Antonio Gramsci,* p. 128 n. 6.

14. Charles Taylor, "The Politics of Recognition" [1992], in Charles Taylor et al., *Multiculturalism: Examining the Politics of Recognition,* ed. Amy Gutmann (Princeton: Princeton University Press, 1994), pp. 25–74; here p. 62.

15. *Selections from the Prison Notebooks of Antonio Gramsci,* p. 350.

16. Hölderlin, "Patmos" [fragment of a late draft, circa 1804], *Sämtliche Werke* (ed. Beißner), 2/1:177–178. "Es ist der Wurf das eines Sinns, der mit / Der Schaufel fasset den Waizen, / Und wirft schwingend dem Klaren zu ihn über die Tenne. / Ein furchtbar Ding. Staub fällt. / Korn aber kommet ans Ende."

17. See Ludwig Stein, "Friedrich Nietzsches Weltanschauung und ihre Gefahren," *Deutsche Rundschau* 6 and 8 (March and May 1893); as cited in Aschheim, *The Nietzsche Legacy in Germany,* p. 38.

18. Compare Paul Ernst, "Friedrich Nietzsche: Seine historische Stellung, seine Philosophie," *Freie Bühne*, 1:18 and 19 (June 4 and 11, 1890), 489–491 and 516–520, respectively, with his *Friedrich Nietzsche* [1900], 2d ed. (Berlin: Gose und Tezlaff, 1904); also cited in Aschheim, *The Nietzsche Legacy in Germany*, p. 43.

19. Mitchell, *The Reconfigured Eye*, p. 85.

20. Balzac and Dumas surface occasionally in Nietzsche's notebooks and correspondence, though not in this context; but Gramsci is not posing a question of influence only. The direct literary sources of Nietzsche's concept and term "Superman" are obviously overdetermined. One of the earliest and most significant came from an account of Hölderlin's dramatic fragment "Empedocles," which Nietzsche read for the first time in 1861 as a boarding-school teenager, plagiarized for a school essay, used as the basis for his own drama fragment entitled "Empedocles," and later appropriated along with *Hyperion* for *Thus Spoke Zarathustra*.

21. See Gramsci, *Selections from Cultural Writings*, pp. 355–359.

22. For two attempts to bring Gramsci up to technocultural speed see Renate Holub, *Antonio Gramsci: Beyond Marxism and Postmodernism* (London and New York: Routledge, 1992), esp. ch. 7: "Gramsci's Intellectual and the Age of Information Technology"; and Marcia Landy, *Film, Politics, and Gramsci,* introduction by Paul Bové (Minneapolis: University of Minnesota Press, 1994); for a more skeptical approach see David Harris, *From Class Struggle to the Politics of Pleasure: The Effects of Gramscianism on Cultural Studies* (New York and London: Routledge, 1992).

23. Gramsci, *Selections from Cultural Writings,* p. 355. Gramsci developed his model of the circulatory movement from "high" culture to "low" in part from Hegel's theory of incorporation as mediated by the Risorgimento social reformer and literary historian Francesco de Sanctis (1817–1883), for whom philosophical notions manifest themselves as a "sinking" (*calarsi*) into concrete cultural forms. Gramsci's model — which has much to do with problems of political hegemony and leadership by consent rather than coercion — was further overdetermined by his adaptation to politics and political theory of the work of his university teacher Giulio Bartoli (1873–1946). Bartoli was a leading "neo-" or "spatio-linguist" who developed a multifaceted theory of "areal normativity" to describe and predict the ways linguistic innovations "radiate" to subaltern groups from "sources of defusion" in dominant groups and regions. Bartoli's theory further bears directly on Gramsci's grasp of the complex relationship between "intellectuals" and "national popular" culture, as well as between communist parties as "collective individuals" and "the people." See the editors' comments in *Selections from Cultural Writings,* pp. 87–91, 164–167, 196–198, and 343–345.

24. Jorge Luis Borges, "Kafka and His Precursors," trans. James E. Irby, in *Labyrinths: Selected Stories and Other Writings,* ed. Donald A. Yates and James E. Irby, preface by André Maurois, augmented ed. (New York: New Directions, 1964), pp. 199–201; here p. 201.

25. See Michael Dummett, "Can an Effect Precede Its Cause?" [1954] and "Bringing About the Past" [1964], in *Truth and Other Paradoxes* (Cambridge,

Mass.: Harvard University Press, 1978), pp. 319–332 and 333–350, respectively. In *The Sublime Object of Ideology*, Žižek spins off Dummett to note that the symptom qua return of the repressed is "an effect that precedes its cause (its hidden kernel, its meaning), and in working through its symptom we are precisely 'bringing about the past' — we are producing the symbolic reality of past, long-forgotten traumatic events" (pp. 56–57). Unsurprisingly, Dummett's answer to the question "can an Effect Precede Its Cause?" involves definition: "There is an immense temptation, which must be overcome, to look for an a priori reason why an event can be counted as a sufficient condition of a previous event only in cases where the later event can be called 'the means of finding out whether the earlier event had occurred,' i.e. in cases where an ordinary causal account can be given of the connection between them; and to give such a reason by saying that past events are already determined. The difficulty of sustaining this objection lies in the problem of elucidating 'is determined' " (Dummett, "Can an Effect Precede Its Cause?" p. 329).

26. *La jetée* (Chris. Marker, France, 1962). "Tel était le but des expériences — projeter des émissaires, appeler passé et l'avenir au secours du présent."

27. See Gabriel García Márquez, *One Hundred Years of Solitude* [1967], trans. Gregory Rabassa (New York: Harper & Row, 1970).

28. Foucault, "History of Sexuality" ["Les rapports de pouvoir passent à l'intérieure des corps," interview with Lucette Finas, 1977], in *Power/Knowledge*, pp. 183–193; here p. 187.

29. See *Shocker* (Wes Craven, USA, 1989). As often happens in junk culture, the resolution of the film — in this case a mishmash of new age, neo-Catholic mumbo-jumbo — has little to do with its Nietzschean philosophical premise.

30. See Nietzsche, "NF, November 1887–März 1888"; *KGW* 8/2:267–270, 313–317, and 335.

31. Cf. Niethammer (with Dirk van Laak), *Posthistoire*, p. 137.

32. David Singer, "Letter from Europe: Algeria Slides into Civil War," *The Nation* 258:7 (February 21, 1994), 217 and 234–236; here 236.

33. See Frederick Winslow Taylor, *The Principles of Scientific Management* [1911] (New York and London: W. W. Norton & Co., 1967), pp. 41–47.

34. See August H. Th. Pfannkuche, *Was liest der deutsche Arbeiter? Auf Grund einer Enquete beantwortet* (Tübingen: J. C. B. Mohr, 1900), p. 23.

35. See Kurt Eisner, *Psychopathia spiritualis: Friedrich Nietzsche und die Apostel der Zukunft* (Leipzig: Verlag Wilhelm Friedrich, 1892). Eisner, later a main protagonist in the German Soviet Republic of 1918, was himself not free from Nietzschean tendencies.

36. See *Friedrich Nietzsche im Urteil der Arbeiterklasse*, ed. Adolf Levenstein (Munich: Ernst Reinhardt, 1912). The response by socialists to Levenstein's anthology seems to have been generally positive, at least when it was reprinted after the war; see, for example, Max Adler, "Arbeiterbriefe über Nietzsche," *Wissen und Leben* 14 (1921), 430–433.

37. For a relevant application of the notion of "reading formation" (the term is

Tony Bennett's) see Geoff Waite, "The Politics of Reading Formations: The Case of Nietzsche in Imperial Germany, 1870–1919," *New German Critique* 29 (Spring/Summer 1983), 185–209. See further Tony Bennett, *Outside Literature* (London and New York: Routledge, 1990), and *Popular Fiction: Technology, Ideology, Production, Reading* (London and New York: Routledge, 1990).

38. Rainer Stollmann, "Fascist Politics as a Total Work of Art: Tendencies of the Aesthetization of Political Life in National Socialism," *New German Critique* 14 (Spring 1978), 41–60; here 55–56.

39. Balibar, "Fascism, Psychoanalysis, Freudo-Marxism" [1990], in *Masses, Classes, Ideas*, pp. 177–189; here p. 188.

40. Elisabeth Förster-Nietzsche, unpublished text of July 10, 1926, Nietzsche-Archive, Weimar; as cited in H. F. Peters, *Zarathustra's Sister: The Case of Elisabeth and Friedrich Nietzsche* (New York: Crown Publishers, Inc., 1977), p. 213. The Nazis undertook serious research into what soldiers actually read in battle. See Willi Lorch, "Bücher im Schützengraben," *Bücherkunde: Organ des Amtes Schrifttumspflege bei dem Beauftragten des Führers für die Überwachung der gesamten geistigen und weltanschaulichen Schulung und Erziehung der NSDAP* 6:11 (1939), esp. 517–519. Nietzsche's *Thus Spoke Zarathustra* is indeed prominently mentioned, along with Goethe's *Faust* and selected poems, Hölderlin's hymns, the *Nibelungenlied*, Johann Peter Hebel's poetry—a particular favorite of Heidegger's—selections from the Brothers Grimm, poems by Stefan George, Rainer Maria Rilke's *Duino Elegies*, and of course Martin Luther's translation of the Bible. These results were basically confirmed by a more systematic work of applied sociology undertaken at this time by Inge Ehringhaus—with the collaboration of major Germanists such as Herbert Cysarz, Paul Kluckhohn, and Hermann August Korff—and published as *Die Lektüre unserer Frontsoldaten im Weltkrieg* (Berlin: Neue Deutsche Forschungen & Junker und Dünnhaupt, 1941). The Nazis duly reprinted these favorite texts in olive drab editions that were sent to all fronts of World War II.

41. Anonymous worker, cited in *Friedrich Nietzsche im Urteil der Arbeiterklasse*, p. 48.

42. See Heinrich Mann, "Geist und Tat" [1910], in *Essays* (Hamburg: Claassen Verlag; Berlin, GDR: Aufbau-Verlag, 1960), pp. 7–14. The lack of precision in Mann's take on Nietzschean ideology—though more precise, astute, and progressive than that of his better-known brother, Thomas—resurfaced in his later writings on Nietzsche. For a representative example in English see his convoluted introductory essay to *The Living Thoughts of Nietzsche*, presented by Heinrich Mann (Philadelphia: David McKay Company, 1939), pp. 1–40, which ends: *"Requiescat in pace."* The classic Western Marxist critique of left-liberalism of the Heinrich Mann type is in Benjamin, "Der Autor als Produzent" [1934], in *Gesammelte Schriften*, 5:683–701. For a translation see *Reflections*.

43. On the former, see George L. Kline, *Religious and Anti-Religious Thought in Russia* (Chicago and London: The University of Chicago Press, 1968), ch. 4: "The

'God-Builders': Gorky and Lunacharsky"; on the latter, see Aschheim, *The Nietzsche Legacy in Germany*, pp. 247–250.

44. Two anonymous workers, cited in *Friedrich Nietzsche im Urteil der Arbeiterklasse*, pp. 87 and 12.

45. Nietzsche to Ruggero Bonghi, end of December 1888 [draft]; *KGB* 3/5:568–569; here 568.

46. See, for example, Gramsci, *Prison Notebooks* (ed. Buttigieg), 1:255 [notebook 2, § 12; 1929–1933].

47. Dick, *Solar Lottery* [rev. ed. of *World of Chance*, 1955] (New York: Collier Books, 1990), p. 76.

48. John McDonald, *Strategy in Poker, Business and War*, illustrated by Robert Osborn (New York: Norton, 1950); as cited by Dick as the epigraph for *World of Chance*, but omitted when the text was reprinted thirty-five years later, with other modifications, as *Solar Lottery*.

49. Douglas Crimp, with Adam Rolston, *AIDS Demo Graphics* (Seattle: Bay Press, 1990), p. 17.

50. See Benjamin, *Das Passagen-Werk*, 1:570–611 [section N]; here esp. 593.

51. Nietzsche, "NF, Frühjahr–Herbst 1881"; *KGW* 5/2:376; emphasis added.

52. Horkheimer and Adorno, "The Culture Industry: Enlightenment as Mass Deception," in *Dialectic of Enlightenment*, pp. 120–167; here p. 167.

53. Descombes, *Modern French Philosophy*, pp. 26 and 177.

54. Deleuze and Guattari, *Anti-Oedipus*, p. 314, but translation modified. *Capitalisme et schizophrénie: L'Anti-Œdipe* (Paris: Les éditions de minuit, 1970), p. 374; last ellipses in original, emphasis added.

55. See Octave Mannoni, *Clefs pour l'imaginaire ou l'autre scène* (Paris: Éditions du Seuil, 1969), pp. 163–164. This is a dominant theme of the work of Sloterdijk and Žižek.

56. Foucault, "Intellectuals and Power" [a conversation between Foucault and Deleuze, 1972], in *Language, Counter-Memory, Practice*, pp. 205–217; here p. 207. Compare also Adorno's notion of the "picture-puzzle" (*Vexierbild*), in which workers "forget" what they best know: namely, *that* they are workers (Adorno, *Minima Moralia*, p. 193).

57. Žižek, *Tarrying with the Negative*, p. 216.

58. Ibid., pp. 216–219.

59. See again Lacan, "Le stade du mirroir," in *Écrits I*, pp. 94–95 and 99; emphasis added.

60. Kristeva, *Tales of Love* [*Histoires d'amour*, 1983], trans. Leon S. Roudiez (New York: Columbia University Press, 1987), pp. 135–136.

61. Gibson, *Count Zero*, pp. 1–2.

62. See Žižek, *For They Know Not What They Do*, pp. 245–249.

63. See again Vaihinger, "Nietzsche and His Doctrine of Conscious Illusion," in *The Philosophy of "As-If*," pp. 341–362.

64. See Russell Neuman, Marian Just, and Ann Crigler, *Common Knowledge: News and the Construction of Political Meaning* (Chicago: The University of Chicago Press, 1992); and John Fiske, *Power Plays Power Works* (London and New York: Verso, 1993), p. 6.

65. Baudrillard, *Simulations*, p. 50. Baudrillard is referring to the "Loud Experiment" in 1971. The everyday life of an American family was shot uninterrupted for seven months: "300 hours of direct non-stop broadcasting, without script or scenario, the odyssey of a family, its dramas, its joys, ups and downs—in brief a 'raw' historical document" in the course of which—a classic case of the "anthropologist's dilemma"—this nuclear family broke apart at the seams.

66. See Podoroga, "The Eunuch of the Soul," pp. 381 and 400. Podoroga is understandably critical of actually exiting socialism, yet this particular thesis is also a lesson of Negri and Guattari in *Communists Like Us*, with their definition of communism as a continuous interface between collectivity and singularity.

67. See Nietzsche, "Versuch einer Selbstkritik," in *Die Geburt der Tragödie. Oder, Griechenthum und Pessimismus; KGW* 3/1:5–16 ["Attempt at a Self-Criticism"].

68. Cf. above all Alexander Nehamas, *Nietzsche: Life as Literature* (Cambridge, Mass. and London: Harvard University Press, 1985). For a critique of Nehamas, see Robert John Ackermann, "Current American Thought on Nietzsche" [1986], in *Nietzsche heute*, pp. 129–136, and his interesting—though perhaps insufficiently frenzied—book *Nietzsche: A Frenzied Look* (Amherst: The University of Massachusetts Press,, 1990), esp. pp. 157–159. Nehamas's work, following that of Walter Kaufmann and Arthur Danto, is one of a long line of deeply misguided Anglo-Saxon appreciations of Nietzsche; among current studies Nehamas's is one of the most respected by philosophers and one of the most politically naïve and obscurantist. Not a significant improvement here, more surprisingly, is Sloterdijk's otherwise much more insightful notion of Nietzsche as a "thinker on stage," which concludes that "nothing in Nietzsche's writing can have as great a continuing effect as his own refutation of this theory of the will to power." Not only did Nietzsche pretty much begin by assuming such refutation to be possible, he did so with very specific political effects in mind, and not merely "self-affirmation" or "liberation" of the post-Marxist, postmaterialist, and supposedly postcynical variety. Cf. Sloterdijk, *Thinker on Stage: Nietzsche's Materialism* [1986], trans. Jamie Owen Daniel, foreword by Jochen Schulte-Sasse (Minneapolis: University of Minnesota Press, 1989), p. 91, and *Critique of Cynical Reason*, pp. xxvi–xxix.

69. Nietzsche, "NF, Winter 1872–73"; *KGW* 3/4:154.

70. Franz Mehring, "Nietzsche gegen den Sozialismus" [Nietzsche against socialism, 1897], *Gesammelte Werke*, ed. Thomas Höhle, Hans Koch, and Josef Schleifstein (Berlin, GDR: Dietz Verlag, 1961), 13:167–172; here 169. See further, in the same volume, Mehring's essays "Zur Philosophie und Poesie des Kapitalismus" [on the philosophy and poetry of capitalism, 1891] and "Über Nietzsche" [on Nietzsche, 1899], 13:159–166 and 173–183, respectively, and his ambivalent review of Eisner's *Psychopathia spiritualis*, in *Die Neue Zeit* 10 (1892), 668–669.

71. Nietzsche, "NF, Frühjahr–Herbst 1881"; *KGW* 5/2:369.

72. Ibid., 5/2:370.

73. Ibid., 5/2:374 and 370.

74. Adorno, *Minima Moralia*, p. 43.

75. Ibid., p. 226.

76. For a more positive assessment of Adorno in this respect see Jameson's *Late Marxism: Adorno, or, The Persistence of the Dialectic* (London and New York: Verso, 1990); for a similar assessment of postmodernism see his *Postmodernism, or, The Cultural Logic of Late Capitalism*.

77. Allan Bloom, *The Closing of the American Mind*, foreword by Saul Bellow (New York: Simon & Schuster, Inc., 1987), p. 222.

78. Strauss, *Thoughts on Machiavelli*, p. 36.

79. Bloom, *The Closing of the American Mind*, p. 159.

80. Lukács, *The Destruction of Reason*, pp. 87–88.

81. Debord, *Comments on the Society of the Spectacle* [1988], trans. Malcolm Imrie (London and New York: Verso, 1990), pp. 2, 6, and 9; emphasis added. See further the analysis of "Integrated World Capitalism" in Guattari and Negri, *Communists Like Us*, pp. 47–92, and of "the world economy of the socialized worker" in Negri, *The Politics of Subversion*, pp. 102–114.

82. Gramsci, *Prison Notebooks* (ed. Buttigieg), 1:234 [notebook 1, § 156; 1929–1930].

83. Althusser, "Is It Simple to Be a Marxist in Philosophy?" in *Philosophy and the Spontaneous Philosophy of the Scientists*, p. 210; emphasis added.

84. Norman Stone, *Europe Transformed 1878–1919* (Cambridge, Mass.: Harvard University Press, 1984), pp. 11 and 45. For a leftist discussion of *trasformismo* see the essays in *Gramsci and Italy's Passive Revolution*, ed. John A. Davis (London: Croom Helm, 1979).

85. Žižek, "The Violence of Liberal Democracy," *Assemblage* 20 (1993), 92–93 (special issue on "Violence and Space," ed. Mark Wigley). Žižek has elaborated his analysis in the last chapter of *Tarrying with the Negative*—"Enjoy Your Nation as Yourself!"—in which he notes: "It is perhaps more than a mere curiosity that, in Yugoslavia, Althusserians . . . were the only ones who remained 'pure' in the fight for democracy: all other philosophical schools at some point or other sold themselves to the regime" (p. 229).

86. Mao, "Combat Liberalism" [September 7, 1937], in *Quotations from Chairman Mao Tse-Tung*, pp. 248–249.

87. See Peter Stallybrass and Allon White, *The Politics and Poetics of Transgression* (Ithaca: Cornell University Press, 1986), p. 14. The authors are here paraphrasing the arguments of Georges Balandier and B. Babcock, with Mikhail Bakhtin hovering in the background.

88. Resch, *Althusser and the Renewal of Marxist Social Theory*, p. 17.

89. Ibid.

90. For the best discussion in English of Gramsci's relationship to Hegel and

Croce see Maurice A. Finocchiaro, *Gramsci and the History of Dialectical Thought* (Cambridge: Cambridge University Press, 1988). Some of Gramsci's critique of Croce has been translated in his *Selections of the Prison Notebooks* and especially in *Further Selections from the Prison Notebooks*, pp. 326–475.

91. "Our perception of the United States has been that of a democracy inside and an empire outside: Dr. Jekyll and Mr. Hyde. We have admired democracy; we have deplored empire. And we have suffered the actions of this country, which has constantly intervened in our lives in the name of manifest destiny, the big stick, dollar diplomacy, and cultural arrogance" (Carlos Fuentes, *The Buried Mirror: Reflections on Spain and the New World* [Boston, New York, and London: Houghton Mifflin Company, 1992], p. 325).

92. Christine Buci-Glucksmann, "State, Transition and Passive Revolution" [1977], trans. Kate Soper, in *Gramsci and Marxist Theory*, ed. Chantal Mouffe (London: Routledge & Kegan Paul, 1979), pp. 207–236; here p. 224.

93. The motto from Spinoza that serves as one epigraph of this chapter, taken from his analysis of coercion and hegemony as the dual dynamic of *nearly* total social control, concludes on a more optimistic note: "Though the powers of government, as thus conceived, are sufficiently ample, they can never become large enough to execute every possible wish of their possessors" (Spinoza, *A Theologico-Political Treatise*, in *A Theologico-Political Treatise and A Political Treatise*, p. 216 [ch. 17]).

94. Negri, "Postscript, 1990," pp. 158–173. It is important to stress that this analysis of socialism, capitalism, and communism is not *post festum* with regard to the collapse of actually existing socialism; rather, it was firmly in place by the late 1970s. See, for example, Negri, *Marx Beyond Marx*, and the special issue of *Semiotext(e): Autonomia: Post-Political Politics*. The otherwise excellent introduction to *Autonomia* begins unfortunately, with a singularly inappropriate quotation from Nietzsche. And one of the authors now adheres to the official party line of Nietzschean *gauchisme*; see Sylvère Lotringer's symptomatically vapid introduction, entitled "Furiously Nietzsche," to the English translation of Bataille's *On Nietzsche*, pp. vii–xv. Of course, there are today any number of critiques and outright rejections of the vanguardist political project implied by the positing of "the multitude" and the ability of others to speak, in effect, on its behalf. Baudrillard, to take perhaps the most cogent case, has called attention to the self-serving, self-legitimating tendency of intellectuals to produce something called "the masses" and "mass culture," only in order to give themselves the illusion of direct, unmediated contact not only with both but with something nostalgically called "the Real." Baudrillard thinks such contact is both logically and practically impossible, given the postmodern hegemony of the simulacrum. See especially Baudrillard, *In the Shadow of the Silent Minorities . . . Or the End of the Social*, trans. Paul Foss (New York: Semiotext[e] Foreign Agents Series, 1983). Nonetheless, as Philip Rosen has noted, Baudrillard does not thereby escape as radically as he tends to think from various subject/object dualisms on which his work is predicated, and hence depends precisely on that Real

that he strives to deny or to dissolve into hyperreality. See Philip Rosen, "Document and Documentary: On the Persistence of Historical Concepts," in *Theorizing Documentary*, ed. Michael Renov (New York and London: Routledge, 1993), pp. 58–89; here esp. pp. 82–87. Yet Rosen does not extricate himself entirely from the liberal political position that he desires, at times, to critique. Although he alludes positively to the work of Gramsci, like Baudrillard he fails to make explicit that the form of "vanguardism" explicitly demanded by Gramscian — and Leninist — political theory and practice involves the recruitment of the vanguard *from* the masses, indeed the *obliteration* of the *bogus* dualist distinction between "multitude" and "elite."

95. Grahame Lock, introduction to Althusser, *Essays in Self-Criticism*, pp. 1–32; here p. 17, where Lock is citing "a thesis advanced by Althusser in a course on Marx's *Zur Kritik der politischen Oekonomie*, given at the École Normale Supérieure, rue d'Ulm, Paris in June 1973."

96. See *Selections from the Prison Notebooks of Antonio Gramsci*, pp. 52–120 and 128–130. Also see Gramsci's reflections on "Croce and Literary Criticism" and "Ethico-political History," in *Selections from Cultural Writings*, pp. 103–107, in addition to the relevant sections of *Further Selections from the Prison Notebooks*.

97. Resch, *Althusser and the Renewal of Marxist Social Theory*, p. 15 (paraphrasing an argument of *The German Ideology*).

98. Ibid., p. 14.

99. *La dialectique peut-elle casser des briques* (René Viénet, Taiwan/France, 1973). Exemplary for situationist "appropriation art," this is a détoured kung-fu film to which a new, politico-philosophical soundtrack was added to an unretouched imagetrack.

100. Debord, *Comments on the Society of the Spectacle*, p. 77.

101. Virilio, *Popular Defense & Ecological Struggles*, p. 92; emphasis added. On this topic and related matters, see also some of Virilio's other — marginally less nihilistic — works: *Speed and Politics: An Essay on Dromology* [1977], trans. Mark Polizzotti (New York: Semiotext[e] Foreign Agents, 1986); *Pure War*, with Sylvère Lotringer, trans. Mark Polizzotti (New York: Semiotext[e], 1983); and *War and Cinema: The Logistics of Perception* [1984], trans. Patrick Camiller (London and New York: Verso, 1989).

102. Marx and Engels, *The German Ideology*, in *Collected Works*, 5:236.

103. Citing from DeLillo's novel *White Noise* (New York: Viking, 1985), p. 9, but thinking also of Baudrillard's *Amérique* (Paris: Éditions Bernard Grasset, 1986). This ambivalent but ultimately oddly loving depiction of America as "the hysterical country" and as "hologram" — which would likely be news to the homeless or workers on strike — is at the same time almost literally reifying. America becomes, in effect, a hyperreal cyberspace after a neutron bomb has hit. There are no living people in Baudrillard's America; what is most hysterical here is things, their relations, and *this* representation of them. Elsewhere, Baudrillard has noted a "Paradox: all bombs are clean — their only pollution is the system of control and security they

radiate *when they are not detonated"* (*Simulations*, p. 79) — news, perhaps, to the inhabitants of Guernica, Coventry, Dresden, Hiroshima, Hanoi, Sarajevo, even Chernobyl and Three Mile Island.

104. Compare and contrast the following sets of remark. First:

Multiculturalism does not lead us very far if it remains a question of difference only between one culture and another. Differences should also be understood within the same culture, just as multiculturalism as an explicit condition of our times exists within every self. Intercultural, intersubjective, interdisciplinarity. These are some of the keywords that keep on circulating in artistic and educational as well as political milieus. To cut across boundaries and borderlines is to live aloud the malaise of categories and labels; it is to resist simplistic attempts at classifying, to resist the comfort of belonging to a classification, and of *producing* classifiable works. Interdisciplinary is, for example, not just a question of putting several fields together, so that individuals can share their specialized knowledge and converse with one another within their expertise. It is to create in sharing a field that belongs to no one, not even to those who create it. What is at stake, therefore, in this inter-creation is the very notion of *specialization* and of *expertise, of discipline and professionalism.* To identify oneself with a position of specialized knowledge, to see oneself as an expert or as an authority on matters, even and especially on artistic matters is to give up all attempts at understanding relations in the game of power. (Trinh T. Minh-ha, "A Minute Too Long" [1988], in *When the Moon Waxes Red: Representation, Gender and Cultural Politics* [New York and London: Routledge, 1991], pp. 107–118; here pp. 107–108)

Second:

What in fact does the slogan of interdisciplinarity mask? 1. Certain real practices, perfectly founded and legitimate: practices that remain to be defined, in cases that remain to be defined. To define them is to distinguish them from others. The first line of demarcation. 2. In the interior of these practices and these real problems, there are new distinctions to be made (application, constitution) and therefore new lines of demarcation to be drawn. 3. Outside these real practices, we encounter the pretensions of certain disciplines that declare themselves to be sciences (the human sciences). What are we to make of their pretension? By means of a new line of demarcation we distinguish between the real function of most of the human sciences and the ideological character of their pretensions. 4. If we go back to the slogan of interdisciplinarity, we are now in a position to state (on the basis of certain resistant symptoms) that it is massively *ideological* in character. (Althusser, "Philosophy and the Spontaneous Philosophy of the Scientists" [1967], in *Philosophy and the Spontaneous Philosophy of the Scientists,* pp. 69–165; here p. 98)

105. See Derrida, *L'autre cap* [*suivi de*] *La démocratie ajournée* (Paris: Les éditions de minuit, 1991). The first title would translate literally as *The Other Cape* or *The Other Heading;* in the second title, the adjective *ajournée* means "adjourned" and

"postponed" as well as "summoned"; but it also means "held back," as in the expression "after failing the exam, the candidate was held back." Derrida weaves a characteristically intricate philosophical text about the possibilities and dangers attending the "New Europe," asking that we interrogate what the notion "new" ever really means. He exploits the semantic resources of a specific etymological and connotative word field. French and Latin *cap-* is coaxed to deconstruct the following nexus of presuppositions and prejudices: (1) the "naturalness" entailed in privileging one geopolitical region ("cape") over others, and one which (2) qua shape has hidden phallocentric and patriarchal connotations, but which is also therefore informed (3) by castration-anxiety ("decapitation"); (4) the knee-jerk need for a politics headed by strong leaders (*caput:* "head" of state); (5) common assumptions about where symbolic and real centers of power are to be located (their "capitals"); (6) the direction Europe as a whole is taking and/or ought to take, its "prow," "bearings," or "heading" (as in the French expression *mettre le cap sur*); (7) the authenticity of the dialogue between rival visions of Europe (*cap à cap* means "head to head," "tête-à-tête"); and (8) the kind of political economy that will rule the postsocialist New Order (some form of "capitalism," undoubtedly, but one with a more or less human face, with a stronger or weaker welfare state safety net?). While marvelous in its own terms, ideologically and politically speaking Derrida's text reinvents the wheel. Readers are left with little more than a well-meaning but empty plea for liberal pluralist restraint. For example, Europeans are enjoined to recognize and thus confront irreducible "Otherness," but at the same time, somehow, they are to integrate "the Other" into "their" Europe — in a manner uncannily reminiscent of Nietzsche's "good European" — a concept that was figured to be anything *but* egalitarian. *L'autre cap* is interesting enough read as one might read a text by Stéphane Mallarmé; read as political philosophy — though Mallarmé can certainly be read this way, too — it is little more than defunct liberalism. And so we would need to ask what ideology *this* particular cape, qua cloak, conceals. Contrast Negri's more charged reflections about "The End of the Century" in his *The Politics of Subversion,* pp. 61–74, as well as Badiou's *D'un désastre obscur.*

106. Think, for example, of "Old World," Jonathan Richman and the Modern Lovers (David Robinson, Jerry Harrison, Ernie Brooks, and Jonathan Richman), *The Modern Lovers,* © 1976 Beserkley Records/Rhino Records, RNC 70091.

107. Milarepa, "The Enlightenment of Rechungpa," in *The Hundred Thousand Songs of Milarepa,* trans. and annotated by Garma C. C. Chang (New Hyde Park, N.Y.: University Books, 1962), 1:225–240; here 225. Abandoning attachment to one's country, ironically enough today for some Tibetans, is a constant theme of Milarepa (1040–1123), arguably Tibetan Buddhism's greatest poet-saint.

108. Žižek, *Tarrying with the Negative,* p. 227.

109. These points have also been made in interviews given by the self-described "computer illiterate" William Gibson — coiner of the term "cyberspace" and inspiration to NASA scientists, plastic surgeons, and inventors, as well as to cyberpunks

and other cyborgs. At the same time, however, Gibson takes care to emphasize that humans continue to exist around most of the globe — often, indeed most typically, in extreme and dehumanizing illiteracy, disease, and poverty. For the time being, most posthumanity is reserved for the capitalist: the man safe in Beverly Hills above the rubble of the City of Quartz, say, who can afford a new kidney, heart, hip, hand, eye, and so on — though not, just yet, brain or spinal column — when the old ones go the way of all flesh; he can even have himself frozen when he dies — perhaps to be reborn again, to return eternally, as the poor person cannot. At the end of *The Difference Engine* — which has traveled back to one of the purported "origins" of cyberspace circa 1855 — others have proposed the inscriptions in Paleolithic caves and elsewhere — it is made clear that the wealthy eat joints of meat prepared by servants who eat tinned beans, and that state-of-the art technology develops only more or less covertly against the backdrop of the Irish famine, the Paris Communards, and Captain Swing. In short: Nothing New Under the Sun, or at any rate Less Than There Often Appears. See Gibson and Sterling, *The Difference Engine,* pp. 324–429. See further Howard Rheingold, *Virtual Reality* (New York: Simon & Schuster/Summit Books, 1991), pp. 378–385; David Tomas, "Old Rituals for New Space: *Rites de Passage* and William Gibson's Cultural Model of Cyberspace," and Michael Heim, "The Erotic Ontology of Cyberspace," both in *Cyberspace: First Steps,* ed. Michael Benedikt (Cambridge, Mass. and London: The MIT Press, 1991), pp. 31–47 and 59–80, respectively; and Philip Hayward, "Situating Cyberspace: The Popularization of Virtual Reality," in *Future Visions,* pp. 180–204; esp. pp. 183–188. Also see Benjamin Woolley, *Virtual Worlds: A Journey in Hype and Hyperreality* (Oxford and Cambridge, Mass.: Blackwell, 1992).

110. Lukács, *The Young Hegel: Studies in the Relations between Dialectics and Economics* [completed 1938, published 1948], trans. from the 2d ed. of 1954 by Rodney Livingstone (Cambridge, Mass.: The MIT Press, 1975), p. 408; emphasis added.

111. See Haraway, "The Actors Are Cyborg, Nature Is Coyote, and the Geography Is Elsewhere: Postscript to 'Cyborgs at Large,'" in *Technoculture,* ed. Constance Penley and Andrew Ross (Minneapolis and Oxford: University of Minnesota Press, 1991), pp. 21–26; and *She, the Inappropriate/d Other,* ed. Trinh T. Minh-ha, special issue of *Discourse* 8 (Fall–Winter 1986–87). See further Trinh, *Woman, Native, Other: Writing, Postcoloniality, and Feminism* (Bloomington: Indiana University Press, 1989); and Haraway, *Simians, Cyborgs, and Women,* esp. part 3.

112. Haraway, "The Actors Are Cyborg," in *Technoculture,* p. 21.

113. Trinh, introduction to *She, the Inappropriate/d Other,* pp. 1–9; here p. 9.

114. Debord, *Comments on the Society of the Spectacle,* p. 11.

115. Consider, for example, Kevin Roberts and Frank Webster, "Cybernetic Capitalism," in *The Political Economy of Information,* ed. Vincent Mosco and Janet Wasko (Madison: University of Wisconsin Press, 1988), pp. 44–75. For an incisive demolition of the claim that Marx himself was a technological determinist see, in addition to virtually the entire œuvre of Althusser, Richard W. Miller, *Analyzing Marx: Morality, Power and History* (Princeton: Princeton University Press, 1984).

116. See Robins and Webster, "Athens without Slaves . . . or Slaves without Athens? The Neurosis of Technology," *Science as Culture* 3 (1988), 7–53.

117. Andrew Ross, "Hacking Away at the Counterculture," in *Technoculture,* pp. 107–134; here p. 125.

118. Haraway, "The Actors Are Cyborg," in *Technoculture,* p. 24.

119. De Certeau, "History: Science and Fiction" [1983], *Heterologies: Discourse on the Other,* trans. Brian Massumi, foreword by Wlad Godzich (Minneapolis: University of Minnesota Press, 1986), pp. 199–221; here p. 214.

120. Michael Balch, then of the industrial/cyberpunk band Front Line Assembly, speaking of the influence on his work of Gibson's novels; as quoted in the documentary video *Cyberpunk* (Marianne Trench and Peter von Brandenburg, USA, 1990).

121. Marcus, *Lipstick Traces,* p. 74. With this thesis Marcus unwittingly links arms with the Allan Bloom who writes of contemporary stars of popular musical culture that they "are singing a song they do not understand, translated from a German original and having a huge popular success with unknown but wide-ranging consequences, as something of the original message touches something in American souls. But behind it all, the master lyricists are Nietzsche and Heidegger" (Bloom, *The Closing of the American Mind,* p. 152).

122. Laurie Anderson, "The Puppet Motel," *Bright Red,* © 1994 Warner Brothers, 9 45534–2.

123. Kroker, *The Possessed Individual* (ch. 2: "Paul Virilio: The Postmodern Body as a War Machine"), pp. 20–50; here pp. 28–29. This book contributes to the task of articulating recent philosophy and current mass culture. Elsewhere, however, Kroker has bought wholesale into a Nietzschean *gauchisme* in which the political dimensions and implications of Nietzsche's thought are inadequately interrogated. Among the many extravagant claims made in Kroker's coauthored *The Postmodern Scene* (1986–1987), for example, is that Nietzsche was/is "the limit and the possibility of the postmodern condition." This is to say: "He is the *limit* of postmodernism because, as a thinker who was so deeply fixated by the death of the grand referent of God, Nietzsche was the last and the best of all the modernists. In the *Will to Power,* the postmodernist critique of representation achieves its most searing expression and, in Nietzsche's understanding of the will as a 'perspectival simulation,' the fate of postmodernity as a melancholy descent into the violence of the death of the social is anticipated. And Nietzsche is the *possibility* of the postmodern scene because the double-reversal which is everywhere in his thought and nowhere more than his vision of artistic practice as the release of the 'dancing star' of the body as a *solar system* is, from the beginning of time, the negative cue, the 'expanding field' of the postmodern condition." From this hyperbolic logic, it eventually follows that "Nietzsche's accusation of a cynical history and his poetic of an embodied power are the fateful forms of critique of the 'referential illusion.' In the postmodern century, the spectre/sign of Nietzsche haunts *Capital* now, and promises to return us, beyond Marx and Nietzsche, to the question of myth and enlightenment" (Arthur Kroker and David Cook, *The Postmodern Scene: Excremental Culture and Hyper-*

Aesthetics [1986], 2d ed. [Montréal: New World Perspectives, 1987], pp. 9 and 188). The problem is not whether any of these claims are "right" or "wrong" exactly. Rather, the problem is that it is unclear how on this argument's *own* terms one might ever know or care deeply one way or the other.

124. Virilio, *The Lost Dimension,* p. 136.

125. Ibid., p. 133.

126. Laurie Anderson, "Speak My Language," *Bright Red,* © 1994 Warner Brothers, 9 45534–2.

127. Gibson, *Neuromancer,* p. 203.

128. As quoted in *Cyberpunk* (Trench and Brandenburg, USA, 1990). In the late 1960s, the Left-Nietzschoid Marcuse, too, had described the transmission of what he variously called "the revolution in perception," "the aesthetic dimension," or "the new sensibility" as a virus. Marcuse wrote: "The new sensibility has become a political force. It crosses the frontier between the capitalist and the communist orbit; it is contagious because the atmosphere, the climate of the established societies, carries the virus" (Marcuse, *An Essay on Liberation,* p. 27). On the use and abuse of metaphors of contagion in political rhetoric, see Susan Sontag, *Illness as Metaphor* (New York: Farrar, Straus and Giroux, 1978), and *AIDS and Its Metaphors* (New York: Farrar, Straus and Giroux, 1989); and especially Grant, "Critical Intellectuals and the New Media."

129. Nietzsche's personal library in the Nietzsche Archive in Weimar contains many books of a scientific and mathematical nature. This "materialist" aspect of his thought is too often overlooked. For two valuable introductions to this problematic from different angles see again Mittasch, *Friedrich Nietzsche als Naturphilosoph,* and Schlechta and Anders, *Friedrich Nietzsche: Von den verborgenen Anfängen seines Philosophierens.* The latter is a particularly interesting, unfairly ignored, but ultimately frustrating book: in part because the authors are required to expend so much effort combating the failings of existing editions of Nietzsche's works, in part because they fail to deliver on their promise to show the ways Nietzsche's philosophy of language was joined not only to his studies of the natural sciences, mathematics, and epistemology but also his political project (see esp. pp. 34, 38–39, 47, 99, and 155). Schlechta and Anders were among the first authors to allude to the possibility that this multiply determined project included a powerful esoteric dimension — but they did not follow this potentially very significant suggestion through, preferring to assert that Nietzsche himself never fully realized or exploited it (p. 14). Whenever confronted with the direct question as to *why* Nietzsche might have began around 1872, as they argue, to combine his various linguistic, scientific, historical, and current interests in a more or less esoteric pattern of thought that then remained remarkably coherent and consistent throughout his career, Schlechta and Anders fall back on vague existential and ad hominem explanations (see, for example, pp. 41, 49, and 156).

130. Metta Winter, "Viral Gene Sabotages Itself and Surprises Researchers," *Agri-*

culture & Life Sciences News [Cornell University] (August 1993), 9. Winter is summarizing the research of teams led by Milton Zaitlin and Dennis Gonsalves, among others.

131. See Deleuze, "Postscript on Control Societies" [1990], in *Negotiations,* pp. 177–182.

132. For a relevant survey of the history of code making and breaking from their major modern inception in World War II to the cyberpunk counterculture of today, see Julian Dibbell, "Code Warriors: Battling for the Keys to Privacy in the Info Age," *The Village Voice* (August 3, 1993), 33–37.

133. Ross, "Hacking Away at the Counterculture," in *Technoculture,* p. 110; emphasis added. Compare Cronenberg's remark: "The artist's duty to *himself* is a culmination of immense responsibility and immense irresponsibility. I think those two interlock." This is also an apt characterization of Nietzsche/anism as a major post/modernist type of ethical interlock, though — as Cronenberg himself goes on to imply — it necessarily leaves the specific *social* dimension of the interlock unclarified. For Cronenberg, the artist qua artist is irresponsible, otherwise art becomes "totally useless and ineffective"; yet the same artist must "of course" be responsible socially, qua citizen, parent, friend, lover, and so on. See the interview with Cronenberg in *Rolling Stone* 623 (February 6, 1992), 68–70 and 96. Nietzsche obliterated very precisely Cronenberg's distinction *socially,* so as to take responsibility with regard to the creation of his future corps, and was more irresponsible with regard to how this corps would take and hold power.

134. Jameson, *The Seeds of Time,* p. 205.

135. Marx, "Preface to the First German Edition," *Capital,* 1:9.

136. See Dick, *Do Androids Dream of Electric Sheep* [1968] (New York: Ballantine Books, 1982) and "We Can Remember It for You Wholesale" [1965–1966], *The Collected Stories of Philip K. Dick,* 2:35–52, which became *Blade Runner* (Ridley Scott, USA/UK, 1982) and *Total Recall* (Paul Verhoeven, USA/Holland, 1990), respectively. In New Bad Future films, cyborgs, advertising, and the films themselves function as "cultural transitional objects" and/or "cultural fetish objects" to tap into and then manage deep-seated fears of impending technoculture. See Fred Glass, "Totally Recalling Arnold: Sex and Violence in the New Bad Future," *Film Quarterly* 44:1 (Fall 1990), 2–13; and, further, Michael Ryan and Douglas Kellner, *Camera Politica: Politics and Ideology of the Contemporary Hollywood Cinema* (Bloomington and Indianapolis: Indiana University Press, 1988); and several essays in *Alien Zone: Cultural Theory and Contemporary Science Fiction Cinema,* ed. Annette Kuhn (London and New York: Verso, 1990).

137. See, for example, Dick, *The Simulacra* (New York: Ace Books, 1964), *The Penultimate Truth* [1964] (New York: Carroll & Graf, 1989), *The Three Stigmata of Palmer Eldritch* (Garden City, N.Y.: Doubleday, 1965), *UBIK* [1969] (New York: Daw Books, 1983), *Flow My Tears, the Policeman Said* [1974] (New York: Daw Books, 1975), *A Scanner Darkly* [1977] (New York: Daw Books, 1984), *The Divine*

Invasion (New York: Timescape Books, 1981), *Valis* (New York: Bantam, 1981), *The Transmigration of Timothy Archer* (New York: Timescape Books, 1982), and *Radio Free Albemuth* [published posthumously] (New York: Avon Books, 1987).

138. See Dick, *Clans of the Alphane Moon* [1964] (New York: Carroll & Graf, 1988), esp. pp. 92–112.

139. De Man, foreword to Carol Jacobs, *The Dissimulating Harmony* (Baltimore: The Johns Hopkins University Press, 1978), pp. vii–xiii; here p. xi.

140. Dick to Claudia Bush, July 16, 1974; cited in Jay Kinney, "Introduction: Wrestling with Angels: The Mystical Dilemma of Philip K. Dick," *In Pursuit of Valis: Selections from the Exegesis,* ed. Lawrence Sutin (Novato, Calif. and Lancaster, Pa.: Underwood-Miller, 1991), pp. xvii–xxxi; here p. xxiv. Dick's cited remarks about Heidegger are on pp. 108, 194, and 228–232.

141. McLuhan, *The Gutenberg Galaxy: The Making of Typographic Man* (Toronton: University of Toronto Press, 1962), p. 66.

142. Heidegger citing Kleist, in the documentary film *Martin Heidegger: Im Denken unterwegs* . . . (Produced by Richard Wisser for Neske Produktion, Stuttgart, 1975).

143. Heidegger in *Martin Heidegger: Im Denken unterwegs.* . . .

144. Nietzsche, "NF, Juli–August 1882"; *KGW* 7/1:9.

145. Nietzsche, "NF, November 1882–Februar 1883"; *KGW* 7/1:195.

146. Nietzsche, "NF, Frühjahr–Herbst 1881"; *KGW* 5/2:406.

147. Peter Tosh, "400 Years," as recorded on Bob Marley and the Wailers (Aston Barrett, Carlton Barrett, Peter Tosh, Bob Marley, Bunny Livingstone), *Catch a Fire,* © 1973 Island Records, Ltd., 7-90030-4. Then listen to Skinny Puppy (cEVIN KEY, Dave Ogilve, and N. Ogre), "200 Years," *Mind: The Perpetual Intercourse,* © 1986 Capital Industries-EMI, Inc., C4-90467.

148. Polish SF writer and critic Stanislaw Lem, to whom Dick alludes in this passage, was viewed by Dick alternatively as a "leftist," even "party expert," or as a dissident. But Dick may also have had in mind Fredric Jameson, whom he knew and on occasion deeply mistrusted as some sort of "agent" or "double agent." Jameson has come to believe that Dick's novels are "paradigmatic . . . for questions of history and historicity" (Jameson, *Postmodernism, or, The Cultural Logic of Late Capitalism,* p. 283). For Jameson's current take on the Dickian world, including his earlier analyses of it, see, for example, *The Geopolitical Aesthetic,* pp. 14, 23–35, 90–93, and 139. For his own part, Lem was at the time in fact much more of a *structuralist* than a Marxist, albeit one with certain prescriptive tendencies, including occasional doses of socialist realism; his notion of "trash," to which Dick refers, is thus overdetermined. Lem's interpretation of Dick, beginning in the early 1970s, was one of the first important ones, has remained symptomatic of Dick criticism to this day, and was quite complicated. On the one hand Lem — rightly — held that Dick had "amplified, rendered monumental and at the same time monstrous, certain fundamental properties of *the actual world,* giving them dramatic acceleration and impetus." On

the other hand Lem's quasi-structuralist — and naïve — assumption that "any work must justify itself either on the level of what it presents literally or on the level of deeper semantic content, not so much overtly present in, as summoned by, the text," led him to assume — mistakenly — that Dick's work lacks "a focal point," that therefore it "*cannot* be rendered consistent," and that "the impossibility of imposing consistency on the text compels us to seek its global meanings not in the realm of events themselves, but in that of their constructive principle, the very thing that is responsible for lack of focus." A major problem with this line of argument stems from Lem's inadequate regard for the epistemological distinction between: (Channel 1) a meaning the text itself is imagined already to lack or possess; and (Channel 2) our ability or inability to impose meaning on it. As a consequence, in terms of the interaction of both epistemological levels — (Channel 3) — Lem overlooked the apparent fact that Dick, as the latter indicated in his notebooks cited here, consciously as well as unconsciously concealed the explicitly political "focal point" of his work and its intended effect; though, ironically enough, it was precisely Lem's misconception, in part, that enabled Dick to theorize what he was doing in the first place, and to program his version of a properly Nietzschean Channel 4 accordingly. Cf. Stanislaw Lem, "Philip K. Dick: A Visionary Among the Charlatans" [1975], in *Microworlds: Writings on Science Fiction and Fantasy,* ed. Franz Rottensteiner, various translators (San Diego, New York, London: Harcourt Brace Jovanovich, 1984), pp. 106–135; here pp. 117 and 119; emphasis added. See further, in the same anthology, Lem's essays "On the Structural Analysis of Science Fiction" [1970] and "Science Fiction: A Hopeless Case — with Exceptions" [1972; expanded 1975], pp. 31–44 and 45–105, respectively. The latter essay deals extensively with Dick's work; indeed, he is the main "exception" to which Lem's title refers. Dick read all three essays when they first appeared in English translation. Though there has never been a consensus on the matter, since at least the mid-1970s the notion that Dick was somehow sympathetic to a "Marxist" analysis of consumer capitalism has been quite common currency. In addition to Jameson's suitably complex take on Dick, see, for example, Thomas M. Disch, "Toward the Transcendent: An Introduction to *Solar Lottery* and Other Works" [1976], and Peter Fitting, "*UBIK:* The Deconstruction of Bourgeois SF" [1975], both in *Philip K. Dick* [Writers of the 21st Century Series], ed. Martin Harry Greenberg and Joseph D. Olander (New York: Taplinger Publishing Company, 1983), pp. 13–25 and 149–159, respectively.

149. Dick, *In Pursuit of Valis,* pp. 131–132.

150. Kermode, *The Genesis of Secrecy,* p. 29.

151. Dick, *In Pursuit of Valis,* p. 140. Dick's work would be much less complex and significant were it reducible to the terms of the preceding discussion. On the one hand his writing seems "normally" informed by the dialectical possibility that *all* the conspiracies and visions he sees and constructs might be paranoid or drug-induced projections. In that case *In Pursuit of Valis* would be an "abnormal" work. On the other hand, however, it is certainly possible to take *In Pursuit of Valis* as an esoteric

work exposing an intent which his exoteric, published work would then "normally" disseminate. And in *that* case poor Dick would be *properly* Heideggereo-Nietzschean and "fascistic" after all.

152. Balibar, *The Philosophy of Marx* [1993], trans. Chris Turner (London and New York: Verso, 1995), p. 4.

153. Nietzsche, *Menschliches, Allzumenschliches II: Der Wanderer und sein Schatten; KGW* 4/3:313 [aphorism 278]. Nietzsche's aphorism is amplified by five linked theses. First, Leonard Cohen: "Now you can say that I've grown bitter, but of this you may be sure: the rich have got their channels in the bedrooms of the poor" ("Tower of Song," *I'm Your Man,* © 1988 CBS Records Inc., CK 44191). Second, Karl Marx: "Modern industry never views and treats the existing form of a production process as definitive. Its technical basis is thus revolutionary whereas that of all earlier modes of production were essentially conservative . . . [O]n the other hand in its capitalist form it reproduces the old division of labor with its ossified particularizations" (*Capital,* 1:486–87; translation modified). Third, Leo Strauss: "Only one thing is certain for Nietzsche regarding the future: the end has come for man as he was hitherto; what will come is either the Over-man or the Last-man. The last man, the lowest and most decayed man, the herd man without any ideals and aspirations, but well fed, well clothed, well housed, well medicated by ordinary physicians and by psychiatrists is Marx's man of the future *seen from an anti-Marxist point of view*" ("The Three Waves of Modernity," in *Political Philosophy,* p .97; emphasis added). Finally, V. I. Lenin: "for a revolution to take place it is not enough for the exploited and oppressed masses to realize the impossibility of living in the old way, and demand changes; for a revolution to take place it is essential that the exploiters should not be able to live and rule in the old way. It is only when the '*lower classes' do not want* to live in the old way and the 'upper classes' *cannot carry on in the old way* that the revolution can triumph"; and "the bourgeoisie sees practically only one aspect of Bolshevism — insurrection, violence, and terror; it therefore strives to prepare itself for resistance and opposition primarily in *this* field. It is possible that, in certain instances, in certain countries, and for certain brief periods, it will succeed in this. We must reckon with such an eventuality, and we have absolutely nothing to fear if it does succeed. Communism is emerging in positively every sphere of public life; its beginnings are to be seen literally on all sides. The 'contagion' (to use the favorite metaphor of the bourgeoisie and the bourgeois police, the one most to their liking) had penetrated the organism and has completely permeated it. If special efforts are made to block one of the channels, the 'contagion' will find another one, sometimes very unexpectedly" (*"Left-Wing" Communism—An Infantile Disorder* [1920], in *Collected Works,* 31:17–118; here 84–85 and 101).

154. The following sentences are appropriated almost verbatim from the conclusion of Balibar's essay "Racism as Universalism," substituting "Nietzsche's corps/e" and "corps/e" for "racism" (Balibar, "Racism as Universalism" [1989], in *Classes, Masses, Ideas,* pp. 191–204; here p. 204).

1. Viacom Networks College Group, "Too Much Nietzsche?" [advertisement], *The Chronicle of Higher Education* (April 29, 1992), A2. Another ad in the series is called "Too Much Freud?" Marx has not made it here—yet. And Viacom is one of the most powerful communications companies in the world.

2. Richard Kadrey, "The Toilet Was Full of Nietzsche" [from *Metrophage (A Romance of the Future)* (New York: Ace Books, 1988)], as excerpted in *Storming the Reality Studio*, pp. 87–97; here p. 94.

3. Althusser, *Journal de captivité: Stalag XA 1940–1945*, pp. 199–200 (diary entry, October 10, 1944).

4. Marx and Engels, *The German Ideology*, in *Collected Works*, 5:27. *Caput mortuum* (Latin for "dead head") in alchemy and later chemistry is the distillate trace remaining at the completion of an analytic reduction.

5. DeLillo, *Mao II*, pp. 235–236.

6. Hegel, *Phenomenology of Spirit*, p. 45 [preface, § 71]; translation modified.

7. Nietzsche, "NF, Juni–Juli 1883"; *KGW* 7/1:383.

8. Lenin, "Our Revolution" [January 17, 1923], *Collected Works* 33:476–480; here 480.

Index

Bäumer, Gertrud, 143
Bebel, August, 350
Becker, Wilhelm Carl, 141
Beckett, Samuel, 400 n.13, 423 n.173
Bell, Daniel, 19
Bellow, Saul, 234
Benjamin, Andrew, 284
Benjamin, Walter, 102–103, 181, 282–
283, 322, 325, 340, 355, 421 n.139, 438
n.293, 444 n.330, 454 n.8
Bergson, Henri, 24, 216
Beuys, Joseph, 72
Bible, 65, 79–82, 132, 221, 268, 388
Binswanger, Ludwig, 214
Bizet, Georges, 239
Black Flag, 330–331
Blasphemy, 67
Bloch, Ernst, 123, 336–337, 444 n.330
Bloom, Allan, 362–363, 547 n.121
Bobbio, Norberto, 197, 404 n.64
Boethius, 220–221
Bonghi, Ruggero, 354
Bordiga, Amadeo, 137–138, 535 n.12
Borges, Jorge Luis, 346
Bourdeau, Jean, 142, 144, 209
Bourdieu, Pierre, 27
Brague, Rémi, 160
Brecht, Bertolt, 64, 352, 444 n.326
Brood, 15, 125, 226, 228, 348, 355, 455
n.14. *See also* Psychoplasmics
Buci-Glucksmann, Christine, 310
Buddha, 6
Burke, Edmund, 183
Burroughs, William S., 6, 289–290, 319,
383, 414 n.112
Bush, Claudia, 385

Caesar, Julius, 319, 322
Caillois, Roger, 193–194
Callinicos, Alex, 110, 418 n.129
Camus, Albert, 297–298, 535 n.12
Cannibalism. *See* Incorporation
Cantor, Paul, 280, 506 n.103
Carey, Henry Charles, 20, 308–309, 363
Caroly, Claude, 400 n.13
Caruso, Paolo, 108

Castiglione, Baldassar, 230
Castoriadis, Cornelius, 99
Causality, 25–26, 34–51, 416–417 n.129,
419–420 n.138, 420–421 n.139
Cave, Nick, & The Bad Seeds, 402 n.33
Cavell, Stanley, 199–205
Chambers, Marilyn, 128
Changeux, Jean-Pierre, 127
Channel 4, 87, 92, 168–175, 178, 184–
185, 188–189, 192, 195, 204, 214–215,
238, 246–251, 271, 286, 292, 479
n.172, 551 n.148. *See also* Esotericism;
Esoteric semiotics; Esoterrorism; Sub-
liminal communication; Subliminal
influence
Channels, 91–92, 168–175, 286–287
Churchill, Winston, 236
Cixous, Hélène, 37–38, 326–327, 423
n.174, 452 n.386
Clash, 192
Clausewitz, Karl von, 59, 115
Cohen, Leonard, 59, 366, 552 n.153
Colli, Giorgio, 218
Common sense, 201–202
Communism, 69–71, 431 n.239, 432
n.241, 451 n.376
Concept, 21–24
Confucius, 6
Congreve, William, 281
Corngold, Stanley, 406 n.57
Corps/e, 26, 51–58, 87–88, 112, 136,
196, 258
Crane, Hart, 285
Crane, Stephen, 227
Crary, Jonathan, 16–18
Craven, Wes, 120, 348–349
Crime & the City Solution, 402 n.32
Croce, Benedetto, 40, 130, 225, 343–344,
368–373, 541–542 n.90, 543 n.96
Cronenberg, David, 8–9, 90, 127–128,
174, 289, 455 n.14, 480 n.184, 549 n.133
Crude thinking, 64
Cyberpunk, 74–75, 377–384, 392, 549
n.132
Cyberspace, 77, 90, 172–173, 242, 375,
377–379, 382–383, 545–546 n.109

Geoff Waite is Associate Professor of German Studies
at Cornell University.

Library of Congress Cataloging-in-Publication Data

Waite, Geoff.
Nietzsche's corps/e : aesthetics, politics, prophecy, or, the spectacular
  technoculture of everyday life / Geoff Waite.
    p.   cm. — (Post-contemporary interventions)
  Includes bibliographical references (p.   ) and index.
ISBN 0-8223-1709-5 (cloth : alk. paper). — ISBN 0-8223-1719-2 (pbk. :
  alk. paper)
  1. Nietzsche, Friedrich Wilhelm, 1844-1900. 2. Nietzsche, Friedrich
  Wilhelm, 1844-1900 — Influence. 3. Philosophy, Modern — 19th
  century. 4. Philosophy, Modern — 20th century. I. Title. II. Series.
                                              B3317W32 1996
        193 — dc20   95-42018   CIP